The Symbol at Your Door

To Alexis and Sophie

The Symbol at Your Door

Number and Geometry in Religious Architecture of the Greek and Latin Middle Ages

Nigel Hiscock
Oxford Brookes University, UK

ASHGATE

Published by
Ashgate Publishing Limited
Gower House
Croft Road
Aldershot
Hampshire GU11 3HR
England

Ashgate Publishing Company
Suite 420
101 Cherry Street
Burlington, VT 05401-4405
USA

Ashgate website: http://www.ashgate.com

British Library Cataloguing in Publication Data
Hiscock, Nigel, 1940–
The symbol at your door: number and geometry in religious architecture of the Greek and Latin Middle Ages
1. Church architecture 2. Symbolism in architecture 3. Geometry in architecture
4. Architecture – Composition, proportion, etc. 5. Architecture, Medieval
6. Architecture, Ancient – Greece 7. Architecture, Ancient – Rome
I. Title
726.5'1'094'0902

Library of Congress Cataloging-in-Publication Data
Hiscock, Nigel, 1940–
The symbol at your door: number and geometry in religious architecture of the Greek and Latin Middle Ages / Nigel Hiscock.
p. cm.
Includes bibliographical references and index.
ISBN 0-7546-6300-0 (alk. paper)
1. Symbolism in architecture. 2. Geometry in architecture. 3. Religious architecture.
4. Architecture, Medieval. 5. Architecture, Byzantine. I. Title.

NA2500.H57 2007
725.509'02–dc22 2007010748

ISBN 978-0-7546-6300-3

Typeset by Manton Typesetters, Louth, Lincolnshire, UK.

Printed and bound in Great Britain by MPG Books Ltd, Bodmin, Cornwall.

Contents

List of Figures

All figures not credited to external sources are by the author.

Acknowledgements

The continuing growth in medieval studies is undoubtedly gratifying, but it generates a volume of research and publication of which many scholars find it difficult to keep fully abreast in their own field, let alone be able to keep an eye on work being done in neighbouring fields. Yet the integrity of medieval culture requires that it be studied in an integrated way in order to approach a true understanding of it. More than multidisciplinary, medieval scholarship needs to be genuinely interdisciplinary. This, together with the difficulty of keeping up to date with developments across the various fields makes it a circle correspondingly difficult to square. Speaking of geometry, an architect's training, such as I had, can help, for the practice of architecture integrates different disciplines into the process of design and construction, disciplines as diverse as cultural, environmental, structural, constructional, legal, and financial, for all of which an architect needs a working understanding. So just as an architect necessarily consults, so does one who is enquiring into medieval architecture, and I continue to be both dependent and thankful for the advice I receive.

Since this present study is intended as a companion to my book, *The Wise Master Builder*, and would not have been achievable without it, it follows that I remain most grateful to everyone who helped me with my earlier volume. In addition to them, I have once again been privileged in the help I have received during this investigation. Since the object of conferences is to confer, I have benefited greatly from conversations with colleagues too numerous to mention, at Kalamazoo and Leeds each year as well as elsewhere, but who notably include, as far as architecture is concerned, Carl Barnes, Bill Clark, Peter Fergusson, Dick Jones, Martin Kemp, Christopher Norton, Richard Schneider, and Harry Titus, and for other matters, Bert Hall and Sophie Page, to name but a few. Others have been generous in sharing their work and exchanging observations, and include Rob Bork for general methodology and the geometry of towers and spires, Karen Britt for St John's Basilica at Ephesos, Paul Crossley for chapter houses and much else, Jean Givens for Southwell Minster, Kalliroe Linardou for the Pentecost miniature in the *Homilies* of Jakobos, Charles McClendon for Germigny-des-Prés, Stephen Murray for Amiens Cathedral, Ellen Shortell for St Quentin, Magdalena Skoblar for baptisteries and hexagonal fonts, Charlotte Stanford for Erwin, supposedly of Steinbach, and Nancy Wu for Reims Cathedral. Bill Clark once again, Murray Fraser, Cyril Mango, and Paul Oliver read and commented on large parts of the text, and the publisher's reader made invaluable comments and suggestions for the whole book.

It is always sobering to discover how the nature of interdisciplinary work constantly places the enquirer in the company of others who invariably know more about their subject and so, above all, one is unusually grateful for patient explanations. For medieval chant – that mirror of medieval architecture – and musicology in general, Susan Boynton, John Caldwell, Vivian Ramalingam, Kay Slocum, Chrysogonus Waddell, and David Wulstan have been unfailingly helpful; and so have David Bell and Kallistos Ware for theology; also Jenny Alexander, John Allen, Glyn Coppack, and Stuart Harrison for medieval building technology; for various acts of kindness, I should add Cyril Edwards, Carolyne Larrington, Jen Stebbing, among others; and for time once spent happily secluded in the library of Lincoln Cathedral, my thanks go to Nicholas Bennett.

An investigation such as this, which places texts alongside architecture for their mutual illumination, would not have been possible without the enthusiastic interest and hard work of several translators. Be the texts Latin, French, sixteenth-century German, or seventeenth-century Spanish, Kate Burton, Alexandra Vinall, Olga Vitale, Duncan Wheeler, and especially Timothy Beech conducted textual searches, explored and explained their meaning and, latterly, assisted in securing numerous permissions to reproduce copyright material. Where their translations are used in the text, they are cited in the Notes but, being unpublished until now, not in the Bibliography.

One of the premises of this book is that the evidence for its thesis is visual and abundant, and so the ability to secure reproduction rights was fundamental to demonstrating the argument. Whilst all copyright holders who responded have been cited in the List of Figures, I am particularly indebted to those institutions and authors who granted permission freely, among the latter notably James Ackerman, Painton Cowen, William MacDonald, Carolyn Malone, Lon Shelby, and Lorna Price on behalf of the late Walter Horn.

Also invaluable to this project has been my own institution, Oxford Brookes University, which has extended support beyond my retirement through a visiting research fellowship. In addition to financial assistance and the use of the University's facilities, I should mention various colleagues in the School of the Built Environment for their interest and support; also the library and its inter-library loans service; finally the graphics workshop and the endless patience of Graham Toon in leading me out of the film age and into the digital.

Finally, I continue to owe a debt greater than I can repay to my wife, Vi, for all her interest, curiosity, and advice, and for continuing to share the whole journey.

Nigel Hiscock
November 2007

Prologue

Part One: The Critical Context

> ... especially in architecture are these two things found: that which signifies and that which is signified.
>
> Vitruvius, *De architectura* I. 1. 3.[1]

One reason for the history and theory of architecture being taught together in architecture schools is that they are so completely intertwined as branches of architectural studies. The history of architecture charts its various theories; its theories are exemplified by its history. Moreover, architectural history is a branch of architectural criticism as much as it is a branch of history. It is for this reason perhaps that the perceptions of architectural historians in recent times so often resemble those of architectural practitioners and critics. A case in point is the attitude of both to the question of signification.

Historians accept that a particular reading of history is partly a reflection of the time the reading is made. Thus it can be seen that, from the middle decades of the twentieth century onwards, the reading of medieval architecture was a reflection of first modern, then postmodern thought and criticism, particularly with regard to signification. Since this book is concerned with symbolism, and since its critical context should help to locate it in the present, a brief outline of that context and its effect on the interpretation of medieval architecture is offered before moving to the historical introduction of the book in the final part of this Prologue.

Modernism and the denial of meaning

The modernist school that descended from the French rationalists of the eighteenth and nineteenth centuries held that architecture was an art sufficient unto itself. What architecture communicated was architecture, nothing more or less. When architectural designs arose from planning grids of squares,[2] it was for the very reason that they were believed to signify nothing external to architecture. The implication was that they were free of any association with the symbolism, religion, and superstition so abhorrent to rational humanism.[3] The early days of the Modern Movement saw building and painting composed of rectangular planes and cubes to define form and space, thereby characterizing Modern Art at its most abstract and, by intention, universal.[4] The teaching of the Bauhaus eventually led to the International Style of architecture because its principles were conceived as being universal. Its architecture could be built anywhere because reference to place, along with any other inbuilt meaning, was avoided as irrelevant. Its famous dictum that 'Form follows Function' could have been re-stated as 'Form only follows Function'.[5] To Mies van der Rohe, 'Less is More' and so he restricted himself to the right angle for defining form and space, to rectilinear grids for planning, and to the rationalized measures of industrial production. His grids consisted of squares and other rectangles, the precise purpose and form of each varying for each project to suit the architect's wider objectives. It was important in providing a discipline; it was a means to an end, not an end in itself.

A partial exception to the neutrality of the Miesian method was Le Corbusier,[6] who published his system of design in *Le Modulor* in 1950,[7] which ingeniously combined human measures with the golden section, the latter because of its apparent recurrence in art and nature. While Le Corbusier was working on his *Modulor*, Colin Rowe published 'The mathematics of the ideal villa' in 1947, which was followed two years later by Rudolf Wittkower's *Architectural Principles in the Age of Humanism*. Both were fully in tune with the prevailing interest in human scale and classical proportion, with Wittkower explaining Palladio's designs in terms of Pythagorean and Platonic mathematics and Rowe attempting to show how Palladio's proportions can be found in the work of Le Corbusier. Not surprisingly, the affinity of the Modern Movement with classical principles of design bred an aversion to the medieval which continued, and still continues fallaciously, to be identified with the romantic. When Wittkower treated architecture as embodying the Platonic ideals of musical harmony, human proportion, and their connection to the universal scheme, the architecture he cited was exclusively of the classical tradition, not the medieval. Even when Scholfield produced his *Theory of Proportion in Architecture* in 1958, which was without chronological or stylistic constraints, its medieval content was negligible and was dismissed in a single sentence of his conclusion.[8] In true modernist spirit, he ignored the question of symbolism altogether, instead making his an account of the mathematics of visual proportion.[9]

According to modernists, where tradition looked back to a past weighed down by obsolete values and beliefs, modernism heralded a fresh start. The intention of its architecture of space, light, form and function was to be free of historical connection and connotation. Notwithstanding the interest of Le Corbusier in proportion and human measures, modernist architects used geometry as a working method, an expression of industrial production, and an abstract ordering principle that meant nothing beyond itself. To a remarkable extent and at the same time, this same attitude to building design was being attributed to medieval master builders by a modernist critique of medieval architecture that can likewise be traced back to the French rationalists of the nineteenth century.

Foremost among these was Eugène Viollet-le-Duc, whose account of medieval architecture is avowedly rationalist, his great work published between 1858 and 1868 being entitled *Le dictionnaire raisonné de l'architecture française*.[10] Although he does have an entry in it for 'symbol', which he partly defines as concealing a metaphysical idea, and he even cites a thirteenth-century work on signification by Durandus,[11] the overwhelming thrust of his analysis of medieval architecture is as a practical response to functional need. Accordingly, geometry was applied to planning and structure as a practical procedure, and vaulting was developed to make its setting-out, construction, and performance more efficient, just as fortifications were improved to meet the progressive threats of siege warfare. His extensive section on the cathedral consists of a digest of different French cathedrals, each with its own plan, yet his curiosity in proportion is mainly confined to the simple application of triangular figures and diagonals to elevations and sections, his interest being in their effect on the performance of Gothic structure.[12]

This is not to suggest that the rationalist school had it all its own way, as some of the literature of William Lethaby and others demonstrates. Yet Lethaby's *Architecture, Mysticism, and Myth*, published in 1891, along with the writings of Baring Gould and others,[13] is very much a miscellany of antiquarian curiosities typical of the Victorian age, rather than a systematic, substantiated treatment of ritual and symbolism. Indeed, when he came to write his history of medieval architecture in 1904, entitled *Mediæval Art*, it was primarily an account of the transmission of architectural ideas to do with typology and building technique. To an even greater extent, Simpson's *History of Architectural Development*, which was first published in three volumes between 1904 and 1911 and repeatedly re-published in various versions for well over half a century, was based on a system of analysis across its volumes devoted to the evolution of architecture in terms of chronology, geography, typology, and the materials and techniques of construction. This was helpful for understanding architecture as physical artefact, but said little about its connection with the beliefs and values it was built to house and express.

For such a connection, it was necessary to go to Germany. In 1902, Joseph Sauer published his monumental *Symbolik des Kirchengebäudes und seiner Ausstattung*, with a new edition coming in 1924. In it, he brought attention to the allegorical interpretations of churches and liturgy by Honorius, Sicardus, and Durandus in the twelfth and thirteenth centuries, yet he believed that these had become detached from their patristic origins. Nevertheless, he followed this with a comprehensive account of church symbolism in medieval literature and in their design and decoration. From the 1940s, with modernism still at its height, the expressive connection between belief and architecture began to be voiced again by scholars, including a number of German emigrés such as Krautheimer, von Simson, and Panofsky. An important landmark was Krautheimer's article, 'Introduction to an "Iconography of Medieval Architecture"', published in 1942, in which numerology and geometry were advanced as the basis of architectural symbolism. Citing, in particular, cruciform churches and octagonal baptisteries, it was obvious to Krautheimer that these structures were intended to convey meaning.[14] This was followed by Frankl in 1945 with his article about the secret of medieval masons, which put forward the equilateral triangle and the square as key figures in architectural design because they had been sanctified by Plato in his *Timaeus*.[15] Consequently, according to him, Gothic architects used them in designing their cathedrals in order to guarantee beauty and perfection.[16] In 1949, Ackerman published his article on the deliberations in Milan at the turn of the fifteenth century over the design of its cathedral, which revealed that the equilateral triangle and the square had been considered.[17] This was taken up by Maria Velte in 1951 in *Die Anwendung der Quadratur und Triangulatur bei der Grund- und Aufrissgestaltung der gotischen Kirchen*, which traced the use of the square in German church towers and spires, and conjectured the use of both figures in plan design. The metaphysical beliefs of Antiquity and their transmission to the Middle Ages were developed by Otto von Simson in 1956, who applied them to Suger's Abbey of St Denis and Chartres Cathedral. In the following year, Panofsky attempted to establish a connection between scholarly learning and architectural design in order to explain how such ideas could have come to be expressed in architecture and in 1963 Conant published a number of schematic layouts generated by number theory and geometry, to which he claimed the plans of the second and third abbey churches of Cluny answered and by which it could be interpreted. Just over a decade earlier, Günter Bandmann, who had remained in Germany, published his *Mittelalterliche Architektur als Bedeutungsträger* in 1951. Building on the work of Krautheimer and others, he proposed that it was the meaning embodied within forms that determined their reception, which had resulted in the Romanesque architecture of the Holy Roman Empire having become a derivation of the Roman *imperium*.[18] At the time, his interest in meaning was not generally shared in Germany, but it is an indication of the current interest being taken in the subject that its translation into English was planned in the mid-1990s and published in 2005.

To pragmatists, however, a number of questions were being begged, the most fundamental being whether master builders and masons actually thought and worked in the manner that was being presumed. To interpret a building in a particular way was one thing, to suggest that this was also the intention of the designer was quite another. What did builders know? How did they think? Since theirs was a craft that was taught through an oral tradition by one generation to the next, where did they obtain the advanced metaphysical ideas they were supposed to be expressing? If, instead, this was handed to them by their patrons, what form did such programming take? And where is the evidence?[19]

The reality and importance of signification in the Middle Ages were not being seriously doubted by others. Art historians, musicologists, liturgiologists and literary historians readily acknowledged the language of symbolism in medieval religious culture, and so did many architectural historians. But to an influential group of them, this was simply something medieval masons did not do, and certainly not with geometry. The teaching of medieval architecture, especially in the Anglo-American world, centred on the building as artefact. The approach was archaeological; the dissertation was a building to be studied, not a thesis to be tested. Issues such as ideas and design theory, being invisible, were ignored and left for others. It was from this environment, during the 1960s and early 1970s, as a reaction against the theories of Frankl, von Simson, Panofsky and others, that Shelby for example asserted that the education of masons was empirical and utilitarian,[20] that it was futile to search for the supposed secret of the masons, or believe it to be esoteric,[21] or universal in significance, for their geometry was extremely simple.[22] The record showed that it consisted of squares, and the rotating of squares within squares known as quadrature. Bucher similarly argued that the masons' use of geometry was practical, without theoretical connotation,[23] that the geometric figures and proportions which they employed were used for their own sake, removed from any connection with symbolism, numerology, or mysticism.[24] The design method of medieval architects was characterized as square schematism and consisted of the addition and subdivision of modules, which comprised the square, the golden rectangle, and the $1 : \sqrt{2}$ rectangle.[25] In asserting the medieval use of geometry as being a purely practical procedure, Bucher[26] supported Shelby,[27] and Harvey[28] supported Bucher.[29] In sum, the use of geometry was simply part of lodge practice; it was variously described as practical, constructive and prescriptive. And it was precisely at this time, during the latter days of the Modern Movement in the 1960s, that architectural practices were embracing a design method based on modular co-ordination and which defined itself as problem-solving, in exactly the way being ascribed by historians at the time to medieval builders in erecting their cathedrals.

Postmodernism and the retrieval of meaning

More than forty years on, it is still possible to encounter the odd unreconstructed modernist in the bowels of quite famous institutions, still in denial that meaning was ever in the mind of master builders when planning and elevating their cathedrals. The authority of Vitruvius is called upon to validate claims that certain ratios and proportions were used devoid of meaning, while the assertion by him that architecture consists of 'that which signifies and that which is signified' is ignored.[30] Yet if modernism entailed the denial of meaning, postmodernism is to do with the retrieval of meaning and its first seeds were being sown as Shelby and others were still writing. In 1966, Robert Venturi published his seminal book, *Complexity and Contradiction in Architecture* and, where modernists had called for the rejection of the past, Venturi returned to it for guidance. In rejecting the puritanical approach of modernist architects, he accused them of reducing architecture to diagrams by oversimplifying their programme. He turned their maxim on its head, proclaiming 'Less is a bore'. Richness and ambiguity are to be preferred to clarity, visual perception needs to be exploited, with multiple layers of meaning permitting plural interpretations.[31] This was followed by other publications reacting to the inadequacies of the modernist manifesto, and calling instead for a return to the past as a reference for contemporary re-interpretation.[32]

The repudiation of modernism for its anonymity and, for that matter, of atonality in serial music for the same reason, recognized the emotional and psychological importance of association above that of autonomy. A large triangular plane mounted above part of a building's ground floor will signify its entrance because it will be associated in the mind of a visitor with the pediment of a portico. Similarly, quotations and ironic pastiche in contemporary music have to do with recollection. In postmodern architecture, connection with place becomes important once more and the intention to communicate meaning is assumed. As a result, the eye and the mind were being engaged, and memory evoked to associate form with symbol in order to convey meaning. Similarly, throughout the 1990s, in their continuing symbiosis with contemporary architectural theory and practice, critiques of medieval architectural history began reflecting postmodern interest in memory and meaning, subjective experience, and association with place.

An interesting comparison was made in *The Craft of Thought* by Mary Carruthers in 2000 between the medieval use of memory by monks and masons, and its connection with imaginary and real architecture.[33] Masons acquired their craft through oral instruction, the learning of exercises, and by practising and imitating their masters. Monks learned their texts by following their own masters and the church fathers, using formulae and memorizing techniques acquired from the study of rhetoric. A familiar building was imagined and material mentally placed in its different rooms, which were connected by a mental map of recollected routes. By the twelfth century, the idea of the building itself became imaginary, and monastic. Qualities were associated with particular spaces, such as happiness with the cloister garden, weakness with the infirmary. The arches of imagined arcading served as frames for remembered texts, just as drawings of them framed the texts of canon tables in manuscripts.[34] Given the manner in which the experience, memory, and imagining of religious architecture merged in the monastic mind, the frequent visions of architecture which led to actual construction, most famously Gunzo's dream and Cluny III, were only to be expected.[35] In his article, 'The man from inner space' in 1998, Paul Crossley shows that the context and placement of altars in a church choir could be read in a liturgical sequence of interrelated themes, combining their dedications, feasts, display of relics, and religious associations, representing both a spatial and devotional journey simultaneously in the church and in the mind.[36] The church's structure of bays and sequence of images provided points for prayer and commemoration along a processional route, each location articulated by pier, arch and vault as a cell within the greater space, and each possessing its own sense of place and content through the event or person commemorated, thereby functioning as a prompt for contemplation.[37]

The focus, it may be seen, has moved from the modernist view of architecture as object, to architecture as a background to subjective experience. In this regard, it has been suggested that the connections made by architectural geometry between thinking, imagination, drawing, building, and eye as an experiential sequence, are by projections in space wherein the relation of architecture to geometry is to be found.[38] Something similar to this has been proposed as an explanation for the re-ordering of urban space around the cathedral and old palace in thirteenth- and fourteenth-century Florence.[39] Trachtenberg's *Dominion of the Eye*, published in 1997, was prompted by observations that bring together spectator, space and monument in a unified scenographic experience.[40] It was found that the Piazza del Duomo and the Piazza della Signoria were enlarged and regularized by the re-alignment of the buildings surrounding them, so that their building lines were made either parallel or perpendicular to the external walls of the cathedral and the old palace. It was argued that the Piazza della Signoria was re-configured as a close approximation to the geometry of two squares and a triangle, with the result that the monument impressed itself on the form of the space around it; the space acquired a formal geometric order; and controlled views of the monument were constructed at entry points into the space, analogous to the portrayal of architecture and urban space in contemporary painting.[41]

The inference drawn is that the geometry of the square was used both in the creation of formal civic space and in the controlled viewing of it and its buildings, the object being to project the authority of the church and state onto the individual citizen. Thus, piazza and palazzo combined as a single scenographic entity, equating civic space with civic power and thence civic order. The formality of the imposed geometry echoed that of Plato in his equation of political order with universal order, the formal rectitude of the piazza literally underlined by being paved as a vast rectilinear grid.[42]

Unlike the square schematism proposed in the 1960s and 1970s by Shelby, Bucher and others as being nothing other than a practical expedient, here the geometry of the square is posited in an application to urban planning and scenography that both possesses and projects meaning, arguing for an importance accorded to visual subjectivity as early as the thirteenth century.[43] The 1990s saw other studies underline the importance of signification, seeking meaning in number, geometry and architectural design. In his *Proportion: Science, Philosophy, Architecture*, published in 1999, Richard Padovan follows Wittkower – whilst challenging some of his conclusions – in relating architecture to cosmological ideas through the mathematics of Pythagoras and Plato, which he extends to the Middle Ages and beyond.[44] Books dealing with architectural design in both the Greek and Latin Middle Ages, in which plan design is interpreted, have appeared with 'meaning' pointedly incorporated in their titles.[45] Recent studies of French churches propose different forms of square schematism for their plans, speculating that the dimensions advanced for their crossings could signify the heavenly city and the perfection of creation.[46] Yet the questions remain. The descriptions of the symbolic content in architecture which survive from the Middle Ages are by churchmen, not master builders, and so it remains possible to argue that, independently of the builders, these were interpretations made of number and geometry in architecture to which the builders attached no meaning themselves. However, what is possible is not necessarily plausible. Only a cursory glance at medieval religious architecture shows that it is replete with all the figures of Platonic geometry – the equilateral triangle, the square, the regular pentagon, and the circle, along with their figurate numbers, 3, 4 and 5, and their derivatives – in architectural form, plan design, the numbering of architectural elements, the design of windows, and in many more instances besides.

Part Two: Structure

Thesis

Taking this to be the case, it seems difficult to believe that architects and builders would only have used number and geometry as mere pattern-making, part of lodge practice and devoid of external meaning, in a process which happened to allow churchmen to interpret the architecture symbolically. If one mind-set working in one way – the ecclesiastic's – was being applied to the work of a mind-set that was working in a completely different way – the builder's – the symbolic associations made by churchmen with the architecture would be no more than fortuitous and haphazard. Bearing this in mind, and how postmodern theory stresses the uncertainties in recovering original meaning, it is an underlying purpose of this study to investigate whether there might be anything systematic in the occurrence of number and geometry in the architecture, and whether this might be corroborated by other factors, such as location, religious function, liturgical practice, metaphysical belief, even popular belief. For if postmodernism teaches anything, it is that it is context which invests the abstract with meaning.

The premise of this investigation therefore is that the historical context of medieval religious architecture suggests that churchmen would have had every reason to express number and geometry in their architecture as part of a programme of intended Christian Platonist symbolism. It will be shown that, in some instances, there is evidence that they did, which in turn indicates that this would also have been the practice in other cases for which no evidence has so far been found. Accordingly, the investigation will attempt to suggest what symbolic intentions could lie behind religious architecture and art, and how these could have been interpreted by others, whether intended or not. In so doing, care will be taken to ensure that any possible meanings that are proposed can be supported by literary and documentary evidence, and that the possible means of achieving them fall within the known competence of the parties involved.

Method of approach

The study will cite examples of the explicit presence of number and geometry, as originating in Neo-Pythagorean and Platonic thought, in the religious architecture of the Greek and Latin Middle Ages. It will also attempt to explain how these examples could have been understood as signifiers at the time, within the terms of surviving medieval texts and by reference to their context. In so doing, it is hoped that this will contribute to the debate about Christian Platonist symbolism in medieval architecture and serve as a companion volume to *The Wise Master Builder* by the present author.[47] This recorded an investigation into plans of medieval abbeys and cathedrals, and it found that they answered to a system of geometric proportioning based on Platonic geometry but, being implicit in the plans, its presence could be open to question. Since the occurrence of number and geometry cited in this current volume is by contrast explicit, its presence is beyond doubt, leaving the way clear to consider whether its use is likely to have been expressive and, if so, what it might have been expressing. In this way, while both volumes have been devised to complement each other, each is a separate study in its own right.

The method adopted for presenting the findings of this investigation will be to summarize in the 'Historical Introduction', which concludes this Prologue, the number theory of the Pythagoreans and the geometry of Plato's cosmology as transmitted to the Middle Ages, in the form of Christian Platonism, and taught in the monastery schools through the liberal arts. This is followed by textual evidence of the motives for expressing Christian doctrine through allegory and images, as taught by Gregory the Great, John of Damascus, Honorius of Autun, and others. A discussion of the possible means by which these ideas could have been used programmatically for architecture will consider the role of patrons and architects, theory and practice, and a possible differentiation between schematic design and constructional design. This section will conclude by returning to the distinction that is necessary to make between original intention and subsequent interpretation, also some problems in evaluating written and oral history in an attempt to gain some understanding of popular belief. An example of the latter will be cited in the form of the creed chant, an excerpt from which this book takes as its title.

The investigation follows in six chapters. The first two deal with the fundamental conceptions of heaven and earth, and of the universal macrocosm and human microcosm, also the expression of both in architectural form through the use of solid geometry. The next three chapters are devoted to the metaphysics and architectural expression of each of the plane figures of Platonic geometry, while the final chapter brings them together in conjunction with the circle as a comprehensive symbol of the Christian universe. Thus Chapter 1 opens with the solid geometry of the sphere and the cube and their representation of heaven and earth as understood in various medieval texts. Prominent among architectural examples is the Great Church of Hagia Sophia in Constantinople, followed by its evident association with Solomon's temple of wisdom. In connection with this, an explanation will be offered for its apparently anomalous column placement. The imagery of the sphere and the cube will then be explored in relation to churches in the form of the Greek Cross on its own and inscribed in a square, also the octagon similarly inscribed. Their form and iconographic programmes will be used to corroborate their declared architectural symbolism.

Chapter 2 is devoted to the interconnected dualities of Christ as God and man, of man as spirit and body, and of the temple as body and building, as well as being a spiritual and material entity. Using textual evidence, the transmission of ideas concerning body and temple will be traced from Antiquity to the medieval association of cruciform man with cruciform church. This will be viewed in parallel with the concept of man as microcosm of the universe. The biblical model offered by Noah's Ark will also be analysed as a further example of associating the human microcosm with sacred structure, leading to an exposition of this relationship in metaphysical and mathematical terms that culminates in their mathematical union.

Having examined number and geometry in the architectural expression of heaven and earth, and of the macrocosm and microcosm, Chapters 3, 4 and 5 consider the occurrence in religious architecture of the equilateral triangle, the square and the pentagon, together with their derivatives and figurate numbers. Chapter 3 will summarize the mathematics and metaphysics of the equilateral triangle, the *vesica piscis* and the hexagon, also the numerology of the numbers 3 and 6, and their association with the Trinity and Creation. This will be set beside their visible expression in architecture and art, leading to the division of circles by 6 and 12, as evidenced by such typologies in popular culture as the wheel of fortune. Chapter 4 outlines the different forms of square schematism in architectural design as attested by medieval documentary evidence and by the biblical models of the New Jerusalem, Moses' Tabernacle, and Solomon's Temple. The mathematics and metaphysics of the square and its derivatives will be summarized, together with their counterparts in the musical consonances. The analysis converges upon the concept of unity, and the essential distinction to be drawn between equality and harmony, findings that could have justified the architectural employment of the square. Chapter 5 commences with an investigation into the number and geometry of the pentagon and continues with their appearance in religious architecture. This brief exposition will serve as an introduction to Chapter 6, which will examine various typologies in architecture and art in which different aspects of belief in the created order of the universe appear to be symbolized.

Thus Chapter 6 sets the 'whole frame of the universe' and its constituent elements as the context for concluding the investigation. In this, the 3 Platonic figures will be seen in conjunction with the circle through the division of circles by their figurate numbers, or multiples of them. Firstly, circular shrines and the radial subdivision of their internal space are analysed, followed by different types of octagonal shrine and, by extension, polygonal chapter houses. The exploration continues with the architectural geometry of chevet design and the various forms of wheel in architecture and art, followed by an examination of geometric tracery in windows. This serves as an introduction to the presence of number and geometry in wheel and rose windows, concluding with an attempt to address the diversity found in their design and placement.

The Epilogue will discuss the survival and loss of Christian Platonist symbolism, which will follow the principal conclusions drawn from the six chapters of the investigation. The findings will include various correlations demonstrated between metaphysical formulae and architectural form, set against contemporary interpretations of architecture consistent with Christian Platonist thought. Evidence of the reception of the same system of thought later in the thirteenth and fourteenth centuries will be evaluated in romance literature and musical developments at the time. The study will end with a summary of the partial loss, survival, and revival of this knowledge adduced from the proceedings of various architectural congresses, the books of Roriczer and Alberti, concluding with an example of symbolism evident in a surviving schematic plan of a church from the end of the Middle Ages.

Terms of reference

From the foregoing outline, it will be apparent that the method of presenting the investigation and its findings is an interplay between the thematic and the chronological, where the thematic takes precedence because the ideas exemplified are relatively timeless. The themes are provided by Pythagorean number theory and Platonic geometry as a system of thought. Its transmission to the Middle Ages is treated historically; its manifestation in architecture and art is treated thematically; within a theme, the treatment may be chronological where appropriate. To illustrate this interplay, it is coincidental that the investigation appears overall to be chronological, commencing with sixth-century Byzantine architecture and concluding with Gothic rose windows of the sixteenth century for, thematically, the Byzantine buildings represent unity expressed by the dome and the cube; the rose windows represent the synthesis of all the Platonic figures within the unity of the circle. At the same time, in viewing circular and polygonal architecture, chronology can be instructive, for it is of undoubted significance that chapter houses evolved through time from the circular to the polygonal, and of probable significance that, beyond a certain time, they were overwhelmingly octagonal.

In an era of micro-specialization, it might be thought reckless for a study to attempt to embrace the Greek and Latin halves of Christendom, and to focus on three centuries within a broader span of fourteen hundred years. Of the numerous themes and typologies, and the countless buildings referred to here, there will be many scholars who have studied and published each in far greater depth than it has been relevant or possible to do here, or even to refer to here. Yet if it is accepted that depth is necessarily achieved at the expense of breadth, so the converse also needs to be accepted. Therefore, rather than challenge the necessity of specialization or its results, this investigation has tried to benefit from them, seeking to add to them a different, broader perspective, one of the symbolism of number and geometry from its transmission from Antiquity to its revival in the Renaissance, as one more critical tool in the understanding and evaluation of medieval religious architecture.

Part Three: Historical Introduction

Pythagoras and Plato

The assertion in Antiquity that Pythagoras (c. 569–500 BC) had declared that 'All is number' and that Plato (c. 429–347 BC) had had inscribed over the portal to his Academy the words, 'Let no one ignorant of geometry enter here'[48] provided the two disciplines by which the universe was understood and explained.[49] The tenets of Plato's cosmology were that the universe had been brought from a state of chaos into a state of order; that this was the work of a creator who was benign; it was accomplished by his application of mathematical laws; it resulted in harmony because its parts were created in proportion to each other and to the whole; an important example of this being that man was fashioned as a microcosm of the universe; and he had been given the capability of apprehending the intelligible, incorporeal world of the universe through the power of his mind and the sensible, corporeal world through his senses.

These beliefs were brought together most completely in Plato's Dialogue *Timaeus*; being transmitted to the Latin Middle Ages by such writers as Chalcidius, Macrobius and Martianus Capella;[50] and made acceptable to Christianity principally through the writings of Augustine (354–430), Boethius (c. 480–524) and Cassiodorus (c. 490–c. 583). *Timaeus* was the only Dialogue of Plato's to enjoy a continuous Latin tradition and it has been observed that every library of importance sought to own a copy.[51] In it, Plato explains the harmonious relationship that was created between the four elements, the universe, and the human microcosm by using number and geometry. This was not easily achieved since, to Greeks, harmony consisted in difference:

> … from such constituents, four in number, the body of the universe was brought into being, coming into concord by means of proportion …
>
> And for shape he gave it that which is fitting … For … the fitting shape would be the figure that comprehends in itself all the figures there are; accordingly, he turned its shape rounded and spherical … a figure the most perfect and uniform of all …
>
> Copying the round shape of the universe, [the gods] confined the two divine revolutions in a spherical body – the head [of the human], as we now call it – which is the divinest part of us and lord over all the rest. To this the gods gave the whole body, when they has assembled it, for its service …
>
> *Timaeus* 32C, 33B, 44D.[52]

Arithmetic

As a result of the transmission and Christian acceptance of the importance of number, Augustine in the fourth century could assert that 'reason is nothing else than number' (*De ordine* II. 18. 48).[53] In the seventh century, Isidore, the bishop of Seville (c. 570–636), wrote: 'Take away the number in all things, and everything perishes' (*Etymologiae* III. 4). In the thirteenth century Robert Grosseteste (c. 1168–1253), who was chancellor of Oxford University and later bishop of Lincoln, acknowledged Augustine's view:

> Measure leads the understanding to the power that contains all things: number to wisdom, since according to Augustine number and wisdom

> are the same thing; weight is a tendency of a thing … that leaves the thing at rest in its proper place and its proper ordering.
>
> *Hexaëmeron* VIII. 4.5.[54]

This is in reference to one of the most frequently quoted beliefs of the Middle Ages about the universal scheme, which is to be found in the apocryphal Book of Wisdom, and which in turn explains why number was so important: 'thou didst order all things by measure and number and weight' (Wisdom XI. 20).[55] A simple example which explains how number, and therefore arithmetic, precedes everything is given by Boethius:

> (Arithmetic) is prior to all not only because God the Creator of the massive structure of the world considered this first discipline as the exemplar of his own thought and established all things in accord with it; or that through numbers of an assigned order all things exhibiting the logic of their maker found concord; but arithmetic is said to be first for this reason, also, because whatever things are prior in nature, it is to these underlying elements that the posterior elements can be referred. … The same thing is seen to occur in geometry and arithmetic. If you take away numbers, in what will consist the triangle, the quadrangle, or whatever else is treated in geometry? All of those things are in the domain of number. If you were to remove the triangle and the quadrangle and all of geometry, still 'three' and 'four' and the terminology of the other numbers would not perish. Again, when I name some geometrical form, in that term the numbers are implicit. But when I say numbers, I have not implied any geometrical form.
>
> *De arithmetica: Praefatio*.[56]

Another example similarly relates number to music in the way that the first four numbers produce unison and the principal harmonies, otherwise known as consonances or musical ratios (Figs 1, 2). Taking a monochord, which consists of a musical string stretched across a movable bridge, if it is tuned so that the bridge divides the string equally, 1 : 1, the two parts of the string will produce the same note, that is, in unison. If the string is divided 1 : 2, the two parts will produce the consonance of diapason, or an octave; when divided 2 : 3, the result is an interval of a fifth, which is the consonance of diapente; and 3 : 4 gives a fourth, which is diatessaron. As noted by Boethius:

> The same relationship which we remarked in geometry can be found in music. The names diatessaron, diapente, and diapason are derived from the names of antecedent numerical terms. …
>
> *De arithmetica* I. 1.[57]

The study of arithmetic, however, had little to do with counting and nothing to do with calculation, which was the subject of *computus*. Arithmetic taught the theory of number. Hugh (1096–1141), the writer and teacher at the abbey of St Victor in Paris, explained:

Fig. 1 The Pythagorean tetract

Fig. 2 Boethius demonstrating a monochord

> The Greek word *ares* means *virtus*, or power, in Latin; and *rithmus* means *numerus*, or number, so that 'arithmetic' means 'the power of number.' And the power of number is this – that all things have been formed in its likeness.
>
> *Didascalicon* II. 7.[58]

The theory and power of numbers were demonstrated by their patterns and meanings. One example of numerical relationships and the inherent harmony to be found in them is given by Augustine when expounding on the first four numbers, upon which the musical ratios are founded (Fig. 1). Because something must consist of a beginning, a middle and an end for it to be whole, 3 is the first whole odd number, consisting as it does of three units with an indivisible middle.

$3 = 1 + 1 + 1$

Similarly 4 is the first whole even number because it consists of three integers with a middle that is divisible.

$4 = 1 + 2 + 1$

Since, $1 + 1 = 2$, which is the next number to 1, and,
$1 + 2 = 3$, which is the next number, but,
$2 + 3 = 5$, which is not the next number,

Augustine reasoned that 'this great harmony is in the first three numbers' (*De musica* I. 12. 22).[59] He then extended the series by the addition of 4, stating that 'one, two, three, four is the most closely connected progression of numbers' (*De musica* I. 12. 23)[60] because,

3 follows 1 and 2, and is the sum of $1 + 2$, whilst,
4 follows 1, 2, 3 and consists of $1 + 3$ and 2×2.

In other words, considering the numbers as a series,

1, 2, 3,

4 equals the sum of the end terms, or extremes, and is the product of the middle term, or mean, when squared.

$1 + 3 = 4$, and $2 \times 2 = 4$

> And this agreement of the extremes with the mean and of the mean with the extremes is by proportion which in Greek is called *analogia*.
>
> *De musica* I. 12. 24.[61]

Finally, the first four numbers were known as the tetract, and the numerical relationships between them were demonstrated by arranging them in descending order in the form of an equilateral triangle (Fig. 1). Most important of all, their sum is ten, the number that contains all the numbers there are.

Accordingly, it was the relationships found between numbers that added to their fundamental importance for, just as numbers were related to each other and were found in things, so they bound all things together in a state of stability. Alan of Lille (c. 1116–1202/3), who studied and taught in Paris, wrote,

> … the whole art of numbers. … bestows its resources, the art which enquires, according to definite laws, into the seeds of things, their compacts, their interpenetration, their causes and their bonds, investigates numbers and every result of theirs by which all things are held fast and are drawn together by their alternations and all things are bound together at once by numbers and keep the peace as agitation disappears. Thus laying bare the secrets … she makes the man her heir, reveals to him all she possesses that can be known, all that her power pours forth, to let him know what is the rationale of numbers, what efficacy and power are in numbers, what force so great holds sway in numbers that a stable bond binds everything by a knot of number.
>
> *Anticlaudianus* III, VII.[62]

Integral with the relationships between numbers are the meanings, or powers, with which numbers were invested and which, according to Augustine, provided a key for understanding God's creation:

> … the theory of number is not to be lightly regarded, since it is made quite clear, in many passages of the holy Scriptures, how highly it is to be valued. It was not for nothing that it was said in praise of God, 'You have ordered all things in measure, number and weight.'
>
> *De civitate Dei* XI. 30.[63]

The meaning of number, as transmitted by the Pythagoreans and adapted by the Church, possessed its own inherent logic similar to that which was demonstrated by Augustine as existing for numerical relationships, and it resulted in a synthesis of the mathematical properties and metaphysical associations of the numbers themselves. Thus according to this tradition, 1, being the generator of all integers, was identified with God, who was the generator of all. Among the host of authors testifying to this, the Syrian mystic Dionysius the Pseudo-Areopagite (fl. c. 500)[64] and John of Damascus (c. 675–c. 750), a monk and prolific writer, were both particularly influential. According to them:

> Every number preexists uniquely in the monad and the monad holds every number in itself singularly.
>
> Dionysius, *De divinis nominibus* V. 6.[65]

> God … is one, perfect, uncircumscribed, the maker of the universe. …
>
> John, *De fide orthodoxa* I. 5.[66]

2 is the first departure from unity and was therefore associated with division and discord. Because it is composed of 2 digits, which lack a middle term, and is therefore not whole, it was regarded as female.[67] In spite of its misogynistic association, several fundamental manifestations of duality were recognized, such as Christ as God and man, and man as soul and body,[68] although, perhaps because of this negative association and of various dualist heresies, they do not appear to have explicitly attached themselves to the broader idea of the dyad.

3 is the first whole number, and is therefore male, and the first that is wholly odd. Not surprisingly, in succession to numerous triads in ancient religions, it soon stood for the Holy Trinity.[69]

4 is the first number that is wholly even and therefore represented equality and stability, thence justice. As Clement of Alexandria (c. 150–c. 215), the Greek philosopher and Christian convert, baldly stated,

> ... righteousness is quadrangular ...
>
> *Stromateis* VI. 12.[70]

Because the universe was believed to exist in a state of equilibrium, it was conceptualized as consisting of 4 elements, divided into the 4 quarters of the compass – even now people speak of the 4 corners of the earth, knowing it to be round – paradise was irrigated by its 4 rivers, time was divided into the 4 seasons of the year, the human microcosm consisted of 4 elements and 4 humours; and when the New Testament began to be established from the second century onwards, the Gospels that were chosen as canonical also numbered 4.[71]

5 stood for marriage, being the sum of the first female and male numbers, 2 + 3. Various forms of marriage which it represented can be identified when it is understood that its properties were interchangeable to some extent with those of 10. For example, whilst 10 was associated with the universe, for reasons which will be explained shortly, 5 also stood for the universe, being the fifth body of the regular polyhedra in succession to those representing the 4 elements, as well as the figurate number of the pentagon, which is also explained below.[72] It was also the number of the human microcosm. Hence there are 5 human senses and the human soul was divided into 5.[73] Being the sum of 2 + 3 underlined how the microcosm embodied both the female and the male. The five-pointed star, or pentagram, was an emblem of identification between the followers of Pythagoras signifying health and their greeting, 'Health to you'.[74] Another marriage of meanings concerned the association of 5 and 10 with the Law. The first 5 Books of the Old Testament, known as the Pentateuch and ascribed to Moses, acquired the status of the Law of Moses[75] and embodied the Decalogue, or Ten Commandments, which were delivered on two tablets of stone. A third marriage joins these two sets of meanings of 5 and 10, namely the universe and the Law, on the grounds that a heavenly state would exist on earth if the Law was kept. To Clement of Alexandria, 'the Decalogue [is] an image of heaven' (*Stromateis* VI. 16).[76]

6 was the number of creation because it is the product of the first female and male numbers, 2×3. It is also the first perfect number, in the sense that it equals the sum of its parts. That is to say,

$$1 \times 2 \times 3 = 1 + 2 + 3 = 6$$ [77]

For this reason, it was believed that God had taken 6 days to create the world because his creation was perfect and 6 was a perfect number. It was also noteworthy that the cube, which represents earth, has 6 sides.[78]

7, it was reasoned, was the virgin number because it alone is neither product nor factor of any other number up to 10. Perhaps it was for this reason that it came to represent the Holy Spirit, rather than the fact that it is the sum of the first wholly odd and wholly even numbers, 3 + 4, which was the explanation offered by Augustine.[79] Akin to this is its association with Wisdom, and the 7 pillars of its temple.[80] Its other-worldly character was further to be found in its connection with the 7 planets[81] and the 7 phases of the moon,[82] also the day of God's rest after the 6 days of creation.[83]

8 is the first cube number, being the product of $2 \times 2 \times 2$, and it represented a new beginning, the journey that leads to heaven, and therefore salvation.[84] Once more, a series of apparently distinct meanings and properties turn out to have unexpected connections, as explained by Clement when interpreting a passage from the Myth of Er in Plato's *Republic*:[85]

> And the Lord's day Plato prophetically speaks of in the tenth book of the Republic, in these words: 'And when seven days have passed to each of them in the meadow, on the eighth day they are to set out and arrive in four days'. By the meadow is to be understood the fixed sphere, as being a mild and genial spot, and the locality of the pious; and by the seven days each motion of the seven planets, and the whole practical art which speeds to the end of rest. But after the wandering orbs the journey leads to heaven, that is, to the eighth motion and day.
>
> *Stromateis* V. 14.[86]

In starting on the eighth day, the journey lasts 4 days and therefore ends on the twelfth, thereby establishing a relationship between the three numbers specific to the idea of the spiritual journey that would find its expression in circular and octagonal shrines.[87] In Plato's geocentric universe, earth was 'the fixed sphere' around which the 7 planets revolved. Thus it could be counted as either the first or eighth sphere. Now the element earth was represented in Plato's abstract model of the universe as a cube, as will also be explained shortly, and this appears to be tied in with the fact that 8 is the first cube number. This was summarized by Clement when he wrote,

> And they call eight a cube, counting the fixed sphere along with the seven revolving ones …
>
> *Stromateis* VI. 16.[88]

The eighth day represents a new beginning after the 'seven days have passed', 'the end of [God's] rest', and marks the start of 'the journey [that] leads to heaven ...' Sunday is both the eighth day of the old week and the first of the new. According to Augustine,

> [8] is signified both by the circumcision on the eighth day in the Old Testament and by the Lord's Resurrection after the Sabbath (which is indeed both the eighth day and the first) ...
>
> *De sermone Domini in monte* I. 4. 12.[89]

By escaping the Flood, Noah's Ark served as a symbol of salvation and renewal, and it was held to be significant that the souls aboard numbered 8.[90] As a result, 8 came to signify baptism and death as preludes to salvation.[91]

9 was revered as the triad multiplied by itself, the religious equivalent being the *Trisagion*, praising God as thrice holy, or repeating the names of the persons of the Trinity 3 times. 9 was also the number of the Muses in Antiquity, who enjoyed the rank of minor goddesses. Although it cannot be stated with certainty, this could betoken an affinity with the 9 orders of angels, for it has been observed that Aristotle would have classified angels as gods. Be this as it may, Dionysius the Pseudo-Areopagite divided the angels into 3 classes of 3.[92]

10, being the Decad, was regarded as perfect because it is the sum of the tetract and it contains all the numbers there are, each with their own powers and their own types of perfection (Fig. 1). In this sense, it is as all-encompassing as the sphere of the universe and was recognized, both for this reason and for being the sum of the tetract, as 'the perfect number in the universe'.[93] By extension, 10 squared, 100, represented totality.[94] As already noted, it was as a model of perfection that 10 was equated with the number of God's Commandments, The Decalogue, which, to Clement, represented 'an image of heaven'. Through its state of perfection therefore, 10 provided the link between the universe and heaven, which, architecturally and iconographically, was to be represented by the dome of the firmament.[95] Beyond the decad, a host of numbers acquired significance but, for the purposes of this study, it may be sufficient to conclude with the number theory surrounding 12, which, perhaps for its duodecimal properties, was hardly less important than 10 as a decimal number.

12 includes the measure and division of time in its associations, as marking the end of the spiritual journey, and as commonly expressed in astrology and the wheel of the zodiac inherited from Antiquity. To Augustine, however, 12 was a mystical number akin to 7, for the one was the product of 3 and 4, the other was the sum. Displaying characteristic ingenuity, he explained that this was because the Apostles had announced the Trinity through the 4 cardinal points of the world, as 3×4.[96] Whatever one may think of such reasoning, this is what was believed at the time, and elsewhere Augustine points to the importance of the Apostles numbering 12 by describing how Judas was replaced. Two candidates were considered – Matthias and Barsabas – who drew lots. Matthias won and joined the 11 Apostles. In other words, it was not thought possible for their number to remain 11, neither could it be allowed

to expand to 13. It had to be made up to 12, a process which, in Augustine's account, also prevented Paul being accorded apostolic status.[97]

An important inducement for early Christianity in accepting the number theory of the ancient world as a foundation for its own beliefs was the recognition that much of it was to be found in both the Hellenic tradition of Pythagoras and Plato and in the Judaic tradition of the Old Testament. Indeed, the correspondence between the two struck some of the early fathers with sufficient force for them to feel compelled to account for it. Clement of Alexandria traced Plato's belief in the immortality of the soul through Pythagoras to Egypt, where Pythagoras had studied for many years. Much of Clement's writing was also devoted to showing how the Greeks, especially Plato, had borrowed from the Hebrews.[98] Similarly, Augustine had Plato studying in Egypt, where he supposed he may have learned Scripture, and he goes on to compare the beginning of Genesis with Plato's *Timaeus*.[99] To this might be added two examples of the way number theory sometimes displays correspondences between the two traditions. The Greek tradition defined 2 as the first departure from unity, representing discord and was female. The Jewish tradition depicts the second human of creation as a female bringing discord to the Garden of Eden. The Greek tradition explains why 2 is female and 3 is male, and therefore why their product, 6, represents creation. It also demonstrates why 6 is mathematically perfect. The Jewish tradition describes how God took 6 days to create the world and how it was good.[100] Even more revealing perhaps, is the correspondence that is apparent in the theory surrounding each number between the mathematics and the metaphysics for, being part of the same universal scheme, they are indivisible.

Geometry

The literal definition of geometry as 'earth measure', *geo-metria*, is not particularly helpful in understanding it fully as a discipline and counterpart of arithmetic. Augustine described it as a tool of reason in observing the universe, distinguishing in so doing between Plato's intelligible and sensible worlds and, interestingly, regarding the creation in terms of design:

> Scanning the earth and the heavens, (reason) realized that nothing please it but beauty; and in beauty, design; and in design, dimensions; and in dimensions, number. It asked itself whether any line or curve or any other form or shape in that realm was of such kind as intelligence comprehended. It found that they were far inferior, and that nothing which the eyes beheld could in any way be compared with what the mind discerned. These distinct and separate realities it also reduced to a branch of learning, and called it geometry. …
>
> *De ordine* II. 15. 42.[101]

In common with arithmetic, geometry combined mathematical properties with metaphysical associations. On the one hand, Euclid (fl. c. 300 BC) described the construction from first principles of geometric figures and their

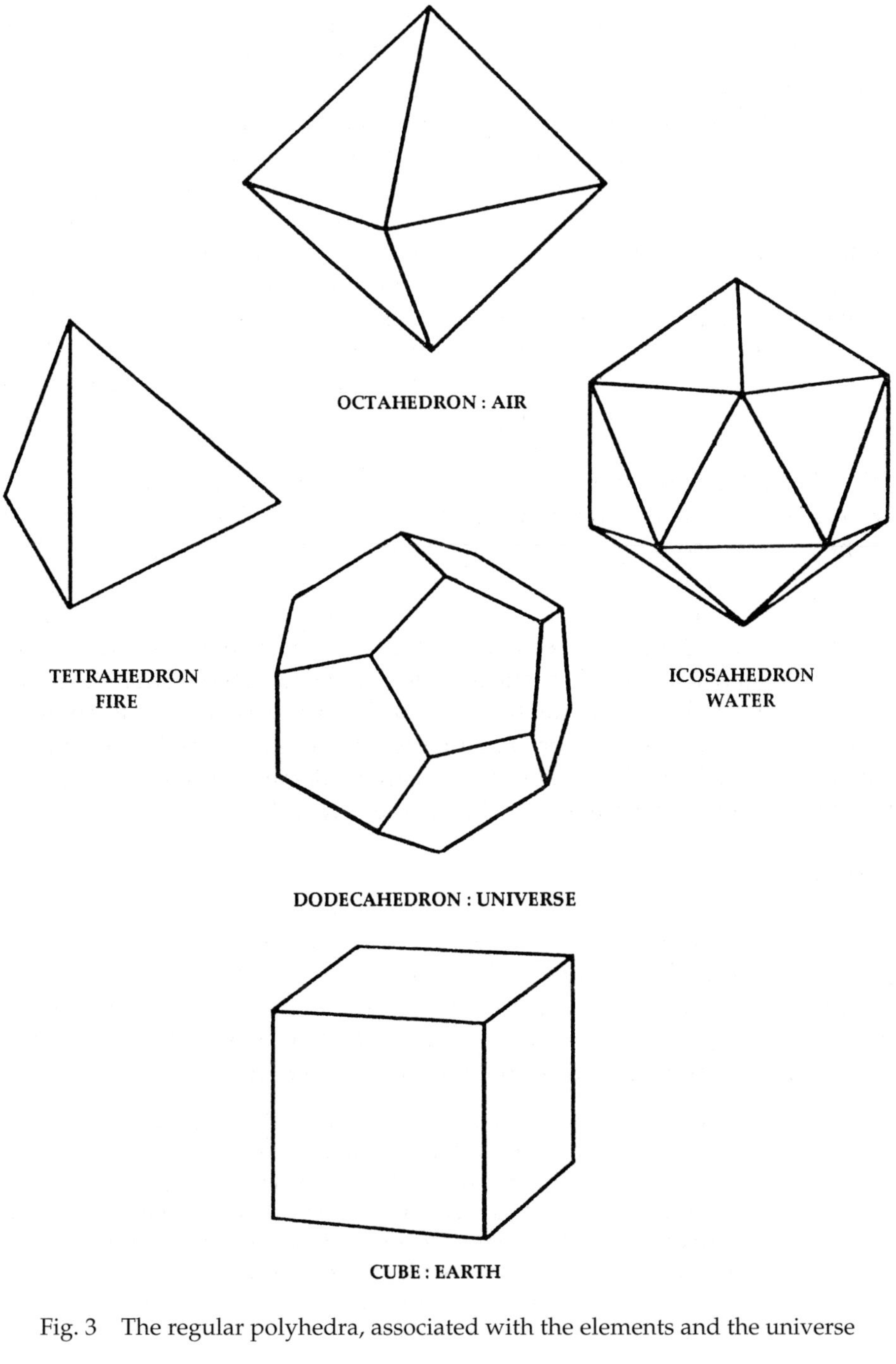

Fig. 3 The regular polyhedra, associated with the elements and the universe

properties. On the other hand, their metaphysical meanings originated in Plato's cosmology, leading Hugh of St Victor in the twelfth century to define the discipline as 'the contemplative delineation of forms … "a fount of perceptions and a source of utterances"' (*Didascalicon* II. 15).[102]

This perception of geometry arose from the conceptual model of the universe that was formulated in Plato's Academy in Athens, which associated the 5 regular polyhedra with the 4 elements and the universe (Fig. 3).[103] The tetrahedron represented fire, the octahedron air, the icosahedron water, and the cube, as already noted, earth. The dodecahedron, which most resembles a sphere, was assigned to the universe, and incorporated all the elements in a similar manner to the way that all the polyhedra could be inscribed within a sphere. As with number theory, their mathematical properties provided the logic for their metaphysics. The tetrahedron, octahedron, and icosahedron are geometrically related by being formed from equilateral triangles – 4, 8 and 20 respectively. The elements they represent are also related, since fire, air, and water are physically interchangeable.[104] They are even chromatically related because Clement of Alexandria records that they were each assigned colours – red for fire, blue for air, and purple for water. Earth, being solid matter, is represented by the stability of the cube and its colour is that of linen – suggesting perhaps the purity produced by the earth.[105] The dodecahedron is formed from 12 pentagons.

Number and geometry

The two disciplines of arithmetic and geometry achieved a union through the association of geometric figures with their figurate numbers. This was demonstrated by arranging numbers into patterns by using pebbles, a practice attributed to the Pythagoreans by Aristotle and still in use when Hugh of St Victor was a boy sixteen centuries later.[106] The simplest of these exercises is to place a pebble at each apex of an imaginary triangle, thereby proving that 3 is a triangular number. Similarly, if pebbles are placed at the corners of an imaginary square and an imaginary pentagon, this will show that 4 is a square number and 5 is pentagonal. The next step is to add pebbles at regular intervals to each side and to the intermediate rows of a given figure, so that the first triangular figure of 3 pebbles becomes enlarged to 6 and then to 10 (Fig. 1).

This latter figure was known as the tetract and would have been used to teach the simple relationships between the first 4 numbers expounded by Augustine.[107] Counting from top to bottom, it can be seen that 1 is unity; 2 lacks a middle and is not whole; 3 has a middle, is whole and odd; 4 is whole and even because its middle is divisible. Likewise, it has already been shown how the first 4 numbers produce the musical ratios (Fig. 2), which can also be read downwards row by row in this same figure as 1 : 2, 2 : 3, and 3 : 4. The tetract also exemplifies the 4 elements of geometry, for 1 is a point; 2 represents a line; 3 is a plane, the triangle being the irreducible of figures; and 4 is solid, the tetrahedron having a triangular base, with the fourth point marking its height, thus making it the irreducible of solids.[108] For these reasons, and above all because,

$$1 + 2 + 3 + 4 = 10,$$

the tetract was especially hallowed, for just as 10 is perfect because it incorporates all numbers, so the tetract embodies 'the most closely connected progression of [the first 4] numbers',[109] also the principal consonances of music, and the elements of geometry. Lucian (c.120–?) was a lecturer and writer on philosophy and he had Pythagoras proclaim in the second century, 'what thou thinkest four is ten, and a perfect triangle, and our oath' (*Vitarum auctio* II. 457).[110]

By a similar process, Plato's construct for the universe may also be expressed by associating the elements with their geometric figures and their figurate numbers (Fig. 4). Accordingly, the equilateral triangle is the plane figure of the tetrahedron, octahedron, and icosahedron representing the atmospheric elements of fire, air, and water, and its figurate number is 3; the square is the plane figure of the cube that is earth, and its figurate number is 4; while 5 is the number of the pentagon, which is the plane figure of the dodecahedron, representing the universe. Expressed in this way, Pythagoras's theorem acquires an additional, fundamental meaning. For the equation,

$$3^2 + 4^2 = 5^2$$

can be interpreted as signifying that the figurate numbers of the atmospheric elements and earth are exactly contained within that of the universe. Bearing in mind that the sum of all three is 50, this must be the intended meaning of Philo Judaeus (c. 20BC–c. 50AD), a Greek-speaking Jew, when writing about the columns inside Moses' Tabernacle:

> … there will then be left that most holy number of fifty, being the power of a rectangular triangle, which is the foundation of the creation of the universe.
>
> *De vita Mosis* III. 3.[111]

The liberal arts

The perceived truths of the universe and its state of created order were taught in the Greek East and the Latin West through the study of the liberal arts, which existed in an early form in Plato's day and were expanded in number by the Romans before being reduced back to their definitive complement of seven.[112] They were divided into two parts, the first being a preparation for studying the second. The literary disciplines of the *trivium* taught how to study: grammar taught the student to read, dialectic taught how to understand, rhetoric how to construct an argument. By mastering the *trivium*, students were equipped to study the mathematical disciplines of the *quadrivium*. These were rationally organized in relation to each other, following most commonly in the East and the West the sequence of arithmetic, music, geometry, and astronomy. As already demonstrated, arithmetic was anterior to everything, and it was defined as dealing with multitude in relation to itself; music dealt with multitude in relation to another multitude, as in the musical ratios; geometry treated of magnitude that is immobile; astronomy was magnitude in motion.[113] It can also be seen that in arithmetic, number is immobile, while

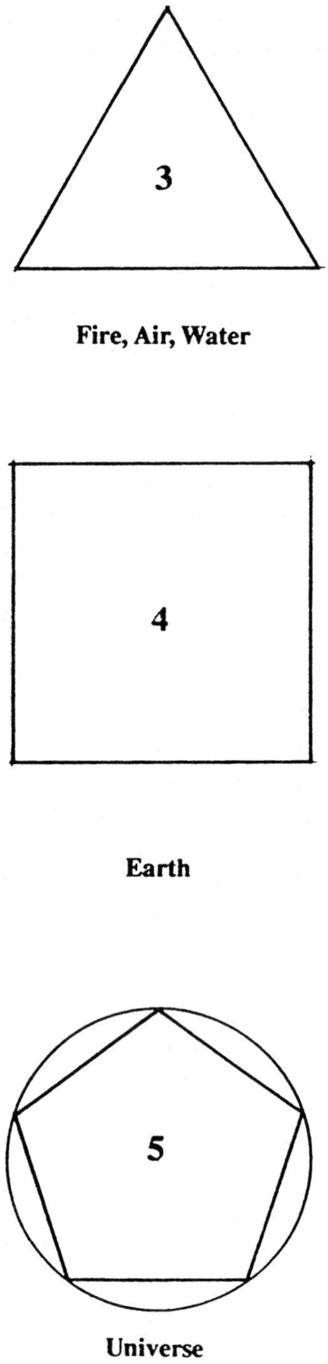

$$3^2 + 4^2 = 5^2$$

Fig. 4 The Platonic figures, their figurate numbers, the elements, and the universe in music it is in motion; also that music is the application of number, astronomy the application of geometry in the configurations and paths of its heavenly bodies, the perfect harmony and unity of which was said to cause the music of the spheres.[114] In other words, these were not the separate subjects of a school curriculum but the *four ways* of apprehending the intelligible universe, which is the meaning of *quadri-vium*.

In the East, the liberal arts had enjoyed a continuing, if uneven, tradition since being taught in Plato's Academy. In the Middle Ages, an education in them was sought after by those destined for the Church and civil service alike, Constantinople possessing one liberal arts school which was, in effect, a palace school, with another located in the courtyard of the Church of the Holy Apostles.[115]

In the West, the acceptance by the Church of liberal arts teaching was largely the result of Augustine's influence, whose writings assume their importance and are permeated by Christian Platonist thought, and that of Boethius, who wrote a treatise on each of them, in part translated from Greek. Their introduction to Western monasticism also followed when Cassiodorus argued their necessity to Christian education and established them in his own monastery.[116] Thereafter their teaching spread throughout monastery schools in the West with the proliferation of numerous copies, summaries and commentaries by such figures as Isidore of Seville in the seventh century, Alcuin of York in the eighth century, and Abbo of Fleury in the tenth.[117] In the twelfth century, the *Heptateuchon* of Thierry (c. 1100–1150), who was chancellor of the school at Chartres, consisted of a collection of books on each of the 7 liberal arts. The first three books of Hugh of St Victor's *Didascalicon*[118] show how the liberal arts illuminate the meaning of scripture and the works of creation.[119] In Alan of Lille's epic tale, *Anticlaudianus*,[120] when a chariot is needed to seek a soul for the perfect man, it is the liberal arts that construct the chariot and instruct the man once his body and soul are joined.[121] Such was the importance of the liberal arts programme to ecclesiastical patrons that it is to be found represented in their architecture, as in the twelfth-century Royal Portal of Chartres Cathedral[122] and in the rose window in Laon Cathedral's north transept at the turn of the thirteenth century.[123]

Image and anagogy

With an abstract construct of the Christian universe to proselytize, the Greek and Latin Churches had every reason to express it in their architecture and art (Fig. 5). The connection was made by the process of signification: as the Church was conceptualized as an image of the world, so it was symbolized by each church in its architecture. This was explained in the East by Maximus the Confessor (c. 580–662), who was for a time abbot of Chrysopolis:

> God's holy Church [is] a figure and image of the entire world composed of visible and invisible essences …
> For the whole spiritual world seems mystically imprinted on the whole sensible world in symbolic forms, for those who are capable of seeing

Fig. 5 Apse mosaic, S. Apollinare in Classe, Ravenna. S. Apollinaris stands as a witness to the Transfiguration

> this, and conversely the whole sensible world is spiritually explained in the mind in the principles which it contains. In the spiritual world it is in principles; in the sensible world it is in figures. …
> Moreover … God's holy Church in itself is a symbol of the sensible world as such, since it possesses the divine sanctuary as heaven and the beauty of the nave as earth.
>
> *Mystagogia* II, III.[124]

The scholar and patriarch of Constantinople, Photius (c. 810–c. 895), described the analogy through his own experience:

> … when … one has … looked into the church itself, with what joy and trepidation and astonishment is one filled! It is as if one had entered heaven itself with no one barring the way from any side, and was illuminated by the beauty in all forms shining all around like so many stars, so is one utterly amazed.
>
> *Homiliae* X. 5.[125]

In the West, Augustine explained the connection between Church and church more pragmatically:

> Whether we call it the 'House of God' or the 'Temple of God,' or the 'City of God,' it is the same thing …
> Indeed this house, the City of God, which is the holy Church, is now being built in the whole world …
>
> *De civitate Dei* VIII. 24, XV. 19.[126]

Honorius of Autun (fl. 1106–1135) was a theologian and writer, and he put this in its simplest terms:

> In the church the Church is symbolized …
>
> *De gemma animae* XXIX.[127]

It was to be expected that teachers and writers would allegorize the sensible in spiritual terms for the benefit of their pupils, and there is evidence that this was also put into practice in church-building. Eusebius (c. 260–c. 340), who was bishop of Caesarea, addressed a panegyric in person to Bishop Paulinus of Tyre upon the church that Paulinus had built. Eusebius describes the embodiment of symbolism as a sequential process, in terms of intent, act, and effect, in this case likening the building to the living temple of the living God. Firstly, he proclaims the potency of Paulinus to create his church as a symbol:

> This living temple, then, of a living God formed out of ourselves, I mean the greatest sanctuary and truly reverend, whose innermost shrine may not be seen by the common eye, for verily holy it is and a holy of holies – who that viewed it would dare to describe? Who is able even to peer into the temple buildings that surround it, save only the great High Priest of the universe, to whom alone it is permitted to search the hidden mysteries of the soul? … looking unto the first as unto a master with the pure eyes of the mind, whatsoever he seeth Him doing, these he useth as patterns and archetypes, and by his workmanship hath wrought their images, as far as in him lieth, into the closest likeness; thus in no wise doth he come behind that Bezalel[128] whom God Himself filled with the spirit of wisdom and understanding and with the knowledge as well of crafts and sciences, and called him to be the workman that should construct the temple of heavenly types in symbolic fashion. After this manner, then, this man also, bearing in his own soul the image of Christ entire, the Word, the Wisdom, the Light, hath formed this magnificent temple of God most high, answering in its nature to the pattern of that which is better, even as the visible answereth to the invisible …

Eusebius follows this with an account of the church's construction.

> Thus, then, the whole area that he enclosed was much larger [than the previous church]. The outer enclosure he made strong with the wall surrounding the whole, so that it might be a most secure defence thereof; while he spread out a porch, great and raised aloft, towards the rays of the rising sun … Now he hath not permitted him that passeth inside the gates to tread forthwith with unhallowed and unwashen feet upon the holy places within; but hath left a space exceeding large between the temple and the first entrances, and adorned it all around with four transverse colonnades, fencing the place into a kind of quadrangular figure, with pillars raised on every side … and in the midst thereof he hath left an open space where men can see the sky … And here he hath placed symbols of sacred purifications, by erecting fountains right opposite the temple, whose copious streams of flowing water supply cleansing to those who are advancing within the sacred precincts. … But verily, passing by this spectacle, he hath thrown open passages to

> the temple by means of innermost porches in still greater numbers, once again under the rays of the sun placing three gates on one side, upon the middle one of which he hath bestowed a height and size that far surpasseth the two on either side …
> Now as to the [basilica] … I deem it superfluous for me to describe here the length and breadth of the edifice, to recount in full the brilliant beauty … and the loftiness that reacheth heaven … Why need I now speak more particularly of the perfect wisdom and art with which the building hath been ordered … ? … having thus completed the temple he adorned it with thrones, very lofty, to do honour unto the presidents, and likewise with benches arranged in order throughout … and … he hath placed in the midst of the holy of holies even the altar, and again surrounded this part also, that the multitude might not tread thereon, with a fence of wooden lattice-work …

Finally, Eusebius demonstrates how the church fulfils its function as a symbol of Christian teaching.

> Building verily in righteousness, he duly divided the whole people according to their several abilities; with some he fenced the outer enclosure … surrounding it with a wall of unerring faith … to others he entrusted the entrances to the house … to … guide the steps of those entering, wherefore they have … been reckoned as gateways of the temple; others he supported with the first outer pillars that are about the quadrangular courtyard, bringing them to their first acquaintance with the letter of the four Gospels. Others he joineth closely to the [basilica] on either side, still indeed under instruction and in the stage of progressing and advancing, yet not far off nor greatly separated from the faithful who possess the divine vision of that which is innermost. Taking from the number of these last the pure souls that have been cleansed like gold by the divine washing, he then supporteth some of them with pillars much greater than the outermost, from the innermost mystic teachings of the Scriptures, while others he illumineth with apertures towards the light. The whole temple he adorneth with a single, mighty gateway, even the praise of the one and only God, the universal King; and on either side of the Father's sovereign power he provideth the secondary beams of the light of Christ and the Holy Spirit. …
> Now there are also in this fane thrones and countless benches and seats, as many as are the souls on which the gifts of the divine spirit find their resting-place; such as long age appeared to the sacred Apostles and those that were with them …
> And the souls of some might be the seats even of angels … But as to the reverend, mighty and unique altar, what might it be save the spotless holy of holies of the common priest of all?
> Such is the great temple which the Word, the great Creator of the universe, hath builded throughout the whole world beneath the sun, forming again this spiritual image upon earth of those vaults beyond the vaults of heaven; so that by the whole creation and by the rational, living creatures upon earth His Father might be honoured and revered. …
>
> *Historia ecclesiastica* X. 4.[129]

It needs to be borne in mind, however, that what may be the case somewhere in the Middle East in the fourth century is not necessarily so in another place, or another time, especially when the dispute over icons is taken into account,[130] for this raged in the Byzantine world for most of the eighth century and half of the ninth, and it specifically questioned the validity of imagery. Nevertheless, when comparing the Greek Middle Ages with the Latin, it seems as easy to exaggerate the differences between them as it is to exaggerate the similarities. Of course the doctrinal and political differences between the two Churches, which led to the Schism between them, and which is traditionally dated to 1054 and continued for the rest of the Middle Ages, were as large and as obvious as the differences in their architecture and art. Yet once the dispute in the East was settled in favour of holy images in 842, the importance of image and allegory was shared by both Churches. Even before the dispute, Gregory the Great (c. 540–604), who had experienced both worlds, explained:

> The picture is exhibited in church, so that those who cannot read may, by looking at the walls, at least read there what they are unable to read in books.
>
> *Epistola ad Serenum* MGH. *Ep.* II. 195.[131]

This was to be echoed by Charlemagne (c. 742–814) when countering what was then the Byzantine position against images:

> ... we allow pictures of the saints in the basilicas, not for adoration, but for the commemoration of events and for the beauty of the walls.
>
> *Capitulare de imaginibus* III. 16.[132]

After the icon dispute, and for the remainder of the Greek Middle Ages, the definitive text of Orthodox theology was the *Πηγη γνωσεωσ*, or *Fount of Knowledge*, a work which was also respected in the West sufficiently for it to be translated into Latin.[133] It had been written in three parts around 743 by John of Damascus, who has already been encountered in this study. The most important part, which was given the Latin title *De fide orthodoxa*, echoes Gregory's words concerning images and recognizes their allegorical function as well:

> Since ... not all know letters ... the Fathers deemed it fit that these [holy] events should be depicted as a sort of memorial and terse reminder. It certainly happens frequently that at times when we do not have the Lord's Passion in mind we may see the image of His crucifixion and, being thus reminded of His saving Passion, fall down and adore. But it is not the material which we adore, but that which is represented. ...
>
> *De fide orthodoxa* IV. 16.[134]

In the West, Gregory's words were elaborated by Honorius of Autun four hundred years later:

> Painting arises from three causes: first, because it is the literature of uneducated men; secondly, in order to adorn the house; and thirdly, in order to recall to mind the lives of those who have gone before.
>
> *De gemma animae* I. 132.[135]

Even more important than the merits of practical instruction to an illiterate congregation was the apprehension of the presence behind the image. Alan of Lille, writing a generation after Honorius, reminded his audience:

> What the tongue cannot tell the picture does: how language, since it fails to reach the essence of God, grows senseless when it tries to express things divine … Sounds die into silence … and words stop quarreling [*sic*] about their connotation; how God himself embraces in himself the names of all things … he conceives everything by means of a trope and by way of a figure …
>
> *Anticlaudianus* V.[136]

The path from figure to God lay in a belief in anagogy, whereby contemplation of the material led the mind to the spiritual. The foremost source for this belief was Dionysius the Pseudo-Areopagite, who has also been cited earlier in this introduction. He wrote at the turn of the sixth century:

> We use whatever appropriate symbols we can for the things of God. With these analogies we are raised upward toward the truth of the mind's vision, a truth which is simple and one. …
>
> *De divinis nominibus* I. 4.[137]

> He revealed all this to us in the sacred pictures of the scriptures so that he might lift us in spirit up through the perceptible to the conceptual, from sacred shapes and symbols to the simple peaks of the hierarchies of heaven.
>
> *De coelesti hierarchia* I. 3.[138]

The spiritual benefit of using the material church anagogically was pointed out by Maximus in the seventh century and, in the twelfth, by Nicholas Mesarites (1163–c. 1220), an official at the Church of Hagia Sophia in Constantinople:

> Whoever has been fortunate enough to have been spiritually and wisely initiated into what is accomplished in church had rendered his soul divine and a veritable church of God. It is perhaps for this reason that the church made by human hands which is its symbolic copy because of the variety of divine things which are in it has been given to us for our guidance toward the highest good.
>
> Maximus, *Mystagogia* V.[139]

> … it is time for us to proceed in our description to the things within the Church and to look at the things there with the eyes of sense and to understand them with the eyes of the spirit. For the spirit is wont to … understand ultimate things and to penetrate to the secret places …

> the paradise which is depicted in the beauty of the Church ... may be opened to it, so that it may enter and gaze on the things within and may ... furnish ... a clear conception ... of the outwardly expressed and inwardly contained meaning.
>
> Mesarites, *Description of the Holy Apostles* XII. 2, 18.[140]

Dionysius was an important source for John of Damascus in the eighth century,[141] who wished his readers,

> to be guided by their sense perceptions up to that which is beyond all sense perception and comprehension, which is He who is the ... Creator of all. 'For by the beauty of his own creatures the creator is by analogy discovered'[142] and 'the invisible things of him from the creation of the world are clearly seen, being understood by the things that are made'.[143]
>
> *Dialectica* I.[144]

John again had Dionysius in mind when writing about symbols in concrete terms:

> The fourth kind of image is when Scripture invents figures, forms and symbols for invisible and incorporeal things, and the latter are represented in bodily form for the sake of a faint understanding of God ... inasmuch as we are unable to contemplate incorporeal beings without figures that correspond to our comprehension, as stated by Dionysius the Areopagite, a man learned in divine things. It is indeed with good reason that forms of the formless ... have been set before us, namely that our condition is unable to rise directly to the contemplation of intelligible things and is in need of aids appropriate to our nature so as to guide us upwards.
>
> *Pro sacris Imaginibus Orationes tres;* III:
> *Adversus eos qui sacras imagines abjiciunt* 21.[145]

It is thought likely that Gregory the Great brought the complete works of Dionysius to the West on his return to Rome around 585, heralding Dionysius's enormous influence on writers in both halves of Christendom. Nearly three centuries later another copy found its way to the royal abbey of St Denis outside Paris, evidently in the mistaken belief that Denis and Dionysius were the same person. The arrival of the Syrian's writings was the result of a gift from the Byzantine emperor to the French king, whereupon they were translated twice into Latin during the ninth century.[146] Abbot Suger of St Denis (c. 1081–1151), who commenced rebuilding the abbey in 1140, described the anagogical import of his work in terms which Dionysius would have recognized when he quoted the verses from the bronze doors in his new west front:

> Bright is the noble work; but being nobly bright, the work
> Should brighten the minds, so that they may travel, through the true lights,
> To the True Light where Christ is the true door.
>
> *De administratione* XXVII.[147]

In adding his new choir to the Carolingian nave, Suger declared:

> Once the new rear part is joined to the part in front,
> The church shines with its middle part brightened.
> For bright is that which is brightly coupled with the bright,
> And bright is the noble edifice which is pervaded by the new light …
>
> *De administratione* XXVIII.[148]

In the choir and chevet of St Denis and elsewhere at the time, a new importance was being given to windows, stained glass, and light, one of which at St Denis Suger typified as 'urging us onward from the material to the immaterial'.[149] Suger's friend, Hugh, of the Augustinian abbey of St Victor in Paris, was one among many who wrote commentaries on Dionysius's works at that time. Writing in the 1120s, Hugh applied Dionysius's anagogy through scholastic method to the contemplation of the word:

> … how profound is the understanding to be sought in the Sacred Writings, in which we come through the word to a concept, through the concept to a thing, through the thing to its idea, and through its idea arrive at the Truth. Because certain less well instructed persons do not take account of this, they suppose that there is nothing subtle in these matters on which to exercise their mental abilities … they do not understand that in Scripture there is anything beyond the bare surface of the letter.
>
> *Didascalicon* V. 3.[150]

Honorius of Autun, writing at the same time, made the same point, but cited architectural form as his exemplar:

> Churches made in the form of a cross show how the people of the Church are crucified by this world; those made round in the form of a circle show that the Church is built throughout the circuit of the globe to become the circle of the crown of eternity through love.
>
> *De gemma animae* XLVII.[151]

Following the construction of his choir in 1144, Suger was to write:

> The midst of the edifice … was suddenly raised aloft by twelve columns representing the number of the Twelve Apostles and, secondarily, by as many columns in the side-aisles signifying the number of the (minor) Prophets, according to the Apostle who buildeth spiritually.
>
> *De consecratione* V.[152]

The association of number with the ordering of architecture was commonplace. In his description of the Church of the Holy Sepulchre in Jerusalem, Eusebius had also likened its ring of 12 pillars to the number of Apostles,[153] as he had the columns of the four-sided atrium at Tyre with the 4 Gospels and its triple portal with the Trinity.[154] As Eusebius was personally addressing Paulinus, his panegyric was doubtless an acknowledgement of Paulinus's own intentions in the design of his church, since he was likely to have had the same associations in mind, their being so commonplace. It might be thought that this would also have been the case with Suger, for he was the author of his own account of his own project, yet the facts suggest something more intriguing. The layout of his choir consists of a double ambulatory with two arcs of, not 12, but 10 round pillars. To make the number up to 12, at least in the inner colonnade, he must have counted the two compound piers east of the crossing as well as the pillars around the apse.[155] Evidently the reason for there being 10 columns is that the chevet is set out with 9 chapels, seven radiating and two rectangular. This is an unusual number, which Suger must have stipulated to his builders, for he lists the saints to whom the chapel altars had been dedicated.[156] Making the number up to 12 in this way is revealing, for he could equally have associated each ring of round pillars with the Ten Commandments. The reason he chose not to suggests a desire on his part to adhere to the accepted type whereby columns, in supporting a vault, were understood to represent the Apostles and fathers of the Church upholding Christ's teaching. Unless it is to be argued that Suger simply could not count to 12, the implications of his artifice would seem to be that the association of the columns with the 12 Apostles was made retrospectively; the determining factor at the time was not to make the columns number 12 but to make the chapels number 9; even though this produced 10 columns, it was not desirable to associate them with the Ten Commandments because the accepted type equated with 12 Apostles; Suger nevertheless wanted the columns to number 12, whether they did or not. The importance of signification to him was such that he had inscribed on the frontal of his high altar a salutary reminder to his monks and, perhaps, to himself:

> That which is signified pleases more than that which signifies.
>
> *De administratione* XXXI.[157]

The architectural programme, patrons, and architects

Since ecclesiastical architecture served as a metaphor variously for the holy Church, the living temple and the Christian universe, and patrons as diverse as Bishop Paulinus in fourth-century Tyre and Abbot Suger in twelfth-century Paris apparently programmed into their projects allegorical content for others to interpret, how was this accomplished?[158] Implicit in this question are the role and status of patrons and their architects. The relationship between the two must have been intriguing, since the ecclesiastical patron looked upon God as the divine architect. John of Damascus asked rhetorically:

> What is it that has ordered the things of heaven and those of earth, the things which move through the air and those which move in the water … ? What is it that combined and arranged them? What is it that set them in motion and put them on their unceasing and unhindered courses? Or is it that they had no architect to set a principle in them all by which the whole universe be moved and controlled? But who is the

> architect of these things? … It is most certainly some other thing than mere chance. What else is this, if it is not God?
>
> *De fide orthodoxa* I. 3.[159]

To be adequately qualified, architects early in the Greek East were expected to acquire an understanding of the created order of the universe through a study of the liberal arts. Not long after Paulinus completed his church in Tyre, the Emperor Constantine (c. 274–337) issued a law calling for students to be recruited to train as architects:[160]

> There is a need of as many architects as possible … Your Sublimity shall encourage to this study those men … who are about eighteen years old and have had a taste of the liberal arts.
>
> *Codex Theodosianus* XIII. 4. 1.[161]

Similarly, at about the same time, the mathematical writer, Pappus of Alexandria (fl. c. 300–c. 350), recalled how,

> … someone who has been trained from a young age in [geometry, arithmetic, astronomy and discourses about nature] and in addition has reached mastery of the aforesaid arts … will be the best architect …
>
> *Collectio mathematica* VIII: *Praefatio*.[162]

It will be seen shortly in this study how the architects of Justinian's cathedral of Hagia Sophia in Constantinople evidently mastered the *quadrivium*, being mathematicians and authors specializing in geometry.[163] In other words, architects were literate and sufficiently qualified to write technical treatises. Consequently, having received an academic education in the liberal arts, they would have been able to understand and implement a patron's brief. This was sometimes conveyed to the architect by handing him a plan. When Gaza Cathedral was to be built in 402, a letter arrived from Empress Eudoxia, the wife of Arcadius, with greetings and a request for prayers:

> On another sheet enclosed in the letter was the plan of the holy church in the form of a cross, such as it appears today by the help of God; and the letter contained instructions that the holy church be built according to this plan.
>
> The holy Bishop had engaged the architect Rufinus from Antioch … He took some chalk and marked the outline of the holy church according to the form of the plan that had been sent by … Eudoxia.
>
> Marcus, *Vita Porphyrii* 75, 78.[164]

Around 560, the design for a martyrium to be built near Antioch was revealed to a monk by Martha, the mother of Symeon the Younger Stylite (521–592), who emulated his predecessor of the same name:

> 'Lo, the great Lady has appeared to me with joyful countenance … and showing me the plan of a chapel having three conches, namely one to the east, and one to the right and one to the left. She explained to me the entire arrangement of the structure and enjoined on me to report

> this to all of you ...' And on the holy day of the Lord God's servant Symeon ... directed that [the outlines of] the triconch chapel be traced in accordance with the form that had been delineated by the Blessed Woman and shown to him.
>
> *Vita sancti Marthae, matris Symeonis stylitae iunioris.*[165]

However, the vicissitudes of the icon dispute and their aftermath brought about several fundamental changes in Byzantine architectural practice, which will be recounted later.[166] Suffice it to note for the present that from the ninth century onwards it appears that the status of architect declined in the East to that of master builder; the term *architekton* virtually disappeared; and, unlike his Western counterparts, he was not depicted in contemporary manuscripts. Instead, instructions appear to have been passed between patron and builder by the patron's secretary, who could even function as a project's overseer. Interestingly, this state of affairs coincided with the apparent adoption of a few standard architectural types, which were widely reproduced with only ancillary variations, and which therefore could have been commissioned and built without the necessity of an architect operating as originator.[167]

The situation in the West, on the other hand, seems to have been the reverse, where the function and even the appellation of architect was sometimes assigned to ecclesiastical patrons early in the Middle Ages, with the lay architect emerging as an identifiable professional from the twelfth century, whereafter his status in society rose.[168] Towards the end of the tenth century, for example, Bishop Æthelwold of Winchester was described as '*theoreticus architectus*', having rebuilt Abingdon Abbey, before going on to build several others around the Fens, including Thorney Abbey in 973.[169] Likewise in the following century, Bishop Argerich of Verdun was 'a good architect and painter' and Benno, the bishop of Osnabruck, was 'an outstanding architect, an expert in masonry work ... [and] planner'.[170] Other ecclesiastics at the time were recorded as if operating as architects. In 934, Archbishop Odo 'directed the assembled craftsmen' in his restoration work at Canterbury; in 969 Bishop Oswald of Worcester passed on 'a beautiful design according to [his] method and plan' for Ramsey Abbey; Anstaeus, a monk who had been schooled in the liberal arts, also produced 'a very beautiful plan' for abbey buildings at Gorze; at the turn of the new millennium, Heriveus, the sacrist at Tours, 'with the Holy Spirit teaching him ... described to the masons how to lay the foundation of a work without equal'; in 1001 Abbot William of Volpiano, who built and rebuilt numerous abbeys in Lombardy, Burgundy, and Normandy, 'with the great genius of his mind', 'hired the master craftsmen and dictated the work [which was] made with a mystical significance' in rebuilding his abbey of St Bénigne in Dijon; and finally, Archbishop Heribert of Cologne was recorded 'imparting ... the science of all building' to his architects in the reconstruction of his abbey at Deutz in 1002.[171] Among others, may also be added Abbot Odilo at Cluny, Bishop Fulbert at Chartres, and Bishop Bernward at Hildesheim.

One point of significance about these activities may be gauged when it is understood that they were part of the Church reforms that were widespread throughout the tenth century in the West under the Ottonian rulers; that the reforms were accompanied by a revival in learning, which included the liberal arts; and that most, if not all, of these clerics were scholars and teachers as well as builders – Æthelwold for example taught the liberal arts at both Abingdon and Winchester,[172] and William urged the study of them at Dijon and elsewhere.[173] Consequently, they were in a position to instruct their builders to produce a building with whatever programmatic, or allegorical content they desired, which as patrons they were entitled to do. Accordingly, Oswald's 'beautiful design' for Ramsey Abbey resulted in a layout 'in the fashion of a cross' after the sign he had made to protect the foundations; Æthelwold's abbey at Thorney was 'tripartite in its unity, to the praise of the Trinity';[174] at the New Minster in Winchester,

> [Abbot] Æthelgar … longing to embark on the course of perfection with his own labours [divided its new tower into 6 stages, being] made up of the sum of its parts, is sufficient for the sacred mysteries and is most perfect by the rules of philosophy …
>
> *Liber vitae* V.[175]

The crypt of St Emmeram's Abbey in Regensburg, which was built in 976,

> [was] very artfully ordered by [Abbot Ramwold, because it] exhibited in threefold and even fourfold notion what was intended. And because the originator of this work loved the holy Trinity and held fast in the faith of the four Gospels he produced thus a kind of credible evidence. The columns, indeed, which hold up this underground church compose wonderfully the duality of his twofold love, namely of God and the neighbour. Also the five altars – in which … relics are arranged … keep in mind foremost respect for the five Books of Moses, and they urge strongly ever to have fivefold circumspection regarding the five bodily senses. The sixth altar, however … announces the perfection of the 'sextuple', comprising everything.
>
> Arnold, *Liber* II. 40.[176]

In the twelfth century, as already noted, Suger wrote that the two arcs of columns around his new choir of St Denis stood the 12 Apostles and minor prophets.[177]

The supposition continues to be made, however, that these are interpretations *ex post facto* and do not necessarily represent the patron's intentions. This may well be the case sometimes, for the search for inner meaning in things was a medieval habit. It will already have been noticed that Augustine displayed this inclination in ascribing the sum of 3 + 4 to the Holy Spirit because 3 is the first whole odd number and 4 is the first that is wholly even; he then explains that 12 is significant as the number of the Apostles because it is the product of 3 × 4, which he justifies elsewhere by citing the Apostles as preaching the Trinity throughout the 4 corners of the world.[178] Suger even went so far as to suggest that the arcs of 10 columns around his choir actually numbered 12 in order to make the association between pillars of the Church and the Apostles.

Finding symbolic connections between the corporeal and incorporeal was a process which William, the abbot of Auberive (†1180) and one of the Cistercian compilers of number mysticism, positively encouraged when he acknowledged that interpretation was partly a matter of personal invention and that many interpretations are possible so long as the faith of the Church is respected.[179] It was after all part of the anagogical function of a church to be a prompt for contemplation leading to higher things, which would be independent of the designer's original intentions, whether it coincided with them or not. As Odo (c. 1116–1161), the abbot of Morimond and the first of the Cistercian compilers, put it,

> The reason why things are represented by other things is that visible things derive from the invisible.
>
> *Analetica numerorum* XVII.[180]

However, it cannot be presumed that all such attributions are a chronicler's interpretation and not a record of the originator's intention, and to insist upon such an argument would in any case risk constructing a false dichotomy. Since a chronicler was usually part of the world he was chronicling, any symbolic connection in his mind was likely to have been in a patron's mind as well. If 3 windows located above a high altar reminded him of the Trinity, it is likely they were placed there for that purpose, since the habit of thought was shared by the community and was commonplace. Finally, in the instances cited above, the chroniclers either assert or imply that they were actually recording the founder's intention and several of the texts were written at the time, or well within living memory of the foundations being made. The description of Thorney Abbey for example was part of its Foundation Charter. Thus it is stated that the abbey buildings at Ramsey were built 'according to the method and plan' of Oswald, which 'he began to construct … in the fashion of a cross', 'since he had protected [the foundations of the church] by the sign of the revered cross'; Æthelwold constructed his abbey at Thorney 'tripartite … to the praise of the Trinity'; the New Minster tower was divided 'by the number of perfection' because Æthelgar '[longed] to embark on the course of perfection with his own labours'; St Emmeram's crypt was 'artfully ordered by [Ramwold]' who 'commanded [its] erection', and it 'exhibited … what was intended' by the meanings attached to the numbers 2 to 6; and it was Suger himself who wrote that his choir 'was suddenly raised aloft by twelve columns representing the number of the Twelve Apostles'. In the light of this, when it was recorded that Odo of Canterbury 'directed [his] assembled craftsmen', Oswald passed on his 'beautiful design according to [his] method and plan', Anstaeus produced his 'beautiful plan', Heriveus 'described to the masons how to lay the foundation', 'with the Holy Spirit teaching him', and when William of Volpiano 'dictated the work … with a mystical significance', 'with the great genius of his mind', and Heribert imparted 'the science of all building to his architects', the evidence is at least suggestive, if not indicative, of clerical patrons conveying an architectural programme to their builders.

Fig. 6 The Divine Architect, creating order from chaos using a pair of dividers

None of this should be surprising for, just as these religious foundations were regarded as models of the Christian universe, so the universe was conceptualized architecturally, and the Creator was repeatedly portrayed as the Divine Architect using the instruments of geometry (Fig. 6). This was at a time, moreover, around the twelfth and thirteenth centuries, when medieval architects were similarly being portrayed with their drawing instruments.

Fig. 7 King and architect. The king issues instructions to his architect, who stands apart from the building site clasping his mason's square and dividers

From the *Eadui Codex* at the turn of the eleventh century,[181] in which the hand of God, bearing scales and proportional dividers, appears to illustrate his ordering of 'all things by measure and number and weight' (Wisdom XI. 20),[182] to the *bibles moralisées* of the late twelfth and early thirteenth centuries, God is shown creating universal order out of chaos by applying the laws of mathematics, specifically geometry, and using the dividers of medieval architects to do so. At the same time, Alan of Lille was putting this into words:

> When God willed to call forth the fabric of the palace of the Universe … as the choice architect of the universe, as the golden constructor of a golden construction … He constructed the marvellous form of the kingdom of the world by the command of His deciding will alone … Accordingly God assigned various species of things to the palace of the Universe and these, though separated by the strife between differing classes, He regulated by agreement from law and order …
>
> *De planctu Naturae* VIII. 4.[183]

In the thirteenth century, Robert Grosseteste appeared to be echoing the words, already cited, of John of Damascus, whose writing he translated:

> I do not understand where [order and beauty in the creatures of creation] come from, if it is not from the supreme measure and number and order, which are to be found unchangeable and eternal in the sublimity of God. … Whenever you see something with measures and numbers and order, look for the craftsman. You will not find one, except where the supreme measure, the supreme number, and the supreme order are: that is with

> God, of whom it was most truly said that he disposed all things with measure, number and weight.
>
> *Hexäemeron* VII. 4. 18.[184]

It was precisely at this time that medieval architects are portrayed as if they were the earthly counterpart of the Divine Architect clasping the same dividers (Fig. 7). These they used in their tracing-houses to inscribe on plaster floors their designs to full size,[185] before cutting templates from them to hand to the masons for execution on site.

It was by the twelfth century that the medieval architect, or master builder, began to emerge in the West as a professional distinct from the rest of the workforce. One such person was Lanfranc, who was rebuilding Modena Cathedral and who was subsequently portrayed, staff in hand, leading a group of visitors towards his building site, complete with disgruntled workmen.[186] In the thirteenth century, the Dominican friar, Nicholas of Biard (fl. mid thirteenth century), complained about the architect being,

> … a chief master who only directs things by word, seldom or never lays hand to the work himself. …
>
> *Distinctiones*.[187]

During the thirteenth century in the West, architects appear to have achieved the full status of lay professional.[188] In such portrayals as already mentioned, they were depicted beside their building sites receiving instructions from kings;[189] their architectural drawings survive from this period;[190] they were commemorated on the pavements of cathedrals and on tombstones in their churches;[191] they were becoming literate, organizing themselves into self-governing bodies of masons with their own statutes, incorporating local lodges under a master lodge for an entire country.[192] Clearly these were professionals as capable of receiving a detailed brief from their patrons as had been their early Christian counterparts prior to the icon dispute.

Returning to the question of the patron's programme, it is easy to imagine patrons providing builders with some form of *schema*, embodying instructions for a building to be tripartite, or cruciform, or round, and supplementing this with a simple justification such as provided by Honorius of Autun, if indeed one were needed. It is equally straightforward to envisage a patron specifying the work, or parts of it, by numbers, such as locating 5 altars in a crypt, dividing a tower into 6 stages, or raising 12 columns around a choir. William Durandus (c. 1230–1296), who was bishop of Mende, effectively provided the allegorical basis for a client's brief when he wrote about the symbolism of churches. Repeating Honorius and his associations between cruciform churches with the crucifixion, and round churches with the circle of the world, he added that Christ is the portal, the 4 walls of the church are built on the teaching of the 4 Evangelists, and its piers are the bishops and doctors who similarly uphold the Church with their teaching.[193] Neither would there be any difficulty in patrons specifying the dimensions of their church, either in terms of numbers that were significant or otherwise. The dimension of 40 feet that was inscribed on the ninth-century plan of St Gall for the width of its nave (Fig. 8) has been explained as possibly signifying the number of days spent by Moses on Mount Sinai or by Christ in the desert, a connection similar to one made by Augustine with the number of days between Christ's Resurrection and Ascension.[194] The Syriac *Testamentum Domini* of the fourth or fifth century sets out the ordering of churches in terms of numbers and dimensions that are significant:

> Let the church be as follows: let it have three entrances for a type of the Trinity. ... Within the front court let there be a *baptisterion* twenty-one cubits in length, for a type of the complete number of the prophets. Let the breadth [be] twelve cubits for a type of those who have been foredetermined to proclaim the Gospel.
>
> *Testamentum Domini* I. 19.[195]

It was also perfectly possible for a patron's *schema* to take the form of a plan, as had been the case in the early centuries in the East. In the seventh century, a Bishop Arculf drew plans of the shrines he had seen in the Holy Land, which he handed to Abbot Adamnan of Iona, who turned his account into *De locis sanctis*.[196] Several copies of this survive from the ninth century, along with the Plan of St Gall, which shows that drawings could incorporate whatever programmatic content a patron wished, including the 40 feet later inscribed on it for the width of its nave. Since there is no evidence that it was ever built, this might well have been intended as a *schema* for other projects to follow as they wished. It was after all sent by one abbot, Heito of Reichenau, to another, Gozbert of St Gall. There are five sketch plans of churches in the thirteenth-century Portfolio of Villard de Honnecourt (fl. 1220s and 1230s) (Fig. 9).[197] If Villard was an architect, as some still believe, then he was in a position to discuss and sketch the requirements for a building with its patron. Indeed, one such sketch is captioned to the effect that it was produced in collaboration with one Pierre of Corbie.[198] If, on the other hand, Villard was a clerk to a building committee, with a keen interest in architecture and the building process, as others believe, then here was a person on the client's side who could sketch plans for an architect to follow.

Four of Villard's sketches are plans of chevets, three of which were recently or currently under construction, the fourth being the Villard-Pierre design. The fifth sketch is a plan of a cruciform church for the Cistercian Order and this stands apart in being unidentified, in consisting of a planning grid of squares and double squares, and is drawn as a near-complete layout (Fig. 78). As a result, this also has the appearance of a schematic design, as distinct from a building plan of a particular project. As if to bear this out, two Cistercian churches followed it very closely in England and France.[199] It is also interesting that the caption draws attention to the grid being made of squares, as if this were novel to Villard, since the grids of his other plans display various proportions. As it happens, an investigation by the present author, which is the antecedent and companion to this volume, shows how a wide range of plans of abbeys and cathedrals up to the thirteenth century answers to geometric

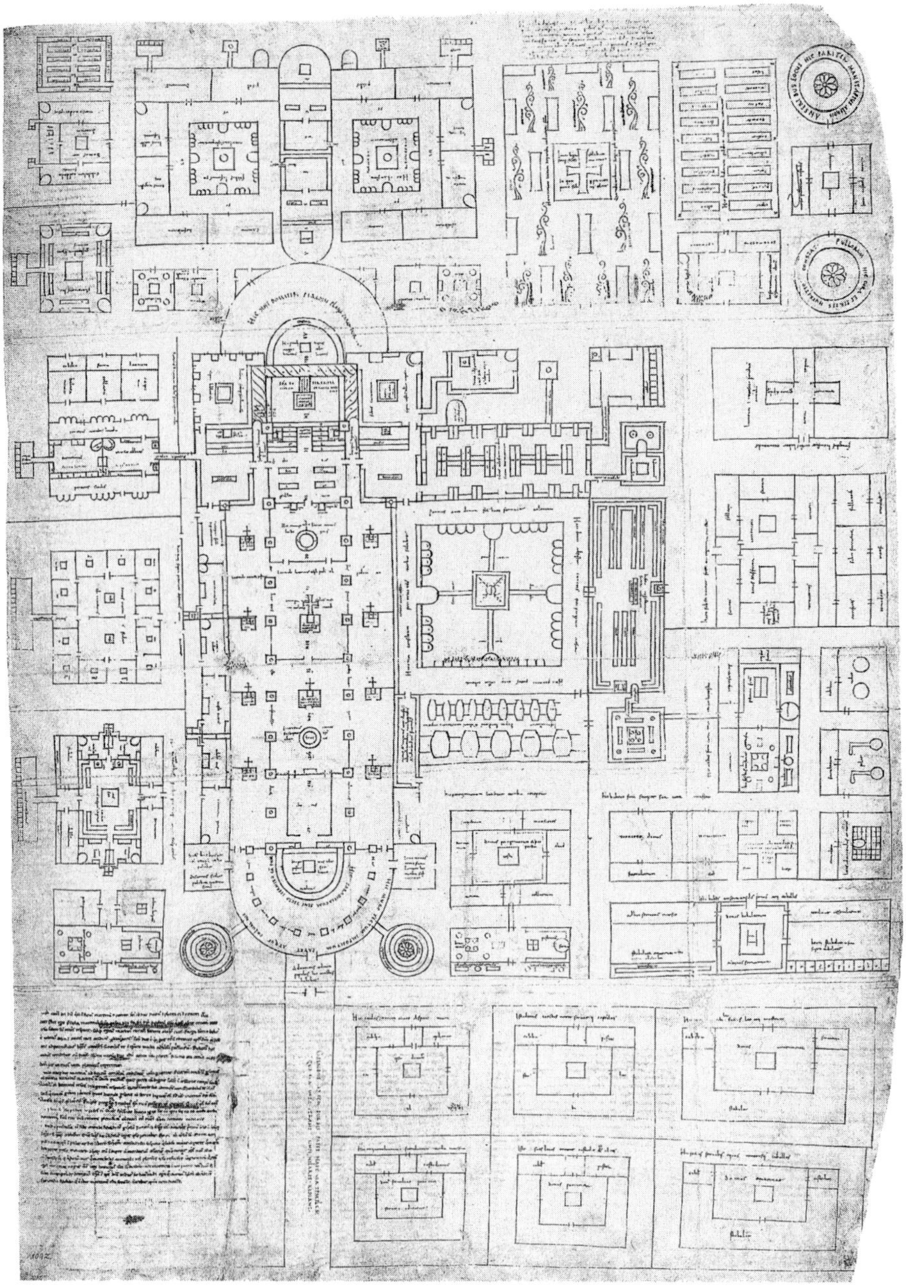

Fig. 8 *The Plan of St Gall*, c. 820. Evidently a master-plan for a complete Benedictine monastery

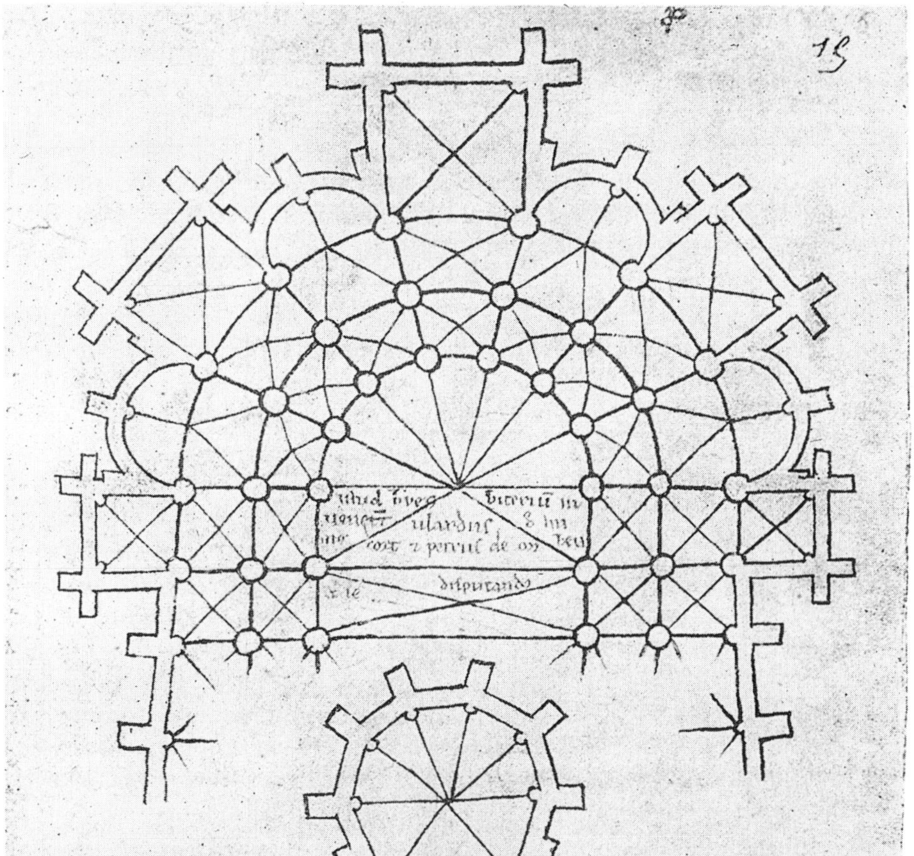

Fig. 9 Church plans, Villard de Honnecourt, Portfolio, fol. 15r. *Top:* A sketch-design for a chevet by Villard and Pierre of Corbie. *Bottom:* The chevet of Meaux Cathedral

proportioning derived from all the figures of Platonic geometry. It also demonstrates various methods, known to the Middle Ages, which could have been used to set out plans, thus proportioned, on site.[200] However, it remains the case that no client instructions have survived until later in the Middle Ages,[201] consequently their content must remain a matter for speculation.

The ability of the architect to carry out instructions, as argued above, cannot be doubted. He could read a plan and he had charge of his lodge, which included overseeing his masons and training apprentices. For most of the masons, whether freemasons, carvers, setters, or layers, and whether lodge-masons or day-workers,[202] their training made them adept at practical geometry, through the use of dividers to inscribe stone for setting out or carving, and the L-shaped mason's square for ensuring the blocks of stone were cut and set square (Fig. 7). The Portfolio of Villard de Honnecourt contains several sketches constructed from the geometric procedure of inscribing and rotating squares within each other known as quadrature.[203] This is employed in the Portfolio both as a guide for drawing faces and groups of human figures, and as a proportioning device for the plans of individual architectural elements, such as a cloister and probably a tower. Towards the end of the Middle Ages, the handbooks of Mathes Roriczer (1430s–1490s), who was the architect of Regensburg Cathedral at the time, and Hans Schmuttermayer (fl. late fifteenth century), a goldsmith, show how quadrature had by then become used for elevating pinnacles and gablets, which Roriczer sets out as an exercise for beginners.[204] In his *Unterweisung*, or Instruction, to his son about how to design and build a choir, Lorenz Lechler (fl. late fifteenth–early sixteenth centuries) uses quadrature as a design module for sizing the details, in his case derived from a given wall thickness, also as a geometric construction for profiling mullions and the jambs of windows and doorways, and for elevating the work (Fig. 10). He explains that this is work that masons can do provided they have the ground plan and dimensions. In other words, along with the templates handed to them by the architect, the square was derived from the plan and was then used as a module of design to dimension, detail and elevate the work. This means that the plan had first to be provided by the architect and Lechler describes how this could also be designed by squaring and by division, the plan of his choir being a double square.[205] But how this might have incorporated the patron's instructions, either then or earlier in the Middle Ages, is barely known. It is this *lacuna* that enabled the modernist view to assert that in the absence of evidence of any other method of design which a master may have used, none is likely to have existed and that the masons' use of geometry was purely practical, derived from the square, and signified nothing beyond itself. However, for masters and masons to be working in one way and churchmen to be thinking in another would require the builders to have been totally isolated from contemporary culture. Yet each mason would presumably have had a Christian upbringing, many if not all would have gone to church and said their prayers, and would undoubtedly have understood that 3 and the triangle symbolized the Trinity, 6 and the hexagram would have reminded them of the 6 days of creation, 12 stood for the 12 Apostles, and that the five-

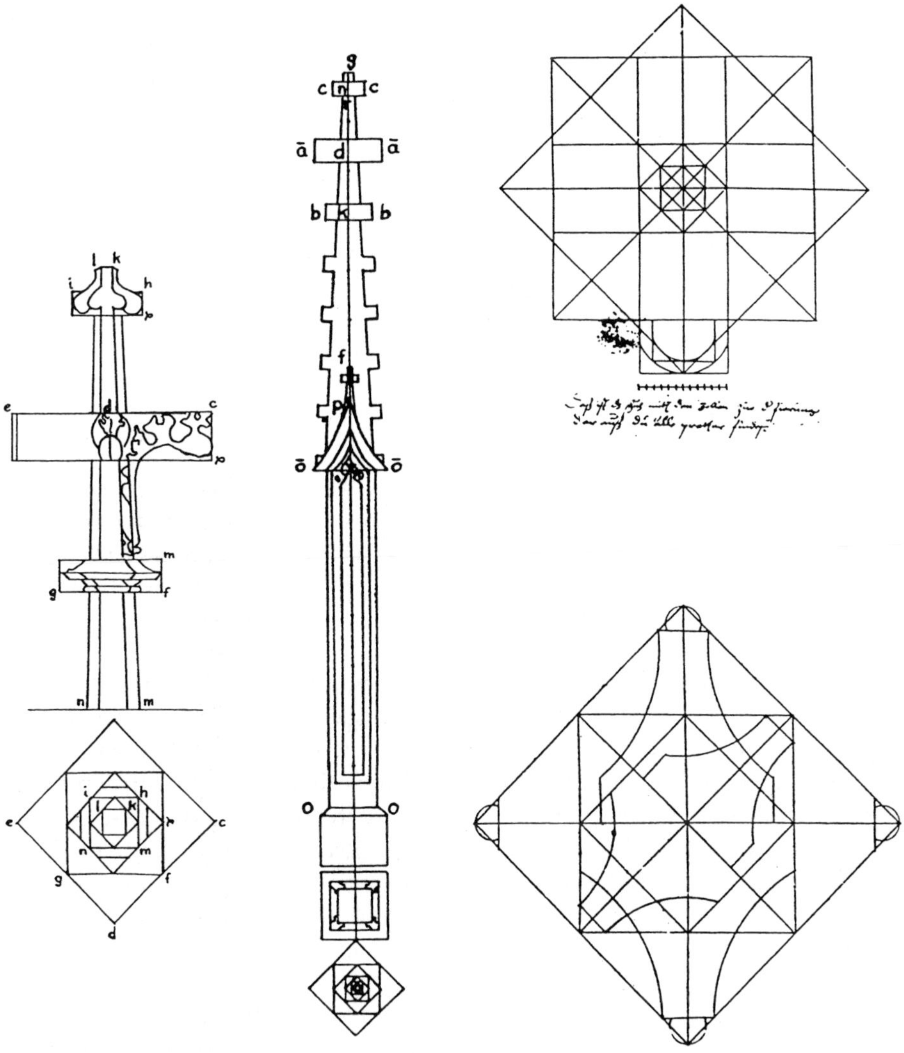

Fig. 10 Examples of quadrature by Roriczer, Schmuttermayer, and Lechler. *Left:* Elevating a gablet from its plan. *Centre:* Elevating a pinnacle from its plan. *Top right:* Obtaining the square, as a module of constructional design, from the wall thickness of the building. *Bottom right:* Profiling window mullions

pointed star averted evil.[206] Even if Suger had instructed his architect to support the vault of his choir on 12 columns, he may not have even needed to explain the reason.

Popular culture

Firm evidence of popular belief in the Middle Ages, however, is scarce for the very reason that it so often lies in the realm of unwritten history, which is supposed to be an oxymoron. Yet it is sometimes possible for evidence to be read between the lines of written history. For example, the growing interest in millennial studies, which the new millennium encouraged, has re-opened the question about the reality or otherwise of apocalyptic fears among the populace at the turn of the previous millennium. With the Church allegedly determined to suppress any thought of the end of the world – and therefore its own end – being imminent, and with the writing of history at the time being the monopoly of churchmen, the possibility appears to have been largely discounted by the Church in both act and report. Nevertheless, it is possible to detect even in its own written record clues to popular anxiety that was probably more widespread than the record suggests.[207] Similarly, it has been conjectured that the popular peace assemblies either side of the year 1000, and the mass worship of relics and surge in pilgrimages which followed, seem to indicate a demotic movement in popular devotion not fully credited to the laity by the Church's own account of events.[208]

Because demotic culture constitutes a valuable and necessary body of evidence that requires it to be taken into account, it is important to try to gauge what it consisted of in a given period. To some extent it is reflected, often unwittingly, in the romance literature of the twelfth and thirteenth centuries surrounding the courts of love, the legends of Arthur and his knights, the quest for the Grail, and the Romance of the Rose. They are all the stuff of fable and by definition openly allegorical. However, they belonged to the castle and the court, if not the cloister, and, although these tales will have enjoyed a vernacular existence around the cottage hearth as well, this illuminates little of the beliefs actually inculcated in its more humble hearers. Other texts can also occasionally provide helpful insights and, for the purpose of this study, four are cited here as examples. They all belong to the fourteenth century and throw light on subjects as diverse as Pyrenean villagers, a Tuscan merchant and his family, a fictional Oxford carpenter, and a legendary knight.[209] In these texts it is possible to detect some of the popular beliefs underlying a range of customs and habits among ordinary folk, where signing the cross and swearing on it punctuated everyday life, before eating, before making contracts, before sleeping, when it was sometimes followed by uttering a spell into the 4 corners of the chamber and across the threshold;[210] a pentagram is a sign of protection on the knight's shield;[211] the moon is consulted for determining a propitious date for a wedding and forecasting rain;[212] fever is treated by taking a sage leaf and saying Our Father and Hail Mary, followed by another two leaves in similar fashion, the 3 leaves having been picked before dawn by a man kneeling and saying 3 Our Fathers and 3 Hail Marys to God and the Trinity;[213] 3 beggars are fed on 3 Fridays by a supplicant to precipitate a pregnancy, or letters written on a belt are traced on the woman's naked belly by a virgin boy, with 3 Our Fathers and 3 Hail Marys incanted to God, the Trinity and St Catherine;[214] after childbirth a coloured candle is lit to the Virgin;[215] in preparation for death, mass should be attended every morning followed by reciting 5 Our Fathers;[216] and a candle is placed above the mouth of the dying, whose soul will be as bright as the light if it is penitent, whence it will go to God.[217]

It may be seen that these practices combine religious devotion, folklore and superstition without commoners necessarily being aware of any difference between them. There can be little doubt, however, given the frequent supplications to God and the Holy Trinity, that doing things by threes was a way of seeking the Trinity's blessing and that the 4 corners of the room that received the carpenter's spell made his room a miniature of the world with its 4 corners. By adding the threshold, the number was made up to 5, evidently as a sign of protection applied to doorways, just as it was, in the form of a pentagram, on the knight's shield. As the number of the human microcosm as well, with its 5 senses and five-fold division of the soul,[218] it is interesting that the preparation of the soul for death involved saying not 3 Our Fathers as in other situations, but 5.

The association of the pentad with protection, as well as other common associations of numbers up to and including 12 are revealed by one of the most popular of creed chants. These are part of the traditional form of verse known as cumulative recitation, which was possibly used for instruction and was often concerned with spells and how to break them in order to complete an undertaking.[219] Commonly included are the properties of numbers, sometimes embodying pre-Christian meanings,[220] whilst creed chants combine number with articles of religious belief. These exist in many versions, Muslim and Hebrew as well as Christian, with many surviving all over Europe, including many parts of Britain.[221] Among the best known is *The Twelve Apostles*, also known as *The Dilly Song*, or *Green Grow the Rushes-O*:

> I'll sing you twelve, oh!
> Green grow the rushes, oh!
> What is your twelve, oh?
> Twelve for the twelve apostles,
> Eleven for the eleven that went up to heaven,
> Ten for the ten commandments,
> Nine for the nine bright shiners,
> Eight for the eight bold rainers,
> Seven for the seven stars in the sky,
> Six for the six proud walkers,
> Five for the symbol at your door,
> Four for the Gospel-makers,
> Three, three for the rivals,
> Two, two for the lilywhite boys, clothèd all in green, oh!
> One and one is all alone, and evermore shall be so.
>
> *The Twelve Apostles*.[222]

This recalls similar exercises, such as those of the Cistercians in the twelfth century and Alcuin's as long ago as the eighth century, in which he set out the biblical meanings of the numbers 10 to 1 as 'the doctrine of numbers, or rather, the comparison which can be found between the ancient law and the authority of the New Testament' (*Epistolae*, 260).[223]

It was only in the early part of the seventeenth century that one version of *The Twelve Apostles* was written down[224] and so, as may be expected from a diverse oral tradition of immeasurable age, many examples of the chant have become thoroughly corrupt, sometimes to the point of nonsense. Yet those which do survive relatively uncorrupted provide an invaluable insight into popular belief. All, for example, agree that the numbers 12 and 10 stand for the Apostles and the Commandments. The nine bright shiners represent the 9 orders of angels of Dionysius. A Danish version associates 8 with the souls saved aboard Noah's ark; most versions agree to an ascription of 7 to the stars, or planets; whilst a Spanish version equates 6 with the days of creation, which might help to explain the inclusion of Solomon's Knot in Spanish window tracery.[225] The traditional Dorset version cited above describes 5 as 'the symbol at your door', thereby providing this book with its title and inspiration. It also accords with the carpenter's spell, already encountered in Chaucer, which he repeated a fifth time across the threshold of his doorway. Other versions of this particular line appear to be corruptions, degenerating for example into 'thimble in the bowl'.[226] Nearly all versions associate 4 with the Gospel-makers; 3 refers to the Trinity in most versions, including the Hereford song, rather than the rivals of the Dorset version, although this is also thought to signify the Trinity, given the medieval sense of rivals actually meaning partners.[227] The 2 lilywhite boys, or babes, are taken to mean Jesus and John the Baptist in childhood, whilst almost all forms of the chant agree with the Dorset version of 1 being all alone and ever more so, signifying God Almighty, the generator of all.[228] In this way the number theory of Antiquity, as adapted by the Church, appears to have been absorbed into popular culture, probably as a means of teaching children how to count by associating number with simple biblical maxims.

Conclusions

To summarize, the number theory of Pythagoras and the geometry of Plato's cosmology, which explained the principles of a perceived universal order, were adapted by the early Church in the form of Christian Platonism and taught in monastery schools through the programme of liberal arts. The need of the Church to teach these truths to its students and to a populace that was largely illiterate led to their transmission in school treatises and their portrayal in religious architecture and art. The evidence of popular culture indicates that some of the rudiments of this teaching were understood by ordinary laypeople, presumably including masons and other artisans involved in the building process, who were able to make simple religious associations with the meaning of numbers and, to some extent, the figures of geometry. It is clear that architects early in the Greek Middle Ages would have been able to receive and implement a patron's brief, sometimes by way of a drawing of a plan, whilst early in the Latin Middle Ages, some reforming abbots and bishops were regarded as architects of their own building projects and that they conveyed some form of architectural programme to their builders. They certainly had the means to do this in a way that could include symbolic content, and their builders likewise had the means to implement it. From the twelfth century onwards, architects in the West are depicted beside their building work, taking instructions from their patrons. Before graduating, their apprenticeship had been shared in the lodge with masons who were trained in practical geometry and who commonly used quadrature for devising their constructional details, work which evidently depended on first receiving the plan and a key dimension from the architect.

How the ground plan embodied the patron's requirements is not known, but it is likely to have been derived from some form of *schema* provided by the patron or commissioning body. It would have been a relatively simple matter for it to have defined the size and architectural form of the work, the layout and positioning of altars and chapels, the location of the chancel in relation to the nave, along with particular numbers of architectural elements, as indicated in the historical examples cited above. The manner of achieving this would have been left to the builders under the supervision of the architect, or master builder, according to their own practices. This suggests a two-stage process involving a schematic design, incorporating the patron's programme in some form or other, as exemplified possibly by the Plan of St Gall and Villard's Cistercian plan, and the constructional design, which was the builders' work in raising it according to current practice.[229] Various methods, for which medieval evidence exists, could have been used to transfer a schematic design, in the form of a ground plan, to the building site. The Plan of St Gall and Villard's sketch plans (Figs 8, 9), together with contemporary accounts of setting out buildings on site (Fig. 11),[230] depict a planning grid representing the axes of walls and arcades, with piers located at their intersections, being laid out across the site with surveyors' cords and pegs. The plan could have been enlarged to full size by modular multiplication, or by the projection of angles, or by numerical ratios approximating to specific proportions (Fig. 12).[231] With the planning grid laid out, the architect would provide the design module on which the construction was to be based, such as the thickness of a particular wall.[232] This would serve as a modular dimension, to be adopted as the side of the geometric square for that project. This was used, through the process of quadrature (Fig. 10), to locate walls over their axis lines, and to size, profile, and elevate the details.[233]

Thus the *schema* might ensure the transmission of tradition, authority, and the unchanging truths of the universal scheme, whilst the constructional design would be progressive, following current practice in building, and current style in the fashioning of details. To return to the elementary examples already cited, churches that were round and cruciform were built throughout Europe and across time. Whilst the form might remain constant, along with such meaning as embodied in the form, each was nevertheless built in the style of its day, whether Byzantine, Carolingian, Romanesque, or Gothic, or at any time within these periods. Likewise, 3 doorways marking the entrance to a church, or 3 windows above an altar, or 12 columns supporting a vault around an altar, would each have been built according to current methods and fashion. A dual process such as this was not only logical, it is difficult to conceive of an alternative. Is it likely, for instance, that a patron would have

Fig. 11 Gunzo's dream, twelfth century. Gunzo dreams of Stephen paying out surveyors' cords for Peter and Paul to lay out the new abbey church at Cluny

had no programmatic requirements, symbolic or otherwise, and would have left the architect and builders to please themselves? Is it likely that an architect would have built a church devoid of symbolic content, divorced from his patron's religious predilections, and confounding literary and documentary evidence to the contrary? Indeed, the two-stage process proposed here seems to be indicated by the record of the great pilgrim church of Santiago de Compostela, which must have been typical of administrative structures for other large-scale building projects. In the years leading up to its foundation ceremony in 1078, two bodies had charge of the work. The building committee administered the project on behalf of Bishop Pelaéz and consisted of Abbot Gundesund and clerics Wicart and Segered, the latter being treasurer, and they would presumably have ensured that instructions were carried out, the cost was monitored and accounts settled. The building team was led by the master builder, Bernard, together with Robert and about fifty masons, who were responsible for the work and its progress, including the organization of labour and the ordering of materials.[234] This was a perfect model for translating a patron's programme into building construction.[235]

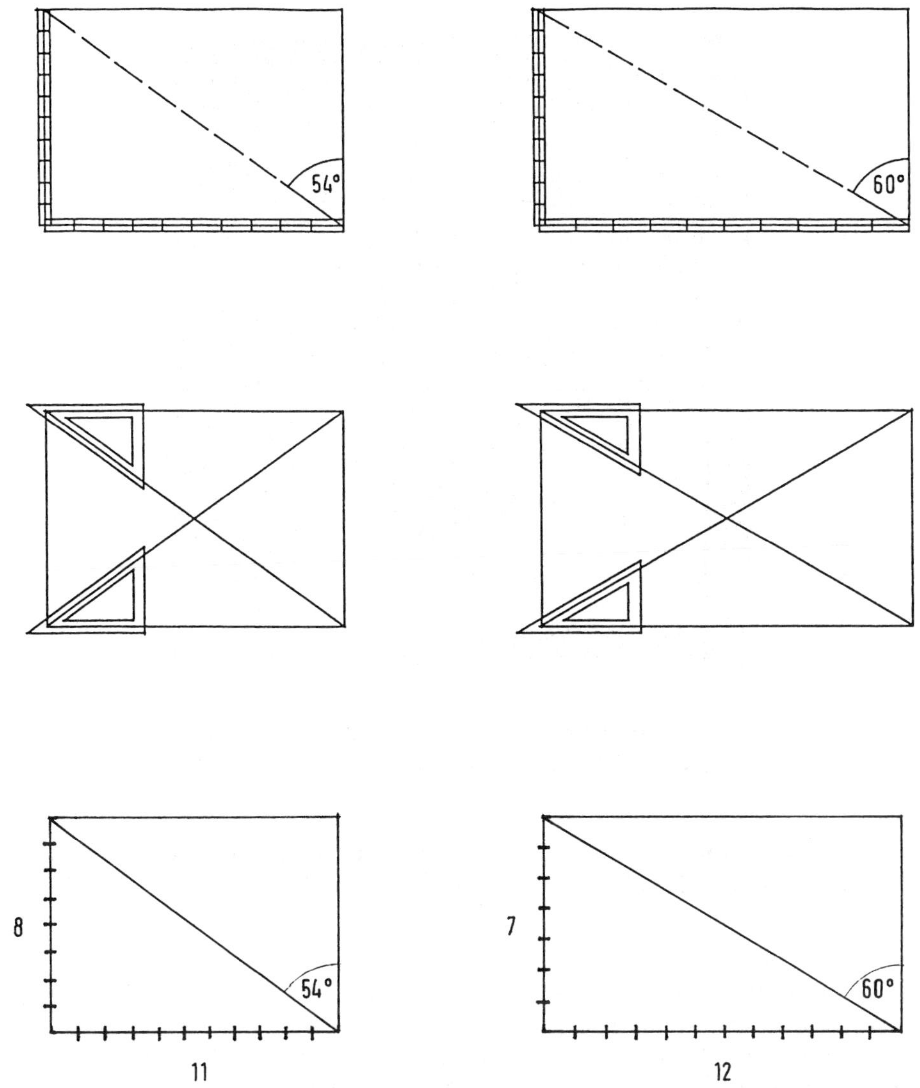

Fig. 12 Translation of schematic plans to site, showing how rectangles proportioned according to the 54° diagonals of a pentagon and the 60° sides of an equilateral triangle can be enlarged from a plan and laid out to full size on site. *Top:* By taking the rectangle from the plan, and enlarging it by a single factor, and marking this on rods or wooden laths for laying out the requisite number of lengths for each side of the rectangle. *Centre:* By taking the rectangle from the plan and reproducing its proportions by projecting the corresponding diagonals on site, using a triangular template. *Bottom:* By using numerical ratios that approximate to the sides of the rectangle

Notes

1 ... *tum maxime etiam in architectura haec duo insunt, quod significatur et quod significat.* Vitruvius (1931), I. 6, 7. For discussion of this, see also note 30.
2 Such as those published by J.-N.-L. Durand in 1809.
3 For a symbolic interpretation of planning grids of squares, see Chapter 4, sections on '*Architectura ad quadratum*' and 'Mathematics and metaphysics of the square and its derivatives'.
4 Examples of this can be seen in Rietveld's Schröder House in 1924 and Mondrian's paintings of the same time. Informing the formal preoccupation with abstraction, the ideology and politics of modernism were concerned with humanity's destiny in a mechanized world, and with the place of belief in a modern society. For example, Mondrian's interest in theosophy led him to recognize common principles underlying various world religions and, to him, abstract art was the expression of these 'great generalities', with the rectangle being the universal form of its expression (Blotkamp, 79). Similarly to van Doesburg, another theosophist member of De Stijl, the square had supplanted the cross as a symbol of universality (Overy, 36).
5 The author of this maxim was Louis Sullivan. Forty years of architectural criticism have led to a re-evaluation of the Modern Movement and it is now recognized that its simplicity of form could only be achieved by deliberately simplifying the definition of its function. See Robert Venturi below.
6 Ernö Goldfinger was another exception, practising in London from the 1930s through to the 70s. He used rectangles of particular proportions, such as the golden rectangle, as an ordering principle in design. However, to Goldfinger they signified nothing other than themselves and their aesthetic pedigree.
7 For a critique of the mathematical fallacy on which the *Modulor* is based, see R. Evans (1995), 279–80. For the antique and medieval connection between the human body and sacred architecture, see Chapter 2.
8 Scholfield (1958), 127.
9 Ibid., v, 1, 3. In another correlation with modernist abstraction, one of the theories examined by Scholfield, that of Hambidge in 1920, represented a mathematical method for producing rectangles of purely abstract proportions, including the golden section. Termed 'dynamic symmetry' by Hambidge from its use in ancient Greek, the sides of these rectangles are incommensurable, typically one being a square root of the other. Yet, as a result, they are commensurable in power. In other words, the squares on the length and width of the rectangle are commensurable in area. Hambidge goes on to demonstrate the presence of these proportions in Greek temples, including the Parthenon, and Greek pottery.
10 See also G. Dehio, *Untersuchungen über das gleichseitige Dreieck als Norm gotischer Proportionen* (Stuttgart, 1894); C. von Drach, *Das Hüttengeheimnis vom gerechten Steinmetzen-grund in seiner entwicklung und bedeutung für die kirchliche baukunst des deutschen mittelalters ...* (Marburg, 1897).
11 Viollet (1864), VIII. 501, 506. Durandus, *Rationale divinorum officiorum*. See Chapter 2, section on 'Cruciform man and his church'.
12 Viollet does include a geometric construction for the chevet of Amiens Cathedral (Vol. II. 331–3) but it demonstrates how it may have been set out, not why, in terms of choice of geometry and numbers of chapels. Similarly, he includes part of a plan of Bourges Cathedral with a grid of squares and diagonals superimposed over it (Vol. VII, 546–7). Of the next generation, von Drach considered the masons'

use of the equilateral triangle to have been practical and, although Gwilt acknowledged certain symbolic connections with geometry as well as the importance of the Platonic figures (for definition, see below), his conclusion when dealing with geometric tracery, was that these figures were chosen for ease in subdividing them (Gwilt, 1039). For interpretations of geometric tracery, see Chapter 6, sections on 'Geometric tracery' and 'The Eyes of the cathedral'.

13 For example, *Strange Survivals* (London, 1892); also William Andrews, *Old Church Lore*, (Hull, 1891) and *The Church Treasury of History, Folk-lore, Custom* ... (London, 1898).

14 Krautheimer (1942), 131.

15 See 'Geometry' in Part Three: Historical Introduction.

16 Frankl (1945), *passim*, 58–9.

17 Ackerman (1949), 89–91, 93, 108. See also introductions to Chapter 3, Chapter 4, and Epilogue.

18 Bandmann's focus in this work is almost exclusively German.

19 See 'Historical Introduction' below, also Hiscock (2000), 158–66.

20 Shelby (1964), 388.

21 Shelby (1970), 24–5.

22 Shelby (1972), 420–21.

23 Bucher (1968), 50.

24 Bucher (1972), 37.

25 Bucher (1968), 50–51; (1972), 37, 43. See Chapter 4, *passim*, especially '*Architectura ad quadratum*'.

26 Bucher (1972), 37, note 2, 42, note 17.

27 Shelby (1972).

28 Harvey (1972), 113.

29 Bucher (1968).

30 Vitruvius I. 1. 3, (1931), I. 7. The commentary on Rowland's translation (1999) argues that Vitruvius is following a convention here, borrowed from natural philosophy, of beginning a discourse with definitions (p. 135). This seems partly borne out by the continuation of Granger's translation:

> That which is signified is the thing proposed about which we speak; that which signifies is the demonstration unfolded in systems of precepts.
>
> Vitruvius (1931), 7.

Another way of putting this seems to be that the signified is the subject of discussion and the terms which refer to it are those which signify it. But then he continues:

> Wherefore a man who is to follow the architectural profession manifestly needs to have experience of both kinds. He must have both a natural gift and also readiness to learn.

It can be seen that his first duality, of subject and reference to subject, does not lead to his second duality, of gift and readiness, which raises several questions. Where is the connection between the two? What does he mean by 'experience of both kinds'? And why in any case is this especially true for architects? If Vitruvius was only making a general point about the need to define terms for discourse, as suggested, this would apply equally to all things. The fact that he singles out architecture 'especially', in relation to signification, seems to imply something more. The commentary mentioned above observes that Vitruvius often takes certain things for granted (p. 11; see also pp. 15–16) and this is also noticeable when he deals with ideas and design. It has been pointed out elsewhere for example that he knew that 6 and 10 were perfect numbers without saying why, just as he understood that buildings should be designed with their parts in proportion to the whole 'after the fashion of the … human body' (Vitruvius III. 1, 2, 4–6; Hiscock (2000), 118). Yet when he comes to describe the proportions of temples and other buildings, he makes no further reference to the human connection (Vitruvius III. 4. 3, IV. 4. 1, V. 1. 2, 8. 2). Perhaps the safest conclusion regarding his reference to signification is that its special connection to the language of architecture is somehow comparable to the importance of definitions to the language of philosophy. For the number theory of 6 and 10 and their relation to human proportions, also for the relationship of human proportions to religious architecture, see Chapter 2, *passim*, and the section on 'Union of the macrocosm and microcosm'.

31 Venturi (1966), 18–20, 22, 24–8.

32 Notable among these were the earlier debates within the TEAM 10 group of architects in 1968. Smithson (1968), 3, 24.

33 See also the collection of medieval texts concerning memory by the same author, *The Book of Memory: A Study of Memory in Medieval Culture*, Cambridge Studies in Medieval Literature, 10 (Cambridge, 1990).

34 Carruthers (2000), 1–2, 7, 13–14, 238, 255, 270.

35 Ibid., 226–7.

36 Crossley (1998), *passim*, 166–7, 170–72, 176–7.

37 Carruthers (2000), 42, 258–61. Curiously, Carruthers does not address the fact of commemoration itself, or religious belief in the living presence of holy figures in sacred space.

38 R. Evans (1995), xxxi. This recalls a description of fractal geometry as existing between the Euclidean dimensions of point, line and plane (M. Batty and P. Longley, 'The Fractal City', in *New Science = New Architecture?* Architectural Design Profile 129 (1997), 74–83: 74. Following Wittkower and Scholfield, Evans's analysis omits the Middle Ages and his observations sometimes appear at variance with each other. Nevertheless, he concludes that in architectural geometry, the geometry is ideal and the architecture functions 'to bring the pure idea to mind' (354). Also the power of symbol transcends knowledge; descriptions of six-pointed stars for example continue in use even though they are not borne out by the way stars actually appear when seen; and domes over Renaissance churches were still read as representing a universe already known to be more complex than that conceptualized by Plato (18, 43). See also Chapter 1.

39 Trachtenberg (1997).

40 Ibid., ix.

41 Ibid., 27–147.

42 Ibid., 163, 178, 181, 214, 216, 252, 256–7, 270.

43 Ibid., ix.

44 Padovan's work is in effect a mathematical history of proportion and its application to architecture in relation to universal meaning. Taking issue with Wittkower, he follows Karl Hopper and the Dutch monk, writer and architect, van der Laan, whose work occupied the latter half of the twentieth century, by inverting the conventional view taken of the universe. In attempting to

understand, the human mind uses its capacity to recognize order, and then imposes this order on nature. It is a postmodern account of proportion, its starting-point being subjective. The mathematics predominantly consist of arithmetic and ratios of whole numbers, even allegedly in the Middle Ages: 'Number, not geometry, rules the Gothic world' (178). This appears to be a false dichotomy, given the integrity of the *quadrivium*, by which the ordered universe was apprehended, also the complementary positions of arithmetic, which defines rational number, and geometry, which describes the irrational, such as square roots and the golden section. This arises from a perceived difficulty in setting out a building, if designed geometrically, by supposedly having to reconstruct the same geometry across the site in order to set out the building. As a consequence, the argument misses the possibility of that building having been designed geometrically, then converted to measures for setting out. Yet it is a possibility which is acknowledged by the author when commenting on Chartres and Milan Cathedrals (183, 190), and implicitly acknowledged when referring to convergent series of numbers, which yield numerical approximations to irrational quantities, which in turn could have been used to convert proportions into whole number measures. On the other hand, if the fundamental influence of Plato's *Timaeus* on medieval thought, together with its geometric implications, recognized by the author, is set beside the conclusive evidence for the use of geometry by medieval architects, the case for ends and means is surely compelling. For a discussion of these matters, see the following section 'Historical Introduction'.

45 Two such studies are Hans Buchwald's *Form, Style and Meaning in Byzantine Church Architecture*, published in 1999, and Eric Fernie's *Romanesque Architecture: Design, Meaning and Metrology* of 1995, to which should be added the English translation of Günter Bandmann's *Early Medieval Architecture as Bearer of Meaning* in 2005 (see reference above). Buchwald's and Fernie's books are both collections of past papers and articles, with Buchwald's containing an exploration of possible meanings underlying the design of middle Byzantine churches, culminating in those composed of the Greek Cross inscribed in a square. For a variant reading of this common archetype, see Chapter 1, section on 'The Greek Cross and Byzantine church design'. Fernie's construction of meaning is architecturally self-referential and confined to suggesting that possible Anglo-Saxon elements in the construction of Durham Cathedral might have been in honour of the Saxon saint, Cuthbert, whose shrine it is (36–8); also that columns with spiral decoration in Anglo-Norman sanctuaries and crypts might be emulating those at St Peter's tomb in Rome (32, 90, 183, 265–6); and that the lengths of such cathedrals as Ely and Norwich might have been imitating the basilicas of St Peter and St Paul in Rome (332). Paradoxically, the proportion which Fernie consistently advances for the plan design of various Anglo-Norman abbeys and cathedrals, to the exclusion of other possibilities, namely the ratio of the side of a square to its diagonal, is invested with no meaning, save for a single attribution to Plato's method of doubling a square as paraphrased by Vitruvius (368). This appears to miss the larger influence of Plato's cosmological ideas on medieval thought, together with their geometrical implications which extend well beyond the limitations of the square and its diagonal. It is hoped that this will be demonstrated in the present volume. Regarding church layouts as a whole, Fernie elsewhere remains sceptical that they might have contained symbolic intent (Wu (2002) 8), despite writings by Honorius, Durandus and others, also such texts as the *Testamentum Domini*. See 'Historical Introduction' and Chapter 2.

46 Amiens Cathedral, in Murray (1996), 43; St Ouen, Rouen, and St Urbain, Troyes, in Davis and Neagley (2000), 172, 174. See also Chapter 3, sections on 'The Trinity and Creation' and '*Architectura ad triangulum*' below.
47 Hiscock (2000).
48 Boyer (1968), 54, 93.
49 This is partly a digest of Christian Platonist thought from Hiscock (2000), 43–136.
50 Chalcidius, *Timaeus a Calcidio translatus commentarioque instructus*; Macrobius, *Commentarii in Ciceronis Somnium Scipionis*; Martianus Capella, *De nuptiis Philologiae et Mercurii*.
51 Klibansky (1939, repr. 1981), 28. The appeal of Plato's teaching to early Christians was partly due to the rational basis it provided to religious faith for Greeks, whilst also having much in common with the Judaic tradition and, finally, its compatibility in describing a Deity in three persons creating order from chaos in the universe, with mankind a microcosm of it, possessing an immortal soul.
52 Cornford (1937), 44, 54, 150.
53 Augustine, tr. Russell (1948), 324.
54 Grosseteste, tr. Martin (1999), 227.
55 Wisdom, tr. Reider (1957), 147. See also Augustine, *De civitate Dei* V. 11; Dionysius, *De divinis nominibus* IV. 4; Isidore III. 4; Grosseteste, *Hexaëmeron* VII. 14. 8. The Book of Wisdom, otherwise known as The Wisdom of Solomon, was written sometime in the first two centuries BC, almost certainly in Alexandria, partly to reconcile Jewish and Greek philosophy; Reider (1957), 1, 10, 14, 16.
56 Boethius, tr. Masi (1983), 74.
57 Ibid., 71.
58 Hugh of St Victor, tr. Taylor (1991), 67.
59 Augustine, *De musica* I. 12. 20–23; tr. Taliaferro (1947), 198.
60 Ibid., 200.
61 Ibid., 201.
62 Alan of Lille, *Anticlaudianus*, tr. Sheridan (1987), 104, 182.
63 Augustine, tr. Bettenson (1984), 465.
64 So called because of his pseudonym for the Dionysius converted by Paul on the Areopagus Hill in Athens.
65 Dionysius, tr. Luibheid (1987), 99. See also Macrobius I. 6. 7, 8; Martianus Capella, 731.
66 John of Damascus, tr. Chase (1958), 173.
67 Clement, *Stromateis* VI. 16; Grosseteste, *Hexaëmeron* III. 13. 1; Macrobius I. 6. 18; Martianus Capella, 732.
68 See Chapter 2.
69 Augustine, *De civitate Dei* XI. 31; idem, *In Iohannis evangelicum* 27. 10. (4); Clement VI. 16; Grosseteste, *Hexaëmeron* VIII. 3. 5; Martianus Capella, 733.
70 Clement, tr. Wilson (1869), 363.
71 Augustine, *De civitate Dei* XI. 31; Eusebius III. 24, X. 4; John of Damascus, *De fide* I. 3, II. 7, 9; Glaber, *Historiarum* I. 1, 2; Martianus Capella, 734; *ODCC* (1997), 279.
72 Martianus Capella, 735.
73 In a further example of the kinship of 5 with 10, Maximus the Confessor explained how the human soul is divided into 5 pairs of properties: mind and reason, wisdom and prudence, contemplation and action, knowledge and virtue, enduring knowledge and faith, Maximus V. See also Clement VI. 16; John of Damascus, *De fide* II. 12; Martianus Capella, 735.

74 Lucian, *Pro lapsu* 5, in Kilburn (1959), 178–9.
75 Alcuin, *Ep*. 260.
76 Clement, tr. Wilson (1869), 383. See also the explanation of the number 10 below.
77 The next perfect number is 28 and there is only one perfect number to be found in each group of numbers of 1, 2, 3, 4 digits, e.g. 6, 28, 496, 8128 ... Boethius, *De arithmetica* I. 20.
78 Augustine, *De civitate Dei* XI. 30; Grosseteste, *Hexaëmeron* IX. 1. 1; Martianus Capella, 280.
79 Augustine, *De civitate Dei* XI. 31; Macrobius I. 6. 7, 8; Martianus Capella, 738.
80 See Proverbs IX. 1; Augustine, *De civitate Dei* XVII. 4.
81 At the time, it was believed that the only planets were the moon, sun, Venus, Mercury, Mars, Jupiter, Saturn.
82 Clement VI. 16; Grosseteste, *Hexaëmeron* IX. 10; Macrobius I. 6. 54–5; Martianus Capella, 738.
83 Augustine, *De civitate Dei* XI. 31.
84 Clement V. 14, VI. 16; John of Damascus, *De fide* II. 1.
85 Plato, *Republic* X. 616B.
86 Clement, tr. Wilson (1869), 284.
87 See Chapter 6.
88 Clement, tr. Wilson (1869), 387.
89 Augustine, *De sermone*, tr. Kavanagh (1963), 29.
90 Alcuin, *Ep*. 259, 260; Augustine, *De civitate Dei* XII. 15.
91 *Sylloge Laureshamensis* III; John of Damascus, *De fide* IV. 9. See Chapter 6, under 'The octagonal shrine'.
92 Dionysius, *De coelesti hierarchia* VI. 1, 2; Gilson (1994), 167; John of Damascus, *De fide* II. 3; Martianus Capella, 741.
93 Grosseteste, *De luce*, tr. Riedl (1942), 17.
94 Clement, VI. 16; Augustine, *De civitate Dei* XX. 7; Macrobius I. 6. 76; Martianus Capella, 742.
95 See Chapter 1.
96 Augustine, *De civitate Dei* XV. 20, *In Iohannis evangelicum* 27. 10. (4); John of Damascus, *De fide* II. 7.
97 Acts I. 24–6; Augustine, *De civitate Dei* XX. 5.
98 Clement I. 25; II. 5, 22; V. 4, 14; VI. 2.
99 Augustine, *De civitate Dei* VIII. 4, 11.
100 The Greeks translated the Hebrew as 'beautiful'; the Latin Vulgate as 'good'; Tatarkiewicz (1970), 5.
101 Augustine, tr. Russell (1948), 318.
102 Hugh of St Victor, tr. Taylor (1991), 71. Hugh may have been quoting either Cassiodorus or Isidore, see 71, note 55.
103 Cornford (1937), 210.
104 Applying sufficient heat to water makes it evaporate and become air; when heat is withdrawn from air it condenses and becomes water.
105 Clement V. 6.
106 Burkert (1972), 72; Hugh VI. 3.
107 See theory and power of numbers in 'Arithmetic' above.
108 Boethius, *De arithmetica* II. 4.
109 Augustine, *De musica* I. 12. 23, tr. Taliaferro (1947), 200.
110 Lucian, tr. Hopper (1938), 42. See also Maximus V.

111 Philo, tr. Yonge (1854–5), 90.
112 For early references to the liberal arts by Christian writers, see Clement VI. 10; Augustine, *De ordine* I. 8. 24, II. 5. 14.
113 Boethius, *De arithmetica, Praefatio*; John of Damascus, *Dialectica* III; Hugh of St Victor, *Didascalion* II. 6.
114 Boethius, *De musica* I. 2.
115 Burkert (1972), 421–2; Mango (1980), 141; Mesarites, in Downey (1957), 894–6.
116 Cassiodorus, *De institutione divinarum litterarum* and *De artibus ac disciplinis liberalium litterarum*. Wagner (1986), 20.
117 For the teaching of the liberal arts in the tenth century, see Hiscock (2000), 32–42, 102–3.
118 Hugh of St Victor, *Didascalicon*, ed. Buttimer (1939).
119 Hugh of St Victor, *Didascalicon*, tr. Taylor (1991), 34–5.
120 Alan of Lille, *Anticlaudianus*, ed. Bossuat (1955).
121 Alan of Lille, *Anticlaudianus* II, III.
122 The liberal arts are personified in the archivolts above the south door.
123 These images are partly original and partly modern reconstructions.
124 Maximus, tr. Berthold (1985), 188–9.
125 Photius, tr. Mango (1972), 185. In this quotation, Photius was describing the Church of the Virgin of Pharos, in the Imperial Palace at Constantinople.
126 Augustine, tr. Bettenson (1984), 335, 629.
127 Harvey (1972), 226.
128 Bezaleel was the builder of Moses' Tabernacle appointed by God, Exodus XXXI. 2.
129 Eusebius, tr. Oulton (1932), 411–15, 421–7, 439–43.
130 The dispute over icons is generally referred to as the Iconoclastic Controversy, a term as long-winded as it is inaccurate, for it was more a long, murderous, internecine feud than a controversy, and it embroiled iconophiles as well as iconoclasts.
131 Tatarkiewicz (1970), 105. After founding several monasteries and entering one of them, Gregory served at the Imperial court at Constantinople between c. 578 and c. 585, before returning to Rome and becoming pope in 590.
132 Charlemagne, *Libri Carolini: Capitulare de imaginibus* III. 16, in Tatarkiewicz (1970), 106.
133 Bell (1996), 221; *ODCC* (1997), 891.
134 John of Damascus, tr. Chase (1958), 372.
135 Tatarkiewicz (1970), 106.
136 Alan of Lille, *Anticlaudianus*, tr. Sheridan (1987), 141.
137 Dionysius, tr. Luibheid (1987), 53.
138 Ibid., 147.
139 Maximus, tr. Berthold (1985), 195.
140 Mesarites, tr. Downey (1957), 867, 868.
141 John of Damascus, tr. Chase (1958), xxxiv; *ODCC* (1997), 891.
142 Book of Wisdom XIII. 5.
143 Romans I. 20.
144 John of Damascus, tr. Chase (1958), 9–10.
145 Idem, tr. Mango (1972), 172.
146 Dionysius, tr. Luibheid (1987), 26–7.
147 Suger, tr. Panofsky (1979), 47–9.
148 Ibid., 51.

149 Suger, *De administratione* XXXIV, tr. Panofsky (1979), 75. In the past twenty years, the reappraisal of von Simson's and Panofsky's view of Suger being in effect the father of the Gothic style through his acquaintance with Dionysius's writings and thence his adoption of anagogy and the metaphysics of light, was initially a necessary, if intemperate, corrective. Yet it goes too far in downplaying the importance of Dionysius generally at the time, also his influence on Suger, and Suger's likely influence on the design of his abbey (Kidson (1987), 1–17; Grant (1998), 4–5, 23–5, 29–30, 255, 265–71). This process has continued more recently with detailed analyses of Suger's texts; see for example, Linscheid-Burdich (2004), 20–78, 200–201, 218–21; Speer (2006), 73–5. Their main findings are that there is no evidence in Suger's writings of a direct influence from Dionysius as the philosophical inspiration for Suger's project, or indeed of any theological or philosophical system being at work in it. Whilst, in anagogical matters, Suger chooses his own words rather than those of Dionysius, there is on the other hand evidence of his knowledge of other writers. The inspiration of the Syrian on Suger is rather as apostle, martyr, and supposed patron of the abbey, whilst Suger's concerns for his project are more practical, mainly in regard to the accommodation of pilgrims and the liturgy. For a recent bibliography of studies on Suger and St Denis, see Clark (2006 (1)), especially notes 32 and 42. Plausible though these findings are as far as they go, they beg the question of Suger's intended readership. Since this was unlikely to have included his builders, his instructions to them and his reasoning behind those instructions can hardly be expected to be found in these texts. Moreover, by choosing his own words and revealing a knowledge of writers other than Dionysius simply demonstrates how widespread anagogical, or Neoplatonic, thinking and Dionysius's influence on it were. Finally, in necessarily conducting microscopic examinations of the text, its context remains equally important. For example, proper weight still needs to be given to the unique connection that existed between the abbey and Dionysius, with the imperial gift of the Greek text of his writings and their Latin translation in its library, at a time when it was generally thought that the abbey had been dedicated to Dionysius; also with the demonstrable link between Dionysius and Suger existing in their promotion of anagogy being so prominent in both their writings, as well as Suger's knowledge of Dionysius, the verses on his west doors even being taken from the Syrian; and with the prevailing importance being given architecturally to windows and light in contemporary architecture, of which his choir is such a notable example. Given this, it is difficult to see how Dionysius's influence can be described as 'pernicious' (Grant (1998), 270).

150 Hugh of St Victor, tr. Taylor (1991), 122.

151 Honorius, in Harvey (1972), 226.

152 Suger, tr. Panofsky (1979), 105.

153 Eusebius, *Vita Constantini* III. 38. Because Eusebius describes the pillars as encircling the hemisphere opposite the doors of the basilica, some scholars have placed them around the apse of the basilica, others inside the rotunda beyond the basilica, and there are problems with either interpretation. For the description to fit the basilica, 'hemisphere' would have to mean 'semi-dome', which it does not; yet it is difficult to see how the description could apply to the rotunda because this would be out of place in Eusebius's account and, in any case, he does not mention the rotunda, having died long before it was finished. See Lethaby/Talbot Rice (1949), 18–20; Mango (1972), 13. One possible solution might

be that he saw the bases for the columns in the rotunda before he died, although this would beg the question of the absence of the rotunda from his account.

154 Eusebius, *Historia ecclesiastica* X. 4. See his panegyric to Paulinus above.

155 For the plan of St Denis' choir, see Crosby (1987), pl. 1.

156 Suger, *De consecratione* VII. 237. Although he makes no reference to it, the number of chapels could allude to the 9 orders of angels in Dionysius's *De coelesti hierarchia* VI. 1, 2, since the work was known to Suger; see Chapter 6, under 'Chevet design'.

157 Suger, tr. Panofsky (1979), 55.

158 One recent account of High Gothic architecture summarizes the influence of the Pythagorean-Platonic system of number and geometry, and presumes its application to cathedral architecture without demonstrating how this might have been achieved. See chapters on design and symbolism, and constructional design; Binding (2002), 27–52, 57–79.

159 John of Damascus, *De fide*, tr. Chase (1958), 170.

160 For further references to architects in the Byzantine world, see the following section, also Chapter 1, Part 1, 'Hagia Sophia, Constantinople'.

161 Mango (1985), 35; see also Cuomo (2000), 40–41.

162 Cuomo (2000), 93.

163 See Chapter 1, section entitled 'Heaven on Earth'.

164 Marcus, tr. Mango (1972), 31.

165 *Vita sancti Marthae, matris Symeonis stylitae iunioris*, tr. Mango (1972), 126–7.

166 See Chapter 1, section on 'The Greek Cross and Byzantine church design'.

167 Ousterhout (1999), 43–7.

168 For an outline of activities of ecclesiastical patrons in the tenth-century monastic reforms and of later medieval architectural practice, see Hiscock (2000), 28–32, 158–67, 171–203.

169 *Historia I. Translationis sanctae Witburgae*, A. SS. II. 604. 1.

170 *Vita Ceolfridi*, ed. Knoegel, 461, in Pevsner (1942), 554; *Vita Bennonis* II, MGH. S. Sep. Ed. 9, in Lehmann-Brockhaus (1938), nos 1364, 3005; see also Pevsner (1942), 554–5.

171 *Vita sancti Odonis*, PL 133. 940. 11, in Lehmann-Brockhaus (1935), 39; *Chronicon abbatiae Rameseiensis* I. 22. 39, in Lehmann-Brockhaus (1935), 38; John of Metz, *Vita Iohannis abbatis Gorziensis* 355–6. 66–7; Glaber, *Historiarum* III. 4, *Vita sancti Guillelmi* XV. 710–11; *Altera vita sancti Guillelmi* 8–9; Lehmann-Brockhaus (1938), no. 270.

172 Yorke (1997), 8.

173 Chevallier (1875), 150, 153.

174 *Vita sancti Oswaldi*, Rolls 71. 434, in Gem (1983), 13; Hart (1966), 167, in Gem (1983), 14.

175 Birch (1892), 9–10, in Gem (1983), 15.

176 Arnold, *Liber*, tr. Stadler (1991).

177 Suger, *De consecratione* IV. It will be recalled that this appears to have been a contrivance on his part, made retrospectively.

178 Augustine, *De civitate Dei* XI. 31, XV. 20; *In Iohannis evangelicum* 27. 10. (4).

179 William of Auberive, *Tractatus de sacramentis numerorum*, in Leclercq (1948), 184–5; see following note.

180 G. Evans (1983), 113. The first Cistercians gave great importance to the mysticism of numbers. Odo was a secretary of Bernard of Clairvaux before becoming abbot of Morimond, perhaps in 1156, and part of his *Analetica numerorum et rerum* was

copied at Clairvaux from 1147 during Bernard's abbacy. Having been taught at the school of Hugh of St Victor, Odo produced his own variation of Hugh's *De numeris mysticis*, setting out to examine the numbers 1 to 10 in scripture and arranging them in different categories of signification. After revising his work several times, Odo only reached the number 3 and the task was eventually taken up firstly by William of Auberive in his *Tractatus de sacramentis numerorum*, in which he proceeded to 12, and then Geoffrey of Auxerre, another secretary of Bernard, who continued to 20 in *De sacramentis numerorum*. Finally, Theobald of Langres organized the material in the single digest, *De quatuor modis*. Odo I. 10; G. Evans (1983), 111–13; Grill (1962), 193, 194; Leclercq (1948), 181–99.

181 *Eadui Codex*, Hanover, Kestner Museum WM XXIa, 36 fol. 9v.

182 For a brief discussion of the dividers God is shown clasping, see Hiscock (2000), 154–5.

183 Alan of Lille, *De planctu*, tr. Sheridan (1980), 144–5.

184 Grosseteste, *Hexäemeron*, tr. Martin (1999), 218.

185 Tracing-houses have survived at York Minster and Wells Cathedral. Elsewhere, architectural details have been inscribed on inconspicuous parts of the building fabric, such as the floor of the crypt at Bourges Cathedral.

186 *'Lanfranc architector'*; *Relatio translationis corporis sancti Geminiani*, Modena, Archivio Capitolare, Cod. 0. II. ii.

187 Nicholas of Biard, *Distinctiones*, Mortet (1906), 268.

188 In the literature, architects are variously referred to as such, or as the master builder, or master mason. For the purposes of this study, 'architect' and 'master builder' are generally regarded as synonymous terms, with perhaps a slightly greater expectation of the role of designer lying with the term 'architect', although it is granted that this is a distinction that should not be pushed too far. As the Middle Ages advanced, the evidence suggests that architects sometimes moved between projects, when presumably the equivalent of today's site architect or foreman would remain in charge of the work on site. Whilst the master mason must have functioned as the chief of masons, there must have been times when his role was wider than this, depending on the circumstances.

189 King and architect; Paris, *Vitae Offarum*, British Museum Cott. MS. Nero D. I. fol. 23v; *Alban*, Dublin, Trinity College Library, MS. 177, fol. 59v.

190 For example, elevations of Reims and Strasbourg Cathedrals.

191 The names of four architects were commemorated on the pavement labyrinth of Reims Cathedral, with three similarly displayed on the Amiens labyrinth; the tombstone of Hugh Libergier stood in his church of St Nicaise in Reims, before being removed to the cathedral, while the tombstones of two other architects can be seen in the choir of St Ouen at Rouen.

192 The Paris Statutes date from 1268, with Strasbourg's following in 1276, its lodge becoming the master-lodge for all Germany a year later. Harvey (1972), 137–8.

193 Durandus, *Rationale divinorum officiorum*, I. 15, 26, 27, in Neale and Webb (1843), 25, 29. It is recognized that Durandus relies much on early sources, yet, in addition to making the material he is transmitting available to his own age, as with most transmitters he attests to the interest taken by one age in the ideas of another. Similarly, his nineteenth-century translators reveal the interest taken in his text by the ecclesiology movement of the time, hence the antiquated tone of the translation.

194 Horn and Born (1979), 103; Augustine, *De Trinitate* IV. 4. 10.

195 *Testamentum Domini*, tr. Sperry-White (1991), 46.

196 See also Horn and Born (1979), vol. 1, figs 41–4.

197 Paris, Bibliothèque national, MS. fr. 19. 093.

198 Villard, fol. 15r.

199 They are the churches at Byland Abbey, which was finished by 1190, and Fontaine-Jean, which was completed by 1240 and was therefore under construction when Villard was active.

200 Hiscock (2000), 207–52, 278–85, pls 21–105; (2002), 100–105.

201 For example, in England, King Henry VI's detailed brief from the 1440s for King's College Chapel in Cambridge. See Harvey (1972), 253–6.

202 These were known as journeymen, from *jornée*, the French for day.

203 See Chapter 4, under '*Architectura ad quadratum*'.

204 Roriczer, *Büchlein von der Fialen Gerechtikait* (Regensburg, 1486), no. 1 fol. 2v; see also *Wimpergbüchlein*, (Regensburg, c. 1488).

205 Lechler, *Unterweisung*, fol. 43, 133; in Reichensperger (1856), 133, 145.

206 See 'Symbol, context, and meaning' in Chapter 6.

207 Landes (2000), 104–5, 118, 123, 131–4.

208 Landes (2003), 250–58.

209 The first of these sources gives a first-hand account of village life between 1294 and 1324 in and around Montaillou, a centre of Cathar heresy, and is drawn from records of the interrogation of suspects and witnesses: Ladurie (1980). These survive in Latin MS. 4030, Vatican Library, and the references cited here follow Jean Duvernoy, *Le Registre d'Inquisition de Jacques Fournier, evêque de Pamiers (1318–1325)*, (Toulouse, 1965). The second source is the private correspondence of Francesco di Marco Datini, a merchant of Prato, which is part of the voluminous Archivo Datini, Prato, and covers the years 1382–1400: Origo (1963). The third source is *The Miller's Tale* from Geoffrey Chaucer's *The Canterbury Tales* which date from around 1386. The genre of the tales is diverse and they originate from different parts of Europe, with only a few original to Chaucer. *The Miller's Tale*, which is about a carpenter, belonged to an oral tradition of story-telling and was evidently heard by Chaucer, who produced his own written version of it: Chaucer (1979), 17–18. The final source is *Sir Gawain and the Green Knight*, the alliterative verse fable dating from the end of the fourteenth century. A single manuscript survives as BM. Cotton MS Nero A. x. *Gawain* (1965), 7, 127.

210 Chaucer (1979), 112; Ladurie (1980), 300; Origo (1963), 311.

211 *Gawain* II. 6, 7 (1965), 49, 50.

212 Chaucer (1979), 113; Ladurie (1980), 289, i. 291;

213 Origo (1963), 302.

214 Ibid., 163.

215 Ladurie (1980), 306, i. 223.

216 Origo (1963), 335.

217 Ladurie (1980), 298, i. 457.

218 See section on 'Arithmetic' above.

219 Eckenstein (1906), 115–16.

220 A popular version of this is *The Twelve Days of Christmas*, Eckenstein (1906), 134–5.

221 Familiar examples of cumulative recitation, in addition to *The Twelve Days of Christmas*, are *The Old Woman and Her Pig* and *The House that Jack Built*, Eckenstein (1906), 117, 134–5.

222 Dorsetshire Traditional, Broadwood and Maitland (1893), 156–8.

223 Unpublished translation by Hubert Stadler.

224 It was entitled *A New Dyall*, MS. Harleian 5937, c. 1625.

225 Eckenstein (1906), 145–7, 163–4. In the version cited here, 'six proud walkers' is thought to be a corruption of 'six proud waters', which would also have denoted creation. See Chapter 3, under 'Solomon's Knot'.

226 Broadwood and Maitland (1893), 159, regard the ascription of 5 to the 'symbol at your door', or 'at your feet', or 'at your call', as the commonest, which they interpret as alluding to the pentagram, with which thresholds were marked in order to avert evil, citing a reference in Goethe's *Faust* as an example.

227 As in 'the rivals of my watch', Shakespeare, *Hamlet* Act 1 Scene 1; *The Dilly Song*, Vaughan Williams Memorial Library, Leaflet 10, 3; for the general interpretation, Broadwood and Maitland (1893), 159.

228 Broadwood and Maitland (1893), 158; Eckenstein (1906), 163.

229 Hiscock (1999), 25; (2002), 86, 92, 100–105.

230 Two twelfth-century accounts of setting buildings out on site are very similar. One occurred in a dream described by Gerald of Wales, while the other was a vision of a new abbey church for Cluny, which came to the monk Gunzo, and which was also illustrated. A conflation of these describes measuring and marking out the plan of each building over the site using surveyors' cords. See Hiscock (2000), 196, 198.

231 Hiscock (2000), 280–82.

232 The thickness of the choir wall provided the dimension for the square in Lechler's *Unterweisung*, fol. 42v, Shelby (1971), 148.

233 Hiscock (2000), 104–5.

234 Harvey (1972), 34, 235–6.

235 In the case of Santiago, any programme is likely to have emanated from the hierarchy of the Benedictine Order, in view of its similarity with other churches built around the same time on the pilgrim roads leading to it. Interestingly, while their constructional design and certain features of their layouts, such as their chevets, are similar, a wide divergence exists in the size and proportions of their layouts, as between Ste Foye at Conques for instance and St Sernin in Toulouse, and this must have been predetermined somehow.

Fig. 13 Hagios Nicholas, Monemvasia. The Byzantine expression of the sphere and the cube at its most uncompromising

CHAPTER 1

The Sphere and the Cube

Part One: Heaven on Earth

Hagia Sophia, Constantinople, and the symbolism of domed churches

Plato's description of the universe, with the earth as the 'fixed sphere' at its centre, encircled by each of the planets, had its counterpart in his abstract model of it. In this, the universe was a sphere composed of the 4 elements. To each of these was assigned one of the regular polyhedra, which were conceptualized as being inscribed geometrically in the sphere.[1] The atmospheric elements of fire, air, and water are unstable, and are composed of equilateral triangles. Earth, the only stable element, is represented by the cube and all are contained by the sphere of the universe.[2] This, it would appear, was the model that John of Damascus, the monk and theologian, had in mind when he wrote in the eighth century,

> … we say that in the creation of the universe we consider as heavens that which the pagan philosophers … call a starless sphere. … [Some] say that [its substance] is made from the four elements. Still others say that it is a fifth body and distinct from the four elements. … They say that the heavens have seven spheres. … For they have said that there are seven planets … They also say that the heavens surround the earth like a sphere.
>
> *De fide* II. 6.[3]

For the architectural expression of the sphere and the cube, and their signification in Christian terms as not only heaven and earth, but heaven on earth, it is necessary to turn to the domed churches of the Byzantine world. At first sight, the manifestation of this symbolism seems simple, even simplistic, with the upper and lower zones of churches being equated with heaven and earth respectively, their domes identified with the dome of heaven atop the cube of earth. Nothing expresses the solid geometry of this symbolism more uncompromisingly than the post-medieval churches of Hagios Nicholas and the Panagia on the sea-lashed rock of Monemvasia (Fig. 13).[4] For churches to be conceived as symbolizing the universe, however, the creation of the universe would have to have been similarly perceived and described. In the fifth century, the Syriac writer Narsai (d. c. 503) did so in these verses:

> He created two dwellings and constructed two worlds.
> He rendered the lower one suitable for mortals;
> He gathered it up and filled it with the fruits appropriate to corporeal beings,

> He made the upper one a beautiful building full of delights,
> So that the spiritual beings might enjoy it spiritually.
>
> *Homilies on the Creation* I. 92–6.[5]

In the seventh century, Maximus the Confessor described the reciprocal symbolism of the Holy Church and the sensible world:

> God's holy Church in itself is a symbol of the sensible world as such, since it possesses the divine sanctuary as heaven and the beauty of the nave as earth. Likewise the world is a church since it possesses heaven corresponding to a sanctuary, and for a nave it has the adornment of the earth.
>
> *Mystagogia* III.[6]

Here he associates heaven and earth, not vertically with the upper and lower parts of the church, but horizontally with its sanctuary beyond the nave, a distinction that was fitting for a basilica more than a centralized domed church. Other writers consistently visualize a church's vertical compartmentation. The hymn in praise of the cathedral of Hagia Sophia at Edessa, rebuilt around 525, is explicit:

> … it is an admirable thing that in its smallness it should resemble the great world,
> Not in size, but in type: waters surround it [situated between two lakes], as the sea [surrounds the earth];
> Its ceiling is stretched like the heavens – without columns, vaulted and closed –
> And furthermore, it is adorned with golden mosaic as the firmament is with shining stars.
> Its high dome is comparable to the heaven of heavens …
> Its great, splendid arches represent the four sides of the world …
>
> *Edessa Hymn* 4–7.[7]

In the eighth century, it is thought to have been Patriarch Germanus I of Constantinople who wrote:

> The church is heaven on earth, where the God of heaven dwells and moves.
>
> *Historia Mystagogica* I.[8]

A tenth-century description of a church near Constantinople recorded that,

> [The Emperor Justinian] erected from the foundations this great church in the name of Our Lady, which he cleverly compacted by means of only four arches and wrought it in a circle so that it seemed to hang in the air – a smaller dome on earth similar to the greater one of heaven.
>
> *De sacris aedibus Deiparae ad Fontem*, ASS Nov. III. 879.[9]

Five hundred years later, the model continued to be proselytized by Symeon, the archbishop of Thessalonica (d. 1429):

> ... the temple ... [expresses] this visible world; and the higher parts of the temple [express] the visible sky, the lower parts however [express] the things which are above earth and [even] paradise itself ...
>
> *De sacro templo ejus consecratione* CXXXI.[10]

Given the quantity and availability of evidence from contemporary sources, it is difficult to understand how it might be thought that the symbolism in Early Byzantine architecture was less important to people than its geometry or the liturgy performed in it.[11] Besides being unsupported by the evidence, such a suggestion appears to be postulating another false dichotomy. Equally, there appears to be greater subtlety in the *ekphrasis* of the dome of heaven and the realm of earth than justifies characterizing the symbolism as banal.[12] Without doubt, the clearest evidence for the association of the sphere and the cube with heaven and earth is provided by descriptions of the principal church of the Byzantine world and palace church of the Emperor, the Cathedral of Hagia Sophia in Constantinople, built by the Emperor Justinian (c. 482–565).

Following the destruction of its predecessor in civil riots, Justinian commissioned the design of the new building, appointing Anthemius (c. 474–c. 534) and Isidorus (fl. sixth century) from the Ionian cities of Tralles and Miletus. Their profession, according to the practice of the time, was that of *mechanikos*, which was regarded as superior to *architecton*, but without translating exactly as engineer. Rather it corresponds more with the role of modern architect, with *architecton* implying master-builder. Their qualifications, however, would be unrecognizable to a modern architect, for Anthemius wrote a treatise on mechanical devices, one on conic sections and had a commentary on conics dedicated to him by someone who may have been a pupil of Isidorus. Isidorus was a professor of geometry or possibly mechanics, revising an edition of Archimedes, commenting on a treatise by Heron on vaulting, while his school translated into medieval Greek works by Apollonius, Archimedes, Heron, and Pappus. One of his pupils wrote a supplement to Euclid's *Elementa*, which demonstrates the inscription of regular solids within others and cites Isidorus for the method of drawing the inclination between faces of geometric solids.[13] Available to them, among other works, were Heron's two-volume *Geometricorum et Stereometricorum reliquiae*, which includes methods of calculating various complex elements of building construction, such as the measurement of curved surfaces and vaults, the volumes of wall sections, columns, arches and beams, and much else. Of particular relevance to the design they were to produce for Justinian, as will be seen shortly, were the determination of spheres in cubes, which enabled a dome to be fitted to a square base, of triangles to spherical surfaces, which facilitated the construction of pendentives, whilst Isidorus's edition of Archimedes involved the calculation of various properties of the circle and the sphere.[14]

Started in 532 and consecrated in 537, Hagia Sophia suffered structural collapses in 558, 986, and 1346. In its reconstructed state, which is essentially

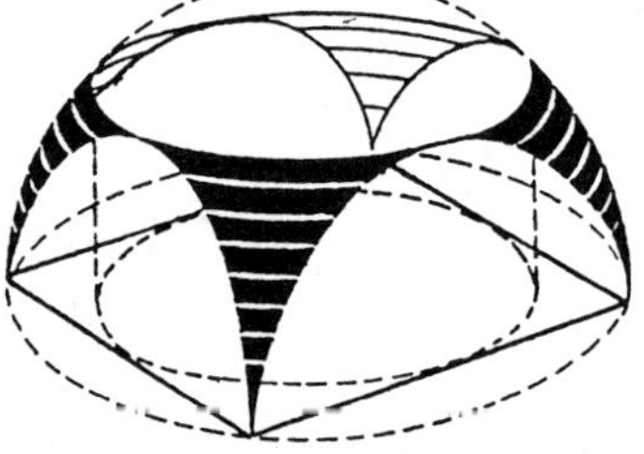

Pendentives.

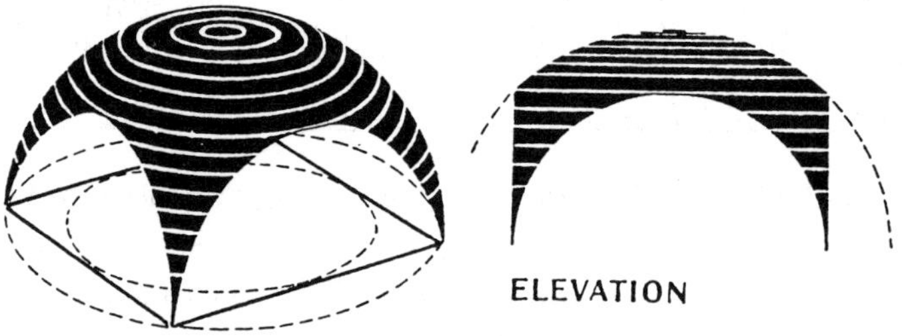

Simple dome, the pendentives and dome being part of the same hemisphere.

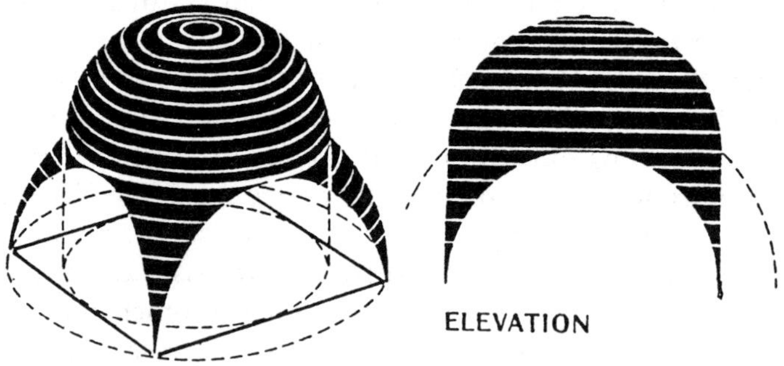

Compound dome, the dome being a hemisphere set above the pendentives.

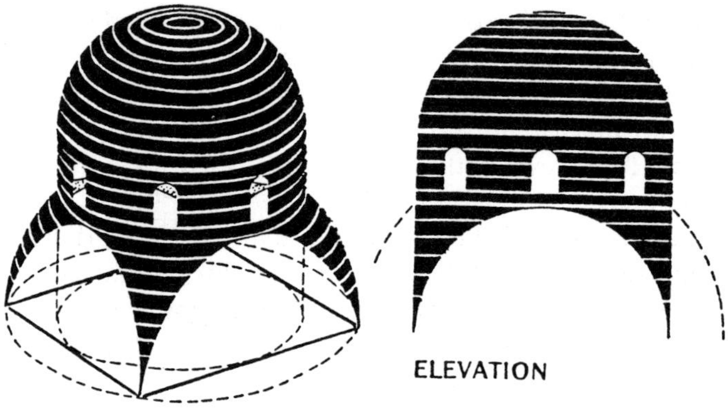

Compound dome with drum.

Fig. 14 The dome on a square base; the compound dome; and the dome raised on a drum

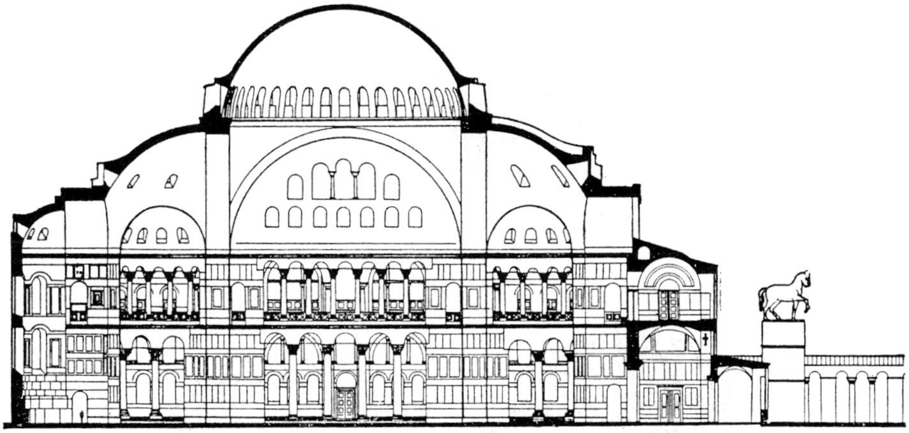

Fig. 15 Longitudinal section, from east to west, Hagia Sophia, Constantinople

that of 558–562, its architectural form can be defined as a dome, placed upon a larger dome which has been reduced by having its top sliced off to form a seating for the upper dome, and by having four similar slices made to it vertically to convert its circular base into one that is square (Figs 14, 15, 16, 17).[15] These four faces are necessarily semi-circular and they sit within, and coincide with, the sides of the cube, of which the square is its top, with the upper dome sitting on it. The cube is marked by four massive piers standing at its corners, extending outwards to the north and south to form buttresses and these support the four main arches that carry the dome. The four vertical slices made to the supporting dome, revealed as semi-circular arches, are walled in to the north and south between the buttresses and left open to the east and west where they are buttressed by half-domes each sitting on a half-cylinder.[16] The internal space of the cube is thereby extended to the east and west by two giant apses, that to the east being enlarged by a further apse for the sanctuary. These main apses are also given two semi-circular *exedrae* each. The space of the double-apsed central cube is flanked to the north and south by large aisles in two storeys, which open into the central space through colonnades at each level. To the west are an inner and outer narthex approached from an *atrium*. Relating this as a schematic design to the geometric model that is evidently underlying it, the four spherical triangles are all that is left of the larger supporting dome, after its top and four sides have been sliced away, and they form pendentives.[17] The diameter of the upper dome equals the side of its square base, which is the top of the cube, the diagonal of which equals the diameter of the supporting dome. Thus the two domes are related to each other proportionally through the square. Agathias (c. 536–582/94), who was a poet and historian writing a few decades later, described the skill of Anthemius as 'the application of geometry to solid matter'.[18]

Taking a Byzantine foot to be 0.312 m, it has been shown that the internal diameter of the dome is 100 feet and so, therefore, is the side of the internal

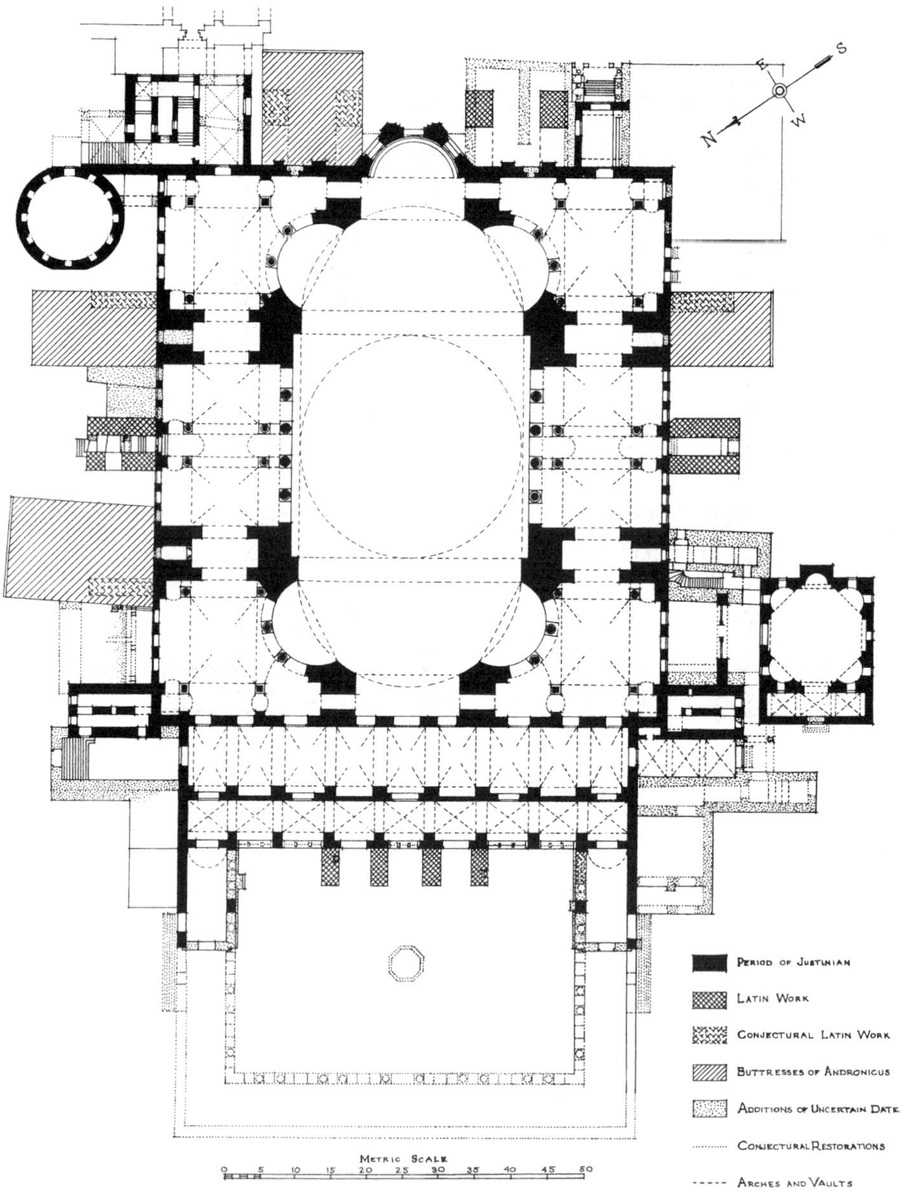

Fig. 16 Ground plan, Hagia Sophia, Constantinople

square beneath it at pavement level.[19] The present dome, however, is the second dome to have been constructed, after the original dome fell in 558 following an earthquake. The height of this first dome therefore can only be estimated and this has been put at 180 feet.[20] Both these governing dimensions possess potential significance, 100 being the decad squared, which is the number associated with the universe, and 180 being the product of 3 × 6 × 10, standing perhaps for the Holy Trinity, Creation, and the universe.[21] The top

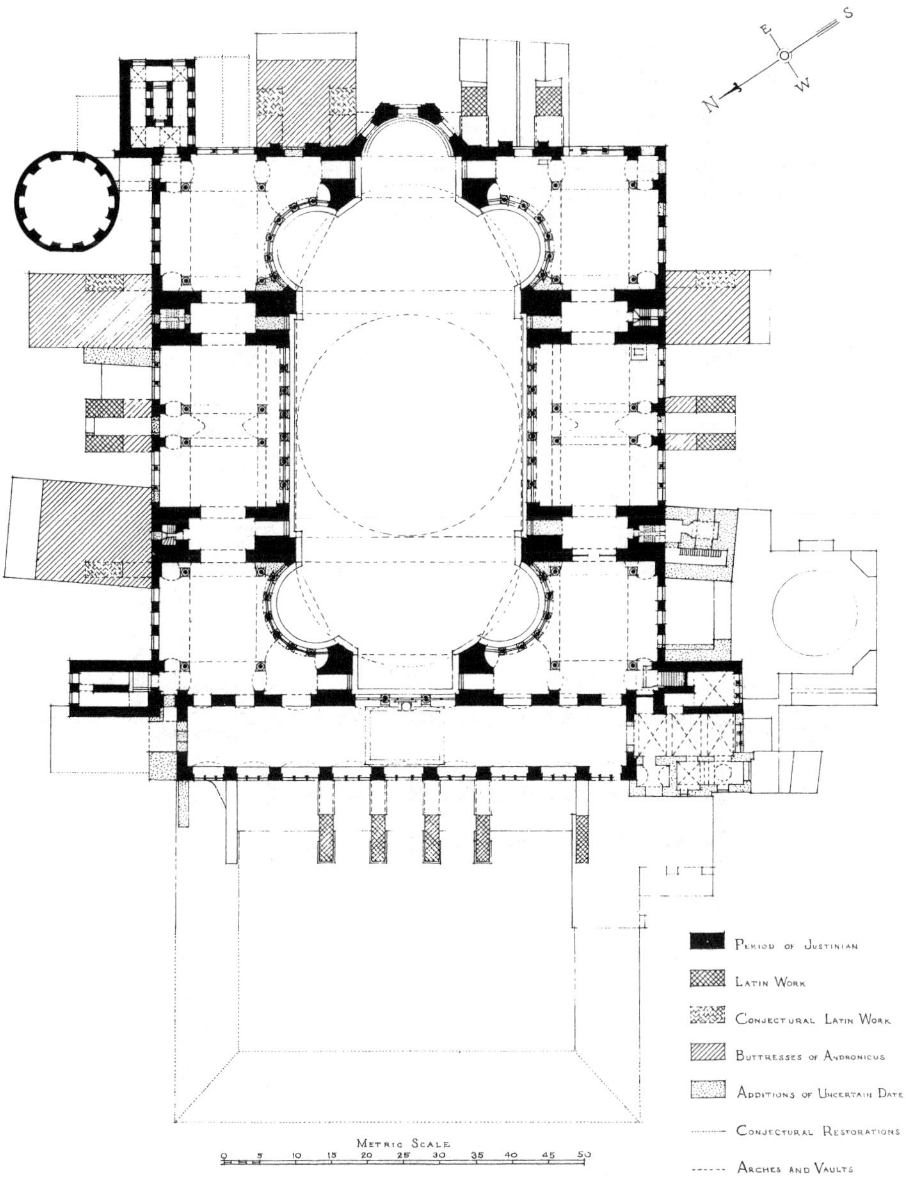

Fig. 17 Gallery plan, Hagia Sophia, Constantinople

of the cube is delineated internally by the third cornice, which is approximately 126 feet above the pavement and, to be a true cube, this would need to be commensurate with its external dimensions. These approximate east–west to 122.5 feet and north–south to 127.5 feet but, since the latter measurement includes the outward leaning of the north and south arches by over 4 feet, which was caused during construction, and by even more subsequently,[22] it would seem that the east–west dimension may be nearer that intended,

Fig. 18 Interior of dome, Hagia Sophia, Constantinople

yielding the side of the cube of 122.5 feet to a height of 126 feet, a divergence of less than 3 per cent.[23]

The collapse that followed the earthquake brought down parts of the original dome along with portions of the eastern arch and semi-dome. As a result, Isidorus's nephew built the present dome to the profile of a hemi-sphere, but with its centre lying some 6 feet below the present cornice (Fig. 18).[24] The original dome had been much shallower and it has been suggested that this might have been the result of trying to reduce its mass and therefore the weight bearing on the supporting structure, without fully realizing how much this would increase the lateral thrust exerted by the dome, in comparison with a hemi-sphere.[25] Although it is impossible to reconstruct the first dome with certainty, attempts have been made and it is thought that it might have continued the curvature of the pendentives, either continuously or raised up by some six to eight feet to provide headroom around the base of the dome above the cornice.[26] In the case of the latter, this would make it the original top slice of the larger dome, slightly lifted above it like a lid above its circular base.[27] Conceptually, the dome and its pendentives are simply the top half of a notional sphere, with its equator level with the springing of the four main arches supporting it, and with its lower part curving beneath the pavement. If this might be thought odd,[28] it will shortly be seen that, just as the top of the cube is open to heaven, as it were, so the bottom of it was also regarded as open, marking the surface of the ocean. This means that there was a single, generating form, that of a sphere, with its sides removed and perhaps its top raised, enveloping a cube, its diagonal on plan being equal to the diameter of the sphere, a singular synthesis of sphere and cube, in total geometric

Fig. 19 Interior, Hagia Sophia, Constantinople

harmony.[29] This would have been fully within the capability of Greek mathematics at the time and the genius of Anthemius and Isidorus (Fig. 19). Whether this was understood by Procopius (?500–?565), who was Justinian's contemporary and biographer, or whether he was paying a more general compliment to the interplay of circular forms, he wrote:

> In the middle of the church there rise four man-made eminences which are called piers, two on the north and two on the south, opposite and equal to one another, each pair having between them exactly four columns. ... Upon these [piers] are placed four arches so as to form a square, their ends coming together in pairs and made fast at the summit of those piers, while the rest of them rises to an immense height. Two of the arches, namely those facing the rising and the setting sun, are suspended over empty air, while the others have beneath them some kind of structure and rather tall columns. Above the arches the construction rises in a circle ... And since the arches are joined together on a square plan, the intervening construction assumes the form of four

> triangles. The bottom end of each triangle, being pressed together by the conjunction of the arches, causes the lower angle to be acute, but as it rises it becomes wider by the intervening space and terminates in the arc of a circle, which it supports, and forms the remaining [two] angles at that level. Rising above this circle is an enormous spherical dome which makes the building exceptionally beautiful. It seems not to be founded on solid masonry, but to be suspended from heaven by that golden chain and so cover the space. All of these elements, marvellously fitted together in mid-air, suspended from one another and reposing only on the parts adjacent to them, produce a unified and most remarkable harmony in the work …
>
> *De aedificiis* I. 1.[30]

Michael of Thessalonica (fl. mid twelfth century), who was a teacher and orator at Hagia Sophia, construed the east and west semi-domes, when added to the main dome, as forming an outer sphere representing invisible heaven, within which the smaller sphere of visible heaven is located, composed of the four semi-domes of the *exedrae*:[31]

> Those piers rising up bear the great roof, the whole of which is made up of two spheres … in this way the spectacle that is here observed may imitate both the first, invisible heaven and the second that is visible. Does it not have too the images of the elements … and a picture of the whole cosmos? Indeed, each arch (they are four in number) is here signifying one element. … accordingly each arch desires to be bent into the form of a circle, and to join with the nearest one, and so does this work of art imitate the whole universe.
>
> *Ekphrasis* 4.[32]

The recognition of Hagia Sophia as the 'Great Church' of the Orthodox faith[33] attracted eulogies in praise of it throughout the Middle Ages, augmented by annual commemorations of Justinian's re-dedication of the church following the earthquake and the completion of its new dome.[34] Those that have survived continue the identification of the sphere and the cube with heaven and earth in a tradition that transcends the simplistic. In order to evaluate these writings, it may be helpful to picture the interior of the building (Fig. 15). The division of the two zones, between the curved upper surfaces of vaults, semi-domes and domes, and the vertical wall planes and horizontal pavement below, was accentuated by everything above the springing line being sheathed in mosaic, and everything at ground level being panelled and paved in marble slabs (Figs 20, 21). Byzantine mosaics consist of small cubes of glass, coloured, or with gold leaf applied, and sometimes interspersed with marble or mother-of-pearl. They were pressed into plaster while it was still soft, often being set at angles for optical effect, producing occasional sparkle as direct and reflected light slowly rotate with the movement of the observer. When applied to the curved surfaces of vaults, light becomes refracted within the skin of its glass so that it glows with its own inner light incandescently and, as will be seen shortly, it was the quality of different effects of light that

Fig. 20 Mosaics and capitals, *exedra* gallery, Hagia Sophia, Constantinople

Fig. 21 Marble panelling, ground storey, Hagia Sophia, Constantinople

caught the Byzantine eye both physically and allegorically.[35] In Hagia Sophia, the original mosaic scheme appears to have been non-figural.[36] This was exceptional, for the display of figurative art was normal, such as seen in S. Vitale in Ravenna, another church in which Justinian was involved. Here figures are integral to the iconography and the sanctuary is flanked by two large mosaic panels of Justinian and his empress Theodora together with Church leaders and courtiers. It has been suggested that the lack of figures in Hagia Sophia's mosaics may have been in deference to Theodora's Monophysite sympathies, although there is no evidence to support this.[37] In contrast with the mosaic of the upper surfaces, varied-coloured marble was used to panel walls and pave the floors in large rectangular slabs or borders. Those on the walls were commonly set in rectangular architraves, having been split in two, then opened up and polished to reveal the symmetrical veining of their inner surfaces. To return to Procopius:

> You might say that the [interior] space is not illuminated by the sun from the outside, but that the radiance is generated within, so great an abundance of light bathes this shrine all round. … The entire ceiling has been overlaid with pure gold which combines beauty with ostentation, yet the refulgence from the marble prevails, vying as it does with that of the gold. There are two colonnades, one on each side, not separated from the church by any structural element, but actually adding to the measure of its width and extending to its whole length … They, too, have a vaulted ceiling adorned with gold. … Who could recount the beauty of the columns and the marbles with which the church is adorned? One might imagine that one has chanced upon a meadow in full bloom. For one would surely marvel at the purple hue of some, the green of others, at those on which the crimson blooms, at those that flash with white, at those, too, which Nature, like a painter, has varied with the most contrasting colors.
>
> *De aedificiis* I.1.[38]

The inner radiance, the golden light of the vault, and the blossoming meadows of marble below form an image repeatedly emulated by other commentators in the *ekphrasis* of Hagia Sophia. Shortly after the first re-dedication in 562, after completion of the rebuilt dome, the poet and court official Paulus Silentarius declaimed:

> Whoever lifts his eyes to the beautiful firmament of the roof can scarcely keep them on its rounded expanse, sprinkled with dancing stars, but soon turns to the fresh green hills below, eager to see there the flower-bordered streams … and the green tendrils of the vine …
>
> *Descriptio ecclesiae sanctae Sophiae* 286–93.[39]

Just as the stars are associated with the dome, so that of the earth with its cube is underlined by reference to the four-sidedness of the realm of earth within the church. This is defined either by 4 arches or by 4 columns, as already encountered in Edessa Cathedral's 'great, splendid arches [representing] the four sides of the world', and Michael's reference to Hagia

Sophia's 4 arches 'signifying one element'.[40] Attention is also drawn to the greenness of the marble and the fact that marble is cut from the earth. Finally, the imagery is extended to the marble veining and colour of pavements resembling the rivers and seas of earth, thereby defining the pavement as the surface of its rivers and the ocean.[41] Later in his panegyric, Paulus describes the great *tympana* filling the north and south arches, supported on their internal colonnades:

> … towards the murmuring south wind and the rainless north there rises a mighty wall up to the chin of the rounded arch, and it is illuminated by twice four windows [before later rebuilding]. This wall rests below on … six Haemonian columns, like the fresh green of emerald … These in turn are heaved upon massive heads by four columns fixed immovable on the ground, glittering jewels of Thessalian marble … Never were such columns … blooming like a grove with bright flowers, cut from the land of Molossis. Yet who … shall sing the marble meadows gathered upon the mighty walls and spreading pavement of the lofty church? … [tools of] toothed steel have cut these from the green flanks of Carystus and have cleft the speckled Phrygian stone, sometimes rosy mixed with white, sometimes gleaming with purple and silver flowers. … You may see the bright green stone of Laconia and the glittering marble with the wavy veins found in the deep gullies of the Iasian peaks, exhibiting slanting streaks of blood-red and livid white; the pale yellow with swirling red from the Lydian headland; the glittering crocus-like golden stone which the Libyan sun, warming it with its golden light, has produced on the steep flanks of the Moorish hills; that of glittering black upon which the Celtic crags, deep in ice, have poured here and there an abundance of milk … and that which the land of Atrax yields, not from some upland glen, but from the level plain …
>
> *Descriptio ecclesiae sanctae Sophiae* 532, 617.[42]

According to a legendary description of the building of Hagia Sophia from the eighth or ninth century,

> … the floor … made visitors marvel for it appeared like the sea or the flowing waters of a river thanks to the great variety of its marble.

The account continues with the replacement of the pavement after the fall of the dome:

> For the floor … [Justinian] sent … to Proconnesus to cut slabs that would denote the earth, while the green ones signify the rivers that flow into the sea.
>
> *Narratio de sancta Sophia* 26, 28.[43]

Thus where the floor is seen as the sea, the walls surrounding it might have been understood as idealized cliffs of marble. Whether the allegorization of Hagia Sophia set the tradition, or whether the tradition incorporated it as its principal exemplar, other religious buildings were invested with similar imagery. Contemporary with the completion of Hagia Sophia, Choricius (sixth century), an orator, spoke of the church of St Stephen in Gaza, presumably at its dedication:

> The curious observer may look high and low in search of a spot bare either of marble or gold: he will not find one here. …
> The river [Nile] itself is nowhere portrayed in the way painters portray rivers, but is suggested by means of distinctive currents and symbols, as well as by the meadows along its banks. Various kinds of birds that often wash in the river's streams dwell in the meadows.
> This charming sight is offered by the walls of the aisles which, furthermore, are well ventilated, there being two breezes that blow into them from two directions and, through them, into the middle [of the church] thanks to the many large windows …
>
> *Laudatio Marciani* II. 49–51.[44]

Late in the ninth century, Emperor Leo VI (866–912) wrote of a church built by his father-in-law, Stylianus Zaoutzas:

> Such, then, are the upper beauties of the church, and they are all made of mosaic … But what of the lower part? Four columns adorned with the green color, such as the earth puts forth … support the pendent arches. The ground is covered all over with the hues of various flowers. … and this, in turn, is surrounded by the purple slabs as if by rivers; the latter, too, are enclosed by a contexture imitating the different flowers of the earth.
>
> *Sermon* 34.[45]

In the middle of the twelfth century, Michael of Thessalonica delivered the annual panegyric in Hagia Sophia at the commemoration of Justinian's rededication of the church, and it summarizes in full the symbolism encountered so far:

> So has the pile of this church 'planted its head in heaven', even though it has cast its roots into the earth; and the gold proves that the hand-wrought roof should not be considered as that of the world, for the cosmic heaven has been named 'the all-brazen', but this roof turns out to be 'all-golden'. Perchance it does indeed imitate heaven and, taking into itself the images of the elements, it hardly falls short of making a cosmos. For the beautiful piers, circuits of finely-finished workmanship, standing apart, four on either side, do not terminate before receiving the roof upon themselves, and in the spaces between are high columns, some going in a straight line, others as it were in a dancing fashion inclining towards each other on a circle, mutually complementing the plan of the building by the difference of their stance. … Some of them are greenish in color, as though they had grown out of the ground just there, others are reddish, and all are lightly speckled with white. …
> As for the sides – all is gold, all flowering stones … These stones nature has dipped in a fast and full-bodied dye, and art, by polishing their roughness, has almost turned them into mirrors. Thus has the stone, which is hard by nature, yielded, and, having emerged from the earth,

> it sparkles brilliantly and agreeably to the eyes. It paves the floors and has been fixed round the walls, and in many respects convicts the flowers of being easily withered, since it is also cut from the mines of the earth, but preserves its flowery dye even after severance from its own root. …
> The floor is like the sea, both in its width and in its form; for certain blue waves are raised up against the stone …
>
> *Ekphrasis* 4, 5, 6.[46]

He then compares the *ambo* to an anchored ship, the *solea* behind it to an isthmus, the sanctuary apse beyond to a gulf, and the stepped *synthronon* to breakers.[47] His two references to the marble having been won from the earth once again underline its elemental connection (Fig. 21), being sawn and polished into thin planes, split open like leaves of a book to reveal the lines of nature, transforming its hewn roughness into ruled rectilinearity, it becomes an abstraction of the element earth, lining the inner faces of its cube, the physics making sensible the metaphysics. And just as motion is suggested in the metaphor of the sea, so it is in the light suffusing the realm above (Fig. 22):

> How its countenance flashes forth like liquid through the gold which is everywhere! … the ceilings, adorned with mosaic cubes. … the brightness of the gold almost makes the gold appear to drip down; for by its refulgence making waves to arise. … in eyes that are moist, it causes their moisture to appear in the gold which is seen, and it seems to be flowing in a molten stream.
>
> *Ekphrasis* 1, 3.[48]

This echoes the words of Procopius and Paulus Silentarius six hundred years earlier:

> All of these elements … produce a unified and most remarkable harmony in the work, and yet do not allow the spectators to rest their gaze upon any one of them for a length of time, but each detail readily draws and attracts the eye to itself. Thus the vision constantly shifts round, and the beholders are quite unable to select any particular element which they might admire more than all the others.
>
> Procopius, *De aedificiis* I.1.[49]

> The roof is compacted of gilded tesserae from which a glittering stream of golden rays pours abundantly and strikes men's eyes with irresistible force. It is as if one were gazing at the midday sun in spring …
>
> Paulus, *Descriptio ecclesiae sanctae Sophiae* 668.[50]

It has been pointed out elsewhere how evident it is in these descriptions of spatial experience inside Hagia Sophia and elsewhere that, in the words of Procopius, 'the vision constantly shifts round', so that, to the sense of motion in the streams of light and the rivers and seas below, is added the motion of the eye and mind of the viewer. Given also the apparent lack of visual focus inside Hagia Sophia that is normally provided by the holy figures of Byzantine

Fig. 22 Dome and pendentive, Hagia Sophia, Constantinople

iconography, the intention appears to be to suggest the presence of God through the representation of divine light, and allowing the architectural form to speak for itself, rather than fixing the attention on any particular.[51] In a similar sense, the idea of movement was an important part of Early Byzantine liturgy, which may be characterized as a liturgy of processions.[52]

The structure of the liturgy fell into two parts, the First Entrance being devoted to the sacrament of the word, followed by the Entrance of the Mysteries celebrating that of the body. The procession of celebrants assembled well outside the church and moved towards the *atrium*, where the congregation were waiting, and entered the narthex (Fig. 16). Here everyone gathered for the First Entrance and, if present, the emperor joined the patriarch. As the procession moved into the church and approached the *ambo*, the *solea*, and sanctuary, the congregation streamed into the nave through numerous doors around the church. There were generally entrances on all sides of Early Byzantine churches, especially Hagia Sophia, where there were four into the outer narthex, seven into the inner narthex, nine into the church, another three to the north and south, even three from the east, either side of the sanctuary, totalling sixteen directly into the church, thirteen of them formally related to the architecture.[53] Once inside, there must have been a palpable sense of fluidity and openness, for Procopius mentions that the nave and aisles were undivided from each other,[54] leaving the congregation to fill the nave up to the sanctuary screen and around the *ambo*, without any physical division beneath the dome, with women occupying the north side, men to the south,[55] the emperor in the south aisle, possibly female members of the court in the north gallery, and the clergy moving about the sanctuary during the liturgy and sitting around the top of the *synthronon*. After the readings and the conclusion of the first part, the catechumens left[56] and the Entrance of the Mysteries commenced, with the bread and wine evidently being carried in procession from the rotunda north of the church,[57] presumably re-entering from the easterly door on the north side, passing through the side of the sanctuary enclosure. This consisted of an open framework of pillars supporting a lintel, with a balustrade in between and openings to the sides and front.[58] Consequently the liturgy was conducted in full view of the people, including the eucharist. Eventually, it ended with the celebrants processing out of the church by the same route as they entered, followed by the congregation, who, in effect, evacuated the church.[59] The permeability of the building is striking, with its multiple openings and the openness of its sanctuary, nave and aisles, the absence of fixity that would have been provided by mosaic figures, the freedom from focus beneath the dome, the fluidity of people making their entries and exits, their gathering before the live action of the liturgy, which ended with everyone retracing their steps, leaving the church empty, like an open vessel, or like 'the framing of the world', in the words of John of Damascus.[60]

One change that arrived with the inauguration of the new dome in 558 was described by Paulus Silentarius:

> At its very summit art has depicted a cross, protector of the city. … the sign of the cross is depicted within a circle by means of minute mosaic so that the Saviour of the whole world may for ever protect the church …
>
> *Descriptio ecclesiae sanctae Sophiae* 489, 506.[61]

Although set in the dome, its effect may not have been unlike the mosaic of the great cross of the same period symbolizing Christ transfigured in the semi-dome of S. Apollinare in Classe outside Ravenna (Fig. 5). Everything, however, was to change once the icon dispute was settled in the middle of the ninth century. At Hagia Sophia, Patriarch Photius (c. 810–c. 895) evidently added mosaics of the Virgin and Child to the sanctuary apse, also various holy figures to the vaults, and a portrait of Christ to the main dome.[62] Although no contemporary description of this appears to have survived, Photius himself described a mosaic of Christ similarly placed in a church dedicated to the Virgin of the Pharos in the Imperial Palace:

> On the very ceiling is painted in colored mosaic cubes a man-like figure bearing the traits of Christ. Thou mightest say He is overseeing the earth, and devising its orderly arrangement and government, so accurately has the painter been inspired to represent … the Creator's care for us.
>
> *Homiliae* X. 6.[63]

At the end of the ninth century, another patriarch, Anthony Kauleas, commissioned work at a monastery, also in Constantinople, which Emperor Leo VI described shortly afterwards:

> Now the [structure] which is above the beautiful pavement and forms the roof is raised in the shape of a half-sphere. In the midst of it is represented an image of Him to whom the craftsman has dedicated the church. You might think you were beholding not a work of art, but the Overseer and Governor of the universe Himself.
>
> *Sermon* 28.[64]

In another sermon, the emperor described a church built by his father-in-law Stylianus, which has already been cited:

> In the center … [that is] the segment of a sphere that rises at the summit, is an image that lacks the lower part of the body. … In this way … has the Creator of the universe been delineated at the summit. And, at the springing of the hemisphere are represented, all round, His servitors …
>
> *Sermon* 34.[65]

It appears from these examples that the new dispensation following the icon dispute continued the architectural symbolism of the sphere and the cube and their identification with heaven and earth, simply adding the figure of Christ as 'the Creator of the universe', his position as 'overseer' being twofold, both in terms of overseeing the act of creation and of overseeing its fruits on earth from the summit of the dome (Fig. 34). This particular mode of representing God as Pantokrator[66] appears to have been prefigured by Gregory (c. 335–c. 395), the bishop of Nyssa and brother of Basil the Great:

> ... because he holds the orb of the earth in his palm, and he measures the depth of the sea with his hand; he includes in himself every spiritual creature in order that all might remain in existence, ruled by his all-containing power.
>
> *Contra Eunomium* II.11.[67]

This was the view followed by Dionysius the Pseudo-Areopagite, writing just over a century later:

> ... because all things reside in him, he contains and embraces all ... he produces all things out of himself as a source that holds all and draws all things back to himself as an all-container ...
>
> *De divinis nominibus* X. 1.[68]

Even before the arrival of the Pantokrator, the sense of space, when standing in a nave beneath its dome, would undoubtedly have conveyed the idea of the 'all-container'. In the last few examples, the spatial experience would have been modest in scale, but there was another great church which the Emperor Justinian rebuilt in Constantinople, which will be examined shortly, for which medieval accounts of its Pantokrator survive, and this is the Church of the Holy Apostles. It was cruciform with a dome over each arm of the cross and a higher one over the central crossing. In the tenth century, the poet Constantine of Rhodes wrote:

> The craftsman has piously ordained that the central [dome] should be elevated and rule over the others, destined as it was to be the Lord's great throne, and to protect His precious image which has been delineated in the middle of the famous church. ...
> In the middle of the costly ceiling, it ... bears a representation of Christ as if He were the sun, a wonder exceeding all wonders; next, like the moon, that of the stainless Virgin, and, like the stars, those of the wise Apostles. The whole inner space has been covered with a mixture of gold and glass, as much as forms the domed roof and rises above the hollowed arches, down to [the] ... multicolored marbles and the second cornice.
>
> *Στυχοι Κονσταντυνου (Poem of Constantine)* 626, 737.[69]

At the turn of the thirteenth century, a church official at Hagia Sophia, Nicholas Mesarites, left this record of it:

> This dome, starting at its very base, exhibits an image of the God-man Christ looking down, as it were, from the rim of heaven towards the floor of the church and everything that is in it.
>
> *Description of the Church of the Holy Apostles* XIV.[70]

References to 'Christ as if He were the sun' and as God, 'the Creator of the universe' logically place him as the source of light in the dome of heaven. John of Damascus explained the orientation of churches thus:

> It is not without reason or by chance that we worship toward the east. ... since God is spiritual light and Christ in sacred scripture is called 'Sun of Justice' ...
>
> *De fide* IV. 12.[71]

Nicholas Mesarites continued his description of the Church of the Holy Apostles with the dome and four arches of its crossing:

> There support and hold up this hall, which can really be called the dome of Heaven since the Sun of Justice shines in it, the light which is above light, the Lord of Light, Christ, four arches, which are ... Atlas-like pillars ...
>
> *Description of the Church of the Holy Apostles* XV. 1.[72]

It has been pointed out that, as Pantokrator, he is invariably shown holding the book, which is generally closed. When it is shown open, the text is usually from John's Gospel (8: 12):

> I am the light of the world; he who follows me will not walk in darkness, but will have the light of life[73]

The image of the Pantokrator peering down upon earth as if through an *oculus* in the sky, or 'from the rim of heaven' in the words of Nicholas, makes a further allusion to divine light in that the circle framing the *oculus* is often depicted in the colours of a rainbow.[74] Thus the symbolic evolution of the sphere and the cube, from the metaphysics of Plato's cosmology to the materialization of architectural space in Early Byzantium before the icon dispute, progressing to the Middle Byzantine period, may be exemplified foremost by Hagia Sophia, from its conception initially as being figure-free, including its great dome, and its *ekphrasis* of heavenly light above earth, to the eventual arrival of the Pantokrator in the dome, perceived as 'the Creator of the universe', whereupon he proclaims, 'I am the light'. Complementing this reading as archetype of heaven on earth, however, Hagia Sophia may also embody another sphere of signification, for its dedication may be translated as Divine, or Holy, Wisdom.

Part Two: The Temple of Wisdom

Hagia Sophia, Constantinople, and the Temple of Wisdom

The predecessor of Justinian's church originated in a large basilica raised around 350 by Emperor Constantius II (317–61) and was known as the Great Church, a tradition which Justinian's church took over and which continued throughout the Middle Ages. Ten years later, Constantius's church was also referred as to Hagia Sophia,[75] or Holy Wisdom, in honour evidently of Christ as the Wisdom of God.[76] To John of Damascus,

> Christ is the subsistent wisdom and truth and in Him are all the hidden treasures of knowledge.
>
> *Dialectica* 1.[77]

> The Son is the counsel, the wisdom, and the power of the Father.
>
> *De fide* I. 13.[78]

To Nicholas Mesarites, Justinian's Church was,

> … the great shrine of the Wisdom of the Logos of God.
>
> *Description of the Church of the Holy Apostles* XL. 4.[79]

Following the partial collapse of the new dome over Justinian's church in 1346, a mosaic of the Pantokrator appeared in the rebuilt dome, which was described by the historian Nicephorus Gregoras (c. 1290–1360) shortly afterwards as,

> … the holy image of the enhypostatic Wisdom of God, I mean Christ our Saviour, that was recently depicted on the inner curved surface of the roof.
>
> *Historia* 29. 47.[80]

Beneath the dome, the liturgy commenced with the invocation, 'Wisdom! Stand!' as did the Gospel reading with the words, 'Wisdom, arise, let us listen to the holy Gospel'.[81]

The connection with the Wisdom of Solomon and his Temple also appears to have been made. According to the partly legendary *Narratio* of the eighth or ninth century, on entering his newly-completed church, Justinian declared:

> Glory be to God who has thought me worthy to finish this work. Solomon, I have surpassed thee.
>
> *Narratio* 27.[82]

In the twelfth century, the historian Michael Glycas wrote of Justinian erecting a statue,

> … representing Solomon as looking at the Great Church and gnashing his teeth with envy.
>
> *Annales a mundi* IV.[83]

In the century of its completion, Flavius Corippus, who was a poet and bishop, wrote:

> Praise of the temple of Solomon is now silenced, and the Wonders of the World have to yield the pre-eminence. Two shrines founded by the wisdom of God have rivalled Heaven, one the sacred Temple, the other the splendid fane of S. Sophia, the Vestibule of the Divine Presence.
>
> *In laudem Iustini* IV. 283–87.[84]

In the eleventh century, the philosopher and statesman, Michael Psellus (1018–c. 1080) evidently described Hagia Sophia as,

> … the very beautiful temple, the incomparable home which the Divine Wisdom built in His own name and which He raised on seven pillars.[85]

In the fifteenth century, a Russian visitor paused at the main door into the church and took the figure in the mosaic above him to be Solomon.[86] If this was in reference to the prostrate figure that is there at present, this is thought to represent Emperor Leo VI dating from the early tenth century. Since the figure lacks identification, which is unusual, the assumption made by this foreign visitor perhaps indicates the currency and strength of the connection linking the building with Solomon.

There is also much in Wisdom literature that resembles descriptions of Justinian's Hagia Sophia, especially with regard to the presence and motion of light (Fig. 22).[87] The Book of Wisdom, otherwise known as the Wisdom of Solomon, contains passages that some of Hagia Sophia's commentators could well have had in mind when writing of their experience of its interior. Here, Wisdom's appearance is as a female personification:

> For Wisdom is more mobile than any motion,
> Yes, she pervades and penetrates all things by reason of her pureness.
> For she is a vapour of the power of God,
> And a pure emanation of the glory of the Almighty.
> For she is a reflection of eternal light,
> And a spotless mirror of the working of God …
>
> Wisdom VII. 24–6.[88]

Importance is also placed on the Law for, by obeying it and understanding it, one obtains wisdom and thus draws near to God. The Wisdom of Jesus, or, The Book of Ecclesiasticus, opens with the words,

> … my grandfather Jesus, having much given himself to the reading of the law, and the prophets, and the other books of our fathers … was drawn … to write somewhat pertaining to instruction and wisdom; in order that those who love learning … might make progress much more by living according to the law. …
> He that feareth the Lord will do this;
> And he that hath possession of the law shall obtain her.
>
> Ecclesiasticus, Prologue, XV. 1.[89]

It is a progression which is explained in The Wisdom of Solomon.

> For the truest beginning of her is the desire for instruction,
> And care for instruction is love for her,
> And love for her is keeping of her laws,
> And adherence to the laws the assurance of immortality,
> And immortality makes to be near unto God …
>
> Wisdom VI. 17–19.[90]

It will be recalled that one connection between the law and heaven is made through the Ten Commandments, or Decalogue.[91] As Clement of Alexandria, the Greek philosopher and convert to Christianity, explained:

> That ten is a sacred number, it is superfluous to say … And the Decalogue, viewed as an image of heaven, embraces sun and moon, stars, clouds, light, wind, water, air, darkness, fire. This is the physical Decalogue of the heaven.
>
> *Stromateis* VI. 16.[92]

Similarly, 10 was associated with the sphere of the universe since, just as the universe contained all things, so the decad contains all numbers. By extension, the literature also describes how Wisdom was believed to have framed the universe, and the house or temple, its archetype, for Solomon. According to The Wisdom of Jesus,

> Wisdom hath been created before all things,
> [The Lord] created her,
> And saw, and numbered her,
> And poured her out upon all his works.
>
> Ecclesiasticus I. 4, 9.[93]

The description of Wisdom accompanying the creation is found in The Proverbs of Solomon:

> When he prepared the heavens, I was there: when he set a compass upon the face of the depth:
> When he established the clouds above: when he strengthened the fountains of the deep:
> When he gave to the sea his decree, that the waters should not pass his commandment: when he appointed the foundations of the earth:
> Then I was with him, as one brought up with him: and I was daily his delight …
>
> Proverbs VIII. 27–30.

The act of creation necessitated calculation on the part of the Creator, of whom it was written:

> … thou didst order all things by measure and number and weight.
>
> Wisdom XI. 20.[94]

And, famously, it was said that:

> Wisdom hath builded her house, she hath hewn out her seven pillars …
>
> Proverbs IX. 1.

The process could be apprehended by analogy to the house or temple of Wisdom:

> The fear of the Lord is the beginning of wisdom; and the knowledge of the holy is understanding.
> Through wisdom is an house builded; and by understanding it is established:
> And by knowledge shall the chambers be filled with all precious and pleasant riches.
>
> Proverbs IX. 10, XXIV. 3, 4.

Sceptics were chided by Clement of Alexandria because,

> … they have not read what is said by Solomon; for, treating of the construction of the temple, he says expressly, 'And it was Wisdom as artificer that framed it …'
>
> *Stromateis* VI. 11.[95]

There may not at first sight be pillars by the 7 to be counted in Hagia Sophia but it could be by counting pillars that their otherwise anomalous disposition may be explained, as will be discussed shortly. There are, however, 7 doorways into the inner narthex at the west end, 7 windows and 7 blank niches along the base of the *tympana* to the north and south, and 7 steps to the *synthronon* in the east. It might be argued that this could have been circumstantial, arising from practical considerations. Yet it has been remarked how awkward the entrance arrangements are at the west end, where the two middle doors in the outer narthex lead to blank walls, requiring people to turn twice in order to enter the inner narthex, where there is also a conspicuous mismatch between the cross-arches of the vaults and the arches over the three end doorways to the north and south.[96] These arrangements appear highly impractical, prompting the suggestion that they could have been determined by factors that are not obvious, such as the significance of number. Although he makes no connection with their signification, Paulus does single out 'the seven holy gates inviting the people to enter',[97] whilst Michael of Thessalonica observed that the 3 central doors symbolized the Holy Trinity.[98] Similarly, it could be argued that the row of 7 windows and niches in the *tympana* could have been the consequence of the gallery colonnade beneath consisting of 6 pillars and therefore 7 arches, with which the window openings and niches were vertically aligned, but the choice of 6 pillars in the first place appears anomalous, for reasons explored below. Finally, since the priests apparently sat on only the top step of the *synthronon*,[99] its bank of steps could have comprised any number, which again suggests the possibility of the choice being allegorical. When Gregory the Great explained the 7 levels to the sanctuary of the Temple, he wrote:

> In our mind the first level of the staircase is the fear of God, the second piety, the third knowledge, the fourth perseverance, the fifth counsel, the sixth understanding, the seventh wisdom.
>
> *Homiliae in Hiezechihelem prophetam* 40.[100]

Returning to the question of column placement, it may be instructive to investigate their disposition and what this may reveal, particularly in view of the importance accorded the 7 pillars of Wisdom and, for that matter, the 50 columns inside Moses' Tabernacle which betokened to Philo Judaeus nothing less than 'the foundation of the creation of the universe' (Figs 16, 17).[101] At ground level in Hagia Sophia, the 4 large monoliths that are referred to repeatedly in contemporary accounts stand between the great piers on each of the north and south sides of the nave, with a further two in each of the 4 *exedrae* (Figs 15, 23). All of them are round, as are the 4 smaller columns in each centre bay of the aisles, with two more in each of the 4 corner bays. Oddly, the remaining two in each corner bay, adjacent to the sanctuary and narthex walls, are square. At gallery level, the colonnades to the north and south between the piers comprise 6 columns, with a further 6 in each of the *exedrae*. There are 12 columns in each of the north and south galleries, the same number as there are below and in the same positions; and they are all round. In the west gallery above the inner narthex, there is a different arrangement, with 4 structural columns, which are paired, and 4 free-standing columns bearing lamps (Fig. 24).

Besides the variety found in the arrangement and type of these columns, mismatches in the internal structure, such as those already pointed out in the inner narthex, have been noted more than once.[102] Above all, the placing of 6 columns in the gallery arcade above 4 below (Fig. 23), and to an even greater degree, standing 6 in each *exedra* upon just two below appears to be without precedent, it was entirely contrary to the classical tradition, and is still to be satisfactorily explained. It was observed without comment by Procopius:

> In the middle of the church there rise four man-made eminences which are called piers, two on the north and two on the south, opposite and equal to one another, each pair having between them exactly four columns. … Upon these [piers] are placed four arches so as to form a square, their ends coming together in pairs and made fast at the summit of those piers, while the rest of them rises to an immense height. Two of the arches, namely those facing the rising and the setting sun, are suspended over empty air, while the others [to the north and south] have beneath them some kind of structure and rather tall columns.
>
> *De aedificiis* I. 1.[103]

The historian Evagrius (sixth century), writing soon after the rebuilding, seems not to notice:

> The divine palace consists of a dome lifted up on four arches and rising to so great a height that those who behold it from the ground are at a loss to comprehend how the cupola was completed … The arches rise free from the ground to the roof-covering. Beside them, on right and left, columns of Thessalian marble are set out in a row, supporting, by means of other, similar columns, galleries which enable anyone who so wishes to look down upon the service …
>
> *Historia ecclesiastica* IV. 31.[104]

Fig. 23 North colonnade and gallery, Hagia Sophia, Constantinople

Paulus Silentarius did notice and put it down to daring:

> Upon the porphyry columns [of the exedrae] stand others from Thessaly, splendid flowers of verdant stone. Here are the fair galleries for the women, and they have the same form that may be seen below, except that they are adorned not with two columns, but with six Thessalian ones. One may wonder at the resolve of the man who upon two columns has bravely set thrice two, and has not hesitated to fix their bases over empty air.
>
> *Descriptio ecclesiae sanctae Sophiae* 362.[105]

Yet when he arrived at the north and south colonnades, he made no similar comment:

> … towards the murmuring south wind and the rainless north there rises a mighty wall up to the chin of the rounded arch … This wall rests below

Fig. 24 West gallery, Hagia Sophia, Constantinople

> on stone props, for, underneath it, six Haemonian columns, like the fresh green of emerald, hold up the tireless sinewy juncture ... These in turn are heaved upon massive heads by four columns fixed immovable on the ground, glittering jewels of Thessalian marble ...
>
> *Descriptio ecclesiae sanctae Sophiae* 532.[106]

Michael of Thessalonica, on the other hand, appears to have composed his text at home without checking it against the building:

> For the beautiful piers ... standing apart, four on either side, do not terminate before receiving the roof upon themselves, and in the spaces between are high columns, some going in a straight line, others as it were in a dancing fashion inclining towards each other on a circle ... The upper galleries which rest on these columns are exactly formed after the fashion of those below, and no task is performed twice for the same purpose, except that column goes on top of column, that is, a smaller

> on a greater … so that you might say that the daughter becomes a sweet burden to her mother.
>
> *Ekphrasis* 4.[107]

Although he is mistaken, he at least describes the arrangement he believes to exist, because placing one column above another is precisely what was to be expected. Modern commentators either fail to comment or struggle to explain. One recent study, like Paulus, notices the misalignment of columns in the *exedrae*, but attributes this to a desire for decoration.[108] Another, in noting the lack of correspondence between the upper and lower columns in the *exedrae* and in the north and south arcades, also observes that the pilaster responds, which are planted against the piers at the ends of the straight colonnades at ground level, are repeated in the gallery above where they rise to a point well above the existing gallery arcade. This clearly indicates that a much taller arcade was first planned for the gallery, more the size of the ground level colonnade, which would probably have resulted in erecting the same number of columns as in the colonnade below. If this is so, the plan must have been changed once construction reached the gallery and one reason offered is that the quarries may have run out of the size of Thessalian marble needed.[109] An alternative explanation could be that it was the porphyry columns of the *exedrae* that could not be repeated in the galleries, causing the north and south gallery colonnades to be reduced in order to follow suit. Be this as it may, there may also have been the realization that a larger number of smaller columns would be easier to erect at gallery level and would also result in the more satisfactory scale that has, in the event, been achieved.[110] Given the importance consistently attached to number, the change in design could equally have been caused by an awareness of the difference in the significance of the number of columns that has resulted (Figs. 16, 17).

Taking the first scheme as it was probably intended, each straight colonnade would have comprised the 4 present columns at ground level with another 4 above, in other words 4 twofold, signifying earth, and perhaps 8, the journey that leads to heaven.[111] The colonnaded *exedrae*, which the congregation faced either side of the sanctuary apse, would each have consisted of 4 columns, two above and two below, again signifying earth; and all at the level in the building that was repeatedly associated with earth in the texts. In the scheme that was built, substituting 6 columns in the gallery for the 4 in the straight colonnades and another 6 for the two in the *exedrae*, if that is what happened, appears to introduce a layer signifying creation between the realm of earth and the dome of heaven. As Clement of Alexandria wrote, at the turn of the third century of the Greek tradition,

> … the Pythagoreans … reckon six the perfect number, from the creation of the world … from its being the middle of the even numbers, that is, of ten and two. … And as marriage generates from male and female, so six is generated from the odd number three, which is called the masculine number, and the even number two, which is considered the feminine.
>
> *Stromateis* VI. 16.[112]

But 6 is also the number of sides enclosing a cube. Although every schoolchild would have known this, Martianus associates this fact with the perfection of 6,[113] whilst Boethius transmits the association with the harmonic median by Nicomachus of Gerasa (mid first–mid second century AD), whose work was well known to the Greeks, by citing the cube as exemplifying the harmonic medial proportion of 6 : 8 : 12 because the cube has 6 sides, 8 corners, and 12 edges.[114]

The architectural composition of the north and south sides of the nave could be described as a colonnade of 4 columns surmounted by another of 6, framed beneath the semi-circular arch of the *tympanum*, the 4 columns representing earth, and the 6 representing the creation of earth and the composition of its cube, coinciding with two of the sides of the cube within the building, and together amounting to 10, the number of the law and the universe.

Considering all the columns and commencing at ground level (Fig. 25), there are 12 in each of the aisles, divided between round and square. The round columns number 16 altogether, or 4 squared, the square columns number 8, or 4 twofold, and this is only achieved as a result of making 8 of the columns square in the first place. There are also 16 columns in the north and south colonnades and *exedrae*, or 4 squared once again. The total number is 40, which is 4 tenfold, or 10 fourfold.

In the galleries, there are 36 columns in all the colonnades, which is 6 squared, and, in the north and south galleries, another 24, which is 6 fourfold, or vice versa. The total is 60, or 6 tenfold, but, once again, this has only been achieved by placing 6 columns over the 4 and 2 below in the first place. It may be reasoned that, where the columns at ground level comprehensively group themselves in fours, those at gallery level can be grouped in either fours or sixes but, either way, their total remains the product of the numbers of both creation and the cube, 6, with the number which represented both 'an image of heaven' and the universe, 10. Similarly, as the ground level total can be expressed as the product of the numbers of earth, 4, and heaven, 10, so the total at gallery level is the product of creation, 6, and heaven, 10.

This analysis does not yet include the west gallery which, with its idiosyncratic columns, might be considered an irrelevance (Fig. 24). However, if the paired columns are added to those in the two other galleries, this brings the total to 64, which is 4 cubed. If the 4 lamp-bearing columns are then added, the total becomes 68 which, intriguingly, is the product of 4 and the sum of the numbers of heaven and Wisdom – 10 + 7.[115] And so 7, the number of Wisdom, is present in the number of pillars after all and, significantly perhaps, it takes the 4 light-giving lamps to bring this about. Located as they are in the gallery above the main entrance, they could well represent the enlightenment shed by Wisdom upon those entering the church below and, being at the level of creation in the supposed schematic composition of the building, could reflect the process of the temple being framed by Wisdom, as foretold by Solomon, in words repeated by Clement.[116]

In the building as a whole, the total number of structural columns that are round is 96, which is the product of 4 squared and 6. The number of all the

Dome: Heaven				
diameter, Byzantine feet		= 100		= **10** × 10
windows		= 40		= **10** × 4
Gallery: Creation and cube of Earth				
colonnades, including *exedrae*		= 36	= **6** × 6	
aisles		= 24	= **6** × 4	
Total		= **60**		= **6** × 10
West gallery				
paired columns	= 4	= 64	= 4 × **4** × 4	
lamp-bearing columns	= 4	= 68	= 4 × (**10 + 7**)	
Ground: Earth				
colonnades, including *exedrae*		= 16	= **4** × 4	
aisles, round columns		= 16	= **4** × 4	
aisles, square columns		= 8	= **4** × 2	
Total		= **40**		= **4** × 10
Totals: Gallery and Ground				
structural columns, round		= 96	= **4** × **6** × 4	
all round columns		= 100		= **10** × 10
column positions		= 106		
Grand total		= 108	= 100 + 8	
			= **4** × 3 × 3 × 3	
			= **6** × 6 × 3	
			= **10** × 10 + 8	

Fig. 25 The numbers 10, 6 and 4 in the dome and arrangement of columns, Hagia Sophia, Constantinople

columns that are round is 100, the number of heaven, or the universe, squared, and the diameter of the dome in Byzantine feet. It has been suggested that square columns were selected for the 4 corners of the building so as to avoid the number of circular columns exceeding 100.[117] Because the paired columns in the west gallery each occupy a single position, the number of different column positions in the building is 106, which is the length of Solomon's Temple measured in cubits, as described in the First Book of Kings,[118] and the number of years Solomon took to build it was 7.[119] The grand total of all columns is 108, which has many divisors,[120] several possessing potential significance. Prominent among them, again, are 4 and 6, yet this number could also have been understood as the sum of 10 squared, standing for heaven and the universe, plus 8, representing the journey that leads to heaven.[121]

Finally, the number of window openings around the base of the dome also amounts to 40 (Figs 18, 25),[122] which, if signifying the dome of heaven, might logically be expressed as 10 fourfold, or 10 quartered. It has already been shown that religious architecture was routinely interpreted numerologically by counting architectural elements, a tradition which includes Hagia Sophia. In support of this, the example of Michael of Thessalonica has already been referred to in passing:

> There being, symbolically, a triple entry … (for the holy places are accessible to those who have been taught that there is one God in the Trinity) …
>
> *Ekphrasis* 4.[123]

Similarly the Emperor Justinian was said to have told his builders:

> I wish that you make me the apse with three lights by means of three arches, in the name of the Father, the Son and the Holy Ghost.
>
> *Narratio* 12.[124]

For Justinian's Church of the Holy Apostles,

> … the colonnades which support the whole Church are twelve in number … a detail arranged by the architect not without purpose, I think, but in order that his might be indeed a living Church of Christ, supported by colonnades and columns equal in number to the Disciples of Christ.
>
> Nicholas Mesarites, *Description of the Church of the Holy Apostles* XXXVII. 6.[125]

The danger of over-interpretation is ever present of course, especially with so many permutations possible, and so is the temptation of juggling with numbers to induce a particular result. However, it is argued here that nothing has had to be forced in this analysis; other meanings are present, such as 3 for the Trinity, 8 for salvation, 9 for the orders of angels, 12 for the Apostles and time, but these are complementary to the proposed paradigm, not contradictory.[126] Conversely the meanings that have been found and advanced here serve as signifiers in the particular context of the formal model in question, and their presence is consistent and structured according to their own logic. To summarize, it seems reasonable to assert that these readings would have served to underline the integrity of the formal scheme, in that the occurrence of number exactly supports the geometric form – 10 for the sphere of heaven, 6 for the creation and the cube of earth, 4 for the square of earth and its corners, incorporating the singular presence of Wisdom herself in the intervening layer of creation.[127] If anything exemplifies Wisdom framing the temple, it is surely Justinian's Great Church of the Holy Wisdom.

Part Three: The Greek Cross and Byzantine church design

The Church of the Holy Apostles, Constantinople

While Hagia Sophia was under construction, Justinian was also building the Church of the Holy Apostles out towards the walls of the city to a completely different design (Figs 26, 27).[128] Like Hagia Sophia, it replaced a predecessor of the same dedication dating from the city's earliest years. According to Eusebius, the Emperor Constantine (?285–337) decided to build a memorial church to the Apostles, with a place for his own sarcophagus in the middle.[129] When he died, he was entombed as planned and, within twenty years, was joined by relics of the Apostles Timothy, Luke, and Andrew. This was presumably done to complement in New Rome, which was Constantine's co-appellation of Constantinople, the

Fig. 26 Ascension miniature, Holy Apostles, Constantinople? Jakobos of Kokkinobaphos, *Homilies on the Virgin*, Constantinople, twelfth century

apostolic shrines of Peter and Paul in Old Rome.[130] It is thought that construction started with Constantine erecting his mausoleum and, with his son Constantius, adding a cruciform basilica. Constantine's building was evidently a rotunda with 7 niches and an entrance in the eighth side,[131] an altar in the middle, and his own tomb occupying the easterly recess opposite the entrance. The basilica followed with the arrival of the Apostles' relics and was consecrated in 370. In the meantime, the mausoleum had been repaired after an earthquake and Constantius was entombed in it beside his father.[132] As the foundation and mausoleum of the first Christian emperor and founder of Constantinople,[133] predating even Hagia Sophia, and as the imperial mausoleum for centuries to come, the Church of the Holy Apostles became second only to Hagia Sophia in importance yet, by Justinian's reign, in the words of Procopius,

> ... it had been shaken by the lapse of time and was not expected to stand much longer. The emperor Justinian demolished it entirely, being eager

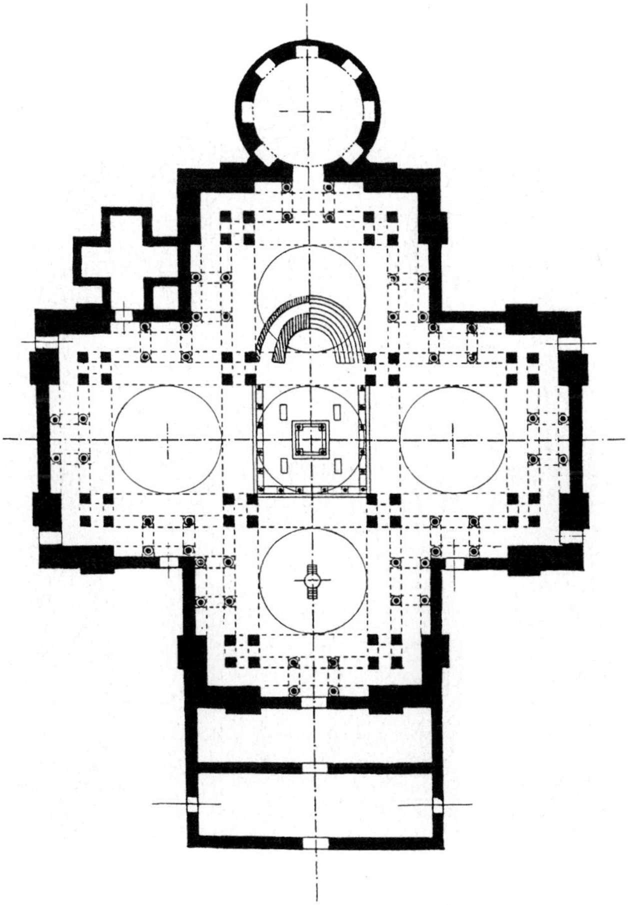

Fig. 27 Plan, Holy Apostles, Constantinople

> not merely to restore it, but to make it more remarkable with regard to size and beauty. He carried out his intention in the following manner. Two straight arms were made, intersecting each other in the middle after the fashion of a cross, the longitudinal one running east and west, while the transverse one was turned to north and south. … At the junction of the two straight arms … a place has been consecrated that … is fittingly called the sanctuary. The transverse arms on either side of the sanctuary are equal to each other, while on the longitudinal axis the western one is that much longer than the other as to form the shape of a cross. The … roof that is above the sanctuary … has been made to resemble that of the church of Sophia – … as regards the middle – except that it happens to be smaller than the latter. The arches, four in number, are suspended … likewise, the circular ring that rests upon them is divided by windows, and the dome that curves above seems to be somehow hovering in the air … and as for the arms which … are four in number, their roof is of the same dimensions as the one in the middle, but lacks this one feature, namely that underneath the circular curvature the masonry is not pierced by windows.
>
> *De aedificiis* I. 4.[134]

At the end of the twelfth century, Nicholas Mesarites summarized the layout thus:

> Now the architect brought each of the stoas (colonnaded arms) to completion in the shape of a perfect hemisphere. … four of them have their foundations in the form of a cross, and face toward the four quarters of our earth … while the other in the center stands up above them, and the direction of this one faces toward heaven, calling on the heavenly God-Man … to descend to it … as though from heaven …
>
> *Description of the Church of the Holy Apostles* XIII. 4, 5.[135]

In the words of Constantine of Rhodes two hundred years earlier, already cited,

> … the central [dome was] elevated … over the others, destined as it was to be the Lord's great throne …
>
> *Στυχοι Κονσταντυνου (Poem of Constantine)* 626.[136]

From the available evidence, a plan of Justinian's church has been reconstructed (Fig. 27),[137] and it consists of a Greek Cross with domes over the crossing and each arm, and an inner and outer narthex to the west, making the nave arm of the cross longer than the others, as noted by Procopius. Each dome surmounts a square compartment opening into its neighbour through deep cross-arches supported on piers. The piers are threaded by cross-passages at floor level and linked by colonnades. Between the cross-arches and the surrounding walls are the aisles with galleries above. The sanctuary, unusually, is situated beneath the central dome which Constantine of Rhodes says was raised over the others, and Procopius says alone had windows around its perimeter as at Hagia Sophia. The east arm leads into Emperor Constantine's

Fig. 28 Interior, St Mark's, Venice

original mausoleum beyond it while, to the east of the north arm is Justinian's tomb-house, which is cruciform.[138]

The church was dedicated in 550 and, following various vicissitudes from the ninth century onwards, was eventually replaced in 1462 by the first of two Ottoman mosques.[139] For an impression of its interior, however, it is only necessary to enter the basilica of St Mark in Venice (Fig. 28). This was closely modelled on the Holy Apostles in the middle of the eleventh century[140] for a number of convergent reasons. As the church of the Doge's Palace, it was a ducal foundation, just as the Holy Apostles was an imperial foundation. Similarly, St Mark's was a ducal burial-place, numbering the founding doge and other early doges, although their whereabouts are unknown. Finally, above all, St Mark's Basilica follows the Holy Apostles in being an apostolic shrine. Differences of doctrine and detail notwithstanding, St Mark's spatial sequence internally of domed, square compartments extending equally in 4 directions, is subtly accentuated by the slightly larger central dome, the whole being linked by colonnaded aisles and galleries, and is entirely sheathed with glass mosaic and marble panelling, thereby materially defining the realms of heaven and earth as in Justinian's Hagia Sophia. The Greek Cross layout, even in Justinian's day, was not new, and precedents have already been encountered in this study – Gaza Cathedral for example, dating from 402, was cruciform and the mausoleum of Galla Placidia from 450 in Ravenna is a small Greek Cross funerary chapel, similar to that shown as being Justinian's at the Holy Apostles. Interestingly, Constantine of Rhodes states that the architects of Hagia Sophia, Anthemius and Isidorus, were also involved in Justinian's Holy

Apostles[141] and, for all the obvious differences between the two buildings, they both share the dome and the cube as their generating idea. Similarly, just as the allusion of the dome to heaven is as obvious as that of the cruciform to the crucifix, there appear to be layers of meaning, not immediately apparent, that enrich the reading of the design of the Holy Apostles' Church in a similar fashion to those already explored for Hagia Sophia.

To begin with, the Greek Cross is itself an abstraction of the supposed cross of the crucifixion with the long vertical post of the original, and shorter cross-arm set near its top. Instead, the equal arms of the Greek Cross seem to lend themselves to a scheme of square compartmentation and domes, which necessarily amount to 5 in number. By raising the central dome over the other 4, the description by Martianus Capella of the pentad is recalled as,

> … the number assigned to the universe. This identification is reasonable, for after the four elements, the universe is the fifth body of a different nature.
>
> *De nuptiis Philologiae et Mercurii* 735.[142]

In addition to signifying the macrocosm of the universe, it has already been shown that 5 also represents the microcosm of the human being, with its 5 senses.[143] Accordingly, the representation of Christ in the central dome of the Holy Apostles and elsewhere, carrying with it his identification with humanity through his incarnation and crucifixion, is surely expressed by this interaction of iconography and architectural form, in which the five-domed Greek Cross can be understood in terms of being both a Platonic and an Orthodox archetype.[144] If this might be thought fanciful, it was John of Damascus who connected crucifixion with creation, in a passage that is easy to imagine as having been inspired by experiencing the architecture of Justinian's Holy Apostles:

> And the word of the Cross is the power of God … because, just as the four arms of the cross are made solid and bound together by their central part, so are the height and the depth, the length and the breadth, that is to say, all creation both visible and invisible, held together by the power of God.
>
> *De fide* IV. 11.[145]

The Greek Cross inscribed in a square

Perhaps less than a century after the completion of Justinian's Holy Apostles, a variation in the architectural application of the Greek Cross produced a schematic design that was to perpetuate itself throughout the Middle and Late Byzantine periods. An early appearance of it can be seen in the layout of Etchmiadzin Cathedral in Armenia dating from 632, the year when the Armenian and Greek Orthodox Churches united (Fig. 29). Here the Greek Cross is inscribed within a square, with a central cupola raised over the crossing and carried internally on 4 pillars, the cross-arms being raised above

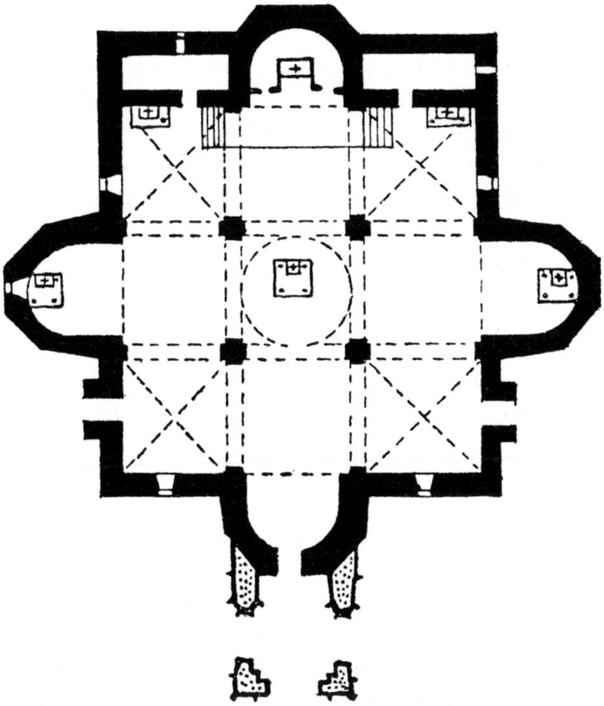

Fig. 29 Plan, Etchmiadzin Cathedral, Armenia

the rest of the square, leaving 4 square bays at the corners. Additionally, and untypically of later examples, an apse projects from each of the 4 sides.[146] Other examples have been noted from the 630s in Armenia at Vagarshapat, Bagavan, and Mren, where the cross-in-square form became elongated.[147] Yet it may not have been until the ninth century that this type of design was introduced to Constantinople,[148] and only after a small version of Etchmiadzin was built on the banks of the Loire at Germigny-des-Prés in 806. This served as an oratory for Theodulf (c. 760–821), who was a leading figure in the court of Charlemagne and was both bishop of Orléans, some distance downstream from Germigny, and abbot of Fleury, along the Loire in the other direction.[149] Then in 880, Emperor Basil I (c. 811–86) built the Nea Ekklêsia in the grounds of his Imperial Palace in Constantinople, to decorate which he raided Justinian's mausoleum at the Holy Apostles for its mosaics. But this was not before he had restored over thirty churches in and around the capital, including the Holy Apostles.[150] The *Vita Basilii* describes his church thus:

> But why do we dwell on his lesser achievements [the restoration and rebuilding of churches in Constantinople] … and not include that admirable work of his which he built in the very imperial palace, himself supervising it and creating it … a holy and beautiful church in which art, riches, an ardent faith and a bountiful zeal were all combined and

> the most beautiful materials were gathered together from every quarter … Its roof, consisting of five domes, gleams with gold and is resplendent with beautiful images as with stars …
>
> *Historia de vita Basilii* 83, 84.[151]

Although its five-domed arrangement could have been a smaller version of the Holy Apostles, it has been surmized that it was probably a Greek cross-in-square design with a central dome and 4 more domes over the corners of the square.[152] If true, this would be of interest. Basil was the first of the Macedonian dynasty of Byzantine emperors, so called because of its geographic origin within the empire. Yet he was not a Macedonian but the son of an Armenian, part of the population which had been resettled there from Armenia in order to dilute the power of the Slavs in Macedonia. He was an Armenian and so was Stylianus Zaoutzas, whose church has been cited above, and who became policy chief and father-in-law of Basil's son, Leo VI (866–912).[153] A generation earlier, Emperor Leo V (775–820), who reigned from 813, was an Armenian; a generation later, so was Emperor Romanus I (c. 870–948), together with his Great Chamberlain, the Patriarch of Constantinople, and the Commander-in-Chief of the armed forces, followed by Emperor John I (c. 925–976), whose reign extended until 976.[154] In 986, it was the Armenian architect Trdat who rebuilt the dome and semi-dome of Hagia Sophia after another collapse. Throughout this period therefore, the Armenian composition of the court was complemented by numerous Armenians such as Trdat operating as artisans and merchants in Constantinople, as well as in other cities of the empire. Such was the ethnology of the Macedonian dynasty.

The reason Basil might have had for choosing for his palace chapel a design that reached back to his homeland of Armenia, if indeed this was his intention, may have been bound up with the same impetus that created the need for him to restore so many of the capital's churches in the first place. This was to be found in the spirit of revival following the settlement of the icon dispute a generation earlier. Such was the upheaval caused by the dispute, it has come to mark the separation between the Early and Middle Byzantine periods, just as the Fourth Crusade and Catholic conquest of Constantinople early in the thirteenth century divides the Middle and Late periods.

Since the consequences of the dispute are of greater relevance to this study than its substance, it may only be necessary to note that it raged intermittently from 726 to 843 between iconoclast emperors with ecclesiastical supporters, and iconophile churchmen, partly led in the first instance by John of Damascus.[155] As might be expected, the iconoclasts accused their opponents of idolatry, of offending against the Commandment not to worship graven images; while iconophiles asserted that they were not worshipping images, but using them as a path to the holy souls they represented. Quoting Basil the Great (c. 329–379), the Bishop of Caesarea, John put the case at its simplest:

> … the honor paid to the image redounds to the original …
>
> *De fide* IV. 16.[156]

The advocates of icons won after a long and bitter struggle riven with vicious persecution and severe disruption of artistic activity, causing monastic artists and craftsmen to flee East and West. To this day their decorative art can be seen as far afield as the Great Mosque of Damascus, the Dome of the Rock in Jerusalem, and in the basilica of S. Prassede in Rome. At one point in the dispute, the Oecumenical Council of 787 in Nicaea set out its provisions for icons, which was confirmed by a later Council in Constantinople at the end of the dispute, and this remained the final word on the subject.[157]

The decades following this second Council have been described as being devoted to the restoration both of images to churches which had been robbed of them by iconoclasts, and of the churches themselves which had often fallen into decay during the dispute. Importantly, it was also accompanied, it seems, by a revival of older architectural models drawn from a more settled time.[158] This might account for the activities of Emperor Basil I in restoring the churches of Constantinople and their images, and in looking to his Armenian heritage for the domed cross-in-square design for his Nea Ekklêsia, if indeed this is what he did.[159] It may also have been a result of the symbolic significance of the design, a possibility which will be explored shortly. Be this as it may, this was a time when, above all, developments in iconography, liturgy and various versions of the Greek cross-in-square design converged to produce an archetype that sufficed for at least the next five hundred years (Fig. 30).[160]

Iconographically, the interior of churches was divided into three zones of descending sanctity, with the Pantokrator in the dome and the Mother and Child in the sanctuary's semi-dome, as already encountered in the mosaics added to Hagia Sophia by Photius at this very time. To provide greater elevation, domes were now raised on drums, around the interior of which were set angels or prophets to be seen above the 4 crossing arches and their supporting pillars. The middle zone consisted of the barrel vaults and the semi-circular ends of the cross-arms, which radiated out from the crossing and portrayed the earthly lives of Christ and Mary. The surrounding walls formed the lowest zone which, being in closest proximity to the congregation, was filled with church fathers, martyrs, patriarchs, and priests; in other words, holy men and women displayed as if part of the company of the congregation.[161]

The liturgy evolved from one of openness, involving processions and lay participation in settings shaped by the linear horizontality of Early Byzantine basilicas, to a liturgy during which the laity stood as witnesses in the domed, vertical space of the nave, separated from clergy who presided over the sacred mysteries out of sight in the sanctuary behind an icon screen, through which they made occasional appearances. For this, the compact, centralized space of the domed Greek cross-in-square layout must have seemed ideal. More particularly, since the liturgy commenced with the appearance of the priest from behind the icon screen once the congregation had taken up their places in the nave, there was no longer a need for processional routes or an atrium, but there was one for a vestry for robing within the church, and this was provided by the *diaconicon*, or apsed chamber adjoining the sanctuary to the

Fig. 30 Plans, cross-in-square churches. *Top and centre:* Examples from Bulgaria. *Bottom:* Examples from Athens and vicinity

south. Similarly, since there was no longer a second entry prior to the eucharist, the holy sacraments also had to be prepared within the church and this was done in the *prothesis*, a corresponding chamber to the north of the sanctuary, thereby perpetuating the practice of bringing the sacraments into the sanctuary of Hagia Sophia from its *skeuophylakion* to the north.[162] Thus the triple-apse arrangement of most Middle and Late Byzantine churches was completed.[163]

Because sermons became read before the door in the icon screen, the *ambo* disappeared; the open structure of the chancel projecting into the nave was moved back to the archway into the sanctuary, becoming in the process a solid screen for the display of icons with a door in it; the altar was moved back with it into the sanctuary and, because the clergy could no longer be seen sitting around the *synthronon* in the apse, it was reduced in height to a step or two, or dispensed with altogether when numbers did not justify it.[164]

The result of all these changes produced a fusion of imagery, liturgy and architectural space into a total religious experience. The geometry of the space was left clearly articulated by the hierarchy of holy images and by the delineation provided by simple cornices and string courses.[165] In eschewing the perspective systems in a painting or mosaic that create the illusion of space beyond the building, with figures located in it, Byzantine skenography induced a sense of the figure and worshipper sharing the same space, shaped as the container of all, in a metaphorical association with Christ, who was shown in the aspect of Pantokrator, the holder of all.[166] Upon entry, the impact of the vaulted cross-arms would have been reinforced by worshippers crossing themselves, also by crosses worn and held by the priests, and the crossings of blessing repeatedly made by them throughout the liturgy. Beneath the dome and the pillared crossing, the space of the nave was shared by the congregation with the Pantokrator gazing from the dome, holding the book, so that when the priest appeared in the nave before the sanctuary door to read the Gospel, he united them with Christ in the same shared space through the sacrament of the word. Similarly, the celebrant commenced the eucharist by censing the altar, before emerging through the icon screen into the nave to cense the icons, then the people, thereby uniting congregation and saints within the same space. A second union with Christ in the nave followed with the eucharist through *theosis*, the belief that the communicant becomes transformed into Christ.[167] As Paul had declared:

> I am crucified with Christ: nevertheless I live; yet not I, but Christ liveth in me …
>
> Galatians II.20.[168]

Also as Athanasius (c. 295–373), the patriarch of Alexandria, had written:

> He became man in order that we might become God.
>
> *De Incarnatione*.[169]

Significantly, it is the dome and the Pantokrator looking down from it that, ultimately, dominate the nave (Fig. 34), situated as they are above the arms of the cross, as if transcending them, and there is evidence that the sight-lines that were necessary to achieve this effect from different parts of the church may have been controlled during the setting out of the building, as will be explored shortly. Many systems of geometric and arithmetic proportioning have been advanced to account for the planning and elevating of Byzantine churches, with a varying number of buildings answering to each of them. Yet there is very little consistency to be found at all, even among a small group of buildings.[170] One possible explanation for this might be the dwindling importance of the architect, which is evident from the ninth century onwards. His place seems to have been taken by the master builder, with the commissioning and supervision of building construction at least sometimes being conducted by the patron's own secretary.[171] With each building being erected as an independent project by its patron and builder, albeit to a familiar model, yet without the body of theory to determine its proportions and dimensions that might have come from the employment of an architect,[172] it is hardly surprising that a consistent, proportional system of design is difficult to find and that there should be so many variations on one particular theme (Fig. 30). For example, a Greek cross-in-square church may have its central cupola supported on pillars or piers. It will usually have apses projecting either side of the sanctuary; but sometimes these are contained within the wall thickness; sometimes they are missing altogether. The layout may be enclosed within a regular square, with apses projecting from it, or it may be irregular, or even a parallelogram, depending on the accuracy of the setting-out. Its corner bays may be barrel-vaulted, or have vaults that are groined or domical, or sometimes domed. The enclosing square of the layout may be elongated westwards by a narthex, or expanded on three sides by a *parekklesion*. Exceptionally, the square may be reduced by omitting the pillars and corner bays along the east side. Conversely, the most common variation is to extend the cross-in-square eastwards by elongating the east arm, flanking it with a second pair of piers, and adding an extra bay between the corner bays and side apses.[173] Nevertheless, at the core of all but the one reduced variation is a central cupola on 4 supports, dominating 4 equal cross-arms, with 4 lower corner bays completing the square.

Whether a cause or consequence of such diversity, another possible explanation for it, in addition to the varied processes of commissioning and building already mentioned, may be that the selection of a particular archetype mattered more than an accurate, standardized reproduction of it. An icon painter of the modern era who was trained and practised in the Byzantine tradition described the artistic and architectural forms of the Orthodox faith as expressing spiritual reality, using symbolic forms and colours, which, because they reach beyond the physical world, do not fit into its measures. Also since the forms themselves may be changeless, whether they be prototypes for an icon or chapel, the artist or artisan, freed from the need to invent and produce novelty, can pour all his experience into the execution.[174]

For all the variations in the execution of the domed cross-in-square model, one determinant has apparently been found to be present consistently across a sizeable sample of Middle and Late Byzantine churches, and it correlates with the cross-section of each building investigated. If lines are drawn diagonally from the crown of the cupola downwards to either side of it, they will intersect the top of the vaults of the cross-arms and reach ground level at the foot of the nave walls, forming an isosceles triangle (Fig. 31). The little church of Hagii Theodorii in Athens is typical of many, and it is a system that

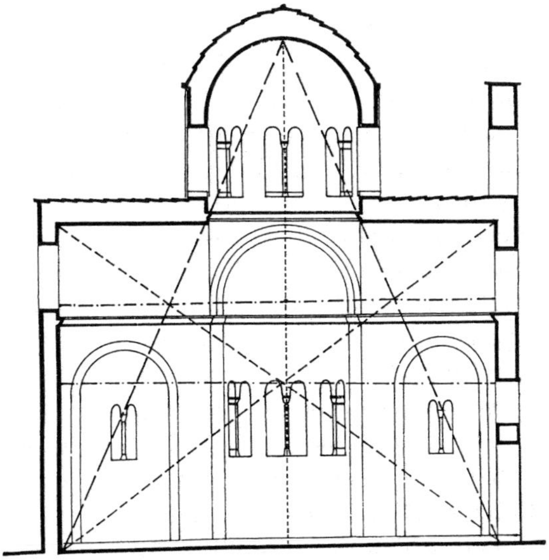

Fig. 31 Section with sight-lines to the dome, Hagii Theodorii Church, Athens

applies both to longitudinal and lateral cross-sections and to buildings with varying layouts and heights, though the proportions of each triangle may consequently vary with each building. The explanation offered is, once again, the creation of a total space shared by holy images and worshippers alike, embracing the Pantokrator in the dome, wherein sight-lines connect the whole of the nave to the dome. This also means that the whole of the nave, being the realm of earth, is visible to the Pantokrator in the dome of heaven.[175] Perhaps somebody had been inspired by the words of Maximus the Confessor when, in the seventh century, he expounded how the church was an image and figure of God:

> It is [Christ] who encloses in himself all beings by the unique, simple, and infinitely wise power of his goodness. As the center of straight lines that radiate from him he does not allow by his unique, simple, and single cause and power that the principles of beings become disjoined at the periphery but rather he circumscribes their extension in a circle and brings back to himself the distinctive elements of beings which he himself brought into existence.
>
> *Mystagogia* I.[176]

At the end of the twelfth century, Nicholas Mesarites translates this same synthesis of geometry, sight-line, and image into the description of the Church of the Holy Apostles and its crossing dome:

> Beginning with Him, as though from a kind of *kentron* … one can see a circle drawn about the edge of the hemi-sphere, and lines drawn … to the outer border of the circle; for if a point or a center is given, and a radius, it is possible to inscribe a circle, as the geometricians say.

> And the lines are not plain, but they please the senses and impress the mind by their varied colors and the brilliance of the gold and the brightness of their hues.
>
> *Description of the Church of the Holy Apostles* XIII. 7, 8.[177]

During this same period of change following the settlement of the icon dispute, these developments were accompanied by what has been described as the miniaturization of church architecture. With public worship being confined to weekends and holy days, and communion being taken only a few times a year, more frequent attendances of the liturgy tended to be conducted in private, for example in the side chapels of churches or in domestic oratories.[178] This custom evidently translated itself into new foundations being either privately endowed for personal or monastic use, or built for small village congregations, and therefore requiring architecture on a reduced scale, to which, once again, the domed Greek cross-in-square church was ideally suited.[179] In the wake of Basil I's Nea Ekklêsia, other examples followed in Constantinople, with one being built in 907 at the monastery of Constantine Lips, followed in about 920 by another at the Myrelaion monastery. The latter was raised initially as a chapel to the private residence of Emperor Romanus I, becoming a funerary chapel for himself and his family. It will be recalled that he, like Basil I, was Armenian and he could well have been following Basil in looking to the architectural tradition of Armenia and the domed Greek cross-in-square design. The pattern of small-scale imperial patronage was to continue in the capital with the Empress Irene and Emperor John II (1087–1143) erecting three churches adjoining each other at the monastery of the Pantokrator, the south church for the monks in 1118, the north church for the citizens a decade or so later, and both conforming to the domed cross-in-square layout, with a domed, imperial mausoleum between the two following later.[180]

The inscribed octagon

Outside the capital, the oldest surviving cross-in-square church in Greece is the one dedicated to the Mother of God, or Theotokos, at the monastery of Holy Luke in Stiris. Dating towards the end of the tenth century, it stands to the north of the monastery's catholicon, which was built early in the following century to a different design,[181] yet it could be construed as an adaptation of the Greek cross-in-square, distinct though it undoubtedly is. This particular type of layout is usually termed an inscribed octagon, or domed octagon, where the cupola, pillars, and cross-arms of the cross-in-square church are replaced by one large, clear-span dome covering the entire cubic space (Figs 32, 33, 34). The internal angles of the cube are bridged across by arches to form an octagon mediating between the square top of the cube and the circular base of the dome. These arches are known as squinches and their inside surfaces are made concave so as to mould themselves into the corners of the cube. Consequently, the formal language of the sphere and the cube that is present in all these Byzantine typologies is maintained here as well. Indeed the monastic church of this layout at Daphni, outside Athens, dating from around 1080, can be shown to incorporate a notional sphere on top of a cube (Fig. 32). The Greek Cross and the square are maintained in this type of church, with cross-arms opening from the 4 cardinal sides of the octagon and projecting outwards from the cube supporting the dome to the sides of the outer square (Fig. 35). Occupying the corners of the square, in the angles of the cross-arms, are 4 double-bay chapels and burial chambers. Finally, to the east is the usual arrangement of sanctuary and side apses, with a narthex to the west.

In addition to the monastic churches of Holy Luke and Daphni, others can be found in Athens, Mistra, Monemvasia, and elsewhere, dating between the eleventh and thirteenth centuries, as well as a variant group. This is described as octaconch, in which it is the octagonal form that is dominant and the cruciform is either suppressed or absent. Four such examples are located on the island of Chios, most notably at Nea Moni – another imperial foundation – dating from 1045, with others on the Greek mainland and one near Constantinople.[182] Because the octagon can be derived from both the square and the circle, this group of domed octagon churches will be discussed further in Chapters 4 and 6. Suffice it to note for the present that both main groups of churches considered so far – the cross-in-square and the inscribed octagon – consist of inserting either a cross within a square, or an octagon within a square, with both being crowned by a dome.

Symbolic interpretations

This entire group of domed octagon churches seems to have made its appearance without interrupting the domed cross-in-square as the principal type.[183] As late as the fourteenth century, examples of the latter were built within a few years of each other in Constantinople and Thessalonica. Around 1310, a cross-in-square chapel was added to the convent Church of the Panagia Pammacaristos in Constantinople, in which Patriarch Gennadius II (c. 1400–c. 1473) was later to explain the tenets of Orthodoxy to Sultan Mehmet following the Ottoman Conquest of Byzantium.[184] Then in 1312, construction started on the Church of the Panagia, which the Patriarch of Constantinople added to the monastery of the Holy Apostles in Thessalonica (Figs 36, 37).[185] Not only does this display the standard arrangement of the domed cross-in-square internally, but it is presented in expanded form externally by there being a *parekklesion* surrounding it on three sides, and this is crowned by domes on tall drums at all 4 corners. If the original precedent for this type of church really was Etchmiadzin Cathedral or one of its Armenian contemporaries, then it had enjoyed a life of nearly seven hundred years by this time, which surely requires explanation.

The common thesis is a perceived conservatism theologically and artistically among patrons and the Church following the settlement of the icon dispute, and there appears to be some substance to this claim. It has already been seen that having established prototypes to follow was

Fig. 32 Section, inscribed with sphere and cube, Daphni monastery

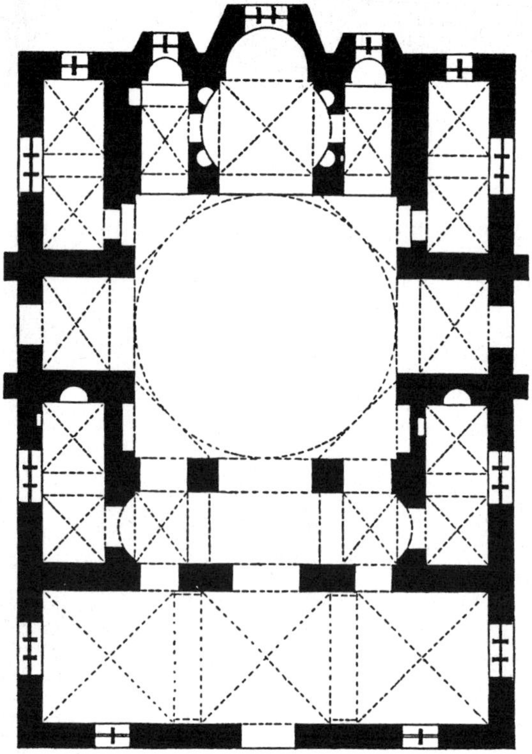

Fig. 33 Plan, Daphni monastery

Fig. 34 Pantokrator, Daphni monastery. Note how the dome is seen to sit over a ring of arches

Fig. 35 Exterior from east, Daphni monastery

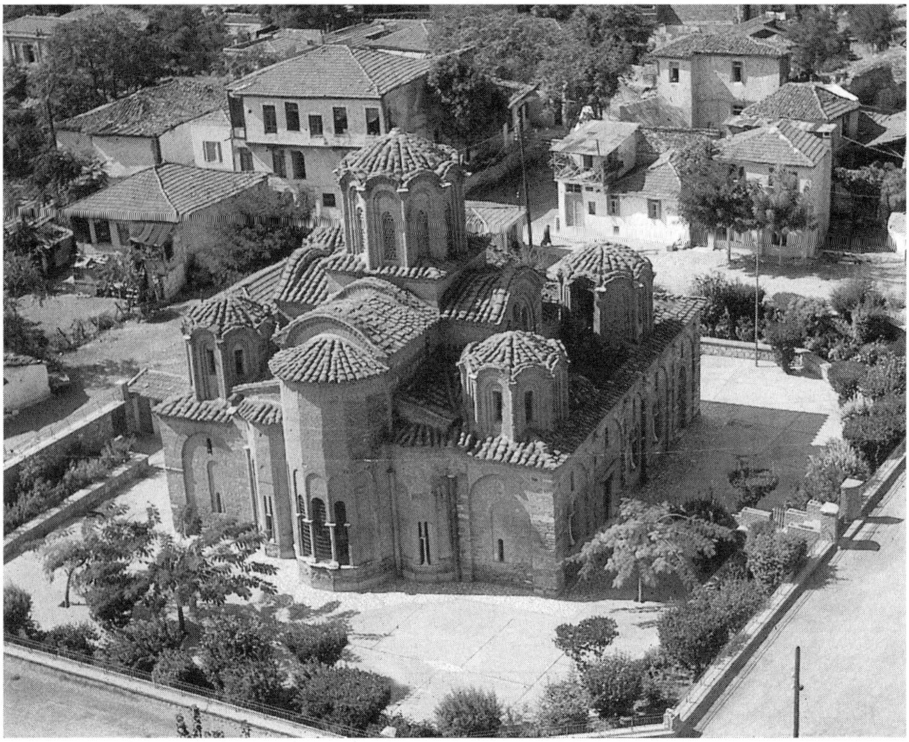

Fig. 36 Aerial view, Holy Apostles, Thessalonica

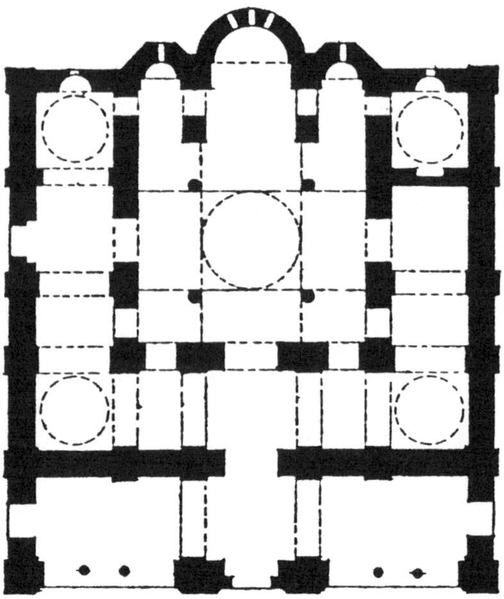

Fig. 37 Plan, Holy Apostles, Thessalonica

recognized as offering the artist a discipline within which to discover the freedoms available in execution. The catharsis of the icon dispute was such that it has been thought unremarkable that it should lead thereafter to a settled iconography and one or two standard church types.[186] If this constituted conservatism, then it was strengthened when, in the eleventh century, first Michael Psellos, professor of philosophy at Constantinople University, then John Italos (c. 1025–post-1082), his student and successor, were forced into monasteries for flirting too closely with the ideas of Plato. Psellos reasoned that because God had existed before the incarnation, it was he who would have influenced the philosophers, including Plato, with the result that much Christian teaching was to be found anticipated in their writings, a position thoroughly in the tradition of Clement of Alexandria and John of Damascus. Italos went further and was condemned for espousing Platonic doctrine heretical to the Church. From the time of their enforced retirement in the 1070s and 1080s, the Church discouraged further philosophical enquiry or academic study into religious faith. The mind and soul of Orthodoxy would reside, not in the universities, but in the monasteries where the practice and experience of religion would be valued more highly than the rational understanding of it, and would be their own reward.[187]

True though this may be, it does not explain why it was the Greek cross-in-square church that became the beneficiary of this supposed conservatism and, presumably as a result, was the most common type to be built from the ninth century onwards. Since its form had been established long before this outbreak of nervousness about the teaching of Plato, it is easy to understand why it should have continued in use. It had become a tradition in its own right.[188] But why was this form continued and others less so, such as the inscribed octagon, the choice of which does not seem to have carried into the late period? Adherence to the cross-in-square is not explained either by the desire to control iconographic space. Hagia Sophia and the Holy Apostles in Constantinople, along with the church at Daphni, all provide high, middle, and low zones for their hierarchical programmes of images, yet none is cross-in-square. Likewise, the manipulation of interior space to ensure sight-lines to the crown of a dome can be achieved with various designs and does not depend on the type being cross-in-square. Shared iconographic space and visibility cannot be the whole story. Instead, a clue might be found in the particularization of the cross-in-square's configuration, which is repeated over and over again – the cupola over the crossing, the 4 crossing arches supported on 4 pillars standing in the centre of the space, the 4 vaulted cross-arms spreading outwards from the centre, the vaults and domes at the 4 corners of the square, or enclosing rectangle. There is a completeness and an implied perfection of this form, which, it has been observed, may simply have been difficult, impossible, or unnecessary to improve.[189] Further, it has been suggested that although the model might be to a certain extent variable, which in itself seems to have been an advantage, it could be that it embodied something essential that goes beyond the practical functions of structure, liturgy and iconography.[190] To investigate this possibility, it may be worth returning to Armenia for sources

Fig. 38 Crossing vault, Mausoleum of Galla Placidia, Ravenna. Symbols of the Evangelists are located in the four corners, at the springing of the vault, as if supporting it in the way they supported the teaching of Christ, who is symbolized by the Cross at the crown of the vault

that may throw light on the way the cross-in-square church might have been perceived at the point of its apparent origin.

John of Odzun (650–729), the Catholicos of the Armenian Church, explains the preparations for a church's foundation ceremony, stipulating that there are 12 foundation stones to represent the Apostles; they are to be set at the 4 corners of the church in resemblance to the 4 corners of the world; the building is to be four-sided for the same reason; the anointing of the doors is to be fourfold because the worshippers passing through them are composed of the 4 elements; whilst the 4 columns supporting the dome stand for the 4 virtues. Early in the eleventh century, Stephen of Tarŏn describes various Armenian churches by identifying their domes with the vault of heaven, which have firm pillars for their support. Elsewhere various holy men are likened to pillars of the church.[191] This recalls the earlier *ekphrasis* of Eusebius on Paulinus's church at Tyre where he likens the pillars of its four-sided atrium to the 4 Gospels,[192] thereby equating the support of the pillars with the support the Gospels lend to the teaching of the Word. A graphic representation of this appeared in mosaic a century later in the domed vault over the cruciform mausoleum of Galla Placidia in Ravenna (Fig. 38). Here the starry mosaic surface of the vault is crowned by the cross of Christ and in the 4 corners, at the springings of the vault, are the symbols of the 4 Evangelists, as if in support of his life and teaching.[193] It was Eusebius in the third or fourth century who asserted that:

> In the first place should be put the holy tetrad of the Gospels.
>
> *Historia ecclesiastica* III. 25.[194]

And it was Maximus the Confessor in the seventh century who reminded his readers that the sum of the tetract is 10, the universal number of perfection, which proceeds from God, when he wrote,

> … the tetrad is the decade in potency, joined together in a progressive series from the one.
>
> *Mystagogia* V.[195]

It is noticeable how these Armenian sources are broadly in agreement with those of their sister Church in Byzantium with regard to architectural form and the meanings attached to it, with the dome of heaven above the 4 corners of the earth, also the importance attached to the representation of the universe, in the guise of heaven, and the elements. It is surely this, underlying the Christian symbolism of the Pantokrator in his heaven, presiding over an earthly liturgy with the support of the 4 Gospels, that explains the longevity and self-sufficiency of the domed Greek Cross inscribed in a square.

One study of Middle Byzantine churches, which includes the cross-in-square, has also proposed a Platonic dimension for them through an analysis of their geometric form. Accordingly, the sphere is the most perfect form and is equated with the universe, the cube the most perfect prism, and the square, of which it is composed, the most perfect rectangle. They are translated into architectural form, with the sphere appearing increasingly fragmented the further down the structure towards earth it occurs, from the dome, which is usually a hemisphere, to the drum, the pendentives, and the semi-dome in the sanctuary, which is apsidal.[196] This is a visualization that seems to be akin to, yet the reverse of, that of Michael of Thessalonica, when he mentally reconstructed the dome and semi-domes in Hagia Sophia into two concentric spheres. In the study in question, the progressive breaking of the sphere into parts down through the structure is a descent that is mirrored by the hierarchy of images, from Christ in the dome down to the figures of patriarchs, priests and monks closest to the congregation. In so doing, the sensible world, portrayed through iconography, is a reflection in Plato's terms of the intelligible world, which is represented formally through the immutable truths of mathematics by architectural geometry.[197] This interpretation certainly appears plausible as far as it goes although, yet again, the analysis can fit various types of domed Byzantine church, including Hagia Sophia, not just the cross-in-square. To be tenable, the hypothesis would also need to be shown to be consistent with the attitude of the Church towards Plato and the pagan philosophers in general.

After the silencing of Psellos and Italos, one of the anathemas pronounced upon Italos could hardly have been clearer:

> Anathema on those who of their own accord invent an account of our creation along with other myths, who accept the Platonic forms as true,

> who say that matter possesses independent substance and is shaped by the forms, who openly question the power of the creator to bring all things from non-existence to existence, and as their creator to impose a beginning and end on all things in the manner of their lord and master.[198]

However, this was one among several anathemas aimed at the professor and it might be argued that the extremism of its terms was designed, even provoked, to counter a particular offence, rather than to serve as a general statement of the Church's position. Plato's writings, after all, were copied, collected and studied throughout the Greek Middle Ages, as were his cosmological ideas taught through the *quadrivium* of the liberal arts and transmitted through the works of Dionysius the Pseudo-Areopagite and John of Damascus, among many others.[199] Leo the Mathematician (c. 790–post-869) studied all 4 subjects of the *quadrivium* before becoming metropolitan of Thessalonica. On returning to Constantinople, he was made head of a new school by Emperor Michael III (836–867) to teach the liberal arts, and he helped to edit Plato. In the middle years of the following century, it was because teaching in the liberal arts had fallen into neglect that Emperor Constantine VII (905–959) appointed new professors and recruited their students into the Church and civil service, using it in effect as a palace school.[200] During this same period, Plato's texts were being copied and collected freely. To cite just a few examples, the identification of a particular group of manuscripts has led to the supposition of a *scriptorium* operating in Constantinople around the middle of the ninth century, and the majority of them are copies of Plato's dialogues, including his *Timaeus*, Proclus's commentary on *Timaeus*, as well as writings by Dionysius the Pseudo-Areopagite. By way of negative evidence, Archbishop Arethas of Caesarea (c. 860–post-932) ordered copies of two dozen dialogues by Plato, not including *Timaeus*, which, given his demonstrated interest in the philosopher, probably means he already owned it. He also acquired Aristotle's *Organon*, indicating his pursuit of the *quadrivium*, and went on to write various introductions to Plato. Photius, patriarch of Constantinople in the ninth century, and already encountered in this study,[201] also makes references to Plato and Aristotle in his writings. In the tenth century, copies of Plato and Aristotle were made by a monk called Ephraem and, at the turn of the eleventh century, a Master Gregory translated *Timaeus* into Armenian.[202] In addition to literary transmission, Plato and other Greek philosophers were sometimes portrayed in the wall-paintings of churches,[203] and it was not unknown for churchmen to adopt the name of Plato.[204] But it was John of Damascus as much as any authority, who carried the ideas and methods of Plato and Aristotle into the Middle and Late Byzantine periods. He has been regarded as the last of the fathers of the Church and his principal work, *The Fount of Knowledge*, or *Fons scientia,* was the first of the great medieval *summae* of the East and West and the definitive theological treatise for the rest of the Greek Middle Ages.[205] Yet he opens it with the declaration:

> First of all I shall set forth the best contributions of the philosophers of the Greeks, because whatever there is of good has been given to men from above by God …
>
> *Fons scientia, Praefatio.*[206]

This is followed by the first of three sections, *Dialectica*, a synopsis of Greek philosophy for use in the study of theology, and contains much of Plato, which John derived from Maximus, as well as Aristotle's systems of universals and categories. Following the second part, which is an account of various heresies, the final section is *De fide orthodoxa*, which has already been cited several times, and which became the accepted definition of Orthodox faith. This is divided into 4 books, the second being an account of creation, which again broadly conveys Plato's cosmology by way of the Cappadocian fathers.[207] The fundamental problem the Church seems to have had with Plato's teaching was his treatment of the soul, along with ideas about resurrection and eternity.[208] In other words, its disagreement with him was theological rather than metaphysical, notwithstanding the anathema on John Italos. Consequently, in the Church insisting on a return and strict adherence to the church fathers, those reading Basil the Great – the most influential of all for the Greek Church – will have found the essence of Plato's cosmology confirmed:

> It is right that any one beginning to narrate the formation of the world should begin with the good order which reigns in visible things …
> 'In the beginning God made heaven and earth.'. . Thus, although there is no mention of the elements, fire, water and air, imagine that they were all compounded together, and you will find water, air and fire, in the earth. … Do not ask, then, for an enumeration of all the elements; guess, from what Holy Scripture indicates, all that is passed over in silence.
>
> *Hexaëmeron* I. 1, 7.[209]

John of Damascus, the last of the fathers, continued the tradition:

> He brought all things from nothing into being: some, such as heaven, earth, air, fire, and water, from no pre-existing matter … we say that in the creation of the universe we consider as heavens that which the pagan philosophers … call a starless sphere. … Still others say that it is a fifth body and distinct from the four elements.
>
> *De fide* II. 5, 6.[210]

In looking down upon the church of the Holy Apostles' monastery in Thessalonica, it would be difficult to add to, or subtract from, its composition of cupola on a tall drum sat on a cube, with cross-arms extending outwards on all 4 sides, its 3 apses facing east, and its narthex and *parekklesion* on the other 3 sides punctuated by similar domes on drums at each corner, features which, belonging as they do to the *parekklesion*, it is worth emphasizing, have no relevance internally.[211] All in all, it seems inescapable to read the dominant dome and its 4 satellites as symbolizing the universe and the 4 elements; as well as reading it in terms of Christ's teaching, figured in the dome, holding the book, and supported by the 4 Evangelists; and finally the dome of heaven above the 4 corners of the earth, the whole marked out as the metaphysical square of earth on the physical surface of earth, a synthesis of the perfect Platonic model with the Orthodox.

Part Four: Conclusions

Having investigated the schematic design of various Byzantine church types, it is possible to recognize in all of them the fundamental unit of Justinian's Great Church, namely the sphere and the cube, whether repeated fivefold in the domed cruciform Basilica of the Holy Apostles; or reconfigured in the domed Greek cross-in-square church which proliferated across the empire and down the centuries; or spanning the structure of inscribed octagon churches in the Middle Byzantine period. In unfailingly signifying heaven and earth, these two geometric forms not only convey the basis of Plato's cosmology into the Greek Middle Ages in Christian guise, they demonstrate the inseparability of Byzantine architectural form, space, and iconography. It was a symbiosis that developed in multivalent layers, from the living brilliance of divine light in the design, decoration, and description of domes as the vault of heaven, to the marble meadows of earth, defined by the rectilinear panelling of marble sheets as a cubist abstraction of earth, lining the insides of the cube of the physical building, with its top open to heaven and its bottom the surface of earth's rivers and seas. Likewise, when in the ninth century the Pantokrator arrived in the dome, it was as the light of the world, while he peered down from heaven holding the book, ready to teach his congregation in the earthly nave below. When the cross-in-square design was taken up, uniting the cross within the square of earth, the figure of Christ was seen as already risen above its cross-arms, there in the dome of heaven.

In all its particularities, the cross-in-square church demonstrates the inseparability too of geometric form and number, in its 3 portals, 4 pillars, 5 domes, and much else. The central dome dominating its 4 satellites is common to the Greek Cross basilica and the cross-in-square church. The reading of their symbolism is supported by contemporary writing directly, both descriptive in the form of topographical accounts and interpretative in the form of *ekphrasis*; also indirectly in theological exegesis, which displays striking parallels with some of the architecture that was erected as its reflection and metaphor. The flexibility of the cross-in-square model, which permitted detailed variations of layout and iconography, although marginal, would have aided individual patronal and artistic expression within the general framework set by a single archetype, as well as permitting the latitude necessary in implementing the archetype by individual patrons and builders when apparently lacking a precise architectural theory.

Other examples of multivalency follow in the next chapter, with a return to the cruciform basilica and further nuances of meaning attaching to ideas of crucifixion and *theosis*, again in the Greek East as well as the Latin West, and again combining the Platonic with the biblical in the signification that is apparent in the architecture.

Notes

1 See Prologue, under 'Pythagoras and Plato', also 'Geometry'. Within the paradigm of the regular polyhedra, the universe was represented, not by the sphere, but by the dodecahedron, which was the regular solid closest to being a sphere. In his dialogue *Phaedo* (110B), Plato likens the universe to a ball made of 12 pieces of leather. The dodecahedron consists of 12 pentagons, which would allow its form theoretically to be inflated into a spherical shape so long as the pentagons were as flexible as leather.

To the 4 elements, some authorities added a fifth, literally the quintessence, which was variously the ether filling the universe, or the universe itself, the model of which was formed by the five-sided figure of the pentagon. Heath (1921), I. 158.

2 The composition advanced by Plato in his dialogue *Timaeus* (53C) depends on bisecting the equilateral triangle and the square, producing two $1 : 2 : \sqrt{3}$ scalene triangles and two right-angled isosceles triangles respectively. The physical instability of the atmospheric elements is reflected in the indeterminate proportions of scalene triangles, which can vary infinitely from acute to obtuse, in contrast to the right-angled isosceles triangle which is constant, thereby representing the stability of the element earth.

3 John of Damascus, *De fide*, tr. Chase (1958), 212.

4 Both these churches date from the beginning of the eighteenth century and, being of the Italo-Byzantine tradition, their domes are elevated on drums as in the churches of the Middle Byzantine period. In contrast to their bareness, the church of Hagia Sophia on the acropolis of Monemvasia is typical of Byzantine construction with its tiled roofs and walls made decoratively of stone and brick.

5 Narsai, tr. McVey (1983), 83, 115.

6 Maximus, tr. Berthold (1985), 189.

7 *Edessa Hymn*, tr. Mango (1972), 57–8.

8 Germanus, tr. Taft (1980–81/95), I. 72; also in Mango (1972), 141–2.

9 *De sacris aedibus*, tr. Mango (1972), 103.

10 Symeon, tr. T. Beech (2003).

11 Mathew (1963), 92–3; Mathews (1971), 177.

12 *Ekphrasis* has been defined as recounting the emotional and spiritual response evoked by a work, rather than presenting a factual description of its physical appearance and composition, thereby representing the spiritual reality underlying it. See James and Webb (1991), 4, 6, 8–12, 14.

13 This appears as Book XV of Euclid. Downey (1948), 108–13; Ousterhout (1999), 44; Warren (1976), 8.

14 Warren (1976), 4–5, 8.

15 A discussion of the original dome follows shortly.

16 There has been some discussion as to whether the four great arches were designed to be true semi-circles, but see Mainstone (1988), 87. Much debate has also surrounded the intended and actual function of the half-domes. Suffice it to say that, during construction, the main dome pushed out the tops of the arches to

the north and south where there are no half-domes and, following the first of several collapses, the east arch moved outwards after its semi-dome fell, probably causing the adjacent part of the main dome to collapse as well. Mainstone (1988), 212–15.

17 Pendentives are the spherical triangles that rise from a square base to form a circular base for the dome.

18 Agathias, *Historiarum* V. 6, tr. Mathew (1963), 67.

19 Mainstone (1988), 179. A Byzantine foot of 0.315 m has also been advanced for the sixth century. See Dwyer (1985), 5, note 5.

20 Mainstone (1988), 179.

21 See Prologue, 'Arithmetic'.

22 Mainstone (1988), 215.

23 The dimensions cited here for the cube are approximate and are the result of scaling dimensions from the measured survey by R. Van Nice (1965). This was published as a large portfolio of drawings with general layout plans, sections, and elevations at a scale of 1 : 250, and with detailed part-plans at 1 : 100. The accuracy of this survey has recently been validated by a digital survey using a 3D long-range laser scanner. This produced the first machine-generated ground plan of Hagia Sophia, which has been superimposed on Van Nice's plan (pl. 31); Hoffmann (2005), x, 14, 15.

This survey formed the basis of an attempted reconstruction of the geometric design of Hagia Sophia which, it is claimed, 'illustrated how architects of the 6th century geometrically developed the ground plan as well as the elevation of the Hagia Sophia out of one single figure', x. Setting aside the stating of supposition as fact, the investigation starts with the square and its inscribed and circumscribed circles, exactly as found in the present relationship between the upper dome, the top of the cube, and the larger dome implied by the pendentives; and it ends with some suggested cosmological connections with these figures. In between, however, this basic system is elaborated by a series of invented constructs that continue to be made until the plan and elevation are completed. This consists of doubling the original square and circles, providing quadruple cross-over points at the four corners, which are used randomly in the constructions that follow, 16, 18; an insertion of two measured lengths of 50 and 100 Byzantine feet into an otherwise geometric system, 20, which produces a matrix of diagonals that are multiplied until intersections with each other and with the main axes produce the centres for the main apses, *exedrae*, and sanctuary apse, 22; and finally, for the geometric construction of the dome, a method of generating a circle from a square of equal area is added, 26, for which no contemporary evidence is cited; neither is any substantiation offered for the procedure as a whole, or for the choice of any of the constructs. Whether the exercise has succeeded in recovering the original design process, or has only reproduced the result of it, must be a matter of individual judgment.

24 Mainstone (1988), 213, 216.

25 Warren (1976), 5.

26 See reconstruction by Antoniades (1907), III. 104, fig. 617; also Mainstone (1988), 127, fig. 154, 210–11, fig. 237.

27 Small domes that are a continuous part of the same hemisphere as their pendentives were common. One can be seen in the funerary chapel formerly attached to the lost basilica of S. Croce in Ravenna, otherwise known as the Mausoleum of Galla Placidia, dating from about 450.

28 In comparison, for example, with a notional sphere that is to be found in the Pantheon, which is exactly inscribed within it; see Fig. 100.
29 Hoffmann also appears to propose that the original dome continued the curvature of the pendentives, although it is not stated in these terms, and he shows it to be part of a circle which passes beneath the pavement, without offering a reason for this; pls 29, 30.
30 Procopius, tr. Mango (1972), 74–5.
31 Michael excludes the semi-dome of the sanctuary apse. The architectural form of the monastic church at Daphni, outside Athens, dating from late in the eleventh century, embodies a sphere on a cube. See 'The Greek Cross and Byzantine church design' below.
32 Michael of Thessalonica, tr. Mango and Parker (1960/95), 238–9.
33 Mainstone (1988), 131–2.
34 For a chronology of sources, see Mango (1992), 51–6, to which should be added Mango and Parker (1960/95).
35 For a summary of the technique of Byzantine mosaic art, its treatment of, and by, light, see James (1996), 2–8. Acknowledgement is also due to Cormack's collection of studies entitled *The Byzantine Eye* (1989).
36 Cormack (1989), VIII. 133–4; Mainstone (1988), 126, 213.
37 Ibid., VIII. 134. I am grateful to Cyril Mango for this qualification.
38 Procopius, tr. Mango (1972), 74, 76.
39 Paulus Silentarius, tr. Mainstone (1988), 219.
40 See *Ekphrasis* 4 above.
41 See Gage (1995), 57.
42 Paulus Silentarius, tr. Mango (1972), 83–6.
43 *Narratio*, tr. Mango (1972), 101, 102.
44 Choricius, tr. Mango (1972), 68, 71–2.
45 Leo, tr. Mango (1972), 203, 205.
46 Michael of Thessalonica, tr. Mango and Parker (1960/95), 237–8, 239.
47 Ibid., 239, 243–4.
48 Ibid., 235, 237.
49 Procopius, tr. Mango (1972), 75.
50 Paulus Silentarius, tr. Mango (1972), 86.
51 Cormack (1989), VIII. 133–5; Mathew (1963), 30.
52 For a description of the early liturgy in Hagia Sophia, see Taft (1980–1/95), I. 49–57. For its relationship to the architecture, see Mathews (1971), 105–8, 144–5, 157–61. See also Mathews (1982/95), III. 125–6.
53 Mathews (1971), 93–5.
54 See *De aedificis* at note 38.
55 For a discussion of ambiguities in the sources about the place for women, see Mathews (1971), 129–33.
56 This was a practice which apparently ceased outside Constantinople but continued in the capital until the seventh century or later. See Mathews (1971), 128–9.
57 This is commonly referred to as the *skeuophylakion* and served as a sacristy and possibly vestry. Taft (1980-81/95), I. 49, 53; idem (1979–80/95), II. 105–6.
58 Sanctuaries may not have become closed until the eleventh century, and then only by curtains at first. Mathews (1982/95), III. 126.
59 Mathews (1971), 93–5, 99, 105–8, 122, 125, 128–9, 144–5, 157–8, 161; Taft (1980–1/95), I. 49–50, 53.

60 John of Damascus, *De fide* II.1, tr. Chase (1958), 204. For a further reference to this expression, see Chapter 6, 'The Whole Frame of the Universe'.
61 Paulus Silentarius, tr. Mango (1972), 83.
62 Cormack (1981/89), VIII. 134–5.
63 Photius, tr. Mango (1972), 186.
64 Leo, tr. Mango (1972), 202.
65 Ibid., 203.
66 The term Pantokrator was associated with this particular type of portrayal of Christ from the ninth century; Mathews (1990/95), XIII. 201.
67 Gregory of Nyssa, *Contra Eunom.* PG 45. 524, tr. Mathews (1990/95), XIII. 194.
68 Dionysius, *De div. nom.* X. 1, in Mathews (1990/95), XIII. 194.
69 Constantine of Rhodes, tr. Mango (1972), 200.
70 Nicholas Mesarites, tr. Mango (1972), 232.
71 John of Damascus, *De fide*, tr. Chase (1958), 352–3.
72 Nicholas Mesarites, tr. Downey (1957), 870.
73 Mathews (1988/95), XII. 18; idem (1990/95), XIII. 210. See also Gage (1995), 45.
74 For a discussion of the rainbow in Byzantine iconography, see James (1996), 91–109.
75 Mainstone (1988), 131–2.
76 See Paul, I Corinthians I. 24; *ODCC* 1755.
77 John of Damascus, *Dialectica* I, tr. Chase (1958), 8.
78 *Idem., De fide* I. 13, tr. Chase (1958), 200.
79 Nicholas Mesarites, tr. Downey (1957), 893.
80 Gregoras, tr. Mango (1972), 249.
81 Taft (1979-80/95), II. 107, 116, 291.
82 *Narratio*, tr. Lethaby and Swainson (1894), 141. See also Mango, in Mark and Çakmak (1992), 45, 50.
83 Glycas, tr. in Lethaby and Swainson (1894), 145.
84 Corippus, tr. in Lethaby and Swainson (1894), 145. It is surprisingly common for the dedication to Holy Wisdom to be misattributed to a female saint called Sophia. The correct Latin version of the dedication would be Sancta Sophia, not Santa Sophia.
85 Psellus, undisclosed source in Lethaby and Swainson (1894), 145.
86 Anonymous Russian writer 1424–1453, in Lethaby and Swainson (1894), 109–10.
87 The body of Wisdom literature is variously defined as comprising the Books of Ahikar, Ecclesiastes, Ecclesiasticus, Job, Proverbs, Tobit, and Wisdom (See for example *ODCC* (1997), 1755; Reider (1957), 39), those of Ecclesiastes, Job and Proverbs being incorporated into the Old Testament.
88 Wisdom, tr. Reider (1957), 115, 117. Compare this with quotations cited above by Procopius, in Mango (1972), 75; Paulus Silentarius 286, in Mainstone (1988), 219; Michael of Thessalonica 3, in Mango and Parker (1960/95), 237.
89 Apocrypha (1895), 230, 261.
90 Reider (1957), 105.
91 See Prologue, 'Arithmetic'.
92 Clement of Alexandria, tr. Wilson (1869), 383.
93 Apocrypha (1895), 231.
94 Reider (1957), 147.
95 Clement of Alexandria, tr. Wilson (1869), 358, citing Wisdom XIV. 2, 3.
96 Mainstone (1988), 29, 32.

97 Paulus Silentarius 438, tr. Mango (1972), 82.
98 Michael of Thessalonica, *Ekphrasis* 4.
99 Mathews (1971), 99.
100 Gregory the Great, in Carruthers (2000), 242–3. Gregory would certainly have become familiar with Hagia Sophia during his service at the Imperial Court before becoming pope. In addition to signifying Wisdom, John of Damascus connects 7 with God's rest and the sabbath, then cites Solomon in pointing to its connection with time, along with 8 (*De fide* IV. 23, Ecclesiastes XI. 2). This latter association is presumably of 8 representing a new beginning, as in the eighth day also being the first (see Augustine, *De serm. Dom.* I. 4. 12).
101 Philo III. 3, tr. Yonge (1854), 90. See Prologue, under 'Number and geometry'.
102 Mango (1985), 65; Mainstone (1988), 32.
103 Procopius, tr. Mango (1972), 74–5. The 'rather tall columns' have been taken by the translator to mean tall mullions, on the supposition that the original form of the *tympana* may have reproduced the great west window, p. 75, note 95.
104 Evagrius, tr. Mango (1972), 79.
105 Paulus Silentarius, tr. Mango (1972), 81.
106 Ibid., 83–4.
107 Michael of Thessalonica, tr. Mango and Parker (1960/95), XVII. 237–8.
108 Ousterhout, in Safran (1998), 89.
109 Mainstone (1988), 36, 42, 191, 194–5, pls 220, 221. In correspondence with the author, Cyril Mango notes that there are wide variations in the size of the ground level columns, suggesting that the quarries might have been finding it difficult to produce any more of the right size.
110 For a reconstruction of what the original arrangement might have looked like, see Mainstone (1988), pl. 222.
111 See Prologue, under 'Arithmetic'.
112 Clement of Alexandria, tr. Wilson (1869), 387.
113 Martianus Capella 736.
114 Boethius, *De arithmetica* II. 49.
115 $4 \times (10 + 7) = 68$.
116 See exposition of Wisdom above; Wisdom XIV. 2, 3; Clement, *Stromateis* VI. 11, tr. Wilson (1869), 358.
117 Lethaby and Swainson (1894), 151.
118 I Kings 6. 2–20.
119 I Kings 6. 38.
120 2, 3, 4, 6, 9, 12, 18, 27, 54.
121 If the original plan had been to duplicate the ground floor column arrangement at gallery level, the corresponding column totals would have been twenty less, that is, 76, 80, 86, 88. None of them is divisible by 6; and the totals of 100 and 106, along with their meanings, would not have been represented. The reason for changing the design can only be conjectured.
122 There is no means of knowing whether there is any resemblance between this and the original dome, although Procopius's description seems suggestive of windows around the base.
123 Michael of Thessalonica, tr. Mango and Parker (1960/95), 237.
124 *Narratio*, tr. Mango (1972), 98.
125 Nicholas Mesarites, tr. Downey (1957), 890.
126 There is no occurrence of 3, 6, 9 or 12 in the dome or in the columns at ground level.

127 For a further layer of possible interpretation regarding 10 and 6, in relation to the idea of Hagia Sophia as representing the Temple, see Chapter 2, under 'Union of the macrocosm and microcosm'.

128 The frontispiece to the twelfth-century *Homilies on the Virgin* by Jakobos of Kokkinobaphos (Vatican MS. Gr. 1162, fol. 2v; BnF. MS. Gr. 1208, fol. 3v) has been taken to portray the Church of the Holy Apostles in Constantinople because of its monumental grandeur and, in particular, its composition of central dome dominating 4 surrounding domes. Against this attribution, it has been argued that the image is likely to have been generic and composed as typical for the scene depicted. For a summary of this discussion, see Linardou (2004), 12–20, and I am most grateful to Kallirroe Linardou for this information. It also needs to be borne in mind that a true portrayal of the Holy Apostles' Church would result in a smaller dome being shown in front of the main dome. This being the case, the artist's model could have been the ubiquitous design of the Greek Cross inscribed in a square (see below), conceived on a grand scale. Alternatively, given the uniqueness of the capital's Church of the Holy Apostles and how well known it was throughout the Byzantine world, second only to Hagia Sophia; given also that the *Homilies* were produced in Constantinople; and given the presence of the Apostles at the Ascension and therefore in this Ascension scene, it must be likely that a connection was made between the event depicted and this particular building. As for the domes, perhaps the artist simply used his licence in rearranging them so that all of them might be visible.

129 Eusebius? *Vita Const.* III. 48, IV. 58–60, in Mainstone (1988), 131. Since Eusebius was visiting Constantinople between 335 and 336, his is probably a first-hand account; Mango (1990), 55.

130 Mainstone (1988), 131; Mango (1990), 55–6, 434.

131 See Chapter 6, under 'The octagonal shrine'.

132 Mango (1990), 54, 56–8.

133 Constantine was the first emperor to recognize the new religion and he converted to it on his deathbed.

134 Procopius, tr. Mango (1972), 102–3.

135 Nicholas Mesarites, tr. Downey (1957), 869.

136 Constantine of Rhodes, tr. Mango (1972), 200.

137 G. Soteriou (1921), in Mango (1990), 62, fig. 1.

138 Mango (1990), 54.

139 Krautheimer (1965), 175; Mango (1990), 54.

140 Mango (1990), 54.

141 Downey (1948), 112.

142 Martianus Capella, tr. Stahl, Johnson and others (1971/91), 279.

143 See Prologue, 'Arithmetic'.

144 The architectural connection between Christ and man will be explored further in Chapter 2.

145 John of Damascus, *De fide*, tr. Chase (1958), 350.

146 Armenia was fertile ground for complex geometric plan forms, often centralized. To Etchmiadzin can be added the palace chapel at Zwarthnotz of the same period, which is quatre-foiled, through to the intricate centralized geometry of the church at Achthamar on Lake Van dating from the tenth century.

147 Mango (1985), 104.

148 Nothing is known for certain about the provenance of the Greek cross-in-square churches of the Middle and Late Byzantine periods, but it has been variously

supposed that they evolved from unidentified antecedents, or were introduced from unspecified sources, which were probably monastic; Mango (1985), 96; Ousterhout (1999), 16. However, Armenia is the likeliest source, in spite of a doubt being raised about its alleged remoteness from Byzantium (McClendon (2005), 131–2), for full weight needs to be given to the union of the Greek and Armenian Churches, and the Armenian influence at the Byzantine Court. As argued in the following passage, there are strong reasons in support of Armenia as their origin.

149 Before the present nave was added later in the Middle Ages, an apse projected from all 4 sides, as at Etchmiadzin. Greek influence on the design of Germigny has been doubted (McClendon (2005), 131–2), again despite the influence of the Armenians on the Greeks. It is interesting to note that the Byzantine Emperor Leo V was both a contemporary of Theodulf and an Armenian. However, any influence on Germigny from the East would be in the face of Theodulf's antipathy towards the Greek Orthodox church. I am grateful to Charles McClendon for this exchange of views.

150 Mango (1972), 181, note 1; Ousterhout (1999), 87.

151 *Historia de vita Basilii* 83, 84, ed. Bekker, 325–6, tr. Mango (1972), 194.

152 Mango (1972), 181; idem (1985), 108.

153 Norwich (1993), 104.

154 Runciman (1933/61), 181, 203, 210.

155 John of Damascus (1958), xiii. Two recent summaries of the dispute are to be found in Bell (1996), 267–80, and Safran (1998), 44–8.

156 John of Damascus, *De fide*, tr. Chase (1958), 370.

157 Mathew (1963), 103–4.

158 Mango (1972), 81; Lange (1986), 106. No particular precursors are offered by Mango other than those that were domed, nor is it suggested what current models might have been abandoned in favour of them. A strong inference must be that the chosen model was the domed cross-in-square church, since this is the type that mainly held sway after the icon dispute, and, if this was not to be found in Constantinople until the ninth century, it must presumably have been imported since antecedents existed outside the capital. For a summary of theories concerning the Greek cross-in-square church, including its possible origins typologically and geographically, see Lange (1986), 94–100, 106–7. This also lists examples that may predate Basil's Nea Ekklêsia and were spread over a wide area, including Georgia, Turkey, and Greece, as well as a few in the West.

159 Given the existence of the Greek cross-in-square type already in its complete form in Armenia from the 630s, and given the Armenian descent of Emperors Leo V, Basil I, Leo VI, Romanus I, and John I, together with the revivalist tendency of the so-called Macedonian renaissance, it is argued here that this connection, first advanced by Strzygowski (1918), remains the likeliest. See Lange (1986), 100, 106–7.

160 The domed cross-in-square church is acknowledged as the most common type to be built in the Middle Byzantine period; see for example, Bouras (1979), 21; Buchwald (1992/99), XI. 303. However, its currency will shortly be seen to extend well into the Late period as well.

161 Mathew (1963), 106; Mathews (1988/95), XII. 14–15; Ousterhout (1999), 23. These sources develop material in a seminal work on Byzantine iconography by Otto Demus, *Byzantine Mosaic Decoration* (London, 1948).

162 See note 57 and text to which it refers.

163 In some exceptional cases, these chambers have been identified as tiny side chapels. See Mathews (1982/95), III. 131–5.
164 Mathews (1971), 144, 178–9; idem (1982/95), III. 126–7; Ousterhout (1999), 13–15.
165 Ousterhout (1999), 25; Buchwald (1992/99), XI. 305, 310–13.
166 The flat, rather cubist rendering of the third dimension in Byzantine art, in which the background and foreground of a painting confront the observer as if in the same space, was evidently derived from a system of skenography transmitted by Proclus in a work on optics; Mathew (1963), 30–31.
167 Bell (1996), 210; Buchwald (1992/99), XI. 303–5, 311–13; Mathews (1988/95), XII. 14, 18–19; (1990/95), XIII. 191, 194, 208, 210; Safran (1998), 40–41.
168 See Mathews (1990/95), XIII. 191.
169 Athanasius, tr. Perl in Safran (1998), 40–41.
170 For a summary and short bibliography of design theories for Byzantine architecture, see Striker (1995), 33–4. One such study proposes the use of quadrature and square grids, with a possible connection to the Pythagorean musical ratios, and is to be found in Buchwald (1992/99), XI. 297–302. This is commented on in another summary of design theories concerning plans, sections, and metrology in Ousterhout (1999), 74–83, and Striker (1995), 34–5.
171 Ousterhout (1999), 44–7; Mathew (1963), 113–14. See Prologue, under 'The architectural programme, patrons and architects'.
172 It has been suggested that the application of geometry to architecture from the ninth century onwards was probably more practical than theoretical; Ousterhout (1999), 72.
173 Lange (1986), 94, fig. 1; Ousterhout (1999), 21, fig. 11; Buchwald (1992/99), XI. 303–4.
174 Fotis Kontoglous in conversation with Constantine Cavarnos (1957), 12, 18, 67–8, 87–8, 101.
175 Mutsopulos (1962), 284–8, figs 1–28; 283, fig. 9; Striker (1995), 35–6. See also Ousterhout (1999), 81, fig. 52, after Mutsopulos. Mutsopulos attributes the geometric correspondence with the cross-sections of churches to an 'architectonic significance'. Striker tested the system against a wide sample of buildings and found it to be present invariably. His conclusion was that it arose from a supposed requirement for the Pantokrator in the dome to 'control' the space of the naos through uninterrupted sight-lines.
176 Maximus Confessor, tr. Berthold (1985), 187.
177 Nicholas Mesarites, tr. Downey (1957), 869.
178 Mathews (1982/95), III. 125–31, 136–7.
179 Ousterhout (1999), 30.
180 Mango (1985), 110, 113; Ousterhout (1999), 15, 19, 104; Ousterhout, in Safran (1998), 110.
181 Ousterhout, in Safran (1998), 100.
182 Mango (1985), 124, 127, 159; Bouras (1979), 21, 28–31; Ousterhout (1999), 97, 116.
183 Mango (1985), 137.
184 Mango (1985), 150; Runciman (1965), 158.
185 Mango (1985), 155. For the application of quadrature to the plan and section of the Holy Apostles, Thessalonica, see Ousterhout (1999), 78, fig. 49, after Striker; Kuniholm and Striker (1990), 14–15, fig. 8. For quadrature in general, see Striker (1995), 34–7; Ousterhout (1999), 76–8.

186 Ousterhout (1999), 24.
187 Wilson (1983), 153–4; 156–60; Bell (1996), 159–62.
188 See Buchwald (1992/99), XI. 319.
189 Demus (1948), 11; Mango (1985), 137; Ousterhout (1999), 12, 38.
190 Ousterhout, in Safran (1998), 97; Ousterhout (1999), 24. Lange notes that the ascription of supposed iconographic and liturgical requirements to justify the domed cross-in-square church can apply equally to other types of layout, as argued above. Instead she calls for an examination of the type as representing an aesthetic ideal. Yet this is to attach a particular meaning to, and role of, aesthetics that may not have been operative in Byzantium at the time. On the other hand, it is perhaps noteworthy that Lange's theoretical enquiry finds no place for geometry or symbolism as possible influences. Lange (1986), 106–10.
191 Thomson (1979), 108–12; citing John of Odzun, *Opera*, and Stephen of Tarŏn, *Patmut 'iwn Tiezerakan*.
192 See Eusebius's panegyric in 'Image and anagogy' in the Prologue.
193 The symbols of the Evangelists were derived from the 4 winged creatures in Ezekiel's vision (Ez. I. 5–10) in a tradition transmitted by Origen and Paulinus. According to this, Mark was symbolized by the lion, Luke the ox, Matthew the man, and John the eagle. Dow (1957), 273–4. See also Chapter 6, under 'Wheels of Fortune and Life'.
194 Eusebius, *Hist. eccles.*, tr. Lake (1949), 257.
195 Maximus Confessor, tr. Berthold (1985), 193.
196 This is only partly correct. The curved surfaces of the vaults and drum are not spherical.
197 Buchwald (1992/99), XI. 317–19; see also 308, 310–14.
198 Uspensky (1893), 420–23, in Wilson (1983), 154.
199 John of Damascus, xxvi–xxviii, 11–13, 107; Mathew (1963), 3; *ODCC*, 406, 891; Bell (1996), 159.
200 Mango (1980), 138–41.
201 See Prologue, under 'Image and anagogy'.
202 Wilson (1983), 86–7, 93–5, 114–15, 120, 123–4, 128–9, 131, 138–9, 164.
203 Saradi-Mendelovici (1991), 6–8, 11.
204 One example was the founder and abbot of the monastery of Saccudion in Bithynia. His nephew was abbot of the Studion monastery in Constantinople, and both were part of the revival of learning in the capital. Plato attended the second Council of Nicaea, which had set out the specifications for icons, died in 814, and was commemorated by Theodore in his *Oratio* XI, PG 99. 804–50. Hussey (1986), 47; Mango (2002), 215.
205 John of Damascus, v; Bell (1996), 221.
206 John of Damascus, tr. Chase (1958), 5.
207 John of Damascus, xxv–xxviii, xxxii–xxxiv; *ODCC* (1997), 891; Bell (1996), 221.
208 Bell (1996), 162.
209 Basil, tr. Jackson (1895), 52, 56.
210 John of Damascus, tr. Chase (1958), 210, 211.
211 Safran (1998), 106.

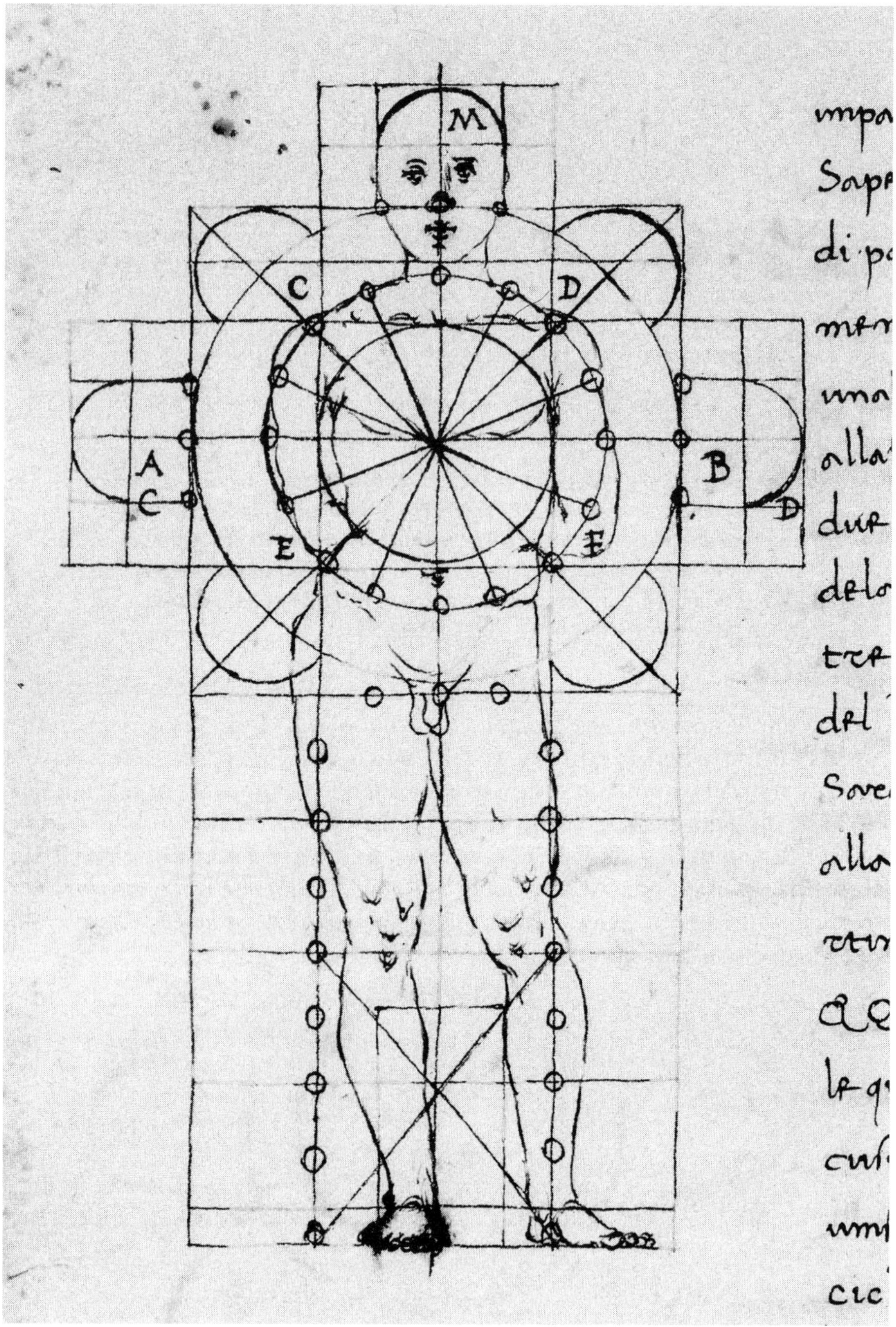

Fig. 39 Temple and body, Francesco di Giorgio Martini, fifteenth century

Chapter 2

Temple and Body

Macrocosm and microcosm

Two tenets of Plato's teaching about the universe were that it was a living creature and man was a microcosm of it. He describes it thus in *Timaeus*:

> … from such constituents, four in number, the body of the universe was brought into being, coming into concord by means of proportion …
>
> And for shape he gave it that which is fitting and akin to its nature. For the living creature that was to embrace all living creatures within itself, the fitting shape would be the figure that comprehends in itself all the figures there are; accordingly, he turned its shape rounded and spherical; equidistant every way from the centre to extremity – a figure the most perfect and uniform of all …
>
> *Timaeus* 32C, 33B.[1]

Just as the sphere of the sensible universe embodies all living creatures, so the sphere of the intelligible universe and its four 'constituents', or elements, are conceptualized in terms of Plato's abstract model, with four of the regular polyhedra being inscribed within the fifth, the dodecahedron and the closest to being a sphere (Fig. 3).[2] Plato continues in almost comical terms. Partly because the human head is notionally spherical, man is a microcosm of the spherical universe, his body being no more than a service pod for keeping the head alive and active:

> Copying the round shape of the universe, they confined the two divine revolutions in a spherical body – the head, as we now call it – which is the divinest part of us and lord over all the rest. To this the gods gave the whole body, when they had assembled it, for its service …
>
> Plato, *Timaeus* 44D.[3]

The interconnection between macrocosm and microcosm was elaborated by Maximus the Confessor, one of many who attest to its Christian acceptance:

> … using a well-known image he submitted that the whole world, made up of visible and invisible things, is man and conversely that man made up of body and soul is a world. … as the soul is in the body so is the intelligible in the world of sense, that the sensible is sustained by the intelligible as the body is sustained by the soul …
>
> *Mystagogia* VII.[4]

The connection was equally accepted in the West and is typified by Hildegard of Bingen (1098–1179), the prolific writer, composer, dramatist, and visionary who, in one of her visions, sees many symmetries between the world and the body and soul. Parts of the macrocosm are shown to be in proportion with each other in a similar fashion to proportions found in the human microcosm. Hildegard demonstrates this by citing measurements, and she continues with a series of analogies, such as between the 4 elements and 4 humours, the 4 winds and the 4 limbs.[5] Alan of Lille, also in the twelfth century, demonstrates the integrity of man with the universe by similar means when he has Nature, God's appointee, declare:

> I am the one who formed the nature of man according to the exemplar and likeness of the structure of the universe so that in him, as in a mirror of the universe itself, Nature's lineaments might be there to see. For … the four elements unite the parts of the structure of the royal palace of the universe, so too … [the] diversity of four combinations bind together the house of the human body. Moreover, the same qualities that come between the elements as intermediaries establish a lasting peace between the four humours.
>
> *De planctu Naturae* VI. 3.[6]

There follows an account of the humours produced in the universe by the sun and moon, and in man by his heart and liver; and this is followed by a correlation between the 4 ages of man – child, youth, adult, elder – with the 4 seasons.[7]

The importance Plato gives to the head in the 'assembling' of the human body was also understood by the Church. The head is the seat of the mind, and it is his mind that makes man rational, and, to Christians in the Greek East and the Latin West, this proved that God had made man in his own image. According to John of Damascus in the eighth century,

> … God intended to fashion man after His own image and likeness from the visible and invisible creation to be a sort of king and ruler over the whole earth and the things in it …
>
> And so God made man … with all good qualities. He made him a sort of miniature world within the larger one …
>
> Through his power of reason man is akin to the incorporeal and intellectual natures … For this reason, man is also a microcosm.
>
> *De fide* II. 11, 12.[8]

This was echoed five hundred years later in the West by John's translator, Robert Grosseteste, the bishop of Lincoln:

> Let us make man to our image and likeness. This expression … includes the most secret thing of God and the most sacred thing of the human being. … for it says that human beings were made in the image of the supreme Trinity. …

> Basil … says that we are not in the image of God according to the form of the body, nor according to anything changeable or corruptible, but are in the image of God according to the soul and according to the reason. …[9]
>
> I am in God's image in that I am rational: I am in God's likeness in that I am made a Christian. …
>
> If it were not so, we could not catch sight of the unchangeable truth with our minds.
>
> *Hexaëmeron* VIII. 1. 1, 5. 6, 8. 1, 9. 4.[10]

John of Damascus also seems to understand that the converse of man being made in God's likeness is man's need perforce to be able to conceive of God in man's own image:

> … in sacred Scripture we find many things said symbolically of God as if He had a body … we are unable to think or speak of the divine, lofty, and immaterial operations of the Godhead unless we have recourse to images, types, and symbols that correspond to our own nature. Consequently, everything that is said of God as if He had a body is said symbolically and has a loftier meaning.
>
> *De fide* I. 11.[11]

As a result, this reciprocal relationship was encapsulated in the West by Thomas Aquinas (1226–1274):

> God was made man in order that man might become God.
>
> *Summa theologica* III. q. 1, art. 2.[12]

The mutual identification between God and man, of course, was completed with the Incarnation. Although it had taken many councils of the early Church, well into the fourth century, to formulate and agree definitions of the three persons of the Trinity and the dual natures of Christ, by the time John of Damascus was writing, the Incarnation could be stated with relative simplicity.

> … God became man. For, while He was by nature perfect God, the same became by nature perfect man.
>
> *De fide*, III. 2.[13]

It is striking how all these inter-relationships are based on various dualities, although they are rarely, if ever, categorized as such. It is easy to imagine the Church wishing to steer clear of explicit references to a principle of duality, given the succession of dualist heresies that juxtaposed God, creator of souls, and the Devil, creator of the material universe, where all matter was evil and the reality of Christ's body was denied.[14] Nevertheless, the postulation of the macrocosm and microcosm, the intelligible and the sensible, also man in the image of God, his bipartite composition of body and soul, also of body and mind, with the Incarnation bringing the divine and human natures of Christ, represents a complex interweaving of dual relationships that became extended by the identification of Christ's body with the Temple, as well as the Temple as a type of the universe embodying the proportions of the human microcosm.

Temple and Body

The prescription that temples be proportioned in the manner of that of the human body was pre-Christian, and was transmitted at length by Vitruvius in his treatise *De architectura*. It is difficult to be certain of his influence on the Middle Ages but over fifty copies of his work date from the medieval period and were often to be found in places of architectural importance.[15] Given its subject matter and vernacular style of writing, he would hardly have been studied for any other reason than for civil engineering, building construction, and architectural design. On the design of temples, he writes,

> ... without symmetry and proportion no temple can have a regular plan; that is, it must have an exact proportion worked out after the fashion of the members of a finely-shaped human body.
>
> *De architectura* III. 1. 1.[16]

He then specifies in exhaustive detail what those proportions are, of which this is an excerpt:

> For Nature has so planned the human body that the face from the chin to the top of the forehead and the roots of the hair is a tenth part ... the head from the chin to the crown, an eighth part; from the top of the breast ... to the roots of the hair, a sixth part; from the middle of the breast to the crown, a fourth part ... The foot is a sixth of the height of the body; the cubit a quarter, the breast also a quarter. The other limbs also have their own proportionate measurements. ...
>
> *De architectura* III. 1. 2.

Having set out the proportional relationships between the detailed parts of the anatomy, he proceeds to the major proportions of the human body by associating it with the circle and the square, summoning the image of Vitruvian man made famous by Leonardo da Vinci and his contemporaries (Fig. 40):

> In like fashion the members of temples ought to have dimensions of their several parts answering suitably to the general sum of their whole magnitude. Now the navel is naturally the exact centre of the body. For if a man lies on his back with hands and feet outspread, and the centre of a circle is placed on his navel, his (fingers) and toes will be touched by the circumference. Also a square will be found described within the figure, in the same way as a round figure is produced. For if we measure from the sole of the foot to the top of the head, and apply the measure to the outstretched hands, the breadth will be found equal to the height, just like sites which are squared by rule.
>
> *De architectura* III. 1. 3.

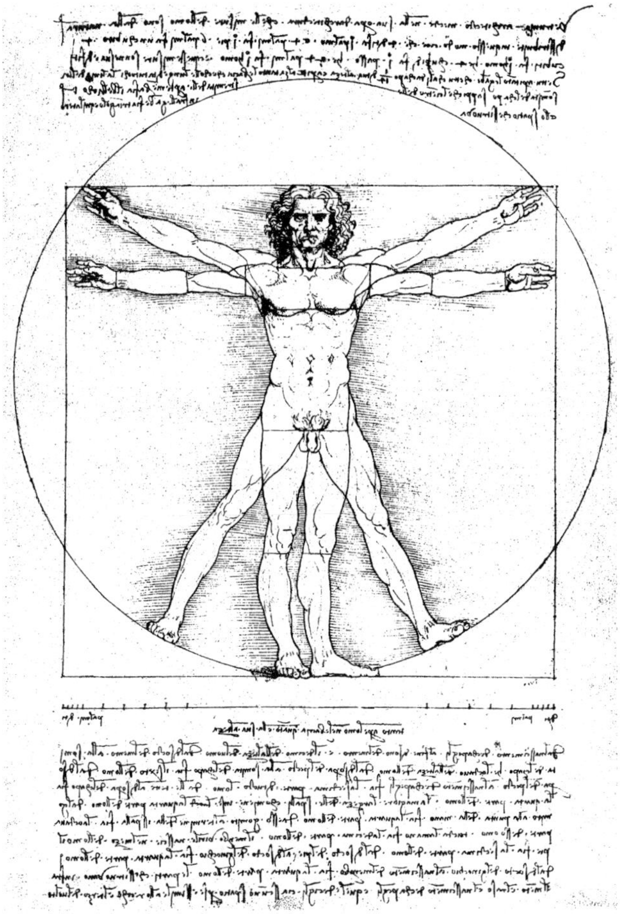

Fig. 40 Vitruvian man, Leonardo da Vinci, sixteenth century

After reiterating that the parts of a temple should be in proportion to the whole just as Nature had fashioned the parts of man, Vitruvius turns to the use of anthropometrics, by which the temple's parts were not only arranged in proportion but, he reminds his readers, each was built using measures which themselves were derived from the human figure:

> Therefore if Nature has planned the human body so that the members correspond in their proportions to its complete configuration, the ancients seem to have had reason in determining that in the execution of their works they should observe an exact adjustment of the several members to the general pattern of the plan. …
> Moreover, they collected from the members of the human body the proportionate dimensions which appear necessary in all building operations; the finger or inch, the palm, the foot, the cubit. …
>
> *De architectura* III. 1. 4, 5.

Among the numbers and ratios in his analysis, he detects the occurrence of 10 and 6, which he recognizes as being perfect numbers, but without attaching any particular significance to them:

> Now the ancients determined as perfect the number which is called ten. … Now while in the two palms with their fingers, ten inches are naturally complete, Plato considered that number perfect, for the reason that … the decad is perfected. …
> But mathematicians … have said that the number called six is perfect for the reason that this number has divisions which agree by their proportions with the number six. …
> Not less also because the foot has the sixth part of a man's height …
>
> *De architectura* III. 1. 5, 6, 7.

Vitruvius rounds off his exposition by returning to the object of the exercise:

> Therefore, if it is agreed that number is found from the articulation of the body, and that there is a correspondence of the fixed ratio of the separate members to the general form of the body, it remains that we take up those writers who in planning the temples of the immortal gods so ordained the parts of the work that, by the help of proportion and symmetry, their several and general distribution is rendered congruous.
>
> *De architectura* III.1. 9.

The biblical association of the temple with the body is found in John's Gospel, where he likens the destruction and rebuilding of Solomon's Temple to the destruction of Christ and his resurrection, again implicating the number 6, though here in relation to time:

> Jesus … said unto them, Destroy this temple, and in three days I will raise it up.
> Then said the Jews, Forty and six years was this temple in building, and wilt thou rear it up in three days?
> But he spake of the temple of his body.
>
> John II: 19–21.

In the Latin tradition, Augustine explained this particular numerological connection, reasoning that the number of years taken to build the Temple, the perfection of Christ's body took in days six-fold:

> … this same number six is taken as the equivalent of a year in the building up of the Lord's body; for he spoke of it frequently as the temple, and said that He would raise up in three days the temple destroyed by the Jews. For they said: 'Forty-six years has this temple been in building.' And forty-six times six makes two hundred and seventy-six. And this number of days completes nine months and six days. This is reckoned as ten months in the case of pregnant women, not because all reach the sixth day after the ninth month, but because the perfection itself of the Lord's body is known to have been brought to birth in so many days … In this number of years the temple was built, because in that number of sixes the Lord's body was perfected, which

> He raised again on the third day after it had been destroyed by the suffering of death. For 'He said this of the temple of his body' …
>
> *De Trinitate* IV. 4. 9.[17]

Commenting on this same passage in John's Gospel, John of Damascus added his own interpretation to the Greek tradition:

> And it is plain that the resurrection of the Lord was the uniting of a soul with an incorrupted body … because He said: 'Destroy this temple; and in three days I will raise it up.' And the holy Gospel is a trusty witness to the fact that He was here speaking of His own body.
>
> *De fide* IV. 27.[18]

It may not be too much of a simplification to see in this two-part metaphor, associating the idea of the temple with Christ's crucifixion and resurrection, the seeds of the two principal types of churches in the East and the West, namely the cruciform expressing crucifixion, and the circular expressing resurrection. The Christian precedent for the latter was the rotunda of the Holy Sepulchre itself in Jerusalem and the type became developed architecturally into various forms, including octagonal baptisteries and martyria where resurrection was equated with the salvation that was thought to be achieved through baptism and martyrdom.[19] The association of the temple with the body crucified, on the other hand, evidently led to the various types of cruciform churches to be seen in the East and West, which were also partly perceived anthropomorphically at the time. Vitruvian man, it seems, had become Cruciform man.

Cruciform man and his church

The principal types of cruciform church in the Greek world have already been encountered in the Greek Cross basilica and the Greek cross-in-square church (Figs 28, 37). The most spectacular example of the former, the Emperor Justinian's Church of the Holy Apostles in Constantinople, was a precursor of St Mark's Basilica in Venice and was doubtless derived from the small cruciform funerary chapel, such as the Mausoleum of Galla Placidia in Ravenna and Justinian's own mausoleum that was attached to the Church of the Holy Apostles. In describing the church at the turn of the thirteenth century, Nicholas Mesarites first invoked each of the Apostles and, when he came to Bartholomew, he wrote,

> … thou art nailed to the Cross through which the gates of paradise were opened for thee. Prepare my mind to be nailed to the sights which are to be seen about this cross-formed Church …
>
> *Description of Church of Holy Apostles* XII. 18.[20]

As it happens, John's tomb was located at Ephesos and had been the site of a succession of churches before Justinian decided to build a new basilica to the Apostle (Fig. 41). In the words of Procopius,

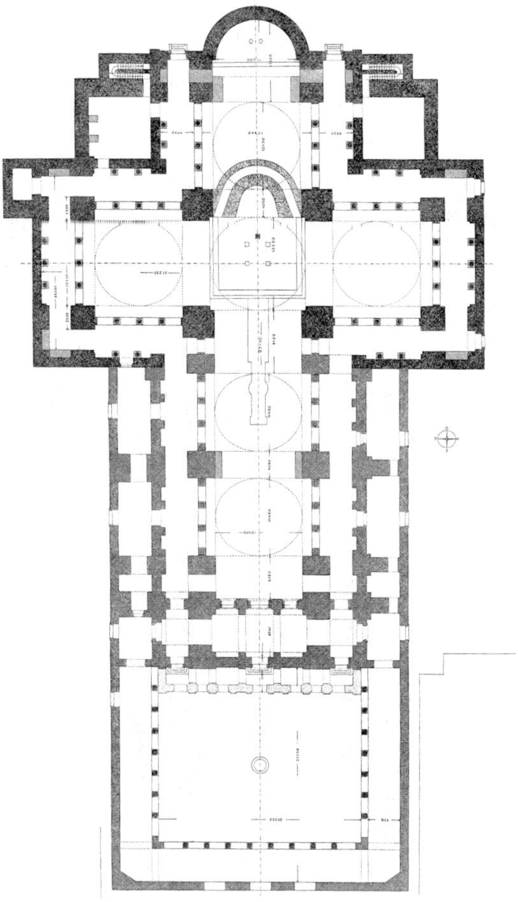

Fig. 41 Plan, St John's Basilica, Ephesos

> [the old] church the Emperor Justinian tore down to the ground and replaced by a church so large and beautiful, that, to speak briefly, it resembles very closely in all respects, and is a rival to, the shrine which he dedicated to all the Apostles in the imperial city …
>
> *De aedificiis* V. 1.[21]

However, whilst the domed sanctuary and cross-arms of St John's Basilica were very similar to the Holy Apostles, there being only differences of detail, the nave extended for two domed bays, making the whole not a Greek but a Latin Cross, foreshadowing those in Romanesque Europe by several centuries (Fig. 42).[22] How this came about is open to conjecture, but there is evidence that the original plan for a Greek Cross basilica was changed during construction before the nave was commenced,[23] and it has been suggested that this was the result of the bishop wishing the basilica to emulate the form of St Peter's Basilica in Rome as well as the Holy Apostles' in Constantinople.[24] Finally, there seems to be no reason why John of Damascus could not have

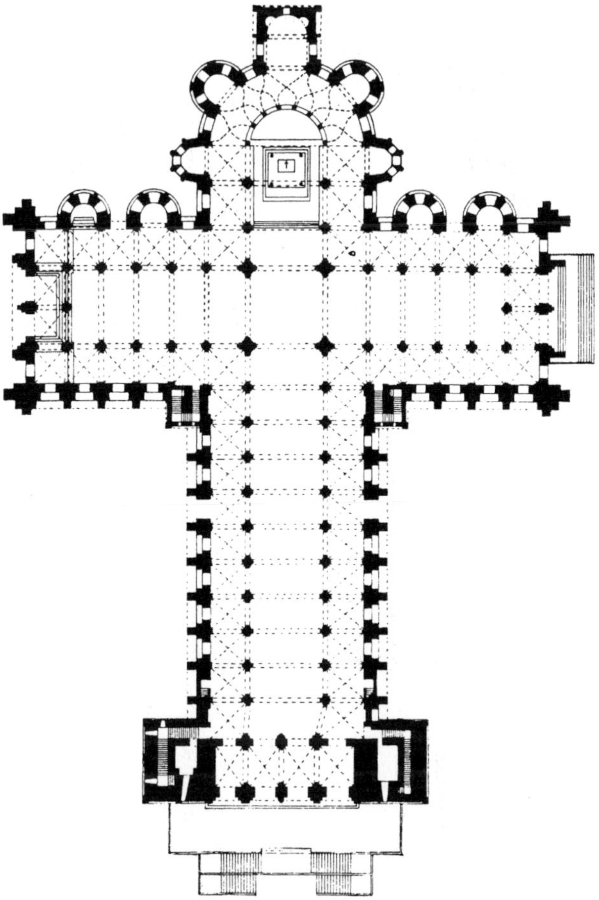

Fig. 42 Plan, Santiago de Compostela

had a cruciform church in mind, along with the crucifix in religious imagery, when he wrote,

> … we also adore the likeness of the honorable and life-giving cross … as a symbol of Christ. Thus when He explained to His disciples: 'Then shall appear the sign of the Son of man in heaven,'[25] He meant the cross.
>
> *De fide* IV. 11.[26]

In the period leading up to Mesarites's description of the Holy Apostles and beyond, associations of the human body with the temple, and of the cruciform church with crucifixion can also be seen in manuscripts surviving in the West, from the middle of the eleventh century to the middle of the thirteenth. This was a period which evidently coincided with intensified interest in Christ and his crucifixion, embracing the example of his life, visions of his resurrection, communion through the sacrament of his body, and meditation upon his Passion in the quest of a spiritual union with him, not unlike the Orthodox belief in *theosis*.[27] In the twelfth century, it has already been observed that Honorius of Autun extended the architectural reference to crucifixion to that of all Christians by the tribulations of this world:

> Churches made in the form of a cross show how the people of the Church are crucified by this world; those made round in the form of a circle show that the Church is built throughout the circuit of the globe to become the circle of the crown of eternity through love.
>
> *De gemma animae* 47.[28]

Composing his metrical *Vita sancti Hugonis* in the 1220s, Henry of Avranches took the architectural symbolism of the crucifixion as read in describing the reconstruction of Lincoln Cathedral:

> With wonderful art [Hugh] built the work that is the cathedral church.
>
> ...
>
> The old mass of masonry was completely demolished and a new one rose. Its state as it rose fitly expressed the form of a cross ...
>
> *Vita sancti Hugonis* 836, 854.[29]

Also in the thirteenth century, William Durandus, bishop of Mende, followed the attributions made by Honorius by specifically connecting the cruciform with Christ's crucifixion:

> ... some churches are built in the shape of a Cross, to signify, that we are crucified to the world, and should tread in the steps of The Crucified ... Some also are built in the form of a circle: to signify that the Church hath been extended throughout the circle of the world ...
>
> *Rationale divinorum officiorum* I. 1. 17.[30]

The symbolic intent revealed in these writings is supported by graphic evidence, for medieval drawings of church plans customarily show them orientated upwards. For example, the ninth-century Plan of St Gall and the sketch plans in the thirteenth-century Portfolio of Villard de Honnecourt (Figs 8, 9) were drawn with their east ends at the top of their sheets of parchment. With plans of cruciform churches being perceived at the time as representations of the cross, an essential point is lost nowadays whenever church plans are reproduced lying on their sides, in deference to the modern cartographic convention of north always pointing vertically up the page. Similarly, medieval maps of the world, or *mappae mundi*, habitually place east at the top of their enclosing circles, with Jerusalem at the centre, the navel of the earth (Fig. 43). Above it, occupying the top half of the circle is Asia, leading to paradise at the very top; below it, in the lower left quadrant is Europe, separated by the Mediterranean Sea from Africa, which lies to the right.[31] *Mappae mundi* belonged to a body of cosmological diagrams in the form of wheels, or *rotae*, for memorizing the physics of the world. This same tripartite division of the world into the three known continents was also the basis of diagrams of the world common in school treatises. The partition of the three continents, shown within the circle of the world, resemble

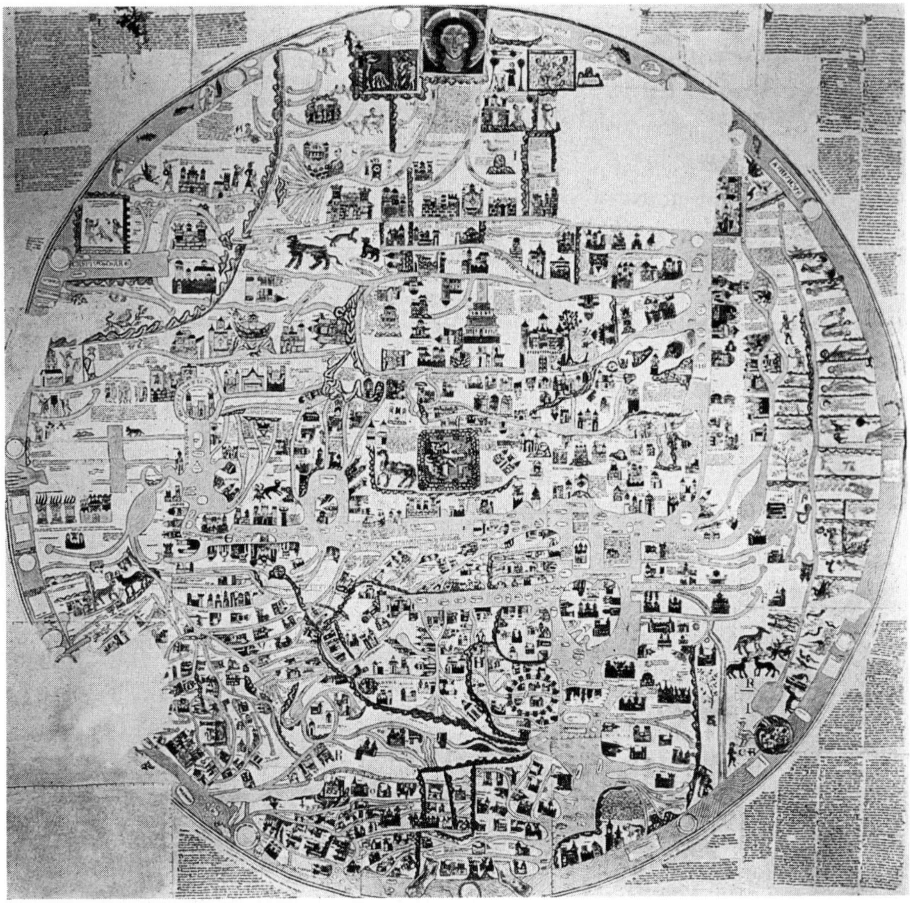

Fig. 43 The Ebstorf World Map, thirteenth century, reconstructed twentieth century

a capital T, again with Asia at the top above the bar of the T, and with Europe to the left and Africa to the right below the bar. In pictorial *mappae mundi*, such as the thirteenth-century Psalter World Map, the figure of Christ is sometimes shown standing behind the circle, as its creator. In the Ebstorf Map, also dating from the thirteenth century, Christ was also shown with the circle of the world in front of him. His head lay to the east at the top, his hands north and south at either side, his feet at the bottom to the west, whilst Jerusalem was positioned once again at the centre.[32] Although his hands and feet lack nail-holes, it is tempting to envisage medieval eyes construing in this a depiction of both Creator and Crucified, thereby concentrating in a single image associations between God and his creation, the human form of God and the macrocosm, as well as Christ crucified and the crucifying world.

Explicit reference to the crucifixion is not always made in the literary sources, yet the descriptions in them of cruciform man overlaying the cruciform church are strongly suggestive. In the eleventh century, the abbey church of St Trond was described thus:

> The building of this church was such that, like all well finished churches, in accordance with the opinion of the doctors, it was said to be formed on the model of the human body. For it had … a sanctuary … in the shape of a head and neck, a choir with stalls in the shape of a chest, the transept extended on both sides of the choir like sleeves or wings in the shape of arms and hands, its nave in the shape of a bosom, and the lower transept projecting to north and south likewise in two wings in the shape of thighs and shins.
>
> *Gesta abbatum Trudonensium* 1055–1058.[33]

In the following century, the church of Santiago de Compostela was similarly described (Fig. 42):

> The church has … nine naves below and six above, and one larger 'head', namely, where the altar of the Holy Saviour is found, and one 'laurel wreath', and one 'body', and two 'limbs' …
>
> *Codex Calixtinus* IX.[34]

In the thirteenth century, Durandus had preceded his architectural allusion of the cruciform church to the crucifixion, cited above, with one that is purely anthropomorphic:

> The arrangement of a material church resembleth that of the human body: the Chancel … representeth the head: the Transepts, the hands and arms, and the remainder, – towards the west, – the rest of the body.
>
> *Rationale divinorum officiorum* I. 1. 14.[35]

It is a tradition that lives on in modern English usage with references to the sanctuary apse, ambulatory and radiating chapels at the east end of a church as the chevet, which in French is derived from *chef*, meaning head, also to the arms of a transept, and the nave as the body of a church. A Baroque version of this was drawn by the artist Francesco di Giorgio Martini (1439–1502) late in the fifteenth century, which combines the two principal forms of church with the human body (Fig. 39).[36] The head still coincides with the east apse but, superimposed over the cruciform crossing is a rotunda, taking the form of a centralized sanctuary. Apses terminate both its diagonals and the north and south axes, leaving most of the nave corresponding with the legs of the human body. The altar is located at the centre of the circular sanctuary, over the heart of the figure,

> [because] it seems suitable that the Sacrament … should be in the centre … being … one and absolute … in similitude of the One who … truly exists …
>
> *Architettura civile e militare* IV.[37]

The identity between the temple and the body of the single human was also extended to all humans, representing the living souls of which the Spiritual Church was constructed. This was described by Eusebius, Augustine and Durandus, among others:

> He looketh into the lively temple which we all compose, and vieweth the house formed of living and firmly set stones, well and securely grounded upon the foundation of the apostles and prophets, Jesus Christ himself being the chief corner-stone. ... This living temple, then, of a living God formed out of ourselves, I mean the greatest sanctuary ... whose innermost shrine may not be seen by the common eye ...
>
> Eusebius, *Historia ecclesiastica* X. 4.[38]

> Indeed this house, the City of God, which is the holy Church, is now being built in the whole world ... [and] those men ... on believing in God, have become like 'living stones' of which the house is being built.
>
> Augustine, *De civitate Dei* VIII. 24.[39]

> ... as the material church is constructed from the joining together of various stones, so is the Spiritual Church by that of various men.
>
> ... the material church, wherein the people assemble to set forth God's holy praise, symboliseth that Holy Church which is built in Heaven of living stones.
>
> Durandus, *Rationale divinorum officiorum* I. 1. 1, 8.[40]

Although the connection between cruciform man and crucified Christ, and between both and the cruciform church is inescapable, the overlaying of Christian symbolism upon the pre-Christian archetype of the temple had hardly disturbed the original, underlying image of Vitruvian man as the human microcosm. Vitruvius had visualized 'a man [lying] on his back with hands and feet outspread'.[41] Hildegard's vision reveals that, just as man's length equals his breadth with his arms outstretched, so the firmament is equal in length and breadth.[42] Similarly, just as the body represented the microcosm, so the temple signified the macrocosm. Maximus the Confessor offered one all-encompassing correspondence:

> ... he used to speak of God's holy Church as a figure and image of the entire world composed of visible and invisible essences because like it, it contains both unity and diversity. ... while [God's holy Church] is one house in its construction it admits of a certain diversity in the disposition of its plan by being divided into an area exclusively assigned to priests and ministers, which we call a sanctuary, and one accessible to all the faithful, which we call a nave. Still, it is one in its basic reality without being divided into its parts by reason of the differences between them, but rather by their relationship to the unity ...
>
> *Mystagogia* II.[43]

Union of the macrocosm and microcosm

The association of Christ with the circle of the world in the Ebstorf Map must be compared with that of Christ, and cruciform man, with the temple, for in both cases the body appears in union with the macrocosm, the world in one

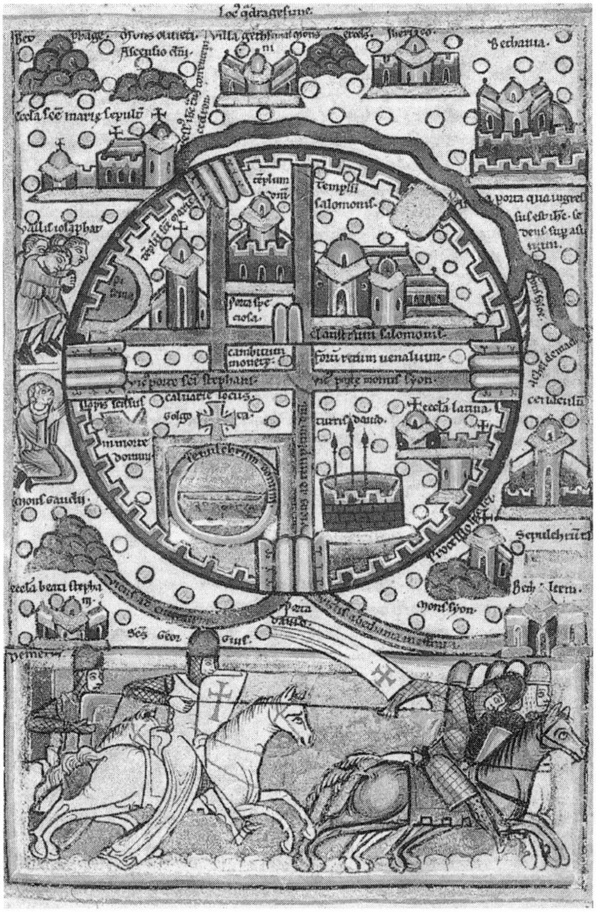

Fig. 44 Map of Jerusalem, twelfth century

case, the church in the other. In addition to *mappae mundi*, cities were also depicted within cosmic circles (Fig. 44). Jerusalem appears at the exact geometric centre of the Hereford World Map and its showing is clearly symbolic, for it is rendered as a walled circle quartered twice over by 4 gates and 4 towers. A twelfth-century map of Jerusalem,[44] which typifies others, combines symbolism with realism for, whilst it too is a perfect circle, quartered, monuments are located in their respective quarters and the east gate is displaced, terminating the street to the north of the east-west axis. Such maps can be seen to take their place in an ascending hierarchy in which the city can be seen as a microcosm of the world, as the world was of the universe, and, like Plato's description of the universe, they were each regarded as living entities. In admiring the choice of site for the Church of the Holy Apostles within the walls of Constantinople, Nicholas Mesarites pointed out that,

> ... instead of the center, and the region about the navel, [Constantius] gave preference to the region a little above the middle and about the heart.

> The first and greatest praise of this Church is that it is rich in possessing such a site and that it occupies the place of the heart in relation to the whole body of the Queen of Cities, from which those who dwell in the city, who are so to speak the remainder of the body, draw … the means for true living.
>
> *Description of Church of Holy Apostles* I. 2, II.[45]

There is another archetype, however, and it embodies the mathematical union of the macrocosm with the microcosm, and that, perhaps surprisingly, is Noah's Ark. In addition to being understood as a symbol of salvation for reasons, both obvious and less obvious, which will be explored in Chapter 6, it too was, in the words of Philo Judaeus, 'an emblem of the [human] body',[46] and the solution is to be found in its measurements.[47] Before citing them, Clement of Alexandria invests the construction of the Ark with the idea of security, perhaps better stated as stability, which is obtained by the cross-section of its timbers being square:

> And let the testimony of geometry be … the ark that was fashioned, – constructed in most regular proportions, and through divine ideas, by the gift of understanding, which leads us from things of sense … to the holy of holies. For the squares of wood indicate that the square form, producing right angles, pervades all, and points out security. And the length of the structure was three hundred cubits, and the breadth fifty, and the height thirty … And the numbers introduced are six-fold, as three hundred is six times fifty; and ten-fold, as three hundred is ten times thirty …
>
> *Stromateis* VI. 11.[48]

In common with Vitruvius before him, Clement identifies the numbers 6 and 10 as important integers, without explaining why. Augustine goes a step further and, in so doing, reveals how Noah is a prefiguring of Christ.

> That Noah, with his family, is saved by water and wood, as the family of Christ is saved by baptism, as representing the suffering of the cross. That this ark is made of beams formed in a square … for a square stands firm on any side. That the length is six times the breadth, and ten times the height, like a human body, to show that Christ appeared in a human body. That the breadth reaches to fifty cubits … That it is three hundred cubits long, to make up six times fifty. … That it is thirty cubits high, a tenth part of the length …
>
> *Contra Faustum* XII. 14.[49]

Later, in his great work, *De civitate Dei*, he completes the analogy and discloses why these two perfect numbers were significant, a fact which Vitruvius had only acknowledged but could not explain.

> Without doubt this is a symbol of the City of God on pilgrimage in this world, of the Church which is saved through the wood … The actual measurements of the ark, its length, height and breadth, symbolize the human body … For the length of the human body from the top of the

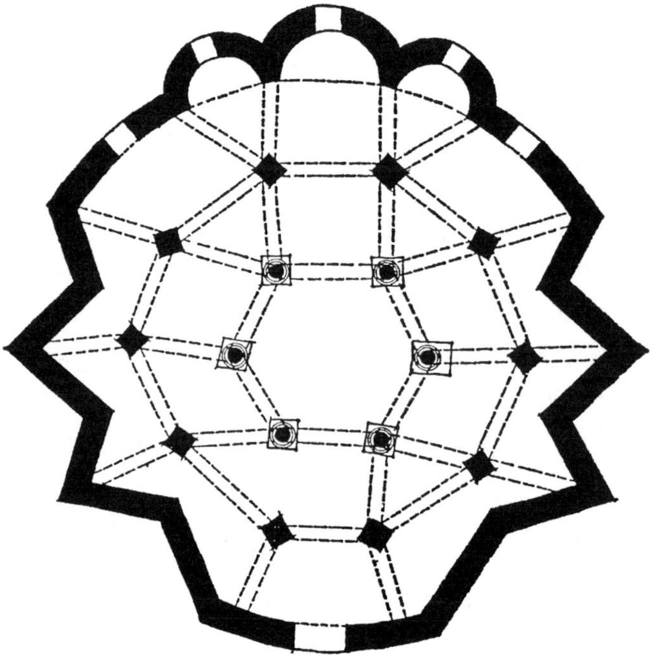

Fig. 45 Plan, Sancta Sophia, Benevento

head to the sole of the foot is six times its breadth from side to side, and ten times its depth, measured on the side from back to belly. … That is why the ark was made three hundred cubits in length, fifty cubits in breadth, and thirty in height. … All the other details mentioned in the construction of the ark are symbols of realities found in the Church.

De civitate Dei XV. 26.[50]

In passing, it is interesting to note an eighth-century church with an apparently unique layout, which is best, or perhaps only, explained in terms of the numbers 6 and 10 (Fig. 45). It is dedicated to Sancta Sophia in the former Lombard duchy of Benevento, south of Rome. Raised by the local duke and consecrated in 762, its plan consists of a curved east end with three apses, a curved west end containing the entrance and, between the two, side walls which stand in 6 angular folds.[51] The interior was arranged around a central core, with a predecessor of the present dome over it, encircled by two colonnades forming an inner and outer ambulatory. Exceptionally, the core is not octagonal but hexagonal, and its 6 columns link to an outer ring of, not 6 or 12 piers, but 10 in an arrangement that has yet to be explained.[52] One clue seems to be that the duke enjoyed close ties with Byzantium and Sancta Sophia's chronicler claimed that the design of the church was a copy of Hagia

Sophia in Constantinople.[53] This would have been partly evident in its centralized space and colonnades beneath the original dome, and in its dedication. Yet given the prominence of the numbers 6 and 10 in the Italian design, was this a reference to their perfection, 6 for being the sum of its parts, 10 for containing all the numbers there are; or for being the key numbers in the proportions of the human body in relation to the temple; or perhaps to the prominence of the same numbers in Justinian's Hagia Sophia, and might not this also have been a way of relating the human microcosm to the macrocosm of the temple in the Great Church itself?

Returning to the measurements of Noah's Ark, in addition to 6 and 10, it can also be seen that the figurate numbers of the elements and the universe – 3, 4, and 5 – are also present.

All three occur in its length:	$300 = \mathbf{3} \times 100 = \mathbf{4} \times 75 = \mathbf{5} \times 60$;
3 is also present in its height:	$30 = \mathbf{3} \times 10$;
5 is also present both in its breadth:	$50 = \mathbf{5} \times 10$; and in its height: $30 = \mathbf{5} \times 6$.

Since these three numbers are recognized as the figurate numbers representing the macrocosm, and 6 and 10 have now been understood as representing the microcosm, it may be thought remarkable that their union with each other is not only metaphysical, but mathematical, for:

$$3 \times 4 \times 5 = 6 \times 10$$

The consideration of the sphere and the cube in medieval architecture has necessarily drawn its evidence from the Byzantine world, for the dome was largely unknown to Romanesque and Gothic architecture. On a different count, it has been shown that an understanding of the macrocosm and microcosm in the guise of the temple and body, together with their architectural expression in literature, architecture, and iconography, are apparent in both the Greek and Latin Middle Ages. Likewise, the figurate numbers 3, 4 and 5 of the triangle, the square, and the pentagon, inherent in Plato's cosmological model, have been seen expressed in the Greek world and will similarly be evident in the Latin. In turning to the presence in medieval architecture of the three geometric figures themselves, it will become apparent that the evidence for this will be found almost entirely in the Latin West, their relative absence from Byzantine architecture possibly being explained by its interest in the sphere and the cube, and, by extension, the octagon. Each of the three chapters that follow will therefore be devoted to one of the three geometric figures, along with its figurate number, and its derivatives. Material relevant to each, and familiar in part from the earlier stages of this study, will be drawn together and expanded in order to provide a conspectus of ideas and applications surrounding each figure.

Notes

1 Cornford (1937), 44, 54.
2 See Prologue, 'Geometry'.
3 Cornford (1937), 150.
4 Maximus, tr. Berthold (1985), 196.
5 Hildegard, *Lib. Div. op.* I: Vision 4.
6 Alan of Lille, *De planctu*, tr. Sheridan (1980), 118–19.
7 Ibid., 122–3.
8 John of Damascus, *De fide* I. 11, tr. Chase (1958), 230, 235, 237.
9 Basil, *Hex.* X. 6–7.
10 Grosseteste, *Hex.* VIII, tr. Martin (1999), 221, 230, 234, 236.
11 John of Damascus, *De fide* I. 11, tr. Chase (1958), 191.
12 Aquinas, *Summa theologica*, tr. Nirenberg, in Clifton (1997), 18.
13 Ibid., 270.
14 The earliest of these beliefs was Manichaeism, originating in third-century Persia. This influenced an early Byzantine sect, the Paulicians, some of whom were to join the Bogomils, a similar sect in the Balkans. During the twelfth and thirteenth centuries, the Cathars in France displayed some of the same heretical characteristics before being suppressed. *ODCC* (1997), 219–20, 301, 1027, 1243.
15 Frankl (1945), 57; Hallinger (1950), 123.
16 This and the following extracts are from the translation by F. Granger (1931), I. 159–67.
17 Augustine, *De Trin.*, tr. McKenna (1963), 141, 142.
18 John of Damascus, *De fide*, tr. Chase (1958), 404.
19 See Chapter 6, 'The octagonal shrine'.
20 Mesarites, tr. Downey (1957), 868.
21 Procopius, *De aed.*, tr. Dewing and Downey (1940), 317–19.
22 It appears that the nave domes would have been ovoid, resembling the oval dome at the west end of Hagia Eirene in Constantinople.
23 Hörmann (1951), 296, pl. LXVIII.
24 Britt (2003), *passim*.
25 Matt. 24. 30.
26 John of Damascus, *De fide*, tr. Chase (1958), 351.
27 Clifton (1997), 18, 20.
28 Harvey (1972), 226. Honorius also encapsulates the two fundamental types of religious architecture referred to above, although he interprets the round, not with the resurrection as commemorated by the Holy Sepulchre, but with the sphere of the world. Implicit in this could be the idea of the world itself as a microcosm of the universe, a possibility which is explored below.
29 Henry of Avranches, tr. Garton (1988), 53, 55. For comment on Lincoln's double transepts, see following note.
30 Durandus, tr. Neale (1843), 26. For a brief comment on Durandus the transmitter, and on his translators, see Prologue, note 196 above. Durandus also likens architectural elements such as the door and the cornerstone to Christ. For a brief outline and context, see Neagley in Clifton (1997), 27.

Lincoln Cathedral, where rebuilding started in 1192, has double transepts in succession to Canterbury's, which date from 1175, and so does Salisbury, which succeeded Lincoln in 1220. This particular form of cross is the Patriarchal Cross, so called because it was the device of the Patriarch of Jerusalem who granted its use to the Order of the Knights Templar, which was founded c. 1120. In Christian art, the upper arm of the cross represents the sign-board of Christ, INRI, standing for Jesus the Nazarene, King of the Jews. It had also been the standard borne by one of the knights at the capture of Jerusalem in 1099, who, being the duke of Lorraine, also gave this name to the cross. If any of this was brought to bear on the choice of layout for these cathedrals, it would have been an addition, not an interference, to the basic meaning of the cruciform, as attested by Henry's description of Lincoln's form; see previous quotation from *Vita S. Hugonis*.

None of this, however, explains why Cluny III was laid out with twin transepts in 1089. Neither does it explain the significance of church layouts lacking transepts altogether. Although well beyond the scope of this study, this may have had something to do with a particular sanctity attaching to the idea of 'hall'. It may be indicative that the dedication inscription around the interior of Charlemagne's chapel at Aachen refers to it as *aula*.

31 This arrangement also applies to the Hereford *mappa mundi*, despite the titles of Europe and Africa being inadvertently switched by the scribe.

32 Kline (2003), 10, 12, 13, 232. The Ebstorf Map was destroyed in 1943 and exists in a modern facsimile. For a brief summary of this and other *mappae mundi*, together with other cosmological diagrams, see Kline (2003), 2–48, 220–39.

33 *Gesta abb. Trud.*, tr. in Tatarkiewicz (1970), 172.

34 *Cod. Calixtinus*, tr. Gerson and others (1998), II. 67. The translators explain that the 'nine naves below and six above' represent one nave with aisles and two transept arms each with aisles, with galleries above all the aisles; the 'head' is the axial chapel and the 'laurel wreath' the ambulatory; the 'body' is the nave and aisles; and the 'limbs' the transept arms and their aisles.

35 Durandus, tr. Neale (1843), 24.

36 Martini, ed. Maltese (1967), fig. 236.

37 Ibid., 409, tr. Vitale (2004).

38 Eusebius, tr. Oulton (1932), 411.

39 Augustine, *De civitate Dei*, tr. Bettenson (1984), 335.

40 Durandus, tr. Neale (1843), 17, 22.

41 Vitruvius, III. 1. 3.

42 Hildegard, *Vision* 4. 15.

43 Maximus, tr. Berthold (1985), 188.

44 Map of Jerusalem, Hague, Koninklijke Bibliotheek, MS 76. F. 5, fol. 1r, in Kline (2001), 212.

45 Mesarites, tr. Downey (1957), 862.

46 Philo, *De plantatione* XI, tr. Yonge (1854), I. 425.

47 The remainder of this chapter is derived from material first explored in Hiscock (2000), 124–6, 134.

48 Clement, tr. Wilson (1869), 353.

49 Augustine, *Contra Faust.* tr. Stothert (1872), 214–15.

50 Augustine, *De civ. Dei*, tr. Bettenson (1984), 643, 644.

51 These are a modern reconstruction of the original walls, following an earthquake and re-modelling at the turn of the eighteenth century; Rusconi (1967), 341–52. See also Rotili (1986), 191–6.

52 The restorer advanced an analysis relating the hexagon, decagon, and outer walls to each other geometrically, but without attempting to explain the choice of polygons and the resultant rings of columns in the first place; Rusconi (1967), 353–4.

53 Verzone (1968), 193, 194, 196; McClendon (2005), 54–7. See also *Chronicon sanctae Sophiae*, ed. Matin (2000), 45–51.

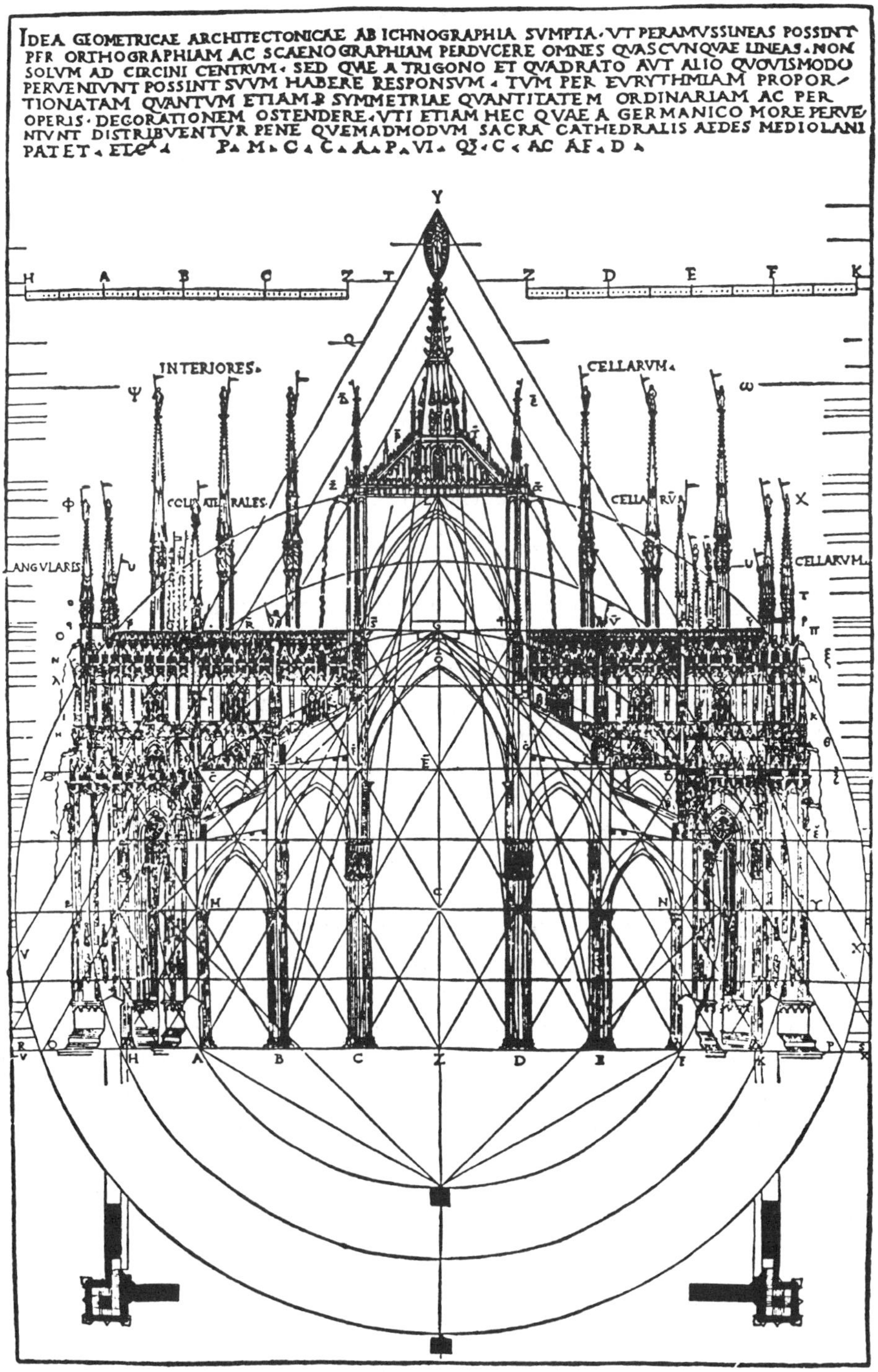

Fig. 46 Cross-section of Milan Cathedral with equilateral triangles superimposed, Cesariano, sixteenth century

Chapter 3

Ad Triangulum

Utrum ecclesia ipsa non computando in mensura tiburium fiendum debeat ascendere ad quadratum an ad triangulum?

Whether this church, not counting within the measurement the tower which is to be built, ought to rise according to the square or the triangle?

Declaraverunt quod ipsa posset ascendere usque ad triangulum sive usque ad figuram triangularem et non ultra.

It was stated that it should rise up to a triangle or to the triangular figure, and not farther.

Annali della fabbrica del Duomo di Milano I. 68.[1]

On 1 May 1392, a conference of architects and engineers was asked if the construction of the new cathedral of Milan 'ought to rise according to the square or the triangle?' The local Lombard masons had laid out the building to a grid of squares and some of the piers had been raised ready to take their vaults, but the building committee had become alarmed at the height that was projected for them. The engineers' response was 'that it should rise up to a triangle or to the triangular figure, and not farther'.[2] This confirmed a written proposal of 12 March the previous year that the cross-section be designed within an equilateral triangle. This was made by Annas of Freiburg and when Heinrich Parler replaced him in December of that year, he too at first proposed the equilateral triangle to determine the heights of the cathedral.[3] In 1521, in the commentary on his translation of Vitruvius, Cesar Cesariano published a drawing of Milan Cathedral with its heights answering to a system of equilateral triangles (Fig. 46), adding that the 'rule of the German architects' stipulated that the length and breadth of a church should be fixed by the *vesica piscis* (Fig. 47) – which is a circumscription of two equilateral triangles base-to-base – and that its heights should also be fixed by equilateral triangles.[4]

The equilateral triangle is the simplest of figures to construct with a pair of dividers and from it may be generated a family of figures, which includes the *vesica piscis*, trefoils, hexagons, hexafoils, hexagrams, and, by dividing circles into 12, dodecagons. Simplicity in drawing, however, does not in itself necessarily justify the engineers' verdict, or explain the reverence with which the figure was held at the end of the Middle Ages,[5] particularly given the importance that was attached to the meaning of things. In this chapter, after recapitulating mathematical and metaphysical material from Antiquity relating to the equilateral triangle, its figurate number 3, and derivatives of both, evidence of their Christian acceptance in literature will briefly be presented, followed by examples of their occurrence in architecture and art.[6]

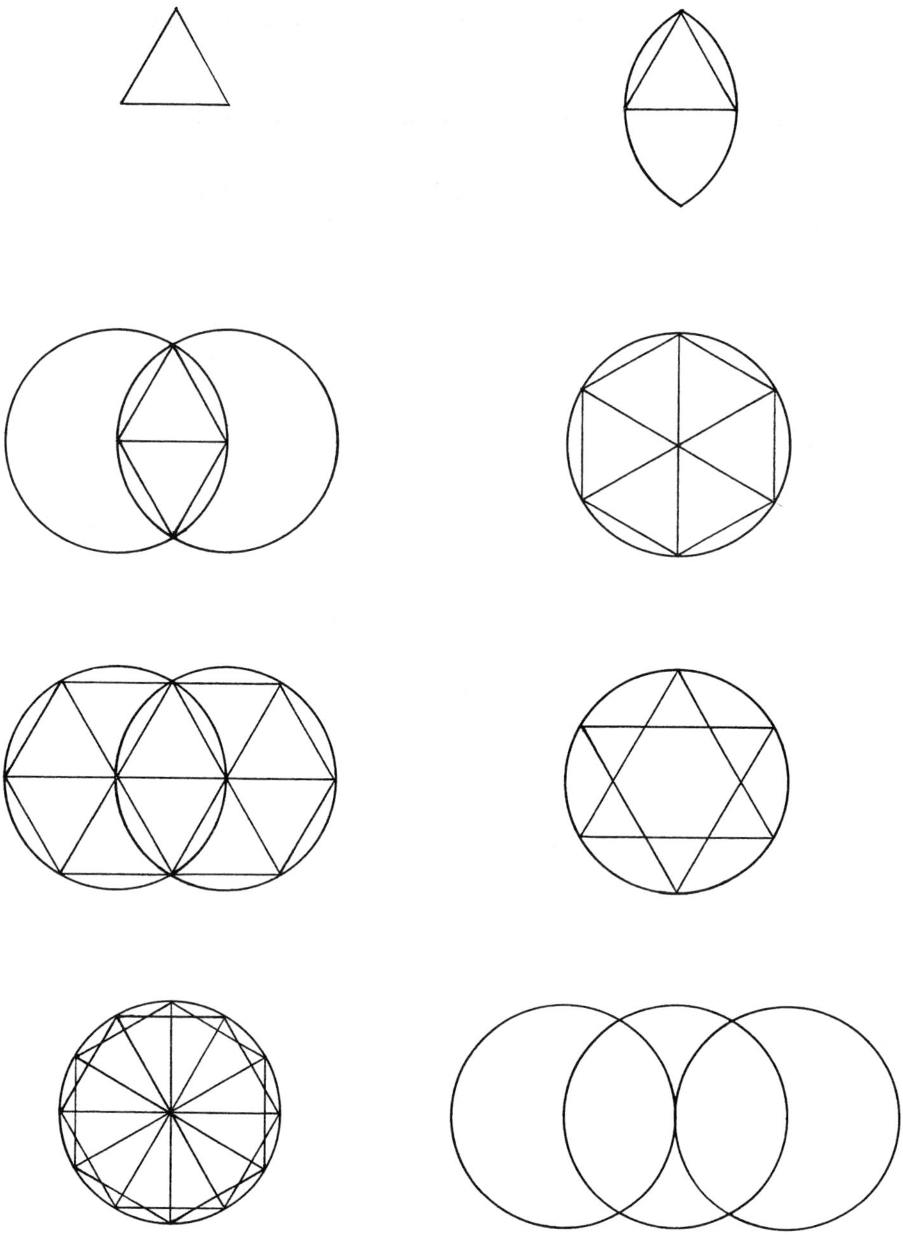

Fig. 47 The geometry of the equilateral triangle and its derivatives. *Top left*, a. Equilateral triangle. *Top right*, b. *Vesica piscis*. *Second row left*, c. Intersection of two equal circles through each centre. *Second row right*, d. Hexagon inscribed in circle. *Third row left*, e. Intersection of two equal circles with hexagons inscribed. *Third row right*, f. Hexagram. *Bottom left*, g. Dodecagon. *Bottom right*, h. Double *vesica piscis*

Mathematics and metaphysics of the equilateral triangle and its derivatives

It will be recalled how the Christian significance of the equilateral triangle is rooted in Plato's cosmology, in which the 3 atmospheric elements of fire, air, and water were assigned to the polyhedra composed of equilateral triangles – 4, 8 and 20 respectively (Fig. 3).[7] Yet in his *Timaeus*, Plato starts the construct of these polyhedra, not with the equilateral triangle, which is isosceles, but with the triangle bisected vertically into two scalene triangles, each in the ratio of 1 : 2 : √3. He reasons that the indeterminacy of scalene triangles, which possess an infinity of shape, equates with the instability of air, fire, and water. This contrasts with the stability of earth, the square of its cube being composed of the regulated form of two right-angled isosceles triangles (Fig. 48).[8] The physical interchangeability of the atmospheric elements and their location in relation to each other and to the earth were well understood, as attested by Augustine and Robert Grosseteste, the thirteenth-century bishop of Lincoln:

> Then, too, this form earth is differentiated from the other elements …
>
> Augustine, *De musica* VI. 17.58.[9]

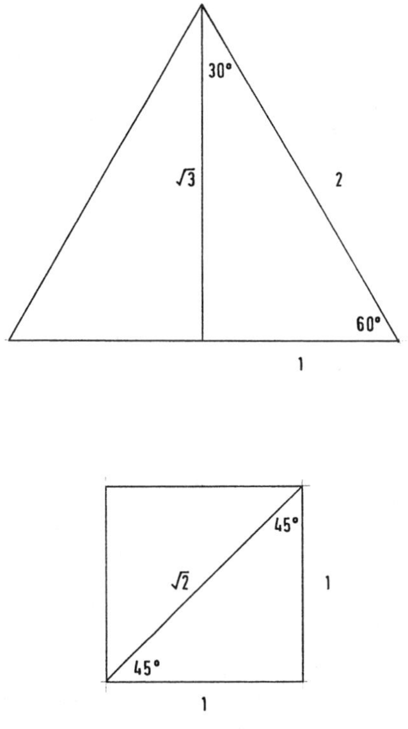

Fig. 48 The geometric root of the equilateral triangle and the square; Plato, *Timaeus* 53C–55C. This demonstrates how the equilateral triangle was conceived as consisting of two right-angled triangles, with sides 1 : 2 : √3; and the square as consisting of two right-angled isosceles triangles, with sides 1 : 1 : √2

> The system by which Plato connects and disposes the four elements in a symmetrical order interposes the two intermediary elements of air and water between the two extremes, fire, the most mobile element, and the motionless earth, in such a way that water is as far above earth as air is above water and fire above air.
>
> Augustine, *De civitate Dei* VIII. 15.[10]

> ... at the same time as the waters were gathered together air came into existence, since to rarefy vaporous waters is to produce air. If the rarefication and thinning down is very great, then even fire and flame are produced.
>
> Grosseteste, *Hexaëmeron* I. 7. 2.[11]

As part of Plato's abstract model, it was a system that incorporated an intrinsic logic that was both physical and metaphysical and, although he could have chosen any figure as an exemplar, it is interesting that it was the triangle that Boethius cited when he differentiated between intelligible structure and sensible matter:

> ... distinguishing it in the mind one contemplates the triangle itself and its property outside matter.
>
> *De hebdomades* IV.[12]

The 4 elements of geometry, where 1 is a point, 2 is a line, 3 is a plane, and 4 is a solid,[13] demonstrate why it is that 3 is a plane, for it is not possible for a plane to have fewer than 3 sides. The triangle, therefore, is the irreducible of plane figures, and similarly its figurate number, 3, is the irreducible of whole numbers, because for any thing to be whole, it must have a beginning, a middle, and an end, which the digits of 3 irreducibly possess.[14]

Turning to the geometric figures related to the equilateral triangle, the *vesica piscis* (Fig. 47b) is fundamental to Euclid since it is used to demonstrate the first proposition in Book I of his *Elementa*: 'On a finite straight line to construct an equilateral triangle'.[15] A version of this appears in the early medieval *Ars geometriae et arithmeticae*, which was attributed in the Middle Ages to Boethius and was widely disseminated across Europe, often being kept in places of architectural importance.[16] It evidently acquired its Latin name through a resemblance to a fish's bladder, and its alternative appellation – *mandorla* – for reminding at least one Italian of the shape of an almond nut. Its figure comprises the intersection of two equal circles through each other's centre, the top and bottom halves therefore each enclosing an equilateral triangle (Fig. 47c). This will also have been understood as demonstrating axioms concerning the radii of equal circles and the geometry of hexagons (Fig. 47d). Just as the figure of the *vesica piscis* constitutes the shared overlap between the two circles, so are its two equilateral triangles shared, and if the two circles are completed, both triangles together will be seen to be one-third of the hexagons inscribed within the circles (Fig. 47e). The equal sides of the triangles become the sides and radii of the two overlapping hexagons. It is a mathematical inevitability, for example, that 6 circles exactly surround a seventh of equal size – they have

Fig. 49 Six equal spheres surrounding a seventh

equal radii (Fig. 49). Taking one of the hexagons, and connecting the alternate angles around its perimeter with each other, a hexagram, or six-pointed star, is obtained (Fig. 47f). This consists of two equilateral triangles overlaying each other and was known as Solomon's Knot. If one hexagon is rotated mid-way over another, a dodecagon is obtained, taking the form of a twelve-spoked wheel (Fig. 47g).

The signification of the numbers attaching to these figures was established in Antiquity and has already been outlined.[17] 3, the figurate number of the triangle, being the first whole number, was male. 6, the figurate number of the hexagon, was perfect because it equals the sum of its parts. A number whose sum of parts is greater than itself was said to be superfluous,[18] and one whose parts are less was said to be diminished,[19] which will be of relevance shortly. 6 also signified creation, since it was the product of the first female and male numbers, which are 2 and 3.[20] Finally 12, the figurate number of the dodecagon, was associated with the measure and division of time, and the zodiac of Antiquity.

The Trinity and Creation

The transmission of these ideas to the early Middle Ages, in the form of Christian Platonist thought, resulted in an additional layering of meaning. In succession to numerous triads in ancient religions, 3 came to stand for the Holy Trinity and sometimes for the spiritual gifts of faith, hope, and charity.[21]

Interestingly, the heavenly nature of the Trinity and its intangibility are somewhat akin to the intangibility and ethereal nature of the 3 atmospheric elements, both in contradistinction to earth and both signified by the triangle.[22] In the twelfth century, the *Heptateuchon* of Thierry of Chartres identified the Trinity with the equilateral triangle,[23] and in the thirteenth century, Jean de Meun combines this with the idea of Christ as a sphere in the womb of the Virgin. This is part of Nature's Confession in *Le Roman de la Rose*:[24]

> From the moment she conceived him, she knew, and this fortified her in her pregnancy, that he was the wondrous sphere that knows no bounds, that has its centre everywhere and whose circumference is not in any place. She knew that he was the marvellous triangle in which the whole is the three angles, while the three angles together make but a single whole. It was the triangular circle, the circular triangle that dwelt within the virgin. Plato ... did not see the triple unity in that single trinity, nor the sovereign deity clothed in human flesh. It was God, who is called the Creator.
>
> Jean de Meun, *Le Roman de la Rose* X.[25]

Also in the thirteenth century, Robert Grosseteste linked the Trinity in his *Hexaëmeron* to Augustine's recognition of the wholeness of the triad:

> It is fitting ... that the number of persons should be three, since the number three is the first ... number that has a beginning, a middle and an end.
>
> *Hexaëmeron* VIII. 3. 5.[26]

Among many coincidences of thought between the Hellenic and Judaic traditions,[27] the association by the Greeks of the number 6 with perfection and creation was matched by the 6 days of Creation recounted in Genesis. In this, Grosseteste again followed Augustine's reasoning:

> So the heavens and the earth were finished, and all the adornment of them. This brings ... a conclusion to ... the perfection of heaven and earth ... For their perfection follows from the perfection of the number six, in which number [of days] they were made. As Augustine says, it is not that the number six is perfect because God completed his works in six days, but rather that he completed his works in six days because the number six is perfect.
>
> *Hexaëmeron* IX. 1. 1.[28]

According to the same reasoning, 12 was to be respected, not because it was the number of Apostles but because its mystical nature was such that it determined that the number of Apostles should be 12:

> The mystical number remained, the number twelve, because through the entire world, that is, through the four cardinal points of the world, they were going to announce the Trinity. Thus three times four.
>
> Augustine, *In Iohannis Evangelicum* XXVII. 10. 4.[29]

This was the reason for Judas to be replaced and, although there were two candidates, it was also the reason only one of them could be chosen. The number had to be 12, even if it left no place subsequently for Paul, as observed by Augustine:

> [The] number twelve ... is significant as being the number of ... the apostles because it is the product of the two parts of seven – that is, three multiplied by four ...
>
> ... and there may be other explanations of the number twelve which could give the same significance. Otherwise, since we are told that Matthias was appointed an apostle in the place of the traitor Judas, there will be no throne of judgment for the Apostle Paul ...
>
> *De civitate Dei* XV. 20, XX. 5.[30]

Architectura ad triangulum

Number

Since the mathematics and metaphysics surrounding the equilateral triangle, the *vesica piscis*, and the hexagon, together with their figurate numbers 3, 6, and 12, evolved from Antiquity into a series of interrelated beliefs that were taught by the Church, starting with the Trinity and Creation, it is hardly surprising to find them present in the architecture and iconography of the Church, or that there should be evidence that their presence expressed these beliefs intentionally. Eusebius, in his fourth-century panegyric to Paulinus on his church at Tyre, attributes the light of the Trinity to its triple entrance portal.

> ... he hath thrown open passages to the temple ... once again under the rays of the sun placing three gates on one side, upon the middle one of which he hath bestowed a height and size that far surpasseth the two on either side ...
>
> The whole temple he adorneth with a single, mighty gateway, even the praise of the one and only God, the universal King; and on either side of the Father's sovereign power he provideth the secondary beams of the light of Christ and the Holy Spirit.
>
> *Historia ecclesiastica* III. 10. 4.[31]

In the sixth-century, the Syriac hymn to Edessa Cathedral proclaimed,

> ... a single light shines in the choir through three open windows,
> Announcing the mystery of the Trinity ...
>
> Hymn to Edessa Cathedral.[32]

In the ninth century in the West, Angilbert incorporated 3 churches around the cloister of his abbey at Centula (Fig. 50), the south range of which,

Fig. 50 Exterior, Abbey of St Riquier; seventeenth-century engraving from lost eleventh-century manscript

unusually, was built at an angle. The main church of St Riquier lay along the north side in the normal manner, with the other two churches – dedicated to Mary and Benedict – located at the corners of an implied triangle. The eleventh-century chronicler explained:

> Since … the faithful should have faith in the most sacred and indivisible Trinity, venerate it and worship it in their mind and firmly believe in it … we have striven to found … three main churches.
>
> Hariulf, *Chronicon Centulense* II. 8.[33]

At Thorney Abbey in the following century, Æthelwold 'constructed a church, tripartite in its unity, to the praise of the Trinity'.[34] In the thirteenth century, Robert Grosseteste's account of Creation associates triple lights with the Trinity.

> … the mind ascends to the contemplation of the Trinity and brings back a light of fear from the power of the Father, a light of knowledge from the wisdom of the Son, and a light of love from the kindness of the Holy Spirit. With these three lights it destroys the darkness …
>
> *Hexaëmeron* IX. 9. 1.[35]

As 3 expressed the Trinity in architectural descriptions, so 6 represented perfection. It will be recalled that at New Minster in Winchester in the tenth century, Æthelgar divided its tower into 6 stages, possibly by inserting string courses into the new construction, because 6 is 'made up of the sum of its parts … and is most perfect by the rules of philosophy' (*Liber vitae* V).[36] Similarly, Ramwold 'very artfully ordered' the crypt of his abbey church at Regensburg so that the 'sixth altar … announces the perfection of the "sextuple", comprising everything' (*Liber* II. 40).[37] Returning to Grosseteste in the thirteenth century, he interprets the number 7 as representing God's rest following the 6 days of creation, associating 6 as a perfect number with 1 as the divinity of God (Fig. 49).

> Seven is … made up of one and six. Unity is the primary attribute of the simplicity of divinity. Six is perfect because it [equals the sum of its parts] and lacks superfluity and diminution.[38]… This is the best perfection, since something that [represents equality] attaches itself and is joined, in its way, to the primary and supreme simplicity. It is in seven that this kind of perfection first appears, [in] that the equality that lacks superfluity and diminution is applied to the first simplicity and hence to rest.
>
> *Hexaëmeron* IX. 10. 4.[39]

Had Grosseteste lived long enough to see Simon of Thirsk's window lighting the end of the Angel Choir of his cathedral (Fig. 151), which dates from the end of the thirteenth century, he would surely have recognized the geometric equivalent of this passage, with its 6 *oculi* surrounding a seventh, in which the circle of 6 *oculi* stands for Creation, the single *oculus* in the centre representing the Creator, to which Grosseteste might have added, incidentally, the sum of 7 symbolizing the Holy Spirit:[40]

> There is a great deal that could be said about the perfection of the number seven … [for] seven is made up of [the numbers 3 and 4]. … For this reason the Holy Spirit is often referred to by this same number …
>
> Augustine, *De civitate Dei* XI. 31.[41]

The vesica piscis

Also profuse in medieval architecture and art is the *vesica piscis*. Increasingly from the ninth century onwards, it was chosen to enclose Christ and certain Holy Roman emperors when seated in majesty, and in the case of Christ, usually attended by the symbols of the 4 Evangelists at the 4 corners of a page or a relief. These derived from the vision of Ezekiel, with Mark being

Fig. 51 Christ in majesty, *Gospels of Lothair*, ninth century

Fig. 52 Christ in majesty, altar frontal, Aachen Chapel

Fig. 53 Christ in judgment, Royal Portal, Chartres Cathedral

Fig. 54 The Bishop's Eye, south transept, Lincoln Cathedral

symbolized by a lion, Luke an ox, Matthew a man, and John an eagle, and they can be seen occupying the angles around the figure of Christ in the ninth-century *Gospels of Lothair* from Tours (Fig. 51),[42] the golden altar frontal at the palace chapel of Aachen early in the eleventh century (Fig. 52), and in numerous sculptural reliefs of the Last Judgment over the west doors of churches, notably Chartres Cathedral in the middle of the twelfth century (Fig. 53). Above this particular portal, another *vesica piscis* crowns the central lancet window, which is devoted to the Life of Christ, this one framing the infant on his mother's lap.[43] In addition to its occurrence in stained glass, the same geometric figure appears in window tracery, one unusual – perhaps unique – instance being the double *vesica piscis* in the south transept window of Lincoln Cathedral (Fig. 54). This dates from early in the fourteenth century and is an interesting case of implied geometry. Whereas a single *vesica piscis* implies a double circle, one overlapping the other, a double *vesica* implies 3 circles overlapping each other, surely signifying the Trinity, as any geometer at Lincoln's cathedral school would have recognized (Fig. 47h).[44] Finally, in plan design, it has already been observed that Cesariano noted the use of the *vesica piscis* by German architects.

The form of the *vesica piscis*, enclosing Christ in the overlap of two circles, sometimes represents in the East his aura of divine light, for example in the fourteenth-century fresco in the Church of St Saviour in Chora, in Constantinople. In the West, the geometric figure appears to express his governance over the two circles of heaven and earth. Among the biblical evidence for this interpretation is this from Isaiah:

> Thus saith the Lord, The heaven is my throne, and the earth is my footstool: where is the house that ye build unto me?
>
> Isaiah 66: 1.

The import of this is that God's head is in heaven and his feet are on earth, and for heaven and earth each to be represented by a circle, this suggests two circles arranged, not horizontally, but vertically. This appears to be borne out by early images before the *vesica piscis* was adopted for this purpose. Among ninth-century examples, *Vivian's Bible* (Fig. 55) shows Christ within two circles arranged vertically, framed by a lozenge of two triangles base to base, with prophets in roundels at each of the 4 apexes.[45] On the cover of the *Codex Aureus*, he is shown within twin circles, one above the other, and with his feet on a third, much smaller, circle.[46] In the *Stuttgart Gospels*, he is shown within an oval, arranged vertically, which is inscribed:

> Here sits the king, the summit and creator of earth and heaven.[47]

By what process Christ came to be depicted within the overlap of the two circles, which are now implied but, were they to be drawn, would be arranged horizontally (Fig. 51), cannot at present be stated. The evidence makes clear, however, that although a great many *vesica piscis* figures appear to be true circumscriptions of two equilateral triangles base to base, many others are drawn with a horizontal axis greater or smaller than this, suggesting their

Fig. 55 Christ in majesty, *Vivian's Bible*, ninth century

artists were either unaware of the underlying geometry, or were simply interested in the geometric figure for representing the intermediate realm shared by heaven and earth, regardless of its exact proportion.

The equilateral triangle

The *vesica piscis* also appears in the thirteenth-century Portfolio of Villard de Honnecourt,[48] which is, in addition to this, a prolific source for the architectural application of the equilateral triangle and its derivatives. The figure appears in the gables of the clock-house[49] and in the window design for Lausanne Cathedral,[50] both in association with the square. It provides the base for the lectern (Fig. 56),[51] which is composed of two equilateral triangles overlaying each other, the lower one being trefoiled. The upper triangle beneath the eagle is also isosceles and seems to be an attempt at a three-dimensional projection of another equilateral triangle. The wheel window for Chartres Cathedral is

Fig. 56 Lectern, Villard de Honnecourt, Portfolio fol. 7r, thirteenth century

Fig. 57 Equilateral arch and hexafoil, Villard, fol. 10v, thirteenth century

Fig. 58 Wheel window, Chartres Cathedral, Villard, fol. 15v, thirteenth century

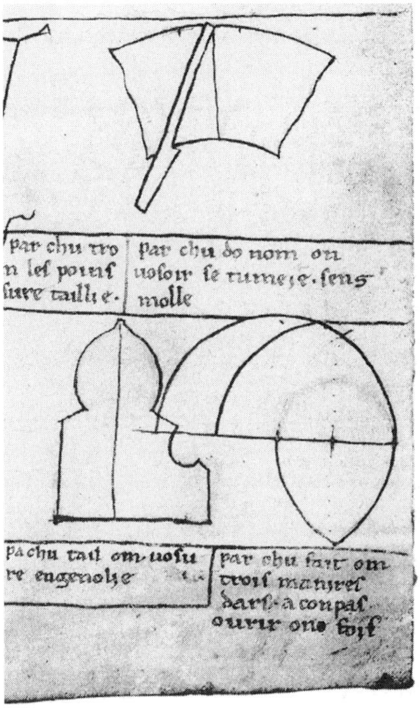

Fig. 59 Sketch of three arches, Villard, fol. 21r, bottom right, thirteenth century

Fig. 60 Interlacing arcades, chapter house, Much Wenlock Priory

a dodecagon (Fig. 58),[52] with a central *oculus* with 12 lobes, surrounded by 12 *oculi*. Each of these is divided into 12,[53] interspersed around the circumference with 12 trefoils in a type of design which paved the way for the Gothic rose window, which was almost invariably twelve-foiled.[54]

In addition to these examples, by far the most frequent occurrence of the equilateral triangle both in Villard's Portfolio and in contemporary architecture takes the form of equilateral arches, the most common form of arch in the thirteenth century and, in tracery, often incorporating the hexafoil (Fig. 57). These are to be seen in the Portfolio with varying degrees of precision, and are sometimes stilted; for example, on the tower elevation of Laon Cathedral,[55] and the windows and arcading on Villard's elevations of Reims Cathedral.[56] Finally, the three related arches in the sketch on folio 21r share a common base divided equally into 4, and include a semi-circular, tiers-point, and equilateral arch (Fig. 59). The base of the latter was also shared by another semi-circular arch formerly drawn above the horizontal, but this has been erased. Even fainter is the mirror-image of the inverted arch, thereby completing the *vesica piscis*, the upper end of its arc still intersecting the larger semi-circle. The caption of this sketch, added by a later master,[57] has been translated thus:

> By this [means] one can draw three kinds of arches with [but] one opening of a compass.[58]

Nothing illustrates better than this the medieval mason's delight in swinging his dividers and describing arcs, which will have provided him with an empirical understanding of the geometry of equilateral arches, and their derivation from interlacing semi-circular arches so popular in Norman architecture. The most extravagant displays of such arcading must be the twelfth-century examples across the west front of Castle Acre Priory and in the chapter-house of Much Wenlock Priory, the latter suggesting a fantasy of arch forms piled upon each other (Fig. 60). The lowest row, incidentally, incorporates semi-circular arches within each equilateral arch, as originally drawn in Villard's sketch of three arches. Yet if the top third of each semi-circle is omitted, arcades of equilateral arches are created. The penny dropped at Southwell Minster sometime between completion of the north tower, which carries interlaced round arches, and the south tower, which has similar arcading, except that the tops of the round arches have now been omitted, resulting in a row of equilateral arches (Figs 61, 62). As the sketch on folio 21r makes clear, every equilateral arch is the top half of a *vesica piscis*, a thought which may have occurred to someone while gazing at an arcade of them in the middle of his offices.

The Wheel of Fortune and the zodiac

Another application of the equilateral triangle in Villard's Portfolio is seen in the division of a circle into 6 to construct a Wheel of Fortune, which is developed into a hexafoil encircling the seated figure of the goddess *Fortuna* (Fig. 63).[59] The 6 figures around the hexafoil illustrate the cycle of fortune as if the wheel is rotating. Above *Fortuna*, one figure sits regally holding a sceptre; on the goddess's left, two others fall; at her feet, another lies downcast; after which the cycle continues with two mortals rising up on her right, back towards the figure of power at the top. In other examples, it was common for there to be 4 figures, with those at the top and bottom being complemented by one figure rising up on the goddess's right, and the other falling on her left, accompanied by the words – *Regnabo – Regno – Regnavi – Sum sine regno.*[60] The association of rising fortune lying on the goddess's right and of declining fortune on her left corresponds with depictions of Judgment Day where the saved appear on the right hand of God and the damned fall to his left. This represents a tradition that can be traced back at least as far as the Myth of Er, with which Plato concludes his *Republic*. Here souls journey after death towards their Judges, who sit between apertures both into the earth and up to the sky. After judgment, the just ascend the path up to the sky, which rises to the right, and the unjust descend to the bowels of the earth, taking the path that falls to the left.[61] It is a connotation that survives in modern English, when it is remembered that the Latin for left is *sinister* and right is *dexter*, the epithet dexterous being a compliment.

A principal source for *Fortuna* and her wheel in the Middle Ages is found in Boethius' celebrated dialogue, *De consolatione Philosophiae*:

> So with imperious hand she turns the wheel of change
> This way and that like the ebb and flow of the tide,
> And pitiless tramples down those once dread kings,
> Raising the lowly face of the conquered –
> Only to mock him in his turn;
> Careless she neither hears nor heeds the cries

Fig. 61 North tower, Southwell Minster. Note the interlacing arcades of round arches in the second storey below the eaves

> Of miserable men: she laughs
> At the groans that she herself has mercilessly caused.
> So she sports, so she proves her power,
> Showing a mighty marvel to her subjects, when
> The self-same hour
> Sees a man first successful, then cast down.
>
> *De consolatione Philosophiae* II. 1.[62]

Among the medieval translations of this was one into French by Jean de Meun towards the end of the thirteenth century and, among its many copies, *Fortuna* and her wheel was a favourite illustration.[63] The topic also formed a large part of the Advice of Reason in Jean's continuation of *Le Roman de la Rose*, which was one of the most popular romances of the Middle Ages.[64] Describing the House of *Fortuna* as well as her wheel, both fall into the duality of opposites as her victims are lifted up only to be cast down, with all their attempts to interfere with the wheel being doomed to failure.[65] The fickleness of *Fortuna* is a theme that had already reappeared in the twelfth-century *Anticlaudianus* by Alan of Lille:

> She keeps her wheel in fast motion and no rest brings an end to the toil of movement ... It envelops mankind, exempts no one from its downward spin but forces all to put up with the antics of fate and drives men down into all kinds of misfortune. It increases the pressure on some, lightens the burden for others; hurls some down, raises others up.
>
> *Anticlaudianus* VIII.[66]

Fig. 62 South tower, Southwell Minster. Note the arcades of equilateral arches in the second storey below the eaves

Belonging to the same century is the Wheel of Fortune window in the north transept of St Stephen's church at Beauvais dating from around 1135, or perhaps between 1140 and 1150 (Fig. 64).[67] This design multiplies the division of Villard's Wheel to 12 and, unusually, portrays the figures of fortune on the right and those of misfortune on the left when facing the window from the outside.[68] Other architectural examples have survived from the beginning of the thirteenth century onwards and include Basel Minster and Trento Cathedral, where they also occur on the north transept, and S. Zeno in Verona, where its wheel dominates the west front. It has been suggested that the location of wheels of fortune on churches may have corresponded with judicial benches sited in the public spaces adjoining them, possibly in order to show how justice challenged the whims of fortune.[69]

The best-known medieval treatment of *Fortuna* and her wheel must be the six verses in the thirteenth-century collection of sacred and secular songs published in the nineteenth century under the title, *Carmina Burana*,[70] and made popular by their musical setting by Carl Orff in the twentieth century. The verses are appended to the foot of two pages of the collection,[71] the final verse concluding:

At the turn of Fortune's wheel,
  one is deposed,
another is lifted on high
  to enjoy a brief felicity.
Uneasy sits the king –
  let him beware his ruin,

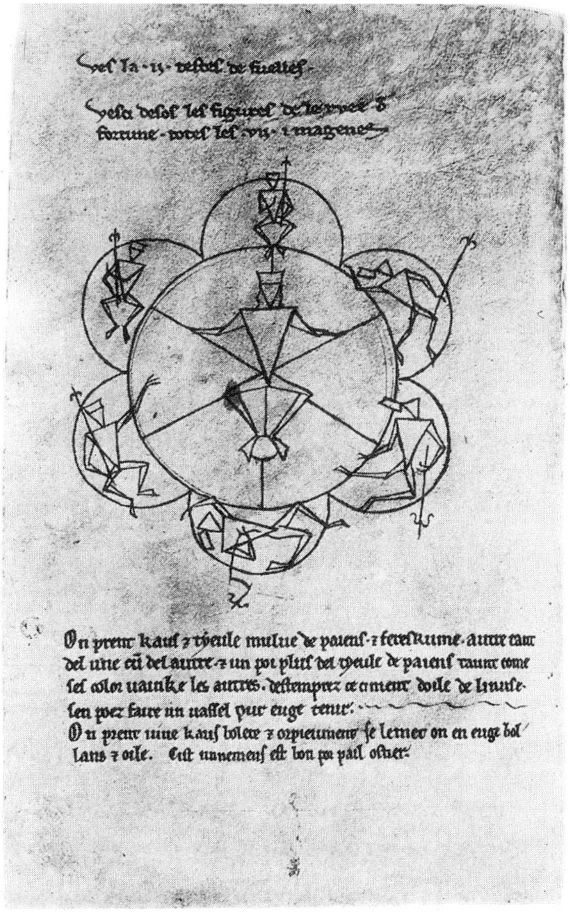

Fig. 63 Wheel of Fortune, Villard, fol. 21v, thirteenth century

for beneath the axle of the wheel
we read the name of Hecuba.[72]

At the head of the first of the two pages is a miniature of *Fortuna* and her wheel in the usual arrangement (Fig. 65), with the goddess inside the wheel and the 4 figures in their familiar positions, each attended by the Latin words denoting the state of their fate.[73] However, this wheel is divided into 8, which was as common as its division into 6, a difference that will be discussed further in the final chapter.[74]

The division of the wheel window of St Stephen's church into 12 makes it a close cousin of another wheel, the zodiac, with its related connotations of fate and time. Early in the Middle Ages, astrology was frowned upon by the Church. Although it understood some of the influences of the celestial bodies on the earth, such as the solar on the seasons and the lunar on the tides, any suggestion of human predestination undermined the theological necessity of free will.[75] To this, Augustine had added a pragmatic objection. Using logic

Fig. 64 Wheel of Fortune window, north transept, St Stephen, Beauvais

Fig. 65 Wheel of Fortune, *Carmina Burana*, thirteenth century

and the example of twins – since simultaneous conception under a single sign is followed by the development of individual difference – Augustine refutes the practice of astrology both for those who believed the influence of the stars had no connection with God's will and for those who accepted its dependence.[76] Showing a concern understandable for a man of the Church, he declaims:

> Those who suppose that the stars decide, quite apart from the will of God, how we shall act, and what blessings we shall enjoy or what disasters we shall suffer, are to be refused any hearing whatsoever ... For can this supposition mean anything but an end to all worship, and all prayer?
>
> *De civitate Dei* V. 1.[77]

Even so, the zodiac and calendar imagery inherited from Antiquity appear to have translated to dome and floor iconography in the Early Christian period[78] and thence to the early Middle Ages. One example from ninth-century Constantinople found its way to the Vatican and shows the 12 signs surrounding Helios, the Sun-god.[79] A turning-point came with the translation of Arabic works on astrology into Latin so that, by the 1120s, Hugh of St Victor could distinguish between astronomy and astrology, and the rational part of astrology that belonged to the natural order and the part that resided in the twilight world of superstition:

> ... astronomy ... treats the law of the stars and the revolution of the heaven, and which investigates the regions, orbits, courses, risings, and settings of stars, and why each bears the name assigned it; it is astrology, however, which considers the stars in their bearing upon birth, death, and all other events, and is only partly natural, and for the rest, superstitious; natural as it concerns the temper or 'complexion' of physical things, like health, illness, storm, calm, productivity, and unproductivity, which vary with the mutual alignments of the astral bodies; but superstitious as it concerns chance happenings or things subject to free choice.
>
> *Didascalicon* II. 10.[80]

The 'natural' and the 'superstitious' in astrology became resolved into its mundane and judicial branches.[81] Encompassing the system were the observations that the sky was divided into 12 houses, which were named after the constellations and their signs encircling the zodiac wheel. Each sign was governed by one of the planets, which included the sun and moon ruling one sign each, and the other five each ruling two, making 12 in all. Their procession through the year linked the idea of motion with time, as in wheels of fortune. In one fourteenth-century zodiac (Fig. 66),[82] the turning of its wheel is suggested by adapting the radial geometry of the dodecagon so that its spokes appear swept. This is achieved by the simple device of dividing its inner and outer circles into 12 and connecting each point on the hub to the one that is one place removed from its opposite number on the rim. The motion of the

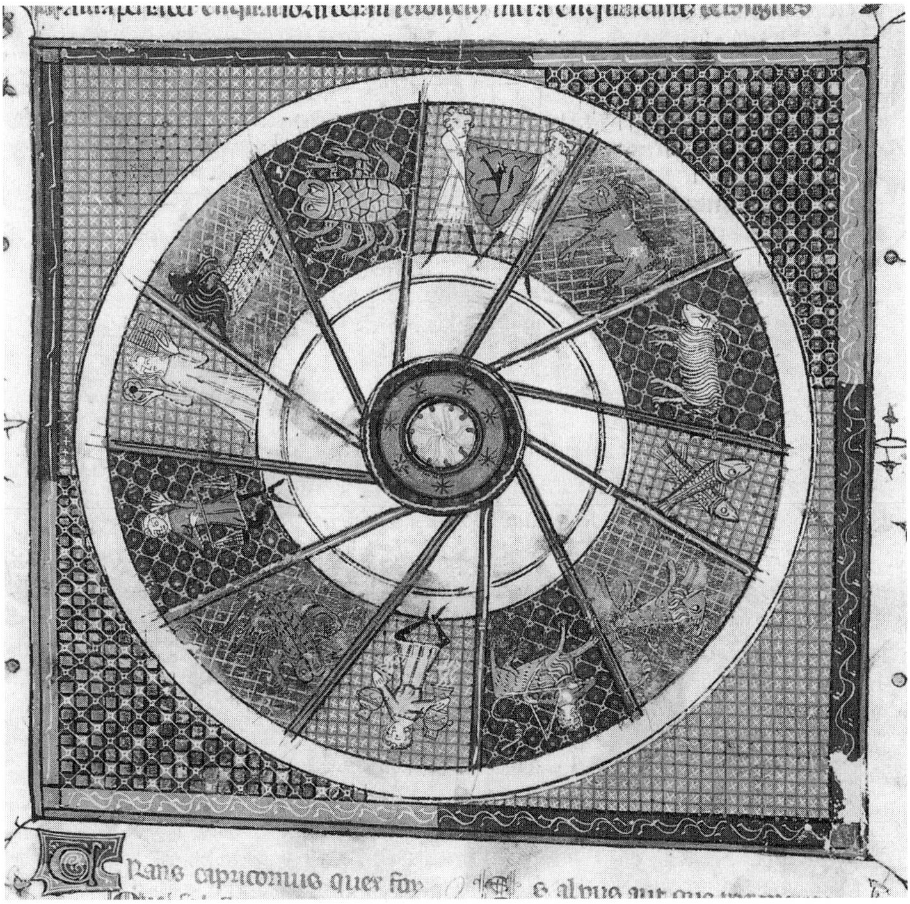

Fig. 66 The zodiac, fourteenth century

zodiac through time led to the calculation of calendars, specifically the Church's calendar, which was needed to fix dates for movable feasts, especially Easter. Two such calendars depicting the 12 signs of the zodiac form part of thirteenth-century mosaic pavements in Florence, at the Basilica of S. Miniato and at the Cathedral Baptistery.[83] With the development of wheel windows into rose windows during the latter part of the twelfth century and into the thirteenth, signs of the zodiac became incorporated into their programmes of stained glass. The west roses of the cathedrals at Paris and Lausanne, dating from around 1220 and 1230, both display signs of the zodiac, those at Lausanne forming part of a complex scheme symbolizing the cosmos (Fig. 67).[84]

Solomon's Knot

Another variant of the hexagon familiar to popular culture is the hexagram, or six-pointed star, known as Solomon's Seal, or Knot, before its adoption as the Star of David (Fig. 47f). This consists of two equilateral triangles interlocked

Fig. 67 Signs of the zodiac, west rose, Lausanne Cathedral. *Left:* Virgo. *Bottom:* Cancer. *Right:* Leo

with each other into a knot. The triangle with its apex pointing upwards was construed as overlaying and locked with the other with its apex pointing down, the first representing the male principle and the element fire, the second the female principle and the element water.[85] Again it was Hugh of St Victor who was among those who transmitted their gender associations,

> … [of] the four elements of which the two upper ones, namely fire and air, are masculine in function and in gender, and the two lower, earth and water, feminine.
>
> *Didascalicon* III. 17.[86]

Thus the hexagram stood for the act of creation and, in so doing, added the discipline of geometry to the established meaning of the number 6. Whilst hexafoils are common in England and France, hexagrams can be found in window tracery in Spain, for example in the fifteenth-century west window of Burgos Cathedral (Fig. 68), also at the cathedrals of Palma and Valencia. Interestingly, the occurrence in popular culture of the Church's teaching on God's Creation, and its duration of 6 days, included Spain. In the creed chant known as *The Twelve Apostles,*[87] the sixth verse exists in several versions, the most common being:

Fig. 68 West window, with hexagram, Burgos Cathedral

I'll sing you six, oh!
Green grow the rushes, oh!
What is your six, oh?
Six for the six proud walkers …

The Twelve Apostles.[88]

Other versions have 'proud waiters', or 'bold waiters' and these are almost certainly corruptions for 'waters' in reference to Christ creating wine in the 6 water-jars for the wedding in Cana (John II. 3–9).[89] Robert Grosseteste recognized this miracle as an act of creation:

> At a wedding in Cana … he changed the water into wine. Six water jugs were standing there, and he commanded them to be filled with water. When the governor [of the feast] tasted the water, he found it to be good wine. … [Jesus] changed the water into wine; and all this was one deed by both God and man. … In all these deeds one can see that he was truly God [who] … created all things.
>
> *Le Château d'amour*.[90]

In support of this reading, one form of *The Twelve Apostles* has 'Six, the echoing waters' and another 'Six, the water-jugs'. Exceptionally, one version has 'Six, the days of creation' which, as it happens, is a variant from Spain.[91]

Given the profusion of hexafoils in tracery design, the possibility of their serving as symbols of God's Creation seems compelling. Geometrically they are variations of Simon of Thirsk's east window at Lincoln Cathedral in that the 6 circles are truncated by the central circle being larger. Yet the reading of them was surely the same, namely the 6 days of Creation, surrounding the single circle in the centre representing the Creator. And if the labyrinth on the

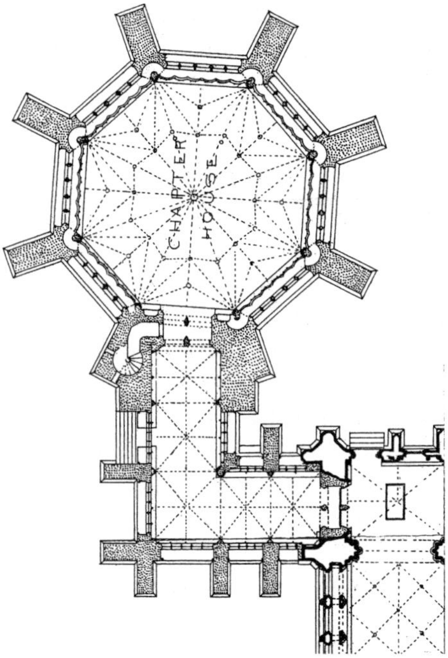

Fig. 69 Plan, chapter house, York Minster, showing 6 seats per side, plus one either side of the entrance

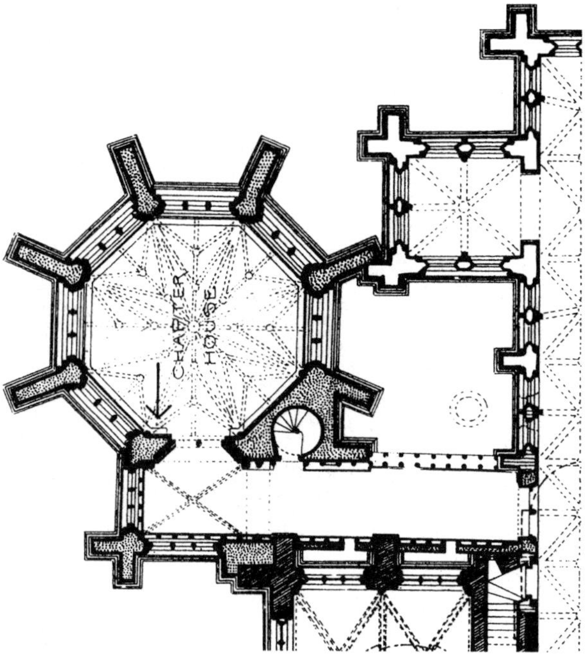

Fig. 70 Plan, chapter house, Southwell Minster, with 5 seats per side, plus one to the north of the entrance

nave pavement of Chartres Cathedral represented the world, then the hexafoil at its centre would have provided a fitting climax to the pilgrim's journey through it.

The power of number

One final example that appears to demonstrate the power of number, in relation to 3 and 12, concerns polygonal chapter houses and their seating layouts.[92] The chapter house at York Minster, dating from about 1280, is an octagon, with 6 stalls built into each of 7 sides, and with 1 either side of the entrance in the eighth side, making 44 stalls in total (Fig. 69). Yet there were only 36 canons, leaving 6 stalls for various assigned dignitaries and possibly 2 for representatives of the king and archbishop; and the complement of canons was evidently held at 36 thereafter, supposedly because this was the number of the Apostles thrice.[93] It was believed that at Pentecost the Apostles became the ideal Christian community and the model for all monastic communities. The *Occupatio* of Odo of Cluny (878–942) chronicles biblical events as the history of salvation, with Pentecost leading to the final stage of the Christian

Fig. 71 Portal, chapter house, Southwell Minster, showing the extra seat to the right of the entrance, which is eccentric to the arch above

life on earth in the form of monasticism, 'the beautiful form of the Church at her birth' (*Occupatio* VI. 572).[94] Consequently, from monks accompanying their abbot to found a new monastery, to inmates of an almshouse living under a warden, the community would number 12, or a multiple of 12. The imperative of achieving this appears borne out by the chapter house of Southwell Minster (Fig. 70). This is also octagonal and was built from about 1295. It has 5 arcaded seats in each of 7 sides, totalling 35. However, an extra seat has been squeezed in beside the entrance to make this up to 36 (Fig. 71), even though this has had the effect of throwing the portal off-centre beneath the three-part blind tracery above. This should have been problematic. According to Augustine:

> In all the arts it is symmetry that gives pleasure, preserving unity and making the whole beautiful. …
>
> If I ask a workman why, after constructing one arch, he builds another like it (alongside) it, he will reply … that in a building like parts must correspond to like. If I go further and ask why he thinks so, he will say that it is fitting … But if I have to do with a man with inward eyes who can see the invisible … I shall ask him whether things are beautiful because … [their] parts correspond and are so joined together as to form one harmonious whole.
>
> If this is so, I shall ask him to tell me where he sees that unity, and what is its source; and if he cannot see it, how does he know what it is that material things imitate but cannot completely achieve. … Whence have you acquired the knowledge of unity according to which you judge material things … With bodily eyes you see nothing but corporeal things. Therefore it is with the mind that we see true unity …
>
> *De vera religione* XXX. 55, XXXII. 59, 60.[95]

The number of prebends at Southwell only amounted to 16 and, even allowing for the attendance of a growing number of chantry priests, if indeed they were admitted to the chapter, the number would fall some way short of 36.[96] This seems to suggest that it was even more important to achieve this number, being the product of 3 × 12, and standing for the Trinity and the Apostles, or simply the Apostles thrice over, than it was to achieve material perfection and unity in the architecture.

Conclusions

To summarize, it has been shown that certain elements of architecture occurring in threes and sixes were understood as signifying the Trinity and the perfection of Creation, and that their geometric counterparts were also commonplace, in the form of triangles, trefoils, hexafoils, hexagons, and hexagrams. It is not necessarily suggested here that every trefoil and hexafoil traced by a mason was intended to represent the Trinity and Creation, although this is possible, but that even a humble Christian upbringing would have meant that masons, as well as their masters, would have understood their meaning while they were constructing them. By extension, the same geometry, generated as it is from equal radii, also produces equilateral arches and the *vesica piscis*, arguably signifying, in the case of the *vesica piscis*, the realm of the Lord shared between heaven and earth. In the case of dodecagons and hexagrams, their meanings entered popular culture as the Wheel of Fortune, the zodiac, and Solomon's Knot; and at the root of them all lay the equilateral triangle, emblematic of the Holy Trinity.

Notes

1 *Annali*, tr. Ackerman (1949), 91, 108.
2 The 'triangle' was the equilateral triangle and the 'triangular figure' was the 3 : 4 : 5 triangle of Pythagoras. The reason for both triangles being considered is explained in the Epilogue, 'Continuing practice and forgotten knowledge'.
3 Ackerman (1949), 89–90, 93, note 37.
4 Scholfield (1958), 86–7. The systems of designing *ad quadratum* and *ad triangulum*, as corroborated by this congress in Milan, was the starting-point for an investigation by Maria Velte (1951), who put forward both figures for the sections and plans of various Gothic cathedrals. This will be discussed in the next chapter.
5 See Epilogue, 'Continuing practice and forgotten knowledge'.
6 The following summary is partly a development of material by Hiscock, in Zenner (2004 (1)) 3–21.
7 Prologue, 'Pythagoras and Plato', also 'Geometry'.
8 *Timaeus* 53C–55C.
9 Augustine, *De musica*, tr. Taliaferro (1947), 377.
10 Augustine, *De civitate Dei*, tr. Bettenson (1984), 321.
11 Grosseteste, *Hexaëmeron*, tr. Martin (1999), 56.
12 Boethius, *De hebdomades*, tr. Schultz (2001), 41.
13 See Prologue, 'Number and geometry'.
14 Augustine, *De musica* I. 12. 20.
15 Euclid, in Heath (1956), I. 241.
16 Ullman (1964), 267–70.
17 Prologue, 'Arithmetic'.
18 12 is superfluous because its factors, 1 + 2 + 3 + 4 + 6 = 16.
19 8 is diminished because its factors, 1 + 2 + 4 = 7.
20 Boyer (1968), 57.
21 I Cor. 13. 13.
22 Augustine, *In Iohan. ev.* XXVII.10.(4); Dante, tr. Sisson (1998), 440.
23 Masi (1983), 33.
24 See Epilogue, under 'Survivals of symbolism'.
25 Guillaume and Jean, tr. Horgan (1999), 295.
26 Grosseteste, tr. Martin (1999), 226.
27 See Prologue, 'Arithmetic'.
28 Grosseteste, tr. Martin (1999), 269; citing Augustine, *De civ. Dei* XI. 30.
29 Augustine, *In Iohannis evangelicum*, tr. Rettig (1988), 286.
30 Augustine, *De civitate Dei*, tr. Bettenson (1984), 634, 901.
31 Eusebius, tr. Oulton (1932), 425, 439.
32 Anon., tr. Mango (1972), 58.

33 Hariulf, tr. Timothy Beech (2003). For the placing of Centula in the development of cloister design, see Horn (1973), 43, 52. For a discussion of the liturgical significance of the three churches at Centula, see Carruthers (2000), 266–8, 273. It should be noted, however, regarding Horn's translation of the chronicle, which Carruthers appears to rely upon, no reference is made in the text to a triangle, obtuse or otherwise.
34 *Vita s. Oswaldi*, tr. Gem (1983), 13.
35 Grosseteste, tr. Martin (1999), 283.
36 *Liber vitae*, tr. Gem (1983), 15. See Prologue, 'The architectural programme'.
37 Translation by Hubert Stadler. See Prologue, 'The architectural programme'.
38 See notes 18 and 19 above on superfluous and diminished numbers.
39 Grosseteste, tr Martin (1999), 288.
40 See Chapter 6, 'Plate and bar tracery' and 'The Eyes of the cathedral'.
41 Augustine, *De civitate Dei*, tr. Bettenson (1984), 466.
42 Paris, Bibl. nat. MS lat. 266.
43 See Chapter 6, 'The Eyes of the cathedral'.
44 See Chapter 6, 'The Eyes of the cathedral'.
45 *Vivian's Bible*, Tours 845–846, Bibl. nat. MS lat.1 fol. 330b; in Holländer (1974), 76, 77, fig. 59.
46 Munich, Staatsbibliothek, Cod. 14000, in Holländer (1974), 108, fig. 86.
47 *Hic mundi caeli que sedet rex summus et auctor*, tr. Bert Hall (2003); Stuttgart, Würtemberger Landesbibliothek II. 40, fol. 1b, in Holländer (1974), 68, 72, fig. 58.
48 Villard, fol. 21r; see Fig. 59.
49 Ibid., fol. 6v.
50 Ibid., fol. 16r.
51 Ibid., fol. 7r.
52 Ibid., fol. 15v.
53 The *oculus* top left of the window is divided by eleven.
54 See Chapter 6, 'The Eyes of the cathedral'.
55 Villard, fol. 10r.
56 Ibid., fols 10v, 30v, 31r, 31v.
57 Hahnloser (1972), 254.
58 'Par chu fait om trois manires d'ars. a conpas ovrir one fois', Bechmann (1986), 125. I am grateful to Carl Barnes for offering this translation.
59 Villard, fol. 21v.
60 I shall rule, I rule, I have ruled, I am without rule. Kitzinger (1973), 353; Sears (1986), 144.
61 Plato, *Republic* X.
62 Boethius, *De consolatione Philosophiae*, tr. Tester (1973), 179, 181.
63 See Courcelle (1967), figs 65–86. See also Chapter 6, under 'Wheels of Fortune and Life', Fig. 134.
64 See Epilogue, under 'Survivals of symbolism'.
65 Guillaume and Jean, tr. Horgan (1999), 74–6, 93–105.
66 Alan of Lille, *Anticlaudianus*, tr. Sheridan (1987), 190–91.
67 For the dating of 1140–1450, see Beretz (2004), 18, which would place this window after the wheel window in the west facade of St Denis' Abbey Church. See also Mersmann (1982), 68–9.
68 One likely explanation for this apparent reversal is that the composition was meant to be read facing towards the window from the exterior, whereas the damned and saved sides in Judgment Day scenes are placed on Christ's left and right sides respectively as he faces outwards to the exterior.

69 Mersmann (1982), 70–78. More research would be required to validate this connection and to determine whether such siting of seats of justice was the cause or consequence of the siting of wheels of fortune.
70 Munich, Bayerische Staatsbibliothek MS. lat. 4660, 4660a; ed. Bischoff (1967).
71 Fols 1 and 48v. These were originally consecutive before being re-ordered so as to set a miniature of *Fortuna* as the frontispiece to the whole collection, thereby making it fol. 1r.
72 *Carmina Burana* fol. 48v, tr. Orff (1953), 4.

Fortune rota volvitur:
descendo minoratus;
alter in altum tollitur;
nimis exaltatus
rex sedet in vertice –
caveat ruinam!
nam sub axe legimus
Hecubam reginam.

73 *Carmina Burana*, fol. 1r.
74 See Chapter 6, under 'Wheels of Fortune and Life'.
75 Page (2002), 30.
76 Augustine, *De civ. Dei* V. 1–8.
77 Ibid., *De civ. Dei*, tr. Bettenson (1984), 179–80.
78 Lehmann (1945), 1–27, but see also Mathews (1982), 12–16.
79 This miniature forms the frontispiece of a copy of Ptolemy's *Syntaxis mathematica*, Rome, Biblioteca Apostolica Vaticana, see Rice (1965), 89, pl. 16.
80 Hugh of St Victor, tr. Taylor (1991), 68.
81 Page (2002), 26, 30.
82 Signs of the zodiac, BM. Harley MS. 4940, fol. 31, in Page (2002), frontispiece.
83 Dow (1957), 259. For the pavement at S. Miniato, which dates from 1207, see Cowen (2005), 52–3.
84 Dow (1957), 294; Cowen (1979), 84–5, 108–9, 128–31. Care needs to be exercised in reading the west rose at Paris, for it has undergone several restorations, especially in the sixteenth and nineteenth centuries; Cowen (1979), 91, 134. See also Chapter 6, 'Wheels of Fortune and Life', and 'The Eyes of the cathedral'.
85 Fontana (2001), 58; Whittick (1960), 188, 197.
86 Hugh of St Victor, tr. Taylor (1991), 100.
87 See Prologue, under 'The architectural programme, patrons, and architects'.
88 Dorsetshire Traditional, Broadwood and Maitland (1893), 156–8.
89 *Dilly Song* 6.
90 Grosseteste, *Château*, tr. O'Carroll (2003), 173–4.
91 Broadwood and Maitland (1893), 155; Eckenstein (1906), 145–6; Sandys (1833), 157; Sharp and Marson (1915), 313.
92 See also Chapter 6, section on 'Polygonal chapter houses'.
93 Norton (2004). I am grateful to Christopher Norton for the opportunity to discuss this question with him.
94 Odo, *Occupatio*; Hallinger, in Hunt (1971), 33–4.
95 Augustine, *De vera religione*, tr. Burleigh (1953), 252, 255.
96 Summers (1974), 20, 22–4. I am grateful to Jean Givens for recommending this source.

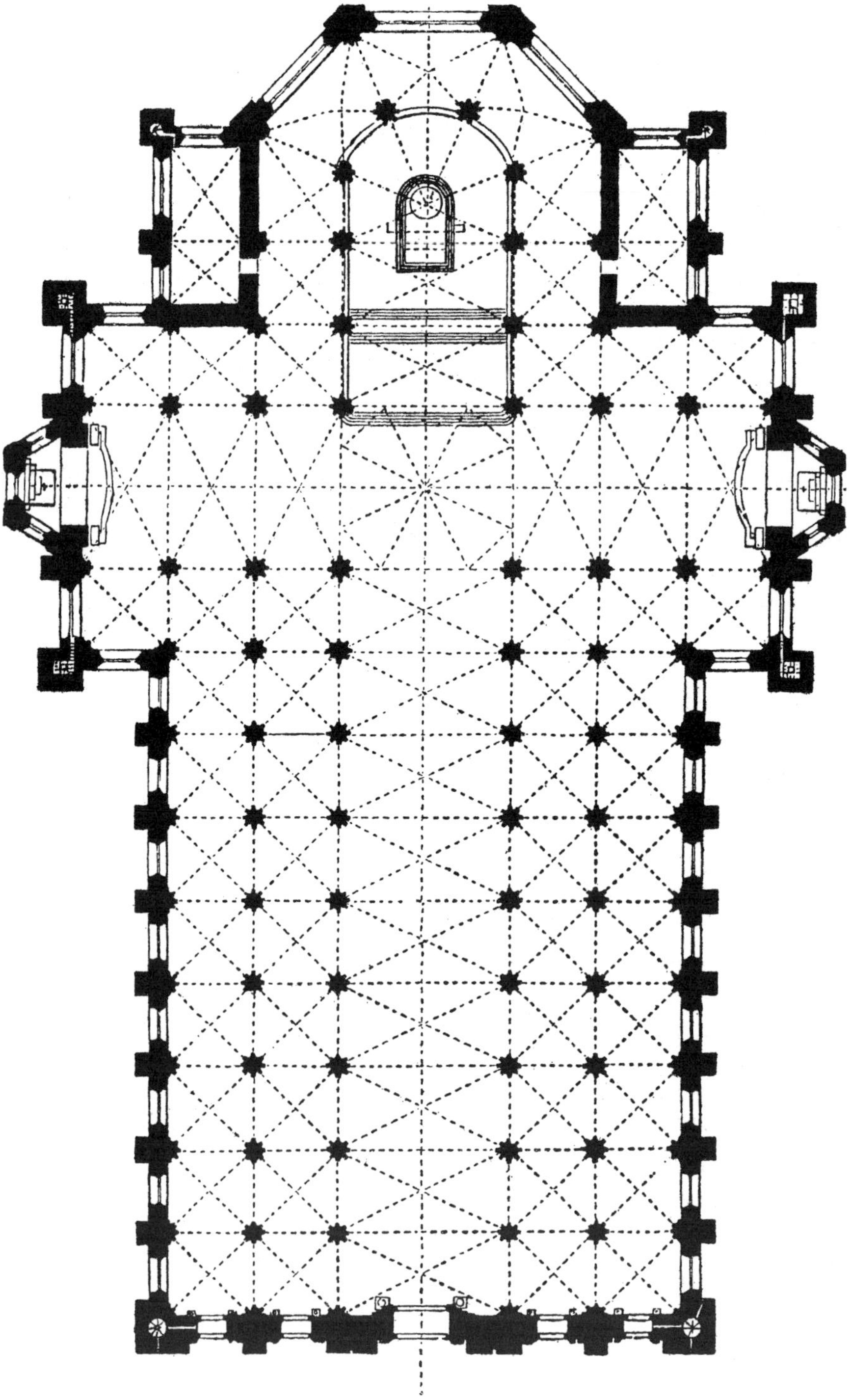

Fig. 72 Plan, Milan Cathedral, laid out to a grid of squares and double squares

Chapter 4

Ad Quadratum

That the building committee of the new cathedral of Milan should have asked whether its construction ought to rise according to the square or the triangle shows that designing *ad quadratum* was also an established method of design. The evidence for its use in architectural planning and constructional design is conclusive, yet the motives for choosing it in the first place are rarely, if ever, sought and the view is still sometimes perpetuated that it was a function of purely practical procedures on the part of medieval masons that had no other meaning. This chapter therefore will summarize the medieval evidence for the architectural use of the square and will review the mathematical and metaphysical properties attaching to it in the Middle Ages in an attempt to suggest how it could have been understood as a signifier in medieval architecture and art.[1]

Architectura ad quadratum

The various forms of square schematism that occur in medieval architectural design may be outlined as consisting of individual squares; planning grids of squares; and squares rotated and inscribed within each other in the system known as quadrature.[2]

The square

The individual square was used for the plans of architectural elements, for example towers, cloisters, and such frequently occurring details as pinnacles.[3] Although not invariably so, the majority of towers and cloisters appear to be square and the plans of two of them are included in the Portfolio of Villard de Honnecourt, one a sketch for a cloister, the other a tower at Laon Cathedral (Figs 73, 81).[4] Since both these drawings also have implications for the practice of quadrature, they will be discussed again shortly, but for the present it is intriguing to notice that on the folio after Laon's tower plan,[5] Villard has drawn a part-elevation of the tower from which, bizarrely, a hand extends delicately holding a tiny object in the shape of a quatrefoil between thumb and finger (Fig. 74).[6] Quatrefoils are as common in Gothic design as trefoils, both in blind tracery and window tracery, and the *motif* is often elaborated into the geometry of wheel and rose windows. The window design for Lausanne Cathedral comprises a central square inscribed with a quatrefoil, with 4 more surrounding it. The north transept window of Lincoln Cathedral contains tracery composed of 4 large circles in the form of a giant quatrefoil,

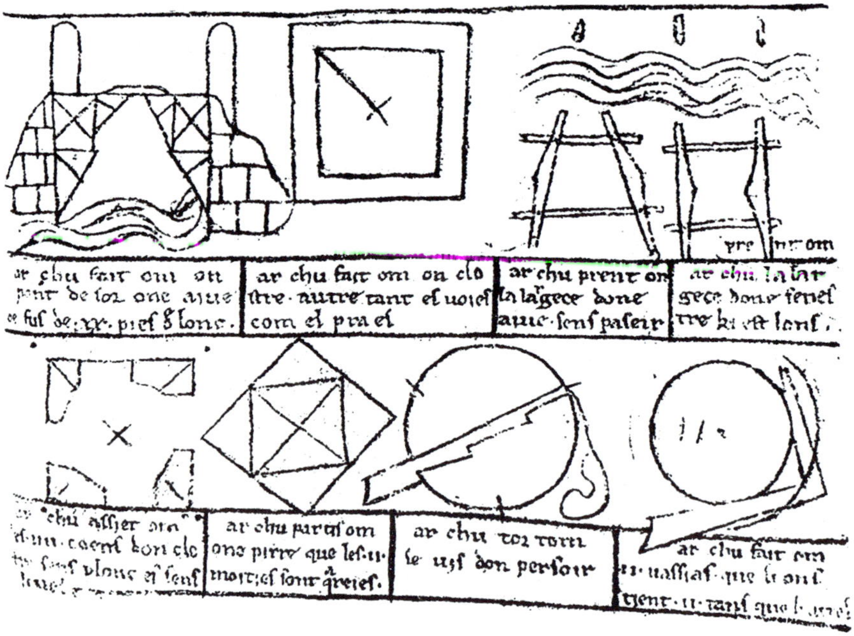

Fig. 73 Cloister plan and doubling square, Villard, fol. 20r, thirteenth century. *Upper row, second left:* The inner square of the cloister is half the area of the outer square. *Lower row, second left:* The inner square is again half the area of the outer square, which is proved by counting the triangles

Fig. 74 Part-elevation, Laon tower, Villard, fol. 10r, thirteenth century. Note the mysterious hand clasping an object in the shape of a quatrefoil

with a small quatrefoil at their centre, and 16 *oculi* around the perimeter (Fig. 75). Interestingly, this window portrays the Last Judgment and 4 was believed to stand for justice.[7] It was Augustine who reasoned, when writing about the equality of the sides and angles of the square:

> ... justice is identical with equity; and equity seems to derive its name from some aspect of equality.
>
> *De quantitate animae* IX.[8]

As a general case, though by no means always, central towers and the crossings beneath them are square.[9] In some Romanesque churches, other compartments of the plan also consist of squares. The abbey church of St Michael at Hildesheim has been cited as an example of this (Fig. 76),[10] although the central bay of its nave is not quite a square. It is generally believed that square compartmentation was an additive process of design by which the plan of a building would be assembled from a series of spatial and structural compartments in the form of modules.[11] If true, the starting-point of the process would presumably have been a single square.

Planning grids of squares

Distinct from a single square is the idea of the starting-point being a planning grid of squares, with the layout of the whole church arising from it. Examples of this survive from the early, middle, and late medieval periods. It has been shown that the church drawn on the ninth-century *Plan of St Gall* answers to

Fig. 75 The Dean's Eye, north transept, Lincoln Cathedral. The Eye sits over five lancet windows externally and an arcade of seven arches internally

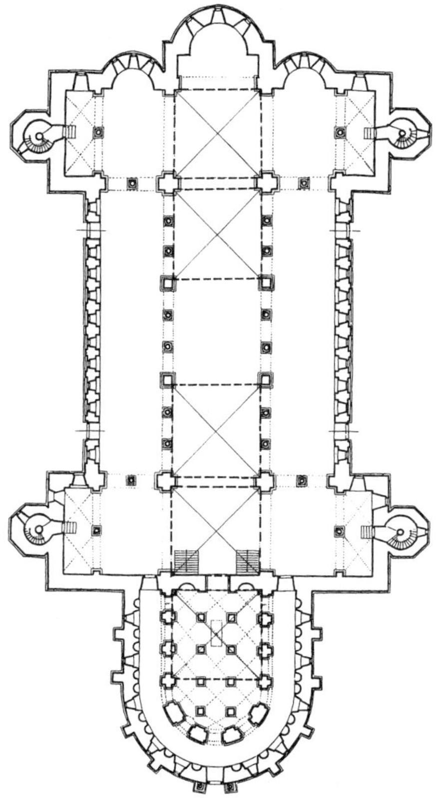

Fig. 76 Plan, with square compartmentation, St Michael's Abbey, Hildesheim

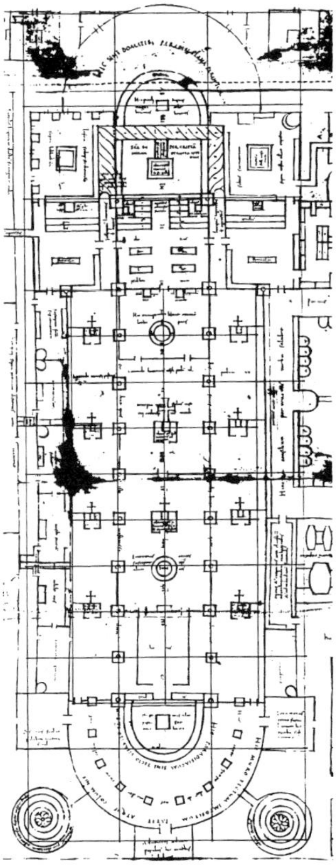

Fig. 77 Plan of church, with grid of squares, *The Plan of St Gall*, c. 820

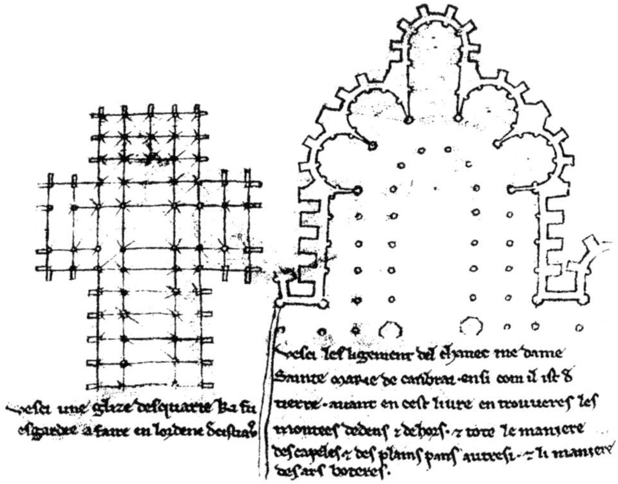

Fig. 78 Left: Plan, Cistercian church, on grid of squares. Right: Plan, choir and chevet of Cambrai Cathedral; Villard, fol. 14v, thirteenth century

such a grid (Fig. 77),[12] although the correlation with the aisles is approximate and there is a large apse at either end. Villard has included a schematic plan of a Cistercian church in his Portfolio (Fig. 78),[13] which he states is composed of squares. Finally, the late fourteenth-century layout of Milan Cathedral consists of a grid of squares (Fig. 72). This is confirmed by measurements recorded at the time of construction,[14] and by a reference in the cathedral's *Annali*,

> … to square out like a net the already mentioned church and its vault, in order that they should correspond with the square according to the laws of geometry …
>
> *Annali* I. 209.[15]

It is important to note that each of these plans consists of square bays for aisles and chapels, combined with double square bays for the main vessels of nave, choir, and transepts.

Quadrature

The geometry of quadrature was known in the twelfth century to the decorator of the Basilica of S. Miniato in Florence, where rows of squares inscribed and rotated within each other are displayed along both sides of the nave above the main arcades (Fig. 79). The Portfolio of Villard provides evidence for quadrature in the thirteenth century, and so do the handbooks of Roriczer and Schmuttermayer late in the fifteenth century in showing how it was practised by masons to develop their architectural details. Early in the sixteenth century, Lechler's *Unterweisung* also taught how masons used quadrature once they were given the ground plan and key dimension, and he described how both could be produced, presumably by the architect, by squaring and simple ratios.

Quadrature, as a term, seems all too often to be employed in the literature with insufficient discrimination, which can cause confusion over claims that are made for it. It can refer, exceptionally, to planning grids of squares, which are otherwise understood from the congresses of Milan as designing *ad quadratum*;[16] it can mean rotating and superimposing a square over another equal to it; also rotating and inscribing squares within each other, which is the accepted basis of the technique; or a combination of these two constructions; or simply rotating squares on their own or in line with others.

Inscribing and rotating squares within each other can be traced back to Plato and his method for doubling a square. He refers to this in his dialogue *Meno*[17] and is paraphrazed by Vitruvius (Fig. 80):[18]

> And first, out of the many and most useful theorems of Plato, I will set out one with its demonstration. If there is a square area, or field with equal sides, and it is necessary to double it, there will be required some number which cannot be found by multiplication …
>
> Since arithmetic does not furnish a solution, let a diagonal line be drawn from angle to angle in the square which was 10 feet long and wide, so

Fig. 79 Nave, S. Miniato, Florence. The frieze between the clerestorey and main arcade displays inner squares inscribed and rotated within outer squares as seen in the technique of quadrature. It also contains the rule for doubling and halving squares as added to fol. 20r of Villard's Portfolio; see Fig. 73

> that two triangles of equal magnitude, each of the area of 50 feet, are described. On the length of the diagonal let a square be described with equal sides. Therefore two triangles of 50 feet in area will be drawn upon the diagonal line in the lesser square; four triangles of the same magnitude and the same number of feet will be described in the larger square. In this manner the duplication is demonstrated geometrically by Plato …
>
> *De architectura* IX. Praefatio 4, 5.[19]

A sketch in Villard's Portfolio shows how the solution is proven simply by counting triangles, without knowing any theory (Fig. 73).[20] The larger square incorporates eight triangles, while the inscribed square consists of four. It is surely no accident that immediately above this sketch is the cloister plan, with its caption stating that the area of its walkways equals the area of its garth; in

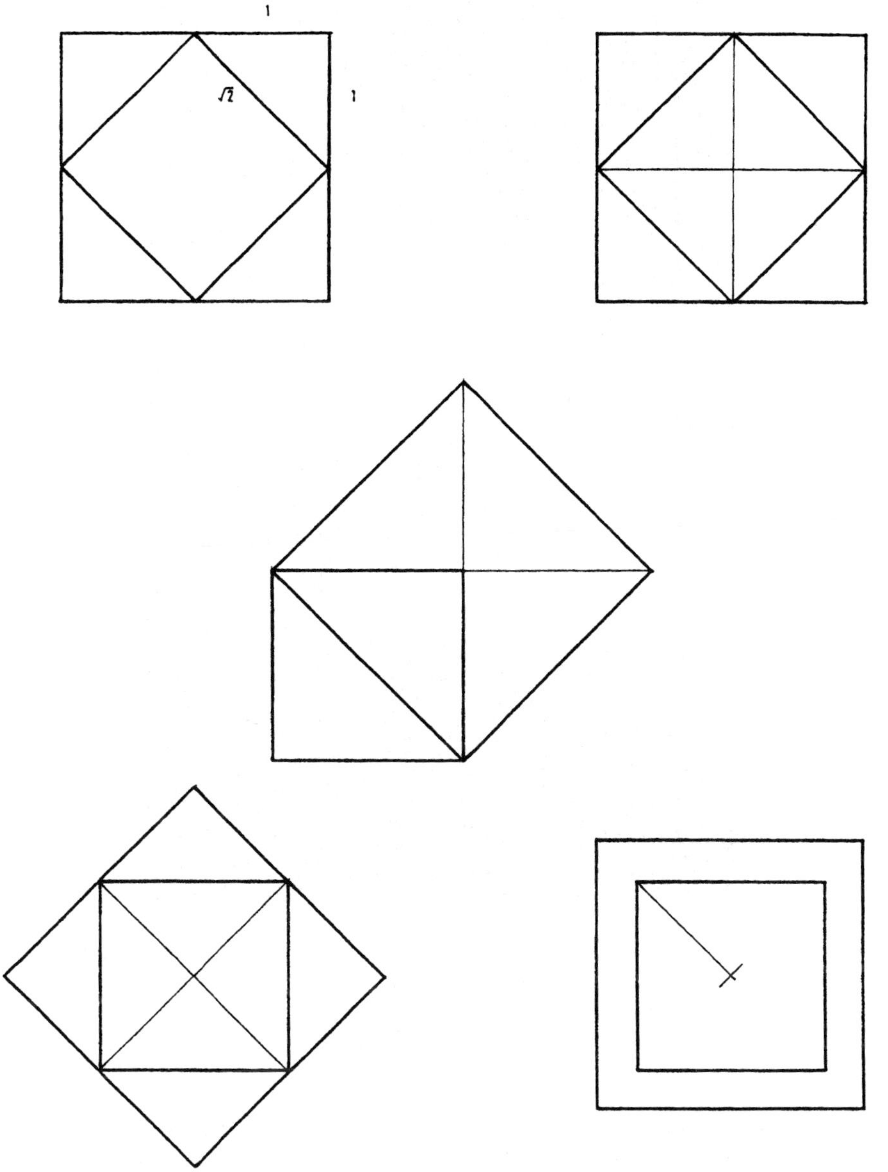

Fig. 80 Doubling a square; Plato, Vitruvius, and Villard. *Upper row:* Quadrature and √2. *Centre:* Doubling a square, after Plato and Vitruvius. *Bottom left:* Doubling and halving a square, after Villard de Honnecourt. *Bottom right:* Cloister plan, after Villard

other words, its inner square is half the area of the outer square. Thus, whilst the square of eight triangles demonstrates the principle of quadrature in halving and doubling squares, the cloister plan demonstrates evidence of its architectural application. The system is to be found elsewhere in the Portfolio in the proportioning of two figures wrestling,[21] as well as being inscribed

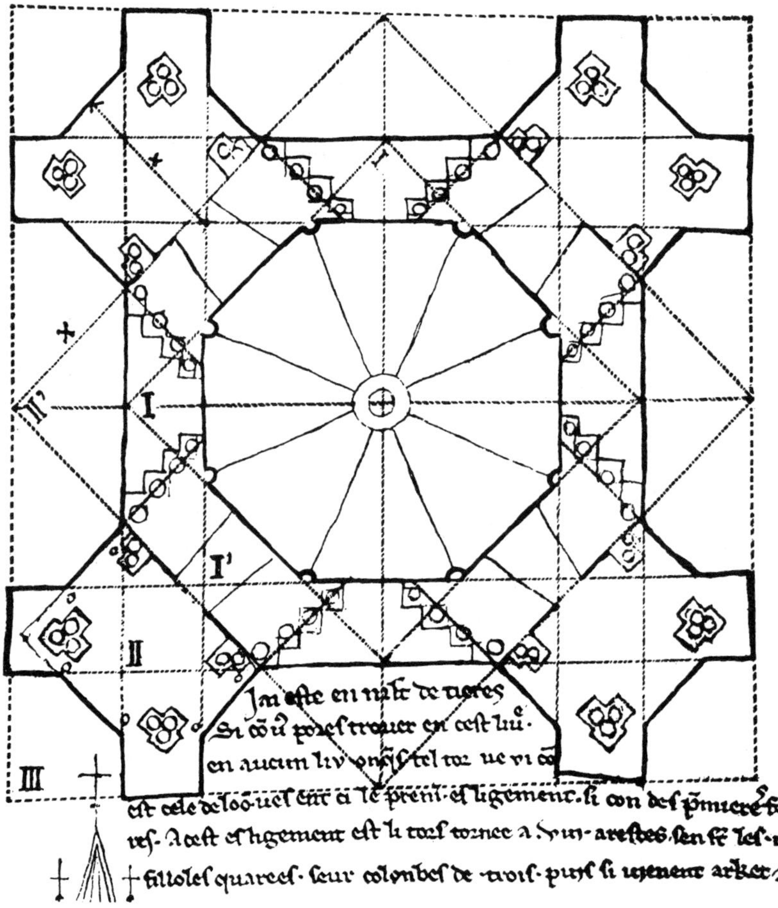

Fig. 81 Plan, Laon tower, after Villard, fol. 9v, demonstrating the application of quadrature

within a grid of squares to proportion a face.[22] Since Villard employs other geometric figures for this purpose as well,[23] the mathematical property of these squares being the half or double of each other may not have been a factor in their choice in these particular instances.[24]

The rotating and superimposing of equal squares over each other was a product of constructing octagons,[25] and is most often encountered in combination with the basic technique of quadrature, that of rotating and inscribing squares. This is implied by Villard's plan of one of the towers at Laon Cathedral, which has been the subject of some contention and can be exemplified by three studies. Because Villard drew the plan without the original geometric construction lines, these were reconstructed in one exercise (Fig. 81), which claimed that the structure of the tower could be derived by quadrature. This the author terms as 'correct measure'.[26] Because of the discrepancy evident between one of the squares and the angled, outer wall-face of the tower,[27] this attempt was criticized for a lack of rigour in the general approach to making such a reconstruction,[28] rather than attributing the discrepancy to the sketch being traced freehand, either without any construction lines on the original to follow, or without attempting to follow any that were there. In making the criticism, a counter-proposal was put forward, which shows very little correlation with Villard's sketch at all.[29] Following this, both attempts were cited as typically misguided in seeking figures of proportion in Gothic architecture in the first place, an endeavour that was to be traced back to the age of Romanticism.[30] This is a view that can be disregarded, for the truth is that, if proper allowance is made for the sketch having been drawn freehand, then quadrature is shown to generate the form, wall thickness, and buttress projections of the tower in five steps.[31] At this point, it is worth emphasizing that the documentary evidence so far dates from the thirteenth century and it supports the use of quadrature only in the planning of discrete architectural elements, such as cloisters and towers, and not whole buildings.

With the publication of the handbooks of Roriczer and Schmuttermayer late in the fifteenth century (Fig. 10),[32] the record attests that by then, and therefore undoubtedly earlier than this, quadrature was being used for extrapolating the heights of architectural elements, in the form of pinnacles and gablets. This, combined with the survival of medieval drawings of cathedral facades, of Strasbourg from around 1260 and 1275, Cologne from around 1300, and Prague from around 1370,[33] have led to numerous studies applying quadrature to the geometry of towers and spires, their being, effectively, giant pinnacles. Not surprisingly, these investigations have suggested, with varying degrees of plausibility, that the technique had developed from the simplest level of the cloister plan in Villard's Portfolio to his tower plan of Laon, before reaching the levels of complexity found in later Gothic structures, as well as from its use as a system for planning to one for elevating.[34]

Lechler's *Unterweisung* from early in the sixteenth century records the next stage that had taken place at some point in the development of the system – its use not only in designing the profiles of such details as window reveals and mullions, and elevating them as well, but also in taking the design module for the work. The subject of his instruction was the design of a choir, and it was the thickness of its wall that provided the side of the square to be used for quadrature.[35] By his stating that the masons can proceed with the work once they have this dimension and the ground plan,[36] it has been presumed, incorrectly, that he used quadrature to produce his ground plan as well. For example, one study of the German architect Matthäus Ensinger applies quadrature to three plans, one of them being Lechler's choir,[37] but there appears to be no support for this in the *Unterweisung*. Lechler does not even use a specific term for it. Instead, he refers to 'this method of squares',[38] which the text makes clear includes different variants of squaring. In his general remarks, he illustrates how to 'realise all layouts and how everything can come from one square'; how to 'raise up the whole layout from the ground, [continuing] on and on with the squares until each high point has been completed'.[39] When he prescribes the proportions of the choir, quadrature does not enter into it. 'The choir should be twice as long as it is wide and twice as high as it is wide';[40] in other words, its plan is a double square and each long wall is a square. The wall-thickness should be one-fifteenth of the choir width; the nave should be twice the length of the choir; and the aisles should each be one-quarter the width of the whole building,[41] in the ratio 1 : 2 : 1.

Two points are worth making. The system of squaring was broader than one confined to quadrature. Secondly, the architectural evidence examined in the host of building studies into plan design that have been prompted by all three German handbooks tends to be late. For example, the study of Ensinger and Bern Cathedral is necessarily of the fifteenth century, as another of St Ouen in Rouen is of the fourteenth.[42] This latter work is one of a group that includes St Urbain in Troyes and Amiens Cathedral from the thirteenth century,[43] and they all put forward a mixture of squaring and swinging arcs from squares and half-squares to lay out their plans. In so doing, these and other studies demonstrate the challenge faced in finding either a complete method for setting out a plan from start to finish, or one that fully accords with the evidence.[44] Among many others, they also advance approximations to a frequent product of squaring, the ratio of the side of the square to its diagonal, as $1 : \sqrt{2}$. However, independent corroboration for the use of this after Vitruvius is again late. For the purpose of this study, since this ratio is an outcome of quadrature rather than a direct application of it, and is one existing in its own right, it will be reviewed separately below. Against the lateness of the documentary evidence for the use of quadrature in the planning of churches, it is worth reiterating that there is much architectural evidence earlier in the Middle Ages for the use of all three Platonic figures,[45] in the system that is also visually explicit in the architecture and the subject of this current volume.

Finally, because the setting of squares on their diagonals along a common axis involves rotation, this variation of squaring can be associated in the mind with quadrature, and documentary support for its possible use has been cited in a miniature of Gunzo's dream (Fig. 11). This dates from around 1180 and depicts Gunzo, a monk visiting Cluny in the previous century, dreaming that the saints Peter, Paul, and Stephen were appealing to him to persuade Cluny's abbot to enlarge his church.[46] By way of specifying the size of the new church, they are shown laying it out on site using ropes, and these have been taken to indicate a line of squares on their diagonals down the length of the building.[47] They could of course equally be delineating, not the sides of squares on their diagonals, but the diagonals of any rectangle set in a line normally. This particular investigation covers several systems, both numerological and geometric, without any being wholly consistent or capable of providing a complete method for setting out the church.[48] Nevertheless, rotated squares can be found in one fifteenth-century manuscript plan in Nuremberg.[49] This sets four squares diagonally to the main axis of its church as angled projections from three main bays, which are also squares. Since the diagonal squares are half the area of the main squares, it is as if the technique of quadrature were being deconstructed in a layout that is quite bizarre. Notwithstanding some of the variations and vagaries to be found in the literature, it can be seen that, in those exercises in applying squaring to plan design that can be properly substantiated, the practice of quadrature in generating the architectural details from the plan and one key dimension ensured that all the parts were related to each other and to the whole, within the controlling figure of a square.

Biblical archetypes

The occurrence and significance of the square in the biblical tradition of sacred construction undoubtedly provided reasons for using it in the Middle Ages and it can be found in literary descriptions of the layouts of the New Jerusalem, Moses' Tabernacle, and Solomon's Temple.

The New Jerusalem

John's Apocalyptic vision of the New Jerusalem was as the heavenly city and it appears to be a reminiscence of Ezekiel's vision. Both cities are square and were entered through 12 gates, 3 in each side facing the 4 cardinal points:

> … and the city shall be in the midst thereof.
>
> And these shall be the measures thereof; the north side four thousand and five hundred, and the south side four thousand and five hundred, and on the east side four thousand and five hundred, and the west side four thousand and five hundred.
>
> And the gates of the city shall be after the names of the tribes of Israel: three gates northward …
> And at the east side … three gates …
> And at the south side … three gates …
> At the west side … three gates …
>
> Ezekiel 48: 15, 16, 31–4.
>
> And I John saw the holy city, new Jerusalem, coming down from God out of heaven, prepared as a bride adorned for her husband.
>
> And there came unto me one of the seven angels … and talked with me, saying, Come hither, I will shew thee the bride, the Lamb's wife.
>
> And he carried me away in the spirit to a great and high mountain, and shewed me that great city, the holy Jerusalem, descending out of heaven from God.
>
> [The city] had a wall great and high, and had twelve gates, and at the gates twelve angels, and names written thereon, which are the names of the twelve tribes of the children of Israel:
> On the east three gates; on the north three gates; on the south three gates; and on the west three gates.
> And the wall of the city had twelve foundations, and in them the names of the twelve apostles of the Lamb.
> And he that talked with me had a golden reed to measure the city, and the gates thereof, and the wall thereof.

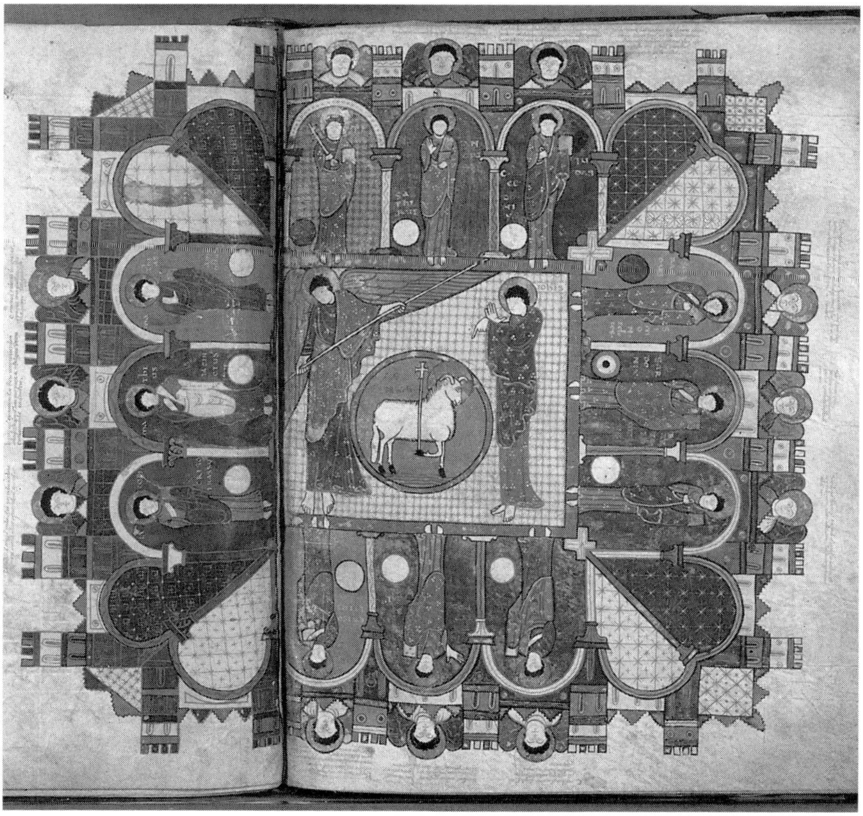

Fig. 82 The New Jerusalem, *Beatus of St Sever*, eleventh century

> And the city lieth foursquare, and the length is as large as the breadth: and he measured the city with the reed, twelve thousand furlongs.
>
> Revelation 21: 2, 9, 10, 12–16.

The description is portrayed in the eleventh-century *Beatus of St Sever*,[50] one of a series of illustrated commentaries on the Apocalypse (Fig. 82). The Lamb of God appears in a circle in the city beside the angel holding the reed. Lining each of the 4 sides are the 3 gates containing the 3 angels, with the figureheads of the 12 tribes of Israel behind them, a cosmic image of a world conceived in a state of order and equilibrium, which was provided by the geometry of squaring. It is therefore tempting to see this cosmic image, alluding to cathedrals as the New Jerusalem, in the dodecagonal geometry of their rose windows, especially those facing west and the faithful as they approach, a possibility which will discussed further in Chapter 6.

The Tabernacle

If the description of the New Jerusalem was a metaphor for the heavenly city, both the Tabernacle and the Temple were also archetypes of the cosmos late in Antiquity, becoming models of the universal Church early in the Middle Ages. Consequently, they were the inspiration for writers who attached great importance to the divine authority and content of the instructions initially given to Moses and David respectively:

> And the Lord said unto Moses, Come up to me into the mount, and be there ...
> According to all that I shew thee, after the pattern of the tabernacle, and the pattern of all the instruments thereof, even so shall ye make it.
>
> Exodus 24: 12, 25: 9.

Philo Judaeus, writing at the beginning of the first millennium, referred to Moses' education, from which it is clear that he would have been well qualified to comprehend his instructions and their significance:

> [Moses] ... speedily learnt arithmetic, and geometry, and the whole science of rhythm, and harmony and metre, and the whole of music, by means of the use of musical instruments, and by lectures on the different arts, and by explanations of each topic; and lessons on these subjects were given him by Egyptian philosophers, who also taught him the philosophy which is contained in symbols ...
> And all the other branches of the encyclical education he learned from the Greeks ...
>
> Therefore Moses now determined to build a tabernacle, a most holy edifice, the furniture of which he was instructed how to supply by precise commands from God, given to him while he was on the mount, contemplating with his soul the incorporeal patterns of bodies which were about to be made perfect ... that it might be an imitation perceptible by the outward senses of an archetypal sketch and pattern, appreciable only to the intellect ...
>
> *De vita Mosis* I. 5, III. 3.[51]

The description of the Tabernacle in Exodus extends over three chapters and amounts to the most detailed specification possible for the structure, materials, fittings, and furnishings, accompanied by their quantities and dimensions.[52] Apart from its Outer Court,[53] no general dimensions are given, and these have to be calculated from the quantities and sizes of the boards with which the structure was made, and the curtains with which it was hung. By contrast, Philo provides a comprehensive account of the numerological significance of the Tabernacle and its details, and this was followed a generation later by an equally detailed physical description by Josephus (c. 37–post-94 AD), a Jewish priest, in his *Antiquitates*.[54] If the profusion of detail in these accounts is stripped away, the basic form of the Tabernacle is surprisingly simple (Fig. 83). The ark of the covenant was housed in the Holy of Holies, which was veiled from an outer sanctuary called the Holy Place. This contained a table and beyond it, in the Outer Court, stood the altar. If dimensions are calculated for the layout, it will be found that the Holy of Holies measured 10 cubits by 10, and the Holy Place which preceded it 10 cubits by 20.[55] In other words, the

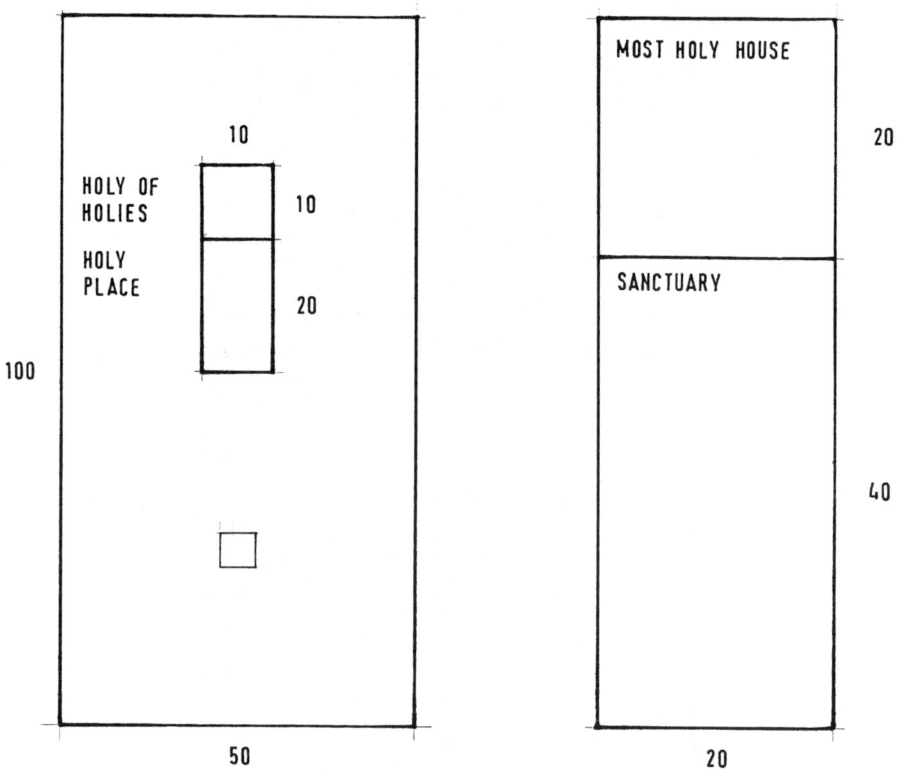

Fig. 83 Diagrammatic plans; Moses' Tabernacle and Solomon's Temple. *Left:* The Tabernacle, according to Josephus, *Antiquitates* III. 6. *Right:* The Temple, according to II Chronicles 3. 1–8

basic plan consisted of a square and a double square. The altar which stood before it was another square, 5 cubits by 5,[56] the enclosing wall of the Court was a double square measuring 50 cubits by 100,[57] even the table inside the Holy Place was a double square, 2 cubits by 1.[58]

The Temple

The description of Solomon's Temple in the First Book of Kings and the Second Book of Chronicles reveals it to be similar in proportions to the Tabernacle:[59]

> And the house which king Solomon built for the Lord, the length thereof was threescore cubits, and the breadth thereof twenty cubits, and the height thereof thirty cubits.
>
> And the porch before the temple of the house, twenty cubits was the length thereof, according to the breadth of the house; and ten cubits was the breadth thereof before the house.
>
> And he built twenty cubits on the sides of the house … even for the oracle, even for the most holy place.

Fig. 84 Plan, Solomon's Temple, *Codex Amiatinus*, eighth century

And the house, that is, the temple before it, was forty cubits long.

I Kings 6: 2, 3, 16, 17.

Now these are the things wherein Solomon was instructed for the building of the house of God. The length … was threescore cubits, and the breadth twenty cubits.
And the porch that was in the front of the house, the length of it was according to the breadth of the house, twenty cubits, and the height was an hundred and twenty …

And he made the most holy house, the length whereof was according to the breadth of the house, twenty cubits, and the breadth thereof twenty cubits …

II Chronicles 3: 3, 4, 8.

Although there are variations in these and other accounts,[60] they mainly concern the side chambers of the Temple, which seem incapable of resolution.

There is no disagreement, however, that the Holy of Holies measured 20 × 20 cubits and the Sanctuary 20 × 40 cubits; in other words, another square and double square. A sketch plan was drawn in the *Codex Amiatinus*, which was commissioned by Abbot Ceolfrith for the Wearmouth-Jarrow community around the turn of the eighth century (Fig. 84).[61] This is thought to have been modelled on the lost *Codex Grandior*, which was used by Bede (672/3–735) when writing his treatises on the Tabernacle and the Temple. The *Codex Grandior* was written under Cassiodorus at his monastery at Vivarum and was evidently the manuscript which Ceolfrith brought to Northumbria from Rome. Among its pages, Bede records that he saw a 'picture' of both the Tabernacle and the Temple.[62] In his own exegesis, which, like Philo's, is a thorough account of the numerology of both structures and their furnishings, Bede makes a connection between the two and, incidentally, between the temple and body:

> The tabernacle that Moses made for the Lord in the wilderness, like the temple that Solomon made in Jerusalem, designates the state of the Holy Church universal … The principal difference between the figures in the construction of the two houses is that the tabernacle designates the building of the present Church … while the temple designates the repose of the future Church … For Moses built the tabernacle while he was still set on the road by which he was proceeding to the promised land along with the people of God, but Solomon constructed the temple after he had already taken possession of the same promised land and the kingship in it.
>
> *De tabernaculo* II. 1.[63]

> The house of God which king Solomon built in Jerusalem was made as a figure of the holy universal Church … It is still partly in a state of pilgrimage from him on earth, and partly … reigns with him in heaven … to it belongs the very mediator between God and men … Christ Jesus, as he himself attests when he says 'Destroy this temple, and in three days I shall raise it up'. To which the evangelist … added: 'But he was speaking of the temple of his own body'.[64]
>
> *De templo* I. 1.[65]

Bede also remarks on the identical proportions of the core of both structures, noting how the Temple is twice the size of the Tabernacle.[66]

The importance of Bede's writing for this study is that renewed interest in the Tabernacle, and in Bede's exegesis of it, was taken during the twelfth century. Several new treatises were written, including commentaries by Peter of Celle, Peter of Poitiers, Richard of St Victor, and Adam of Dryburgh, all of which relied upon the Northumbrian. In the following century, William Durandus followed Bede's ascription of the influence of the Tabernacle and Temple on the earthly church:

> For the Lord commanded Moses in Mount Sinai, that he should make a tabernacle … This was divided by a veil into two parts: the outer, called the Holy Place, where the people attended the sacrifices: the inner,

> the Holy of Holies, where the priests and Levites ministered before the Lord.
> This tabernacle having decayed through age, the Lord commanded that a temple should be built, which Solomon accomplished with wonderful skill: this also had two parts, like the tabernacle. From both of these, namely, from the Tabernacle and the Temple, doth our material church take its form. In its outer portion, the laity offer their prayers, and hear the word. In the Sanctuary, the clergy pray, preach, offer praises and prayers.
>
> *Rationale divinorum officiorum* I.1.4, 5.[67]

He then follows this – and Bede – by viewing the Tabernacle 'as a type of the world which passeth away', with the Temple superseding it at the time of triumph.[68] The two-part division of the Tabernacle and Temple is similar to those made by Josephus about the layout of the Tabernacle, also by Maximus the Confessor about two-cell churches in general, and both as images of the world:

> However, this proportion of the measures of the tabernacle proved to be an imitation of the system of the world; for that ... part thereof which was within the four pillars, to which the priests were not admitted, is, as it were, a heaven, peculiar to God: but the space of twenty cubits, is, as it were, sea and land, on which men live, and so this part is peculiar to the priests only.
>
> Josephus, *Antiquitates Judaicae* III. 6.[69]

This appears to have translated to the two-part division normal for churches in the East and the West:

> On [another] level of contemplation he used to speak of God's holy Church as a figure and image of the entire world composed of visible and invisible essences because like it, it contains both unity and diversity.
> ... while [God's holy Church] is one house in its construction it admits of a certain diversity in the disposition of its plan by being divided into an area exclusively assigned to priests and ministers, which we call a sanctuary, and one accessible to all the faithful, which we call a nave. Still, it is one in its basic reality without being divided into its parts by reason of the differences between them, but rather by their relationship to the unity ...
>
> Maximus, *Mystagogia* II.[70]

A further similarity between these biblical models and some medieval church layouts is that they consist exclusively of squares and double squares, where in medieval plans the aisle bays are square and the main bays are double square. Finally, it is possible to analyse the basic layout of Solomon's Temple described in Kings as a planning grid of squares, each measuring 10 × 10 cubits (Fig. 83). Furthermore, by including the porch, the squares number 7 along each side, the number associated with the Wisdom of Solomon, and already found embedded in the column arrangement of Hagia Sophia in

Constantinople. It may also be significant that Solomon was recorded as having taken 7 years to build it.[71]

Whilst the reverence in which these archetypes were held would explain why some medieval churches could have been modelled on them, it does not explain the significance of the square in the models themselves, and for this it may be worthwhile to return to the Greek tradition.

Mathematics and metaphysics of the square and its derivatives

According to Plato's model of the universe, the element earth was represented by the cube (Fig. 3). Yet, just as his geometric formulation for the polyhedra of the atmospheric elements started, not with the equilateral triangle, but with the figure bisected vertically to produce two scalene triangles, so he commenced construction of the cube, not with the square, but with the square bisected along its diagonal (Fig. 48). This produces two right-angled isosceles triangles, which, being constant, represented stability.[72] Thus the square and its figurate number 4 each took on the quality of stability, balance, thence justice. Accordingly, the year is divided into 4 seasons, and the world, such as portrayed in a tenth-century copy of the *Commentarii* by Macrobius,[73] is quartered into the 4 cardinal points, the 4 elements, the 4 humours, and the 4 virtues (Fig. 85). Similarly, when the New Testament distinguished between which Gospels were to be accorded canonical status and which were to be 'hidden' in the *apocrypha*, the authorized Gospels numbered 4. As they became seen as the 4 primary parts of Christ's teaching, they and the Evangelists' symbols became integrated into the established manifestation of wholeness divided 4 ways. According to the scholar and ascetic, Jerome (340/2–420), and Gregory the Great, the Evangelists' 4 symbolic beasts matched the elements, the seasons, the quarters of the world, and the virtues.[74] Bede expanded Augustine's identification of the Evangelists' symbols with the 4 stages of Christ's life, explaining that Matthew's symbol, being a man signifying the Lord made mortal, represented the incarnation; Luke, the ox, symbolized the Lord sacrificed on the cross, signifying the passion; Mark, the lion, was the Lord conquering death, symbolizing the resurrection; while John's eagle completed the cycle as the Lord ascending to heaven.[75] The monk and chronicler, Rodulfus Glaber (c. 980–c. 1050), associated each of the Gospels with one of the elements. Earth is Matthew's element because of his association with the incarnation; water is Mark's element because of the importance of baptism in his Gospel; air belongs to Luke's Gospel, being the longest; while fire, or ether, is John's, his Gospel being the most spiritual. Glaber also associates the 4 rivers of Paradise with the 4 virtues, all of which he uses to introduce his history of the world, explaining:

> Since we are to treat of events in the four quarters of the earth; it will be well to touch first upon the power of divine and abstract quaternity.
>
> *Historiarum* I. 1.[76]

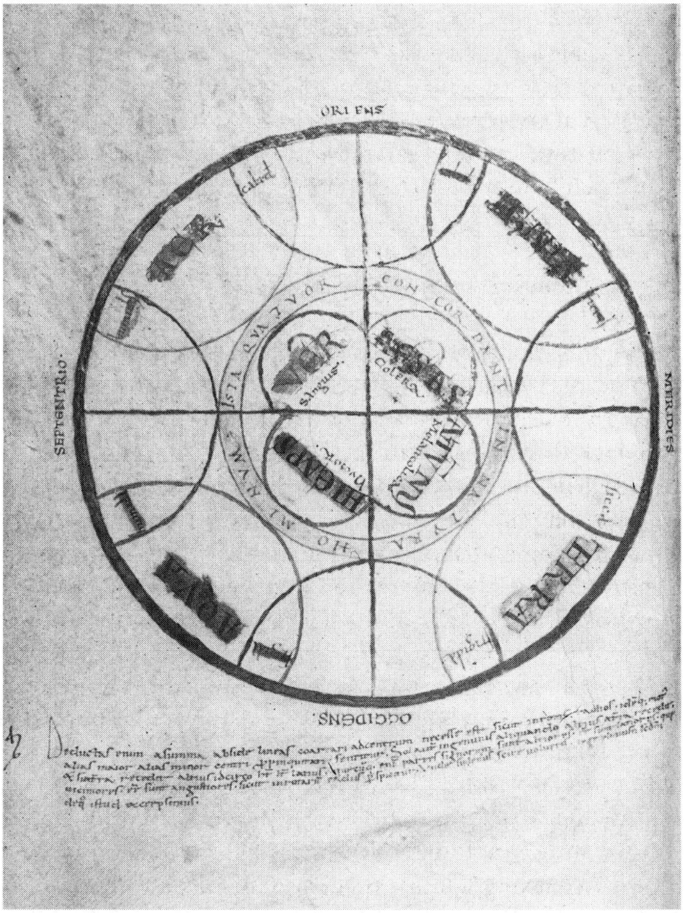

Fig. 85 The quadripartite division of the world; Macrobius, *Commentarii*, tenth-century copy

Expressing 'divine quaternity' most frequently are the Evangelists and their symbols when shown quartered around images of Christ, as already seen on the fifth-century vault of Galla Placidia's Mausoleum, where Christ is symbolized by his cross (Fig. 38); also around Christ seated in majesty in the ninth-century *Vivian's Bible* (Fig. 55),[77] and around the twelfth-century carved relief of Christ over the west portal of Chartres Cathedral (Fig. 53), a symbolic connection gaining added point with the 4 symbols surrounding Christ, specifically when sitting in judgment. Being shown surrounding Christ so often, the Evangelists' symbols acquired the aspect of being his 4 guardians. In describing the west front of Charlemagne's Church of St Denis, Dungal observes that its 'window shows the hand of God. The four Evangelists guard the whole Body'.[78] And the original design for the square crossing tower of Milan Cathedral was said to include a turret at each of its 4 corners like the 4 Evangelists surrounding God.[79]

The square and the octagon

The integrity of the *quadrivium*, literally the 4 ways of apprehending God's creation, may be demonstrated by the mathematics and metaphysical meaning which unite the square and one of its principal derivatives, the octagon (Fig. 86a). An octagon can be constructed from a square by describing arcs, with compass point at each of its corners and radius set to its centre, to cut each of the sides of the square. If the sides of the octagon, so constructed, are then produced to meet each other, a square will be formed, rotated and superimposed over the original. The geometric kinship between the square and the octagon is also reflected arithmetically. The first figurate number of the octagon, 8, is also the first cube number, 2 × 2 × 2, of which the square is the plane figure. According to Plato's geocentric universe, the earth is the eighth planet. It is 'the fixed sphere' around which the remaining 7 planets circle in orbit.[80] Thus, through the number 8, planet earth is associated with the cube that represents the element earth. It is a connection that was encapsulated by Clement of Alexandria:

> And they call eight a cube, counting the fixed sphere along with the seven revolving ones …
>
> Clement, *Stromateis* VI. 16.[81]

The architectural legacy of the octagon is vast, numbering baptisteries, martyria, palace chapels, and chapter houses in its family (Fig. 87). Because they have so much in common with each other, both in terms of architectural form and geometric and numerological meaning, and because the octagon may be generated from the circle as well as from the square, they will be discussed in the final chapter.

The square, the double square, and the golden section

A more direct derivative of the square is the double square, which is also half a square, both existing in the ratio 1 : 2 (Fig. 86b). Known as the masons' long square, it has been shown recurring in the Tabernacle and the Temple alongside the square. A crucial property of the double square is its diagonal, which is the square root of 5. This is the root from which can be constructed the golden section, known to the Greeks simply as 'the section' and to modern mathematics as extreme and mean ratio.[82] Constructions for extending a line according to the golden section, and for dividing one by the same section, depend on the diagonal of the double, or half, square (Figs 86c, d).[83] A line is cut in the golden section when the lesser part is to the greater, as the greater part is to the whole. A rectangle with its sides so proportioned is known as a golden rectangle (Fig. 88). When a square is added to its long side, it remains a golden rectangle, in an example of mathematical self-similarity. An isosceles triangle so proportioned is known as a golden triangle, and its base angles, 72°, are twice the angle of its apex, which is 36° (Fig. 89a). It describes the base and apex of a pentagon, which, as the plane figure of the dodecahedron, has

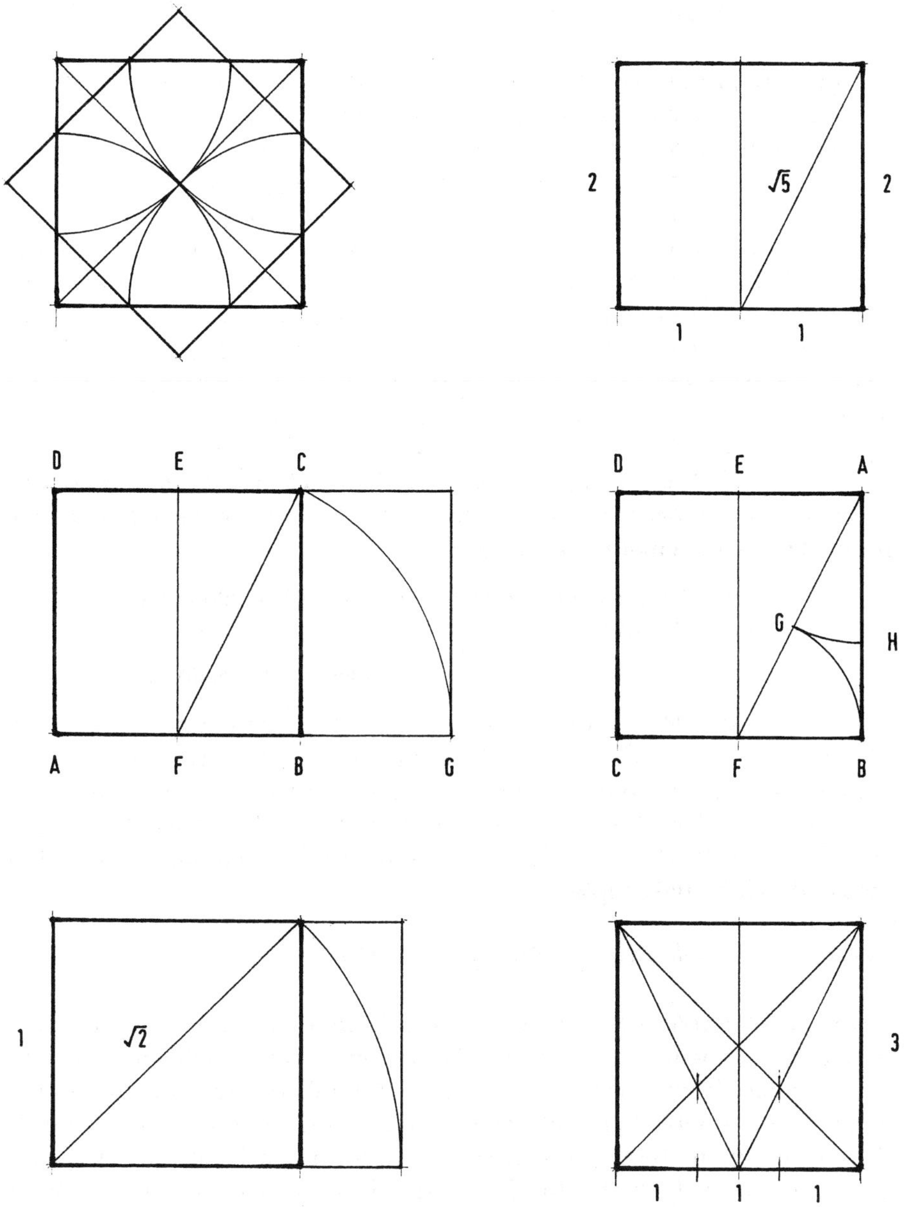

Fig. 86 The geometry of the square and its derivatives. *Top left,* a. The square and the construction of an octagon. *Top right,* b. The double square and its $\sqrt{5}$ diagonal. *Centre left,* c. Extending a line by the golden section. *Centre right,* d. Dividing a line by the golden section. *Bottom left,* e. $1 : \sqrt{2}$ rectangle. *Bottom right,* f. Division of the sides of a square by three

Platonic associations with the universe and the human microcosm (Fig. 89b). It is, therefore, also a tenth part of a decagon, with similar associations with the universe (Fig. 89c). If the diagonals of the pentagon are completed, a

Fig. 87 Aerial view, baptistery, Florence Cathedral

pentagram, or five-pointed star, is the result, with 5 golden triangles radiating from the sides of its inner pentagon.

These constructions, and others related to the section, are arranged in Book XIII of Euclid's *Elementa*, which was known to the Middle Ages. A brief reference is made to the golden section in the *Ars geometriae et arithmeticae*, which was mentioned in the previous chapter in relation to the *vesica piscis*. This was formerly attributed to Boethius, with over twenty manuscripts surviving from the ninth to the thirteenth centuries.[84] In the middle of the twelfth century, Adelard of Bath translated Euclid's *Elementa* from Arabic into Latin and at least one other translation was made from Greek in the thirteenth century.[85] In the same century, the mathematician Leonardo filius Bonacci (1170–1250) published his *Liber abaci* in which he set out his celebrated series of numerical approximations to the golden section. When asked how many rabbits there would be in December if, in the previous January, one pair produced another pair in February, and each pair thereafter bred another pair

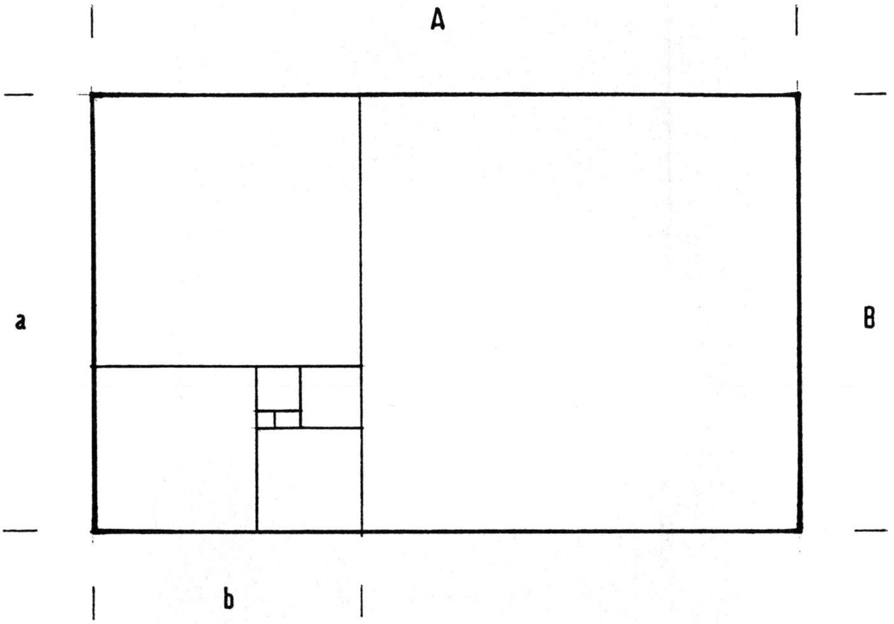

Fig. 88 The golden rectangle. The addition of a square to the long side of a golden rectangle produces a larger golden rectangle

from the second month following their own birth, and continued for the rest of the year, he demonstrated the solution with the series, starting with 1, where each number is the sum of the preceding two numbers, as,

1, 1, 2, 3, 5, 8, 13, 21, 34, 55, 89, 144 ...

The singular influence of the Fibonacci series rests on the fact that it contains the golden section within it. If any number in the series is divided by the number either preceding it, or succeeding it, the result will be the numerical equivalent to the section.[86] Thus, with the ratio for the golden section approximating to 1 : 0.618 ...

21 : 34 : : 1 : 1.618 ... and 55 : 34 : : 1 : 0.618 ...

The geometric demonstration of this arithmetical inversion, whereby the section is present as both 1 : 0.618 and 1 : 1.618, has already been made, in that if a square, being in the ratio 1 : 1, is added to, or subtracted from, a golden rectangle, the proportion will still obtain. Such was the influence of the series that individual numbers from it acquired special importance as Fibonacci numbers, and it may be of passing interest that two of the ratios cited by Vitruvius for proportioning domestic *atria*, 2 : 3 and 3 : 5, are from the Fibonacci series and therefore approximate to golden rectangles. Even more remarkable is the fact that the series does not have to start with 1 + 1. Any series beginning with any two numbers, chosen entirely at random, when added to produce their sum, and so on, will embody the golden section when

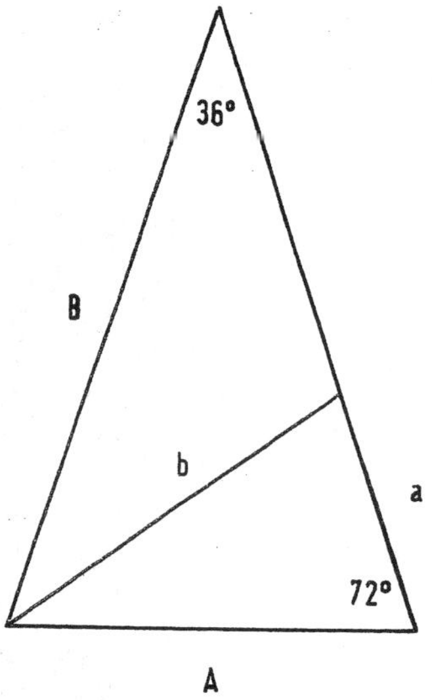

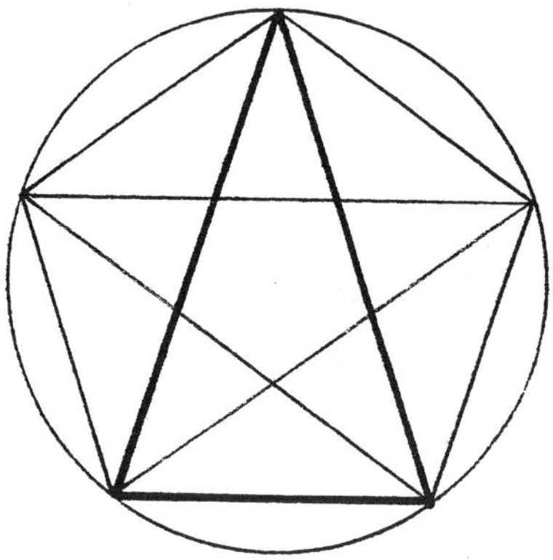

Fig. 89 The golden triangle and its derivatives. *Top,* a. The golden triangle. *Bottom left,* b. The golden triangle, the pentagon, and the pentagram. *Bottom right,* c. The golden triangle and the decagon

similarly divided. When this became known cannot be stated but, at least from the thirteenth century, it must have been as striking that the section is present in the simplest series of numbers starting with 1, as it was that the geometric root of the section is the diagonal of a double square.

Given the universal significance of the golden section, ecclesiastical patrons had every reason to include it in their instructions to their architects, and medieval architects had every reason to include it in their designs. Although various studies have found circumstantial evidence of it in medieval buildings,[87] the only firm evidence for its architectural use is implicitly in the construction of pentagons and decagons, which will be discussed in Chapter 5.

The 1 : √2 rectangle

Self-similarity, or a constancy of proportion, akin to that of the golden rectangle, is the chief property of a rectangle constructed in the ratio of the side : the diagonal of a square, which is 1 : √2 (Fig. 86e). When the rectangle is halved or doubled, it retains its proportion, which is why it was chosen for the European standard for stationery. Given the importance of integrity in the universal scheme, it might be expected that the 1 : √2 rectangle, in common with the golden rectangle, would have found a place in medieval architectural design, yet there is no documentary evidence to support this apart from a single reference in Vitruvius. This relates to the proportioning of *atria* in Roman houses in the ratio of the side and diagonal of a square,[88] but it is only one of three ratios Vitruvius advocates – the others already noted being 2 : 3 and 3 : 5 – and he gives no reason for using any of them.[89] On the face of it, it is difficult to see why the proportioning of medieval cathedrals should have been based on the *atrium* of a Roman house, or why this particular ratio should have been preferred to the other two cited by Vitruvius.[90] If it was because of its proportional integrity, no evidence has so far been encountered that this was appreciated in the Middle Ages, either in relation to this rectangle or the golden rectangle. On the other hand, the 1 : √2 ratio and various permutations of it have been found in a large number of buildings, often with surprising precision. One possible explanation for this has been suggested elsewhere and derives from the actual procedure for constructing the rectangle.[91] This starts with a square and, with compass point on one corner and radius equal to the diagonal, an arc is swung from it to extend the side of the square to form the side of the rectangle. Bearing in mind that the *Plan of St Gall* and four of Villard's plans consist of grids of axis lines, with piers located at their intersections, this same geometric procedure could have been used to convert such a linear grid, when set out on site, into the plan of the building to be erected, thereby converting axis lines into walls with their resultant thicknesses. In other words, as dividers might describe arcs on parchment in a tracing house to produce a schematic plan, so the same procedure could have translated the schematic plan into the building plan. By using a peg and cord to swing similar arcs on site, the lines of the grid could have been converted into the thicknesses of walls and piers, also the distances between them. It would have been a method indistinguishable from the practice of quadrature that the same masons would have used to generate their architectural details once the structure began to rise, similarly ensuring that all the parts were related proportionally to the whole.

One final piece of evidence that appears to have been overlooked in the debate about the 1 : √2 rectangle is that Palladio cites it as a room proportion in the first of his *I quattro libri dell' Architettura*, which was published in Venice in 1570.[92] However, once again it is only one of several proportions enumerated by him, and it is also difficult to know whether he is transmitting a late medieval tradition or resurrecting Vitruvius. A hiatus of a millennium and a half in the documentary record is considerable, and the range of ratios offered by Vitruvius and Palladio hardly justifies the single-minded pursuit in building studies of one to the exclusion of others that are equally present in the architecture of the intervening period. One example of the plurality of possible systems appears in a study of Salisbury Cathedral where, in addition to √2 relationships, √3, √5, and approximations to the golden section were also found, as well as three different planning grids.[93]

Diagonals of the square and double square

The interplay between the diagonals of the square and the double square provides a method of dividing a line according to thirds (Fig. 86f). If a square is halved vertically to produce two double squares, the diagonals of the square and each double square intersect each other at a distance equal to one third of the side of the original square. The architect Sebastiano Serlio (1475–c. 1554) ends his *Libro primo d'architettura*, which is devoted to geometry, with an application of this to a doorway (Fig. 90). The opening of the doorway is proportioned in the ratio of 1 : 2, a double square. The side of the square, which is taken from the main width of the nave inside, measures 3 units and is reproduced as the height of the pediment. Since this could have been accomplished just as easily arithmetically using dimensions, it must have been of significance to Serlio that a precise geometric construction existed derived from the square. In other words, the parts of this design were related to each other and to the whole, within the square, in a similar fashion to the system of quadrature. And since Serlio published this construction in 1545,[94] it may well have been known to the Middle Ages.[95]

The musical consonances

Numerical ratios between the first 4 numbers are also fundamental to the consonances and intervals in music, as reportedly discovered by Pythagoras and transmitted by Boethius, among others (Fig. 2).[96] One important medieval source for them is the anonymous *Dialogus de musica* of the eleventh century.[97] Demonstrated on a monochord with a movable bridge, the division of its musical string equally into two halves, in the ratio 1 : 1, produces unison; 1 : 2 produces the consonance of diapason; 2 : 3 is the consonance of diapente; and 3 : 4 is diatessaron.[98] Just as a diagonal is a line *through* an angle, diapason is the division of the musical string *through* all the tones. Both parts, when played concurrently, produce the consonance of diapason; when played consecutively, they produce the interval of an octave. Likewise, diapente means through 5 tones, which, played concurrently, is the consonance of that name, and consecutively, is the interval of a fifth. Finally, the consonance of

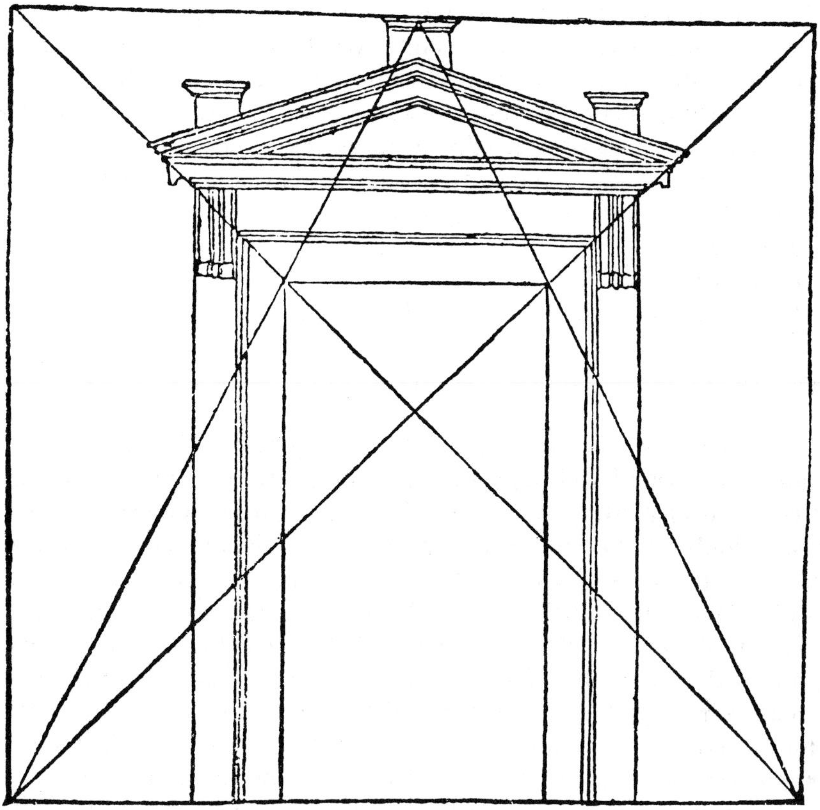

Fig. 90 A doorway and the division of a square into three; Serlio, sixteenth century. The intersection of the diagonals of the square with the diagonals of the half-square divide the sides of the square into three. Thus the head of the doorway is one-third of each side of the enclosing square

diatessaron, through 4 tones, produces the interval of a fourth.[99] It will be observed that the geometric equivalent of the ratios of unison and diapason, 1 : 1 and 1 : 2, are the square and the double square.

Even by the time Boethius wrote *De musica*, the musical theory of the Pythagoreans had become greatly elaborated,[100] with the result that the scope for composition had increased the possibilities for invention and complexity. Yet in spite of this, in writing his *Regulae de arte musica*, which codified the chant reform of the Cistercians in the twelfth century under Bernard of Clairvaux (1090–1153), Guy d'Eu reiterated that,

> The extreme notes of the diatessaron, the first and the last, joined together, produce an agreeable consonance; the diapente a more agreeable one; and the diapason the most agreeable.
>
> The diapason does not only produce a similarity but an ineffable identity in the different voices.
>
> *Regulae de arte musica* 79, 80.[101]

The reason for the omission of unison from Guy's exposition was probably that it consists of the repetition of the same note and is therefore to be identified with equality. It is different from the harmony that is inherent in the other consonances. In addition to the square, the musical ratio of 1 : 1 also represents two people singing the same note. Writing in the fourteenth century, Jacques de Liège described it as the most perfect concord.[102] Augustine, however, sets unison beside diapason in a discussion of harmony:

> 'What is it we love in sensible harmony?' Nothing but a sort of equality and equally measured intervals … that is, either into two equal parts … or into one part single and the other double … so the greater part is twice the less and is in this way divided equally by it …
>
> *De musica* VI. 10. 26.[103]

Another example of the single and double in music was to be found in the measures permitted for chant, where each note in a line was to be equal in length, except for the last note which could be doubled. According to the ninth-century *Scolica enchiriadis*,

> … it must be seen that any melody is sung rhythmically. … one must use longer and shorter durations … so that a song is beaten in the manner of metrical feet. …
> Only the last [syllable] in [these] … phrases is long … If … you wish to change the tempo … do it by a factor of two …
>
> *Scolica enchiriadis* I. 86, 87.[104]

It can be seen, therefore, that, accompanying unison in the ratio of 1 : 1, the consonance and interval of diapason, in the ratio of 1 : 2, was 'the most agreeable' in harmony and melody, as were the single and double in the measures for chant. According to Augustine:

> This correspondence … describing how one is joined to two, is of the greatest importance … this co-adaptation is what the Greeks call *harmonían*. … [The] harmony between the single and the double … has been naturally so implanted in us … for by means of it the treble and the bass voices blend together … one familiar with the subject can demonstrate it … on a properly-adjusted monochord.
>
> *De Trinitate* IV. 2. 4.[105]

The relevance of music theory to architectural design lay in the understanding that aural harmony and visual proportion were two manifestations of the same truth. In his treatises on arithmetic and music, Boethius explains that this is so because they have the same numerical ratios in common:

> The same relationship which we remarked in geometry can be found in music. The names diatessaron, diapente, and diapason are derived from the names of antecedent numerical terms. …
>
> *De arithmetica* I.1.[106]

Fig. 91 Gafurio's discourse; Gafurio, sixteenth century. He is declaring, 'Harmonia est discordia concors', or 'Harmony is discord made concordant.' To the left are three musical pipes, to the right three linear measures, each in the medial proportion of 3 : 4 : 6, thereby demonstrating that the harmony that is heard is equivalent to the proportion that is seen

> … as the ear is affected by sound or the eye by a visible form, in the same way the judgment of the mind is affected by numbers …
>
> *De musica* I.32.[107]

The identification of the aural with the visual is shown in the frontispiece of a treatise, *De Harmonia musicorum instrumentorum* (Fig. 91). This was published by the musical theorist and composer Franchino Gafurio (1451–1522) in 1518, and portrays him lecturing to his students. To the left are displayed three musical pipes along with the ratio of their lengths, which is 3 : 4 : 6. To the right are a pair of dividers and three lines, together with the ratio of their lengths, which again is 3 : 4 : 6.[108] As in all things, it was understood that harmony and proportion proceed from numbers. Thus the numbers forming the root of unison and diapason in harmonics, and the single and double in metrics, are 1 and 2, and their geometric figures are the square and the double square. It may be recalled that Villard's schematic plan of a Cistercian church consists only of square and double square bays (Fig. 78), and, excepting its polygonal chapels, so does that of Milan Cathedral (Fig. 72); whilst the plan and elevation of Lechler's choir also consist of a square and double square.

Unity, equality, and harmony

The architectural application of the square has the additional, practical advantage that plans can be set out on site using a single dimension, possibly in a measure that is numerologically significant. The 40-foot module inscribed on the *Plan of St Gall* could have been explained by Augustine as,

> … meaning … the fasting of forty days which was accomplished not only by Moses and Elijah, but also by the Lord himself. No answer will be found to the meaning of this phrase without becoming acquainted with this number, and contemplating it.
>
> *De doctrina Christiana* II. 16. 25.

It will be recalled that the fourth- or fifth-century *Testamentum Domini* shows that, at least sometimes, a church could be dimensioned numerologically, with the length of 21 cubits for its baptistery standing for the Prophets and its width of 12 cubits the Apostles.[109]

Yet the practical advantage of embodying the square in architectural design was more than matched by the potency of its signification. Displaying the ratio of 1 : 1 identified it with the unity of 1. The importance of this was fundamental not only to an understanding of God the Creator but to the monastic ideal of unity in community. Augustine connected the idea of unity with equality:

> … number also begins from one, and is beautiful in equality and likeness, and bound by order. And so, whoever … desires unity … must confess all things whatever … are made from one beginning through a form equal to it and like to the riches of His goodness, by which they are joined together in charity as one and one gift from one.
>
> *De musica* VI. 17. 56.[110]

John Cassian (c. 360–c. 435), the monk and writer, applied the idea of unity to the monastic community:

> And we will come at last to that objective which I have mentioned, the goal which the Lord prayed to be fulfilled in us: 'That they may be one as we are one, as I am in them and you in me so that they are utterly one …'[111] This, then, is the goal of the monk.
>
> *Collationes patrum* X. 7.[112]

Benedict of Nursia (c. 480–543), whose *Regula* was to form the basis of western monasticism, stated simply,

> … we are all one in Christ. … Therefore let the abbot show an equal love to all.
>
> *Regula Benedicti* 2.[113]

In the twelfth century, Bernard of Clairvaux spoke in similar fashion for Cistercians:

> And perchance the rest of the disciples were present when ... he would commend to all unity in one flock and in one shepherd ... Where unity is, there is perfection.
>
> *De consideratione* II. 8. 15.[114]

Villard's Cistercian plan of squares could well be expressing the Cistercians' ideal of unity and equality of brothers in one spirit (Fig. 78). Furthermore, within his planning grid each individual square possesses its own equality. Augustine's dialogue, *De quantitate animae*, which uses the example of geometry to demonstrate equality, gives the square special importance above triangles and other quadrilaterals because its sides and angles are equal.[115]

Nevertheless, the repetition of equal sides, or the repetition of squares in a grid, or of a single dimension as a signifier, may produce equality but it does not amount to achieving an agreement of different measures – the original meaning of *symmetria* – as understood by Augustine, or by Vitruvius before him:

> Symmetry ... is the appropriate harmony arising out of the details of the work itself; the correspondence of each given detail among the separate details to the form of the design as a whole.
>
> ... symmetry ... arises from proportion ... (which) consists in taking a fixed module ... both for the parts of a building and for the whole, by which the method of symmetry is put into practice.
>
> *De architectura* I. 2. 4, III. 1. 1.[116]

Adding to the writing about symmetry, Augustine alludes to the importance of difference:

> In all the arts it is symmetry that gives pleasure, preserving unity and making the whole beautiful. Symmetry demands unity and equality, the similarity of like parts, or the graded arrangements of parts which are dissimilar.
>
> *De vera religione* XXX. 55.[117]

Here Augustine seems to be making a distinction between the equality present in the similarity of like parts, and the agreement, or harmony, that comes from the reconciling of dissimilar parts. It is this that is the essential element of *harmonia*. Returning to Gafurio, the axiom he is enunciating is, 'Harmony is discord made concordant',[118] and the ratio 3 : 4 : 6 is displayed as his exemplar (Fig. 91). It is an example of a harmonic mean, one of three principal medial proportions set out by Boethius, the other two being the arithmetic and geometric proportions.[119] An arithmetic mean exists in a series of numbers in which the difference between them is equal, for example, 1 : 2 : 3, where the next number would be 4. A geometric mean occurs in a series of numbers in which the proportion of each to the next is equal, for example, 1 : 2 : 4, where the next number would be 8. Boethius explains that the harmonic proportion,

> … asks that just as there be extreme terms in a ratio to each other, so the difference of the larger to the smaller stands compared to the difference of the median to the final term.
>
> *De arithmetica* II. 48.[120]

Thus for Gafurio's numbers, 3 : 4 : 6,

3 : 6 : : (4 – 3) : (6 – 4) : : 1 : 2

Boethius then connects harmonic medial proportions with the musical consonances:

> Of those musical consonances which they call symphonies, you will find practically all the ratios of the harmonic medial proportion.
>
> *De arithmetica* II. 48.[121]

He illustrates this connection with Gafurio's series. In it, diapason is present as 3 : 6, diatessaron as 3 : 4, and diapente as 4 : 6. In other words, octave is achieved from the dissonance of sounding diatessaron and diapente together. In doing so, they also combine to produce the consonance anterior to them as well for,

(2 : 3) × (3 : 4) = 6 : 12 = 1 : 2.[122]

In the previous chapter, it was noticed how, through the powers of observation and reason, differences between the 4 elements within the universe were reconciled into one harmonious whole, to which might be added the geometric differences of their polyhedra, composed as they are of the triangle, the square, and the pentagon. Plato made reference to this in describing the act of creating the universe:

> … the fitting shape would be the figure that comprehends in itself all the figures there are; accordingly, he turned its shape rounded and spherical … a figure the most perfect and uniform of all …
>
> *Timaeus* 33B.[123]

In this case, the elements can be reconciled into a state of harmony not only physically, but mathematically, one proof of this being,

$3^2 + 4^2 = 5^2$

If Gafurio might be thought late for a medieval authority, it can be seen that he was continuing the transmission of a tradition that stretched back to Boethius and beyond. Alan of Lille, at greater length and in the twelfth century, similarly referred to the work that is required to accomplish harmony:

> When God willed to call forth the fabric of the palace of the Universe … He constructed the marvellous form of the kingdom of the world by

> the command of His deciding will alone ... Accordingly God assigned various species of things to the palace of the Universe and these, though separated by the strife between differing classes, He regulated by agreement from law and order; He imposed laws on them, He bound them by sanctions. ... He leagued together things hostile to one another by generic opposition, things whose position had placed them on opposite sides, and He changed the strife of contrariety into the peace of friendship. When all things, then, were harmonised by the fine chain of an invisible connection, in a peaceable union plurality made its way back to unity, diversity to identity, discord to concord.
>
> *De planctu Naturae* VIII. 4.[124]

To summarize, equality exists in similarity; harmony exists in difference, and is achieved with effort, not ease. This perhaps offers a key for understanding the significance of the square and its relatives. The individual square exemplifies unity and equality, thence the 'divine and abstract quaternity' of the world. The double square, in Augustine's words, displays 'sensible harmony' with the square because, as the greater part, it is twice the lesser and is divided equally by it. Grids of squares can be read as embodying equality by repetition, and in measures that are themselves significant. Yet just as unison is not a consonance, so equality is not harmony. Harmony is achieved by resolving difference. It is found in the different ratios of the square's derivatives, in the single and the double, and in the different proportional relationships inherent in quadrature and other constructions derived from the square, such as Serlio's division of a square into 3 (Fig. 90).

Put at its simplest, the agreement of measures, understood by Augustine and by Vitruvius before him as *symmetria*, embraced on the one hand the unity and equality of like parts, exemplified by the square, and on the other hand the harmonizing of dissimilar parts by means of proportion, within the rule of the square. The number 4, the square, and unison exemplify unity and equality; the square's derivatives and the consonances result in harmony, generated from the unity that is the square.

Notes

1 Part of this chapter is a development of material in Hiscock (2004 (1)) 3–21, and (2004 (2)) 157–72.
2 Prologue, 'The architectural programme, patrons, and architects'.
3 The reader is reminded of the evidence Trachtenberg (1997) advances to suggest that the square was also used in reconfiguring principal *piazzi* in Florence at the turn of the fourteenth century; see Prologue, 'Postmodernism and the retrieval of meaning'.
4 Villard, fols 9v and 20r.
5 Ibid., fol. 10r.
6 This detail has yet to receive a conclusive explanation, one attempt being that it might be the hand of God, possibly holding a jewel. I am grateful to Carl Barnes for this report.

7 See Prologue, 'Arithmetic'. There is an image of Christ sitting in judgment in the quatrefoil at the centre of the Lincoln window.

8 Augustine, *De quantitate animae*, tr. Colleran (1950), 30.

9 Of the churches with crossings that were examined in the investigation that led to the publication of *The Wise Master Builder*, eleven crossings out of twenty-two appeared to be square.

10 Bucher (1972), 50 note 5.

11 Bucher (1968), 51, 70; (1972), 37.

12 Horn and Born (1979), 82, 90, fig. 61.

13 Villard, fol. 14v.

14 Notes and sketches of Antonio di Vicenzo (1390). See Fig. 185 of this book, also Ackerman (1949), 88, note 14.

15 *Annali*, tr. Lund (1921), 4. Cesariano's plan of Milan is also drawn *ad quadratum*; Cesariano (1521), fol. XIV.

16 Velte (1951) confuses the two methods, in spite of the starting-point of her study being the evidence of designing *ad quadratum* and *ad triangulum* referred to in the Milan *Annali*, and the absence in them of quadrature.

17 Plato, *Meno*, tr. Jowett (1953), 82ff.

18 Vitruvius I. 1. 4.

19 Vitruvius, tr. Granger (1934), 199, 201.

20 Villard, fol. 20r.

21 This application seems somewhat gratuitous since the construction leaves unanswered more than it answers; Villard, fol. 19r.

22 Villard, fol. 19v.

23 Ibid., fols 18r–19v.

24 It has also been found that the drawing of these geometric figures sometimes precedes and sometimes succeeds the sketches associated with them. I am grateful to Carl Barnes for this information in advance of the publication of his facsimile of Villard's Portfolio.

25 See 'The square and the octagon' later in this chapter.

26 Ueberwasser (1935), 254, fig. 7, 261. According to the caption, the sequence extends from square I to square III.

27 Between squares I^1 and II^1.

28 Velte (1951), 16.

29 Ibid., 53–6. Velte's construction does not account for either the inside or outside of the tower's octagon, or the outer wall or outer buttress faces.

30 Instead, it was argued that the solution is to be found in the application of units of measurement, in the service of form, function, and building construction, a purely modernist view; Hecht (1979), 1–2, 204–12.

31 The sequence followed is square I, rotated; square I^1, equal to square I, rotated to normal and superimposed over it; square II, rotated and circumscribed around square I; square II^1, equal to square II, rotated and superimposed over it; square III, rotated to normal and circumscribed around II^1.

32 M. Roriczer, *Büchlein von der Fialen Gerechtikait* (Regensburg, 1486), *Wimpergbüchlein*, (Regensburg, c.1488); H. Schmuttermayer, *Fialenbüchlein* (Nürnberg, c.1488).

33 The Prague drawings cover the south front and transept.

34 Velte's (1951) study examines the towers at Vienna, Strasbourg, Freiburg, and Basle, in addition to Villard's sketch of the Laon tower. In spite of her criticism of Ueberwasser, her own geometric analysis, if made today, would need to follow

a more rigorous methodology. Among recent studies, see, in relation to Strasbourg and Prague, Bork (2005, 2006).

35 Lechler (1856), 135.
36 Ibid., 133.
37 Mojon (1967), 46, fig. 11.
38 Lechler (1856), 145, tr. Vinall (2006).
39 Ibid.
40 Ibid., 153.
41 Ibid., 146, 153.
42 Davis and Neagley (2000).
43 Ibid.; Murray (1996).
44 The study of Amiens is put forward as a complete design method involving a repetition of square and double square modules. It would be interesting to discover how this could respond to irregularities in Amiens' layout, which appear to be systematic, for the great square, from which the rest of the layout is generated, is not a true square, and the pier spacing in the nave, transepts, and choir is different in each case. Finally, the proof of the system, as proposed, depends upon measurements having been taken to different datum points, whereas the builders are likely to have laid out their design by measuring from one consistent referent, such as axis lines, or inner wall-faces.

The investigations of St Urbain and St Ouen do not set out to propose a complete design method, yet individual correspondences between geometry and structure are interesting in their own right, not least that for fixing the width of the choir aisle from the crossing. This is not only identical in all three buildings, but involves the golden section (see 'The square, the double square, and the golden section' later in this chapter).

45 See Hiscock (2000), 205–63.
46 This allegedly led to the building of Cluny III; Raynaldo, *Vita s. Hugonis*, PL 895–906. For an account of Gunzo's dream in the context of dream theory and dedication liturgy, with reference to Jacob's dream of the heavenly ladder, see Carty (1988), 113–23.
47 Conant (1963), 1–45, 7–10, 31 top figure, 45. Surprisingly, quadrature is the one system Conant does not call upon to explain his theoretical reconstruction.
48 To make the diagonal squaring work, the end square has had to be reduced to fit the plan; the measuring points were changed in an attempt at a mathematical proof; and the system was admitted to be approximate and incomplete.
49 Nuremberg, Nat. Mus. Hz. 3818. 333; see Bucher (1972), 38 fig. 3.
50 *Beatus of St Sever,* Paris, Bibl. nat., MS. lat. 8878, fols 207v–208r.
51 Philo, *De vita*, tr. Yonge (1855), 6, 90.
52 Exodus 25–7.
53 Ibid. 27: 18.
54 Josephus, *Antiquitates* III. 6.
55 Josephus quotes the breadth as 12 cubits, but this appears to be a miscalculation on his part.
56 Exodus 27: 1.
57 Ibid. 27: 18.
58 Ibid. 25: 23.
59 I Kings 6; 2 Chronicles 3. 1–8.
60 See Ezekiel 40, and Josephus, *Antiquitates* VIII. 3.
61 Bede, in Connolly (1995), lii.

62 Bede, in Holder (1994), 92, note 1; Connolly (1995), lii.
63 Bede, *De tabernaculo*, tr. Holder (1994), 45.
64 John 2: 19, 21.
65 Bede, *De templo*, tr. Holder (1995), 5, *et seq*.
66 Bede, *De tabernaculo* II. 8.
67 Durandus, tr. Neale and Webb (1843), 20.
68 Ibid., I. 1. 6.
69 Josephus, tr. Whiston (1876), 52.
70 Maximus, tr. Berthold (1985), 188.
71 I Kings 6: 38.
72 Plato, *Timaeus* 53C–55C.
73 Macrobius, *Commentarii*, Oxford, Bod. MS. Auct. T. 2. 27, fol. 12v.
74 Dow (1957), 274–5.
75 Bede, *De tabernaculo* I. 4; Augustine, *In Beatus Joannis Apocalypsim* III.
76 Glaber, *Historiarum* I. 1, tr. Thorndike (1923), 674–5. This is a somewhat minimalist reading of the Latin which conveys the force of the idea. For a lengthier, more literal, translation, see France (1989), 5.
77 *Vivian's Bible*, Paris, Bibl. nat. MS. lat. 1. fol. 330b.
78 Dungal, tr. Baldwin Smith (1956), 83.
79 *Annali* I: App. 3, in Ackerman (1949), 100.
80 The sequence consisted of the earth, moon, sun, Mercury, Venus, Mars, Jupiter, Saturn, then the realm of fixed stars, as transmitted by Aristotle and Ptolemy.
81 Clement, in *Stromata*, tr. Wilson (1869), 387.
82 See also Chapter 5, under 'The mathematics and metaphysics of the pentagon and its relatives'.
83 To extend a given line according to the section, draw the line AB horizontally; construct a square ABCD on it; bisect the square vertically at EF; produce its base line AB ready to be cut in the section. With compass point at F, and with radius FC, describe an arc to cut the base line so produced at G. The ratio between the line and the extension of the line will be in the golden section, so that BG : AB :: AB : AG.

To divide a given line according to the section, draw the line AB vertically; construct a square ABCD laterally on it, bisect the square vertically at EF; and draw the diagonal of the half-square AF. With compass point at F, and with radius FB, describe an arc to cut the diagonal at G. With compass point at A, and with radius AG, describe an arc to cut the given line at H. The ratio between the two parts of the line AHB will be in the golden section, so that,
HB : AH :: AH : AB.

84 Masi (1983), 33, note 24; Ullman (1964), 267–9.
85 Shelby, in Wagner (1986), 204–5.
86 Huntley (1970), 158–9.
87 Lund (1921), 27–8, 36, 148–9, 183–97; Cocke and Kidson (1993), 66; Davis and Neagley (2000), 167, fig. 10, 170, fig. 16a.
88 Vitruvius VI. 3. 3.
89 Although the 2 : 3 and 3 : 5 ratios approximate to golden rectangles, Vitruvius makes no such connection.
90 For a discussion of this problem, see Hiscock (1999), 20–27.
91 Hiscock (2002), 83–121.
92 *I quattro libri* I. 21.
93 Cocke and Kidson (1993), 63, 66–78.

94 Serlio, *Libro primo d'architettura* (1545).

95 Although the provenance of the material publicized by Serlio is largely, and unsurprisingly, of the Renaissance, given the various practices of squaring late in the Middle Ages, it is at least possible that this particular construction is medieval. Theoretical support for this was found in the geometric investigation in *The Wise Master Builder*, Hiscock (2000), where the proposed system sometimes divided naves into modules of three bays; as at Old St Peter's Basilica, Rome, pl. 42. 9; St Pantaleon's Abbey, Cologne, pl. 24; St Michael's Abbey, Hildesheim, pl. 29; Norwich Cathedral, pl. 71; and Peterborough Cathedral, pls 73, 77.

96 This section and the next are partly a development of material in Hiscock (2004 (2)) 168–70.

97 *Dialogus de musica*, ed. Gerbert (1784), in Strank (1952).

98 *Dialogus* I, II, IV.

99 Boethius, *De musica* IV. 18. I am grateful to Vivian Ramalingam and John Caldwell for explaining this and other matters concerning the medieval theory and practice of music. I am similarly grateful to Kay Slocum for discussing musical material in this section, and the *ars nova* in the Epilogue.

100 The number of consonances had been extended from three to five; they were applied in three genera (diatonic, chromatic, enharmonic); the three Greek modes had been expanded to eight; and the strings of the ancient tetrachord had been increased to eleven.

101 Guy d'Eu, in Maître (1995), 116, 118, tr. Beech (2000).

102 Slocum, in Surles (1993), 19–20. Although Jacques' seven-volume *Speculum musice* is a relatively late source, his purpose in compiling it was to perpetuate Boethian music theory in the face of the *ars nova*; Slocum, in Surles (1993), 11–12. See Epilogue.

103 Augustine, *De musica*, tr. Taliaferro (1947), 351–2.

104 *Scolica enchiriadis*, tr. Erickson (1995), 50, 51.

105 Augustine, *De Trinitate*, tr. McKenna in FC 45 (1963), 133.

106 Boethius, *De arithmetica*, tr. Masi (1983), 71.

107 Boethius, *De musica*, tr. Bower (1989), 49.

108 Wittkower (1988), 117.

109 *Testamentum Domini*, tr. Sperry-White (1991), 46.

110 Augustine, *De musica*, tr. Taliaferro (1947), 375.

111 John 17: 22–3.

112 Cassian, tr. Luibhéid (1985), 129.

113 Benedict, tr. McCann (1952), 19, 21.

114 Bernard, *De consideratione*, tr. Williams-Wynn (1953), 247.

115 Augustine, *De quantitate animae* IX, X.

116 Vitruvius, tr. Granger (1931), I. 27, 159.

117 Augustine, *De vera religione*, tr. Burleigh (1953), 252.

118 *Harmonia est discordia concors.*

119 Boethius, *De arithmetica* II. 43–8.

120 Boethius, *De arithmetica*, tr. Masi (1983), 177.

121 Ibid.

122 Slocum, in Surles (1993), 18.

123 Plato, *Timaeus*, tr. Cornford (1937), 54.

124 Alan, *De planctu*, tr. Sheridan (1980), 144–5.

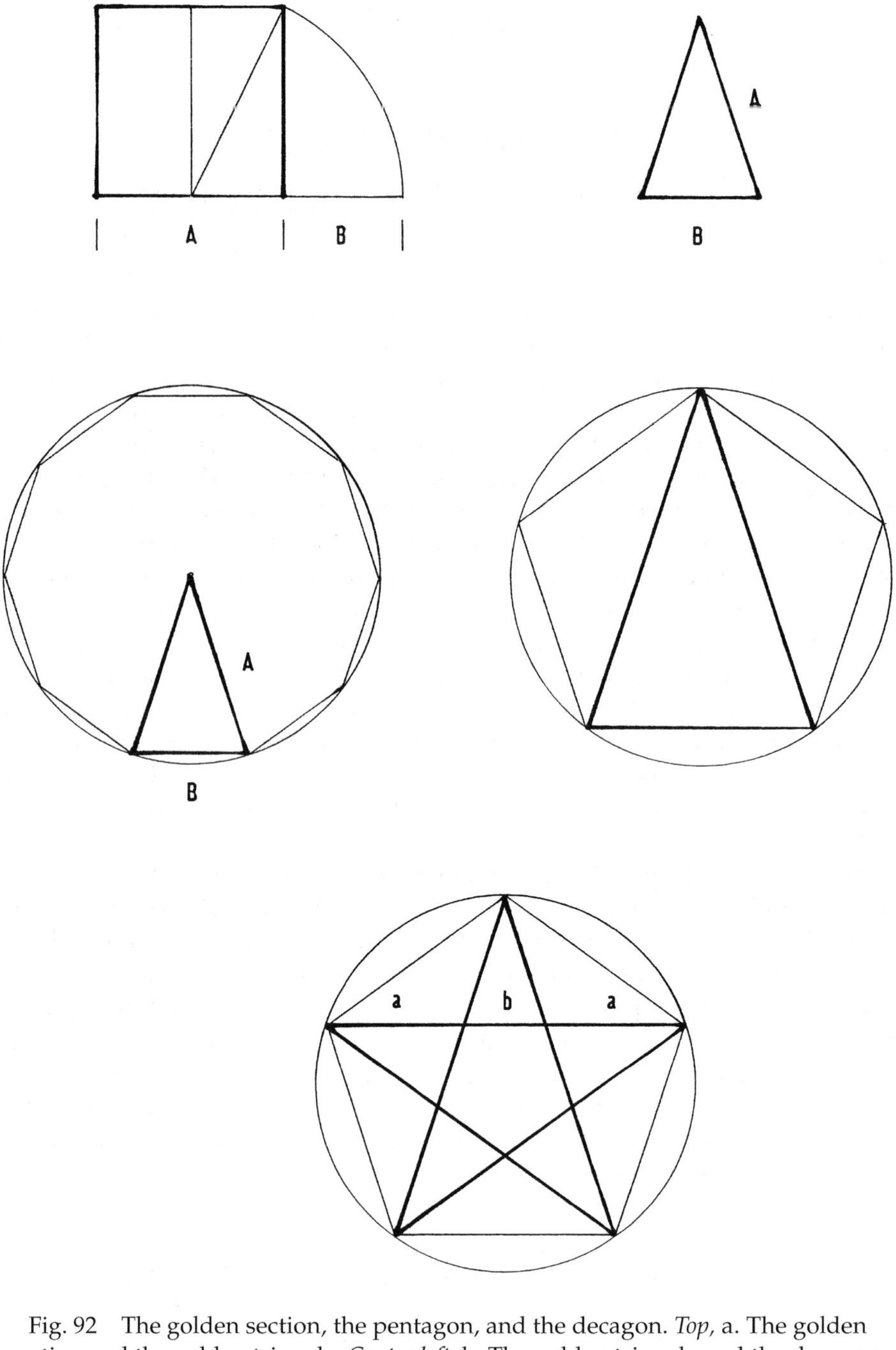

Fig. 92 The golden section, the pentagon, and the decagon. *Top,* a. The golden section and the golden triangle. *Centre left,* b. The golden triangle and the decagon. *Centre right,* c. The golden triangle and the pentagon. *Bottom,* d. The golden section and the pentagram

CHAPTER 5

The Architectural Geometry of the Pentagon

It is interesting, and perhaps revealing, that the various design solutions, that were proposed by those architects and engineers who were called to Milan at the end of the fourteenth century to advise on the heights for the construction of its new cathedral, were proportioned according to the triangle and apparently the square, but not the pentagon, for there is abundant evidence of the architectural use of the pentagon throughout the Middle Ages. From Theodoric's Mausoleum in sixth-century Ravenna to the thirteenth-century chapter house at Lincoln (Fig. 122b), the building of ten-sided, or decagonal, structures would almost certainly have required knowledge of the pentagon and so would construction of the pentagram, which was commonplace, from being known originally as an emblem of the Pythagoreans to its appearance on the shield of Sir Gawain in the fourteenth century[1] and the north transept window of Amiens Cathedral around 1400.[2] Its absence from the Milan debate might simply be explained that it continued in use, as the evidence in the next chapter proves, but not for elevating cathedral structures,[3] or that it did, but not among the few lodges represented by those consultants who were called to Milan.

In medieval metaphysics, the fundamental connotation of the equilateral triangle and the square – underlying their philosophical association with perfection, unity, and stability, and their theological identification with the Trinity, the Creation, and 'divine quaternity'[4] – was cosmological. Being the plane figures of the polyhedra representing the 4 elements (Fig. 3), their metaphysical connection was with the fifth element, the encompassing universe, a connection demonstrated arithmetically by the equation, $3^2 + 4^2 = 5^2$. In Plato's cosmology, the fifth element was represented by the fifth of the regular polyhedra, the dodecahedron, and its structure consists of the pentagon, 12 in number.

The mathematics and metaphysics of the pentagon and its relatives

To Pythagoreans, the figurate number of the pentagon stood for marriage, being the sum of the first female and male numbers, 2 + 3; and both its sum and its geometric figure may be understood as exemplifying several instances of marriage. As the number of the fifth element and the plane figure of the dodecahedron, 5 represented the universe. In the words of Martianus Capella early in the fifth century:

> The pentad [is] the number assigned to the universe.
>
> *De nuptiis Philologiae et Mercurii* 735.[5]

and Macrobius, possibly at the turn of the same century:

> The possession of unusual powers came to the number five because it alone embraces all things that are and seem to be.
>
> *Commentarii in Ciceronis Somnium* I. 6. 19.[6]

The pentad also represented the marriage of the macrocosm and the human microcosm. This was made up, arithmetically and physically, of the male and the female, each with its 5 senses, and its 4 limbs ruled by its head. The emblem of the Pythagoreans, who greeted each other with the words, 'Health to you', was the pentagram.[7] Another marriage existed through the universal connection of the pentad with the decad which was 'the perfect number of the universe' because it contains all the numbers there are.[8] Similarly, the pentad was connected with 10 through the Law, in the form both of the Pentateuch of the Old Testament, or the Five Books of Mosaic Law, and the Decalogue, or the Ten Commandments, which the Pentateuch contains. It was of note, moreover, that the Decalogue was delivered on two tablets of stone. In the words of Albrecht von Scharfenberg in the thirteenth century, 'God himself gave … that writing to Moses … observing all those commandments, five times paired'.[9] To complete the circle, the Decalogue was regarded as 'an image of heaven', since a heavenly state would exist on earth if the Law were kept.[10]

Geometrically, the marriage of 5 with 10 is effected through the golden section, alternatively known as extreme and mean ratio, for the isosceles triangle which has its sides and base in the ratio of the section lies at the root of both the pentagon and the decagon.[11] Indeed, Euclid's construction of a pentagon in his *Elementa* commences with the division of a line in the golden section in order to construct the triangle, and thence the pentagon (Fig. 92a).[12] In addition to the special property of being a triangle in extreme and mean ratio, it is also the triangle that has base angles that are twice its apex angle, namely 72° and 36° respectively. With an apex of 36°, a tenth of 360°, the golden triangle therefore forms one-tenth of a decagon (Fig. 92b). This means that the side and radial of a decagon are in extreme and mean ratio. It also describes the base and apex of a pentagon (Fig. 92c), and if a pentagon is constructed with all its diagonals joined, these will form 5 golden triangles overlaying each other, taking the form of an inscribed pentagram (Fig. 92d). In other words, the side and diagonal of a pentagon are in extreme and mean ratio. It is also a mathematical corollary that each diagonal will be intersected by the other diagonals with the middle part of each being in the golden section with either of its two outer parts.

Fig. 93 The Five Sisters, north transept, York Minster

Fig. 94 West front, Ripon Cathedral

The pentad and the pentagon in medieval architecture

Along with other numbers, it was customary for architectural elements to be arranged according to the number 5, one example being the tenth-century crypt of St Emmeram's Abbey church in Regensburg which,

> [was] ... very artfully ordered by [Abbot Ramwold ... as a result of which] the five altars ... keep in mind foremost respect for the five Books of Moses, and ... have fivefold circumspection regarding the five bodily senses.
>
> Arnold, *Liber* II. 40.[13]

Windows were also commonly arranged in groups of 5, notably the mid thirteenth-century lancet windows in the north transept of York Minster, known as the Five Sisters, together with an earlier group installed in two rows of 5 above the west door of Ripon Cathedral (Figs 93, 94). Whether these intentionally carried the numerological significance ascribed to Ramwold's altars cannot be presumed in the absence of equivalent documentary evidence. To draw even tentative conclusions will need some form of circumstantial corroboration and the possibility of the existence of this will be examined in the next chapter.

Returning to the construction of pentagons, it is not suggested that medieval architects knew Euclid's *Elementa*, or the geometric theory necessary to construct them correctly. The measurement of angles by degrees might have been known to astronomers and to scholars reading astronomy in the liberal arts, but there appears to be no evidence that this was conveyed to medieval architects, and even less to masons. Lodge practice in the early and high Middle Ages tended to be empirical, craft-based, and handed down through an oral tradition. Yet architectural instances of the pentagon, such as the five-part radiating geometry of the chevet of Cambrai Cathedral, which was drawn by Villard with great precision (Fig. 78),[14] also the decagonal chapter house of Lincoln Cathedral (Fig. 122b) and the large pentagram in the north transept rose window of Amiens Cathedral already mentioned (Fig. 163),[15] all of which appear to be regularly set out, prove that a method existed. In contrast to the ease with which the equilateral triangle and the square can be constructed with a pair of compasses, it also demonstrates that architects must have had a compelling reason for incorporating the pentagon in their work. There is also evidence that this sometimes involved a knowledge of the golden triangle, for its repeated use has been noted in Romanesque reliefs and friezes, such as those around the apse of the church of S. Donato on the island of Murano (Fig. 95).[16]

An empirical method for constructing a pentagon is shown on a folio of sketches which has been added to Villard's Portfolio (Fig. 96).[17] It appears to involve rotating right angles until they approximate to the required figure, in this case for setting out a five-sided tower, but the method can be shown to be incomplete and flawed (Fig. 97).[18] The significance of this sketch, however, is twofold. Firstly, it could not be completed because the ratio used is wrong,

Fig. 95 The golden triangle and architectural frieze, Church of S. Donato, Murano

and it was not corrected. Secondly, notwithstanding the error, the sketch strongly suggests the existence of an empirical method for masons to set out regular polygons, in this case pentagons, without any knowledge of the requisite geometric theory, or of the measurement of angles by degrees. The implications are considerable, for it is a method that could have been used, for example, for setting out the piers around the circumference of Cambrai's five-sided apse and the plan of Lincoln's ten-sided chapter house. Whichever method was used, one would also have been needed to set out the main apse and three chapels of the now lost chevet of Meaux Cathedral, which Villard also sketched,[19] for each of these apparently consisted of a half-decagon beyond its diameter, identical to Cambrai's (Fig. 78).[20] As it happens, towards the end of the Middle Ages, the architect of Regensberg Cathedral, Mathes Roriczer, published constructions for the basic polygons including, surprisingly, the heptagon. The pentagon was also among them, which he constructed from two overlapping circles and a *vesica piscis*, yet this is inaccurate by more than 5 per cent.[21]

Notwithstanding these uncertainties, Villard's Portfolio also contains a number of pentagrams (Fig. 98),[22] one probably – and enigmatically – a mason's mark on a sketch of a tabernacle.[23] Others are sketched with varying degrees of accuracy, apparently as constructs for figure drawing. Sometimes these and other geometric constructions in the Portfolio were drawn before the faces and figures, and sometimes afterwards,[24] which would appear to challenge both the conflicting explanations given for their purpose. The conventional interpretation has been that the geometry acts as a mnemonic guide for drawing the figure in question, and this remains the reading that is

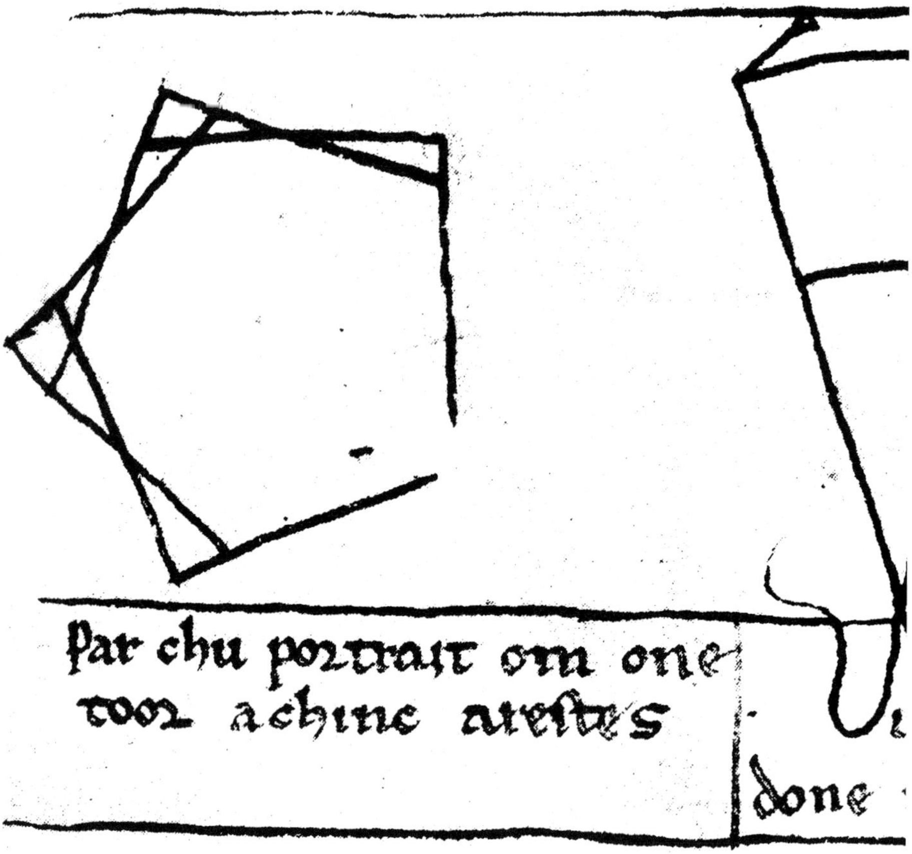

Fig. 96 A five-sided tower, Villard, fol. 21r, thirteenth century. This shows a construction of a pentagon empirically, which appears to be incomplete

still generally accepted. However, the reverse theory has also been put forward; that is, that the faces and figures of animals and humans serve as an aid for remembering the geometric figures, much as is the case for associating constellations with common objects, such as the Plough. According to this theory, the purpose of the geometric figures was to serve as masonic devices for use within the lodge, a practice evidently still in use by modern *compagnons de devoir*.[25] Yet it seems difficult to substantiate a medieval provenance for this, and some of the applications that are advanced seem to take too literally sketches that were probably drawn hurriedly in freehand for the author's own reference. A similarly esoteric interpretation has been proposed for a pentagram that has been shown to correspond with the principal proportions of the Saracen's tomb.[26] Although the width of the pentagram does not apparently coincide with anything, the closeness of the other parts of the figure to the tomb suggests there is a case to answer.

The most accurately drawn pentagram in the Portfolio is the only one to show an architectural application. It provides the roof-form for a cross-gabled

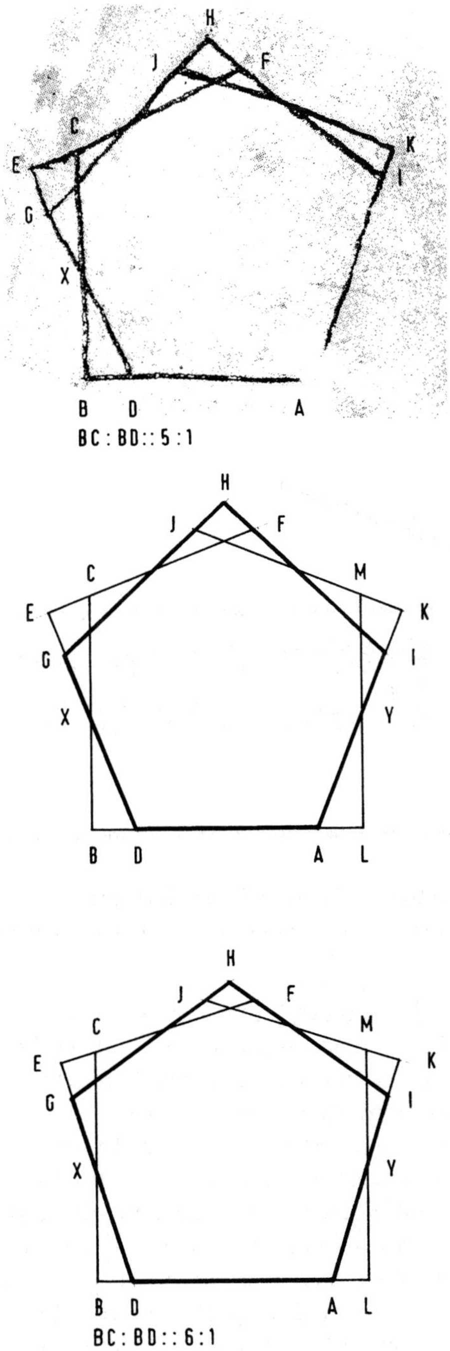

Fig. 97 Geometry of five-sided tower, after Villard, fol. 21r. *Top,* a. Right-angled lines rotated clockwise and off-set 5 : 1, as in Villard, fol. 21r. *Centre,* b. Right-angled lines rotated symmetrically, and off-set 5 : 1, to produce symmetrical, but irregular pentagon. *Bottom,* c. Right-angled lines rotated symmetrically, and off-set 6 : 1, to produce approximation to regular pentagon

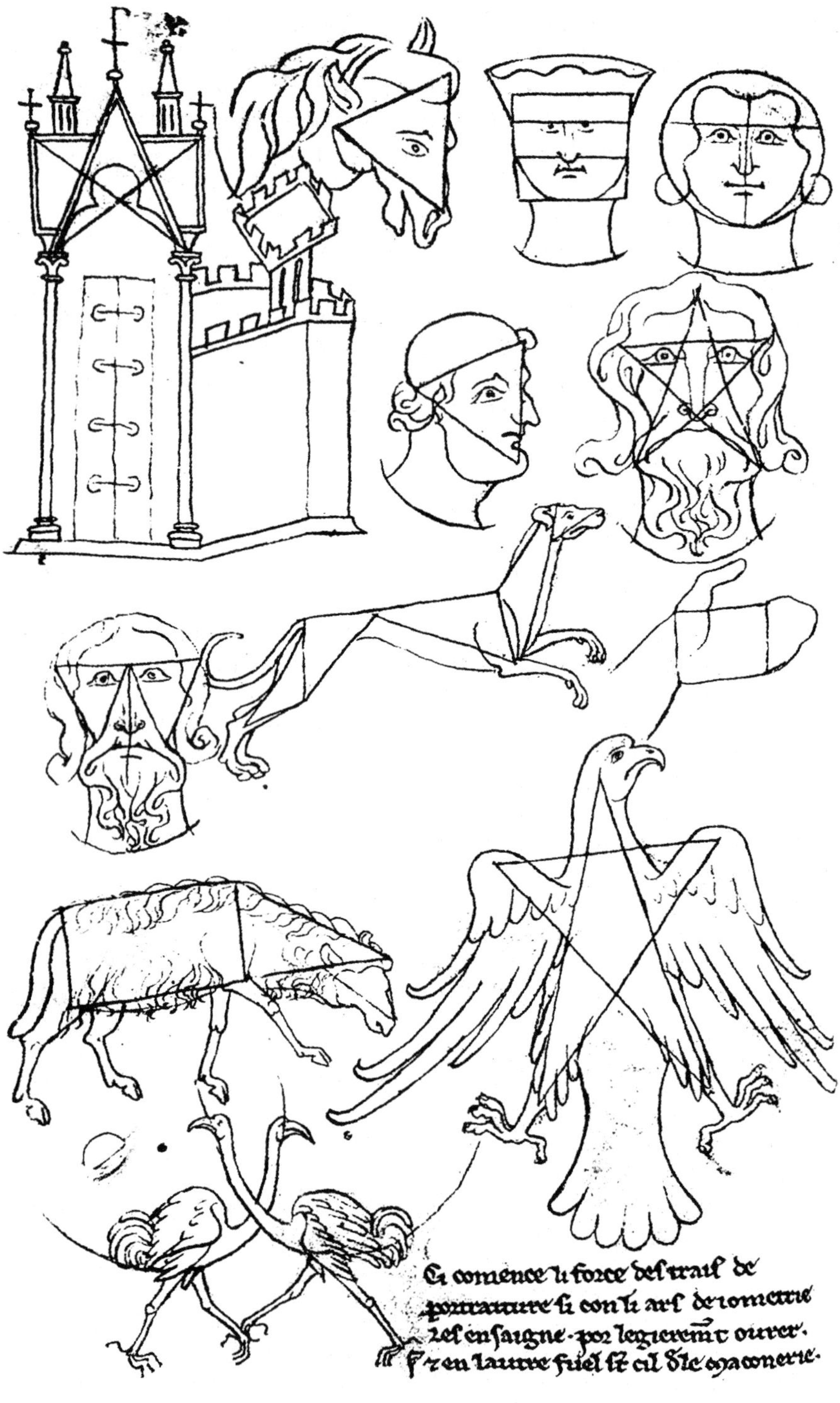

Fig. 98 Platonic geometry and figure drawing, Villard, fol. 18v, thirteenth century. The circle, square, equilateral triangle, and pentagram appear along with other geometric figures, notably the pentagram over the gateway, top left

gateway to a fortified enclosure,[27] in which the upright triangle conforms to its front gable, its two lower points coinciding with the centres of the capitals of the supporting pillars, and the horizontal diagonal determining the ridge of the cross-gable. This part of the sketch showing the correlation between the roof and the pentagram seems to have been drawn with particular deliberation.

One likely point of significance of this sketch will be pursued in the following chapter, for which this present chapter has served as a brief introduction. Similarly, since by far the most numerous occurrences of the pentagon in religious architecture are cinquefoils in geometric tracery, these will also be considered in the next chapter for, in geometric tracery, all the figures of Plato's cosmology are found in conjunction with the circle, as if in celebration of the created order in the universe.

Notes

1 See Prologue, 'Popular culture'.
2 See Chapter 6, 'The Eyes of the cathedral'.
3 One study of geometric proportioning in medieval architecture posited the use of the pentagon in the vertical plane, which would have established various heights for the elevations and cross-sections of cathedrals. However, for its findings to receive serious consideration now would require them to be tested against the more rigorous methodology that has been evolved since its publication. See Lund (1921), 27–8, 34–82, 129–31, 147–9, 188–97.
4 Glaber, *Historiarum* I. 1.
5 Martianus Capella, tr. Johnson (1991), II. 279.
6 Macrobius, tr. Stahl (1990), 104.
7 Lucian, *Pro lapsu* 5.
8 Grosseteste, *De luce*, tr. Reidl (1942), 17.
9 Albrecht, tr. Barber and Edwards (2003), 92.
10 Clement, *Stromateis* VI. 16. See 'Arithmetic' in the 'Historical Introduction' of the Prologue.
11 See Chapter 4, 'The square, the double square, and the golden section'.
12 Euclid, II. 1, IV. 10, 11. Book XIII is also largely devoted to the golden section and the properties of pentagons and decagons.
13 Arnold, *Liber*, tr. Stadler (1991).
14 Villard, Portfolio, fol. 14v.
15 These examples, and others, will be examined in Chapter 6.
16 Moessel (1931), 79, fig. 128.
17 Villard, Portfolio, fol. 21r.
18 On advice, Hahnloser correctly identifies the problem as one of constructing a pentagon by joining together five right angles in sequence according to certain proportions but, because he does not put this to the test, he concludes that the fifth corner of the sketch was left incomplete to make the procedure clearer, rather than realize that it could not be completed because of an error in the construction, as will be demonstrated below. Instead, he suggests, inexplicably, that a pentagram could be constructed from a pentagon using angles of 45°; Hahnloser (1972), 41c.

Bucher also appears to accept the principle behind the procedure, but confuses it with quadrature, in presuming that the right angles are rotated by 22½° whereas the angle would have to be 18° for a regular pentagon to be the result; Bucher (1979), 125, 127V41.

Starting with two lines of equal length at right angles to each other, ABC, drawn as if they were two sides of a square (Fig. 97, top), BC is bisected at an angle by one of another pair of right-angled sides, DEF, at X. This second construction connects with BA at D.

The angle of inclination between lines BC and DE could have been determined by a simple numerical ratio, as BC : BD, such as appears calibrated twice on the previous folio for setting out the sloping sides of a spire; Villard, Portfolio, fol. 20v. The height : base of the spire is 4 : 1, and the side inclines at 8 : 1. Intriguingly, for a method devised for setting out a tower that is five-sided, the ratio in the sketch between BC and BD is 5 : 1 (Fig. 97, top).

However, it can be seen that the sketch is asymmetrical and incomplete. This is due to an accumulated error caused partly by rotating the right-angled constructions in only one direction, in this case clockwise. If they were to be rotated symmetrically (Fig. 97, centre), firstly clockwise with ABC, DEF, and GH; then anti-clockwise with DLM, AKJ, and IH, a complete pentagon would be obtained.

This would be symmetrical but irregular because its upper two sides would be longer than the others, which is due to the inaccuracy of the 5 : 1 ratio employed. The degree of error is more than 18 per cent.

If this is increased to 6 : 1 (Fig. 97, bottom), a near-regular pentagon is obtained, accurate to 97.5 per cent. Although this is reasonably close, even closer approximations have been found in the architectural evidence, suggesting the knowledge of other methods.

To be a regular pentagon, angle BXD = 18°; the 6 : 1 ratio means that XB = 3, and BD = 1:

$$\frac{BD}{BX} = \tan 18^\circ = \frac{BD}{3}$$

$$BD = 3 \times 0.3249 = 0.9747$$

$$\frac{0.9747}{1} \times 100 = 97.5\%$$

19 Villard, fol. 15r.
20 Ibid., fol. 14v.
21 Shelby (1977), 116–18. See Epilogue, under 'Continuing practice and forgotten knowledge'.
22 Villard, Portfolio, fols 9v, 18v, 19r. Another pentagram has been shown to underlie the Saracen's tomb on folio 6r. See below, also Bechmann, in Zenner (2004), 131–3, especially 132, fig. 6. 7.
23 For a discussion of this and other masons' marks in the Portfolio, see Alexander, in Zenner (2004), 53–69.
24 Barnes, *The Portfolio of Villard de Honnecourt* (forthcoming, 2008).
25 Bechmann, *Pensée* (1991), 305–60.

26 Villard, Portfolio, 6r, see Bechmann, in Zenner (2004), 121–34.
27 Villard, Portolio, fol. 18v.

Fig. 99 Interior, the Pantheon, Rome

Chapter 6

'The Whole Frame of the Universe'

The Platonic figures and the circle

It is evident that Plato's abstract model of the universe, represented together with its elements by the regular polyhedra, shaped the way the universe was perceived in the Christian Platonist Middle Ages. To the Greek world in the eighth century and the Latin world in the thirteenth, the universe was visualized as a frame. John of Damascus wrote,

> Before the framing of the world ... there was no measurable age ...
>
> *De fide* II. 1.[1]

This may have been in the mind of John's translator, Robert Grosseteste, the bishop of Lincoln, when he contrasted,

> ... a point in relation to a line, or a single pebble in relation to the sand of the sea ... or one speck of dust to the whole frame of the universe.
>
> *Hexaëmeron* VIII. 1. 2.[2]

In the twelfth century, Alan of Lille also understood the universe as a structure, and man as a microcosm of it:

> I am the one who formed the nature of man according to the exemplar and likeness of the structure of the universe so that in him, as in a mirror of the universe itself, Nature's lineaments might be there to see.
>
> When God willed to call forth the fabric of the palace of the Universe ... as the choice architect of the universe ... He constructed the marvellous form of the kingdom of the world ...
>
> *De planctu Naturae* VI. 3, VIII. 4.[3]

The dodecahedron, enclosed as it is by 12 pentagons, was understood as an abstraction of the physical universe because it is the regular solid that, of the 5, most closely resembles a sphere, which the universe was held to be. In his Dialogue *Phaedo*, Plato, when talking of the earth's sphere, puts these words into the mouth of Socrates:

> ... the true earth, when looked at from above, is in appearance like one of those balls which are made of twelve pieces of leather ...
>
> *Phaedo* 110B.[4]

Thus, if the 12 pentagons of the dodecahedron were flexible, and not rigid, the polyhedron could be inflated into a sphere. Further evidence of the relationship that was made between the two solids appears in Euclid, where a construction is given of a dodecahedron within a sphere.[5] The transmission of this understanding to the Middle Ages, however imperfect it may have been, is attested by Walter of Speyer late in the tenth century, when writing of Geometry personified.

> Then she has joined together surfaces setting down several in turn,
> Triangular, tetragonal and pentagonal,
> Vigorously about to bring the idea of the pyramid in the sphere below the heavens.
>
> *Vita et passio sancti Christophori martyris* I. 173–8.[6]

Just as the pentagon expressed the macrocosm and microcosm, being the plane figure of the dodecahedron, so the circle enjoyed a corresponding significance as the plane figure of the sphere. And as the universe was perceived as consisting of the 4 elements, so the plane figures representing the elements appeared in association with the pentagon and the circle in architectural typologies as varied as circular and octagonal shrines, polygonal chapter houses, chevets, wheels of fortune, tracery design in general, and rose windows in particular. As explained in the Terms of Reference for this study, these types exemplify ideas that will continue to be investigated thematically first and foremost, and chronologically only where relevant to the argument.

Part One: Circular and Polygonal Structures

The circular shrine

The simplest architectural manifestation of the circle in the Graeco-Roman tradition originated in the *heroön* of Ancient Greece, taking the form of round tombs and *tholoi*. The identification of the *heroön* with the functions of burial and commemoration survived well into the Greek Middle Ages with the twelfth-century description by Nicholas Mesarites of Justinian's mausoleum, even though its architecture was cruciform.

> Let us go … to [Justinian's mausoleum], which is called a *heroon*, and is named by some a place of mourning because there are buried in it the emperors, who are, one might say, heroes.
>
> *Description of the Holy Apostles* XL. 1.[7]

The most famous rotunda of the Roman world is the Pantheon in Rome (Figs 99, 100, 101). Built by the Emperor Hadrian in the 120s, its function is neither clearly recorded nor fully understood,[8] but its dedication to *All the gods* suggests that it was at least partly to do with commemoration and the assumption of divinity, a preoccupation of Roman emperors. It also assumes a cosmic significance with its dome forming the upper half of a sphere exactly inscribed within it, unusually coffered into 28 parts presumably in reference to the lunar month,[9] with its crowning *oculus* open to the sky, and with the entire edifice orientated. Its interior is eight-sided, with 7 niches alternately

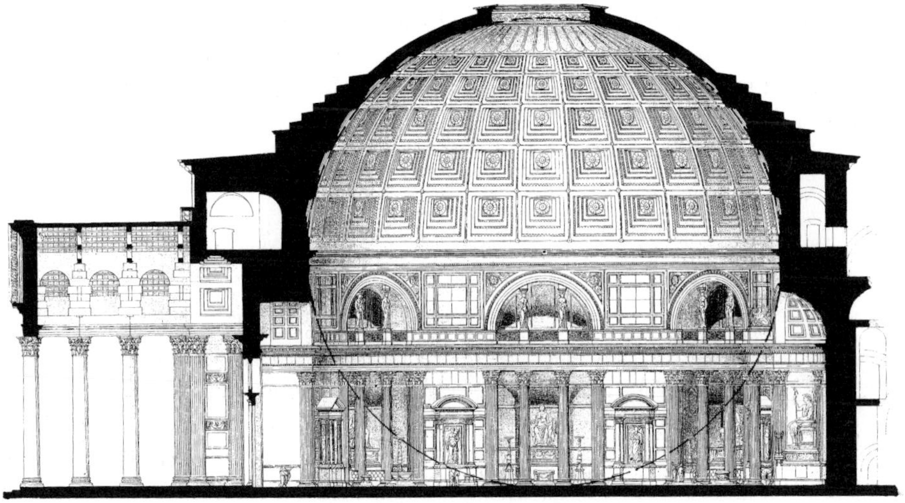

Fig. 100 Section, with circle inscribed, the Pantheon, Rome

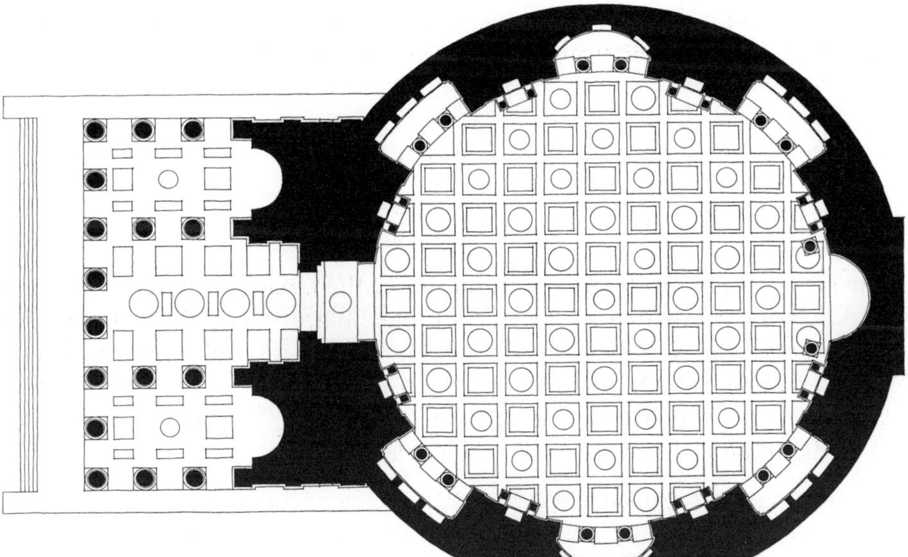

Fig. 101 Plan, the Pantheon, Rome. Round niches on the main axes alternate with squared niches on the diagonal axes

rounded and rectangular, starting and finishing with the entrance in the eighth side. This has led to suggestions that the dedication refers to the 7 planetary gods, although no firm evidence has been found to support this. Of interest to this study is its conversion early in the seventh century into a church.[10]

The rotunda of S. Costanza in Rome was built around 350 by Constantine as a tomb-house for his daughter Constantia, and was only converted into a church in the thirteenth century (Figs 102, 103). The round church of St George in Thessalonica is thought to have been built as a Roman mausoleum at the turn of the fourth century before becoming a church a century later. It was then that its dome was decorated with mosaics of martyrs (Figs 104, 105). These are located above the 8 massive niches in the walls of the rotunda, the westerly now the entrance and the easterly opening into the sanctuary. Each mosaic scene consists of an architectural fantasy of a heavenly choir, domed and pillared, curtained, hanging with holy lamps, and each flanked by a pair of martyrs.[11]

Whatever cosmic connection there may have been between the enshrining of commemorative space and the dome of heaven, or, in the case of the Pantheon, the sphere of the universe, it was a connection augmented in the spread of round churches in northern Europe by an association between the circle of the martyr's crown and the sphere of earth. To recall the words of Honorius in the twelfth century and Durandus in the thirteenth:

> Churches … made round in the form of a circle show that the Church is built throughout the circuit of the globe to become the circle of the crown of eternity through love.
>
> Honorius, *De gemma animae* XLVII.[12]

> … some churches … are built in the form of a circle: to signify that the Church hath been extended throughout the circle of the world …
>
> Durandus, *Rationale divinorum officiorum* I. 1. 17.[13]

In the wake of pilgrimages to the Holy Land throughout the eleventh century, followed by the First Crusade in 1099 and the foundation of the Order of the Knights Templar in 1118, the principal architectural model for these circular shrines was undoubtedly the Rotunda of the Anastasis at the Church of the Holy Sepulchre in Jerusalem, and it was in the twelfth century that its church was being constructed by the Crusaders (Figs 106, 107).[14] Part of a complex dating back to Constantine and which included, to the east of the Rotunda, the open Court of the Cross and the Basilica of Constantine, the Rotunda followed later in the fourth century and encircled the supposed tomb of Christ. It consisted of a ring of piers and columns, surrounded by an ambulatory, with the central space crowned by a dome which, like the Pantheon's, was apparently open to the sky.[15] A connection has been proposed between such structures and later Byzantine domes where the Pantokrator looks down as if from heaven through an aperture in the sky, thereby implying direct contact between God and the worshipper inside.[16] One of several examples of the Holy Sepulchre's progeny in England and the Continent is the church of the same name in Cambridge, which dates from around 1130 (Figs 108, 109). This is a much smaller version of the Jerusalem rotunda, with an ambulatory around a circular colonnade of 8 piers, an entrance in the west side, and possibly an apse originally to the east. Other twelfth-century survivals in England are to be found in Northampton, Ludlow, and the Temple Church in London. Over a century earlier, William of Volpiano had raised a three-storeyed rotunda to

Fig. 102 Interior, S. Costanza, Rome, from the entrance towards the sanctuary. Note the arches are wider on the main axis

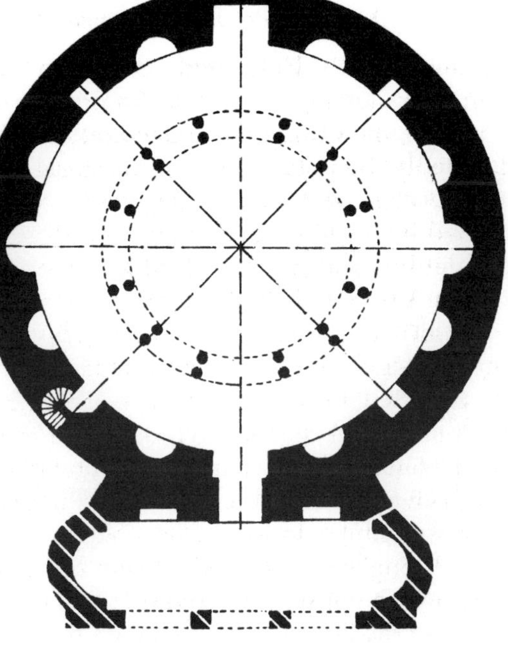

Fig. 103 Plan, with diagonal axes, S. Costanza, Rome. The colonnade consists of 12 pairs of columns, with wider spacing on the main axes and columns on the diagonal axes. The interior of the rotunda is sixteen-sided, with square and round niches alternating, and with niches on both the main and diagonal axes

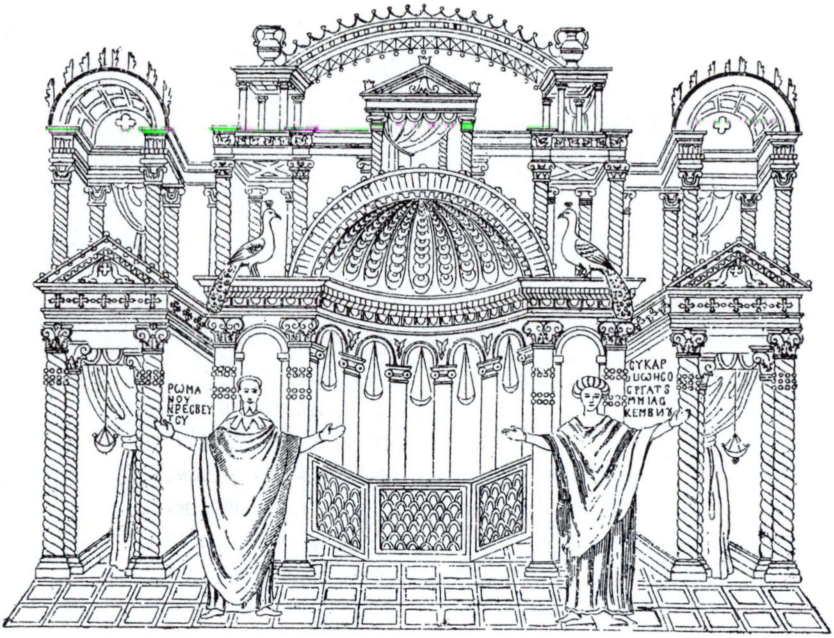

Fig. 104 Image of sanctuary, or choir, dome mosaics, St George, Thessalonica. This portrays one of the eight sanctuaries around the dome, despite the drawing being reconstructed as if it was on a flat surface

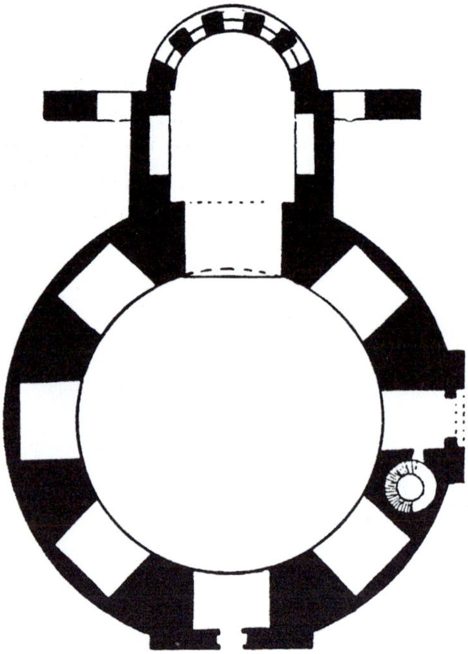

Fig. 105 Plan, St George, Thessalonica. Fourth-century rotunda, with sanctuary added in the fifth century

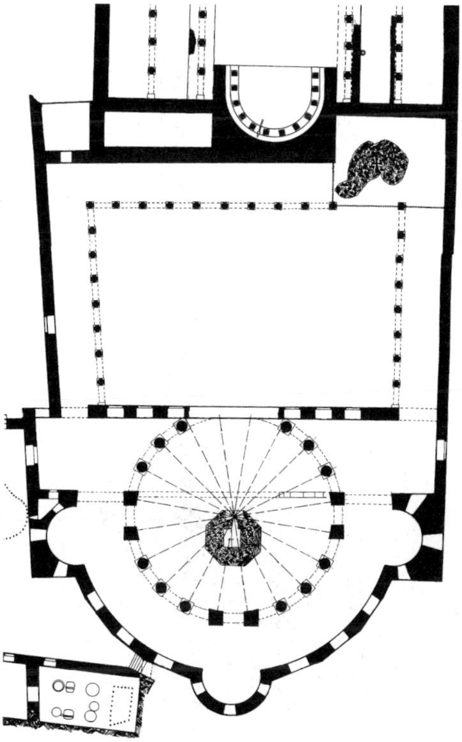

Fig. 106 Plan, fourth century, Holy Sepulchre, Jerusalem, with applied geometry. Three pairs of piers stand on the main axes, with three columns between each pair, making twelve. In place of a fourth pair of piers, the portal interrupts the colonnade tangentially. The underlying geometry depends on the division of a circle by twenty, with the columns nearest the portal being eased back to avoid it

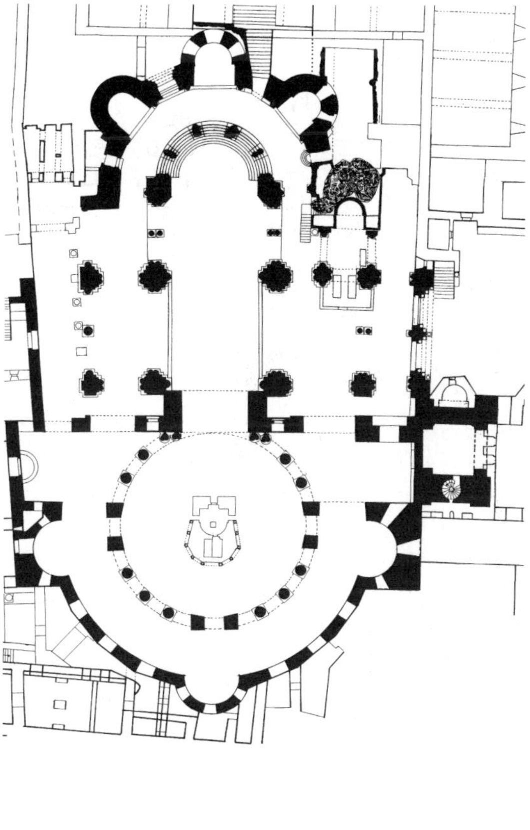

Fig. 107 Plan, twelfth century, Holy Sepulchre, Jerusalem. The original portal has been replaced, and the two columns nearest to it have also been replaced by twin pilasters either side of the doorway, leaving ten columns in the colonnade

Fig. 108 Exterior, Holy Sepulchre, Cambridge

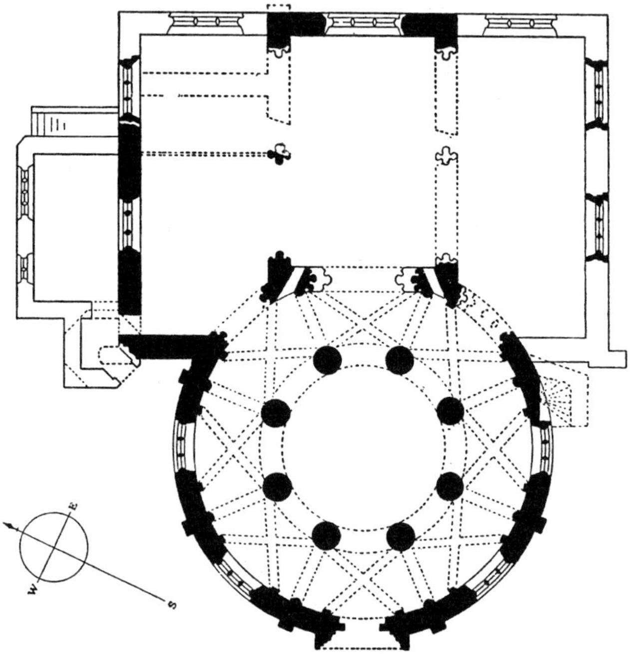

Fig. 109 Plan, Holy Sepulchre, Cambridge. The structures to the east of the rotunda are later

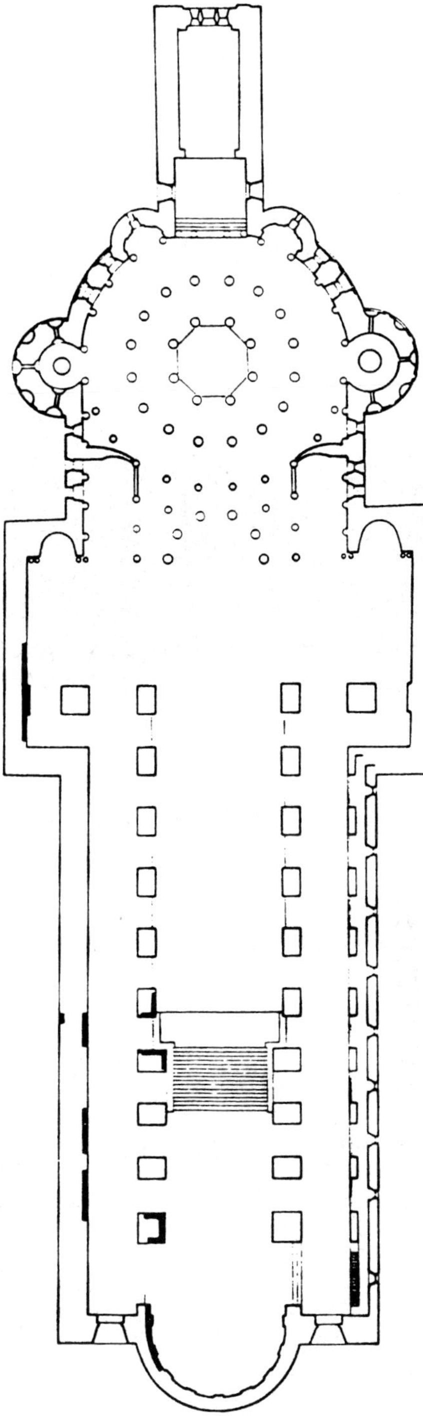

Fig. 110 Plan, St Bénigne, Dijon. Only the crypt of the rotunda survives

house the relics of St Bénigne as part of the rebuilding of his abbey church in Dijon (Fig. 110). This was much larger and surpasses the Jerusalem shrine with two concentric rings of columns and double ambulatories, and its inspiration was said to be Rome more than Jerusalem. During the preparations for its rebuilding, William had travelled to Rome, when he must have visited the converted Pantheon, and, on the way home, stopped at Ravenna where he called at the Church of S. Vitale, returning to Dijon with various skilled craftsmen.[17] The precedent of the Pantheon, and possibly the Holy Sepulchre by reputation, is strongly suggested in William's shrine of St Bénigne for this too was crowned by a dome which had an *oculus* open to the sky, and its inner and outer colonnades of 8 and 16 columns and the central eight-sided opening formerly in each floor above the tomb follow the octagonal geometry of both the Pantheon and S. Vitale.

At the Holy Sepulchre in Jerusalem, the circular colonnade of the fourth-century Rotunda was parted to the east by an entrance portal through a wall running north–south, tangential to the colonnade, and originally fronting onto the open Court, thereby interrupting the ambulatory (Fig. 106).[18] This was an unusual juxtaposition, though not unknown.[19] The colonnade consisted of 3 pairs of piers at the cardinal points to the north, west, and south, with the portal taking the place of an easterly pair, and, with 3 columns standing between each pair of piers and the portal, the piers numbered 6 and the columns 12. However, the *schema* underlying the geometry of the colonnade relies on the division of the Rotunda's circle, unusually and interestingly, by 20, and rotated to avoid piers on its principal axes. This would require the circle to be divided either into 10, then bisecting each angle radiating from its centre, or into 4, then dividing each quadrant into 5. Either way, the radials will be 18° from each other, and 18° is one of the angles of the pentagon. It is also the apex angle of a golden triangle bisected, and it may be recalled that Constantine's project came at a time when he was calling for recruits to the architectural profession who had a knowledge of the liberal arts, which would have included the mathematical subjects of the *quadrivium*.[20] The division of the Holy Sepulchre's colonnade by 20 was not only unusual, it must have been the result of deliberate choice, for which there must have been a reason. If the reason was numerological, the sum could be construed as 10 twofold, standing for the universe and the law, or 5 fourfold, again as the number of the macrocosm, beneath the dome of heaven which the columns supported; also the microcosm, perhaps in reference to the humanity of Christ at the place of his Passion; with 4 in both cases representing 'divine quaternity'. However, this is a reading that is only relevant to the schematic geometry of the Rotunda. As built, a difference was caused by the tangential east wall and portal interrupting the colonnade. As already noted, this resulted in 3 pairs of piers rather than 4, with 12 columns between them and, if Eusebius was referring to these columns rather than 12 in the basilica,[21] they stood for the Apostles in his eyes, with the 3 pairs of piers at the cardinal points doubtless representing the Holy Trinity in their midst, perhaps an allusion to Pentecost.

Over a century before the Crusaders' work on the church, the Byzantine administration rebuilt the Rotunda and Court after the destruction of the holy complex by Arabs in 1009. It involved renovating the fourth-century Rotunda, retaining the same column positions, and adding a sanctuary apse to the east in place of the portal. This entailed modifying the east wall and the opening in it by reducing the number of columns in the circular colonnade by one on each side, and planting a pair of columns against the east wall either side of the entrance to the new sanctuary.[22] The result is the Rotunda essentially in its present form, for the Crusaders' intervention in the twelfth century concentrated on superimposing three parts of a standard Romanesque church over the site of Golgotha to the east of the Rotunda, complete with crossing, transepts, and a choir with 3 radiating chapels (Fig. 107). Thus, the colonnade inside the Rotunda follows the Byzantine reconstruction of the original fourth-century layout, minus two columns. There are still 3 pairs of piers dividing the colonnade, but the number of columns in between is now reduced to 10. Whether this too was considered for its symbolic significance, or whether it was the result of adaptive necessity, the 10 columns could have been understood as representing the macrocosm and the law once again, the 3 pairs of piers the Trinity, and the sum of piers the perfection of Creation. Interestingly, the whole configuration embodies the two numbers seen at the root of the human microcosm, which, it may be recalled, are 6 and 10,[23] perhaps in continuing reference to Christ's humanity on the site of its passing.

The Rotunda's schematic geometry, combining its division by 20 with the juxtaposition of the colonnade and wall, and the complex of number and meaning this produced, make the Church of the Holy Sepulchre exceptional. This should not be surprising, for not only was it an imperial foundation with the best expertise available to it, it was also the holiest shrine in Christendom. In Rome, a slightly earlier project by Constantine is hardly less sophisticated, despite being much smaller. At the rotunda of the Church of S. Costanza, formerly the tomb-house of Constantine's daughter, the 12 columns of its circular colonnade inside anticipated those at the Holy Sepulchre (Fig. 102). Although they are not divided into quadrants by pairs of piers on the cardinal axes, the axes are nevertheless subtly accentuated by the spacing between the columns being wider here than elsewhere in the colonnade, thereby implying a cruciform within the circular space. The increased spacing at the main axes is achieved by placing columns on the diagonal axes; determining the major spacing desired at the main axes; and locating columns either side of the diagonal axes to achieve this. The result is that on the main axes there are no columns, and on the diagonal axes there are; also the geometry determining the placement of niches around the wall of the rotunda is sixteen-sided, and so is the geometry of the colonnade, despite consisting of 12 paired columns. Its underlying geometry is octagonal, and it takes its place in a line of circular shrines incorporating the octagon that stretches at least from the Pantheon, through St Bénigne at Dijon, to the Holy Sepulchre in Cambridge, and beyond.

The octagonal shrine

The mathematics and metaphysics of the numbers 8 and 12, which recognized 8 as the first cube, 'the fixed sphere' of earth, and 12 as the measure and division of time, the mystical number to which the complement of Apostles had to adhere, were well understood and attested.[24] The construct that connected the two numbers can be found in the Myth of Er in Book X of Plato's *Republic*, which Clement of Alexandria explained at length and which is worth repeating:

> 'And when seven days have passed to each of them in the meadow, on the eighth day they are to set out and arrive in four days'. By the meadow is to be understood the fixed sphere, as being a mild and genial spot, and the locality of the pious; and by the seven days each motion of the seven planets, and the whole practical art which speeds to the end of rest. But after the wandering orbs the journey leads to heaven, that is, to the eighth motion and day. And he says, that souls are gone on the fourth day, pointing out the passage through the four elements. But the seventh day is recognised as sacred, not by the Hebrews alone, but also by the Greeks …
>
> *Stromateis* V. 14.[25]

Thus the journey that leads to heaven starts on the eighth day and ends after 4 days on the twelfth. The eighth day follows the 6 days of Creation and the day of the Lord's rest on the Sabbath, and because it marks a new beginning, it is at once the eighth day and the first, as observed by Augustine in his *City of God* and other texts:

> For what does circumcision [on the eighth day] symbolize but the renewal of nature … And what does the eighth day symbolize but Christ, who rose again after the completion of seven days, that is, after the Sabbath?
>
> *De civitate Dei* XVI. 26.[26]

> [8] is signified both by the circumcision on the eighth day in the Old Testament and by the Lord's Resurrection after the Sabbath (which is indeed both the eighth day and the first) …
>
> *De sermone Domini in monte* I. 4. 12.[27]

For Christians, the spiritual journey that led to heaven was the promise of salvation made possible by Christ's Resurrection, and an important symbol of salvation was Noah's Ark. This is made clear again by Augustine in his *City of God* where he draws a double analogy between the Flood and the water of Christian baptism, and the wood of the Ark with that of the Cross, and, in so doing, has Noah prefiguring Christian salvation:

> Without doubt [the Ark] is a symbol … of the Church which is saved through the wood [of the Cross] …
>
> *De civitate Dei* XV. 26.[28]

> ... Noah, with his family, is saved by water and wood, as the family of Christ is saved by baptism, as representing the suffering of the cross.
>
> *Contra Faustum* XII. 14.[29]

It was of significance that Noah and the members of his family aboard the Ark numbered 8 and that, as a result of surviving the Flood, the future of the human race was saved. According to Alcuin, writing in the ninth century,

> ... we read that there were eight souls in the Ark, from whom the multitude of the whole human race sprouted forth ...
>
> *Epistola* 259.
>
> Eight souls were saved in the Ark. The souls of the faithful in the church were saved by eight blessings.
>
> *Epistola* 260.[30]

Thus the path to salvation lay through baptism and death, a connection found in Paul's Epistle to the Romans:

> Know ye not, that so many of us as were baptized into Jesus Christ were baptized into his death?
> Therefore we are buried with him by baptism into death: that like as Christ was raised up from the dead by the glory of the Father, even so we also should walk in newness of life.
>
> Romans VI. 3, 4.

It is not surprising therefore that, from the fourth century, baptisteries, fonts, and *martyria* are customarily octagonal; in the case of baptisteries well into the twelfth century, and fonts, together with the steps on which they were placed, throughout the Middle Ages.[31] A causal connection between intent and design is provided by an inscription that was recorded on the octagonal baptistery of Milan Cathedral, and attributed to Ambrose:

> He erected an eight-choired temple for use by the saints
> and an octagonal font is worthy of its number.
> This number proved fitting for the elevation of a housing of the
> holy baptism, which gave back to the people true deliverance,
> Raising them again in the light of Christ, who loosened the bonds
> of death, and (who) from their graves raised the lifeless ...
>
> *Sylloge Laureshamensis* III.[32]

Clement's purpose in citing the passage from the *Republic* was to demonstrate how, in his estimation, the Greeks had borrowed certain beliefs from the Hebrews. Whether this was true, or whether both traditions shared a common source, the passage can be taken to point to an antique tradition that led to the association of 8 with the architecture of renewal. There is also a practical connection that sees the transposition of the idea of the shrine from pagan Roman to early Christian, where the octagonal mausoleum of the Roman world, such as Diocletian's Mausoleum of around 300 (Fig. 111), leads to the octagonal *martyrion* of the early Christian and Byzantine world, such as the sixth-century Church of S. Vitale in Ravenna (Figs 112, 113), and where octagonal chambers in some Roman baths become the form adopted for Christian baptisteries. Ravenna's octagonal Orthodox Baptistery was first a Roman bath-house (Figs 114, 115, 116). It stands with apses projecting from the cardinal points in a correlation of form with function that was obviously not lost on its Christian inheritors. Similarly, when the Pantheon was converted into a church in 608, it cannot be a coincidence, given its eight-sided interior, that it was dedicated specifically to Mary and All Martyrs. When Gregory of Nyssa wrote to his superior in the 380s requesting workmen to build a church (Fig. 117), he described an octagonal *martyrion* with round and square niches alternating around its 8 sides, similar to the interior of the Pantheon, except that Gregory's design had the square niches at the cardinal points so that it would be cruciform, and round niches on the diagonal axes. Significantly, his church was also dedicated to the Martyrs, and it will also be shown to be

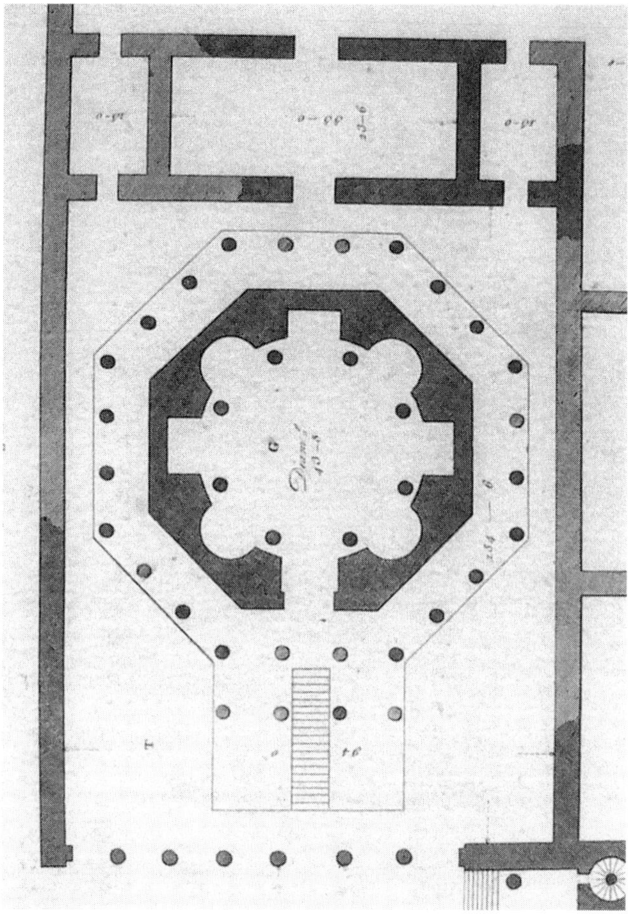

Fig. 111 Plan, Diocletian's Mausoleum, Spalato

Fig. 112 Exterior, S. Vitale, Ravenna

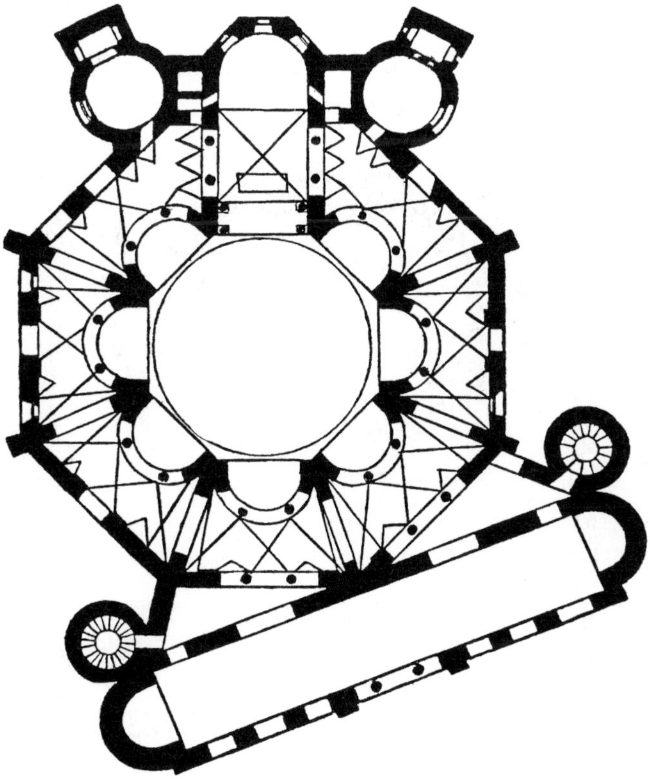

Fig. 113 Plan, S. Vitale, Ravenna

Fig. 114 Christ's baptism, dome mosaics, Orthodox Baptistery, Ravenna

Fig. 115 Exterior, Orthodox Baptistery, Ravenna, originally a Roman bath-house

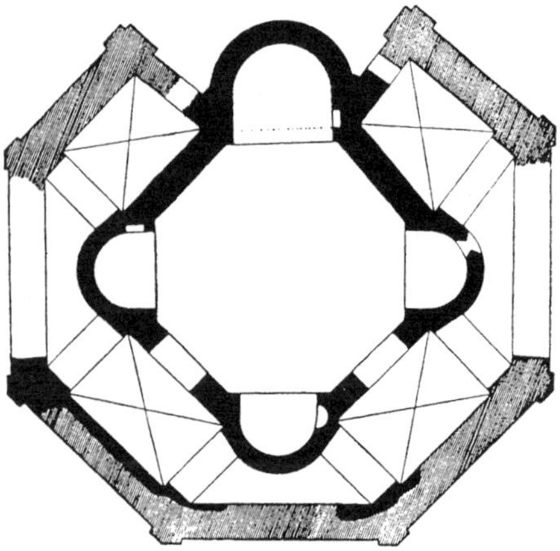

Fig. 116 Plan, Orthodox Baptistery, Ravenna

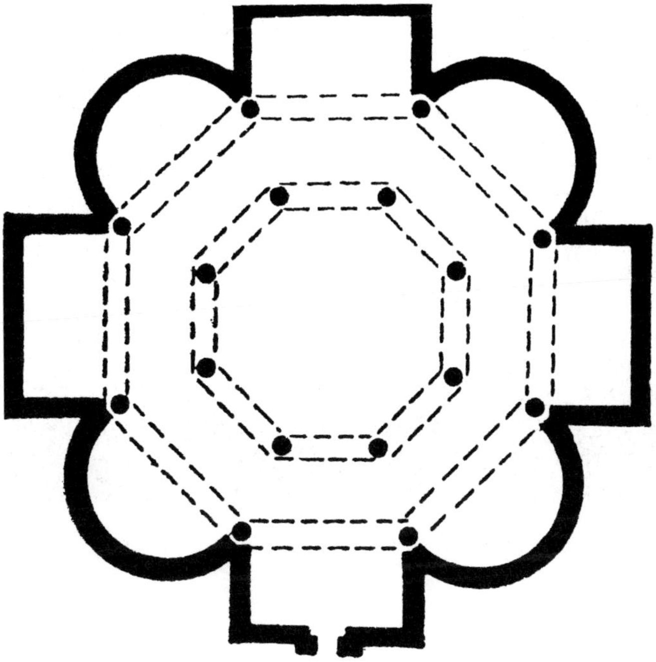

Fig. 117 Plan, Church of the Martyrs, Gregory of Nyssa. Round and squared niches again alternate

relevant that the only measures he specifies for its construction happen to be 4 and 8 cubits.[33]

The fifth-century conversion that produced Ravenna's Orthodox Baptistery was accompanied by a comprehensive scheme of mosaics in the late Classical tradition that, notwithstanding restoration, has survived virtually intact (Fig. 114). The scene of Christ's baptism crowns the dome, with Christ standing in the Jordan beneath the dove of the Holy Ghost, while John blesses him from the bank with the personification of the river looking on as a witness. Encircling this scene in the middle zone of the dome are the 12 Apostles and, surrounding them, in the lowest zone is another ring of 8 'temples'. In comparison with those around St George's dome, these mosaic images are of pillared niches alternately housing an empty throne awaiting the Second Coming and a lectern holding one of the Gospels. The latter occur on the diagonal axes of the baptistery, with the thrones on the cardinal facades, each centred over one of the Baptistery's eight windows. The synthesis in geometry, between the division of the dome into 12 for the Apostles and into 8 both for the circle of temples and the form of the Baptistery itself, might recall the layout of S. Costanza to some extent, except here the two systems are unified by quartering the circle, then dividing each quadrant into 3 for the dodecagon

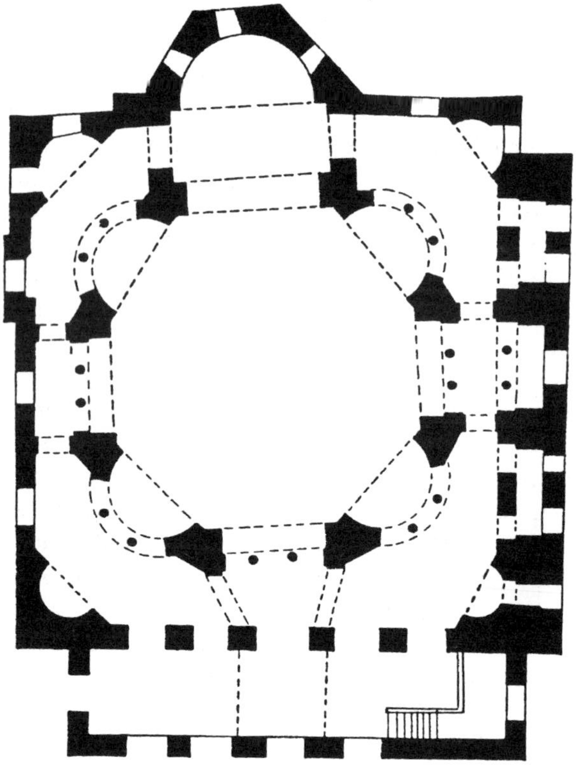

Fig. 118 Plan, SS Sergios and Baakhos, Constantinople

and 2 for the octagon.[34] In the following century, the Arian Christians erected their own Baptistery in Ravenna, which is also octagonal and originally built with a surrounding ambulatory. Only the dome mosaics survive, Byzantine in tradition, and with a similar baptismal scene in the central medallion, surrounded by the 12 Apostles once again. This time, they flank a single empty throne located above the head of Christ. It seems inescapable to see in the iconography of these two domes the 12 Apostles partaking in the spiritual journey that ends after 12 days, when Christ will assume the empty throne as his seat of Judgment, the ring of Apostles a simile for the ring of columns in the Holy Sepulchre, which was also identified with the Apostles. In both of Ravenna's Baptisteries, the Apostles carry the crowns of their martyrdom, thereby conflating once again baptism with death through salvation, the journey that leads to heaven on the eighth day, the whole being expressed by the association of the numbers 12 and 8, and the geometry of the dodecagon with the octagon.

The sixth-century octagonal Church of S. Vitale in Ravenna was dedicated to a slave who was martyred, and it makes an interesting comparison with its counterpart and contemporary in Constantinople, which is dedicated to the Syrian martyrs Sergios and Baakhos (Figs 113, 118). Both were built around an open-sided octagonal core, supporting a central dome, surrounded by an ambulatory and gallery above, which are parted by the apsidal sanctuary. Between the piers of the inner octagon of both churches are colonnades in two storeys, with two columns to each opening supporting arches between the piers, but where those in S. Vitale are in the form of curved *exedrae* on each side, except the sanctuary, those at SS. Sergios and Baakhos alternate between being straight-sided at the cardinal points and curved on the diagonal axes. Another important difference is that the octagonal ambulatory in Constantinople is inscribed within a square enclosure, with *exedrae* in the 4 corners, whereas the external form of S. Vitale follows the octagonal outline of its ambulatory.[35] Common to both, however, is the identification of their octagonal form with their martyrial function.

Two hundred years before William of Volpiano called at the Church of S. Vitale on his way back from Rome to Dijon, Charlemagne had stopped at Ravenna on his return to Aachen to build his Palace Chapel (Figs 119, 120). There were several reasons for Ravenna and its Church of S. Vitale impressing him, all of them pertinent to his own imperial aspirations. Soon to be proclaimed the Emperor of the Romans in the Basilica of St Peter, Charlemagne emulated Constantine as the first Christian emperor of Rome, and venerated the city's Christian shrines. He also admired Theodoric, the barbarian Goth who, three hundred years earlier, had ruled Italy from his capital in Ravenna, had become the adopted son of Byzantium, and very nearly unified the Germanic immigrants with the descendants of ancient Rome. Among the materials the pope donated for Charlemagne's project, were some from Theodoric's palace in Ravenna, and Charlemagne carried Theodoric's statue back with him to Aachen. He also formed an alliance with the Byzantine Empress Irene in pursuit of imperial recognition, and this had brought Byzantine builders to Germany for his palaces. Finally, the martyrial form of S. Vitale's church might have been of interest to him, for his Chapel was to be his burial-place and, even though his precise intentions about this may be in some doubt, he can at least be expected to have had his own personal salvation in mind. While visiting S. Vitale, its form and details would doubtless have been explained to him and he would have been in a good position to understand them. According to his biographer, Einhard,

> [Charlemagne] took great pleasure in the books of Saint Augustine and especially those which are called the City of God.
>
> [He] paid the greatest attention to the liberal arts ... [and] for all the ... subjects [apart from grammar] he was taught by Alcuin ...
>
> *Vita Caroli* III. 24, 25.[36]

It was Alcuin who was master of the palace school, tutor to the royal family, and who, in setting out the biblical meanings for the numbers of the decad, noted that, 'Eight souls were saved in the Ark', declaring that the 'souls of the faithful [are] saved by eight blessings'.[37] Alcuin was still in Aachen when Charlemagne's Chapel was being planned around 790 and its kinship with S. Vitale's Church in Ravenna is obvious. Once again, a two-storeyed octagonal

Fig. 119 Interior, Charlemagne's Chapel, Aachen.

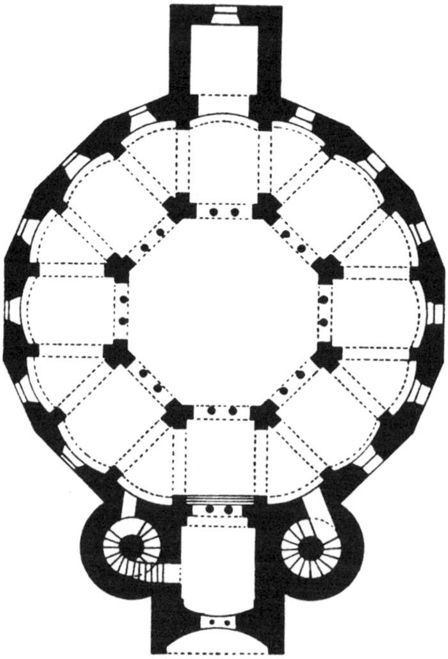

Fig. 120 Gallery plan, Charlemagne's Chapel, Aachen, before Gothic additions

core supporting a dome is surrounded by an ambulatory, which here is sixteen-sided externally. A modest sanctuary extended to the east, opposite the present entrance block. Unlike S. Vitale, the open sides of the inner octagon are straight and there are no intermediate pillars between the piers at ground level. Above, the gallery opens into the central core through 8 arches, each containing a screen of 4 pillars, two above the other, and there is another pair standing between the gallery and the chamber above the porch at the west end. This means that the number of columns around the octagon is 32, or 8 × 4, presumably in reference to salvation by way of the start of the journey that leads to heaven, and its duration. The total number is 36, or 12 × 3, which could represent the end of the spiritual journey after 12 days, also the 12 Apostles and the Holy Trinity. It is interesting to discover the presence of 12 again in association with 8, and the construction of the entire building has been shown to answer to dimensional modules of 12 Carolingian feet,[38] recalling Gregory's specification of 4 and 8 cubits for his Church of the Martyrs. The consecration inscription which runs, in a modern facsimile, around the interior of Charlemagne's rotunda, states:

> As the living stones are bonded in a fabric of peace, *and all come together in matching numbers*, the work of the lord who has built the entire hall[39] shines forth brightly ...[40]

Charlemagne's Chapel was to exert a substantial influence of its own, with other palace chapels and churches being modelled on it at Mettlach, Ottmarsheim, and Nijmegen well into the twelfth century, and several others besides,[41] thereby establishing the octagonal shrine firmly within the western medieval tradition. It was also during this period that another manifestation of the type appeared in the Greek East, taking the form of the inscribed octagon and octaconch types of church that were encountered in Chapter 1, dating from the eleventh to the thirteenth centuries (Figs 32–35).

It will be recalled that churches with the inscribed octagon layout incorporate the cube and cross-arms of the Greek cross-in-square design, but with the cube of its interior dominated by one clear-span dome and drum rising from an octagonal base around the top of the cube. The base is formed by squinches arching across its 4 corners. The different variations of the octaconch type of church sometimes express and sometimes suppress the cruciform but all are crowned by a similar large dome carried on arches on the 4 sides of the cube and squinches across the angles. The use of squinches is interesting, given the existence of the pendentive in Byzantine construction. Both offer surfaces for religious imagery but, whereas pendentives are simply spherical triangles rising to the base of the dome's drum between its side arches, squinches are in the nature of arched niches which frame their images, intervening in between the side arches, and together forming an octagon of arches supporting the dome (Fig. 34). The preference for a squinch over a pendentive may therefore suggest a preference for the octagonal form for these monastery churches, in addition to the symbolism of the sphere and the cube and the cruciform that is also present.[42] The connection of 8 with the journey that leads to heaven and salvation may surely be presumed, yet lacking as it does the synthesis here with the number 12 observed in other types of octagonal shrines, the geometry of the inscribed octagon produces instead a division into 16. In the catholicon of Daphni of around 1080, this has led to a drum of 16 windows with the same number of prophets between them, despite there being no single canonical number for the prophets, as there is for the Apostles.[43] If the surviving mosaics at Daphni are studied, they appear to present a narrative totality. The Pantokrator looks down from the dome, holding the book, ringed by various prophets of the word; the scenes in the squinches, a cycle commencing with Christ's baptism and Transfiguration either side of the entrance into the church, and continuing with the Annunciation and Nativity either side of the sanctuary arch; fittingly, his Passion and Resurrection are placed in the cross-arms of the cruciform; with Mother and Child in the apse, beyond the empty throne on the sanctuary vault, awaiting his Second Coming, flanked by the Archangels in the wings. It is a totality that might recall the words, three hundred years earlier, of John of Damascus:

> A first baptism was that of the flood unto the cutting away of sin. A second was that by the sea and the cloud, for the cloud is a symbol of the Spirit, while the sea is a symbol of the water. A third is that of the Law, for every unclean person washed himself with water and also washed his garments and thus entered into the camp. A fourth is that of John, which was an introductory baptism leading those thus baptized to penance, so that they might believe in Christ. 'I indeed,' he says, 'baptize you in water: but he that shall come after me he shall baptize you in the Holy Ghost and fire'.[44] Thus, John purified with water in advance to prepare for the Spirit. A fifth is the Lord's baptism with which He Himself was baptized. He, however, was baptized not that He Himself stood in any need of purification but that by making my purification His own He might 'crush the heads of the dragons in the water',[45] wash away the sin and bury all of the old Adam in the water, sanctify the Baptist, fulfil the Law, reveal the mystery of the Trinity, and become for us a model and example for the reception of baptism. And we, too, are baptized with the perfect baptism of the Lord, which is by water and the Spirit. Christ is said to baptize in fire, because He poured out the grace of the Spirit upon the holy Apostles in the form of tongues of fire, as the Lord Himself says: 'John indeed baptized with water; but you shall be baptized with the Holy Ghost and fire, not many days hence'.[46] Or it is because of the chastising baptism of the fire to come that He is said to baptize with fire. A sixth is that which is by penance and tears and which is truly painful. A seventh is that which is by blood and martyrdom. Christ Himself was also baptized with this for our sake. It is exceedingly sublime and blessed in so far as it is not sullied by second stains. An eighth, which is the last, is not saving, but, which being destructive of evil, since evil and sin no longer hold sway, it chastises endlessly.
>
> *De fide* IV. 9.[47]

Oddly, his eighth baptism is 'not saving', but the triumph over evil, which others might equate with salvation. In support of this, John prefaces his exegesis by describing how the water of baptism prefigures the grace of the Spirit, which in the fifth baptism appears as fire, 'renewing ... and ... producing the guarantee of life'.[48] Moreover, that John's baptisms should number 8, associating the water of baptism with the fire of Pentecost, pain with renewal and, significantly, the fifth baptism bringing the fulfilment of the law, the revelation of the Trinity, and the eighth the destruction of evil, seem as all-encompassing as any great dome over an inscribed octagon church (Fig. 34), ringed by its 8 arches, embodying the Greek Cross, the cube and the sphere, and echoing the 8 temples surrounding Ravenna's Orthodox Baptistery, the 8 choirs encircling the dome of St George in Thessalonica, the eight-choired temple of Milan Cathedral's Baptistery, the 'eight blessings' of Alcuin, and arguably Aachen's 'matching numbers'.

It is noticeable how the schematic designs of the circular shrine and the octagonal shrine are related to each other and are often one and the same, with the geometry of the octagon inscribed within rotundas as far apart as the Pantheon, St George's Church in Thessalonica, St Bénigne's Abbey in Dijon, and the Holy Sepulchre in Cambridge. It is also of interest how often the symbolism incorporates the representation of 12, presumably as the end of the journey and as the number of Apostles, in the number of columns around the Rotunda of the Anastasis in a scheme which otherwise divides its circle by 20, or S. Costanza where the division is by 8, also in the portrayal of the 12 Apostles in octagonal baptisteries. It is also present implicitly as the sum of 8 and 4, readable as the beginning and the duration of the journey, in the measures of Gregory of Nyssa's Church of the Martyrs, the pillars around the octagon at Aachen, and in its proposed dimensional module. Fundamental to these designs was the division of schematic circles into specific numbers of parts, each capable of being interpreted as signifying meaning consistent with their liturgical function.[49] In order to pursue the possibility of such a correlation, this investigation will proceed by examining other examples drawn from the Latin West where the division of a circle, both notionally and physically, appears to be conceptually fundamental to the design process, and will include polygonal chapter houses, the layouts of chevets, wheels of fortune and other *rotae*, and the design of geometric tracery.[50]

Polygonal chapter houses

The architectural application of the octagon is particularly common among polygonal chapter houses, which are only found in Britain, and for which a connection between form and meaning embodies function and liturgy.[51] It is also a type that draws on all three figures of Platonic geometry – the triangle, the square, and the pentagon – for their architectural form. A sample of twenty-five polygonal chapter houses was investigated, formerly belonging to Benedictine, Cistercian, Augustinian, and Premonstratension houses as well as secular colleges of canons, dating from late in the eleventh century to the middle of the fifteenth (Figs 121, 122).[52]

Fig. 121 East end, Lincoln Cathedral. The chapter house lies to the right of the east end of the Angel Choir and Simon of Thirsk's window

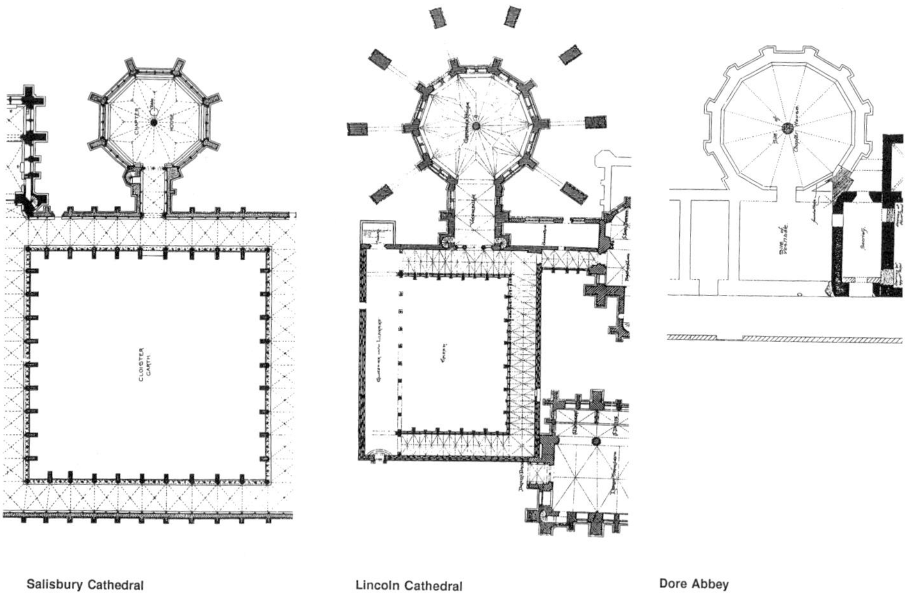

Fig. 122 Plans of polygonal chapter houses. *Left,* a. Salisbury Cathedral. *Centre,* b. Lincoln Cathedral. *Right,* c. Dore Abbey

Various attempts to explain their form and their confinement to Britain remain inconclusive. It has been pointed out that some of the grandest chapter houses, such as those at Lincoln, Wells and York, were raised beside secular cathedrals at a time when chapters were asserting independence from their bishops,[53] yet this does not in itself explain the choice of a polygonal form, or its precedence and continuing use among foundations that were monastic.[54] One contemporary description of the chapter house as 'the workshop of the Holy Spirit in which the sons of God are gathered together'[55] has led to a suggested connection with Pentecost, at which the Virgin was said to be present and which was commonly depicted taking place inside a centralized building. One of several examples can be seen in *St Paul's Bible* of about 870, which shows the 12 Apostles gathered around the interior of a polygonal chamber, with the Virgin standing in their midst (Fig. 123).[56] Although this again does not in itself fully explain the choice of a centralized structure in the first place, a connection with the Virgin may nevertheless be suggested from rotundas, such as the Pantheon and the Aachen Chapel, which were in part dedicated to her, and the thirteenth-century Church of the Virgin, or Liebfrauenkirche, in Trier has a highly unusual centralized layout (Figs 179, 180).[57] Additionally, one function of chapter houses was sometimes to receive the burial of abbots and to commemorate deceased brethren, for whom the Virgin was their principal intercessor.[58] Whilst this is both revealing and true, it again leaves unanswered the reason for choosing a polygonal form, still less one having a particular number of sides. Although the Virgin is undoubtedly an attendant figure iconographically both at Pentecost and at prayers for the deceased, and was associated in romance literature with the rose, she bears no other obvious symbolical association by which a form for chapter houses might be generated from the division of a circle by certain numbers, or with the particular polygonal geometry which resulted.

From their earliest appearance on the Continent in the middle decades of the eleventh century, chapter houses were simple rectangular chambers, sometimes subdivided by arcading, sometimes terminating in an apse. Here was set the abbot's throne, around the perimeter sat the monks, and in the middle stood a lectern. The predecessors of Britain's polygonal chapter houses were rotundas, at Pershore, Worcester, and Margam, the walls of the latter two being divided internally into 10 and 12 bays respectively. Among the earliest octagonal chambers was the chapter house of Beverley Minster, dating from around 1230. After this, the chapter houses at Evesham, Hereford, and possibly Bridlington were alone in being decagonal; all the others are or were octagonal, including those at Cockersand, Westminster, Salisbury, Elgin, Belvoir, York, Thornton, Southwell, Carlisle, London, Bolton, Howden, Whalley and Manchester, a collection extending into the fifteenth century.[59] Their foundations represent a mixture of secular colleges with Augustinian houses, one that was Cistercian, and another that was Premonstratension. Since a secular cathedral was not residential, its lack of conventual buildings around the cloister provided an opportunity for new formal arrangements between both cloister and chapter house. At Salisbury Cathedral, the cloister appears to serve as an atrium to its chapter house, which is set beside its east axis (Fig. 122a). That at St Paul's Cathedral was actually placed within the cloister.[60]

The employment of an octagon in all these cases, however, does require explanation and may well relate to a principal function of chapter houses that

Fig. 123 Pentecost, *St Paul's Bible*, ninth century. Mary and the Apostles occupy an eight-sided chamber

has already been mentioned. The lectern standing in the middle of each was used for readings not only of the Rule but of the community's necrology as well. During the chapter's liturgy, the names of deceased brethren and benefactors were commemorated from it on the anniversary of their deaths. Moreover, from the very first, abbots were buried either at the chapter house door in the cloister or in the chapter house itself. Nineteen are buried inside the chapter house at Fountains Abbey.[61] It would have been recognized that 8 was associated with salvation and renewal which, Augustine reminds his readers, follows circumcision and resurrection on the eighth day. Because Pentecost represented a type of salvation as well, Augustine connected the two with each other, and numerologically with 8 with characteristic ingenuity:

> [The number eight] is signified … by the Lord's Resurrection after the Sabbath … It may also be signified by the very word, Pentecost, for, if

Fig. 124 Chapter house, York Minster. The wide clear span of the vault was achieved by constructing it in timber. Note also the unusual novafoiled tracery in the triple *oculi* of each window

> what may be called an eighth unit is added to the product of seven times seven, a kind of return to the beginning is made on the day when the Holy Spirit was sent.
>
> *De sermone Domini in monte* I. 4. 12.[62]

Accordingly, just as salvation was believed to come with the re-birth of the soul at baptism and at death, so that baptisteries and *martyria* came to be habitually octagonal, so too for chapter houses, for which salvation was believed to result from the recitation in their liturgy of the names of souls departed, including those actually buried in them or at their doors. In this sense, chapter houses functioned partly as commemorative shrines and it should not be surprising that most of them followed the architectural form of *mausolea* and *martyria*. Since they were also described as the 'workshop of the Holy Spirit', which was represented by the number 7, it may also have been of significance that the enclosure of octagonal chapter houses consists of 7 walls enveloping their entrance.

It also seems relevant that chapter houses took their name from the chapters of the Rule that were read in them day by day from the lectern, and that the brethren confessed their offences and pleaded for pardon, were punished and even flogged there before the assembly, the prior and, if in residence, the abbot.[63] In addition to the transaction of the monastery's business, this association of the chapter house with obedience to the Rule is preserved in a description by the abbot of Westminster, Richard de Ware, whose allusion to the 'workshop of the Holy Spirit' has already been cited,

> It is the house of confession, the house of obedience, mercy, and forgiveness, the house of unity, peace, and tranquility, where the brethren make satisfaction for their faults.
>
> *Consuetudines* IV. 311.[64]

Ware became abbot in 1258 on completion of Westminster's chapter house and, notwithstanding its octagonal form, being Benedictine, the abbey's 'house of obedience' had particular importance, for not only was compliance with the *Rule of St Benedict* expected, so was observance of the Law as contained in the Pentateuch of the Old Testament. In the tenth century, Odo of Cluny had treated the Bible as history in his seven-volume *Odonis abbatis Cluniacensis Occupatio*. According to Odo, because Pentecost saw the visitation of the Holy Spirit upon the Apostles, this marked the creation of the ideal Christian community, which in turn lived on in the monastic life.[65] Pentecost represents a union between the Old and New Law in that it commemorates the first Christian community on the fiftieth day after Passover when Moses had initially presented the law of the Old Testament, in the form of the Ten Commandments.[66] Later in the tenth century, a colophon was added to the Bible of William of Volpiano and this is thought to refer to a work that set corresponding passages from the Old and New Testaments alongside each other, which it introduces as, 'Commands from either law this little book doth hold'.[67]

The earliest surviving centralized chapter house, dating from around 1120, is Worcester's, another Benedictine abbey and, although this is circular, its enclosure is divided internally by blind arcading in 10 bays. Two neighbouring abbeys, also Benedictine, are Pershore which also had a round chapter house and so could well have been ten-bayed as well, and Evesham, which was decagonal. This was started in about 1290. In the meantime, Lincoln's had been built and, whilst this is a secular cathedral, its architect had been working at Worcester up to that time, and Lincoln's is also decagonal (Figs 121, 122b).[68] Further north, the undated chapter house of Bridlington's Augustinian Priory may have been decagonal but this is by no means certain. One example of regional similarity is provided by the chapter house at Hereford Cathedral, which is decagonal and was built in the 1350s. This was at about the time Worcester's ten-bayed rotunda was being given its decagonal, Gothic exterior. Bearing in mind the obedientiary function of the chapter house, the importance of the law, and the significance of 10 in relation to it, a connection between them seems irresistible.

Completing the different forms adopted by chapter houses, there are two early examples where the geometry was twelve-sided. They are situated either side of Offa's Dyke at Margam Abbey in Glamorgan and further north at Dore Abbey in Herefordshire (Fig. 122c), and they were both built by the Cistercian Order. It will be recalled that Richard de Ware described the chapter house as 'the house of unity' in expression presumably of the idea of community, which could well explain the choice of a centralized form in the first place, although not its absence from the Continent; and Odo had regarded the 12 Apostles as the first Christian community. It may also be remembered that, following the departure of Judas, 12 was important enough to be maintained as their number seemingly at all costs. Consequently, monastic communities at least in the first instance commonly numbered a minimum of 12 and an abbot, just as other religious communities did later in priests' colleges and almshouses, and so it need not be surprising if this association sometimes extended to the architectural form of their chapter houses.

Among the various orders and colleges to have built polygonal chapter houses, no invariable pattern is apparent in the choice of design. Regarding their structural design, variations can be explained in practical terms. Smaller buildings, such as the chapter house at Southwell Minster, were vaulted in one clear span (Fig. 70); larger structures, such as those at Salisbury and Wells, are supported on a central pillar; York's chapter house is large, yet unsupported inside because it has a lightweight vault made of wood (Figs 69, 124). Regarding their geometric form, those of the Benedictines, Augustinians, and secular colleges could be either octagonal or decagonal, whilst those of the Cistercians were octagonal and dodecagonal.[69] If chronology is taken into account, a general pattern of geometric choice does emerge. The earliest chapter houses in the sample were decagonal and dodecagonal[70] whereas, from their first appearance perhaps around 1230, nearly all chapter houses were octagonal.[71] This seems to indicate the octagonal form being adopted as customary, for which there must have been reasons. If these were to do with expressing the commemorative function of chapter houses, why was this now preferred to the functions and geometries of the earlier structures that were not octagonal? Again, it might be expected that a single practice would be found within a particular Order, yet once two Cistercian abbeys had built dodecagonal chapter houses at the turn of the thirteenth century, another followed later that was octagonal. This might similarly be explained by chronology, since this latter example was built in the middle of the wave of octagonal chapter houses that were being erected during this later period. It was also a move that was followed by all the secular colleges, except one, this being Hereford's, which was decagonal and built around 1370. In considering the reasons for choosing one form rather than another, given the knowledge of number symbolism each chapter would have had from Augustine and others, not least from their own schooling, it is difficult to see in the polygonal geometry of their buildings anything other than a symbolical intent, both behind individual choices and behind the adoption of custom in the first place. In support of this, the three forms employed for polygonal chapter houses – the octagonal, the decagonal, and the dodecagonal – express meanings of direct relevance to their function in relation respectively to commemoration and salvation, obedience to the rule of law, and the ideal Christian community. And underlying them, once again, are the three figures of Platonic geometry, the square, the pentagon, and the equilateral triangle. Another common application of a schematic division of circles – or more particularly semicircles – and the polygonal geometry which results, and which also includes the Platonic figures, underlies the architectural geometry of chevet design.

Chevet design

Sometime shortly after 1220, Villard de Honnecourt visited the building site of Cambrai Cathedral, sixteen kilometres north of Honnecourt, and sketched the plan of its new chevet as it rose from the ground (Fig. 78).[72] The layout consists of a semicircular apse and ambulatory divided equally into 5 parts, with an inner and outer ring each of 5 columns standing on the radials of the apse and its chord, the columns in the outer ring marking the openings into 5 radiating chapels. The plan, which is preserved on folio 14v of his Portfolio, is very carefully drawn, with the compass points and arcs of its geometric construction still visible on the parchment underneath Villard's drawing of the plan.[73] The division of a semicircle into 5 parts of course is geometrically equivalent to the division of a notional circle into 10, as in the design of decagonal chapter houses and, as with the other types of polygonal chapter house, it will be seen that the design of chevets involved divisions into other numbers of parts as well (Fig. 125).[74]

Initially, the design of chevets evolved over some five decades from the plain Romanesque apse to one with an ambulatory, allowing pilgrims and processions to circulate from one side of the sanctuary to the other by passing behind the high altar; then finally to a layout with an ambulatory and chapels opening off it. The first stage in this development, which can be seen in the abbey church at Jumièges around 1037 (Fig. 126), replaced the solid wall of the apse with a semicircular colonnade, thereby requiring the division of a semicircle, and therefore its notional circle, into a specific number of parts.[75] The second stage in the development of the chevet, seen at the abbey church of St Sernin in Toulouse in the 1070s (Fig. 127),[76] called for the geometry of the apse colonnade to be harmonized with the placement of the chevet chapels around the ambulatory. That the setting out of chevets was difficult to achieve on the ground with accuracy is demonstrated by Suger's choir of St Denis' Abbey as late as 1144. Thus to be required to set out curves with a predetermined number of radial lines intersecting them at regular intervals and to have other elements, such as chevet chapels, which are themselves curved or polygonal, to be set out from the main curve of the ambulatory must have been daunting in the extreme, even with such empirical methods as implied by the five-sided tower in Villard's Portfolio. It is perhaps not

a. Division by 8, unrotated.

b. Division by 12, unrotated.

Division by evenly even numbers, eg. 8 and 12, when unrotated, produces axial columns both on the chord of the apse and behind the high altar.

By rotating circles divided by evenly even numbers, as below, the axial column behind the altar is avoided, but so also are the columns on the chord of the apse.

c. Division by 8, rotated; eg. Rouen Cathedral, Westminster Abbey.

d. Division by 12, rotated; eg. Ste Foye at Conques, Cologne Cathedral.

Division by unevenly even numbers, eg. 10 and 14, as below, produces columns on the chord of the apse, avoids the axial column behind the altar, and does not require rotation.

e. Division by 10, unrotated; eg. St Stephen at Nevers; Reims Cathedral.

f. Division by 14, unrotated; eg. St Benoît at Fleury, Santiago de Compostela.

Fig. 125 Division of the circle in the design of colonnaded apses. *Top left,* a. Division by 8 unrotated. *Top right,* b. Division by 12 unrotated. *Centre left,* c. Division by 8 rotated. *Centre right,* d. Division by 12 rotated. *Bottom left,* e. Division by 10 unrotated. *Bottom right,* f. Division by 14 unrotated

surprising therefore that many of the formal relationships examined in this survey are approximate at best, including the chevet of St Sernin.

There is also evidence that difficulties in setting-out on site were initially preceded by uncertainty over the geometric relationships that were to be desired at design stage. For example, in the early chevet of St Stephen's Priory at Nevers (Fig. 128), which dates from around 1083, the mismatch between the division of its apse colonnade according to the decagon and the alignment of its chapels according to the hexagon has produced severe distortion in the bays of the ambulatory.[77] This was soon to be improved upon, as shown by the church of Ste Foy at Conques where an earlier apse was replaced by its chevet around 1100 (Fig. 129).[78] Here the arrangement of chapels and ambulatory vaulting results from their projection outwards, however imprecisely, from the centre of the apse through its colonnade, which appears at first sight to be

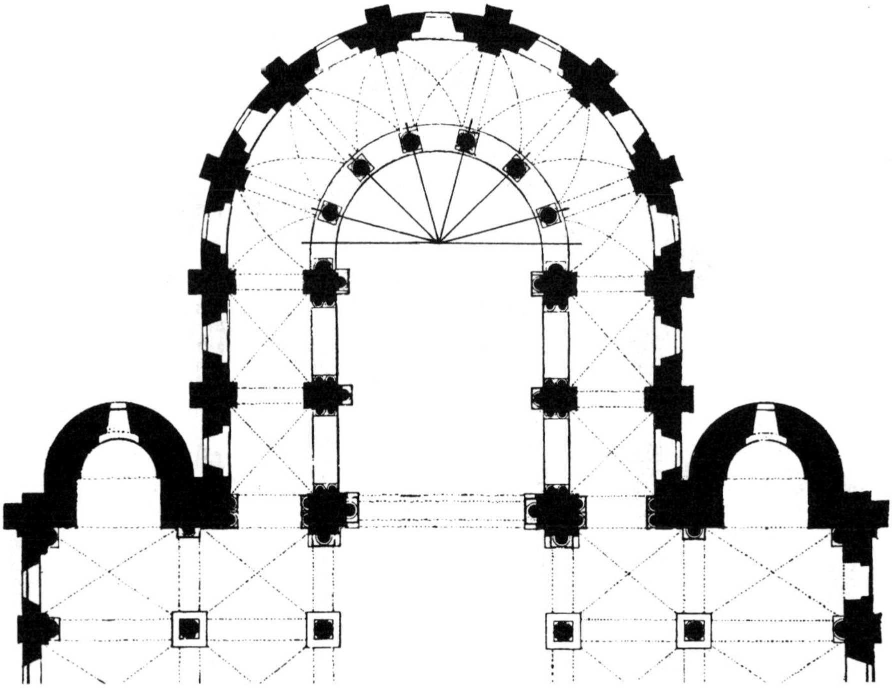

Fig. 126 Plan, east end, Jumièges abbey church, with its apse colonnade divided by seven

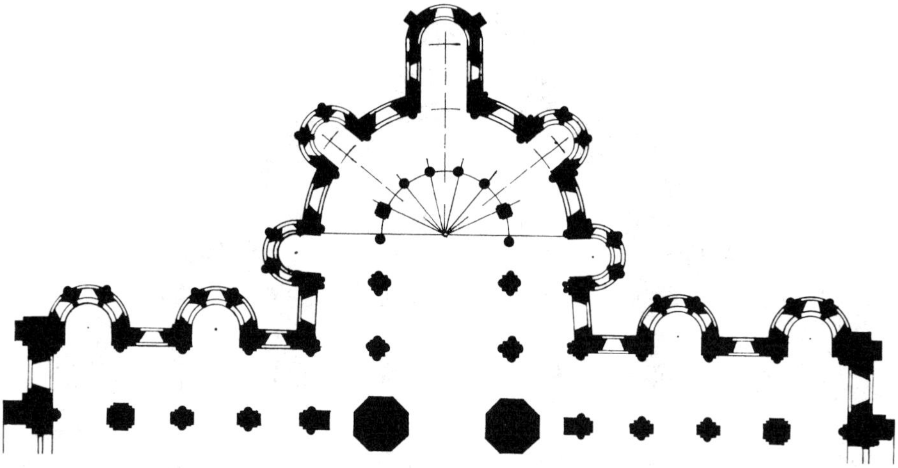

Fig. 127 Plan, chevet, St Sernin's abbey church, Toulouse. Both the apse colonnade and the three chapels east of its chord radiate from the same point. The colonnade is divided by seven, and the chapels are centred on its second, fourth, and sixth bays. The original copies of the plans used in Figs 127–30 were obtained from the architects in charge of the monuments and have not been regularized for publication. The geometric constructions applied to them are regular and show the correlation between the structures as built and possibly as meant

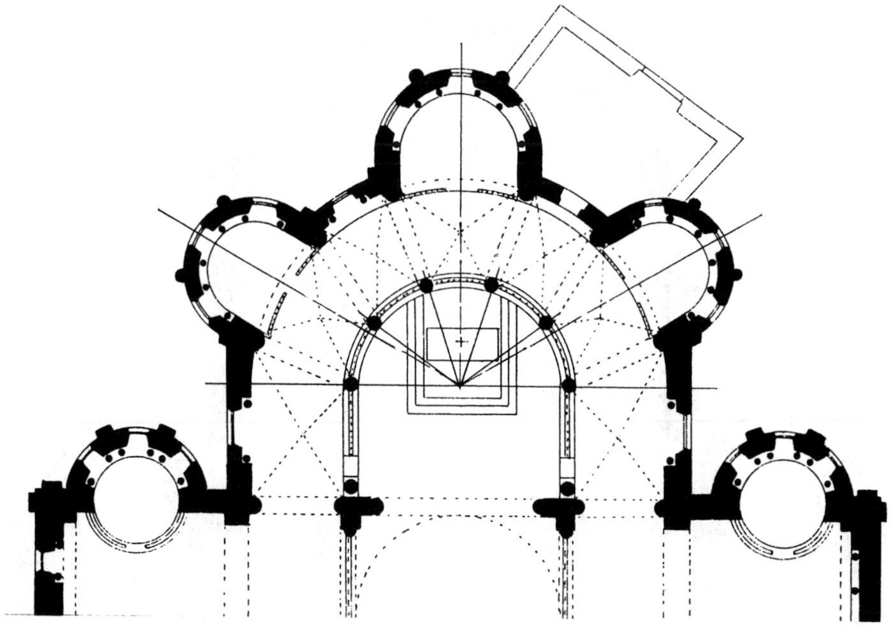

Fig. 128 Plan, chevet, St Stephen's priory church, Nevers. The semicircle of the apse colonnade is divided by five, whilst the chapels radiate from a half-hexagon at 30° and 90°. It can be seen that the mismatch between the two geometries causes severe distortion in the vaulting bays of the ambulatory

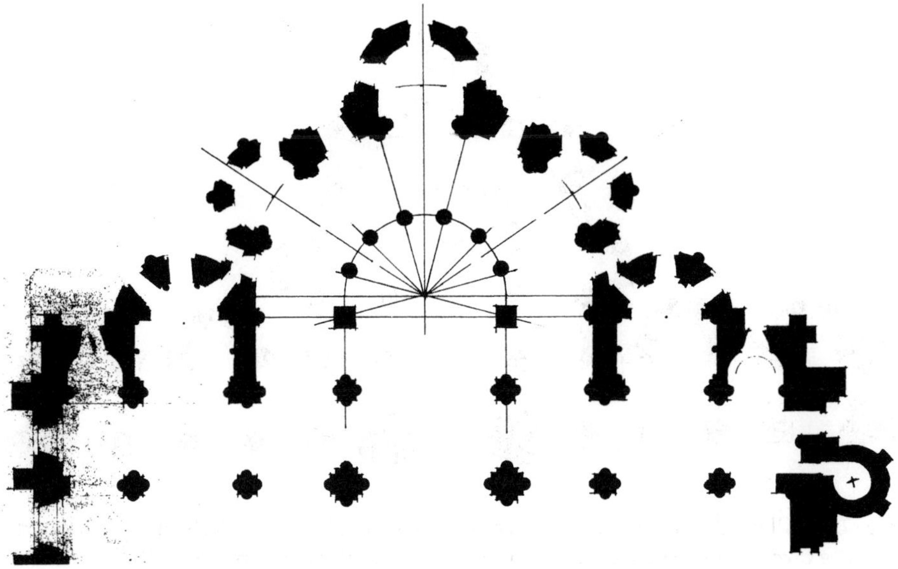

Fig. 129 Plan, chevet, Ste Foye's abbey church, Conques. The apse colonnade is set out from a rotated dodecagon. The chapels radiate from the same centre but their positioning was apparently fixed empirically, rather than from a regular division of a circle, their angles being 90° and c. 34°

divided into 7. However, the centre-point of the apse lies between the easterly piers of the choir and the first columns of the apse. Once this is taken into account, it turns out that the geometry of the chevet is derived from the division of a circle into 12. This produces a semicircle in 6 parts which has been rotated so as to avoid a column standing on the main axis behind the altar, a solecism that was hardly ever allowed to happen outside the Cistercian Order and Germany. However, rotating a dodecagon also fails to locate columns on the chord of the apse (Fig. 125d). Indeed, in many instances, the chords of apses lie forward of the last straight bay of choir arcades. This means that the east–west axis of the choir arcades has to project beyond their last pier, then turn into the curve of the apse as it crosses the chord, without there being another pier to articulate the change in direction (Figs 125c, d). It was a discrepancy that could be made good between the last pier in the choir arcade and the first pier in the apse. The same dilemma arose when chevet design employed the geometry of the octagon. This was invariably applied rotated, for the same reason that this avoids an axial column behind the altar, so there is none marking the chord of the apse either. As a corollary, because the diameter of a polygon is less than the diameter of the circle circumscribing it, the distance between the first piers of an octagonally-generated apse is less than the width of the straight bays of the choir to the west of it. This difference was again made good in the bay bridging the straight bays and the apse, either by the curvature of the arcade wall or by canting the wall in towards the first apse piers, as in Rouen Cathedral around 1202 and Westminster Abbey from 1245 (Fig. 125c, 131a).

According to the evidence of these examples at Conques, Nevers, Toulouse, Rouen, and elsewhere, it can be seen that various manipulations in chevet design were being tried that addressed, at least empirically, some of the geometric principles involved in the dividing of circles and the generating of polygons necessary in the design of chevets. Evidently emerging from these experiments was a realization that dividing a circle by 12, being an evenly even number that is quartered, produces axial columns when unrotated (Fig. 125b). Therefore to avoid an axial column behind the altar, it was necessary to rotate the dodecagon, and this was the chosen method in a number of cases despite this also having the effect of foregoing columns on the chord of the apse (Fig. 125d). To produce columns here but not behind the altar, it was necessary to divide the circle by unevenly even numbers, such as 10 and 14, which also dispenses with the need to rotate the geometry (Fig. 125e, f).

Such a solution appears at the Cluniac abbey of Fleury perhaps around 1100 (Fig. 130), at about the time of Conques' new chevet.[79] Here the geometry of the apse colonnade produces not only columns parted either side of the main axis but also places a pair on the chord of the apse as well, thereby articulating the first straight bay of the choir and the first radial bays of the chevet, as it had at Nevers. This was made possible by dividing the circle by an unevenly even number, in this case 14, thereby avoiding the necessity to rotate the geometry.[80]

The dome of the Pantheon, it may be remembered, is divided into 28 segments, which, along with the division of a circle into 14, requires it first to

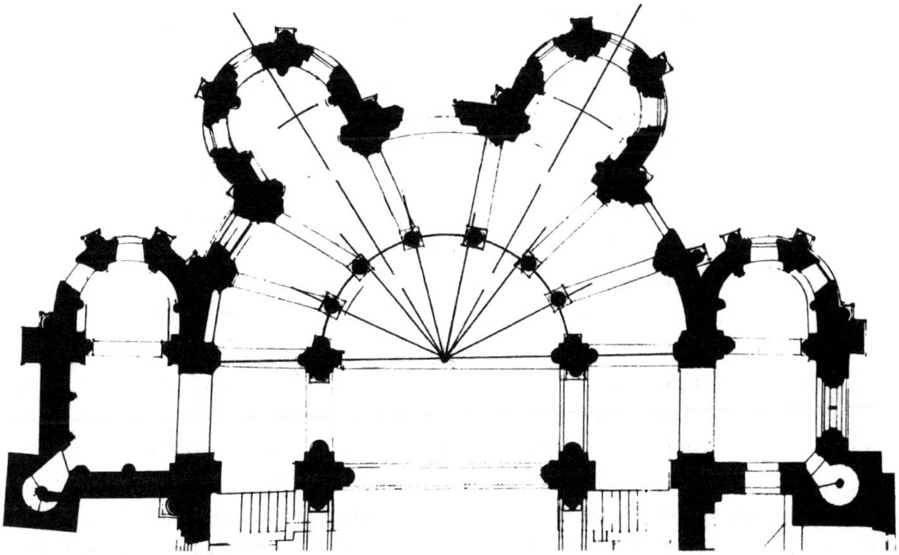

Fig. 130 Plan, chevet, St Benoît-sur-Loire abbey church, Fleury. The apse colonnade is divided by seven, whilst the two chapels are set out from a rotated half-hexagon

be divided into 7. This would have had to depend on non-Euclidean geometry, for which empirical procedures existed. By knotting a cord into 13 equal parts, a 5 : 4 : 4 triangle can be constructed, the base angles of which are virtually a seventh part of a circle, as 51°19' to just over 51°25'.[81] Another method for constructing a heptagon was among those published by Roriczer late in the fifteenth century.[82] Although this division of a circle does not accord with Platonic geometry, the Pythagorean association of the number 7 as the number neither begetting, nor begotten by, any other number in the decad, thence in Christian terms signifying the Holy Spirit, might have made such a division legitimate to anyone concerned. However this may have been justified, it was certainly common in chevet design, although not necessarily so easily executed in other contexts. The *oculus* in the south transept window of Laon Cathedral is, exceptionally, an attempt at a design around a seven-pointed star that is seriously botched.[83]

For the purposes of this study, a sample of thirty-four churches and cathedrals was analysed where construction commenced between the 1030s and 1270s. They were drawn mainly from France, where the chevet was first developed, and other areas of particular French contact (Fig. 131).[84] The earlier examples were mainly Benedictine abbeys, followed by most of the principal cathedrals around the Ile-de-France. The findings were that the chevet of only one in the sample was based on a hexagon;[85] the apses of all the others were semicircles which resulted from dividing a circle into 8, 10, 12, or 14 parts. Those derived from the octagon were four in number and their starting dates are relatively late, between 1174 and 1245 (Fig. 131a).[86] Fifteen chevets were generated by the decagon and were by far the most numerous (Fig. 131b).

Figs 131a–e The geometry of chevet design
a. Division by 4, Westminster Abbey. The apse colonnade is half a rotated octagon. The chapels originally numbered five before the replacement of the axial chapel. Despite their number, the setting-out ingeniously extends the geometry of the rotated octagon, with their centres aligned to 45°, 90°, and the chord of the apse

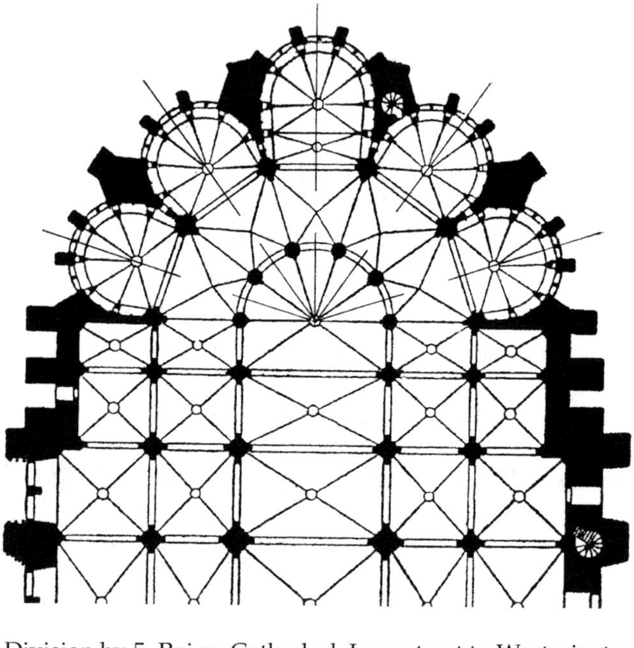

Fig. 131b Division by 5, Reims Cathedral. In contrast to Westminster Abbey, the apse colonnade and chapels conform to the division of the apse by five, with the chapels centred on each bay of the colonnade

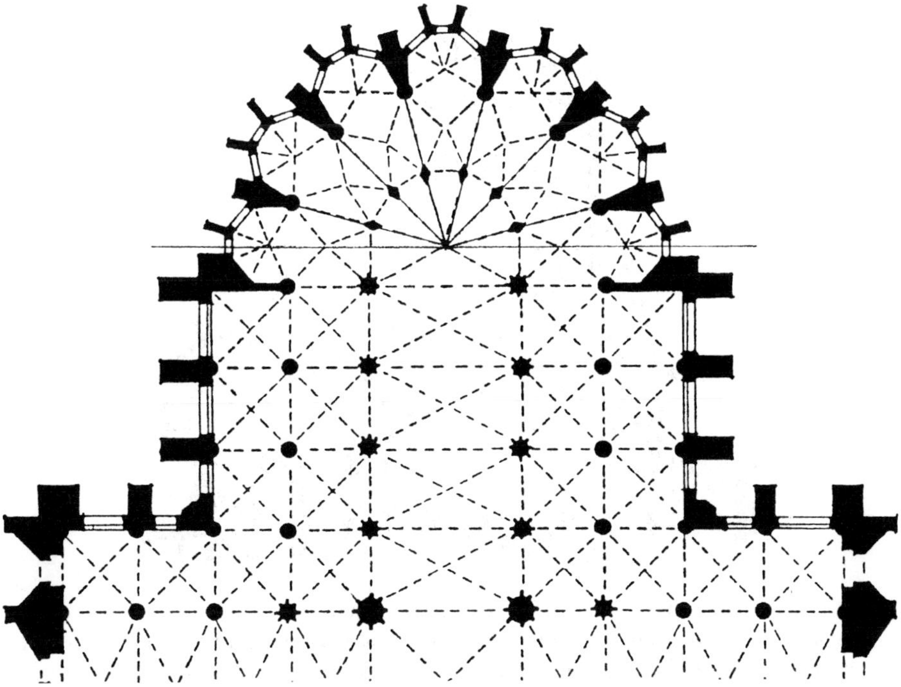

Fig. 131c Division by 6, Cologne Cathedral. Like Reims, the apse colonnade and chapels conform to a single geometric system, this time employing a rotated dodecagon

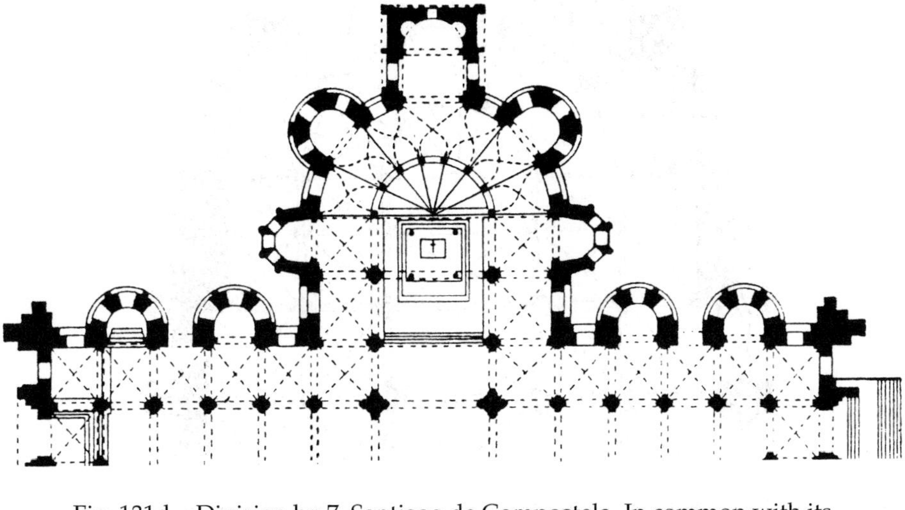

Fig. 131d Division by 7, Santiago de Compostela. In common with its contemporary, St Sernin in Toulouse, Santiago's apse colonnade is divided by seven, with the three chapels east of its chord centred on the second, fourth, and sixth bays

Fig. 131e Division by 7 and 12, Chartres Cathedral. The keystone of the apse vault lies forward of the chord of the apse, which coincides with the last straight bay of the choir. To avoid confusion, the keystone and its radiating ribs have been replaced on the drawing by the geometry of the chevet at floor level. This consists of a division by seven for the apse colonnade, combined with two rotated dodecagons for the intermediate ambulatory colonnade and chapels, i.e. at 15°, 30°, 45°, and 60°. All radials are shown in their correct alignments as distinct from the alignments as built

Although not among the earliest in the sample, commencement of construction ranged from 1083 to 1277.[87] The dodecagon featured in seven examples, including the earliest,[88] but with the greater concentration occurring among Gothic monuments (Fig. 131c).[89] Another six displayed a division by 14 and, with the exception of one,[90] all are Romanesque (Fig. 131d).[91] Finally, one combined a division by 12 with one of 14 (Fig. 131e).[92]

The early experiments in harmonizing the radial geometry of apse colonnades with chevet chapels largely resulted in the straightforward application of the regular geometry that is evident in most of the layouts in the sample, but the adjustments did not end there. It has been shown, for example, that the circuit of chapels at St Denis consists of two arcs, each with its own centre and radius.[93] This has the effect of making the axial chapel and the one either side of it deeper than the pairs to the north and south, which remain concentric with the double colonnades, but without affecting the underlying polygonal geometry. Two further instances of geometric adjustment have been demonstrated at the cathedrals of Amiens and Beauvais,[94] and these appear to have resulted in modified dodecagons. Being rotated, the centre-point of each chevet lies forward of the last straight bay of the choir and, in order to satisfy compositional requirements that can only be conjectured, the middle five of the seven chapels have been bunched more closely together than if they had been segments of a regular dodecagon. The unseen result of this is that the segments to the north and south that are bisected by the chord of the apse are wider than they would be in a regular figure.[95] This recalls the similar, but visible, adjustment made to the colonnade around the interior of S. Costanza, where the radials are widened either side of its main axes to imply a cruciform within its sixteen-sided figure (Fig. 103). In succession to Amiens and Beauvais, Westminster Abbey combines an apse, which is a rotated octagon, with the layout of five chapels found, significantly, at Reims, where the apse is half a decagon (Fig. 131b).[96] This is an example of geometric synthesis reminiscent of earlier experiments, which might also explain the example of Chartres (Fig. 131e). Here, the Gothic building was largely rebuilt over its Romanesque predecessor, the chevet of which had three chapels; one axial and two radiating from its centre at 45°. The Gothic chevet followed the outline of these, adding new chapels in between them. These range around a double ambulatory and an apse colonnade with seven openings. Thus the basis of the apse geometry is half a fourteen-sided polygon, but its radials do not correlate with the intermediate piers around the ambulatory. Allowing for irregularities that are undoubtedly the result of adapting the Gothic layout to the Romanesque, these piers can be positioned by two dodecagons, one rotated over the other and, because dodecagons are quartered, these automatically harmonize with the 45° axes of the original radiating chapels.[97]

Among other variations in the sample were the mixture of columns and piers around the apse and in the choir arcades, also the number of chevet chapels. Sometimes, the apse and choir arcades share a similar type of column;[98] at other times, columns in the apse are differentiated from piers in the choir arcading; in other examples, there are no columns or piers on the chord of the apse, which is when the dodecagon has been adopted, being invariably rotated.[99] The number of chevet chapels also varies, and there seems to be a fairly loose correlation between their number and the generating geometry of the chevet.

In viewing the sample as a whole, it is only to be expected that such variations should lead to the proliferation of different layouts found in the sample. Yet there is a remarkable degree of consistency present in at least one respect. With the exception of only two buildings, and notwithstanding the different variations possible, if the columns standing around each apse are counted, they always number 4, 6, or 8.[100] When the geometry is octagonal, there are 4 columns, without any on the chord; when it is decagonal, there are 4 columns, plus 2 more on the chord, making 6; dividing the apse into 6 and rotating it produces 6 columns, without any on the chord; and dividing it by 7 also gives 6 columns, plus 2 on the chord, making 8. From this, it may be of a significance yet to be determined that apses divided into 5 were twice as numerous as any other; that all but one apse divided into 7 were Romanesque in origin; and all but two, when divided by 6, were Gothic. Whilst most of the later cathedrals showed division by 5 or 6, one of these two exceptions is Chartres (Fig. 131e). However, it has been observed that the Gothic cathedral was largely rebuilt over the plan of its Romanesque predecessor, which dated from the 1020s. At this earlier period, division by 7 was much more common and this is precisely the geometry revealed by Chartres' present apse. Some consistency can also be seen between the modified geometry of the chevets at Amiens and Beauvais, which was begun by a master from Amiens, and between the five-part division of the apses at Reims and Cambrai (Figs 131b, 78), which was in the archdiocese of Reims and where construction commenced only a decade after work on Reims began.

Just as a limited variation is possible between a particular number of chapels and the subdivision of apses, so there is between the subdivision of apses and the number of columns around them. There will be 4 columns in an apse if the geometry is octagonal, or if it is decagonal and there are piers marking the ends of the apse chord. There will be 6 in a decagonal apse if the columns on the chord are similar, or if the geometry is dodecagonal and rotated. The columns will also number 6 if the apse is in 7 parts and there are piers on the chord, or 8 if the columns around the apse and on the chord are the same. This means that the choice of geometry, the choice in the number of columns, and the differentiation between column and pier design could be made independently of each other, but only to a limited extent. One reason why the octagon occurs in such a small minority of plans in the sample could be that, being a relatively low subdivision of a semicircle, the columns are the most widely spaced apart including, crucially, the bay spanning across the apse chord between the last pier in the straight bays and the first in the apse. This could have been regarded as a constructional disadvantage.[101] It is also easy to see that an odd number of columns would be avoided, given the evident aversion to an axial pier behind the altar.[102] It is perhaps understandable therefore that when part-octagons became commonly adopted later in the Middle Ages and mainly in the German world, they were solid apses without ambulatories, and so did not inherit these problems. This leaves the common occurrence of 4 and 6 columns around the apse itself, with or without another pair on the chord. On examining the plans of chevets, constructionally it seems difficult to do with fewer than 4, or to fit any more than 6 into even the widest of apses, as may be demonstrated by the chevet of Beauvais Cathedral.

An interesting correlation has been pointed out among French cathedrals between the geometry of their chevets and the number of bays in the nave.[103] The apses at Paris and Reims (Fig. 131b) depend on a division of their schematic circles by 10, which is also the number of their nave bays; there are 7 bays around Chartres' apse and 7 bays in its nave; at Amiens, the 7 bays around its apse are also matched by 7 in the nave. This could either be a coincidence, given the small number of examples, or it might have been an idea that was highly localized and short-lived. If so, it may be reasonable to speculate a desire to achieve a form of harmony between the sacral and lay halves of the cathedral. Important though this may have been, however, the focus of the internal space remained the high altar and its setting, where the spirit of Christ was believed to reside (Fig. 132). Consequently the details of that setting, including the design of the apse, would most certainly have mattered, not least as an aid to contemplation. It has been seen that 3 windows above a high altar might remind a worshipper of the light of the Holy Trinity, and were therefore probably placed there for that same reason. Likewise, since Suger reported that the columns around his sanctuary at St Denis stood for the 12 Apostles, even though there are only 10, there is no reason why 4 columns around apses elsewhere should not have signified the 4 Evangelists upholding the teaching of Christ, or 6 the celebration of God's Creation, or 8 the hope of salvation. With the arches joining them and the windows above them numbering 5 or 7, this would complete a matrix of meaning with references to the Law or the Holy Spirit, all concentrated upon the sanctuary, the most holy place in the house of God. Since there is firm support for number and geometry being used expressively in architectural design and monumental art, it would be anomalous for them to be deployed elsewhere in a church and not around its high altar. Neither is it impossible that the divisions of the notional circles underlying different chevets may sometimes have been of formative interest.

Complex though the evidence is, it seems to suggest, not surprisingly, a collaboration between the builders and the chapter or building committee. It might be expected that the number of chevet chapels would have been a matter of choice by a chapter. It is conceivable, for instance, that the somewhat unusual number of 9 chapels inferred from Suger's description of his sanctuary at St Denis, could have been inspired by the 9 Orders of Angels famously envisioned by Dionysius.[104] His writings after all were the prized possession of an abbey which thought it had been named after him, and Suger knew the text in question.[105] A prescribed number of chapels would lead the builders to the required division of the apse and ambulatory, whereafter other constructional considerations, such as the question of the axial pier and the need or otherwise to have columns on the chord of the apse, would have determined the particular choice of polygon and whether or not it was to be rotated. It is easy to imagine that the plan, in whatever form, would then have been approved by the chapter, possibly seeing in it the interpretive possibilities of the composition of arcade and windows around the high altar. It would always incorporate 4, 6, or 8 columns, each possessing clear connotations for contemplation, just as the solid part-octagons of later apses could be understood as enclosing their altars with the geometry associated with salvation. This is not to argue that this was the only process possible for evolving and approving a design and it is a question that will be taken up again in the discussion of tracery design below. To continue this investigation, a comparable typology exists where the division of circles is explicit; is often

Fig. 132 Sanctuary, Norwich Cathedral

tied to specific meaning; and it is to be seen in portrayals of the wheel of fortune, the zodiac, and the wheels of life and Scripture.

Part Two: The Circle as Wheel

Wheels of Fortune and Life

The wheel in the iconography of Antiquity was recognized not only as a symbol of the sun, with its spokes suggesting rays, but the passage of the sun and the turning of the wheel also made the wheel a symbol of time and, by extension, the fluctuations of fortune.[106] It has already been shown that wheels of fortune were depicted with spokes numbering 6 or 12, as well as 8 (Figs 63, 65),[107] and examples can be found dating from the twelfth century – notably the wheel window of St Stephen's Church at Beauvais (Fig. 64) – with more divided by 6 and 8 extending into the fifteenth century.[108] However, other examples from the fourteenth and fifteenth centuries, many of them illustrating the relevant passage from Boethus's *De consolatione Philosophiae*,[109] show wheels of fortune divided into 5, 7, 9, and 13 parts as well,[110] which might challenge the supposition of any consistent expression of intended meaning. Across the complete range, some wheels are drawn with obvious deliberation, others less so, while some seem almost incidental to the scene in which they appear.[111] One example from the French translation of *De consolatione* by Jean de Meun, of around 1460, is drawn divided into 6 with great precision as a geometric abstraction of a wheel composed of equilateral triangles (Fig. 134).[112]

A similar diversity is met in the theme that lies behind an off-shoot of the wheel of fortune. This is the wheel of life, which depicts the 10 ages of man, such as seen in the *De Lisle Psalter* (Fig. 135).[113] There is a large wall-painting of one in St Mary's church at Kempley in Gloucestershire, also of the fourteenth century (Fig. 133) and another nearby in Leominster Priory, possibly of the thirteenth century.[114] Unlike the wheel of fortune, which the goddess turns 'this way and that',[115] engulfing 'mankind ... with the antics of fate',[116] the wheel of life turns but once during a mortal's time on earth, marking the rise and decline in its stages as a prelude to the next life.[117] Yet if the 10 couplets around the wheel of life in the *De Lisle Psalter* are examined, there is only an approximate correlation between verse and image, and the ages that are exemplified up to death arguably amount to 7:

> Meek am I and humble, I live on pure milk.
> Never shall I stumble, I measure my age.
> A life worthy of the world is tested by the mirror.
> Not the mirror's image, but life itself delights.
> I am king, I rule the world, the entire world is mine.
> I take up a staff for myself, at death's door.
> Given over to decrepitude, death shall be my lot.
> Given over to feebleness, I begin to fail.

Fig. 133 Wheel of Life, St Mary's church, Kempley

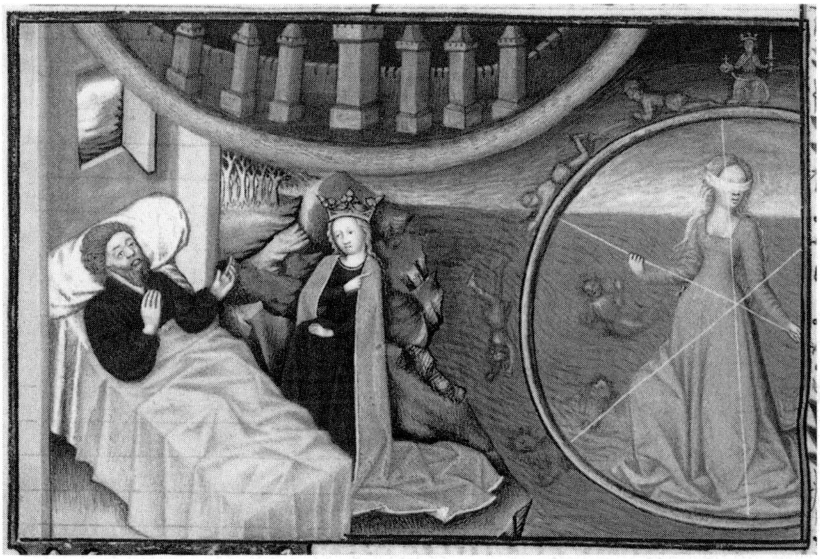

Fig. 134 Wheel of Fortune, Boethius, *De consolatione*, tr. Jean de Meun, c. 1460

Fig. 135 Wheel of Life, *De Lisle Psalter*, fourteenth century

> I thought that I would go on living, life has deceived me.
> I have been turned to ashes, life has deceived me.[118]

It may be noticed that the sixth, seventh, and eighth verses hardly represent stages in life that are truly distinct from each other and, in the tenth verse, the person is already dead. Another wheel of life, in an Irish manuscript dating from late in the thirteenth century, similarly appears to be making up the numbers to the decad, leading to the geometry of the decagon in the showing of the wheel.[119]

The habit of rounding up the quantities of things to a number that was significant generically was well established. Following the defection and death of Judas, the number of the Apostles had to be restored to the original 12; Suger made up the rings of 10 columns around his sanctuary to 12 to represent the Apostles; yet, conversely, at both the south portal of Chartres and the west portal of Amiens, column figures of only 10 Apostles stand in two groups of 5 either side of each door.[120] The decad was likewise a number that represented completeness and, both as the sum of the tetract and the number embodying all numbers, perfection as well. Approaching the end of his *Historia ecclesiastica*, Eusebius announced that,

> ... having now added ... the tenth tome ... we shall dedicate this ... to thee, my most holy Paulinus (bishop of Tyre). ... and fitly in a perfect number we shall here place the perfect and panegyrical discourse on the restoration of ... churches.
>
> *Historia ecclesiastica* X. 1.[121]

Boethius explained how the three basic types of medial proportion came to be expanded to 10:

> ... these are the three ways to knowledge: arithmetic, geometric, harmonic. After these relationships of proportions there are three others, which are conveyed to us without names ... Then later thinkers, on account of the perfection of the number ten, which was pleasing to Pythagoras, added four other kinds, so that in these proportionalities they brought together a body of proportions ten in number.
>
> *De arithmetica* II. 41.[122]

With a slightly different line of reasoning, yet reaching a similar conclusion, Guy d'Eu, the monk who was put in charge of the Cistercians' chant reform in the twelfth century, explained the expansion of the octave, or diapason, into the decachord. This was argued partly on the grounds that the first and last voices of the octave lack the 'dignity' of the intermediate notes because, unlike them, they can only descend or ascend respectively, an argument which Guy also partly based on the authority of the Psalm:[123]

> I will sing a new song unto thee, O God:
> Upon a psaltery and an instrument of ten strings will I sing praises unto thee.
>
> Psalm 144. 9.

> So the authority of the psalter agrees with this number because it is known to be the decachord; and the equality of dignity mentioned above, which is given to the voices of the diapason; and the necessity of notation, which finds such certainty in this number that no chant of ten voices or less can exist which cannot be written down …
>
> Guy d'Eu, *Regulae de arte musica* I. 6. 294.[124]

With regard to the decagonal wheel of life, the rather loose associations between the distinguishable ages of man and the decad noted above are matched by the somewhat diffuse traditions behind the idea of the different stages in human life, which can number 4, 5, 6, 7, or 12 as well as 10. One architectural example demonstrates a further variation. Around the top half of the rose window in the south transept of Amiens Cathedral a relief of the rim of a half-wheel, dating from about 1300, has been carved with 8 figures either side of the usual figure at the top (Fig. 136). To the left, facing the front, the figures rise, and to the right they fall, indicating the wheel turning clockwise.[125] Not surprisingly, this has been taken to be another wheel of fortune,[126] yet, because the rising figures are unbearded and those falling are bearded, they may also be referring to the ages of man,[127] which, in this case, would be numbering 16, discounting the figure at the top. Given such diffusion, consistency is difficult to establish, as is the case with wheels of fortune. Nevertheless, whilst each variation justified its own number, carrying with it its own logic, variations in the geometry of other *rotae* may similarly derive from different systems of thought and individual circumstances. It seems perfectly possible for instance to envisage an artist focusing on the allegorical content involved in portraying the legend of *Fortuna* without this necessarily extending always to the construction of her wheel. Dividing it, for example, into 6 or 8 could sometimes have been a personal preference, or draughting habit, as might apply to illustrating the tread-wheel of a lifting machine on a building site (Fig. 137);[128] it would be difficult to see the execution of a subject as mundane as this being meant to express a universal truth. On the other hand, the hexagonal wheel in the 1460 copy of Jean de Meun's translation of *De consolatione* (Fig. 134) is definitely illustrative of the geometry of the hexagon as an abstraction, there being no attempt at realism at all in its presentation; its radials are the lines of theoretical geometry, not the spokes of a wheel. Similarly, the correspondence seen in the wheel of fortune in the *Carmina Burana* between its octagonal geometry and its 4 figures and 4 inscriptions also has an integrity which must have been meant (Fig. 65). A case might be made therefore for alternative systems of thought being in operation, which could be used to explain these two principal divisions of Fortune's wheel, by 6 and by 8, which at least on certain occasions might have been intended by the artist.

Fortune and the zodiac

The division of wheels of fortune by 6 and 12, as attested by the manuscript evidence cited here, also by the drawing of one in Villard's Portfolio (Fig. 63),

Fig. 136 South transept rose, Amiens Cathedral. The half-wheel of fortune and life encircles the upper half of the rose window

Fig. 137 Treadwheel, building site; *Old Testament*, France, thirteenth century

and by the north transept wheel window at St Stephen's, Beauvais (Fig. 64), connects the turning wheel with the passing of time, and, when divided by 12, with the measure and division of time. It also juxtaposes the related ideas of fortune and fate, governed, as the latter was believed to be, by the 12 houses of the zodiac (Fig. 66). Any other division of a circle would not work in expressing these concepts and so its choice must at least sometimes have been deliberate, beyond that of being a draughting expedient. Alongside these examples, the wheel of fortune divided into 8 parts describes a world in balance; between ruling and ruled, rising and falling, as *Fortuna* 'hurls some down, raises others up',[129] thereby defining the 4 conditions of man. There are no others; anything else is intermediary, and they equate with the quadripartite composition of astrological man, the zodiac cousin of fate, with the 4 elements of which he is composed in their 4 states, his character formed by the 4 humours producing the 4 temperaments.[130] Furthermore, emphasizing the principle of quartering are the descriptions of those 4 conditions – *Regnabo* –

Regno – Regnavi – Sum sine regno – circling the wheel, regardless of the number of figures or spokes shown in a particular image. It is a quartering at one with that of the world in *mappae mundi*, and the connection between the two was made at least once. Possibly late in the twelfth century, a mosaic floor was laid in the Church of S. Salvatore in Turin in which a wheel of fortune is the centrepiece of a geometrically stylized map of the world, and Isidore of Seville (c. 570–636) had likened the earth to a wheel rotating at the centre of the universe.[131]

Ezekiel's Wheel

Within a few years of the wheel of fortune being incorporated into the north transept window of St Stephen's Church at Beauvais, Suger started rebuilding the west block of his abbey Church of St Denis in 1140 and, dominating its central bay, another wheel window was constructed. This, evidently, was also divided into 12 and has been likened to Ezekiel's Wheel from the part played by wheels in the prophet's vision.[132]

> And I looked, and, behold, a whirlwind came out of the north, a great cloud, and a fire infolding itself, and a brightness was about it … out of the midst of the fire.
> Also out of the midst thereof came the likeness of four living creatures. And this was their appearance; they had the likeness of a man.
> And every one had four faces, and every one had four wings.
> And their feet were straight feet …
> And they had the hands of a man under their wings on their four sides; and they four had their faces and their wings.
> Their wings were joined one to another; they turned not when they went; they went every one straight forward.
> As for the likeness of their faces, they four had the face of a man, and the face of a lion, on the right side: and they four had the face of an ox on the left side; they four also had the face of an eagle. …
> And they went every one straight forward: whither the spirit was to go, they went …
> As for the likeness of the living creatures, their appearance was like burning coals of fire, and like the appearance of lamps: it went up and down among the living creatures; and the fire was bright, and out of the fire went forth lightning.
> And the living creatures ran and returned as the appearance of a flash of lightning.
> Now as I beheld the living creatures, behold one wheel upon the earth by the living creatures, with his four faces.
> The appearance of the wheels and their work was like unto the colour of a beryl: and they four had one likeness: and their appearance and their work was as it were a wheel in the middle of a wheel.
> When they went, they went upon their four sides: and they turned not when they went.
> As for their rings, they were so high that they were dreadful; and their rings were full of eyes round about them four.

> And when the living creatures went, the wheels went by them: and when the living creatures were lifted up from the earth, the wheels were lifted up.
> Whithersoever the spirit was to go, they went, thither was their spirit to go; and the wheels were lifted up over against them: for the spirit of the living creatures was in the wheels.
>
> Ezekiel I. 4–20.

Dionysius the Pseudo-Areopagite ends his mystical treatise, *De coelesti hierarchia*, with his own anagogical interpretation of these passages:

> ... it is possible that the iconography of the wheels of the mind be explained by another uplifting [of the mind from perceptible images to intelligent meanings]. For, as [Ezekiel] has pointed out, they are called 'Gelgel', which in Hebrew signifies both 'revolving' and 'revealing'. Those Godlike wheels of fire 'revolve' about themselves in their ceaseless movement around the Good, and they 'reveal' since they expose hidden meanings, and lift up the mind from below and carry the most exalted enlightenments down to the lowliest.
>
> *De coelesti hierarchia*, 339D, 340A.[133]

In their commentaries on Ezekiel, Jerome and Gregory the Great transmitted the prefiguring of the Evangelists' symbolic beasts in Ezekiel as well as their integration into the quaternity of the world and man.[134] They also underline the wheel's function in carrying the Word,[135] which Jerome likens to the Lord's chariot being drawn by the 4 Evangelists as if they were a team of horses.

> Matthew, Mark, Luke and John are the Lord's team of four, the true cherubim or store of knowledge. With them the whole body is full of eyes, they glitter as sparks, they run and return like lightning, their feet are straight feet, and lifted up, their backs are also winged, ready to fly in all directions. They hold together each by each and are interwoven one with another; like wheels within wheels they roll along and go whithersoever the breath of the Holy Spirit wafts them.
>
> *Epistola* LIII. 9.[136]

Gregory then explains that the wheel divided into 4 symbolizes Scripture and its 4 phases of teaching, namely that imparted by the Law, the Prophets, the Evangelists, and finally the Acts of the Apostles. The wheel also represents the 4 mysteries of Christ – his Incarnation, Sacrifice, Resurrection, and Ascension – represented respectively by the Evangelists' symbols of man, ox, lion, and eagle.[137] The wheel therefore was seen as a symbol of Scripture, associated with the 4 Evangelists, with Ezekiel's wheel within another wheel being interpreted as the New Testament foretold by the Old.[138] Whether or not this was the intended message of St Denis' wheel window, it surely was in various Italian examples. Besides the wheel of fortune windows already cited at Verona and Trento,[139] and other wheel windows at Fossanova and Orvieto,[140] those at S. Ruffino in Assisi, also at S. Maria Maggiore and S. Pietro, both in Tuscania, all date from the thirteenth century, are quartered into 12

Fig. 138 Wheel of Scripture, west front, S. Ruffino, Assisi. Readable as a wheel within a wheel, the inner wheel being divided into twelve, the outer wheel, curiously, into thirty-three. In the corners of the enclosing square are the symbols of the four Evangelists

parts, and incorporate reliefs of the 4 Evangelists' symbols in the corners of the square enclosing each window (Fig. 138).[141] It will be recalled how the idea of God being surrounded by the 4 Evangelists gave them the aspect of being his guardians and how, in the planning of Milan Cathedral at the end of the fourteenth century, its square crossing tower was to have a turret placed at each corner, expressing how 'the Lord God is seated in Paradise … and around the throne are the four Evangelists'.[142]

Wheel and rose windows

The characteristics of a wheel window consist of the open ring in its centre, analogous with the hub, from which the spokes radiate; the frequent fashioning of the spokes as colonettes, each complete with its base and capital, and carrying a circle of arches around the inside of the rim in the form of a radial arcade; and the concentric rings of the moulded rim itself, encircling the glazing as wheels within wheels. With the evolution of the wheel into the rose window and the Rayonnant Style, the spokes and their representation as circular arcades gave way to the radial geometry of undifferentiated bars of tracery (Fig. 160), before even these morphed into the curvilinear geometry of the Flamboyant Style (Fig. 167). As a later stylistic term, 'Flamboyant' appears to have been aptly chosen, as if suggesting the flames of Ezekiel's fiery wheel, even the wheel's ancient symbolism of the sun.[143] The alternative reference to them as rose windows, it has been suggested, is also a post-medieval appellation, possibly the result of a corruption of *roue*, or *roe*, which meant wheel in Old French,[144] although it is difficult to explain the arrival of the 's'. If there were any corruption, it is perhaps more likely to have been a misreading of *rota*, the Latin for wheel.[145] However, there is strong circumstantial evidence supporting both the petals of a rose and the tongues of flame being seen in the design of these windows, when it is remembered that their transformation from wheel designs coincided, from the middle years of the thirteenth century onwards, with popular associations being made in romance literature between the rose, the Virgin Mary, and the flame of love; an apparent connection which will be discussed shortly.[146]

Returning to the iconography and geometry of wheels, it may be seen that, underlying the hexagon and the octagon in wheels of fortune, the dodecagon of the zodiac, the quadripartite division of the wheel of Ezekiel and Scripture, and the decagon of the wheel of life, are the Platonic figures of the equilateral triangle, the square, and the pentagon, extending their expressive possibilities into popular culture. It is proposed now to continue the investigation with geometric tracery, being a form of linear design with an even wider public, and which associated the figurate numbers and figures of Platonic geometry with the circle.

Part Three: Tracery Design

Fig. 139 Plate and bar tracery, Bourges Cathedral. The change from one form of tracery to the other marks either a break or a progression in the building campaign

Plate and bar tracery

Literally instrumental in the design of wheel and rose windows, pointed arches of various types, and tracery, were the medieval architect's dividers. These he shared with the Divine Architect when depicted creating order out of chaos, and in portrayals of himself receiving instructions from his patron. It was in his tracing-house that he described the arcuated geometry of his designs, sometimes inscribing them on a floor or a wall for the production of templates (Fig. 140). And it was the mechanics of this activity that determined the geometric tracery of the work that resulted, consisting as it does of the abstract transformations of equilateral triangles, squares, pentagons, hexagons, and octagons into foliated versions of themselves by describing circles centred on their external angles (Fig. 141). The practice was established before the end of the twelfth century, with geometric designs cut into thin slabs of stonework known as plate tracery, when normal fenestration was otherwise left devoid of it, prompting the epithet 'lancet', and when circular windows were still constructed as wheels with radial spokes. How uncertain this practice could be in its beginnings can be seen in the gallery arcading of St Hugh's Choir in Lincoln Cathedral, dating from the 1190s. Yet within a few years, by the turn of the thirteenth century, the circular window over the west front of Chartres Cathedral shows a complete mastery of the technique (Fig. 142), being precisely cut and set as a dodecagon, its inner part a wheel, its outer part an

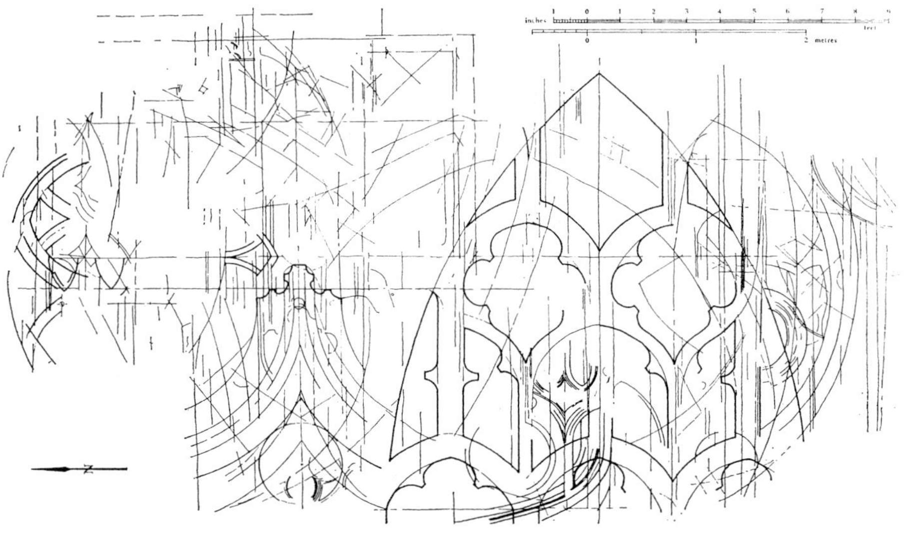

Fig. 140 Inscribed details, tracing floor, York Minster. The tracing-house at York is in the roof-space of the vestibule between the north transept and chapter house. Its floor was laid with plaster so that the architect could literally trace his working details in the plaster with the giant dividers with which he was portrayed; see Fig. 7. Among the various arcs, setting-out lines, and a moulded profile, is a large tracery design for a window

Fig. 141 Geometric tracery. The presence of the triangle, square, and pentagon, along with their derivatives, the hexagon and octagon, as generators of geometric tracery, demonstrates how profuse the Platonic figures were in Gothic architecture and art. *Top left,* a. Trefoil. *Top right,* b. Quatrefoil. *Centre left,* c. Cinquefoil. *Centre right,* d. Hexafoil. *Bottom,* e. Octafoil

orbiting of 12 octafoils interspersed by as many quatrefoils. Only a decade after this, with the invention of bar tracery came the chapel windows around the chevet of Reims Cathedral, complete with their hexafoil tracery and sketched at the time by Villard de Honnecourt. Word arrived on the building site of Bourges Cathedral soon after 1215, when the plate tracery of its

Fig. 142 West rose, Chartres Cathedral

clerestorey windows changed to bar tracery one bay into the nave (Fig. 139). While constructional design had advanced, schematic design remained constant – triple lancets, crowned by a hexafoil – in plate and bar tracery either side of the break.

Geometric tracery

The liberating influence of bar tracery unleashed a host of geometric designs on both sides of the English Channel, regular at first in the Rayonnant Style of northern France and the Geometric Decorated of England, before becoming freer and more naturalistic towards the fourteenth century with the Flamboyant and Curvilinear Decorated Styles either side of the Channel. It was produced variously as open tracery, or glazed, or as blind tracery articulating the surfaces of walls to frame the compositions of their paintings. Along with the cusping of arches, the most common geometric *motif* was the circle, whether surmounting a two-light aisle window or dominating the main facades of choir, nave, or transepts. Here the great *oculi* and roses of these windows were themselves usually filled with the tracery of smaller circles, recalling Ezekiel's 'wheels within wheels' and his 'rings full of eyes'. Construction of the choir of Beauvais Cathedral followed that of Bourges (Fig. 143), with the two-light glazed passage of its apse ringed inside by open cinquefoils, each bay of the soaring clerestorey above crowned by a hexafoil and two quatrefoils, thereby embodying the three Platonic figures. Meanwhile the Angel Choir was being added to Lincoln Cathedral, with a full range of foliated geometry in its clerestoreys, galleries, aisles, and east window, including triangles of blind *vesica piscis* figures in the spandrels of the main arcade implying Trinities of interlacing circles (Figs 151, 153). At the same time, around 1270, two pairs of three-light windows were being inserted into the square east end of Romsey Abbey (Fig. 144), where the tracery of each upper window displays a quatrefoil above two cinquefoils – curiously, the northerly pair of cinquefoils is inverted – whilst the lower windows are composed of a hexafoil above two quatrefoils. Into the second decade of the fourteenth century, the choir of St Ouen's Abbey in Rouen was being built and its aisle windows consist of six lights, crowned by a cinquefoil and two trefoils, above a pair of quatrefoils and another of trefoils (Fig. 145). The trefoils are again an interlocking of *vesica piscis* figures, overlaid by a circle. Running through all these designs are the circle and the three figurate numbers of Platonic geometry, coming together as foliated versions of their geometric figures, extending also to hexafoils and octafoils.

Amidst the profusion, some patterns of composition may sometimes be discerned. It is common, for example, for different foliated circles to be paired, such as the trefoils and quatrefoils in the glazed passage of Beauvais Cathedral's choir (Fig. 143);[147] the quatrefoils and cinquefoils in the aisle windows of Lincoln Cathedral's Angel Choir; and the cinquefoils and hexafoils alternating around the cloister of Salisbury Cathedral (Fig. 146), built between 1258 and 1265, each set above a pair of quatrefoils in the sub-arches of the arcading. Hexafoil tracery appears predominant in northern France, notably in Reims Cathedral; octafoil tracery can be found, but is less common; novafoil tracery is rare, yet it provides the scheme for the windows of York Minster's Chapter House, dating from the 1280s (Fig. 124); decafoil tracery is also rare, yet it heads the thirteenth-century choir windows of the Church of St Quentin (Fig. 147).

Masons, glaziers, and iron-workers

As was initially the case with the diversity of geometry in chevets and in wheels of fortune, the question arises whether tracery design as variegated as this could ever have been intended to signify particular meaning, or was it simply the result of free pattern-making? If tracery was meant as a signifier, was this part of a chapter's programme to its builders? If not, was it nevertheless part of a programme, but left to the architect to instruct his masons? Did masons enjoy any freedom to make such decisions themselves? Was the design of window tracery made independently of decisions about the content and composition of its glass? How did the work of masons, glaziers, and the metalworkers making the iron frames for the glazing, fit together? Few of these questions can be answered with certainty, or at all, because few have been thoroughly explored, and the dynamics of decision-making must in any case have differed with each project, through time, from place to place, and with each particular collection of individuals, making generalizations difficult, impossible, or meaningless. Yet it must be reasonable to assume, given the growing volume and complexity of ecclesiastical building, and the

Fig. 143 Sanctuary, Beauvais Cathedral. The three Platonic figures are represented, with the hexafoils and twin quatrefoils in the clerestorey windows, and the pairs of cinquefoils in the arcading of the glazed passage beneath them

Fig. 144 East end, Romsey Abbey. The three *oculi* in each main window comprise a quatrefoil above two cinquefoils, those to the right and south pointing upwards whilst those to the left and north are inverted

Fig. 145 Choir aisle window, St Ouen, Rouen. The Platonic figures are present again in its four trefoils, two quatrefoils, and one cinquefoil

Fig. 146 Cloister arcading, Salisbury Cathedral. Cinquefoils alternate with hexafoils, beneath a pair of quatrefoils at the top of each bay

Fig. 147 Upper choir, St Quentin's collegiate church. Unusually, the *oculi* of the clerestorey windows are decafoiled

consolidation by the thirteenth century both of the building process and of the architect's profession, that working practices must have been sufficiently developed and organized, and sufficiently flexible, to accommodate variations both in the degree of patronal programming and in the discretion this will sometimes have allowed the workforce.

Regarding the question of connection between the design of window tracery and the iconography of its glass, since the masonry arches, tracery, and mullions of windows serve as a structural frame within the wall opening, they would presumably have been designed and built as the work proceeded. Conversely, glass, being fragile, would have been fitted later, perhaps years later before the scaffolding came down. This could have made its design a separate part of the process, distinct from the design of the tracery, to which it would have been anterior. Although this is necessarily speculative, there are certain clues that suggest this may have been the case. It can be argued that tracery exists as an entity in its own right because the geometric *motifs* and method of construction of window tracery, excepting rebates for the glass, are indistinguishable from those of unglazed tracery. Another clue is that when patrons commissioned windows, stipulating content, layout and other matters of design, they are recorded instructing the glass-painters who will create the windows, not the master mason who designs and supervises the construction of the tracery, having presumably done so years before.[148] The tracery appears to be a given condition which is left unmentioned. Other evidence shows glaziers duplicating their designs for different projects, sometimes reversing them and adapting them in the process. The record also shows glass frequently being removed and re-arranged in different windows. This implies a practice which accepts the masonry frame and tracery of a window as pre-existing, with the composition of the glass in it being interchangeable.[149] This is not to rule out any co-ordination between tracery design and the iconographic content of the glass, but one study has shown a lack of integration between architectural context and image during the early decades of bar tracery,[150] whilst another postulates a distinction between the meaning behind the geometric form of tracery, as being legible to an educated churchman, and the stories in the glass meant as instruction to an illiterate laity.[151]

Later in the thirteenth century, a greater degree of integration reflected a growing influence of the architectural context of the windows themselves on the imagery in the windows, often as a result of glass-painters making use of lodge drawings. When glaziers drew up their sketches, the tracery was often drawn freehand, without any setting-out of its own, as if it were already in position. The closest collaboration glaziers would have had in the making of their windows in such cases would have been with the iron-workers who fabricated the metal frames to which the leaded glass was to be wired, and it was these frames that had to be made to fit their stone surrounds. However, from the fourteenth century, windows began to be replaced by larger up-to-date designs ordered by individual benefactors, guilds, and other organizations.[152] Each window, or series of windows, would therefore be regarded as a discrete project, combining the design of the stone tracery, the metal frame, and the glass as a single collaborative enterprise.[153] Until then, everything seems to point to a process where the tracery might be designed first, and the glass designed to fit. If this was generally the case, it suggests that tracery was important enough to determine, to some extent, not the theme of the glass, but its pictorial composition. If this was the case, what was it that determined the design of the tracery?

Symbolism in tracery

Among numerous studies of this subject, which tend to be descriptive, or concerned with the transmission of geometric *motifs*, one has concluded that the figures of Platonic geometry were chosen for tracery for the ease of constructing and subdividing them;[154] another advances a purely ornamental use of geometry;[155] while a third confines itself to wheel and rose windows, presuming a connection between their number and geometry with the Christian Platonist tradition.[156] The architectural evidence sampled here suggests a degree of variety even greater than that found in chevet design,

Fig. 148 West front, Reims Cathedral

making the attempt to discover anything schematically systematic the more difficult. On the other hand, every three-light window or trefoil could stand for the Trinity to any worshipper gazing up at it, every quatrefoil could represent the Gospels to some or 'divine quaternity' to others, every cinquefoil the law or heaven, every hexafoil the Creation, and every octafoil salvation, as a means to contemplation independently of the stories told in the glass. As a result of the variety found in different combinations of geometric figures, however, the interpretative possibilities are so wide as to make the deduction of any specific intent elusive. Nevertheless, as with the design of chapter houses and chevets, choices in tracery design were being made, either by the chapter, or the lodge, or by both. It was suggested in the case of chevet design that the decision-making was a collaboration between chapter and lodge, initiated sometimes by the chapter stipulating their requirements, then developed into a constructional design by the builders for the chapter's approval. This would have accommodated at least two distinct approaches, each with implications for symbolic content. In the case of tracery design, one would depend on the chapter including in their requirements particular themes to be represented, and possibly the means of achieving this, which the masons incorporated in their work. Another possibility allows the builders to take the initiative in making proposals based on the established practice of their lodge and possibly on recent projects elsewhere. In their response, the chapter might consider any symbolism inherent in the design, and its appropriateness, in eventually granting approval. Either way, there must have been reasons for choosing, or agreeing, the geometric design of the window tracery.

In order to try to make sense of the diversity evident in the results, it will be useful to start where consistency is pronounced, for behind an apparent system of design, there should be a system of thought to justify it. The greatest geometric coherence in tracery design perhaps is provided by Reims Cathedral, the coronation church of the Royal Domain, which was dedicated to the Virgin Mary and begun in 1211 (Fig. 148). It was completed, except for its upper towers, in 1290 and sketched extensively while under construction by Villard de Honnecourt. It is no coincidence that such consistency in design is to be found at Reims, for the whole process of its construction was systematized to a new level, with the first, or early, adoption of bar tracery only one facet of the simplification and standardization of the building process.[157] Consequently, its tracery design is unusually consistent, and the most restricted, for it is derived exclusively from the equilateral triangle. The windows of its chapels, aisles, and clerestoreys consist of two lights crowned by a hexafoil, and all three rose windows are dodecagonal. The quatrefoils and quadripartite tracery in the glazed *tympana* at the west end are insertions made much later in the Middle Ages. It would be interesting to discover if the geometric proportioning of the plan design also answers to the equilateral triangle, for this is certainly the case at Chartres on which so much of Reims is modelled.[158] The symbolism inherent in its tracery seems easy enough to conjecture, of the Trinity, the Creation, and the community of the Apostles, with whom Mary was associated in portrayals of Pentecost. Paradoxically, in view of the apparent absence of two of the three Platonic figures, it is the uncompromising consistency of the window design at Reims that suggests that there must have been a system of thought driving it.

It could well be pertinent therefore that the range of tracery design in Westminster Abbey is nearly as consistent, for it was modelled on Reims while the French church was still under construction, and Westminster's first master, significantly, was Henry of 'Reyns'. In deciding to replace the Romanesque abbey of Edward the Confessor, Henry III combined the royal functions of Reims Cathedral and St Denis' Abbey, for his building would become both the coronation church and burial place of England's monarchs, incorporating, in so doing, a new shrine for Edward, England's last native king. Commencing in 1245, construction continued until shortly after Henry's death in 1272, when the east end, transepts and first bays of the nave stood complete (Fig. 149). The second campaign would not resume for another century when the nave was extended to the original design, except for some differences of detail.

Fig. 149 Upper presbytery, Westminster Abbey. Inverted cinquefoils crown the clerestorey windows, whilst in the arches around the gallery arcading below are cinquefoils pointing upwards

Fig. 150 Window tracery, east end, Westminster Abbey. The clerestorey windows incorporate inverted cinquefoils, the external windows to the gallery are octafoils above the hexafoiled tracery of the aisle windows

Fig. 151 Angel Choir, Lincoln Cathedral. The Platonic figures are represented in the aisle windows, with a quatrefoil above two cinquefoils, crowning three lights each with trefoiled arches. The main *oculus* of Simon of Thirsk's east window consists of six equal circles surrounding a seventh, the central *oculus* being a hexafoil, the others being quatrefoils. Below and either side, a hexafoil and two quatrefoils crown twin windows, each of four lights, numbering eight in total

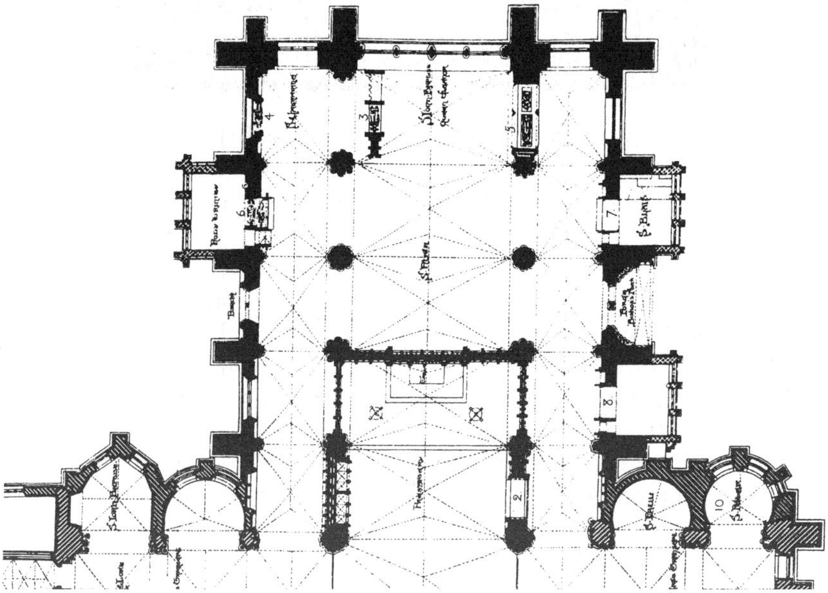

Fig. 152 Plan, Angel Choir, Lincoln Cathedral. Lying east of the east transept, the Angel Choir extends for five bays, marked by four pairs of piers, numbering eight in total

Fig. 153 Aisle and clerestorey windows, Angel Choir, Lincoln Cathedral. Each clerestorey window comprises an octafoil above two trefoils, whilst the aisle windows complete the scheme with a quatrefoil above twin cinquefoils

Considering the tracery design of Henry's campaign, the rose windows in each of the transepts were quartered into 16 parts, and could be seen as the Wheels of Scripture.[159] In the body of the church, the clerestorey windows have twin lancets surmounted by a cinquefoiled *oculus* which is inverted; the gallery arcades have two main arches per bay, each with an open cinquefoil pointing up;[160] the chapel and aisle windows in the chevet and transepts are also given twin lancets, but these are crowned by a hexafoil; the aisle windows in the first four bays of the nave have cinquefoils, inverted on the south side.[161] The insistence on the numbers 5 and 6, which will also be seen elsewhere, was clearly systematic and, if meant symbolically, could signify the microcosm and macrocosm, together with creation. Bearing in mind Alan of Lille's reference to 'the palace of the universe' only a few decades earlier, perhaps the structure of the king's abbey was intended to stand as his palace celebrating the created order of the universe. Another connection might be made in an expansion of this basic scheme, seen in the external gallery windows which sit immediately above the aisle windows for, almost without exception, these are octafoils (Fig. 150).[162] Any church would have cause to project the message of salvation through the expression of the octad but, as the shrine of Edward the Confessor, Westminster Abbey was designed to accommodate a particularly important commemorative function and, sure enough, the termination of its sanctuary is a semi-octagon rotated, which was very unusual (Fig. 131a).[163] It is even more unusual, as noted above, because the geometry between the apse and the ambulatory is hybridized in order to fit in the 5 chevet chapels present in its model at Reims.[164]

Thus a high degree of coherence in tracery design has been found in these two buildings as originally designed, to which could be added the cathedrals of Chartres, Amiens, and others, but it can also be present in major additions to churches which can also contain an equivalent integrity. The Angel Choir of Lincoln Cathedral by Simon of Thirsk is such an example (Figs 121, 151, 152, 153). Built as a new shrine for Hugh of Avalon, the late bishop of Lincoln, between 1256 and 1280, it stands as a five-bayed extension of his choir, aisled and square-ended. As a monk of the strict Order of Chartreuse, the rule of law would have been especially important to Hugh and is perhaps reflected by the number of bays matching the Pentateuch, the 8 piers once again drawing attention to the commemorative function of his shrine. The composition of the tracery design also appears co-ordinated, with octafoils only in the clerestorey windows, trefoils and quatrefoils in the clerestoreys and galleries, and quatrefoils and cinquefoils in the aisle windows (Figs 151, 152). Since the latter are placed over triple lights, each window embodies the 3 basic figurate numbers – 3, 4, 5 – as in St Ouen's aisle windows a little later (Fig. 145).[165] It may be noticed that the expression of the number 6 is absent, for this was reserved for the great east window. This is dominated by an *oculus* of six quatrefoiled circles surrounding a central hexafoiled circle, its two side lights each displaying a hexafoil and two quatrefoils. In considering the intention behind this design, was Simon simply demonstrating the geometric axiom that 6 equal circles exactly surround a seventh of equal diameter, or was he also knowingly projecting a symbol of the Creator and his Creation of the world and, at the same time perhaps, Ezekiel's wheels within wheels? In this reading, the Creator is the single circle in the centre, formed as a hexafoil, the 6 circles surrounding him, formed as quatrefoils, representing the 6 days taken to create the world. Given the integrity of this reading, is it really tenable that Simon was only playing with his dividers, and that the bishop, the dean, and the chapter were happy for him to do so, in a work terminating the entire interior of their cathedral?

Of a different order of structural modification was the Gothic remodelling of the Norman Cathedral of Hereford, lasting just over a hundred years from late in the twelfth century.[166] In largely continuous and sometimes overlapping phases, it commenced with a new east end, including east transepts, retrochoir, and a Lady Chapel of about 1220, followed by a new choir vault and clerestorey in the 1230s, a new north transept in the 1250s and 1260s;[167] then,

Fig. 154 South nave aisle, Hereford Cathedral. The tracery of the aisle windows again represents the three Platonic figures, with a cinquefoil crowning two trefoils over four lights

after an interval of some twenty years, it was completed with a new porch and aisles to nave and choir between the 1280s and about 1310, and new towers over the crossing and west end during the latter part of this period.[168] Of interest to this study are the windows in the new aisles and east transept, for these mostly consist of a pentagram above two trefoils crowning 4 lights (Fig. 154).[169] Being a generation later than the aisle windows in Lincoln's Angel Choir, the geometry is freer; the trefoils are again made of *vesica piscis* figures, but these appear attenuated, and the pentagrams are of a somewhat droopy, floral variety, polygonally irregular. French influence and high fashion have been conjectured, with suggested connections with Hereford, in which case, this influence spread locally.[170] This in itself may have been sufficient reason for the masons to import it and for the chapter to welcome it, but it is striking how each window again embodies the 3 figurate numbers of Plato's cosmology, in the pentagram, trefoils, and 4 lights, akin to the Angel Choir aisle windows at Lincoln preceding it, and at St Ouen succeeding it.

One counter-argument to the connections being suggested so far might be prompted by questioning whether other choices could have been made, or, more to the point, why other choices were not made. For example, why was the tracery of St Ouen's choir aisle windows confined to trefoils, quatrefoils, and one cinquefoil, the three figures of Christian Platonist cosmology? Could the cinquefoil have been a hexafoil instead? Could the geometry of Lincoln's and Hereford's aisle windows have been different, and could the open tracery around Salisbury's cloister (Fig. 146) have been quatrefoils and cinquefoils,

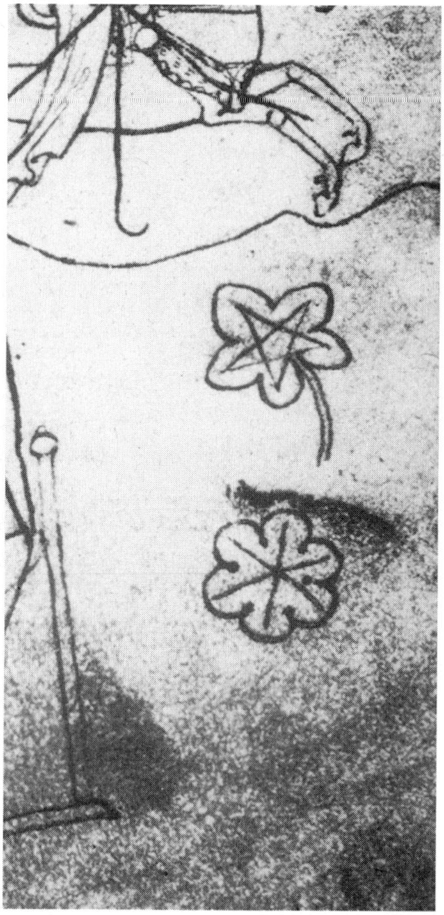

Fig. 155 Five- and six-petalled flowers, Villard, fol. 19r. If this was an innocent doodle, as it probably was, what was in Villard's mind when he structured the flowers with the geometry of the pentagon and hexagon?

instead of cinquefoils and hexafoils? Interestingly, on the margin of one of his leaves, Villard sketched a cinquefoil and a hexafoil as the structure of five- and six-petalled flowers, with a pentagram and the diagonals of a hexagon superimposed on them (Fig. 155). What might have been in his mind?[171] The coupling of these two numbers recalls the internal ordering of Westminster Abbey around this time, and it will be seen shortly how the number and geometry of 5 and 6 often confront each other across the interior space of churches from the north to their south transepts. With regard to Westminster's cinquefoils, is there a reason for those in its gallery arcading pointing up, when all the others in the initial campaign are pointing down? Why were the two northerly cinquefoils at the end of Romsey's choir inverted (Fig. 144), and the two southerly ones set upright? In such a prominent position, how could this possibly have been a mistake? Five was also common in the grouping of lancet

Fig. 156 Lady chapel, Wells Cathedral. Although the net tracery in each window is notionally continuous, the arches cut through it so as to leave a tetract of trefoils, totalling ten, above five lights

windows, with two rows of 5 windows at both Ripon and York dating from around 1250 and 1260 respectively (Figs 94, 93).[172] Yet Ripon's were built across its west front, York's Five Sisters are in the north transept, as are the single group at Lichfield, whilst a similar group at Ely appear at the east end above 3 lancets, making 8.[173] Was this simply the prevailing composition at the time, regardless of their location in a given project and devoid of other meaning? Conversely, the tracery in York's Chapter House is so unusual, this must have been the outcome of deliberate choice, even specific commissioning (Fig. 124). Each window displays three large circles, each divided into 9, presiding over two cinquefoils and an elongated trefoil above the middle light. If number and geometry constituted a picture language, what statement was the York Chapter making to itself? The 9 orders of angels, threefold, may come to mind, but what is their relevance in this context? Could each have been meant to

Fig. 157 West rose, Paris Cathedral. Strictly a wheel window, divided by twelve

signify the Holy Trinity threefold, a Catholic equivalent of the *trisagion*? Did the master of Wells Cathedral's Lady Chapel realize that the way the arches of its windows cut through their reticulated tracery leaves a graphic representation of the Pythagorean tetract (Fig. 156), its rows of whole trefoils ordered as 1, 2, 3, and 4, over 5 lights? If he did not, it would have been known to anyone schooled in the *quadrivium*, such as the bishop or dean perhaps. The same design is also found not that far away, in a pair of clerestorey windows in the nave of Exeter Cathedral.

Because examples of individual architectural designs such as these invite individual explanations, does this mean that the process of decision-making itself was completely individuated, and that it conformed to no general system at all? The national characteristics and regional similarities in northern European window tracery, which have been treated comprehensively in the literature, definitely point to consistent approaches to design and an espousal of particular geometric *motifs* that are assuredly evidence of the practice of individual lodges. Yet each will only have succeeded in flourishing with patronal consent. However, just as it is difficult to disentangle the web of influences between patron, chapter, tracing-house, and lodge, even in individual cases, so it is to advance beyond individual cases when attempting to discover correspondences between tracery design and meaning in a general sense. Bearing this in mind, also that it is the context of an object that can illuminate its meaning, this investigation will conclude with a brief examination of rose windows in the context of their facades and related windows, in order to ascertain whether any systematic schematism is suggested (Fig. 157). In so doing, all the figures of Platonic geometry will be seen incorporated within the circle, and sometimes the square.

Part Four: 'The Eyes of the Cathedral'

Symbol, context, and meaning

It is thought that the metrical *Vita sancti Hugonis* honouring Hugh of Avalon and Lincoln was composed in the 1220s by the wandering poet, Henry of Avranches.[174] Of the new cathedral at Lincoln, Hugh's Choir and the main transepts stood complete and the work was proceeding westwards with the rebuilding of the nave. To the east, the lancet windows in the clerestorey were evidently glazed, for Henry writes,

> ... the top range of windows shines illustrious with flower-petals, signifying the varied beauty of the world ...
>
> *Vita sancti Hugonis* 934–5.[175]

He focuses greater attention on the two circular windows in the transept facades, the northerly known as the Dean's Eye for being located above the door from the deanery, the southerly the Bishop's Eye because its transept contains the entrance from the bishop's palace across the way. In his verse,

Henry explicitly perceives these two Eyes as signifiers in several respects, not least in associating the temple with the body once again:

> And there are two larger windows, like two luminaries; their circular radiance, looking to north and south, outshines all the other windows with these twin lustres. The others are comparable to common stars, but these two are, the one like the sun, and the other like the moon.
>
> These parts, though they have been described with a child's simplicity, import an allegory.
>
> The twin windows that offer a circular light are the two Eyes of the cathedral; and rightly the greater of these is seen to be the bishop and the lesser the dean. For north represents the devil, and south the Holy Spirit and it is in these directions that the two Eyes look. The bishop faces the south in order to invite in, and the dean the north in order to avoid; the one takes care to be saved, the other takes care not to perish. With these Eyes the cathedral's face is on the watch for the candelabra of heaven and the darkness of Lethe.
>
> *Vita sancti Hugonis* 900, 910, 937–45.[176]

The description of these two windows as eyes is as striking as it is unusual.[177] It at once suggests an anthropomorphic figure, as well as the 'rings … full of eyes' in Ezekiel's vision,[178] which led Jerome to write of the Evangelists, '[with the Lord's team of four] the whole body is full of eyes'.[179] As it happens, the root of 'window' is 'wind-eye' and it has been pointed out that Early Christian disc-symbols and wind-eyes in the form of small round apertures, some of them traceried, are found adjacent to doorways in buildings and may well have had a protective function against evil from entering.[180]

Henry's reference to 'the candelabra of heaven' is also interesting, for church candelabra could be suspended or standing, taking the form of a corona, or the circuit of city walls in miniature, or wheel-like discs which were pierced to hold rings of glass oil lamps (Fig. 158). Probably derived from the Byzantine *polycandelon* and mostly made in bronze, medieval examples are recorded in France, Italy, and Spain and were even referred to at the time as wheels. Although their geometric design may have been partly determined by a practical choice about supporting them at either three or four points around their circumference, their medieval identification as wheels, their circles of flame, radial geometry and concentric rings of *motifs*, above all their function as sources of light, make a connection in the medieval mind between the fiery wheel and the rose window seem irresistible, being seen in conjunction with each other, the one in the horizontal plane, the other in the vertical, and illuminating the same space.[181]

It has already been argued that the possibility of the popular perception of circular windows evolving during the thirteenth century from *rota* to *rosa* is likely and, in some examples shortly to be examined, seems certain. At the very time rose windows were being constructed and reconstructed in cathedrals around the Ile-de-France, one of the most popular works of romance literature was being written and read. *Le Roman de la Rose* was started

Fig. 158 Bronze candelabra, London, British Museum, No. 529. The geometry of this type of candelabra was analogous to rose windows, and both were functionally associated with light

by Guillaume de Lorris around 1230 and, after an unexplained interval of forty years, it was taken up and completed by Jean de Meun, evidently in the Paris region around 1270.[182] Central to the poem is a rose-bud in the Garden of Pleasure, which to the Lover becomes 'the sole object of [his] heart's desire'.[183]

> Nature's masterly hand had arranged its four pairs of leaves, one after the other.
> When I approached the rose, I found that it was a little larger and saw that it had grown since the time I first saw it. … but I was pleased that it had not opened enough to reveal the seed but was still enclosed by the rose leaves, which stood up straight and filled the place within … May God bless it, it was even more beautiful and redder as it opened than it had been before …
>
> Guillaume de Lorris, *Le Roman de la Rose* II, III.[184]

Despite its eroticism, or even because of it, the rose became identified with the Virgin Mary, its crimson petals a symbol for the flames of love. A few decades after the completion of *Le Roman*, in the 1300s, Dante started writing his *Paradiso*, where he describes his vision of the Virgin Mary:

> Here is the rose in which the divine word
> Was made flesh …

The name of the fair flower which I invoke
Morning and evening, compelled my whole mind
To fix my eyes upon the greatest flame.

So every one of these brilliances stretched up
With its flame, so that it was patent
How exalted was the love they bore to Mary.

Dante, *Paradiso* XXIII. 73–4, 88–90, 124–6.[185]

Thus, as argued above, the tongues of flame, the petals of the rose, and their mutual colour of fire and love would surely have been seen combined as a single image. Anyone at the French Court familiar with this imagery could have recognized it in the original west rose of La Sainte Chapelle dating from the late 1240s.[186] If *Les Très Riches Heures* of the Duke of Berry portrays it correctly, it could be read equally as an eight-petalled rose, with all its attendant connotations, and, with the 4 quatrefoils in the corners of its enclosing square, as Ezekiel's fiery wheel as well.

The rose window has produced a sizeable literature[187] and, insofar as it deals with geometry, it is variously concerned with exercises in descriptive geometry and geometric reconstructions from archaeological fragments,[188] the classification and transmission of geometric *motifs*,[189] the cataloguing of examples,[190] or their analysis as elements within specific buildings.[191] Among studies in the modern era which deal with design and symbolism, one source argues for an Islamic origin for the rose window, alleging it to have been purely ornamental, which led to Christian usage that was either decorative or symbolic in various ways.[192] Another source suggests possible antecedents in different typologies of wheel, also the *oculus* as the Eye of God. While acknowledging that some studies postulate the presence of Neoplatonic ideas in the Gothic cathedral – conceding that there may have been a place for number symbolism – these ideas, it is argued, are transcended by Christ as the Incarnation of the Word and by the Bible as the primary authority.[193] The geometry and symbolism of wheel and rose windows are central to another study, which charts their chronological development against the current state of scholarship. Yet the geometric content is reconstructive and symbolic readings are largely derived from the iconography of the glass, rather than from the possible meaning of number and geometry in the design of the tracery as well.[194] A fourth study associates the circle of the rose window with the circle and dome of heaven in the architecture and art of Antiquity onwards, especially in relation to the window's circular aperture and the *oculi* in domes that are open to the sky. Various wheel and rose designs are cited, including wheels of fortune, but without any specific treatment of number and geometry in their design.[195]

To return to Henry of Avranches, while the north and south transept windows at Lincoln Cathedral put him in mind of the two 'Eyes [of] the cathedral's face', French cathedrals generally possess 3 rose windows, which can be seen joined in harmony with each other when viewed from beneath the crossing, thereby unifying the spatial and religious experience. Notwithstanding numerous exceptions, sometimes caused by later replacements, a thematic pattern can sometimes be detected between the iconography of the glass in the windows facing north, south, and west, with the Old Testament and the Virgin common to the north, the New Testament and Christ to the south, and the last Judgment in the west.[196] Facing the setting sun, the west facades of French cathedrals resonate with the end of the world and the day of judgment, as worshippers approached and entered 'the palace of the Universe'[197] on their spiritual journey towards paradise in the east. The glass in the west rose of Chartres Cathedral portrays Christ at the Last Judgment, surrounded by 12 stars (Fig. 142). It is dodecagonal in design, combining 4 perhaps for justice and 3 for the Trinity, with 12 standing for the end of the journey, if not the Apostles as well; its circle of octafoils signifying salvation and combining 8 with 12 once again. Under reconstruction between 1194 and 1220 behind its pre-existing west front, the cathedral was completed in a continuous campaign with a corresponding uniformity in general design. Its other two circular windows, terminating the transepts, are also dodecagonal, and both sit over a row of 5 lancet windows, which will shortly be seen to be of possible relevance. The north transept incorporates a circle of squares, radiating on their diagonals, whilst the south transept window has a ring of circles, octafoiled at the cardinal points, with pairs of circles in between, all possessing meaning that would be straightforward to interpret. The fact that all three of Chartres' roses are dodecagonal is noteworthy and they raise an additional possibility of meaning. Akin to 'the palace of the universe' was the heavenly city of the New Jerusalem with its 12 gates for the 12 tribes of Israel, its 12 foundations for the 12 Apostles, and its sides measuring 12 thousand furlongs.[198] For a cathedral to proclaim itself as symbolizing the heavenly city to all who approached it would be eminently understandable.

Other dodecagonal rose windows are found in different combinations at the cathedrals in Paris, Amiens, and Reims. The first of these is at the west end of Notre-Dame in Paris, and it dates from around 1220 (Fig. 157). At about the same time, the original north and south transept roses were dismantled, evidently after developing serious problems and were eventually replaced during the 1260s. This has resulted in an octagonal rose to the north and a south rose that is also dodecagonal but which was subsequently rebuilt.[199] The numerical root of these roses is therefore 4, recalling Gregory's 4 phases of teaching and the 4 mysteries of Christ, threefold in the south window as rebuilt, fourfold in the north. Whilst the hexagonal system underlying the south and west roses is common in France, the octagonal north rose differs in the combination of this particular geometry with the location of the window, but the original rose windows may well have conformed to a different collective scheme. Whatever the truth, the two new roses, as they have survived, register salvation and creation. A collective pattern such as may have obtained originally at Paris can be seen in the three rose windows of Amiens Cathedral, for each of the three Platonic numbers provides the mathematical root for one of these windows. The north and south roses are based on the familiar coupling of the numbers 5 and 6 respectively (Figs 136, 163) and will

Fig. 159 West rose, Amiens Cathedral, divided by eight

Fig. 160 West rose, Strasbourg Cathedral, based on the numbers 4 and 5

be discussed shortly, whilst the west rose is generated by the number 4, expanding to 8 (Fig. 159). Not only does this complete the three figurate numbers between the three facades of the cathedral, but the dependence of the west rose on the number 8 can be interpreted as offering the promise of salvation to all who enter its principal portal, or perhaps the spiritual journey that commences on entry, if not the Wheel of Scripture as well. The latter, along with the heavenly city, might also have been suggested by all three rose windows at Reims Cathedral, which are dodecagonal (Fig. 148), with a row of 3 hexafoiled *oculi* and 3 lancets below those on the north and south transepts. As already noted, this arrangement forms part of a comprehensive scheme of tracery design rooted in 3 and the equilateral triangle, extending to 6 and 12 in the form of hexafoils and the dodecagonal roses, with probable associations with the Holy Trinity, Creation, and the Apostles.

A similar consistency may be seen within individual windows when viewed in their particular context. The west rose of Strasbourg Cathedral, from around 1290, is entirely based on the numbers 5 and 4 (Fig. 160), with each of its 16 petals ending in a cinquefoil, and with another in the centre. Four more cinquefoils are set in open tracery in the corners of the square, which exactly frames the circumference of the window, and these are each flanked by a pair of quatrefoils. Thus the sum of quatrefoils in the angles is 8, the number of cinquefoils 4, representing perhaps the spiritual journey to salvation and the duration of that journey. The teaching of the Gospels is also indicated by the 4 cinquefoils, located as they are in the 4 corners of the enclosing square where, it will be recalled, the symbols of the Evangelists are conventionally shown in reliefs, also in miniatures of Christ in majesty, and in windows designed in the form of Ezekiel's wheel. The cinquefoils and quatrefoils in Strasbourg's window, being derived from the plane figures of the dodecahedron representing the universe, and the cube representing earth, reinforce the same meaning as that attaching to the circle of its rose and its enclosing square, the whole proclaiming the cathedral as the palace of the universe on earth, repeatedly, like the pealing of bells, to those who approached and could comprehend. When the 16 cinquefoils around the edge of the rose are added to the 4 in the angles and the one in the centre, the sum is 21, or 3 sevenfold and 7 threefold, the numbers of the Holy Trinity and the Holy Spirit. It might be argued that the symbolism apparent in Strasbourg's rose would be equally appropriate elsewhere in the cathedral, but the occasion did not arise. The east end and transepts had been built in the twelfth century, the sanctuary ending in an apse, making a large east window impossible to accommodate, and the transepts were divided internally north to south axially, and unusually, by a line of piers. This results in each transept facade also being divided in two by a central wall-buttress, which has allowed only a small wheel window to be fitted in either side of them. It was only when Strasbourg's building campaign reached the west front that the opportunity arose for the first time for the Gothic cathedral to proclaim itself to the outside world from its main facade in a manner of its choosing.

Fig. 161 West rose, Laon Cathedral. The central *oculus* is surrounded by twelve curved pentagons, each containing a circle

A variation on the same numbers, 5 and 4, underlies the geometry of Laon Cathedral's west rose, dating from the turn of the thirteenth century (Fig. 161). This is quartered into 12 segments, with Christ depicted in a twelve-foiled circle in the centre. He is surrounded by 12 angels, each circled in a curved pentagon, the sum of pentagons which form a dodecahedron. Accordingly, the design is capable of being interpreted as Christ seated in majesty in the centre of the universe as its governor. This same tracery design is repeated at the opposite end of the cathedral for its east window, which is highly unusual, and it may again be explained by the particular circumstances surrounding the completion of the cathedral (Fig. 162). The first campaign had started with the original choir sometime between 1155 and 1160 and was concluded with the erection of the west front, complete with its circular window, by 1200.[200] No sooner had this been accomplished, within only five years or so, the first choir, which had consisted of three straight bays and a single apse without ambulatory or chapels, was carefully dismantled stone by stone and replaced by the present choir by about 1220. This second choir is unusual, being very long and, exceptionally for a French cathedral, square ended, with an ambulatory and provision for 5 east-facing chapels. Instead of the original 3 bays, it extends for 10, or 5 double bays each covered by a six-part vault, and is identical to the nave, which, except for a single four-part vault at the west end, also consists of 5 double bays of six-part vaults. This places the crossing, with the light flooding down from its lantern, virtually at the mid-point of the interior. No record has been discovered accounting for the reasons for this

Fig. 162 Interior, Laon Cathedral. The square east end is a reflection of the west front, with a similar rose window, and three lancets looking out towards the east, the counterpart of the three portals at the west end through which the church is entered

second campaign, although they must have been compelling to justify such a dramatic and sudden change of mind so soon after the completion of the cathedral. One suggestion was the need for a large presbytery, but this does not in itself explain the square end and the matching number of bays, whilst another theory was a desire for the choir to balance the nave either side of the crossing.[201] Why this should have been so important here, and not elsewhere, cannot be hazarded. Nevertheless, it is a suggestion borne out by the matching number of bays and the flat wall terminating both ends of the building; also by the deliberate mirroring of the west window by that at the east end within only twenty years; and by the triple portals marking the entry through the west front being reflected by the triple lancets looking out towards paradise from beneath the east window.

Having considered some of the rose windows of French cathedrals which can be read collectively in threes, and others individually, it will be instructive to return to Amiens Cathedral and examine its north and south transept rose windows in relation to each other (Figs 163, 136). The tracery of the north transept window is divided into 15 parts, with a large inverted pentagram as its centre-piece. Its south transept rose has a six-pointed centre expanding to 12 around the circumference. Bordering this is the half-wheel of fortune and life already discussed. Installing the north transept rose, a replacement of the

Fig. 163 North rose, Amiens Cathedral. An inverted pentagram at its centre, the window sits above an open screen of five triple-light arches. Compare this with the hexagonal geometry of the south rose in Fig. 136

original, was a major undertaking in terms of both its schematic and constructional design, and so the decision to execute this particular scheme is unlikely to have been taken lightly. Dating from around 1300,[202] its geometry is complex. From the pentagon at its centre, project the 5 points of the pentagram, each a golden triangle, and these are enclosed by pairs of parallel-sided mullions, 5 in number, extending outwards to the edge of the circle and ending in pointed foils. In between them, larger pairs of traceried lights radiate from each external angle of the pentagon. Around the circumference, 5 trefoils in the arches of the parallel lights alternate with 5 pairs of quatrefoils in the radial lights, thereby embodying the numbers 3, 4, and 5 in the tracery. The circle of the window sits on a glazed screen of 10 lights, the mullions of which descend to a row of 5 three-light windows, recalling the 5 lancet windows in a similar position in both transepts at Chartres. At Amiens, the middle light of the second and fourth windows is blank because of the external buttressing that had to be added to the window soon after completion.[203] Thus two large mullions, fashioned as buttresses, rise independently of the glazing in these positions and are linked at the top by three arches. The hexagonal geometry of the south rose, the third in this position and dating from around 1500,[204] is simpler and more straightforwardly radiating, albeit in floriated fashion. Like the north rose, it sits on a glazed arcade, this time of 8 lights, which again becomes a row of 5 two-light windows.

Not only is the pairing of 5 and 6 and their geometry across the church intriguing, especially in relation to their prominence at Westminster, Salisbury, and elsewhere, the same combination is repeated in other churches in northern France, including St Ouen in Rouen to the west of Amiens (Figs 164, 165), Sens Cathedral to the south (Figs 166, 167), and partly so at the collegiate Church of St Quentin, to the east of Amiens, which displays another pentagram in its main north transept faced by octagonal geometry in its south rose (Figs 168, 169).

The north rose in the main transepts of St Quentin followed about a century after Amiens' window, around 1400.[205] It is also pentagonal, but differs from Amiens' in pointing upwards, generated as it is from a cinquefoil at its centre which is upright. From it, and characteristically for the period, parallel-sided lights project outwards to the circumference, thereby implying a pentagram. In between these lights, trefoiled *oculi* are placed, 5 in number. Even more so than Amiens, the rose is in effect the giant *oculus* of a window nearly filling the gable-end of the transept and, like Amiens, it is divided by two bold mullions. Beneath it is a glazed screen and both this and the window consist of 8 lights, with an extra one in blind tracery at either end, making 10 altogether. The south rose, of about the same date, differs from the other churches in this group in being octafoiled over 4 lights. Yet it was clearly designed to be a pair with the north rose, with a cruciform of similar parallel-sided lights quartering the circle of the window, this time with 4 quatrefoils in between.[206]

St Ouen's north transept rose, of around 1440, is similar to Amiens' in being a regular, straight-sided pentagram, although pointing upwards, with trefoils and quatrefoils alternating around the circumference, and set over a row, once

Fig. 164 North rose, St Ouen, Rouen. A large pentagram within a circle encloses seven stars in the pentagon at its centre, and sits over a screen of seven arches

Fig. 165 South rose, St Ouen, Rouen. Hexagonal geometry again confronts the pentagonal geometry of the north transept, but expands, unusually, into eighteen petals

Fig. 166 North rose, Sens Cathedral. An inverted pentagram sits above five lights

Fig. 167 South rose, Sens Cathedral. The hexagonal geometry of the rose again sits over five lights as a counterpart to the pentagonal rose in the north transept

Fig. 168 North-west rose, St Quentin's collegiate church. A straight-sided pentagram sits over an arcade of ten arches

Fig. 169 South-west rose, St Quentin's collegiate church. As a reflection of the straight-sided pentagram facing it in the north-west transept, a cruciform of tracery describes a quatrefoil design, instead of the hexagon usual for south transept windows

again, of 5 two-light windows. Internally these are screened by open tracery divided into 7, possibly to harmonize with the 7 stars filling the pentagon at the centre of the window. The south rose, constructed later in the fourteenth century, is slightly unusual, in that its hexagonal geometry resolves itself into 18 foils, not 12, terminating with large pairs of quatrefoils alternating with smaller single quatrefoils. Once again, the rose sits on a glazed screen, here of 10 lights. The similarities of both these designs with the north and south roses at Amiens Cathedral are the more interesting, coming as they do in between the installation of Amiens' two windows. This is to be explained by a hiatus caused at St Ouen between the completion of its choir in 1339 and the commencement of its nave in 1469.[207]

The two rose windows at Sens Cathedral are even later, for the crossing and transepts were only inserted into the twelfth-century building at the end of the fifteenth century. In the north transept, the circle of the window, with its inverted floral pentagram, nestles among the stepped arches of a glazed screen of 5 traceried lights, each divided in two. The south rose, generated from another six-petalled figure, sits in identical fashion on the arches of another five-light glazed screen. In sum, despite differences of detail, all four of these churches have north transept roses displaying large pentagrams, three of them facing hexagonal roses in the south transept. With the exception of St Quentin's south transept, all of these roses sit above traceried screens of 5 or 10 lights, in common with Chartres, and to these may be added the north and south transept roses at Beauvais and, almost certainly, Laon.[208] The only substantive difference in the four projects examined here, apart from St Quentin's octagonal south rose, is in the setting of pentagrams either apex up or down. Knowledge of the later identification of these two aspects of the figure with witchcraft and black magic respectively is unlikely to take the enquirer back to the fourteenth century,[209] and so the grounds for making this choice at the time must remain a mystery for the present, both here and at Westminster and Romsey (Fig. 144). It certainly raises the question of intent and the possible reasons for it. Likewise, regarding the apparent system behind the pentagonal and hexagonal twinning of the north and south transept windows in three of these French churches, what was important enough about this to ensure its perpetuation at Sens two hundred years after appearing at Amiens?

To attempt to answer this, it may be helpful to turn once again to Henry of Avranches, who was a Frenchman. He contrasts the northerly and southerly eyes of Lincoln Cathedral as being the opposites of each other, as between 'the darkness of Lethe' to the north, which in Greek mythology was the river that flows through the underworld,[210] and the light of heaven to the south. The present Bishop's Eye is a later replacement and will be discussed shortly, but it is hardly surprising that Lincoln's original window facing south should have been associated by Henry with the sun and heaven, nor possibly the same window and south-facing roses elsewhere being associated by others with creation, through the geometry of the hexagon. God's first act in his creation of the world was the invocation, 'Let there be light',[211] and the masons' elaboration of the hexagon into six-foiled roses reads persuasively as an allusion to rose petals and thence the perfection of creation in nature, or, in Henry's words describing the clerestorey windows, 'signifying the varied beauty of the world'. Henry's identification of the south with the Holy Spirit can be explained by a connection between the fire of the Holy Spirit at Pentecost with the fire of the noonday sun burning in the south rose. Elsewhere, it is Christ who is identified with the sun. John of Damascus may have had the verse of Malachi in mind:

> But unto you that fear my name shall the Sun of righteousness arise with healing in his wings …
>
> Malachi IV: 2,

when he wrote,

> God is spiritual light and Christ in sacred scripture is called 'Sun of Justice' …
>
> *De fide* IV. 12.[212]

To Honorius, Christ was also *Sol Justitiae*,[213] in succession to the *Sol Invictus* of the Roman world.[214] As it happens, John's translator, Robert Grosseteste, had a longstanding connection with Lincoln Cathedral before becoming its bishop in 1235,[215] during which time he wrote *Le Château d'amour*.[216] The castle is Robert's metaphor for the Virgin Mary, protecting her unborn child whom he describes in the words of Malachi and John:

> This woman is very beautiful since she had more beauty than any other creature. But when the sun of righteousness took shelter in her holy body, he enhanced it a thousandfold. Through the closed door he entered, and on leaving left it closed.
>
> *Le Château d'amour*.[217]

Facing the midday sun, it is also possible that, in the usual expansion of sexpartite geometry to 12, there may have been an additional connection with the dial of time. It may be significant that when the creed chant, *The Twelve Apostles*, was first published, it appeared under the title, *A New Dyall*.[218]

Henry's association of the Dean's Eye with the characteristics of the north is equally evocative. As the south represents the sun, the fire of the Holy Spirit, the light of heaven, and the invitation to enter, so the north is equated with the moon, the devil, and the darkness that must be avoided in order not to perish. Synonymous with the devil was Lucifer, the fallen angel, the 'light-bearer' of light that is never sunlight. In the twelfth century, Hildegard of Bingen envisions Lucifer trying to set up his throne in the North before being cast down.

> I who am showed my works in East, South and West, leaving the North empty. In that northern zone, beyond the firmament, is a hell … and the darkness there serves the brightnesses of my praise – for how should light be known except through darkness, or darkness except through light?
>
> *Liber Divinorum operum* I. 4. 12.[219]

It was customary for the subjects of the Old Testament to be displayed on the north side of churches, with the New Testament stories catching the sun along the south side, representing a passage through time across the space of the church, and recalling the words quoted by Abbot Suger,

> What Moses veils the doctrine of Christ unveils.
>
> *De administratione* XXXIV.[220]

Because the north side lies to the left on entering a church, Isidore of Seville, in tabulating the 4 parts of cruciform churches, defines it as *sinistra*,[221] carrying with it no doubt the pejorative connotations popularly attaching to the epithet. In this context, it is tempting to see in the pentagrams so prominent in north transept windows the original Pythagorean emblem of health continuing as a medieval sign of protection. In *Le Roman de la Rose*, the fifth arrow shot by the God of Love at his victims was called 'Fair Seeming' and:

> Anyone struck by this arrow could expect protection and to regain his health …
>
> Guillaume de Lorris, *Le Roman de la Rose* I.[222]

It cannot be a coincidence either that it was a pentagram that emblazoned the shield of Sir Gawain in the fourteenth-century poem and protected him against the Green Knight:

> Then they showed him the shield with its shining gules,
> With the Pentangle in pure gold depicted thereon. …
>
> And I intend to tell you …
> Why the Pentangle is proper to this prince of knights.
> It is a symbol which Solomon conceived once
> To betoken true faith, which it is entitled to,
> For it is a figure which has five points,
> And each line overlaps and is locked with another;
> And it is endless everywhere, and the English call it,
> As I have heard, the Endless Knot.
> Therefore it goes with Sir Gawain and his gleaming armour,
> For, ever faithful in five things, each in fivefold manner …
>
> Thus this Pentangle new
> He carried on coat and shield,
> As a man of troth most true
> And knightly name annealed. …
>
> Thus on his shining shield the shape of this knot
> Was royally rendered in red gold on gules.
> That is the pure Pentangle, so called by people wise
> In lore.
>
> *Sir Gawain and the Green Knight* II. 6, 7.[223]

At Durham Cathedral, 3 cinquefoils crown the north window of the east transept, known as the Chapel of Nine Altars and dating from the late 1280s;

Fig. 170 North-east transept window, Durham Cathedral. Two cinquefoils crown the interlaced arches of this six-light window

3 floral pentagrams figure in its north transept window, from around 1360 (Figs 170, 171); next to it is another pentagram in the window which lights the outermost transept chapel; and none of these is repeated on the south side. The 5 great lancet windows in the slightly earlier north transept of York Minster – the Five Sisters – have already been mentioned (Fig. 93), and these are countered in the south transept by 3 lancets, not 5. The same is true of Lichfield Cathedral, where the 5 lancets in its north transept, dating from around 1240, are faced by a different, albeit later, window to the south.[224] It would be a mistake, however, to suggest anything resembling uniform practice. The Dean's Eye at Lincoln, from early in the thirteenth century, is a large quatrefoil in design surrounded by 16 circles, north-facing though it is. In this, it closely follows the north-east and south-east transept windows of Canterbury Cathedral, with which Lincoln has much in common, suggesting other influences at work.[225] Nevertheless, the Dean's Eye does sit over a row

Fig. 171 North-west transept window, Durham Cathedral. Three pentagrams crown this six-light window

of 5 lancet windows, matching the similar arrangements seen at Laon,[226] Chartres, Amiens, St Quentin, Beauvais, Rouen, and Sens,[227] and it is also faced by geometry generated by the hexagon in the south transept's Bishop's Eye of around 1330 (Fig. 54).

In outline, the circle of the Bishop's Eye encompasses two *vesica piscis* figures taking the form of giant leaves, or possibly twin plants complete with central stems, in a clear celebration of the perfection, even idealization, of nature. These, at least, cannot be confused with tongues of flame. Before the end of the thirteenth century, Gothic architecture, particularly in England, was already being garlanded with the sculptural representations of nature with increasing realism. Not that far from Lincoln at the end of the century, work commenced on the chapter house of Southwell Minster, a campaign which has left its internal capitals and bosses covered with the leaves and fruit of common English *flora* as if intended as botanical specimens.[228] This trend, seen best at Southwell though widespread elsewhere across England, has been accounted for in terms of a growing interest in the natural world throughout the thirteenth century. This in turn has been attributed to one effect of the spread of Scholasticism across Europe following the rediscovery and translation of so many of Aristotle's texts that had been lost to the West. Where Plato started with an abstract model of the universe and assimilated its parts in relation to it, Aristotle started with its parts and deduced the structure of the world from them. Posing the simplest questions of any natural object or phenomenon – what is anterior to it, and what posterior? – the world became scientifically ordered according to the system of genera, species, and individuals. The volume of encyclopaedic literature this generated during the thirteenth century, for example William of Auvergne's *De universo*, *De natura rerum* by Thomas of Cantimpré, Vincent of Beauvais' *Speculum naturae*, and *De animalibus* and *De vegetalibus* by Albert the Great,[229] not only laid the foundations for later scientific thought but focused minds more immediately on the fruits of creation itself. Seen in this light, the Bishop's Eye of Lincoln, with the abstract geometry of its double *vesica piscis* implying the equilateral triangle and the overlapping of 3 equal circles, thence the theology of the Holy Trinity, transformed as it is into the leaves of nature thriving in the sun in their south-facing window, surely amounts to a perfect synthesis of Platonic-Aristotelian method, appreciable not least to the masters and scholars of Lincoln's noted cathedral school at the time. In contrast to all the twelve-petalled roses adorning the south transepts of French cathedrals, the twin *vesica piscis* of the Bishop's Eye, for which an earlier window had made way, remains unique and unequivocal.

Although the north-facing Dean's Eye at Lincoln carries no reference to the pentad other than the 5 lancet windows beneath it, the deep central arch of the cathedral's west front is filled with an intricately carved, glazed cinquefoil dating from about 1240 (Fig. 172) and it raises the possibility of a different, though related, contextual connection from the link suggested between the pentagram and north-facing locations. Two pentagrams are set either side of the west door of Binham Priory in Norfolk, and these may belong to the 1230s (Fig. 173).[230] The west front of Ripon Cathedral (Fig. 94), under construction from about 1220 to 1250, has already been encountered with its double row of 5 lancet windows over its triple doorways. Undoubtedly the most dramatic example is the large floral pentagram at the centre of the fourteenth-century window that glazes the west front of Exeter Cathedral, the pentagram consisting of 5 trefoils radiating from an inverted pentagon (Fig. 174).[231] Although this too cannot be confused with sheets of flames and is clearly another image of nature, it is set within a circle surrounded by another circle, which could refer to Ezekiel's wheels within wheels and his 'rings full of eyes' for, in between the two circles, cinquefoiled *oculi* alternate with quatrefoils. This is also reminiscent of Strasbourg Cathedral's west rose (Fig. 160), where the figurate numbers are confined to 5 and 4, readable as the palace of the universe on earth. Unlike Strasbourg, the division of each circle at Exeter is different, for the geometry of the inner circle is pentagonal while the outer

Fig. 172 West front, Lincoln Cathedral. A cinquefoiled *oculus* and a later window sit above the west door

Fig. 173 West door, Binham Priory, marked by two inverted cinquefoils

Fig. 174 West front, Exeter Cathedral. Another wheel within a wheel, the inner one containing a floral pentagram, the outer ring consisting of twelve *oculi* with quatrefoils alternating with cinquefoils

circle is dodecagonal. The latter results in the quatrefoils and cinquefoils numbering 6 each, thereby adding the dimension of creation to the message of the window. To complete the composition of the inner circle, quatrefoils fill the interstices between the 5 trefoils, which, together with the pentagon at the centre, make up the 3 basic numbers of Plato's cosmology, 3, 4, and 5.

The prominence of the pentad present at the west ends of cathedrals at Lincoln, Ripon, Exeter, and Strasbourg for that matter, invites explanation, and in order to make the attempt it is necessary to remember the distinction drawn in the medieval mind between the sanctity believed to exist within the house of God, even though it was not always upheld, and the corruption of the temporal world without. Since the Fall of Man, the world was full of evil, danger, and disorder. Numerous animals and plants, harmless to humans before the Fall, had become dangerous and poisonous.[232] The world was riven by the evil men do to each other and to the Church. The Church had every reason to protect itself and its faithful from the evil without, as it proclaimed for example by offering sanctuary. As the figure of Christ sitting in judgment above the west door reminded worshippers that leaving the everyday world to enter church was a rehearsal for leaving earthly life to enter paradise, so the west door, the principal portal of the cathedral, needed to protect those inside from evil entering. At the very time of the cathedral crusade during the thirteenth century, advances in castle design were recognizing the vulnerability of defences at the point where they had to be breached in order to enter. This caused the fortified gatehouse to challenge the keep for strategic importance, with an increasing number of defensive devices being concentrated at the point of entry, even cordoning off safe ground before it with a barbican, in the case of Grosseteste's imaginary Castle of Love, 7 in number. Just as the fortified gateway had to counter physical danger, so the west door of a cathedral had to defend against spiritual danger. In his verses about Charlemagne's Church of St Denis in the ninth century, Dungal describes the window then over the west door thus:

> Lest the shrewd temptor enter ... , this window shows the hand of God. The four Evangelists guard the whole Body, and the omnipotent spirit the interior. ... the great hand of God guards the church from the enemy ...
>
> Dungal, *Verses on the Church of St Denis.*[233]

Though the protective imagery is different at this date, the impulse was clearly the same, and by the thirteenth and fourteenth centuries it would be understandable if certain patrons thought of the pentagram as a recognized sign of protection. In the words of *The Twelve Apostles*:

> I'll sing you five, oh!
> Green grow the rushes, oh!
> What is your five, oh?
> Five for the symbol at your door ...
>
> *The Twelve Apostles*, Dorset version.[234]

also the five-part nightly ritual of Chaucer's carpenter:

> And he began the spell for use at nights
> In all four corners of the room and out
> Across the threshold too and round about:
> *Jesu Christ and Benedict Sainted*
> *Bless this house from creature tainted,*
> *Drive away night-hags, white Pater-noster,*
> *Where did you go, St Peter's soster?*
>
> *The Canterbury Tales: The Miller's Tale.*[235]

It is interesting to recollect that the only accurately drawn pentagram in Villard's Portfolio, and the only architectural application of one, is constructed above a gateway (Fig. 98).[236]

It can be seen that the architectural evidence and the literary sources, when taken together, demonstrate a connection, not only between number, geometry and recognized meaning, but between meaning and location. To pursue this line of enquiry, if the displaying of pentagrams on north transepts and at the west ends of naves really is evidence of a response to related ideas, then how was it decided which of the two locations to use, and why not in every church? Part of the answer is likely to be that their occurrence may be more common than might be supposed, which will only be ascertained through a comprehensive study of the architectural evidence, or that the expression of the pentad may have extended beyond the design and arrangement of windows, a possibility that will be explored shortly. Another explanation is that different design decisions were implemented as a result of different customs and patronal preferences being exercised on different projects. This would explain the distinct geometric systems in evidence in the tracery of Chartres and Reims in comparison with each other and with English examples. Equally, it might be thought that nothing could interfere with the requirement for a new French cathedral to have a radiating chevet, given its customary adoption across the Royal Domain, yet there were clearly overriding reasons that led to Laon Cathedral's polygonal apse being replaced within twenty years by a choir and ambulatory that are square-ended. Chronology would also have played a part and might explain the apparent anomaly of the quatrefoil windows at Canterbury and their north-facing counterpart at Lincoln, for their designs date from the end of the twelfth century and the beginning of the thirteenth, whereas the examples of cinquefoils and pentagrams cited above on both sides of the English Channel date from much later in the thirteenth and fourteenth centuries and beyond. Finally, different priorities may sometimes have been dictated by the individual circumstances obtaining in a particular building. In common with Strasbourg Cathedral, for example, the reason why Exeter's rose window is its only rose window, and why its pentagram faces west and not north, is probably because its transepts remain the makeshift internal conversions of its original, and unusual, Norman flanking towers (Fig. 174). Likewise, a similar explanation might lie behind the difference in location of the double row of 5 lancet windows over the west door of Ripon Cathedral compared with the Five Sisters, subsequently, in York Minster's north transept. They were both executed under the auspices of the same archdiocese within a decade or so of each other and it has been argued that either location might be equally propitious. One determinant at Ripon therefore was probably the decision to leave the original Norman transepts unreconstructed, as with Exeter's towers, thereby ruling out a design there on the scale eventually achieved across its west front.

There is one church where the choice between expressing the pentad on the north or west fronts may not have had to be made, for the Cistercian abbey at Ebrach, near Würzburg, has both.[237] In the early 1230s, a wheel window was constructed in each of its north and south transept facades, to the familiar pairing of root numbers 5 to the north, expanding to 20, and 6 to the south, expanding to 12. Half a century later, around 1280, a rose window was added to the west front and this was composed of two sets of 10 foils overlapping each other in refined Rayonnant tracery, producing overall a subdivision of 20, in common with the earlier north transept window (Fig. 175).[238] Subdivision by this number is highly unusual and has been attributed to German builders being ignorant of current practice in France,[239] but Ebrach's west rose has been likened to its counterpart at Strasbourg from about 1290 (Fig. 160), except for the different numbers involved,[240] and herein might lie a clue to the thinking

Fig. 175 West rose, Ebrach Abbey; a modern copy of a thirteenth-century window. Ten overlapping foils produce a division of the rose into twenty, quartered. Thus the root numbers of this design are 4 and 5, in resemblance to the west rose at Strasbourg Cathedral with which this has been compared; see Fig. 160. In addition to the refinement of the tracery, other similarities are the enclosing of the circle within a square, with three roundels in each corner, though here they are hexafoils flanked by cinquefoils

behind both windows. In addition to their Rayonnant tracery, both roses are exactly enclosed by a square frame, with a circle in each of the 4 corners flanked by two smaller circles. At Ebrach, the larger circles are hexafoils flanked by cinquefoils, whereas Strasbourg's combine cinquefoils with quatrefoils. Strasbourg's master at the time was Erwin and, according to one report, he came from Steinbach. If this is true, and if this is the town of that name near Frankfurt, then it is not impossible that he knew the abbey church at Ebrach.[241] Regarding the differing numbers and geometry of the two windows, it has already been observed that the division of Strasbourg's west rose is into 16 parts, rather than the 20 at Ebrach. Yet the root is the same, for

Fig. 176 East window, Ripon Cathedral. An *oculus* of two sets of triple trefoils, alternating with each other, crowns two sets of triple cinquefoils and two triple lights separated by one in the centre

the design of both windows is based on the numbers 5 and 4 signifying, conceivably, heaven on earth, in addition to the sign of protection, for it remains the case that Ebrach's two windows face north and west and they both express the decad twofold. This, incidentally, is akin to the lancets of Ripon's west facade, which number the pentad twofold.

Returning to Ripon, it is interesting that, at the opposite end of the cathedral, the east window of around 1300 displays the number and geometry combined in a single window that was seen throughout Westminster and in the north and south transept windows at Amiens, Rouen, Sens, and Ebrach, namely 5 and 6 (Fig. 176). A smaller and slightly earlier version of it fills the east end of Exeter's Lady Chapel. At Ripon, the *oculus* contains 6 trefoils, 3 foliated alternating with 3 each of 3 *vesica piscis* figures, whilst the two sub-arches of the window are each filled with 3 cinquefoils, 6 in all. Being an east-facing window, its composition may be expected to have connotations distinct from those already discussed for the other three facades of cathedrals, and the absence of any reference to 4 in both windows, either representing the Gospels or earth, requires an attempted explanation. The employment of the figurate numbers 3, 5, and 6 readily suggests the Trinity, the universe or heaven, and Creation; also, facing east as they do, they therefore face the next life, which is beyond earth, possibly accounting for the absence of 4. If this is true, it might also explain the 5 lancet windows facing east from Hereford's Lady Chapel dating from the 1220s, as well as those a couple of decades later at the east end of Ely Cathedral above its main group of 3, and elsewhere. Is it possible that, in associating the pentad with the Christian universe – the fifth element, thought by some to consist of ether, and therefore literally ethereal – all these windows, looking out from the easterly termination of their churches, were offering the prospect of the next world that lies beyond? It is worth remembering that, in the presence of multivalency, it is context that can confer specific meaning.

The arrangement of windows in groups of 5 and 10 beneath transept roses also bears examination, especially those windows immediately above the doors into the transepts. Whether occurring in rows of early Gothic lancets or later screens of Rayonnant tracery and, whether it is simply a coincidence or evidence of a symbolic connection, there is certainly a correlation in such cases of 5 as 'the symbol at your door'. It could be argued that there might have been other compositional reasons for choosing to have 5 windows, for example the desire to avoid the duality of an even number. But there could have been 3, as there are at the west end of Chartres. This cannot be argued, however, for the 5 lancets in the south transept of Chartres (Fig. 177). These show Mary holding the baby Jesus in the central window, with the 4 Evangelists either side of her being carried on the shoulders of Old Testament prophets. Thus the number here is finite. In view of this, was the theme chosen to fit 5 windows; are there 5 windows because of the chosen theme; or was this the result of another inspired synthesis of two ideas that are complementary? Whatever the answer, the fact remains that there are 5 windows 'at the door' of Lincoln's north transept and in both transepts at Chartres, Amiens, Beauvais, Rouen, Sens and, almost certainly, originally at Laon. To a modern eye, Ripon's west front might be the better composed if its upper row of 5 windows were reduced to 3 (Fig. 94), for the arches of the outer lancets come uncomfortably close to the base angles of its gable. Three, moreover, would harmonize with the triple lancets in the gable, the triple archways below, and the triple arcading in the 3 upper stages of the towers; it would also announce salvation through the sum of the facade windows numbering 8. Thus there would appear to be every reason why the upper row should contain 3 windows, not 5. Yet two rows of 5 windows were evidently a requirement both here and at York, tempting a possible association of 10 with the Decalogue and 'the perfect number of the universe', in addition to 'Five for the symbol at your door', twofold.

Finally, there is evidence that the expression of the pentad at entrances did not depend on window design alone. With reference to the 5 lancet windows

Fig. 177 South transept facade, Chartres Cathedral. The circle of the dodecagonal rose sits over five lancet windows. The arch of the portal consists of five archivolts above five column figures on each side, which, curiously, represent the Apostles. Five figures also stand either side of the main door in the north front, and another five formerly stood either side of the main west door

Fig. 178 West front, St Maclou, Rouen. Of the five portals of this facade, only the middle three lead into the church

above the south transept portal at Chartres, and whether the theme of the glass determined their number or was the consequence of it, the composition of its central portal suggests that number was the determinant, for either side of it stand column figures of the Apostles, but they number, not 12 but, improbably, 10 (Fig. 177). On each side, one occupies the corner of the front face of the portal, with another four arranged next to it on the splay, making 5. An archivolt rises above each figure on the splay but, presumably because another could not rise from the front figure, a fifth archivolt was fitted in between the fourth and the tympanum, rising from a shaft in the angle with the door post. Furthermore, 5 archivolts rise above 5 column figures each side of the main door of the north portal, this time representing prophets and patriarchs, and 5 figures originally stood either side of the central door of the west front, before two were replaced by plain shafts. There are niches for 5 figures either side of the west door at Sens, and its arch also consists of 5 archivolts, as do the corresponding arches at Laon and Reims. Although nine figures stand either side of the west door at Amiens, they again include a group of 5 Apostles either side, while reliefs of the 5 Wise Virgins and 5 Foolish Virgins rise up the door post either side.[242] Other occurrences of the pentad, such as the extraordinary five-portal facade of St Maclou in Rouen, finished by 1490 (Fig. 178), where the outer portals lead only to a blank wall, and the pentagram set in the paving at the west door of the church at Montreuil, surely testify to a continuing tradition of belief.

Returning to the design and arrangement of windows, one obvious question arises from such a wealth of evidence: such is the diversification of potential meaning, almost anything could be proved given sufficient ingenuity. However, the different layers of meaning examined here are not different in kind. Sticking with the pentad for example, it can be argued that if a pentagram is a medieval sign of protection, it is because it was derived from the sign of recognition among followers of Pythagoras; if 5 represents man through his 5 senses, it is also because of the Platonic relationship between the human microcosm and the macrocosm of the universe; if it represents heaven, it is through the ethereal aspect of the universe, which is the fifth element; if it is the Law, it is through the idea of the Law being an image of heaven, and through its marriage with the decad, which again represents the universe. The root is the universe and the different meanings are complementary to each other, not contradictory. And if they shift with shifts in context and still maintain observable consistency, this may actually point to the place of symbolism in tracery design and more broadly as well. For it would mean there were systems of thought behind symbols and their locations, however mutable they may have been, which would enable a patron, chapter, or building committee to incorporate them into their requirements, or to approve them if they happened to be present in the builders' proposals. This could have enabled York's archbishops to commission, or sanction, lancet windows grouped in fives in Ripon's west front and in York's north transept; they both worked symbolically in those locations, just as they would have done for Ebrach's chapter. There will undoubtedly be exceptions that are difficult or impossible to explain but it is contended that the architectural evidence nevertheless demonstrates a degree of consistency between number, geometry, and meaning, and between content and context, corroborated by external evidence, that suggests patterns of thought and practice that make exceptions noticeable.

Conclusions

This final chapter has attempted to show that a correlation exists between known metaphysical formulae, understood and documented at the time as exemplifying the created order of the universe, and architectural form, designed in expression of it. Both the pentagon and the circle, being the plane figures of the dodecahedron and the sphere, were representative of 'the whole frame of the universe'. From Antiquity, the sepulchral function of the circular shrine evolved beneath its dome of heaven, eventually becoming fused with the octagonal geometry of the 'eight-choired temple', as evidenced by the intrinsic presence of the figurate numbers 4, 8, and 12 in both types. These signified the duration, start, and end of the spiritual journey that led to salvation through baptism and death, and which can be seen overlaid by associations with 'divine quaternity', the teaching of the Gospels, and the community of the Apostles. Of all examples, the intended symbolism of the various types of architectural octagon is borne out by the literary and iconographic evidence. Similarly, the octagonal chapter house, along with its decagonal and dodecagonal relatives, indicate both a self-imposed restriction on the choice of geometric form and programmatic reasons for making it that accord with their functions.

By contrast, the range of geometric subdivision in chevet design reveals a diversity across the sample studied, yet there stands out the predominant division of apses and ambulatories into 5 parts, followed by others divided into either 6 or 7, with invariably 4, 6, or 8 columns around each apse. This will have arisen from the builders' constructional considerations in determining the geometry of the apse and ambulatory, and the placement of columns and chapels, presumably in answer to the chapter's requirements. The results again suggest a degree of consistency and possibly a connection with specific meaning appropriate to a sanctuary of a major church that could have been intended at least sometimes, and which was certainly capable of being interpreted in such terms. Negative evidence may equally be suggestive of a conscious exercise of choice. Whilst the division of the circle by 12 was used for chapter houses and chevets, the hexagon was not for either,[243] despite the hexagon being the simplest polygon of all to construct and common to wheels of fortune. Although division by 7 was common for chevets, no chapter houses are seven- or fourteen-sided. This is despite their being regarded by Abbot Ware as the workshop of the Holy Spirit, which was symbolized by 7. Consequently, this leaves the enclosure of octagonal chapter houses – by far the most common type – by the 7 walls enfolding their entrances a distinctly plausible explanation. Clearly, separate sets of considerations were being made which, for the geometric and architectural form of chapter houses and chevets, will have followed custom, or local tradition, or sometimes will have been a matter of individual choice. Whichever was the case, it will presumably have required an agreement between chapter and lodge with whatever reasoning lay behind these choices in the first place. For the design of chevets, any intended symbolism would doubtless have been incorporated but, even in the absence of anything prescribed, the chapter could well have been interested in the potential for it in the builders' proposals and based their acceptance partly on this.

The division of the circle inherent in the schematic design of these types extended to a corresponding division in the linear designs of wheels of fortune, the zodiac, life, and Scripture as well as geometric tracery, all carrying possible meaning connected with their function and context. In surveying the different divisions of the circle in wheels of fortune, the range of choice seems at first sight to be so wide as to appear arbitrary, as in some cases it may have been. Yet emerging from the apparent diffusion, the common division by 6 or 8 reveals a degree of consistency that is matched by two distinct sets of meaning, each relevant to the idea of fortune, about the passing of time and about lives in the balance, independent though they may be from each other. The design of tracery in its many forms also appears to be bewilderingly diverse at first sight yet, in common with chevets and wheels of fortune, certain patterns of application become discernible. With the three basic Platonic figures combining with the circle and taking the form of trefoils, quatrefoils, and cinquefoils, extending to hexafoils and, less commonly, octafoils and decafoils, these figures also occur in the design of circular windows. They are generated from divisions of circles by 4, extending to 8 and 16 parts; by 5, expanding to 10, 15, or 20; and most commonly 6, expanding to 12 and occasionally 18. Combining the underlying meaning of eye, wheel, and probably rose with the symbol of the sun and time; the circle and square of heaven and earth, the palace of the universe on earth and the heavenly city; the number and geometry of Christian Platonist truths; the start, duration, and end of the spiritual journey; the fiery wheel of Scripture and the Evangelists; fortune, the zodiac, and judgment; the symbol of protection and the perfection of creation; the wheel and rose window and the great *oculi* illuminating these churches stand as the ultimate model of medieval multivalency.

Because the permutations of geometry in tracery design, combined with their locations in a building and with the meanings that can be ascribed to them, are so numerous, it would be theoretically possible to prove almost anything were it not for those cases where a consistency of applied design suggests systematic thought and practice. This is seen in complete buildings such as Reims Cathedral and Westminster Abbey as first designed, and in additions such as the Angel Choir at Lincoln and Hereford's aisles. Although it is rarely possible to be certain that any particular meaning was intended and, if it was, what it was, it is nevertheless possible to detect an observable coherence in design and posit the meaning it may have carried. It certainly seems possible for Strasbourg Cathedral's west rose. Of the multitude of variables in the evidence, intended symbolism is often indicated by its context, especially its location in a building. There is firm evidence for a protective function for the pentad when sited to the north, or to the west, or both, or when it is otherwise associated with entrances, marked as it is in popular chant as 'the symbol at your door'. It is also possible to infer from the internal evidence a heavenly aspect to the pentad when facing east, although no independent corroboration has so far been found for this. On the other hand, hexagonal geometry in south roses is almost the rule, and it seems irresistible to see a connection between light and creation, for which there is both internal and documentary evidence. The connection between the numbers 4, 8, and 12 with the notion of the spiritual journey that leads to heaven means that a similar reading can be suggested for both octagonal and dodecagonal rose windows when facing west above a principal portal, not least because they each divide into quarters, which in turn offers an additional connection with wheels of Scripture. There is no doubt, however, that many variations appear exceptional, such as Westminster's gallery windows overlooking its cloister, uniquely cinquefoiled in a scheme of octafoils; the octagonal geometry of Paris's north rose and St Quentin's south rose; the decagonal geometry in the south-facing window of Anselm's Chapel at Canterbury, also in the south rose at Burgos; and the seven-pointed star in the south transept window at Laon. Unless the argument is to be seriously entertained that the tracery design of the major windows of cathedrals and of other important projects was no more than arbitrary pattern-making that meant nothing, these apparent exceptions must represent different preferences being exercised, arising perhaps from differing patronal insights and interests.

Among the imponderables in this chapter, a few certainties may be ventured. All the architecture and art described here was open to interpretation at the time, regardless of intent. Given the importance assigned to signification in the Middle Ages, much of it would undoubtedly have been intended. All the indications are that this was the case with Charlemagne's Chapel. In this, he was adopting custom for, while 8 is explicitly identified with salvation, baptisteries and *martyria*, which stand as specific models of salvation, are almost always octagonal. The restriction to 8, 10, or 12 sides for polygonal chapter houses, Laon Cathedral's square-ended choir, and Amiens Cathedral's north rose are so particularized that they must be evidence of specific commissioning or approval. The process by which the intention would have been conceived, formulated, communicated to the builders and implemented in the workshop and on site would have been complex and variable. It may safely be assumed that there would have been a wide variation in the degree of programming, with some chapters active, others reactive to builders' proposals. There might well have been delegation on both sides, with decisions about key elements of the work being taken higher up the command structure than the mass of routine repetitive work, some of which might have been left to the masons. There would certainly have been a variation in the level of interest shown in a project, with some bishops, such as Hugh of Avalon, being actively identified with their building work, and others like Robert Grosseteste apparently showing no interest at all in the same project. The preferred design methods and working practices of individual lodges would have played an equally important part, for if the patron or chapter prescribed what was to be done, it was the builders who were left to decide how it was done, or even to make proposals in the first instance. Schematic design and constructional design would have constituted the two sides of a single process, the objective being to emulate 'the choice architect of the universe, ... [constructing] the marvellous form of the kingdom of the world', that is 'the whole frame of the universe'.[244]

Notes

1 John of Damascus, *De fide*, tr. Chase (1958), 204.
2 Grosseteste, *Hexaëmeron*, tr. Martin (1999), 222.
3 Alan of Lille, *De planctu*, tr. Sheridan (1980), 118, 144.
4 Plato, *Phaedo*, tr. Jowett (1871/1953), I. 469.
5 Euclid XIII. 17.
6 Walter of Speyer, tr. Stadler (1991).
7 Mesarites, tr. Downey (1957), 892.
8 See Godfrey and Hemsoll (1986), 196–201; see also MacDonald (1976), *passim*.
9 28 is also a perfect number in succession to 6, being the sum of its parts.
10 See also Hiscock (2000), 128–9.
11 Sadly, the loss of mosaic, caused by cracks in the dome being repaired and left without the mosaics being restored, makes it difficult to reconstruct the intended coherence of the overall scheme in the mind's eye. The line drawing shown at

least reconstructs one of the 8 heavenly choirs, even though it is presented as if applied to a flat surface.

12 Honorius, in Harvey (1972), 226.

13 Durandus, tr. Neale (1843), 26.

14 For modifications to the *aedicule*, see Ousterhout (1990), 46 fig. 3.

15 Biddle (1999), 66, fig. 62, 67, fig. 63A; Coüasnon (1974), 14–16.

16 Mersmann (1982), 10–11, 16–19.

17 Williams (1934), 533.

18 See also Biddle (1999), 66, fig. 62, 67, fig. 63A.

19 The third-century round temple at Ostia had a similar arrangement although the articulation between its tangential portico and entrance into its rotunda was better handled. See MacDonald (1976), fig. 104.

20 See Prologue, 'The architectural programme, patrons and architects'.

21 See Prologue, note 154.

22 The foundations of the lost two columns still exist beneath the pavement. Coüasnon (1974), 28; see also Biddle (1999), 78–80, fig. 65.

23 See Chapter 2, 'Union of the macrocosm and microcosm'.

24 See Prologue, 'Arithmetic'; also Hiscock (2000), 127–32, 146–8.

25 Clement, *Stromateis*, tr. Wilson (1869), 284, quoting Plato's *Republic* X. 616B.

26 Augustine, *De civitate Dei*, tr. Bettenson (1984), 687.

27 Augustine, *De sermone Domini*, tr. Kavanagh (1963), 29.

28 Augustine, *De civitate Dei*, tr. Bettenson (1984), 643.

29 Augustine, *Contra Faustum*, tr. Stothert (1872), 214.

30 Alcuin, *Epistolae*, tr. Stadler (1990).

31 Notable exceptions are the hexagonal fonts common around Aquileia and Dalmatia up to the sixth century, before being supplanted by cruciform fonts under Justinian, and a baptistery in Zadar, also of the sixth century. The numerological justification proposed for them is that, as an extension of 6 representing creation, man was created on the sixth day and baptism creates in him the Christian, also Christ was crucified on the sixth day, thereby linking baptism with death once again; Skoblar (2005), 2–6. This paper reported the work of P. Chevalier, E. Marin, D. di Manzano, and others on Early Christian basilicas, baptisteries and fonts in the regions of Aquileia and Dalmatia. I am most grateful to Magdalena Skoblar for this information.

32 *Octachorum s(an)c(t)os templum surrexit in usus,*
octagonus fons est numere dignus eo.
Hoc numero decuit sacri baptismatis aulam
surgere, quo populis vera salus rediit
luce resurgentis Chr(ist)i, qui claustra resolvit
mortis et e tumulis suscitat exanimes …

Ambrose? in *Sylloge* (1934), 155, tr. Stadler (1996).

33 Gregory of Nyssa, *Epistola* XVI, tr. Wilson (1893), 540–41.

34 The alignment of the Apostles and the baptismal scene in the centre with the ring of temples and the centres of the window arches is not exact, but it was clearly meant to be.

35 Another obvious difference between the two churches is their entrance and narthex arrangements.

36 Einhard, tr. Thorpe (1969), 78, 79.

37 See above, Alcuin, *Epistolae*, 260, tr. Stadler (1990).

38 Hugot (1990), 8–10.

39 In the context of Aachen's documentary sources, this is generally interpreted as 'church'.

40 Author's italics, tr. H. Stadler from site notes by author: CUM LAPIDES VIVI PACIS COMPAGE LIGANTUR INQUE PARES NUMEROS OMNIA CONVENIUNT CLARET OPUS DOMINI TOTAM QUI CONSTRUIT AULAM.

41 Other examples include the chapel at Groningen, St Lambert at Muizen, and St John in Liège. The inner core at Aachen was also adapted for the three-sided apse of Essen Minster's west choir.

42 See Chapter 1, under 'The Greek Cross and Byzantine church design'.

43 Suger assigns the 12 inner piers of his choir at St Denis' Abbey to the Apostles and the 12 outer piers to prophets; *De consecratione V*.

44 Matthew 3. 11.

45 Psalm 73. 13.

46 Acts 1. 5.

47 John of Damascus, *De fide*, tr. Chase (1958), 346–7. It is not suggested here that the mosaics of Daphni follow John's 8 baptisms but that each represents a totality within its own terms encompassed by the number 8. As it happens, John's reference to Pentecost, through the tongues of fire alighting on the Apostles, finds expression in the mosaics of the catholicon of Holy Luke, Daphni's counterpart, where it is to be found in the saucer dome over its sanctuary.

48 John of Damascus, *De fide*, tr. Chase (1958), 345.

49 In a notable study, the division of the circle into different numbers of parts was claimed to provide the geometric proportioning for buildings from Ancient Egypt through to the Middle Ages. The system proposed was different from the applications noted in this chapter, for the use of radial geometry was shown to generate the rectangles of ground plans by connecting selected radial points on the circumference of circles so divided. Principal among these was the division of the circle by 10, but also included were the other denominations up to 12, excepting 9 and 11. It will be seen shortly that, very rarely, a wheel of fortune could be drawn divided into 9 parts. Although the methodology involved in testing such theories against specific buildings, and in demonstrating the evidence, has advanced in recent years, the basis of Moessel's geometric thesis may still be worth considering in itself. Moessel (1926), I. *passim*, especially 4–10, 16, 19–20, 69–76; idem (1931), II. 11, 139–41.

50 A distinction is postulated here between a schematic division of a circle that may have been executed at design stage by using dividers, and a separate, empirical method that might have been part of lodge practice for setting out polygons on site, for instance for chapter houses and apse colonnades, such as the setting-out of the five-sided tower in the previous chapter.

51 For a general survey of English chapter houses, see Götz (1968), 299–321.

52 The survey included examples that are extant, ruined, or recorded before removal. They are, or were, situated at Abbey Dore, which was Cistercian and twelve-sided; Belvoir, Benedictine and eight-sided; Beverley, secular and eight-sided; Bolton, Augustinian and eight-sided; Bridlington, Augustinian and may have been ten-sided; Carlisle, Augustinian and eight-sided; Cockersand, Premonstratension and eight-sided; Elgin, secular and eight-sided; Evesham, Benedictine and ten-sided; Hereford, secular and ten-sided; Howden, secular and eight-sided; Lichfield, secular and is an elongated octagon; Lincoln, secular

and ten-sided; St Paul's, London, secular and eight-sided; Manchester, secular and eight-sided; Margam, Cistercian and twelve-sided; Pershore, Benedictine and circular; Salisbury, secular and eight-sided; Southwell, secular and eight-sided; Thornton, Augustinian and eight-sided; Wells, secular and eight-sided; Westminster, Benedictine and eight-sided; Whalley, Cistercian and eight-sided; Worcester, Benedictine and circular, subdivided internally by 10; York, secular and eight-sided.

53 Braunfels (1972), 169.

54 Götz (1968), 313.

55 Richard de Ware, in Stanley (1868), 388.

56 *St Paul's Bible*, Rome, St Paul, f. 1. m, fol. 308v; Götz (1968), 317, pl. 120; Crossley (1986), 12–13.

57 See Epilogue, 'Survivals of symbolism'.

58 Crossley (1986), 13–15.

59 Lichfield Cathedral's chapter house is an elongated octagon.

60 Braunfels (1972), 171; engraving by W. Hollar, in Dugdale (1658).

61 Ibid., 58; Butler and Given-Wilson (1979), 68–9; Cook (1961), 64–5, 109–10.

62 Augustine, *De sermone Domini*, tr. Kavanagh (1963), 29–30. In other words, $(7 \times 7) + 8/8 = 50$!

63 Braunfels (1972), 11, 58; Butler and Given-Wilson (1979), 68–9; Cook (1961), 109–10.

64 Richard de Ware, in Stanley (1868), 388.

65 Odo of Cluny, in Hallinger, in Hunt (1971), 334.

66 *ODCC* (1997), 1062.

67 MS. Ham. 82, Berlin; Vregille, in Hunt (1971), 86.

68 Götz (1968), 310; Braunfels (1972), 170.

69 The chapter house at Whalley Abbey was octagonal.

70 This includes the walls of circular chambers divided internally by 10 or 12.

71 Evesham, Hereford, and possibly Bridlington, were decagonal. A partial exception is also Lichfield Cathedral's chapter house, dating from the 1240s, which is an elongated octagon.

72 This is confirmed by Villard's inscription beneath his plan.

73 Barnes, *The Portfolio of Villard de Honnecourt* (forthcoming, 2008).

74 Readers are reminded of the discussion about possible methods for masons to set out pentagons, decagons, and other polygons in the previous chapter.

75 The need to divide an apse into a certain number of parts did not arise for the first time with the introduction of ambulatories and apse colonnades, for many solid apses are divided internally and externally by pilasters. Nevertheless, it was the arrival of the apse colonnade that made the geometric division of apses imperative.

76 Hiscock (2000), 242–4, pls 85–90.

77 Hiscock (1994), 155–7; idem (2000), 241.

78 Hiscock (1994), 149–51; idem (2000), 239–40.

79 Hiscock (1994), 152–4; idem (2000), 240–41.

80 An earlier division by 14 is found terminating the choir of St Stephen's priory church at Vignory, dating from the 1050s but, exceptionally, this polygon is rotated so that there is an axial pier behind the altar and none on the apse chord.

81 Critchlow (1979), 100–101, fig. 71.

82 Shelby (1977), 119. See Epilogue, under 'Continuing practice and forgotten knowledge'.

83 See Cowen (2005), 261.

84 The sample included the churches at Caen (St Stephen), Clermont-Ferrand (Notre Dame), Conques, Fleury, Jumièges, Nevers, St Denis, St Quentin, Santiago de Compostela, Tewkesbury, Toulouse (St Sernin), Vézelay, Vignory, and Westminster; and the cathedrals at Amiens, Beauvais, Bourges, Cambrai, Canterbury, Chartres, Clermont-Ferrand, Cologne, Evreux, Laon, Narbonne, Norwich, Noyon, Paris, Reims, Rodez, Rouen, Sens, Soissons, and Toledo.

85 Tewkesbury 1092; its chevet was rebuilt in the fourteenth century.

86 Canterbury Cathedral 1174, Rouen Cathedral 1202, Toledo Cathedral 1226, and Westminster Abbey 1245. For the geometric synthesis between the sanctuary apse and chevet chapels at Westminster, see explanatory text in 'Symbolism in tracery' below.

87 Nevers Priory 1083, the cathedrals of Norwich 1096, Evreux 1119, Sens 1143, Noyon 1148, Laon 1160, Paris 1160, Vézelay Abbey 1185, Bourges Cathedral 1192, the collegiate Church of St Quentin c. 1195, and the cathedrals of Soissons c. 1200, Reims 1211, Cambrai 1220, Narbonne 1271, and Rodez 1277.

88 Jumièges c. 1037.

89 Jumièges c. 1037, Conques c. 1100, St Denis 1144, and the cathedrals of Amiens 1220, Beauvais 1230s, Cologne 1248, Clermont-Ferrand 1248. For the modified geometry at St Denis, Amiens, and Beauvais, see following explanatory text.

90 St Stephen, Caen 1200s.

91 Vignory 1050s, Fleury 1067/1108, Santiago de Compostela 1075, Toulouse (St Sernin) 1080s, Clermont-Ferrand (Notre Dame) 1185, and Caen (St Stephen) 1200s.

92 Chartres Cathedral 1194. For the geometric synthesis between its Romanesque and Gothic layouts, see the explanatory text that follows shortly.

93 Crosby (1966) 4, 5, 8. Crosby later published more accurate survey drawings, but this did not affect the two-centred geometry of the ambulatory and central chapels, despite the fact that he did not repeat the earlier demonstration of the geometric construction; Crosby (1987), 235–8, pls 1, 2. His later plan also demonstrates how the underlying division of the chevet, however inaccurately it was set out, is dodecagonal. A line drawn north–south through the keystone of the sanctuary vault, parallel with the transverse arch of the first straight bay, describes the diameter of the dodecagon. To the east is half a radiating bay on each side and five full radiating bays in between, completing half the twelve-sided figure.

94 Murray and Addiss (1990), 58–60, fig. 22; Murray (1996), 35–6, 41, figs 40a, 40b; idem (1989), 15, figs 6, 8, 9.

95 The studies in question alternatively argue for an empirical subdivision of the circle into thirteen equal parts, not twelve (Murray and Addiss (1990), 59; Murray (1989), 15, fig. 9), but this is not the only conclusion possible. A simple test of this is that, if the diagram of the Amiens *schema* (Murray and Addiss (1990), 60, fig. 22) is mirrored to the west of its chord, a dodecagon is the result, not a thirteen-sided figure. By measuring the angles on the published plan, those dividing the five equal segments fall almost exactly half-way between the angle of a thirteen-sided polygon, c. 27.69°, and that of a regular dodecagon, 30°, and so the case might be argued either way. In correspondence with the author (24. 8. 2006), Stephen Murray states that the choir geometry may be explained 'in several different ways'. It may equally be argued for instance that, since the dodecagon already existed as an established figure for laying out chevets, it is more likely

that the architects at Amiens and Beauvais adapted a figure they knew rather than invent another for which there may not have been precedent. This would also explain the position of the centre-point of each apse lying forward of the last straight bay, for this is an inevitable product of rotating dodecagons.

96 See also 'Symbolism in tracery' below. The continuing difficulty in laying out chevets, nearly a century and a half after St Sernin, has recently been demonstrated for Reims, where its centre-point is displaced, the arcs of the apse and ambulatory are not concentric, and the piers around the apse are spaced irregularly; Wu (2007), *passim*.

97 The geometry of the choir apse at Chartres is further complicated by the setting out of its vault, for its compartments radiate from a keystone lying forward of the last straight bay, but this should not be confused with the radiating geometry used to lay out the apse colonnade at ground level.

98 Generally columns around apses are similar in design to each other, and only occasionally alternate with piers, such as at Vignory, Toulouse, and Sens.

99 The geometry at Vignory, as already noted, alone among the rest of the sample, is rotated, despite the division of its apse into 7, which produces an axial column behind the altar and none on the chord.

100 The exceptions were Vignory, which has 7 columns and piers, and Tewkesbury, which has 2, both arising from the unusual application of their geometry.

101 The half-octagon apse became more common later in the Middle Ages.

102 Except for Vignory, which has 7 columns and piers.

103 Gwilt (1903), 1006–7.

104 See Dionysius, *De coel. hier.* VI. 1, 2.

105 Linscheid-Burdich (2004), 56. As already observed, when Suger lists the altars of these chapels (*De consec.* VII. 237), it is evident that he adds the two chapels at the ends of the last straight bay to the seven around the chevet. However, if this number was significant, he does not say so, and it does not appear to be reflected in the dedication of the chapels.

106 Dow (1957), 265, 269; Cowen (2005), 203.

107 See Chapter 3, section 'The Wheel of Fortune and the Zodiac'.

108 For a graphic sample of wheels of fortune, see Courcelle (1967), figs 65–86.

109 Boethius, *De consol.* II. 1.

110 Courcelle (1967), pls 73. 1, 74. 1, 76. 2, 82. 1, 85. Care needs to be taken generally in distinguishing the spokes of a wheel from its axle and sometimes the supporting posts.

111 An example of the latter is in Courcelle (1967), pl. 77. 1.

112 London, BM Add. 10,341, fol. 31v, in Courcelle (1967), pl. 76. 1. See also Mersmann (1982), 44–5.

113 London, BL MS. Arundel 8311, fol. 126v.

114 Sears (1986), pls 87, 89.

115 Boethius, *De consolatione*, tr. Tester (1973), 179.

116 Alan of Lille, *Anticlaudianus*, tr. Sheridan (1987), 190.

117 Kline (2003), 38.

118 Sears (1986), 147.

119 Dublin, Trin. Coll. Lib. Cod. 347, fol. 1r. See Sears (1986), 144–9.

120 An explanation for this will be attempted shortly.

121 Eusebius, tr. Oulton (1932), 391.

122 Boethius, *De arithmetica*, tr. Masi (1983), 165.

123 Maître (1995), 272, 277–8.

124 Guy d'Eu, in Maître (1995), 154, tr. Beech (2000).
125 There appears to be no correspondence with the tracery or glass of the rose window, which is the third in this position and dates from around 1500; Murray (1996), 100–101.
126 Sears (1986), 145.
127 Mersmann (1982), 78; Murray (1996), 99; Kline (2003), 44.
128 *Old Testament*, French, c. 1240. New York, Pierpont Morgan Library, MS. 638, fol. 3r.
129 Alan of Lille, *Anticlaudianus* VIII, tr. Sheridan (1987), 191.
130 Page (2002), 53.
131 Isidore, *Etymologiae* XIII. 1. 1, II. 3, XIV. 1. 1, 2. 1. Isidore's image is taken to be allegorical, rather than a postulation of a new theory about the earth rotating. Kitzinger (1973), 347–54, 365–6.
132 Dow (1957), 277. The grounds for claiming this association for the St Denis window are the wheel design combined with reliefs of the 4 Evangelists' symbols in the corners of the enclosing square. These, however, are now attributed to Debret's restoration early in the nineteenth century (Crosby (1987), 170). Although the present window tracery also belongs to the nineteenth century, Scamozzi's drawing of around 1600 shows a twelve-spoked wheel and this is also suggested by Martellenge's sketch of 1741. Following these, Martinet (c. 1780), Céllerier and Legrand (c. 1815), and Rouarque show a clock face filling the round aperture of the window. See Gerson (1986), 141, 208, fig. 11; Crosby (1987), frontispiece, 190, fig. 82, 193, fig. 83.
133 Dionysius, *De coelesti hierarchia*, tr. Luibhéid (1987), 190.
134 See Chapter 4, under 'Mathematics and metaphysics of the square and its derivatives'.
135 Jerome, *Commentariorum in Ezechielem Prophetam*; Gregory the Great, *Homiliarum in Hiezechielem Prophetam*.
136 Jerome, tr. *NPNFCC* (1893), 101.
137 Gregory, *Homiliarum in Hiezechielem* I. 6. See also Augustine, *In Beatus Joannis: Hom*. 3.
138 Dow (1957), 273–7, 279.
139 See Chapter 3, under 'The Wheel of Fortune and the Zodiac'.
140 The west window at Fossanova Abbey, dating around 1200, is divided into 12, whilst the west window at Orvieto Cathedral of 1356 is exceptional in having 22 spokes. Mersmann (1982), 87, fig. 81, 89, fig. 83.
141 Mersmann (1982), 87–91, 94–5; Cowen (2005), 126, 203–5.
142 *Annali* I. App. 3, in Ackerman (1949), 100.
143 Dow (1957), 269, 285–6.
144 Ibid., 268–9.
145 Ibid., 269.
146 See 'The Eyes of the cathedral' below, and the Epilogue.
147 As distinct from its apse.
148 Brown and O'Connor (1991), 34–43.
149 Ibid., 43–4, 53–5.
150 Becksmann (1967), 11.
151 Dow (1957), 294.
152 Becksmann (1967), 11, 15, 23–4, 41–2; (1995), 26–8. Although Becksmann's field of study is the Upper Rhine between 1250 and 1350, the architectural,

iconographic, and practical development of stained and painted windows is observable in its general trends elsewhere in Europe.

153 The east window of York Minster, dating from the 1400s, was supervised by the glazier John Thornton in collaboration with the stonemasons; Brown and O'Connor (1991), 11–14.

154 Gwilt (1903), 1039.

155 Artmann (1991), 45–6.

156 Cowen (1979), *passim*.

157 For a recent summary of the construction process at Reims, see Clark (2006), 85–114, especially 93–8.

158 Hiscock (2000), 244–7, pls 91–5.

159 The north rose, despite being entirely replaced in the nineteenth century, nevertheless retains the sixteen-part division of the original, and the same applies to the twentieth-century renovation of the south rose.

160 The design of the internal gallery arcading is uniform throughout the church.

161 The clerestorey and aisle windows of the second campaign in the nave are given quatrefoiled *oculi*.

162 In the first four bays on the south side of the nave, overlooking the cloister, these windows have triple cinquefoils, inverted. In the second campaign, there are also triple cinquefoils along the nave, north and south, but all pointing up.

163 This form of chevet became popular in Germany.

164 This has had the effect of skewing the first turning bays of the ambulatory, but this was not inevitable. It is possible to project 5 chapels from a rotated half-octagon regularly, provided the westerly pair are centred on the chord of the apse, but this leaves a half bay at the end of the choir arcade. It was presumably to avoid this that regularity in the ambulatory was sacrificed.

165 See 'Geometric tracery' above.

166 Morris, in Aylmer and Tiller (2000), 208–21, 227.

167 Although work on the north transept was under way by 1255, it was planned in the 1240s; Morris (2000), 212, 215, 216.

168 It is not suggested that this was a programme which was premeditated from the outset, yet as it progressed, those concerned must have been aware that they were contributing to a general modernization of the cathedral around its Romanesque core.

169 As with Westminster Abbey, there are anomalies. The windows in the south-east transept are similar in style but not geometry, having three elongated quatrefoils, probably as a result of a mid-fourteenth-century rebuilding of this transept; Morris (2000), 224. Also the two east windows of the north nave aisle are altogether different due to the different bay conditions there between the porch, its vice, and transept.

170 Morris (2000), 233, 235.

171 Villard, Portfolio, fol. 19r. Bechmann suggests that these two figures could have been representing the decimal and duodecimal systems; Bechmann (1991), 320–21.

172 Ripon's windows were constructed with twin lights and tracery, which were later removed.

173 Those at the east end of Worcester Cathedral and in the south transept of St Alban's Abbey belong to the nineteenth century.

174 Garton (1988), 1, 4–5. Hugh died in 1200.

175 Henry of Avranches, tr. Garton (1988), 59.

176 Ibid.
177 See discussion in Dow (1957), 279–81.
178 Ezekiel I. 18.
179 Jerome, *Ep.* LIII. 9.
180 Dow (1957), 251–3.
181 Ibid., 260–65, especially 263; Mersmann (1982), 33–4.
182 Guillaume and Jean (1999), ix.
183 Guillaume and Jean, tr. Horgan (1999), 43.
184 Ibid., 26, 51–2.
185 Dante, tr. Sisson (1998), 452–3.
186 The present window is a fifteenth-century replacement.
187 For recent bibliographies, see Beretz (2004), 23–4); Cowen (2005), 273–4.
188 One example of both is Meyer (1977), 103–6.
189 For example, Franz (1956), 1–22; idem (1957), 253–70; Mersmann (1982), *passim*.
190 Kobler (1987), cols 65–203.
191 For example, Suckale (1985), 59–86.
192 Franz (1956), 1–22; idem (1957), 253–70. Among the symbolic possibilities acknowledged is the wheel of fortune, also rose windows framed by symbols of the Evangelists. These the author accepts as symbolizing Christ Triumphant, stopping short of Dow's convincing argument, made in the same year, connecting them with Ezekiel's fiery wheel, then developing into windows symbolizing the wheel of Scripture; Franz (1957), 270; Dow (1957), 273–9.
193 Dow (1957), 248–97.
194 Cowen (2005), *passim*, especially 195–261. An earlier work by the same author does show how the application of number and geometry to the design of rose windows can be read in expression of Christian Platonist thought, but the connection is presumed rather than substantiated, the understanding of the literary and documentary record seems at times questionable, and is conflated with oriental and Jungian thought. In the tabulation of number theory from 1 to 12, the omission of 10 is inexplicable, as is the omission of the Holy Trinity from the meaning of 3, the Gospels from 4, the universe from 5, perfection and creation from 6, and the Holy Ghost from 7; Cowen (1979), *passim*, especially 81–6, 91–4.
195 Mersmann (1982), *passim*.
196 See Dow (1957), 291, 293–5; Cowen (1979), 82–3; idem (2005), 200; Mersmann (1982), 84. One unexplained anomaly in Dow is the ascription of the west rose, rather than the north, to evil; see below.
197 Alan of Lille, *De planctu*, tr. Sheridan (1980), 144.
198 Rev. 21. 12–16. See Chapter 4, under 'The New Jerusalem'. See also comments on the east rose of the same period, c. 1225, at the Cistercian church at Ebrach, in Suckale (1985), 65.
199 Cowen (1979), 26, 27, 35, 36; idem (2005), 90, 101–3.
200 Laon's north rose is composed of 8 octafoils around a large octafoil in the centre. This contains a modern copy of the figure of Philosophy, who is surrounded by personifications of the liberal arts, five of them original, their number being made up to 8 by the addition of Medicine. The south rose was replaced around 1350 by the present large window, with the badly flawed execution of its *oculus* around a seven-pointed star; see Cowen (2005), 70, 227, 260–61.
201 Clark and King (1983), 26, 48, 54; idem (1987), 61.
202 Murray (1996), 101–2.

203 Cowen (2005), 126.

204 Murray (1996), 100–101.

205 I am most grateful to Ellen Shortell for details of St Quentin and for allowing me to see extracts of her unpublished thesis (2000). See also Héliot (1959), 48.

206 The tracery design in the different parts of St Quentin is extremely diverse, undoubtedly reflecting a spasmodic building history that spread over more than three centuries. Of particular interest, nevertheless, in addition to its rose windows, are the thirteenth-century clerestorey windows around the choir, which are crowned by a ring of 5 *oculi* that are decafoiled (Fig. 147).

207 Wilson (1992), 248.

208 Laon's north transept rose, celebrating the liberal arts, sits over four lancet windows and part of a fifth, which is blocked up. This must have occurred when work was started in the fourteenth century on a new gable-end window, perhaps in succession to the one installed in the south transept, which was then stopped, leaving the westerly lancet truncated. Bearing in mind the deliberation behind the design of this cathedral, not least in the matter of its west and east roses facing each other down the length of the church, the present fourteenth-century window in the south transept, with its disastrous *oculus*, must have replaced a facade similar to the north transept, with a rose window above 5 lancets.

209 Guiley (1989), 265–6. Until its subversion by the black arts, the pentagram appears to have enjoyed no more prominence in medieval magic than other geometric symbols, apart from necromantic literature; see for example Page (2004), *passim*, especially 29–52. I am grateful to Sophie Page for this information.

210 Cotterell (1989), 216.

211 Genesis I: 3.

212 John of Damascus, *De fide*, tr. Chase (1958), 353. In this passage, John was explaining the principle of orientation in worship and why 'the East should be dedicated to God', which nevertheless leaves his ascription of Christ to the sun intact.

213 Honorius, *Speculum ecclesiae: De nativitate Domini*, PL 172. 833–4.

214 Dow (1957), 286.

215 Robert's first recorded connection with the cathedral was as a witness to a document near the year 1190 and he later held a prebend at the cathedral; McEvoy (2000), 21.

216 This is the title that was given to the first printed edition, since none appears on any of the manuscripts, and it is taken from the text; Mackie, in O'Carroll (2003), 156–7.

217 Grosseteste, *Château d'amour*, tr. Mackie, in O'Carroll (2003), 168. See also Epilogue, under 'Survivals of symbolism'.

218 *A New Dyall*, BM. MS. Harleian 5937. See Eckenstein (1906), 143.

219 Hildegard of Bingen, tr. Dronke, in Derolez and Dronke (1996), LI; Latin text, 144.

220 Suger, *De administratione*, tr. Panofsky (1979), 75.

221 Isidore of Seville, *Etymologiae* XV. 4.

222 Guillaume and Jean, tr. Horgan (1999), 16.

223 *Sir Gawain*, tr. Stone (1965), 49, 50. See also Epilogue, under 'Survivals of symbolism'.

224 Lichfield's lancet windows in its north transept were reconstructed late in the nineteenth century, faithfully it is believed.

225 There could well be a connection, for example, between the quadripartite design of the Lincoln window with justice, for the theme of its glass, which alone in the

cathedral survives in its original position, is devoted to the Last Judgment (Morgan (1983) 14). As it happens, the north-east window at Canterbury, which is also quadripartite, represents the Law of the Old Testament, and this could have served as the precedent for the Lincoln window, regardless of its northerly siting being contrary to the customary location of Judgment imagery at the west end. Confusingly, the Last Judgment also appears to have been the subject of the glass in the later Bishop's Eye at Lincoln (Morgan (1983) 20), indicating perhaps the particularization of which individual commissions could be capable.

226 See note 208.

227 It will be recalled that all but St Quentin, but probably formerly including Laon, incorporate the pentad in the glazing below the rose windows of their south transepts as well.

228 The realism of these carvings does not extend to a consistent scale.

229 Pevsner (1945), 20–23, 31–3, 52–5.

230 Uncertainty surrounds the west front of Binham for it was reportedly finished before 1244 and yet its lowest stage stylistically has suggested that it should be dated to the 1270s.

231 Notwithstanding a report in 1817 of the reconstruction of this window, which must have been meant as a report of an intention to rebuild it, no trace survives and the internal masonry of the window is original to the medieval period. It was completed some time after 1342 in its present form, as shown in an illustration of 1825. No survival of any remodelling was noticed during the reglazing of the window in 1904. I am most grateful to John Allan for this information.

232 See Grosseteste, *Hexaëmeron* IV. 27. 1, 2; VII. 6. 1, 7. 1.

233 Dungal, tr. Baldwin Smith (1956), 83.

234 Ashbee (1903), 2–3.

235 Chaucer, tr. Coghill (1979), 112–13.

236 Villard, Portfolio, fol. 18v.

237 See Suckale (1985), 59–86.

238 The present west rose is a modern copy, the original being kept at the Bavaria National Museum in Munich. The church also has an east rose in plate tracery, slightly predating the transept windows, and this is dodecagonal in common with the south transept window.

239 Suckale (1985), 66.

240 Ibid., 69.

241 Ebrach is roughly seventy miles east of Steinbach. However, the origins of Erwin and the correct identification of Steinbach, if this was his home-town, have yet to be agreed. I am most grateful to Charlotte Stanford for her advice.

242 A similar display of the Wise and Foolish Virgins dating from the nineteenth century appears on the jambs of the west door at Paris, although for this to count as evidence would depend on their being copies of medieval originals.

243 Except for the chevet of Tewkesbury Abbey.

244 Alan of Lille, *De planctu* VIII. 4, tr. Sheridan (1980), 144; Grosseteste, *Hex.* VIII. 1. 2, tr. Martin (1999), 222.

Epilogue

Part One: Conclusions

Summary of findings

The starting-point of this study lay in the contention that the historical context of medieval religious architecture suggests that the explicit presence of number and geometry in it is evidence of intended symbolism. The record shows that Pythagorean number theory and Platonic geometry were understood as exemplifying the fundamentals of the universe. This was absorbed by the early Church and transmitted to the Middle Ages in the form of Christian Platonist thought, being taught in the schools through the liberal arts and communicated to churchmen and laity alike through religious architecture and art. Texts from late Antiquity through to the High Middle Ages repeatedly confirm the Christian Platonist view that was taken of the universe.

Architects early in the Greek Middle Ages, schooled in the liberal arts, were capable of working to a patron's programme, including any desired symbolical content, whilst various abbots and bishops early in the Latin Middle Ages were regarded as operating as the architects of their own building projects, instructing builders, and producing results that were recorded at the time as embodying number and architectural form symbolically. Suger, who commissioned the chevet of his own church, construed its columns as standing for the 12 Apostles and, where others associate the 3 portals at the entrance to a church, or 3 windows over a high altar as signifying the Holy Trinity, it is likely they were placed there for that reason. By the thirteenth century in the West, the architect had become established as a lay professional and is portrayed taking instructions from the project's patron, advancing the development in the relationship between patron, programme, architect, and building that suggests a dual process involving schematic design and constructional design. The *schema*, in whatever form, would embody the patron's programme and could be expected to involve the transmission of ecclesiastical tradition, based on authority, and including the eternal truths of religious belief. The Plan of St Gall, together with the basic types of round and cruciform churches identified by Honorius, as well as Villard's Cistercian plan can all be seen as *schemae* for individual projects to follow. As such they would have conveyed to the builders what the programmatic content of the building should be, leaving the builders to determine how this was to be achieved by developing the constructional design through their architectural skill and lodge practice.

Literary and graphic evidence attest to planning grids of churches being drawn up and laid out on site, with a dimensional module being handed to the masons for translating into a building plan through the technique of quadrature, which was also used for producing the necessary details.

The correlation between metaphysical formulae and architectural form is nowhere more explicit than in the various types of domed church in the Byzantine world. Whether the building is the Great Church of Hagia Sophia, or the Greek Cross type of basilica, or the Greek Cross inscribed in a square, or the inscribed octagon type of church, a hemisphere surmounts a supporting cube, with the dome unifying the external form and the internal space. Together they symbolize the dome of heaven above the cube of earth, as described repeatedly in contemporary literature and iconography. And of all these archetypes, one flourished for at least seven centuries, namely the Greek cross-in-square church, and stands as the perfect synthesis of the Platonic-Orthodox model, the central cupola on its 4 pillars, its 4 corner cupolas, the square enclosure, signifying at once the universe and heaven, the elements and the Gospels, set on the square of earth.

As explicit as the symbolism of the sphere and the cube in the East, was that of the cruciform church in the East and the West. Embodying the dualities of temple and body, God and man, macrocosm and microcosm, documentary evidence in both halves of Christendom makes it clear that the form symbolized the crucifixion not only of Christ, but of man by the tribulations of the world. Similarly, Christ appears outstretched behind maps of the world which, in common with contemporary church plans, were habitually orientated vertically. Behind these two types was the Biblical notion that the temple was Christ's body, the temple representing the macrocosm and the body the human microcosm, reaching back to Plato's concept of the universal scheme. Each possessed symmetry, according to which their parts were in proportion to each other and to the whole. Furthermore, the union between the two is demonstrated mathematically by the product of the three figurate numbers of the macrocosm – $3 \times 4 \times 5$ – being in union with the product of the two perfect numbers – 6×10 – proportioning the microcosm.

The architectural geometry of the equilateral triangle, the square, and the regular pentagon, together with their derivatives and figurate numbers, are so integral to the experience of medieval religious architecture that it is difficult to avoid a conclusion that they were fundamental to its schematic, as well as its constructional, design. That the equilateral triangle and its derivatives were employed in art and architectural design is amply borne out by the documentary evidence of Villard de Honnecourt, the Milan Congress, and the writing of Cesariano, among others, as well as abundant evidence in art and architecture, replete as they are with equilateral arches, the *vesica piscis*, trefoils, hexafoils, and hexagrams. With the number 3 recognized in Antiquity as the first complete number and 6 the first perfect number, their Christian association with the Holy Trinity and the perfection of Creation is confirmed not only in exegetical writing but also in architectural description, where they are seen symbolized in the numbers of portals, windows, and altars. By extension, 12 is associated with the Apostles in the numbers of sanctuary piers, as described by Eusebius and Suger, and in the creed chant of the same name. In so doing, the latter source provides evidence of much the same number symbolism existing in popular culture, including another aspect of 12, as the dial of time in wheels of fortune and the zodiac, together with the hexagram of Solomon's Knot signifying the act of creation.

The Milan Congress is also an authority for designing *ad quadratum* and, by the time it started convening, its cathedral had already been laid out to a planning grid of square and double square bays. Although this was not the only system of plan design, for other plans display different proportions,[1] it was nevertheless a practice going back over half a millennium, through Villard's Cistercian grid of squares, to the *Plan of St Gall*. And if the whole layout of a church may be regarded as a macrocosm in its own right, then the square, by which its details were created through the process of quadrature, was its microcosm. Ultimately, designing *ad quadratum* can be traced back to the Old Testament, where the New Jerusalem is described built on a square, and the Tabernacle and the Temple were planned with a double square Sanctuary leading to a square Holy of Holies, undoubtedly equating the unity of the square with the unity of God. As the plane figure of the cube, representing earth in Plato's cosmology, the square was identified with stability and justice, with diagrams of the world quartered by the 4 elements, the 4 winds, the 4 seasons, and much else, just as man consisted of the 4 elements, the 4 humours, and the 4 temperaments. With the adoption of this construct by the Church and its assumption of the 4 authorized Gospels, came the concept of 'divine quaternity', with symbols of the 4 Evangelists depicted, as if in support, in the corners of vaults and around images of Christ in judgment and Ezekiel's Wheel, all being matched by the proliferation of the quatrefoil in tracery. As the Pythagorean tetract, implying the universal decad, 4 encompassed the basic musical consonances, and primacy of these was given to unison, in the ratio 1 : 1, and diapason, which is 1 : 2. The reason given was that diapason is the most closely related consonance to unison, which is 'the most perfect concord' because it consists of unity and equality. Unison and diapason exemplify similarity and difference respectively, and therefore equality and harmony. Harmony is hard won and the Cistercian Order was not alone in understanding that the harmony heard is the proportion seen, when it gave importance to both chant reform and architectural design. The architectural equivalent of unison and diapason is the square and double square in its layout, and the square of quadrature in its details, rendering them in proportion to the whole, and showing another correlation between the documentary and the architectural record.

The pentad and the pentagon, as the fifth element in Plato's scheme, stood for the macrocosm, signified by the dodecahedron as an abstraction of the universal sphere, as well as the human microcosm, with its 5 senses, the pentagram being worn as an emblem of health by the followers of Pythagoras. This evolved into the medieval sign of protection on Gawain's shield, and 'the symbol at your door' to avert evil, whether from north or west; with the pentagram, the cinquefoil, and windows by fives found in these locations in churches, and above the gateway in Villard's drawing. In its universal aspect, because the Law was potentially 'an image of heaven', the pentad also bore a relation to the decad, as the Pentateuch embraces the Decalogue. And so it may be in this sense too that cinquefoils and windows grouped in fives are found facing east, beyond the earthly church to the next life in the sphere of heaven, thereby bringing the chain of meaning full circle.

As the dodecahedron is to the sphere of the universe, so the pentagon is to the circle, signifying 'the whole frame of the universe'; and as the universe comprised the elements, so the Platonic figures representing the elements are found associated with the circle. The architectural expression of this was achieved in two ways. One lay in the division of the circle radially into numbers of parts conforming, with one exception,[2] to the figurate numbers of Platonic geometry, which themselves held potential significance. This resulted not only in the subdivision of circular shrines, chevets, and various *rotae*, but also in the form of polygonal structures typified by baptisteries, *martyria*, and chapter houses. The second means was to compose Platonic figures and circles in relation to each other, as in geometric tracery. This reached its climax in the rose window, where the two methods achieved a synthesis of radial subdivision and concentric rings of foliated figures.

Given the wide range of interpretive possibilities behind the occurrence of number and geometry in these examples, it has often been their context that has helped in suggesting specific meanings that could have been intended. Included in such an analysis is the function of the object, its location, documentary support, other forms of support, and various combinations of these factors. The divisions of the Pantheon's dome by 28 and its rotunda by 8 cannot have been accidental. The dome, being the upper half of a notional sphere inscribed within the rotunda, open to the sky, and directed toward midday, strongly suggests, at least in part, an astronomical-*cum*-astrological function that would justify referencing 28 to the lunar month.[3] The octagonal division inside the rotunda suggests in part a memorial function, bridging the Roman mausoleum and Early Christian *martyrion*. The octagonal and dodecagonal geometry overlaying each other in the former tomb-house, now S. Costanza, reflects the beginning and end of the spiritual journey to heaven on the eighth and twelfth days, as enunciated by Plato and transmitted by Clement of Alexandria. It is an explanation and combination that apply equally to those baptisteries which are eight-sided and portray the 12 Apostles around the empty throne. The key is 8 being the signifier of salvation, as taught by the early fathers and inscribed over the baptistery in Milan, reportedly by Ambrose. It is an association that extends logically to octagonal chapter houses which commemorated their deceased brethren and entombed their deceased superiors at the door. Similarly, number and geometry correspond with the other functions of chapter houses, 10 with obedience to the rule of law, 12 with the first Christian community of Apostles. Despite variations, wheels of fortune are generally divided by 6 or 12, or by 4 or 8, the former undoubtedly in reference to change coming with time, the latter with life in balance. All circles divided by 8 or 12 are quartered and could represent the wheel of Scripture, but when they are placed as windows on the west front of a church, facing worshippers as they approach, and are supplemented by the symbols of the Evangelists in the 4 corners of an enclosing square, then it can be certain that the programmatic intent was Ezekiel's wheel. Likewise, the connection between the decagonal wheel of life with the 10 ages of man, and between the dodecagonal wheel and the 12 houses of the zodiac, positively link number and geometry with belief, and complete the incorporation of the Platonic figures.

In view of the weight of evidence in favour of signification in these examples, the absence of corroboration for it so far in the geometry of chevet design cannot mean that sanctuaries alone were exempt from the symbolism of number and geometry. The number of chapels would certainly have been agreed with patron and chapter, if not the arrangement of columns around the high altar. This was the foremost focus for contemplation of the whole church, and they invariably number, 4, 6, or 8, with obvious symbolic connotations, although which was causal and which effect cannot be hazarded. Geometric tracery is markedly diverse in possible meaning, so that it too needs to be considered in context, even though this will often leave questions unanswered. Nevertheless, despite the exceptions, for which individual explanations remain to be discovered, the beckoning function of west facades could only be reinforced by installing Ezekiel's wheel of Scripture, promising the teaching of the Word to all who enter, such as those cited in Italy; or the octagonal geometry of windows promising salvation, perhaps as at Amiens; or the circle of 12 octafoils in Chartres' window marking the beginning and ending of the spiritual journey, with judgment at the gates of paradise in its glass and above its west portal; or Strasbourg's cinquefoils and quatrefoils proclaiming the cathedral to be heaven on earth; or finally in offering sanctuary by passing beneath the pentagram's sign of protection at Lincoln and Exeter. In like manner, the pentagram averting evil from the north, and the hexagonal geometry of south transept windows celebrating the perfection of creation in the noonday sun, as 'the light of heaven' and the 'Sun of justice', growing into dodecagons of rose petals, or tongues of flame recalling those alighting at Pentecost on the 12 Apostles; in such cases, the varied symbolism of number and geometry appears to fuse into specific meaning pertinent to their physical location.

Main conclusions

Two important questions have emerged from this study, and neither is capable of yielding a conclusive answer. The first concerns the dynamics of decision-making. It has been remarked throughout the latter part of this investigation that patrons, chapters, architects, builders, and artisans were faced with making multiple choices during the life of a project, whether it be the architectural form of the building, its structural requirements, liturgical needs, or any desired symbolic content, such as the number of entrances, the number of sides for a chapter house, the number of columns behind an altar, the composition of an aisle window, the choice of a wheel window for a certain position and the number of its spokes. Without knowing how the choice was made, it is not possible to affirm that its symbolic content was intended, which leads to the second question.

This has been concerned with distinguishing between intention and interpretation. There can be little doubt that they were often one and the same in the Byzantine world, given the correspondence between architectural form, its iconography, and *ekphrasis*, and similarly in the West with the cruciform church. In other cases in the West, such as Æthelwold's tripartite church at Thorney Abbey 'in praise of the Trinity', Oswald's church 'in the fashion of a cross', and the turreted crossing tower proposed for Milan to resemble God surrounded by the Evangelists, the patron's intention has been recorded, however much the stated symbolism might have coincided with satisfying other requirements. Elsewhere, the intention may reasonably be inferred; for example, the number symbolism of Ramwold's crypt was recorded within living memory of the work being done as being part of Ramwold's plan, and when Eusebius praised Paulinus for the 3 portals of his church standing for the Holy Trinity, he did so in person, and so this was likely to have been the reason Paulinus had for following custom in the first place. Nevertheless, in the vast majority of cases, there is no record of intent, which leaves them open to conjecture, yet there are two powerful indicators of deliberate symbolism that lie either side of a design being formulated. On the one hand, the overwhelming body of exegetical and encyclopaedic literature shows Christian Platonist symbolism to be a habit of thought, whilst on the other hand, the body of eulogistic interpretation of architecture in precisely the same terms strongly suggests that number and geometry were intentionally incorporated into work for their symbolic meaning. Whilst the literature proves that patrons had the motive, the fact that the work was executed in this fashion proves that builders had the means.

There might still remain one doubt. Since the permutations of meaning surrounding a particular figure produce multiple possibilities of specific meaning, it might be theoretically possible that a choice of number and geometry could be made in a design purely pragmatically, or even arbitrarily, and still be interpreted symbolically. To anticipate a suggestion that this might be the case, numerous examples have been presented here where systems of design can be seen to correspond to particular systems of thought. These instances can be categorized into designs for complete buildings; recurrent patterns in different buildings; and individual elements within buildings. Belonging to the first category is the dome of heaven and the cube of earth, the cruciform church, octagonal baptisteries, *martyria*, and chapter houses. The second category includes similarities in signification between the window designs of different projects, such as in the aisles of Lincoln's Angel Choir, Hereford, and St Ouen; also transepts where pentagrams in north-facing rose windows confront the hexagonal geometry of south roses; the correlation between the pentad and doorways; and architectural elements grouped in threes. Thirdly are those individual elements which contain their own schematic integrity, such as the west rose at Strasbourg and the Bishop's Eye at Lincoln. The window design of Reims Cathedral, taken as a whole, is a particularly coherent example of systematic design, being rooted in only one of the figurate numbers of Platonic geometry, and manifesting itself in the numbers 3, 6, and 12, in its portals and window arrangement, and in its geometry of equilateral arches and hexafoils. The expression of the Trinity, Creation, Time, the first Christian community of Apostles, and the Heavenly City might be thought more than adequate for the framework of a cathedral to contain its programmes of glass and sculptures, serving, as it were, as its own 'frame of the universe'. But in view of the occurrence of the same system, albeit in more varied forms, elsewhere in northern France, might not this also be the result of general lodge practice, potentially devoid of inherent meaning? The answer must be that this is possible, but unlikely, for it is inconceivable that everything about a cathedral – its programmes of sculpture and stained glass, the content of the liturgy and composition of sacred chant, above all the choice of architectural form – should be designed to convey meaning, and yet the number and geometry used by the builders in the design of the architectural frame alone did not. Though the scale and scope of their understanding of God's creation will have varied from the advanced to the elementary as between patrons, architects, and builders, they nevertheless belonged to the same Christian society and, while patrons were indeed educated churchmen and often scholars, from the twelfth century onwards, architects were increasingly literate and capable of interpreting and implementing a brief, and the Christian upbringing of even the most humble builders will undoubtedly have taught them that 3 stands for the Trinity, 6 for the Creation, and 12 for the Apostles.

In view of all the evidence presented, it may reasonably be claimed that a correlation exists between the articles of Christian Platonist teaching and a corresponding symbolism in medieval religious architecture. This is also consistent with the findings in *The Wise Master Builder* by the present author, which investigated the geometric proportioning of plan design in medieval abbeys and cathedrals. From a wide sample, and with a few exceptions of detail, it was found that each plan can be generated in stages by using the sides of the equilateral triangle and the diagonals of the square and the regular pentagon. Each could be commenced around the crossing, with each of the geometric figures used in the first three steps. Similarities in the application of this system were found between projects that were historically or geographically related to each other and, of those tested mathematically for accuracy, all showed a correspondence between the geometric system and the dimensions of the building in question to within 98.5 per cent degree of accuracy, and this in a *milieu* where, it is generally accepted, the degree of building error can be 3 per cent and more.[4] Thus the geometric system that could have been used to lay out medieval abbeys and cathedrals is consistent with the system investigated here – the one implicit, the other explicit – they are the same. Accordingly, it is argued that the literary evidence of medieval thought adduced here would have justified the choice of number and geometry that is evident in the resulting architecture. The presence of intent is also either shown or strongly suggested by much of the documentary evidence, or by the context of the work in question. To substantiate its presence any further in individual cases would need more work on the documents.[5]

If the thesis of this book is correct, there should be evidence of the symbolic use of Pythagorean number theory and Platonic geometry in fields of medieval culture other than architecture and art, and there should also be evidence of this symbolism being perpetuated as the Middle Ages advanced. The latter will be interesting to determine given the gradual supplanting of the Platonic tradition by Aristotelian Scholasticism up to the middle of the thirteenth century, accompanied by the supplanting of cathedral schools by universities, following the rediscovery of so many of Aristotle's texts. To conclude this investigation therefore, it is proposed to examine romance literature and musical composition for evidence of a continuing Christian Platonist tradition, for this would lend additional support for its presence in the ecclesiastical architecture of the earlier period, and then return to architectural design and practice in order to determine its continuity. The whole exercise will be done on the basis of sampling, and presented as a series of test cases; it is in no sense intended to be a comprehensive late or post-medieval history of architectural symbolism, for that is not the purpose of this book.

Part Two: Inferences and Implications

Survivals of symbolism

Evidence from literature and music has been cited during the main part of the investigation, from the chant reform of the Cistercian Order in the twelfth century, and from Chaucer and *Sir Gawain* in the fourteenth century. It is now intended to enquire into the romance literature of the twelfth century onwards, especially the architecture as imagined in it, since this coincides with the period of the architectural investigation; also sacred chant from the thirteenth and fourteenth centuries, focusing on the contest between the *ars antiqua* and *ars nova*, and the implications this had for Boethian music theory.

Romance literature

In writing *Le Château d'amour*, Robert Grosseteste created an imaginary castle that either refutes contemporary expression of Christian Platonist thought or demonstrates its polyvalency. The castle symbolizes Mary protecting her unborn child. It has a tower keep built on rock; 4 turrets rise from its battlements; 7 steps lead up to an ivory throne inside; 3 wards surround the keep outside and these are protected by 7 barbicans. Robert details the meanings of these numbers, which seem more Christian than Platonist. The 3 wards stand for the Virgin's maidenhood, chastity, and marriage; the 4 turrets represent the cardinal virtues of strength, temperance, justice, and prudence; the 7 barbicans, the virtues vanquishing the vices.[6] That it is no more Platonist than this is probably to be explained by the nature of this part of his treatise. It is a meditation upon Mary, written in the vernacular for members of the Franciscan community in Oxford, including local noblemen.[7] It is devotional, not metaphysical. Had Robert wished to turn *Le Château* into a metaphysical work, few could have been in a better position to do so, for he was chancellor of Oxford University before becoming bishop of Lincoln, and was one of the leading scientific thinkers and teachers of his day whose writings, especially his *Hexäemeron*, were thoroughly Christian Platonist in outlook. This being the case, it would have been equally fitting for the castle's 7 barbican's to represent the protection given by the Holy Ghost, having brought about the Virgin's immaculate conception; the 7 steps, which Robert does not explain, the path to wisdom attained by the one who attains the ivory throne;[8] the 4 turrets, 'divine quaternity', of which the cardinal virtues were a frequent manifestation; the 3 wards, the Holy Trinity, in the furtherance of whose work Mary was labouring.

The most famous of literary castles belonged to the succession of grail legends from late in the twelfth century through the thirteenth and beyond, and these are suffused with numerology. Among them, *Le conte du Graal* is the earliest to have survived and was commenced in the 1180s by Chrétien de Troyes who died without completing it. *Perceval* followed shortly afterwards from the hand of Robert de Boron and, perhaps in the 1200s, Wolfram von Eschenbach produced his own Germanic adaptation entitled *Parzival*. In this, he mentions the Temple of the Gral, which was elaborated by Albrecht von Scharfenberg in *Der jüngerer Titurel* around 1270. In the accounts by Chrétien, Robert, and Wolfram, the castle, as may be expected, is described as superlative, yet it is not endowed with any obvious symbolism involving number and geometry, apart possibly from Chrétien's structure possessing a tower and a hall that are each square. Rather it is the accoutrements of the castle and the activities in the tale that are specified by number. The castle, after all, was the setting for the procession of the lance and the grail and, in Chrétien's *Conte*, the pentad and decad are found to be pervasive. The two golden candelabra which precede the grail hold 'at least' 10 candles each; Gawain wins a duel and gives his victim's horse to a young maiden, and when she says:

> 'Five hundred thanks, good sir'.
> [Gawain] knew exactly what she meant …
>
> Chrétien de Troyes, *Le conte du Graal*.[9]

By the time Perceval met his hermit-uncle on Good Friday, he had forgotten God for 5 years; another castle is 'very well designed' with 500 windows guarded by 500 archers.[10] There is much less in Robert's *Perceval* but this is compensated by the *Parzival* of Wolfram, for here the specification of numbers is comprehensive, largely involving 4, 25, and 100 and centering upon the castle. Its hall was hung with 100 chandeliers and, within its 4 walls, 100 couches were set, each seating 4 knights, each served by one chamberlain from 100 tables placed before them, each knight being proffered a drinking cup from one of 4 trolleys drawn along the 4 walls, with 100 pages dispensing loaves in white napkins. Surprisingly perhaps, central though the grail is to each tale, it changes with each. To Chrétien, it is a serving dish which is subsequently disclosed to hold a single host which is all that has sustained the hermit's brother for 12 years; to Robert, it is the vessel which holds Christ's blood and which had been given to Joseph of Arimathea; to Wolfram, it is the stone that provides food and drink for the Company of Gral Knights[11] and which is otherwise kept in the Temple. His description of the procession of the lance and the grail is both elaborate and detailed, with great attention given to the numbers of celebrants. After the arrival of the lance, which a page carried around the 4 walls of the hall, maidens entered by twos and fours bearing the golden candelabra, two ivory trestles, candles, the table formed of a single precious stone, followed by two knives, and a light, at which point Wolfram makes sure his audience has counted 18 ladies. These are followed by another 6, making 24, and finally the princess bearing in the grail, which is set before the lord, making 25.

No explanation is offered here or in the other versions reviewed for the significance of these numbers, or if indeed any particular significance were intended. Specifying 500 windows, or 500 archers, or 100 pages may simply have been meant to indicate very many. In other cases, it may be reasonable to conjecture a connection, for example, between 12 and the number of Arthur's knights, as being analogous with the Apostles. Yet why does Wolfram draw his audience's attention to 18 ladies at that particular interval in the procession, or to the final complement of 25? After Parzival's first visit to the castle, he made a point of telling his hermit-uncle,

> I saw five-and-twenty maidens of excellent bearing standing there before the King.
>
> Wolfram, *Parzival* IX.[12]

And again on his return, the grail was brought in as before,

> … [by] maidens … in due order … to the number of five and twenty.
>
> Wolfram, *Parzival* XVI.[13]

Several interpretations are possible, but one, that of 5 squared, might be supported by that other Arthurian romance, *Sir Gawain and the Green Knight*.

This was written late in the fourteenth century in the dialect of the northwest of England.[14] The pentagram that is borne on Gawain's shield is part of a complex of properties and powers assigned to the pentad that can be set out as 5 × 5, or, in the words of the poem when describing Gawain,

> … ever faithful in five things, each in fivefold manner …
>
> *Sir Gawain* II. 6.[15]

These are his 5 wits, derived no doubt from his 5 senses; his 5 fingers; the 5 wounds of Christ in whom he trusted; the 5 joys of Mary on whom he also depended, namely the Annunciation, Nativity, Resurrection, Ascension, and her own Assumption; and his 5 virtues of liberality, lovingkindness, continence, courtesy, and above all his piety. In other words, the poem puts him forward as the perfect example of the human microcosm, the 'prince of knights … devoid of all villainy', and overlays his 5 categories of pentadic perfection upon the 5 points of the pentagram, 'the Endless Knot' and emblem of protection:[16]

> … These pure five
> Were more firmly fixed on that fine man
> Than on any other, and every multiple,
> Each interlocking with another, had no end
> Being fixed to five points which never failed …
>
> *Sir Gawain* II. 7.[17]

It is a connection that is equally relevant to the grail legends, for Perceval's quest for the grail was also, necessarily, a quest for human perfection, hence surely the recurrence of not only the pentad but also its association with the decad of the macrocosm as well.

The number 5 is also present, both overtly and covertly, in the Grail Temple, which is described in *Der jüngerer Titurel* by Albrecht von Scharfenberg. Titurel was the ancestor of the grail kings, an angel having entrusted the grail to him. He was over four hundred years old when he started building the temple and it took 30 years to complete.[18] It was located on a cliff of onyx on the mountain taken from Wolfram's *Parzival*. After Titurel cleared the site,

> … the Grail sent the king guidance in writing. Whatever was needed was found before the Grail, according to the master builder's every desire.
>
> [It enabled] him to create the temple in the form, dimensions and ornament that he desired, He found these sketched out all around the onyx.
> He found the foundations sketched out on the stone in elegant proportion …
>
> Albrecht von Scharfenberg, *Der jüngerer Titurel,* 370, 339–40.[19]

There follows a description of the temple, which has a dream-like character given to it because, although it is highly detailed, the detail is rarely related to a context, its sequence wanders, as if in a dream, and the meaning is frequently obscure. Such attempts as have been made to reconstruct it fall short because they presuppose the existence of a *schema,* which probably did not exist in Albrecht's mind. In his words, but re-sequenced here, the temple was '[round] like a rotunda … broad and high'; the foundation was six feet high and there was a distance of 'thirty feet all round, from the outer wall to where the steps ascended'.[20] It was encircled by choirs, 'all octagonal and projecting forwards',[21] and these have been construed as 22 in number, although in the source regarded by the translators as the 'best manuscript', this evidently reads as 72,[22] surely a sum more plausible numerologically. 'The choirs … all had dividing walls'[23] with two doors into each.[24] 'The greatest of the choirs pointed to the Orient … [and was] dedicated to the Holy Ghost … since he was the patron of the whole temple'. The Virgin's choir was next to it, John's may have been the other side, with those of the 12 Apostles nearby.[25] 'Wherever the choirs projected at the corners [Titurel] … placed on top of each pair high belfries, six such chambers, all identical … The belfries matched the noble choirs, forming a circular garland to the honour of the Grail, beyond the means of ten kings. … There were eight walls, and just as many corners, equalling the numbers of the choirs. … Each chamber had three windows in every wall'.[26] There were 3 portals which faced north, south, and west,[27] and '[before] each of [them] were placed all the different kinds of stones which formed part of that great, rich edifice. … How many kinds of stones were carved? Five broad circles were formed from them'.[28] Inside, there stood 4 massive statues of the Evangelists,[29] and all the arches of the temple, 'supported by flying buttresses, met at a central point, converging from four directions, and where the corner points were formed there was no lack of archangels and evangelists in splendour',[30] whilst above, '[one] tower stood in the midst of all this … crafted of gold … together with many thousand radiant, bright, pure stones … the equal in height and breadth of two others'.[31]

The interior was equally rich and filled with wonders. 'This elegant edifice [made of red gold] was borne by pillars of bronze. My heart would rejoice if I were ever to see a temple so rich in all its interior ornament. Each precious stone shone forth in its own colour from the red gold. Where the arches rose to meet the sweep of the flying buttresses many rich designs could be espied, curling above the pillars, beautifully carved, skilfully executed with elaborate ornament. The work was luxuriously embellished with pearls and corals';[32] 'many bright stones there gave off an excess of red light. The glare of the stones lit up the bright gold so that it reflected back their brilliance'.[33] The windows were fashioned from pearls and bright crystals and were embellished with precious stones.[34] 'Over all the vaulting was the blue of sapphires',[35] and the floor was a sea of crystal with fishes moving 'as if they were living in the waves'.[36] Much attention is lavished on the choirs, Albrecht reminding his audience that, 'God himself gave in the form of a sapphire that writing to Moses which frees man from all sin … observing all those commandments, five times paired. For this reason the altar stones were entirely of sapphires'.[37] The choirs were provided with vats of balsam, 6 inside and another 2 outside each choir;[38] 'the walls were well furnished with emeralds',[39] and filled with 'wondrous foliage', '[the] flowers of all plants', vines and 'leaves hung in thick clusters' rustling in the wind and, '[flying] over the vines many bands of angels, [who] responded with absolutely life-like motions' to the rustling of the leaves;[40] and 'whenever the priest sang, a silken string was pulled. A dove brought an angel, who came flying down from the arch. A wheel took him back again'.[41] Clocks, with their '[golden] bells announced … the times of the seven days',[42] and, above the west gate was installed an organ with singing birds in a tree of gold, and 4 angels on the ends of its branches, each with a horn of gold.[43] Above the choirs, each bell-tower around the circle was crowned by a ruby supporting a cross of crystal and a golden eagle[44] and, on top of the central tower, a carbuncle shone as a beacon for the templars.[45] As with the bejewelled interior, they irradiated their own mystical light and to this was added the light of the Grail itself. 'This same rich temple was devoted to the Grail, so that it could be kept there every day and when it was raised on high a broad and radiant sacristy was visible below'.[46]

Descriptions of architectural fantasies such as this demonstrate how much easier it was for a writer to give full rein to his imagination, not least through the use of exaggeration, than it was for an architect, and the same was true of those artists who delighted in portraying architecture that could only exist in the mind. For the material realization of fantasy, it was mainly left to the production of micro-architecture in tombs, shrines, and chantry chapels that achieved the richness, slenderness, and delicacy of detail impractical in a structure built to full size. However, although Albrecht's vision is pure architectural fantasy, the form of his temple bears an uncanny resemblance, albeit on a reduced scale, to the Liebfrauenkirche in Trier, which may have just been completed when he wrote his poem (Figs 179, 180).[47] Its form is a tall Greek Cross, with polygonal terminations to the cross-arms, an extended choir, and a high central tower. These are set within a faceted circle made up of peripheral chapels, 8 in number and half-octagonal in plan inserted diagonally in pairs between the cross-arms. The round form and centralized space of the structure, encircled by 'choirs, all octagonal and projecting forwards', together with the large axial chapel dedicated to the Virgin, must have been very similar to the form Albrecht was to imagine. As one of the first Gothic churches to appear in Germany, the Liebfrauenkirche must have seemed fantastic indeed to its citizens, especially when it is remembered how rich the interiors of High Gothic churches were, being gilded and painted throughout and illuminated by candelabra, banks of candles, and windows glowing with jewel-like stained glass. Furthermore, the mechanical devices that would have been needed to realize Albrecht's fantasy already existed. With this in mind, it might follow that both imaginary and material architecture at the time will have shared much the same systems of symbolism. The circular form of the Grail Temple hardly needs further explanation, and perhaps Albrecht should not be taken too literally when he described it as a model of the New Jerusalem,[48] for this would suggest a square. Numbering the ring of choirs at 72, if this is correct, would make them numerologically prolific, for 2, 3, 4, 6, 8, 9, and 12 are all multiples, with obvious meanings which could be assigned to each of them. Of particular relevance to the function of the Grail Temple and to Albrecht's description of it are 3 for the portals, and the windows in the bell-towers, which, to Titurel, stood for faith, hope, and charity;[49] 4 for the Evangelists guarding the Grail; 6, as the height of the foundation, and as a multiple present in the number of choirs, bell-towers and their chambers, also the bowls of balsam inside each choir, connecting the idea of creation with the particular generative powers of the Grail; 8, in the eight-sided choirs and their total of balsamic bowls, also the eight-sided towers, for the salvation offered by the blood of the Grail; 9 in the choirs and the towers for the angelic host attending the Grail; and 12, possibly

Fig. 179 Interior, Liebfrauenkirche, Trier. The unusual design of this church, unique for its time and locality, was being completed around the time of Albrecht von Scharfenberg's poem of the Grail Temple, and might have been the inspiration of his description of the Temple

for the company of knights, also the 12 Apostles, and almost certainly for the New Jerusalem. It is also intriguing that the numbers given to the choirs and bell-towers conform to the angles of the golden triangle, 72° and 36°, from which a pentagon is constructed. There is much astronomy in the grail legends and the measurement of angles by degrees in popular culture is substantiated in the contemporary *Roman de la Rose*:

> That is the sun that … creates the everlasting day … that has neither ending nor beginning … without passing through a zodiacal sign or a degree or a minute or any other fraction into which an hour could be divided.
>
> Jean de Meun, *Le Roman de la Rose* XI.[50]

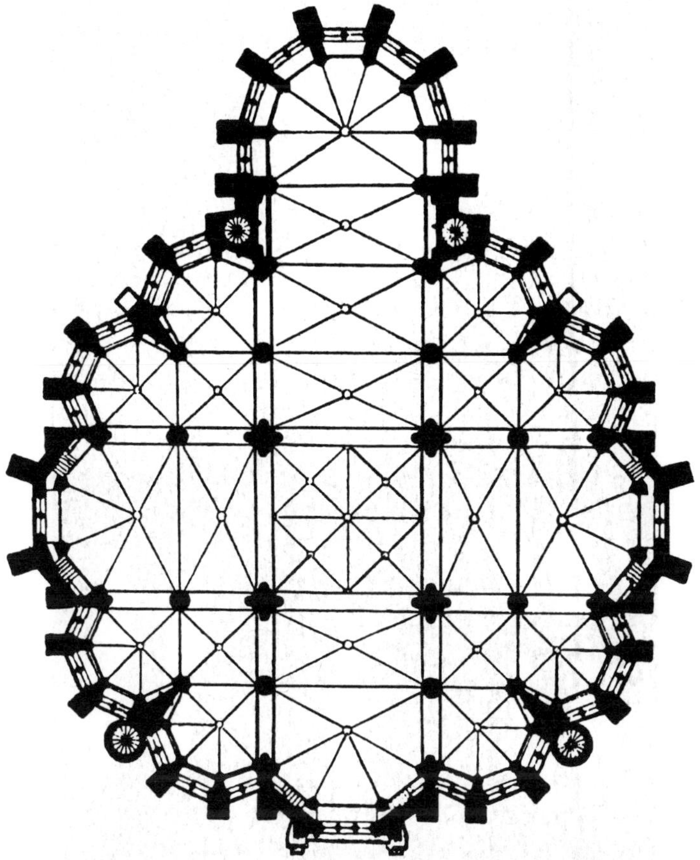

Fig. 180 Plan, Liebfrauenkirche, Trier. The uncanny resemblance between this church and Albrecht's description of the Grail Temple can also be seen in its layout, if allowance is made for poetic exaggeration

Whether or not Albrecht was able to translate this to the measurement of angles in geometry cannot be stated but if he was, the radial geometry of his circular temple, with its 72 choirs and 36 towers would necessitate the division of its circle by increments of 5° and 10°, the numbers of the microcosm and macrocosm that run through these romances. Other numbers specified by Albrecht are 7, for the days marked by the astronomical clock, and 30, as the outer band of the temple's platform, measured in feet, and the number of years taken to build the temple. Describing the clock '[announcing] the times of the seven days' instead of the hours, or the offices, might be thought odd and could reveal Albrecht drawing attention to this number, conceivably in reference to the Holy Ghost to whom the temple was dedicated. The number 30, by resolving itself into both 3 tenfold, and 10 threefold is simple enough to interpret. The decad is also in the text in the number of kings, and the Commandments which Albrecht is at pains to stipulate are 'five times paired'.

Significantly, 5 is also found in the '[five] broad circles' of different stones '[before] each of the portals'. These have been taken to be archivolts,[51] which could be so, but equally Albrecht could have been picturing cinquefoils. Either way, here the pentad appears again at the portal as yet another example of 'the symbol at your door'.

When *Le Roman de la Rose* appeared, it was an immediate success and has left over two hundred manuscripts. Commenced by Guillaume de Lorris in the 1220s and completed by Jean de Meun in the 1270s,[52] the two parts are noticeably different in tenor, the first being rooted in courtly love, centering on the garden of Pleasure, while the second part seems to move to the streets of Paris and the world of academic discourse and disputation.[53] Although the authors' motives, and whether they were even the same, are far from settled, and interpretations of the work are legion,[54] it is ostensibly about the triumph of love over adversity. The metaphor for this is a rosebud in the garden of Pleasure, surrounded by a thorn hedge. After being shot by 5 arrows, the Lover surrenders to the God of Love, later recalling how:

> I suffered greatly from my wounds, knowing that I could only be cured by the rose-bud which was the sole object of my heart's desire.
>
> Guillaume de Lorris, *Le Roman de la Rose* III.[55]

Yet, of the many obstacles the Lover has to overcome, the one given the greatest airing by far is provided by the lady Reason, who was 'perfectly proportioned' and 'made in paradise … by God in his own image'.[56] During her lengthy Advice to the Lover, which belongs to the continuation by Jean de Meun,[57] Reason cites Pythagoras, Plato, and his *Timaeus*. She also calls extensively upon Boethius and *De consolatione Philosophiae*, and it may be recalled that Jean went on to translate this into French, prompting the illustrations of the poem about Fortune and her wheel. In arguing how deceitful Fortune is, Reason's conclusion might appear to be persuasive, and it has caused some commentators to interpret this as Jean's intended message, but which he chooses to deliver concealed by irony.

> … whoever is at one with Reason will never [engage in courtly love], nor value Fortune. … Socrates was … my true friend. He never feared the God of Love, nor was he moved by Fortune.
>
> Jean de Meun, *Le Roman de la Rose* IV.[58]

Later in the poem, Nature's Confession underpins the metaphysical framework of Reason's Advice with a summary of God's creation of the world.[59] This he ordered by number, shape, and weight, composing it of the 4 elements; heaven consists of the stars and the 7 planets moving in the revolution of the great year, following 'the circumference of the great circle of the Zodiac, which turns upon itself like a wheel', producing the music of the spheres.[60] More Christian Platonist thinking is found beneath the rose imagery. The rose garden is defended by 4 guardians;[61] the fifth arrow of the God of Love offers the promise of protection and the regaining of the victim's health;[62]

and when the Lover cries that he suffered greatly from the wounds of the 5 arrows, this seems to be an unmistakable allusion to the 5 wounds of Christ;[63] and among the many instances of the decad is Love's Ten Commandments,[64] yet there is a little more to this than first meets the eye. When these are referred to again by the Old Woman,[65] she urges the Lover to observe only the first 8 because 'the last two … are not worth a brass farthing'.[66] This underlines the truth that is already apparent in the poem, that the rose is to be the Lover's salvation,[67] which probably explains an earlier, isolated detail that is otherwise odd. When the Lover first finds and falls for the rosebud in the garden, the text explains that 'Nature's masterly hand had arranged its four pairs of leaves, one after the other'.[68] Finally, when Jealousy fortifies the garden at the end of Guillaume's text, the quaternity of its structure is completed by its wall enclosing a perfect square, by its 4 gateways and its 4 corner towers, and a round tower in the middle.[69] In addition, as if to reinforce the theme of the microcosm which seems suggested by the Lover's 5 wounds, and its relationship to the macrocosm as apparent in the grail legends, the dimension chosen for the sides of the square garden is 600 feet, 6 and 10 being not only perfect numbers, but also the numbers of the human microcosm,[70] with 10 again representing the macrocosm of the universe. Other interpretations of course are possible and need not exclude this one, consistent as it is with the metaphysical content running through the poem.

The circumstances leading to the third and final poem of *La Divina Commedia* by Dante, his *Paradiso*, differ from *Le Roman de la Rose*, yet they can nevertheless be compared. Both contain conspicuous rose imagery; they chart the course of a journey, in the case of *Paradiso* culminating in a vision of the heavenly court and of God himself; and both attest to a continuing tradition of Christian Platonist symbolism. Following *Le Roman* by a few decades, *Paradiso* was probably begun by Dante around 1308 and completed shortly before his death in Ravenna in 1321.[71] Having been guided through *Inferno* and *Purgatorio* by Virgil, personifying human wisdom, Beatrice, who is divine wisdom, takes his place for Dante's ascent to the tenth heaven, which is the essence of Paradise beyond space and time.[72] His geocentric universe, although scientifically outdated, follows Plato in that the first 7 heavens belong to the planets; the eighth is that of the constellations; whilst the ninth is the last material heaven, the Crystalline Sphere, the rotation of which moves the other heavens.[73] This was God's plan:

> … Everything that is created
> Is part of a mutual order, and that is the shape
> Which makes the universe resemble God.
>
> Here the superior beings see the traces
> Of the eternal power, which is the end
> For which the rule I have spoken of was made.
>
> In this order all natures are arranged
> According to their conditions, more or less
> In the vicinity of their beginning;

So it is that they move to different harbours
On the great sea of being, and each one of them
By the instinct which is given it to bear it on.

Thus did I see that emblem [the imperial eagle], which was formed
Only of praises of the divine grace,
With songs known to those who rejoice there.

Then it began: 'He who drew with compasses
The boundaries of the world, and within it
Ordered so much both hidden and manifest,

His worth could not mark itself upon
The whole of the universe, that his word did not
Remain in its infinite excess'.

Dante, *Paradiso* I. 103–14; XIX. 37–45.[74]

Its constituents inevitably were the 4 elements[75] and, although Dante shows some confusion over Plato's idea concerning souls and the stars, his authority remained *Timaeus*.[76] Dante also has a particular way of dealing with number, whether simply counting or hinting at some ulterior significance. When someone was required 'to account for his actions … he gave seven and five for every ten';[77] also referring to God as 'the first, as out of unity … may be derived five or six …';[78] and writing of the fire of Mars and Leo: 'This fire came back five hundred times, and fifty, and thirty, to its Lion …'.[79] He follows tradition by associating 7 with wisdom, when approaching the castle of the famed, 'I entered seven gates with those wise men';[80] and 9 with the orders of angels.[81] But it is towards the conclusion of his final canto,[82] and therefore the climax of the entire *Commedia*, that Dante's imagination is at its most revelatory, in more than one respect. He has witnessed the heavenly court, guided by Bernard of Clairvaux, whence Beatrice returns to take her place and, following Bernard's prayer to the Virgin, Dante's journey ends with a vision of God:

I saw gathered there in the depths of [his glory],
Bound up by love into a single volume,
All the leaves scattered through the universe;

Substance and accidents and their relations,
But yet fused together in such a manner
That what I am talking of is a simple light.

The universal form of this knot
Is what I think I saw, because when I say that
I feel that my gladness becomes more ample.

So my mind, held in complete suspense,
Gazed fixedly, motionless and intent,
And always as if on fire with the gazing.

In that light a man becomes such
That it is impossible he should turn away
Ever to look upon any other thing.

Dante, *Paradiso* XXXIII. 85–93, 97–102.[83]

He then becomes unduly modest about his power with words.

My language now will be more inadequate,
Even for what I remember, than would that
Of a child still bathing his tongue at the breast.

Not that there was more than a simple appearance
In the living light which I gazed upon
And which is always as it always has been;

It was my sight which was growing stronger
As I was looking; so what looked like one
Worked on me as I myself changed.

In the profundity of the clear substance
Of the deep light, appeared to me three circles
Of three colours and equal circumference;

And the first seemed to be reflected by the second,
As a rainbow by a rainbow, and the third
Seemed like a flame breathed equally from both.

That circle which, conceived in this manner,
Appeared in you as a reflected light,
When my eyes examined it rather more,

Within itself, and in its own colour,
Seemed to be painted with our effigy;
And so absorbed my attention altogether.

Like a geometer who sets himself
To square the circle, and is unable to think
Of the formula he needs to solve the problem,

So was I faced with this new vision;
I wanted to see how the image could fit the circle
And how it could be that that was where it was;

But that was not a flight for my wings:
Except that my mind was struck by a flash
In which what it desired came to it.

Dante, *Paradiso* XXXIII. 106–20, 127–41.[84]

Thus when he supposedly felt that words were failing him, as he looked upon the face of God, Dante turned to the abstract clarity of geometry. Only geometry could express the inexpressible. As it happens, his vision of the 3 circles of the Holy Trinity preceded only by a decade or so the 3 circles implied by the twinned *vesica piscis* of the Bishop's Eye at Lincoln Cathedral.

Music

During this same period, a threat to the Pythagorean-Boethian tradition of music theory was being perceived to be coming from certain modernist composers. From the second half of the thirteenth century, various moves had been made to liberalize the composition and performance of music from its traditional discipline, which, among other manifestations, saw a rise in the popularity of the motet, especially in French universities and cathedrals. The traditional position at the time, becoming known as the *ars antiqua*, was led by Franco of Cologne (fl. mid-thirteenth century) and his treatise, *Ars cantus mensurabilis* of about 1280. The modernists were represented by Philipe de Vitry (1291–1361) and his treatise, *Ars nova*, was written about 1322, giving its name to the new movement. The principal innovations of the *ars nova* were harmonic, in the treatment of discant, and rhythmic, through the introduction of duple meter.[85] This provoked a massive reaction from Jacques de Liège (fl. mid-fourteenth century) in his *Speculum musice*, dating probably from the 1340s. More than a defence of the *ars antiqua*, the *Speculum* ran to seven volumes, the first five being an exposition of the discipline of music as transmitted by Boethius, the sixth concerned chant, while the seventh rejected the teaching of the *ars nova* on discant and rhythm.[86] In so doing, Jacques uses the tenets of the music tradition to uphold the *ars antiqua* and to criticize the modernists. According to him, as the divine order is founded upon number, so is music based on numbers, specifically the tetract, the sum of which is the decad. This produces the musical consonances, the most perfect being unison because it exemplifies unity and possesses the highest degree of simplicity. The other consonances are also favoured because of their closeness to unison. Jacques reasons that, because the *ars nova* freed discant from these consonances, it created discord and departed from simplicity, which is why it should be condemned. Similarly, tradition in metrics based itself on triple meter, either as 1 - 1 - 1, or 1 - 2, and was known as 'the perfection' because of the perfection of the Holy Trinity. By adding duple meter, the *ars nova* was introducing the dyad, which, being the first departure from unity, was by definition imperfect.[87] Despite this condemnation, the *ars nova* flourished alongside the *ars antiqua*, even appearing in the same treatises. This, it has been observed, was not so much a question of the new supplanting the old, but more a matter of taste and, for the *ars nova*, there was now a connection between music theory and practice which ensured its future. For the *ars antiqua*, tradition was also to continue, with Boethius remaining the primary text in universities through the Renaissance and into the seventeenth century.[88]

Continuing practice and forgotten knowledge

Contemporary with the popularity of the rose, as reflected in *Le Roman de la Rose* and Dante's *Paradiso*, were many of the rose windows already encountered in this study. With the flourishing of the Flamboyant Style, the floral metamorphosed into the florid where, as in the south rose of Beauvais Cathedral, although still basically hexagonal, there is barely a straight line to

Fig. 181 South rose, Beauvais Cathedral. A Flamboyant version of the hexagonal geometry typical of south roses

be seen (Fig. 181). Window design became more individualistic, such as the Bishop's Eye in Lincoln. Here, in addition to the clarity of its geometric scheme, are the early signs, in its twin leaves, of the pictorial. The west window of York Minster, dating from 1338 (Fig. 182),[89] is dominated by a heart in its tracery, prompting its popular sobriquet of 'The Heart of Yorkshire'. A century later, in 1446, three hearts appear in the window tracery of Bourges Cathedral's sacristy (Fig. 183), but this was no reference to the Sacred Heart, but the equivalent of a *rebus* of the donor,[90] who was Jacques Cœur. He was the father of the new bishop and, more to the point, both banker and quartermaster to the 'Little King of Bourges', Charles VII, in his struggle to rid France of the English. This made Jacques the richest banker and merchant in the land, and around the parapets of his house then under construction in Bourges, scallops alternate with hearts, repeating his name over and over,[91] whilst two hearts support the *fleur-de-lys* of the king in the tracery of Jacques' own chapel at his house (Fig. 184). Facing onto a city street for all to see, this was meant to broadcast the king's dependence on him. It also marked the degeneration of symbol into sign, a sign moreover in this case of pride in personal wealth and status.[92]

The erosion of Christian Platonist symbolism among masons is also evident in the proceedings of the cathedral council in Milan, which was formed in 1386 to oversee the construction of the cathedral. It will be recalled that the

Fig. 182 West window, York Minster. While geometry was becoming freer, symbol was turning into sign, in this case, that of the heart

Fig. 183 Sacristy window, Bourges Cathedral. Each heart in the centre of the quatrefoils is a rebus for the bishop's family name, which was Cœur, meaning heart, for the money for the sacristy was donated by his father Jacques

Fig. 184 Jacques Cœur's house, Bourges. The full rebus of Jacques' name consisted of a scallop and a heart, the scallop being the emblem of St Jacques and known in French as *coquille St Jacques*. Jacques was both purchaser and banker for the French king, Charles VII, and he advertised the king's dependence on him by displaying two hearts in the tracery of his chapel window supporting the fleur-de-lys of the monarchy. Around the traceried parapets of his house and beneath the windows, scallop shells alternate with hearts

local Lombard builders had laid out the work to a grid of square and double square bays;[93] the foundations were complete and a few of the piers had been started. Doubts soon arose, however, about the competence of local practice to realize the aspirations of the Duke of Milan, Gian Galleazzo Visconti, which were for the building to emulate a northern Gothic cathedral.[94] Over the coming years many questions were to be raised, about the strength of the foundations and piers, the buttressing, and the number of roofs, but of particular interest to this study was the debate about the desired height of the vaults and the means for determining it. To advise the council, a succession of architect-engineers from northern Europe were invited to report, only, in most cases, to be summarily dismissed. The first was a Frenchman, Nicolas de Bonaventure, who, if sketches made by a visiting Italian architect at the time are an indication, proposed raising the structure by increments of 10 cubits to a height of 90 for the main vault (Figs 185, 186a).[95] Since the planning grid consists of square bays of 16 cubits and double square bays measuring 32, there is no recognizable ratio between height and width. For whatever reason, another conference was called and Nicolas was followed by Annas of Freiburg, who advised elevating the church according to the equilateral triangle. Because the builders did not know how to calculate the height of one, a mathematician called Stornaloco was called in to do it for them (Fig. 186b). As a result, it was seen that Annas's scheme had the virtue of reducing Nicolas's dimension for the high vault to 84 cubits, and so work began to implement it in the outer aisles.

Notwithstanding this decision, it may have been a Lombard reaction against the novelty of the equilateral triangle that led to the dismissal of Annas and, eventually, the appointment of Heinrich Parler of Gmünd. He initially upheld the same figure, occasioning the response already quoted:[96]

> Whether this church … ought to rise according to the square or to the triangle?
> It was stated that it should rise up to a triangle or to the triangular figure …
>
> *Annali* I. Appendix 1.[97]

Nevertheless, Parler then seems to have advocated raising the building *ad quadratum*,[98] thereby bringing it into conformity with its planning grid (Fig. 186c). Unfortunately for him, this would have resulted in a high vault of 96 cubits and, for this and for other reasons, he was sacked. The council continued to back the equilateral triangle but, if the heights they specified are compared, it is evident that, although they retained Stornaloco's dimension for the outer aisles, they reduced the others by applying the 3 : 4 : 5 Pythagorean triangle to the scheme (Fig. 186d). Its numerical ratios meant the Lombards could calculate the heights for themselves and achieve the lowest vaults of all, with a main vault of 76 cubits. A final decision was still postponed; another German came and went; and after an interval of five years a French delegation arrived, whose spokesman emerged in the person of Jean Mignot. Like Parler, he reported on a multitude of perceived faults in the construction and in the

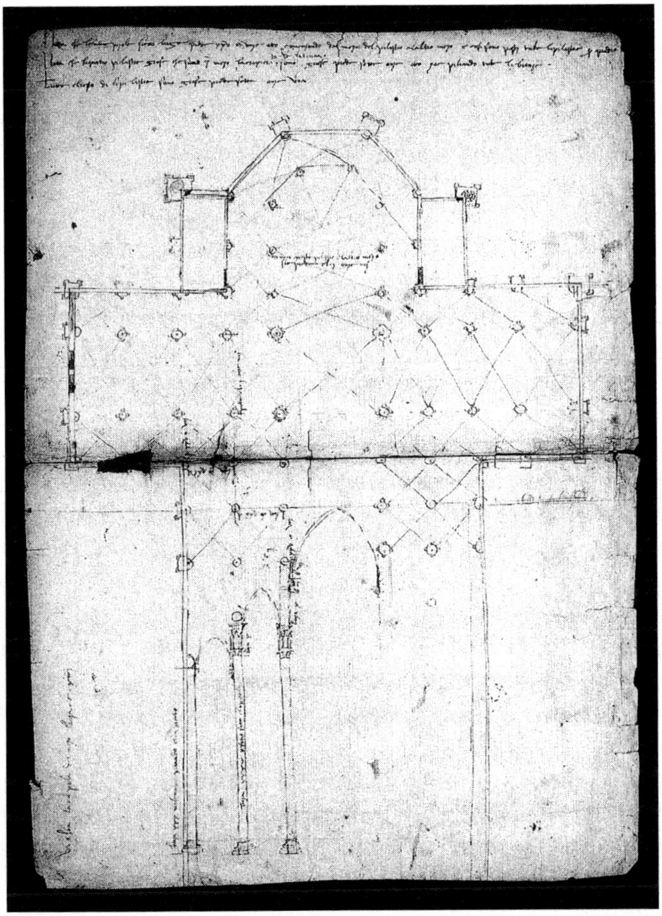

Fig. 185 Plan and section, Milan Cathedral; Antonio di Vicenzo (1390)

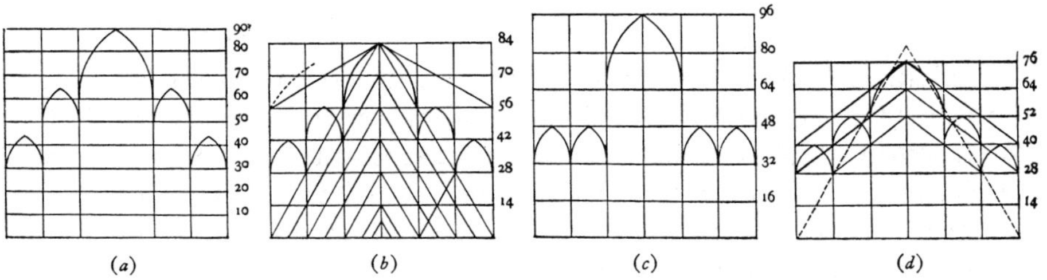

Fig. 186 Proposed sections, Milan Cathedral
a. Proposal of 1390 by Nicolas de Bonaventure, after sketch by Antonio di Vicenzo; Fig. 185
b. Proposal of 1391 by Annas of Freiburg and calculations by Gabriele Stornaloco
c. Probable proposal of 1392 by Heinrich Parler of Gmünd
d. Accepted proposal of 1392, combining equilateral triangles for the outer aisles with Pythagorean triangles for the inner aisles and main vault

builders' plans for carrying it forward. In making their recommendations, one implication was to be to reinstate Stornaloco's scheme, the French arguing for the 'correct order' it possessed in contrast to the 'false order' of the Pythagorean triangle compromising the equilateral.[99] They failed and Mignot was also dismissed, leaving the hybrid scheme to proceed to completion. It was 1401.

During the arguments between the north Europeans and Lombards, especially those involving Parler and Mignot, the gap between the two traditions in thought and practice appeared unbridgeable and produced mutual incomprehension and hostility. It also produced astonishing assertions from the Lombards such as that 'pointed arches do not exert a thrust on the buttresses'[100] and 'what is vertical cannot fall'.[101] Countering this, perhaps the most significant observation came from Mignot, which was that 'art without science is nothing'. This meant, in modern terms, that craft without theory is nothing,[102] for all the northerners had brought their own lodge practice with them which, with the exception of Nicolas, entailed raising the work according to a prescribed geometrical figure, either the equilateral triangle or the square. It had been established as lodge practice in the first place because it was believed that correct proportion would propitiate stability, yet it is possible that even then such Platonic thinking was being challenged by a new appreciation of Aristotelian physics.[103] Even so, this glimpse of north European practice, which the congress provides for the later Middle Ages, reveals that different lodges still used different geometric figures, but without knowing any longer why one should be preferred to another; and why not the pentagon, in view of its widespread use in architectural design; or why it was first believed that any figure should ensure stability. No-one had been able to win an argument with a theoretical justification. Thus, while knowledge of the requisite geometry among these builders continued to be applied, knowledge of the reasoning behind it had apparently become lost. The proceedings also reveal that the Lombards were designing *ad quadratum* and therefore had no empirical method for calculating the heights of triangles, nor saw the futility, in northern eyes, of adulterating one type of triangle with another. Finally it shows a cathedral council, familiar with the conventions of Christian symbolism in associating a square tower and corner turrets with God and the Evangelists, but apparently not being aware any longer of the deeper significance of the geometrical figures that were being reviewed, or their Platonic origins.

Another insight into lodge practice does involve the pentagon, along with the other principal figures, and it is in a work produced by Mathes Roriczer in about 1487 and republished ten years later entitled *Geometria deutsch*.[104] At the time, Roriczer was a citizen of Regensberg and its cathedral architect. He also ran a printing press and had published his handbooks on elevating pinnacles and gablets by using quadrature.[105] His *Geometria deutsch* was intended for craft use as a booklet for solving geometrical problems through practical constructions; it was not a work of theory with necessary proofs.[106] Of the part devoted to the construction of polygons, his methods for the hexagon and octagon are correct,[107] but those for the pentagon and heptagon are not.[108] Interestingly, he constructs a pentagon from two circles overlapping each other to form a *vesica piscis* (Fig. 187). But the method is inaccurate by more than 5 per cent,[109] a margin visible to the naked eye, yet Roriczer states: 'Thus you will have a correct pentagon …'[110] Either he believed it to be correct and was mistaken, or, more likely, he meant it was correct according to the method used in his lodge.

Roriczer is chiefly known of course for publishing the technique of quadrature for elevating architectural details, along with Schmuttermayer and Lechler. It has been pointed out that such use of quadrature as there is in Villard's Portfolio does not extend to extrapolating heights and that there is only documentary support for this late in the fifteenth and early sixteenth centuries with these handbooks, and the same is true of Lechler's reference to 'this method of squares'[111] in designing the ground plan. However, since it can hardly be the case that they had invented these procedures, they had clearly been in use before this date, although how long before it is not possible to state. With the evidence for the use of the other two Platonic figures, the equilateral triangle and the pentagon, at best patchy, it is worth considering whether the square really did enjoy this apparent ascendancy and, if so, why? Deriving everything from the square, from the ground plan to the architectural details, meant that all the parts were in proportion to each other and to the whole, a purely Platonic principle. Yet what was the relevance and meaning of the square, when used on its own, in contrast to Plato's integrated system? All that can be affirmed for the present is that the freeing of design from the regular figures of Platonic geometry, for example in Flamboyant and Curvilinear tracery, accompanied by the increasingly inventive use of the square, coincided with the eclipsing of Platonic theory by Aristotelian Scholasticism, though whether this is merely a coincidence of events or a causal connection can only be conjectured. From a practical point of view, on the other hand, it is easy to see how the use of squares in late medieval plan design was a logical extension of their use in planning individual architectural elements, such as the tower and cloister in Villard's Portfolio, or the increasingly complex planning of towers and spires at Strasbourg and elsewhere, or as a counterpart of planning *ad quadratum*, perhaps by way of filling a vacuum left by the supposed demise of a Platonic system. However, it would be a mistake to overstate the predominance of the square, when it is remembered that it was Annas of Freiburg who proposed elevating Milan Cathedral according to the equilateral triangle; that Cesariano published the elevation of the cathedral with a system of equilateral triangles superimposed on it; and that he reported that the rule of German architects was to use the *vesica piscis* for planning churches, which necessitated the use of equilateral triangles.

Under the circumstances, it is perhaps understandable that Europe's lodges should continue some of their traditions and practices even if they had become remote from their origins and from an understanding of their justification, and that ecclesiastical patrons in the Scholastic Age should also have become remote from the importance of Christian Platonist thought and its symbolism

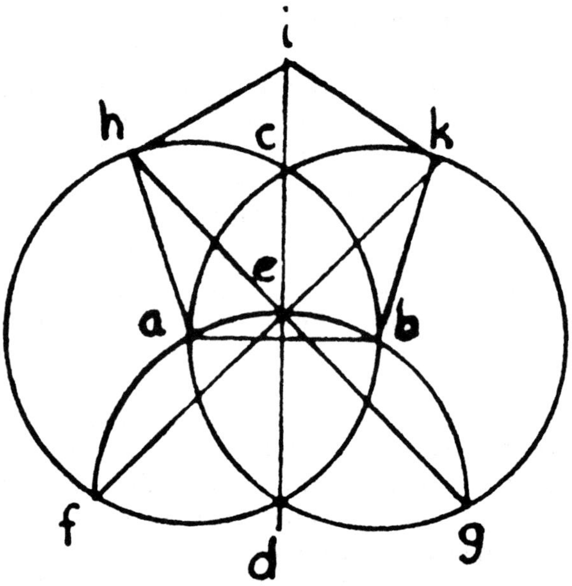

Fig. 187 Construction of a pentagon, Roriczer (c. 1487). This is an empirical construction generated, interestingly, from a *vesica piscis*

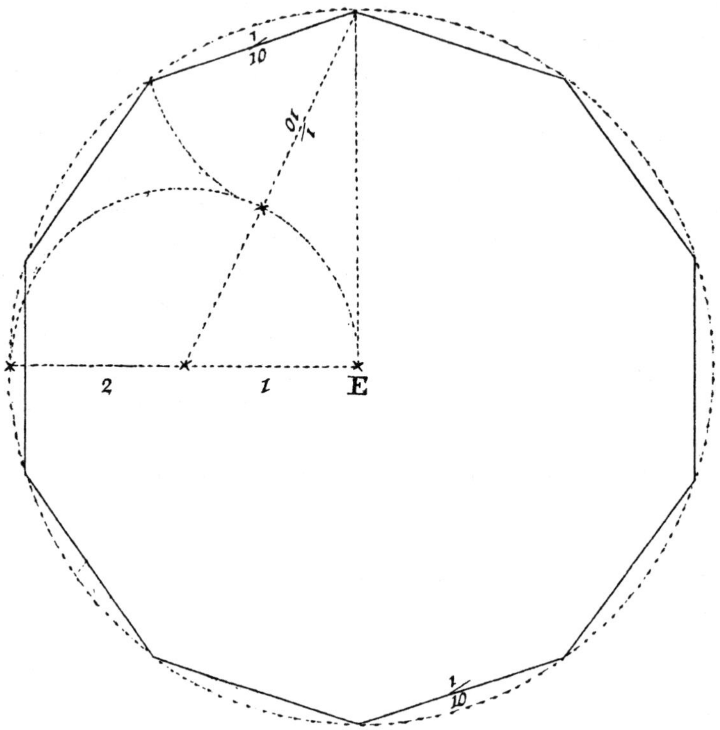

Fig. 188 Construction of a decagon; Alberti VII. 4. Unlike Roriczer's method, this construction is correct according to geometric theory

in their projects. This appears borne out by two more convocations that discussed the building of new cathedrals at Seville and Salamanca. While the congress in Milan was still sitting, in 1401 the cathedral chapter of Seville resolved to build a new cathedral, which 'shall be made so good that there shall be none its equal'. Size, it seems, was to be the principal means of achieving this as, in the words of one member of the chapter, the church would be 'so great and of such kind that those who see it finished shall think we were mad'.[112] Early in the next century, in 1512 a commission of notable Spanish architects met at Salamanca University to agree a design for its city's new cathedral.[113] As appears largely the case with the Milan congress, their conclusions concentrated on practical matters, mainly about siting, but also the dimensions of the nave and aisles, the size of piers and buttresses, and the thickness of walls. They also set up a building committee and appointed an architect, who was Juan Gil (fl. 1500, d. 1526), but there was nothing from the chapter touching on anything philosophical or theoretical.[114] It is as if the church as artefact had arrived, less now the palace of the universe, more the palace of the Church and its prelates. If this was the case, the sensible had now supplanted the intelligible. This poses big questions, which are not susceptible necessarily to short answers, and a comprehensive explanation will not be attempted here. Suffice it to say that due weight does need to be given to how in the fourteenth century the Black Death had changed the Christian outlook on life, death, and faith; how, for most of the same century, the French papacy at Avignon and the papal schism that attended it had changed the state of the Church; how it was increasingly despised for its worldliness by the populace and by the first voices of reform, who saw their holy fathers living the lives of worldly princes. This coincided with the revival of classical humanism in Italy and the Renaissance, also its spread throughout Europe. Crucially, this was accompanied by a Platonic revival, initially centering on the Medici's Florence and the events surrounding the Council held there with the Byzantine Court in 1439. Within a dozen or so years, Alberti had completed his ten books, *De re aedificatoria*, prior to their posthumous publication in Florence in 1485.

Although it is also beyond the scope of this study to investigate Alberti's sources, in what measure medieval, and in what Vitruvian, his treatise nevertheless amounts to a design theory derived from Pythagorean and Platonic principles, however imperfectly remembered, transmitted, and understood. In this, he acknowledges the Divine Architect and his creation, how the ancient masters 'in their Works propose to themselves chiefly the Imitation of Nature, as the greatest Artist at all Manner of Compositions'.[115] They sought beauty and harmony 'in such a Manner as to join and unite a certain Number of Parts into one Body … by an orderly and sure Coherence and Agreement of all those Parts'.[116] The liberal arts are 'indeed absolutely necessary to the Architect', and include now numbers, lines and angles, and painting.[117] He summarizes surviving knowledge of number theory, including numerical ratios and medial proportions,[118] recounting, in slightly altered form, how the numbers 6 and 10 relate to proportions of the human body, according to which Noah's Ark had been built.[119] Indeed, he prefaces his books with the observation that, 'We consider that an edifice is a Kind of Body …',[120] proportioned accordingly,[121] 'as the Members of the Body are correspondent to each other, so it is fit that One Part should answer to another in a building'.[122] He also outlines the musical consonances,[123] stating:

> I am every Day more and more convinced of the Truth of Pythagoras's Saying, that Nature is sure to act consistently, and with a constant Analogy in all her Operations: From whence I conclude that the same Numbers, by means of which the Agreement of Sounds affects our Ears with Delight, are the very same which please our Eyes and our Mind. We [architects] shall therefore borrow all our Rules for the finishing our Proportions, from the Musicians, who are the greatest Masters of this Sort of Numbers …
>
> Alberti, *De re aedificatoria* IX. 5.[124]

For the proportioning of plans,

> … it will not be inconvenient to explain those Things first whereof that Design consists. Every Design therefore is composed of Lines and Angles …
>
> Alberti, *De re aedificatoria* I. 7.[125]

This was certainly confirmed by the geometric investigation into plan design that was conducted in *The Wise Master Builder*.

Just two years before Roriczer published his booklet on empirical methods for constructing polygons, including the pentagon, Alberti's treatise was published, containing correct constructions, informed by theory, for doing the same (Fig. 188).[126] Although empirical procedures would continue in use in the craft guilds and builders' yards, as far as the theory of architectural design was concerned, precision now mattered. In commenting on the setting out of building plans, Alberti complained that, 'in all these quadrangular Platforms the greatest Blemish is for the corners to be not exactly rectangular'.[127] In contrast to Roriczer, whose father had headed the lodge of masons at Regensberg before Mathes became its cathedral architect, Alberti was the son of a merchant and studied law at Bologna University. Thus he came to architecture from outside the lodge tradition and guild system of the Middle Ages, as did Brunelleschi, who had studied literature and mathematics, and whose father was a civil servant, also other Renaissance masters such as Michelozzi, Leonardo da Vinci, and Michelangelo, who were the sons of a tailor, a notary, and a magistrate respectively.[128] As a result, academic theory now overlay craft empiricism.

Given the early modern categorization and separation of Gothic and Renaissance architecture, it may be instructive to learn something of the mental processes and practices that might have been found in the overlap between them. With the Gothic tradition still at its height in Spain a hundred years after the Florentine Renaissance began, by way of a postscript one example is presented here of a residue of Christian Platonist symbolism to be seen in plan design, though whether this is due to its survival from the Middle Ages or its

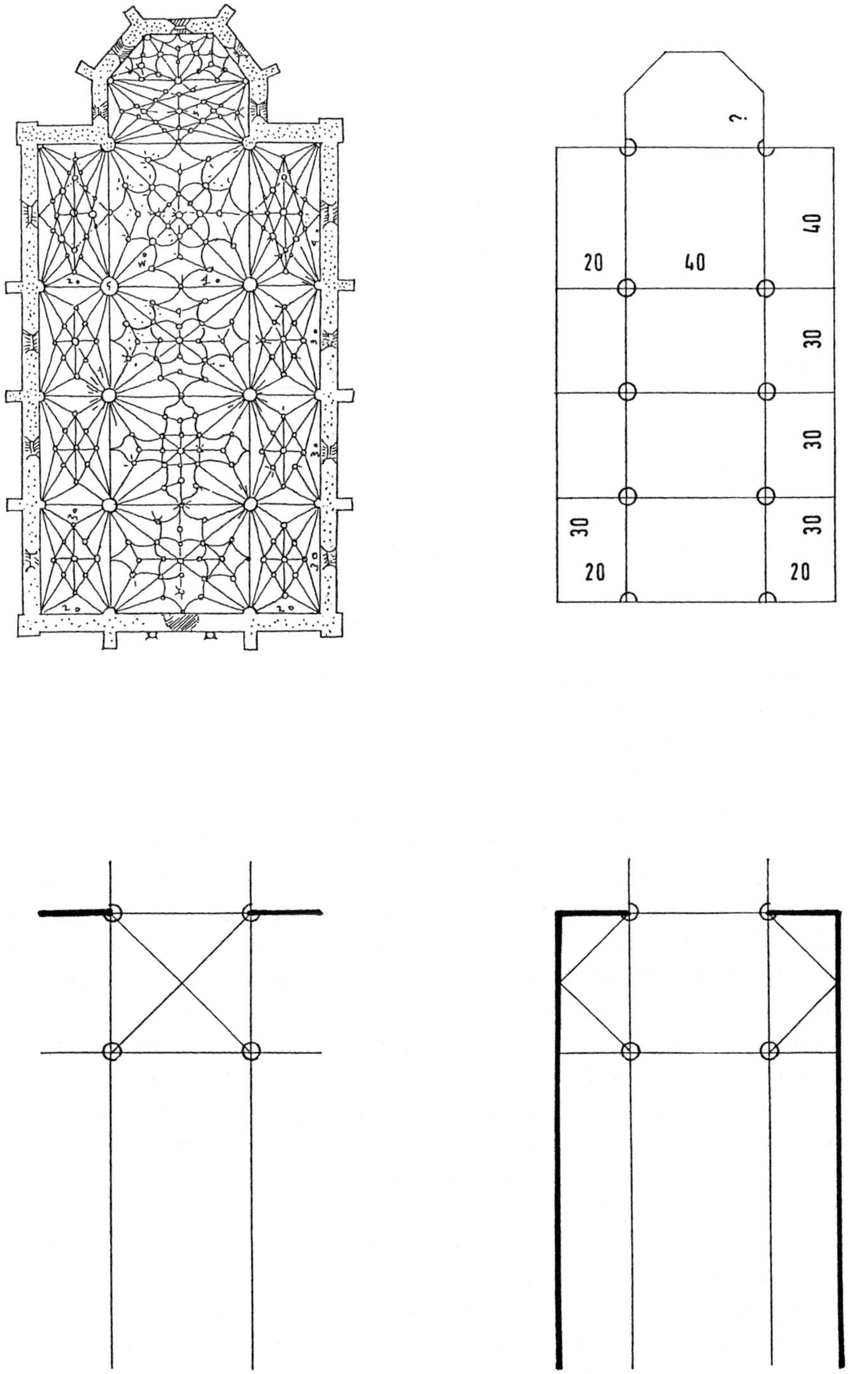

Fig. 189 Plan of church, Rodrigo Gil, with setting-out. *Top left,* a. Rodrigo's plan. *Top right,* b. Diagram of plan, with Rodrigo's dimensions. Note: no dimension is given for the depth of the sanctuary. *Bottom left,* c. Setting-out for body of church, step 1. *Bottom right,* d. Setting-out, step 2

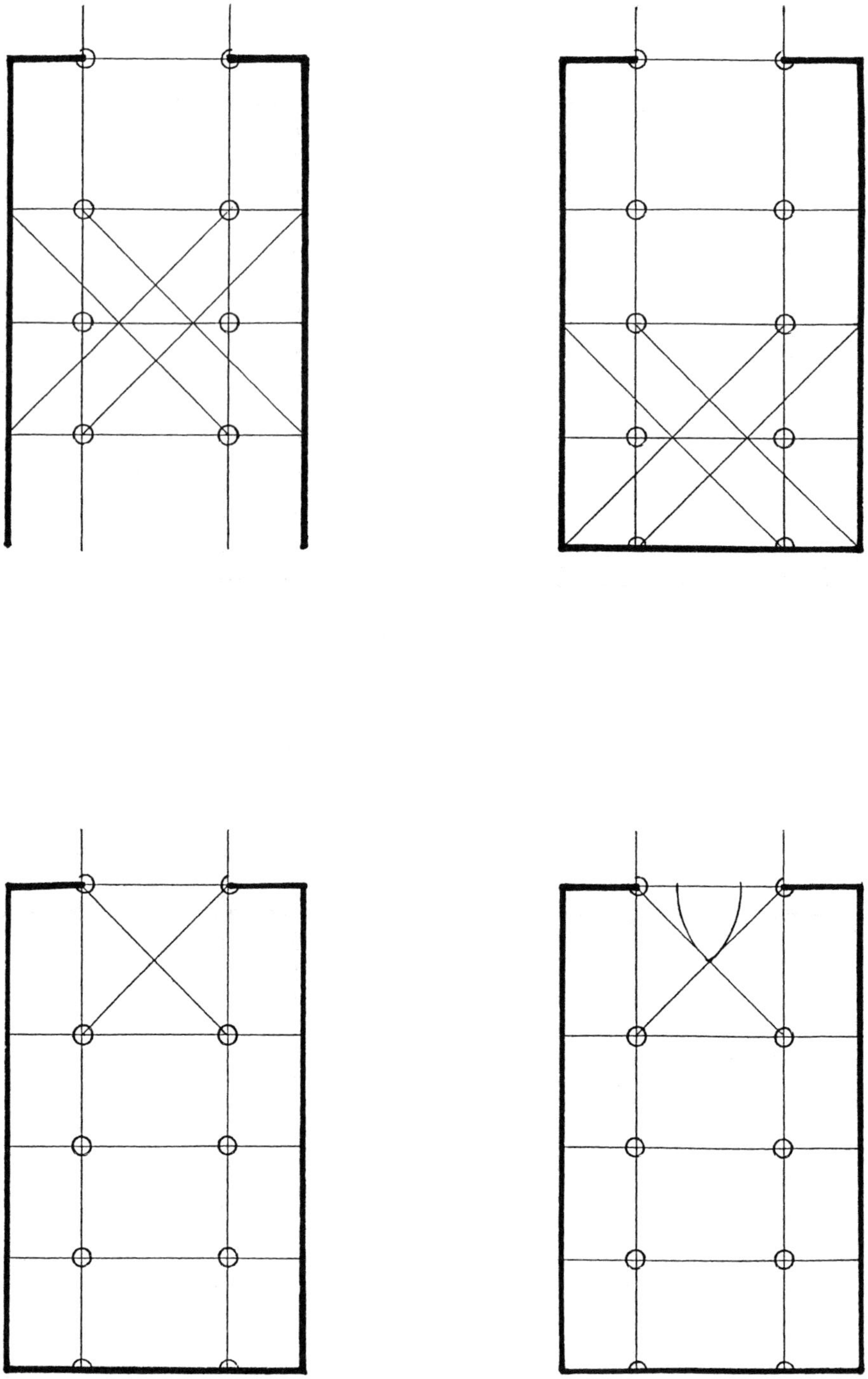

Fig. 190 Plan of church, Rodrigo Gil, with setting-out. *Top left*, e. Setting-out, step 3. *Top right*, f. Setting-out, step 4. *Bottom left*, g. Setting-out for sanctuary, step 5. *Bottom right*, h. Setting-out, step 6

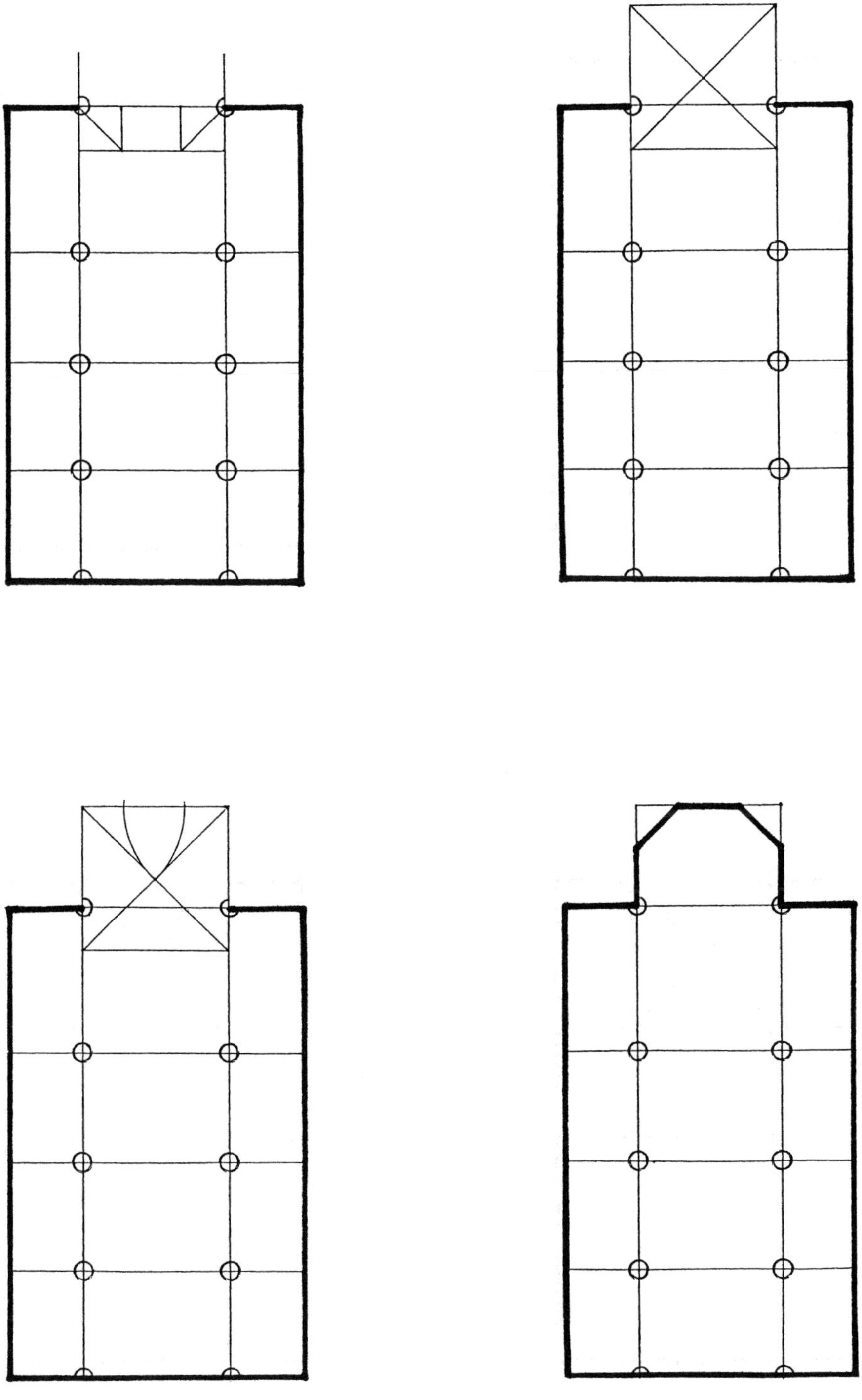

Fig. 191 Plan of church, Rodrigo Gil, with setting-out. *Top left,* i. Setting-out, step 7. *Top right,* j. Setting-out, step 8. *Bottom left,* k. Setting-out, step 9. *Bottom right,* l. Setting-out, step 10

revival in the Renaissance may be open to conjecture. It also possesses a theoretical precision that surely belongs to the Renaissance, despite the architecture being Gothic. After Juan Gil, the architect of Salamanca Cathedral, died, his son Rodrigo (fl. 1521, d. 1577) took over the project, as indeed he did at Segovia Cathedral, which his father had also started. On Rodrigo's death, he left a manuscript containing design methods for plans and sections of different types of church. Some of these became incorporated, somewhat haphazardly, into the *Compendio de arquitectura y simetría de los templos* by Simón García in 1681, a commentary on which appeared in a modern edition.[129] One plan in particular is of interest because it has dimensions in unidentified measures inscribed on it, and it consists of an aisled basilica, with a square crossing, three nave bays, and a sanctuary enclosed by five sides of an octagon (Figs 189a, b).[130] The nave is 40 units wide, and the aisles 20 units;[131] the length of the nave bays is 30 units, and the crossing 40. At first sight, this might resemble a simple application of numerical ratios in the form of design modules – without meaning being attached to them – in the Vitruvian manner, his treatise being repeatedly published during the Renaissance, but this is far from being the case. All the bays in the main body of the church represent the musical consonances: 1 : 1 for the crossing, 1 : 2 for its side bays, 2 : 3 for the aisle bays, 3 : 4 for the nave bays. Moreover, the whole is a golden rectangle, exactly based on the Fibonacci numbers 8 : 13, tenfold, at a time when the golden section was being celebrated in Renaissance literature as the divine proportion.[132] Intriguingly, no dimension is given for the depth of the sanctuary. Apart from this missing dimension, the whole plan could be laid out either in the tracing-house or on site using the dimensions provided without the aid of geometry, but there is no way of similarly setting out the sanctuary. Since geometry is needed for this, it follows that the whole layout should be capable of being set out geometrically and this can be achieved by using only the square in two stages, the first comprising just four steps for the body of the church, the second for setting out the sanctuary in six steps. The first stage starts with the square crossing, followed by a series of overlapping squares, in a system not to be confused with quadrature (Figs 189c, d; 190e, f). Once the main body of the church is drawn, the octagonal sides of the sanctuary can be constructed (Figs 190g, h; 191i–l)[133] Being incommensurable, this is probably why Rodrigo did not assign a dimension to it; he did not have to, except to provide one later for setting out the plan on site, presumably empirically. As a result, the body of the church precisely incorporates all the ratios of the musical consonances, together with the divine proportion and, to delineate the sanctuary, the place of the high altar, in common with numerous late medieval churches, he uses a figure beyond measure, one that for centuries had signified salvation.

Notes

1 See Hiscock (2000), 207–63.

2 The exception is the division of apses and their colonnades into 7.

3 Hadrian, the builder of the Pantheon, took an avid interest in astrology.
4 The buildings tested were chosen to represent the full historical period under review, and included Old St Peter's Basilica, Rome; St Michael's Abbey, Hildesheim; St Maclou in Rouen; and, subsequently, Norwich Cathedral; Hiscock, in Wu (2002), 83–121.
5 These are likely to consist of the less promising material of patronal grants, building accounts and the like, since documentary evidence for architectural practice generally only survives from the fifteenth century onwards, by which time this also appears to concern itself with the practical, as will be shortly shown.
6 Mackie, in O'Carroll (2003), 166–8.
7 Ibid., 153–6.
8 Compare this with Gregory, *Hom. in Hiez.* 40, in Chapter 1, under 'Hagia Sophia, Constantinople, and the Temple of Wisdom'.
9 Chrétien, tr. Kibler (2004), 450.
10 The Rock of Champguin.
11 Commonly translated as Templars from Wolfram's *templeis*; Wolfram, tr. Hatto (2004), 438.
12 Wolfram, tr. Hatto (2004), 251.
13 Ibid., 401.
14 *Gawain*, tr. Stone (1965), 127. The literature on the poem *Sir Gawain* is considerable. For one brief summary of some of the numerology apparent in the text and in the structuring of the text, see Greenwood (1956), 7–12. To his treatment of the pentad should be added the pentagram as the Pythagorean emblem of health, thereby explaining its presence indirectly on Gawain's shield.
15 *Gawain*, tr. Stone (1965), 49.
16 Ibid., 49, 50.
17 Ibid., 50.
18 Albrecht, 383, tr. Barber and Edwards (2003), 95.Titurel also provided the title given to fragments of an epic started by Wolfram; Frankl (1960), 179.
19 Albrecht, tr. Barber and Edwards (2003), 91.
20 Albrecht, 340, 341, tr. Barber and Edwards (2003), 91.
21 Albrecht, 341, tr. Barber and Edwards (2003), 91.
22 Albrecht, tr. Barber and Edwards (2003), 87, note 2, 91, note 15.
23 Albrecht, 373, tr. Barber and Edwards (2003), 94.
24 Albrecht, 396–7, tr. Barber and Edwards (2003), 96.
25 Albrecht, 381, 382, tr. Barber and Edwards (2003), 95.
26 Albrecht, 424–7, tr. Barber and Edwards (2003), 99.
27 Albrecht, 386–90, tr. Barber and Edwards (2003), 95.
28 Albrecht, 389, 390, tr. Barber and Edwards (2003), 96.
29 Albrecht, 377, tr. Barber and Edwards (2003), 95.
30 Albrecht, 419, tr. Barber and Edwards (2003), 98–9.
31 Albrecht, 430, tr. Barber and Edwards (2003), 99–100.
32 Albrecht, 342, 343, tr. Barber and Edwards (2003), 91.
33 Albrecht, 372, tr. Barber and Edwards (2003), 94.
34 Albrecht, 356–64, tr. Barber and Edwards (2003), 92.
35 Albrecht, 374, tr. Barber and Edwards (2003), 94.
36 Albrecht, 436, 437, tr. Barber and Edwards (2003), 100.
37 Albrecht, 350, 351, tr. Barber and Edwards (2003), 92.
38 Albrecht, 409, tr. Barber and Edwards (2003), 97.

39 Albrecht, 402, tr. Barber and Edwards (2003), 97.
40 Albrecht, 400–404, tr. Barber and Edwards (2003), 97.
41 Albrecht, 352, 353, tr. Barber and Edwards (2003), 92.
42 Albrecht, 376, tr. Barber and Edwards (2003), 95.
43 Albrecht, 391–4, tr. Barber and Edwards (2003), 96.
44 Albrecht, 427–9, tr. Barber and Edwards (2003), 99.
45 Albrecht, 431, tr. Barber and Edwards (2003), 100.
46 Albrecht, 385, tr. Barber and Edwards (2003), 95.
47 Construction of the church was probably started in 1227, was largely completed in 1253, and was finished sometime before 1283. Albrecht is thought to have written his poem in about 1270. Frankl (2000), 161; Albrecht, in Barber and Edwards (2003), 87.
48 Frankl (1960), 192.
49 Ibid.
50 Guillaume/Jean, tr. Horgan (1999), 316.
51 Frankl (1960), 181.
52 See Chapter 6, under 'The Eyes of the cathedral'.
53 Guillaume/Jean, tr. Horgan (1999), ix–xiv.
54 Ibid., xxi–xxii.
55 Ibid., 43.
56 Ibid., 46.
57 *Le Roman* IV.
58 Guillaume/Jean, tr. Horgan (1999), 105.
59 *Le Roman* X.
60 Guillaume/Jean, tr. Horgan (1999), 260, 262, 347, 348.
61 *Le Roman* III.
62 Ibid., I.
63 Ibid., III.
64 Ibid., VI.
65 Ibid., VII.
66 Guillaume/Jean, tr. Horgan (1999), 200.
67 With irony intended, or not.
68 Guillaume/Jean, tr. Horgan (1999), 26.
69 *Le Roman* III.
70 See Chapter 2, under 'Union of the macrocosm and microcosm'.
71 Dante, intro. Higgins (1998), 1, 17, 18.
72 Ibid., 16.
73 Ibid., 6, 709.
74 Dante, tr. Sisson (1998), 354, 432.
75 Canto VII. 124–6, 133–48.
76 Ibid., IV. 22–4, 49–60.
77 Why not, for example, 6 and 6, or 9 and 3? Canto VI. 137–8, tr. Sisson (1998), 377.
78 Canto XV. 56–7, tr. Sisson (1998), 415.
79 Ibid., XVI. 37–8, tr. Sisson (1998), 419, 693.
80 Dante, *Inferno* IV. 110, tr. Sisson (1998), 63.
81 Canto XXVIII.
82 Ibid., XXXIII.
83 Dante, tr. Sisson (1998), 498.
84 Ibid., 498–9.

85 Slocum, in Surles (1993), 11, 22; *New Grove Dict.* (2001), IX. 199–200; Bell, in Petersen (2004), 363–4.
86 *New Grove Dict.* (2001), XII. 734.
87 Slocum, in Surles (1993), 12, 15–24; Bell, in Petersen (2004), 369.
88 *New Grove Dict.* (2001), III. 785; Bell, in Petersen (2004), 364, 366.
89 The original window has recently been replaced by a completely new one that attempts to recreate the original.
90 A *rebus* is a visual pun representing the sounds of a person's name, and was common on roof bosses. One, for example, in Winchester Cathedral shows a long note in music inscribed on a barrel, or tun, standing for Bishop Longton.
91 The scallop shell was the emblem of St James, whose French name is Jacques.
92 It represented a display of hubris, incidentally, which soon contributed to his downfall.
93 Ackerman (1949), 88 note 14.
94 For a summary of the proceedings, see *Annali* I (Milan, 1877), in Ackerman (1949), 85–101.
95 The sketches were made by Antonio di Vicenzo in 1390, at the time of Nicholas' visit, in preparation for work on the Church of S. Petronio in Bologna; Ackerman (1949), 88 note 14.
96 Chapters 3 and 4.
97 *Annali*, in Ackerman (1949), 91.
98 Ackerman (1949), 93, note 37.
99 *Annali* I. Appendix 7, in Ackerman (1949), 103–4.
100 Ibid., Appendix 2, in Ackerman (1949), 97.
101 Ibid., Appendix 3, in Ackerman (1949), 100.
102 Ibid., in Ackerman (1949), 100, 101.
103 It has recently been argued that there appears to be evidence in the choice of certain words by Mignot and even the Lombards suggesting an awareness of Aristotle's principles concerning bodies falling and in equilibrium and, as a result, an understanding that forces in a structure are dynamic, not static; Boothby and Walton (2006), 2–8.
104 Shelby (1977), 33, 38, 40.
105 Ibid., 31–2. See Prologue, under 'The architectural programme, patrons and architects'.
106 Ibid., 62–3.
107 Roriczer, *Geometria*, no. 6, fol. 2v, fig. 29; no. 8, fol. 3, fig. 31, in Shelby (1977), 118–20. His method for constructing an octagon is the same as the one shown in Chapter 4, under 'The square and the octagon'.
108 Roriczer, *Geometria*, no. 4, fol. 2, figs 26, 27; no. 7, fol. 2v, fig. 30, in 116–19.
109 I am grateful to my great friend, the late Allan Whitcombe, for developing a proof of this.
110 Roriczer, *Geometria*, tr. Shelby (1977), 117.
111 Lechler, tr. Vinall (2006), 145.
112 Harvey (1957), 230, 233. At the time of going to press, Robert Bork reported that the medieval drawing of Seville's plan displays the geometry of the hexagon and octagon. This remains to be investigated.
113 The council first decided to build a new cathedral in 1491, but it was only in 1512 that the design was finally agreed.
114 Chueca (1951), 17–34, especially 25–30 for a transcript of the architects' recommendations.

115 Alberti IX. 5, tr. Leoni (1755), 195.
116 Ibid., 194.
117 Ibid. 10, tr. Leoni (1755), 206.
118 Ibid. 5, 6, Leoni (1755), 196–200.
119 Ibid. 7, Leoni (1755), 200.
120 Alberti, Pref., tr. Leoni (1755), 112.
121 Alberti IX. 7, Leoni (1755), 200.
122 Alberti I. 9, tr. Leoni (1755), 13.
123 Alberti IX. 5, Leoni (1755), 195–7.
124 Ibid., 196–7.
125 Alberti I. 7, tr. Leoni (1755), 10.
126 Alberti VII. 4.
127 Ibid., tr. Leoni (1755), 138.
128 I am grateful to Martin Kemp for the opportunity to discuss this question.
129 Camón (1941). Although it is difficult to disentangle the contributions of Gil, García, and Camón from each other in this edition, particular plans in the *Compendio* are accepted as being either Gil's, or belonging to the manuscript which he possessed.
130 Camón (1941), 54, fig. 24.
131 As on the Plan of St Gall.
132 Interest in the golden section was prompted by Luca di Pacioli's treatise, *De Divina proportione*, published in Venice in 1509.
133 For the construction of octagons from squares, see Fig. 86.

Bibliography

List of abbreviations

ACW	*Ancient Christian Writers*
ANCL	*Ante-Nicene Christian Library*
A.SS	*Acta sanctorum*
CIMA	*Cahiers de l'Institut de Moyen-Age Grec et Latin*
CSHB	*Corpus scriptorum historiae byzantinae*
FC	*Fathers of the Church*
JSAH	*Journal of the Society of Architectural Historians*
MGH	*Monumenta Germaniae Historica*
NPNFCC	*Nicene and Post-Nicene Fathers of the Christian Church*
ODCC	*Oxford Dictionary of the Christian Church*
PG	*Patrologia Graeca*
PL	*Patrologia Latina*

Classical, early Christian and medieval sources

Acta sanctorum ordinis S. Benedicti, ed. J. Mabillon (Paris, 1668–1701).

Agathias, *Historiarum*, in Mathew (1963), 67.

Alan of Lille, *Anticlaudianus de Antirufino*, ed. R. Bossuat in *Alan de Lille, Anticlaudianus: Texte critique avec une Introduction et des Tables* (Paris, 1955); tr. J. Sheridan in *Alan of Lille: Anticlaudianus or The good and perfect man*, Medieval Sources in Translation 14 (Toronto, 1973/87).

—— *De planctu Naturae*, tr. and commentary J. Sheridan in *Alan of Lille: The Plaint of Nature*, Medieval Sources in Translation 26 (Toronto, 1980).

Albrecht von Scharfenberg, *Der jüngere Titurel*, in Barber and Edwards (2003), 85–102.

Alcuin, *Epistolae*, in Bibliotheca Rerum Germanicarum 6, *Monumenta Alcuiniana*, eds E. Wattenbach and E. Duemmler (Berlin, 1873).

Altera vita: ex chronico sancti Benigni Divionesis excerpta, PL 141, 855–7.

Ambrose?, Baptistery inscription, in *Sylloge Laureshamensis*.

Annali della fabricca del Duomo di Milano dall'origine fino al presente, ed. C. Cantù (Milan, 1877–85).

Ante-Nicene Christian Library: Translations of the Writings of the Fathers down to AD 325, eds A. Roberts and J. Donaldson (Edinburgh, 1867–72).

Apocrypha, The, ed. 1611, rev. 1894 (Cambridge, 1895).

Aquinas, Thomas, *Summa theologica*, ed. Leon, *S. Thomae Aquinatis Opera Omnia* vols 4–12 (Rome, 1888–1906).

Arnold of Emmeram, *Liber II*, MGH. Script. IV. 556–74.

Ars geometriae et arithmeticae in *De institutione arithmetica libri duo, De institutione musica libri quinque, accedit geometria quae fertur Boetii*, ed. G. Friedlin (Leipzig, 1867).

Athanasius of Alexandria, *De Incarnatione*, ed. R. Thomson (Oxford, 1971).

Augustine, *Contra Faustum*, in *Reply to Faustus the Manichaean*, tr. R. Stothert, in *The Works of Aurelius Augustine, Bishop of Hippo*, ed. M. Dodds (Edinburgh, 1872).

—— *De civitate Dei*, in *The City of God*, tr. H. Bettenson (London, 1984).

—— *De doctrina Christiana*, tr. J. Gavigan in FC 2, 2nd edn (1950).

—— *De musica*, in *On Music*, tr. R. Taliaferro in FC 4 (1947).

—— *De ordine*, in *Divine Providence and the Problem of Evil (De ordine)*, tr. R. Russell in FC 1 (1948).

—— *De quantitate animae*, in *St. Augustine: The Greatness of the Soul: De Quantitate Animae*, tr. J. Colleran in ACW (1950).

—— *De sermone Domini in monte*, tr. D. Kavanagh in FC 11 (1963).

—— *De Trinitate*, tr. S. McKenna in FC 45 (1963).

—— *De vera religione*, in *Augustine: Earlier Writings, Of True Religion*, tr. J. Burleigh, Library of Christian Classics 6 (London, 1953).

—— *In Beatus Joannis Apocalypsim Expositio*, PL 35, 2417–52.

—— *In Iohannis evangelicum*, tr. J. Rettig in FC 79 (1988).

Basil the Great, *Hexaëmeron*, in *The Treatise De Spiritu Sancto, The Nine Homilies of the Hexaëmeron and the Letters of Saint Basil the Great, Archbishop of Caesarea*, tr. B. Jackson, NPNFCC 8 (1895).

Bede, *De tabernaculo*, in *Bede: On the Tabernacle*, tr. A. Holder (Liverpool, 1994).

—— *De templo*, in *Bede: On the Temple*, tr. S. Connolly (Liverpool, 1995).

Benedict of Nursia, *Regula Benedicti*, tr. J. McCann in *The Rule of Saint Benedict* (London, 1952).

Bernard of Clairvaux, *De consideratione*, tr. W. Williams-Wynn in *Saint Bernard of Clairvaux* (Manchester, 1935; repr. 1953).

Boethius, *De consolatione Philosophiae*, in *The Consolation of Philosophy*, tr. S. Tester, 2nd edn (London, 1973).

—— *De hebdomades*, in Schultz and Synan (2001).

—— *De institutione arithmetica*, in *Boethian Number Theory; A translation of the De Institutione Arithmetica (with Introduction and Notes)*, tr. M. Masi, Studies in Classical Antiquity 6 (Amsterdam, 1983).

—— *De institutione musica*, tr. C. Bower in, *Fundamentals of Music: Anicius Manlius Severinus Boethius* (New Haven, CT, 1989).

Capella, Martianus, *De nuptiis Philologiae et Mercurii*, tr. W. Stahl and R. Johnson, in *Martianus Capella and the Seven Liberal Arts*, 2 vols (New York, 1991).

Carmina Burana, facsimile edn, B. Bischoff (Munich, 1967).

Cassian, John, *Collationes patrum*, tr. C. Luibhéid, in *John Cassian: Conferences* (Mahwah, NJ, 1985).

Cassiodorus, *De artibus ac disciplinis liberalium litterarum*, PL 70, 1149–219.

—— *De institutione divinarum litterarum*, PL 70, 1106–49.

Chalcidius, *Timaeus a Calcidio translatus commentarioque instructus*, ed. J. Waszink, in Corpus Philosophorum Medii Aevi: Corpus Platonicum 4, ed. R. Klibanksy (London, 1962).

Charlemagne, *Capitulare de imaginibus*, PL 98, 990–1248, in *Beati Caroli Magni imperatoris scripta sive omnium ejus operum* 2, *sectio* 2: *Libri Carolini*, PL 98, 942–1248.

Chaucer, Geoffrey, *The Canterbury Tales*, tr. N. Coghill (Harmondsworth, 1979).

Choricius of Gaza, *Laudatio Marciani* II, in *Choricii Gazaei opera*, eds R. Foerster and E. Richsteig (Leipzig, 1929).

Chrétien de Troyes, *Le Conte du Graal*, in *Chrétien de Troyes: Arthurian Romances*, tr. and intro. W. Kibler (London, 2004).

Chronicon abbatiae Rameseiensis, ed. W. Macray, Rolls Series 83 (1886).

Chronicon sanctae Sophiae, ed. J.-M. Martin, *Istituto Storico Italiano per il Medio Evo: Fonti per la Storia dell'Italia Medievale: Rerum Italicarum Scriptores* 3 (Rome, 2000).

Clement of Alexandria, *Stromateis*, in *Stromata*, tr. W. Wilson, ANCL 4 and 12 (1867 and 1869).

Codex Calixtinus, in Gerson, P., Shaver-Crandell, A., and Stones, A., *The Pilgrims' Guide: A Critical Edition II, The Text: Annotated English Translation* (London, 1998).

Codex Theodosianus, ed. A. Marville, comm. J. Godefroy (Lyons, 1665).

Constantine of Rhodes, *Στυχοι Κονσταντυνου*, in ed. E. Legrand, *Description des Oeuvres d'Art et de l'Eglise des Saints Apotres de Constantinople: Poème en vers Iambiques par Constantin le Rhodien* (Paris, 1896).

Corippus, Flavius, *In laudem Iustini Augusti minoris libri quattuor*, CSHB 11 (Bonn, 1836).

Dante, Alighieri, *Paradiso*, in *Dante: The Divine Comedy*, intro. D. Higgins, tr. C. Sisson (Oxford, 1998), 349–99.

De sacris aedibus Deiparae ad Fontem, A. SS Nov. III. 879.

Dialogus de musica, ed. M. Gerbert, *Scriptores de musica sacra potissimum* 3 (St Blasien, 1784), I. 252–64, partial tr. O. Strank, *Source Readings in Music History* (New York, 1952), 103–16.

Dionysius, Pseudo-Areopagite, *De coelesti hierarchia*,

—— *De divinis nominibus*, in *The Complete Works*, tr. C. Luibhéid (London, 1987).

Distinctiones, in V. Mortet, 'La maîtrise d'oeuvre dans les grandes constructions du XIIIe siècle et la profession d'appareilleur', *Bulletin Monumental* 70.2 (1906), 263–70.

Dungal, *Verses on the Church of St Denis*, in Schlosser (1892), nos 910, 911; tr. Baldwin Smith (1956).

Durandus, William, *Rationale divinorum officiorum*, eds A. Davril and T. Thibodeau (Turnhout, 1995); tr. and intro. J. Neale and B. Webb, in *The Symbolism of Churches and Church Ornaments: A Translation of the First Book of the Rationale Divinorum Officiorum, Written by William Durandus* (Leeds, 1843).

Edessa Hymn, ed. and German tr. H. Goussen, *Le Muséon* 38 (1925), 117–36.
Einhard, *Vita Caroli*, tr. L. Thorpe (Harmondsworth, 1969).
Euclid, *Elementa*, in *The Thirteen Books of Euclid's Elements*, tr. T. Heath, 2nd edn (Cambridge, 1956).
Eusebius, *Historia Ecclesiastica*, in *Eusebius: The Ecclesiastical History*, 2 vols:
—— Vol. 1, bks I–V, tr. K. Lake (London, 1949);
—— Vol. 2, bks VI–X, tr. J. Oulton (London, 1932).
——? *Vita Constantini*, ed. I. Heikel, *Eusebius Werke* I (Leipzig, 1902).
Evagrius, *Historia ecclesiastica*, eds J. Bidez and L. Parmentier, *The Ecclesiastical History of Evagrius* (London, 1898).
Fathers of the Church, ed. L. Schopp (New York, 1947–, Washington DC, 1962–).
Gawain and the Green Knight, Sir, tr. B. Stone (Harmondsworth, 1965);
—— Ibid., tr. O. Greenwood (London, 1956).
Geoffrey of Auxerre, *De sacramentis numerorum a tredenario usque ad vicenarium*, CIMA 29 (Copenhagen, 1979), 1–21.
Germanus of Constantinople, *Historia Mystagogica*, PG 98. 384.
Gesta abbatum Trudonensium, PL 173, 11–438.
Glaber, Rodulfus, *Historiarum*, PL 142, 613–98,
—— *Vita sancti Guillelmi abbatis Divionensis*, PL 142, 697–720, in *The Five Books of the Histories*, ed. and tr. J. France (Oxford, 1989).
Glycas, Michael, *Annales a mundi exordio usque ad obitum Alexii Comneni Imperatoris*, CSHB 59 (Bonn, 1836).
Gregoras, Nicephorus, *Historia*, eds L. Schopen and I. Bekker, CSHB 19 (Bonn, 1829–55).
Gregory the Great, *Homiliae in Hiezechihelem*, ed. M. Adriaen, Corpus christianorum, series Latina 142 (Turnhout, 1971).
Gregory of Nyssa, *Contra Eunomium*, PG 45. 466–572.
—— *Epistolae*, tr. H. Wilson, in *Select Writings and Letters of Gregory, Bishop of Nyssa*, in NPNFCC 2nd Series 5 (Oxford, 1893).
Grosseteste, Robert, *Le Château d'amour*, tr. E. Mackie, in O'Carroll (2003), 151–79.
—— *Hexaëmeron*, in *Robert Grosseteste: On the Six Days of Creation*, tr. C. Martin (Oxford, 1999).
—— *De luce*, in C. Riedl, *Robert Grosseteste: On Light (De Luce)* (Milwaukee WI, 1942).
Guillaume de Lorris and Jean de Meun, *Le Roman de la Rose*, in *The Romance of the Rose*, tr. and intro. F. Horgan (Oxford, 1999).
Guy d'Eu, *Regulae de arte musica*, tr. C. Maître, *La Réforme cistercienne du plain-chant: Etude d'un traité théorique* (Brecht, 1995).
Hariulf of St Riquier, *Chronicon Centulense*, ed. F. Lot, *Hariulf, Chronique de l'abbaye de Saint-Riquier (Ve siècle – 1104)* (Paris, 1894).
Henry of Avranches?, *Vita sancti Hugonis Episcopi Lincolniensis*, tr. C. Garton in *The Metrical Life of Saint Hugh of Lincoln* (Lincoln, 1988).
Heron of Alexandria, *Geometricorum et Stereometricorum reliquiae*, ed. F. Hultsch (Berlin, 1864).

Hildegard of Bingen, *Liber Divinorum operum*, tr. P. Dronke, in A. Derolez and P. Dronke, eds, *Hildegardis Bingensis: Liber Divinorum operum simplicis hominis*, Corpus Christianorum 92 (Turnhout, 1996).

Historia de vita et rebus gestis Basilii inclyti imperatoris, in Theophanes Continuatus, *Chronographia* V, ed. I. Bekker, CSHB 4 (Bonn, 1838), 211–353.

Historia I. Translationis sanctae Witburgae, A.SS. II. 604.1.

Honorius of Autun, *De gemma animae*, PL 172, 541–738.

—— *Speculum ecclesiae*, PL 172, 807–1108.

Hugh of St Victor, *Didascalicon: De studio legendi*, ed. C. Buttimer, Studies in Medieval and Renaissance Latin 10 (Washington, 1939).

—— *The Didascalicon of Hugh of St. Victor*, tr. J. Taylor (New York, 1991).

Isidore of Seville, *Etymologiae sive origines*, ed. W. Lindsay (Oxford, 1911).

Jakobos of Kokkinobaphos, *Homilies on the Virgin*, I. Hutter and P. Canart, eds, *Das Marienhomiliar des Mönchs Jakobos von Kokkinobaphos, Codex Vaticanus Graecus 1162*. Codices e Vaticanis Selecti 79 (Vatican City, 1991).

Jerome, *Commentariorum in Ezechielem Prophetam*, PL 25, 15–490.

—— *Epistolae*, NPNFCC 2nd Series VI, *St. Jerome: Letters and Select Works* (New York, 1893), 1–295.

John of Damascus, *De fide orthodoxa, Dialectica*, in *Fons scientia* in *Saint John of Damascus: Writings*, tr. F. Chase, FC 37 (New York, 1958).

—— *Pro sacris Imaginibus Orationes tres*, III: *Adversus eos qui sacras imagines abjiciunt* 21, PG 94. 1342.

John of Metz, *Vita Iohannis abbatis Gorziensis: auctore Iohanne abbate sancti Arnulfi*, MGH. Script. IV. 335–77.

Josephus, Flavius, *Antiquitates Judaicae*, in *The Complete Works of Flavius Josephus*, tr. W. Winston (London, 1876).

Lechler, Lorenz, *Unterweisung* (1516), ed. A. Reichensperger, *Vermischte Schriften über christliche Kunst* (Leipzig, 1856), 133–55.

Leo VI, Emperor, *Sermons*, ed. Akakios, *Leontos tou Sophou panêgurikoi logoi* (Athens, 1868).

Liber vitae, in W. Birch, *Liber vitae: Register and Martyrology of New Minster and Hyde Abbey*, Hampshire Record Society 5 (1892).

Lucian, *Pro lapsu inter salutandum*, tr. K. Kilburn in *Lucian* 6, Loeb Classical Library (London, 1959), 171–89.

—— *Vitarum auctio*, in *Lucian* 2, tr. A. Harmon (London, 1915).

Macrobius, *Commentarii in Ciceronis Somnium Scipionis*, tr. W. Stahl, in *Commentary on the Dream of Scipio* (New York, 1990).

Marcus diaconus, *Vita Porphyrii*, eds H. Grégoire and M. Kugener (Paris, 1930).

Maximus, Confessor, *Mystagogia*, in *Maximus Confessor: Selected Writings*, tr. G. Berthold, Classics of Western Spirituality (London, 1985).

Mesarites, Nicholas, 'Description of the Church of the Holy Apostles at Constantinople', ed. and tr. G. Downey, *Transactions of American Philosophical Society* NS 47: 6 (1957), 853–924.

Michael of Thessalonica, *Ekphrasis*, *Εκφρασις τής άγιωτάτης τού Θεού μεγάλης έκκλησίας*, in Mango and Parker (1960), 233–45.

Monumenta Germaniae Historica, ed. G. Pertz (Hanover, 1826–).

Narratio de structura templi sanctae Sophiae, in T. Preger, ed., *Scriptores originum Constantinopolitanarum* (Leipzig, 1901).

Narsai, *Homilies on the Creation*, in McVey (1983), 115.

Nicholas of Biard, *Distinctiones*, Paris, Bibliothèque nationale de Paris 16490, see V. Mortet, 'La maîtrise d'oeuvre dans les grandes constructions du XIIIe siècle et la profession d'appareilleur', *Bulletin Monumental* 67 (1906), 268).

Odo of Cluny, *Odonis abbatis Cluniacensis occupatio*, ed. A. Swoboda (Leipzig, 1900).

Odo of Morimond, *Analetica numerorum et rerum in Theographyam* 1, in CIMA 40 (Copenhagen, 1981).

Pappus of Alexandria, *Collectio mathematica*, see Cuomo (2000).

Paulus Silentarius, *Descriptio ecclesiae sanctae Sophiae et ambonis*, PG 86; ed. P. Friedländer, *Johannes von Gaza und Paulus Silentarius* (Leipzig, 1912).

Patrologiae cursus completus, Series Graeca, ed. J. Migne (Paris, 1857–98).

Patrologiae cursus completus, Series Latina, ed. J. Migne (Paris, 1844–65).

Philo, *De plantatione*, in *The Works of Philo Judaeus* I, tr. C. Yonge (London, 1854), 416–52.

—— *De vita Mosis*, in *The Works of Philo Judaeus* III, tr. C. Yonge (London, 1855), 1–136.

Photius of Constantinople, *Photiou homiliai*, ed. B. Laourdas, *Hellênika* Suppl. 12 (Thessalonika, 1959).

Plato, *Meno*, tr. B. Jowett, 4th edn (Oxford, 1953).

—— *Phaedo*, tr. B. Jowett (Oxford, 1871).

—— *Republic*, tr. F. Cornford, *The Republic of Plato* (Oxford, 1941).

—— *Timaeus*, in *Timaeus and Critias*, tr. D. Lee (Harmondsworth, 1979), also Cornford (1937).

Procopius, *De aedificiis*, ed. J. Haury, *Procopii Caesariensis opera* III. 2 (Leipzig, 1913); eds and tr. H. Dewing and G. Downey, *Procopius* VII: *Buildings* (London, 1940).

Psellus, Michael, in Du Cange, 'Notes on Bondelmontius', in Lethaby and Swainson (1894), 145.

Raynaldo, *Vita sancti Hugonis*, PL 159, 844–928.

Richard de Ware, *Consuetudines*, BM. MS Cotton, see Stanley (1868).

Roriczer, Matthes, *Büchlein von der Fialen Gerechtikait* (Regensburg, 1486),

—— *Geometria deutsch, (Aus der geometrey)* (Regensburg, c.1487),

—— *Wimpergbüchlein* (Regensburg, c.1488), all in Shelby (1977).

Schmuttermayer, Hans, *Fialenbüchlein* (Nürnberg, c.1488), see Shelby (1977).

Scolica enchiriadis, ed. H. Schmid, *Musica et scolica enchiriadis una cum aliquibus tractatulis adiunctis* (Munich, 1981); intro. and tr. R. Erickson, ed. C. Palisca, *Musica Enchiriadis and Scolica Enchiriadis* (New Haven CT, 1995).

Silentarius, Paulus, *Descriptio ecclesiae sanctae Sophiae et ambonis*, PG 86; ed. P. Friedländer, *Johannes von Gaza und Paulus Silentarius* (Leipzig, 1912).

Suger, *Liber de rebus in administratione sua gestis*,

—— *Libellus alter de consecratione ecclesiae sancti Dionysii*, both in E. Panofsky, *Abbot Suger on the Abbey Church of St.- Denis and its Art Treasures*, 2nd edn (Princeton NJ, 1979).

Sylloge Laureshamensis, Vatican Cod. Palat. 833, in F. Dölger, 'Zur Symbolik des altchristlichen Taufhauses I: Das Oktogon und die Symbolik der Achtzahl. Die Inschrift des hl. Ambrosius im Baptisterium der Theklakirche von Mailand', in *Antike und Christentum* 4.3 (Münster, 1934), 153–87.

Symeon of Thessalonica, *De sacro templo ejus consecratione*, in *Symeonis Thessalonicensis archiepiscopi opera omnia*, PG 155.

Testamentum Domini, in G. Sperry-White, tr., *The Testamentum Domini*, (Nottingham, 1991).

Theobald of Langres, *De quatuor modis quibus significationes numerorum aperiuntur*, CIMA 29 (Copenhagen, 1978), 29–108.

Villard de Honnecourt, Portfolio, Paris, Bibl. Nat. MS. fr. 19.093.

Vita sancti Marthae, matris Symeonis stylitae iunioris, *Acta Sanctorum* 3rd edn May V, 399– (1863–).

Vita sancti Oswaldi archiepiscopi Eboracensis, in *Historians of the Church of York and its Archbishops 1*, ed. J. Raine, Rolls Series 71 (London, 1879).

Vitruvius, *De architectura*, in *Vitruvius on Architecture*, tr. F. Granger (London, 1931, 1934).

—— *Vitruvius: Ten Books on Architecture*, tr. I. Rowland, commentary T. Howe (Cambridge, 1999).

—— Idem, tr. Giocondo, G., *De architectura* (Venice, 1511).

Walter of Speyer, *Vita et passio sancti Christophori martyris*, ed. W. Harster (Munich, 1878).

William of Auberive, *Tractatus de sacramentis numerorum a ternario usque ad duodenarium*, extract in J. Leclercq, Studia Anselmiana 20 (Rome, 1948), 181–99.

Wisdom, The Book of, tr. J. Reider (New York, 1957).

Wolfram von Eschenbach, *Parzifal*, tr. A. Hatto (London, 2004).

Post-medieval sources

Ackerman, J., '"Ars sine Scientia nihil est": Gothic Theory of Architecture at the Cathedral of Milan', *Art Bulletin* 31 (1949), 84–111.

Adam, R., *Ruins of the palace of the Emperor Diocletian at Spalatro in Dalmatia* (London, 1764).

Adams, W., *The Round Church of Cambridge: A Short History* (Cambridge, 1930).

Adler, F., *Das Pantheon zu Rom* (Berlin, 1871).

Alberti, Leon, *De re aedificatoria*, in *The Ten Books of Architecture*, (Florence, 1485), tr. G. Leoni, 3rd edn (London, 1755), facsimile edn (New York, 1986).

Antoniades, E., *Ekphrasis tes Hagias Sophias*, 3 vols (Athens/Leipzig, 1907–9).

Artmann, B., 'The Cloisters of Hauterive', in *The Mathematical Intelligencer* 13.2 (New York, 1991), 45–6.

Ashbee, C., and J., *The Essex House Song Book* 10 (Campden, 1903).

Aylmer, G., and Tiller, J., eds, *Hereford Cathedral: A History* (London, 2000).

Baldwin Smith, E., *Architectural Symbolism of Imperial Rome and the Middle Ages* (Princeton NJ, 1956).

Bandmann, G., *Mittelalterliche Architektur als Bedeutungsträger* (Berlin, 1951). *Early Medieval Architecture as Bearer of Meaning*, tr. K. Wallis (New York, 2005).

Barber, R., and Edwards, C., 'The Grail Temple in Der jüngere Titurel', in *Arthurian Literature* 20 (2003), 85–102.

Barnes, C., *The Portfolio of Villard de Honnecourt (Paris, Bibliothèque nationale de France, Ms Fr 19093): A New Critical Edition and Color Facsimile* (Aldershot, forthcoming, 2008).

Batty, M., and Longley, P., 'The Fractal City', in *New Science=New Architecture?* Architectural Design Profile 129 (1997), 74–83.

Bechmann, R., *Villard de Honnecourt, la pensée technique au XIIIe siècle et sa communication* (Paris, 1991).

—— 'The Saracen's Sepulcher: An Interpretation of Folio 6r in the Portfolio of Villard de Honnecourt', in Zenner (2004), 121–34.

Bechmann, R., A. Erlande-Brandenburg, R. Pernoud, and J. Gimpel, eds, *Le Carnet de Villard de Honnecourt* (Paris, 1986).

Becksmann, R., *Deutsche Glasmalerei des Mittelalters*, 2 vols (Berlin, 1992, 1995).

—— *Die architektonische Rahmung des hochgotischen Bildfensters: Untersuchungen zur oberrheinschen Glasmalerei von 1250 bis 1350* (Berlin, 1967).

Bell, D., *Many Mansions: An Introduction to the Development and Diversity of Medieval Theology* (Kalamazoo MI, 1996).

Bell, N., 'Signs of Change from ars antiqua to ars nova in Polyphonic Music of the Early Fourteenth Century', in N.H. Petersen, C. Clüver, and N. Bell (2004), 363–72.

Beretz, E., 'Adjustments for the Innovative: Installing a Rose Window into the North Façade of Saint-Étienne, Beauvais', *AVISTA Forum Journal* 14. 1 (2004), 17–24.

Beseler, H., and Roggenkamp, H., *Die Michaeliskirche in Hildesheim* (Berlin, 1954).

Biddle, M., *The Tomb of Christ* (Stroud, 1999).

Binding, G., *High Gothic: The Age of the Great Cathedrals* (Cologne, 2002).

Blotkamp, C., *Mondrian: The Art of Destruction* (London, 1994).

Boothby, T., and Walton, S., 'What did they know and when did they know it? Scholastic Interpretations of Architectural Dynamics', paper given at International Congress on Medieval Studies, Western Michigan University (2006).

Bork, R., 'Geometrical Design Strategies in East Central European Architecture', paper given at International Congress on Medieval Studies, Western Michigan University (2006).

—— 'Plan B and the Geometry of Façade Design at Strasbourg Cathedral, 1250–1350', *JSAH* 64. 4 (2005), 442–73.

Bouras, C., 'Twelfth and Thirteenth Century Variations of the Single Domed Octagon Plan', *ΔΕΛΤΙΟΝ ΤΗΣ ΧΡΙΣΤΙΑΝΙΚΗΣ ΑΡΧΑΙΟΛΟΓΙΚΗΣ ΕΤΑΡΕΙΑΣ* 9 (Athens, 1979), 21–34.

Boyer, C., *A History of Mathematics* (New York, 1968).

Braunfels, W., *Monasteries of Western Europe: The Architecture of the Orders* (London, 1972).

Britt, K., 'The Church of St. John Theologos: A Reevaluation of an Architectural Copy', paper given at International Congress on Medieval Studies, Western Michigan University (2003).

Broadwood, L., and Maitland, J., eds, *English County Songs: Words and Music* (London, 1893).

Brown, S., and O'Connor, D., *Medieval Craftsmen: Glass-Painters* (London, 1991).

Bucher, F., *Architector: The Lodge Books and Sketchbooks of Medieval Architects* (New York, 1979).

—— 'Design in Gothic Architecture – A Preliminary Assessment', *JSAH* 27.1 (1968), 49–71.

—— 'Medieval Architectural Design Methods 800–1560', *GESTA* 11.2 (1972), 37–51.

Buchwald, H., *Form, Style and Meaning in Byzantine Church Architecture* (Aldershot, 1999).

—— 'The Geometry of Middle Byzantine Churches and Some Possible Implications', orig. in *Jahrbuch der Osterreichischen Byantinistik* 42 (Vienna, 1992); in Buchwald (1999), XI, 293–321.

Builder, The (London, 1842–1966).

Burkert, W., *Lore and Science in Ancient Pythagoreanism*, tr. E. Minar (Cambridge MA, 1972).

Butler, L., and Given-Wilson, C., *Medieval Monasteries of Great Britain* (London, 1979).

Camón, J., *Compendio de arquitectura y simetría de los templos por Simón García* (Salamanca, 1941).

Campbell, L., ed., *Twentieth-Century Architecture and its Histories*, Society of Architectural Historians of Great Britain (2000).

Carruthers, M., *The Craft of Thought: Meditation, Rhetoric, and the Making of Images, 400–1200* (Cambridge, 2000).

Carty, C., 'The Role of Gunzo's Dream in the Building of Cluny III', *Gesta* 27. 1/2 (1988), 113–23.

Cavarnos, C., *Byzantine Sacred Art: Selected Writings of the contemporary Greek icon painter Fotis Kontoglous on the Sacred Arts according to the Tradition of Eastern Orthodox Christianity*, tr. C. Cavarnos (New York, 1957).

Cesariano, C., *Di Lucio Vitruuio Pollione de Architectura Libri Dece* (Como, 1521).

Chevallier, G., *Le vénérable Guillaume, abbé de Saint-Bénigne de Dijon: réformateur de l'ordre Bénédictin au XIe siècle* (Paris, 1875).

Chueca, F., *La Catedral Nueva de Salamanca: Historia documental de su construcción* (Salamanca, 1951).

Clark, W., 'Context, Continuity, and the Creation of National Memory in Paris, 1130–1160: A Critical Commentary', *Gesta* 45/2 (2006(1)), 161–75.

—— *Laon Cathedral: Architecture (2): The Aesthetics of Space, Plan and Structure*, Courtauld Institute Illustration Archives, Companion Text 2 (London, 1987).

—— *Medieval Cathedrals* (Westport CT, 2006(2)).

Clark, W., and King, R., *Laon Cathedral: Architecture (1)*, Courtauld Institute Illustration Archives, Companion Text 1 (London, 1983).

Clemen, P., *Gotische kathedralen in Frankreich: Paris, Chartres, Amiens, Reims* (Zurich, 1937).

Clifton, J., ed., *The Body of Christ in the Art of Europe and New Spain, 1150–1800* (Munich, 1997).

Cocke, T., and Kidson, P., *Salisbury Cathedral: Perspectives on the Architectural History* (London, 1993).

Conant, K., 'Medieval Academy Excavations at Cluny, IX: Systematic Dimensions in the Buildings', *Speculum* 38.1 (1963), 1–45.

Cook, G., *English Monasteries in the Middle Ages* (London, 1961).

Corbo, V., *Il Santo Sepulcro di Gerusalemme: Aspetti archeologici dalle origini al periodo crociato*, 3 vols, *II: Tavole* (Jerusalem, 1981).

Corbusier, Le, *Le Modulor* (Paris, 1950).

—— *The Modulor*, tr. P. de Francia and A. Bostock, 2nd edn (London, 1954).

Cormack, R., *The Byzantine Eye: Studies in Art and Patronage* (London, 1989).

—— 'Interpreting the Mosaics of S. Sophia at Istanbul', in Cormack (1989), VIII, 131–49, orig. in *Art History* 4 (London, 1989) 131–49.

Cornford, F., *Plato's Cosmology* (London, 1937).

Cotterell, A., *The Illustrated Encyclopedia of Myths and Legends* (London, 1989).

Coüasnon, C., *The Church of the Holy Sepulchre in Jerusalem* (London, 1974).

Courcelle, P., *La Consolation de Philosophie dans la tradition littéraire* (Paris, 1967).

Cowen, P., *Rose Windows* (London, 1979).

—— *The Rose Window: Splendour and Symbol* (London, 2005).

Critchlow, K., *Time Stands Still: New Light on Megalithic Science* (London, 1979).

Crosby, S., 'Crypt and Choir Plans at Saint-Denis', *Gesta* 5 (1966), 4–8.

—— *The Royal Abbey of Saint-Denis, from Its Beginnings to the Death of Suger, 475–1151* (New Haven, CT, 1987).

Crossley, P., 'The Man from Inner Space: Architecture and Meditation in the Choir of St Laurence in Nuremberg', in Owen-Crocker (1998), 165–82.

—— 'The Workshop of the Holy Spirit: The English Medieval Chapter House', unpubl. paper given to Oxford University Architectural Society (1986).

Cuomo, S., *Pappus of Alexandria and the Mathematics of Late Antiquity* (Cambridge, 2000).

Davis, M., and Neagley, L., 'Mechanics and Meaning: Plan Design at Saint-Urbain, Troyes and Saint-Ouen, Rouen', *GESTA* 39. 2 (2000), 161–82.
Demus, O., *Byzantine Mosaic Decoration* (London, 1948).
Dilly Song, The, Vaughan Williams Memorial Library, Leaflet 10 (London, repr. 1977).
Dow, H., 'The Rose-Window', *Journal of Warburg and Courtauld Institutes* 20 (1957), 248–97.
Downey, G., 'Byzantine Architects, their Training and Methods', *Byzantion* 18 (1948), 99–118.
Dugdale, W., *History of S. Paul's Cathedral* (1658), ed. H. Ellis (1818).
Durand, J.-N.-L., *Précis des leçons d'architecture données à L'Ecôle Polytechnique* (Paris, 1809).
Dwyer, R., 'A Mathematical Interpretation of the Decorative Elements of the Haghia Sophia', *SCINTILLA* 2–3 (1985/6), 1–18.
Eckenstein, L., *Comparative Studies in Nursery Rhymes* (London, 1906).
Evans, G., 'Number-Symbolism and the Theory of Signification in Odo of Morimond and some of his Successors', *Cîteaux: commentarii cistercienses* 34 (1983), 111–20.
Evans, J., ed., *The Flowering of the Middle Ages* (London, 1966).
Evans, R., *The Projective Cast: Architecture and Its Three Geometries* (Cambridge MA, 1995).
Fernie, E., 'Introduction', in N. Wu (2002), 1–9.
—— *Romanesque Architecture: Design, Meaning and Metrology* (London, 1995).
Fontana, D., *The Secret Language of Symbols: A visual key to symbols* (London, 2001).
Frankl, P., *Gothic Architecture*, rev. P. Crossley (London, 2000).
—— *The Gothic: Literary Sources and Interpretations through Eight Centuries* (Princeton NJ, 1960).
—— 'The Secret of the Mediaeval Masons', *Art Bulletin* 28 (1945), 46–60.
Franz, H., 'Die Fensterrose und ihre Vorgeschichte in der islamischen Baukunst', *Zeitschrift für Kunstwissenschaft* 10 (1956), 1–22.
—— 'Les fenêtres circulaires de la cathédrale de Cefalù et le problème de l'origine de la "rose" au moyen âge', *Cahiers archéologiques* 9 (1957), 253–70.
Gafurio, F., *De Harmonia musicorum instrumenntorum* (Milan, 1518).
Gage, J., *Colour and Culture: Practice and Meaning from Antiquity to Abstraction* (London, 1995).
García, S., *Compendio de arquitectura y simetría de los templos* (Salamanca, 1681).
Garton, C., *The Metrical Life of Saint Hugh of Lincoln* (Lincoln, 1988).
Gem, R., 'Towards an Iconography of Anglo-Saxon Architecture', *Journal of Warburg and Courtauld Institutes* 46 (1983), 1–18.
Gerson, P., ed., *Abbot Suger and Saint-Denis: A Symposium* (New York, 1986).
Ghyka, M., *Geometry of Art and Life* (New York, 1946).
Gilson, E., *The Christian Philosophy of Thomas Aquinas*, tr. L. Shook (Notre Dame IN, 1994).

Godfrey, P., and Hemsoll, D., 'The Pantheon; temple or rotunda?' in *Pagan Gods and Shrines of the Roman Empire*, eds M. Henig and A. King, Oxford University Committee for archaeology Monograph 8 (Oxford, 1986), 195–209.

Goldfinger, E., 'Criticism: The Architect Replies', *Architects' Journal* (25 July 1957), 133–4.

Götz, W., *Zentralbau und Zentralbautendenz in der gotischen Architektur* (Berlin, 1968).

Gould, S. Baring, *Strange Survivals* (London, 1892).

Grant, L., *Abbot Suger of St-Denis: Church and State in Early Twelfth-Century France* (London, 1998).

Grill, P., *Die Epistola defensionis des ersten cisterciensischen Zahlenmystikers Odo von Morimond*, Studia Anselmiana 50 (Rome, 1962), 193–203; also in CIMA 40 (Copenhagen, 1981), 83–5.

Guiley, R., *The Encyclopedia of Witches and Witchcraft* (New York, 1989).

Gwilt, J., *An Encyclopaedia of Architecture: Historical, Theoretical, and Practical*, rev. W. Papworth (London, 1903).

Hahnloser, H., *Villard de Honnecourt, Kritische, Gesamtausgabe des Bauhüttenbuches*, (Graz, 1972).

Hallinger, K., *Gorze-Kluny: Studien zu den monastischen Bebensformen und Gegensätzen im Hochmittelalter* (Rome, 1950–51).

—— 'The Spiritual Life of Cluny in the Early Days', in Hunt (1971), 29–55.

Hambidge, J., *The Elements of Dynamic Symmetry* (New Haven CT, 1920).

—— *The Parthenon and other Greek Temples: Their Dynamic Symmetry* (New Haven CT, 1924).

Hamburger, J., and Bouché, A.-M, eds, *The Mind's Eye: Art and Theological Argument in the Middle Ages* (Princeton NJ, 2006).

Hart, C., *The Early Charters of Eastern England* (Leicester, 1966).

Harvey, J., *The Cathedrals of Spain* (London, 1957).

—— *The Mediæval Architect* (London, 1972).

Heath, T., *A History of Greek Mathematics* (Oxford, 1921).

Hecht, K., *Maß und Zahl in der gotischen Baukunst* (Hildesheim, 1979).

Héliot, P., 'Chronologie de la Basilique de Saint-Quentin', *Bulletin monumental* 117 (1959), 7–50.

Hiscock, N., 'Architectural Geometry and the Portfolio of Villard de Honnecourt', in M.-T. Zenner (2004(1)), 3–21.

—— 'Making Sense of √2', *AVISTA Forum Journal* 12.1 (1999), 20–27.

—— 'Platonic Geometry in Plans of Medieval Abbeys and Cathedrals', PhD thesis, Oxford Brookes University (1994).

—— 'A Schematic Plan for Norwich Cathedral', in N. Wu (2002), 83–121.

—— 'The Two Cistercian Plans of Villard de Honnecourt', in Kinder (2004 (2)), 157–72.

—— *The Wise Master Builder: Platonic Geometry in Plans of Medieval Abbeys and Cathedrals* (Aldershot, 2000).

—— Ed. and introduction, *The White Mantle of Churches: Architecture, Liturgy and Art around the Millennium* (Turnhout, 2003).

Hoffmann, V., *Der geometrische Entwurf der Hagia Sophia in Istanbul: Bilder einer Ausstellung* (Bern, 2005).

Holländer, H., *Early Medieval Art* (London, 1974).

Hopper, V., *Medieval Number Symbolism: Its Sources, Meaning, and Influence on Thought and Expression* (New York, 1938).

Hörmann, H., Keil, J., Miltner, F., Sotiriu, G., 'Die Johanneskirche', *Forschungen in Ephesos: veröffentlicht vom Österreichischen Archäologischen Institut* 4. 3 (Vienna, 1951).

Horn, W., 'On the Origins of the Medieval Cloister,' *Gesta* 12 (1973), 13–52.

Horn, W. and Born, E., *The Plan of S. Gall: A Study of the Architecture and Economy of, and Life in a Paradigmatic Carolingian Monastery* (Berkeley CA, 1979).

Hugot, L., *Aachen Cathedral: A Guide* (Aachen, 1990).

Hunt, N., ed., *Cluniac Monasticism in the Central Middle Ages* (London, 1971).

Huntley, H., *The Divine Proportion* (New York, 1970).

Hussey, J., *The Orthodox Church in the Byzantine Empire* (Oxford, 1986).

Jackson, T., *Gothic Architecture in France, England, and Italy*, 2 vols (Cambridge, 1915).

James, L., *Light and Colour in Byzantine Art* (Oxford, 1996).

James, L., and Webb, R.,'To understand Ultimate Things and Enter Secret Places': Ekphrasis and Art in Byzantium, *Art History* 14. 1 (1991), 1–17.

Kidson, P., 'Panofsky, Suger and St Denis', *Journal of the Warburg and Courtauld Institutes* 50 (1987), 1–17.

Kinder, T., ed., *Perspectives for an Architecture of Solitude: Essays on Cistercians, Art and Architecture in Honour of Peter Fergusson*, Medieval Church Studies 11, Studia et Documenta 13 (Turnhout, 2004).

Kitzinger, E., 'World Map and Fortune's Wheel: A Medieval Mosaic Floor in Turin', *Proceedings of the American Philosophical Society* 117 (1973), 344–73.

Klibansky, R., *The Continuity of the Platonic Tradition during the Middle Ages* (London, 1981).

Kline, N., *Maps of Medieval Thought: The Hereford Paradigm* (Woodbridge, 2003).

Kobler, F., 'Fensterrose', *Reallexikon zur deutschen Kunstgeschichte* 8, ed. O. Schmitt (Stuttgart, 1987), cols 65–203.

Krautheimer, R., *Early Christian and Byzantine Architecture* (Harmondsworth, 1965).

—— 'Introduction to an "Iconography of Medieval Architecture"', *Journal of the Warburg and Courtauld Institutes* 5 (1942), 1–33.

Kuniholm, P., and Striker, C., 'Dendrochronology and the Architectural History of the Church of the Holy Apostles in Thessaloniki', *Architectura* 2 (1990), 1–26.

Ladurie, E., *Montaillou: Cathars and Catholics in a French Village 1294–1324*, tr. B. Bray (Harmondsworth, 1980).

Landes, R., 'The Fear of an Apocalyptic Year 1000: Augustinian Historiography, Medieval and Modern', *Speculum*, 75 (2000).

—— 'The White Mantle of Churches: Millennial Dynamics, and the Written and Architectural Record', in Hiscock (2003), 249–64.

Lanfrey, G., *L'Abbaye de Jumièges: plans et documents* (Rouen, 1954).

Lange, D., 'Theorien zur Entstehung der byzantinischen Kreuzkuppelkirche', *Architectura* 16.2 (1986), 93–113.

Leclercq, J., *L'Arithmétique de Guillaume d'Auberive*, Studia Anselmiana 20 (Rome, 1948), 181–99.

Lehmann, K., 'The Dome of Heaven', *Art Bulletin* 27 (1945), 1–27.

Lehmann-Brockhaus, O., *Die Kunst des 10. Jahrhunderts im Lichte der Schriftquellen* (Strasbourg, 1935).

—— *Schriftquellen zur Kunstgeschichte des 11. und 12. Jahrhunderts für Deutschland, Lothringen und Italien* (Berlin, 1938).

Lethaby, W., *Architecture, Mysticism, and Myth* (London, 1891).

—— *Mediæval Art: From the Peace of the Church to the Eve of the Renaissance 312–1350* (London, 1904).

—— Ibid., rev. D. Talbot Rice (London, 1949).

—— *Westminster Abbey and the King's Craftsmen: A Study of Mediæval Building* (London, 1906).

Lethaby, W., and Swainson, H., *The Church of Sancta Sophia, Constantinople: A Study of Byzantine Building* (London, 1894).

Linardou, K., 'Reading two Byzantine Illustrated Books: The Kokkinobaphos manuscripts (Vaticanus graecus 1162 and Parisinus graecus 1208) and their illustration', unpubl. PhD dissertation, University of Birmingham (2004), 12–20.

Linscheid-Burdich, S., *Suger von Saint-Denis: Untersuchungen zu seinen Schriften*, Beiträge zur Altertumskunde, 200 (Munich, 2004).

Lübke, W., and Lützow, C., *Denkmäler der Kunst* (Stuttgart, 1884).

Luca di Pacioli, *De Divina proportione* (Venice, 1509).

Lund, F., *Ad Quadratum* (London, 1921).

McClendon, C., *The Origins of Medieval Architecture* (New Haven CT, 2005).

MacDonald, W., *The Architecture of the Roman Empire I: An Introductory Study* (New Haven CT, 1982).

—— *The Pantheon: Design, Meaning, and Progeny* (London, 1976).

McEvoy, J., *Robert Grosseteste* (Oxford, 2000).

Mackie, E., 'Robert Grosseteste's Anglo-Norman Treatise on the Loss and Restoration of Creation, commonly known as *Le Château d'amour*: An English Prose Translation', in O'Carroll (2003), 151–79.

McVey, K., 'The Domed Church as Microcosm: Literary Roots of an Architectural Symbol', *Dumbarton Oaks Papers* 37 (1983), 91–121.

Mainstone, R., *Hagia Sophia: Architecture, Structure and Liturgy of Justinian's Great Church* (London, 1988).

Maître, C., *La Réforme cistercienne du plain-chant: Etude d'un traité théorique*, Cîteaux: Studia et Documenta 6 (Brecht, 1995).

Malone, C., 'Les fouilles de St. Bénigne de Dijon', *Bulletin Monumental* 138.3 (1980), 253–91.

Mango, C., *The Art of the Byzantine Empire 312–1453: Sources and Documents* (Englewood Cliffs NJ, 1972).
—— *Byzantine Architecture* (New York, 1985).
—— 'Byzantine Writers on the Fabric of Hagia Sophia', in *Hagia Sophia from the Age of Justinian to the Present*, eds R. Mark and A. Çakmak (Cambridge, 1992).
—— *Byzantium, The Empire of New Rome* (London, 1980).
—— 'Constantine's Mausoleum and the Translation of Relics', *Byzantinische Zeitschrift* 83 (1990), 51–62, 434.
—— Ed., *The Oxford History of Byzantium* (Oxford, 2002).
—— 'The Revival of Learning', in *The Oxford History* (2002), 214–29.
Mango, C., and Parker, J., 'A Twelfth-Century Description of St Sophia, *Studies* XVII, orig. in *Dumbarton Oaks Papers* XIV (Washington DC, 1960) 233–45.
Mark, R. and Çakmak, A., eds *Hagia Sophia from the Age of Justinian to the Present*, (Cambridge, 1992).
Martini, Francesco di Giorgio, *Architettura civile e militare*, in C. Maltese, ed., *Trattati di Architettura Ingegnaria e Arte Militare* II (Milan, 1967), 293–506.
Masi, M., tr., *Boethian Number Theory; A translation of the De Institutione Arithmetica (with Introduction and Notes)*, Studies in Classical Antiquity 6 (Amsterdam, 1983).
Mathew, G., *Byzantine Aesthetics* (London, 1963).
Mathews, T., *Art and Architecture in Byzantium and Armenia: Liturgical and Exegetical Approaches* (Aldershot, 1995).
—— *The early churches of Constantinople: architecture and liturgy* (University Park PA, 1971).
—— 'Private Liturgy in Byzantine Architecture: Toward a Reappraisal', in *Art and Architecture* III, orig. in *Cahiers Archéologiques* 30 (Paris, 1982), 125–38.
—— 'The Sequel to Nicaea II in Byzantine Church Decoration', in *Art and Architecture* XII, orig. in *Perkins Journal of Theology* 41, 3 (Dallas TX, 1988), 11–21.
—— 'The Transformation Symbolism in Byzantine Architecture and the Meaning of the Pantokrator in the Dome', in *Art and Architecture* XIII, orig. in *Church and People in Byzantium*, ed. R. Morris (Birmingham, 1990), 191–214.
Mersmann, W., *Rosenfenster und Himmelskreise* (Mittenwald, 1982).
Meyer, G., 'Le tracé régulateur des rosaces du transept de l'Eglise St-Léger de Guebwiller', *Cahiers alsaciens d'archéologie, d'art, et d'histoire* 20 (1977), 103–6.
Moessel, E., *Die Proportion in Antike und Mittelalter* (Munich, 1926).
—— *Unformen des Raumes als Grundlagen der Formgestaltung* (Munich, 1931).
Mojon, L., *Der Münsterbaumeister Matthäus Ensinger* (Bern, 1967).
Morgan, N., *The Medieval Painted Glass of Lincoln Cathedral* (Oxford, 1983).
Morris, R., 'The Architectural History of the Medieval Cathedral Church', in Aylmer and Tiller (2000), 203–40.
Murray, S., *Beauvais Cathedral: Architecture of Transcendence* (Princeton NJ, 1989).

—— *Notre Dame, Cathedral of Amiens: The Power of Change in Gothic* (Cambridge, 1996).

Murray, S., and Addiss, J., 'Plan and Space at Amiens Cathedral: With a New Plan Drawn by James Addiss', *JSAH* 49.1 (1990), 44–66.

Mutsopulos, N., 'Harmonische Bauschnitte in den Kirchen vom Typ kreuzförmigen Innenbaus im Griechischen Kernland', *Byzantinische Zeitschrift* 55 (1962) 274–91.

Neagley, L., 'Architecture and the Body of Christ', in Clifton (1997), 26–36.

New Grove Dictionary of Music and Musicians, The, 29 vols, ed. S. Sadie, 2nd edn (London, 2001).

Nirenberg, D., 'The Historical Body of Christ', in Clifton (1997), 17–25.

Nordström, C.-O., *Ravennastudien: Ideengeschichtliche und ikonographische Untersuchungen über die Mosaiken von Ravenna* (Stockholm, 1953).

Norton, C., 'The Lost Paintings of the Chapter House [at York]', unpubl. paper, International Medieval Congress, Leeds University (2004).

Norwich, J., *Byzantium: The Apogee* (London, 1993).

O'Carroll, M., ed., *Robert Grosseteste and the Beginnings of a British Theological Tradition* (Rome, 2003).

Orff C., *Carmina Burana: Cantiones Profanae* (London, 1953).

Origo, I., *The Merchant of Prato* (Harmondsworth, 1963).

Ousterhout, R., 'The Holy Space: Architecture and the Liturgy', in Safran (1998), 81–120.

—— *Master Builders of Byzantium* (Princeton NJ, 1999).

—— 'The Temple, the Sepulchre, and the *Martyrion* of the Savior', *Gesta* 29. 1 (1990), 44–53.

Overy, P., *De Stijl* (London, 1991).

Owen-Crocker, G. and Graham, T., eds, *Medieval Art: recent perspectives. A memorial tribute to C. R. Dodwell* (New York, 1998).

Oxford Dictionary of the Christian Church, eds F. Cross and E. Livingstone, 3rd edn (London, 1997).

Padovan, R., *Proportion: Science, Philosophy, Architecture* (London, 1999).

Page, S., *Astrology in Medieval Manuscripts* (London, 2002).

—— *Magic in Medieval Manuscripts* (London, 2004).

Palladio, Andrea, *I quattro libri dell'Architettura* (Venice, 1570).

Panofsky, E., *Gothic Architecture and Scholasticism* (New York, 1957).

Papahadjis, N., *Monuments of Thessalonike*, 2nd edn, rev. tr. A. Sanford, repr. S. Molho (Thessalonica, 1962).

Petau, P., *De Nithardo Caroli magni nepote, ac tota eiusdem* (Paris, 1613).

Petersen, N., Clüver, C., and Bell, N., eds, *Signs of Change: Transformations of Christian Traditions and their Representation in the Arts, 1000–2000* (New York, 2004).

Pevsner, N., *The Leaves of Southwell* (London, 1945).

—— 'The Term "Architect" in the Middle Ages', *Speculum* 17 (1942), 549–62.

Rice, D., ed., *The Dark Ages: The Making of European Civilization* (London, 1965).

Richter, J., *The Literary Works of Leonardo da Vinci*, 2 vols, 2nd edn (Oxford, 1939).
Rotili, M., *Benevento romana e longobarda. L'immagine urbana* (Naples, 1986), 184–201.
Rowe, C., 'The Mathematics of the Ideal Villa', *Architectural Review* 101 (1947), 101–04.
Runciman, S., *Byzantine Civilization* (London, 1933/61).
—— *The Fall of Constantinople* (Cambridge, 1965).
Rusconi, A., 'La chiesa di S. Sophia di Benevento', *Corso di cultura sull'arte Ravennate e Byzantina* 14 (1967), 339–59.
Safran, L., ed., *Heaven on Earth: Art and the Church in Byzantium* (University Park PA, 1998).
Sandys, W., *Christmas Carols, Ancient and Modern* (London, 1833).
Saradi-Mendelovici, H., 'Representations of Plato in Byzantine Churches: From Heretical Cult to Cultural Acceptance', paper given at International Congress on Medieval Studies, Western Michigan University (1991).
Sauer, J., *Symbolik des Kirchengebäudes und seiner Ausstattung* (Freiburg, 1924).
Schlosser, J., *Schriftquellen zur Geschichte der Karolingischenkunst* (Vienna, 1892).
Scholfield, P., *The Theory of Proportion in Architecture* (Cambridge, 1958).
Schultz, J., and Synan, E., tr., *St. Thomas Aquinas: An Exposition of the 'On the Hebdomads' of Boethius* (Washington DC, 2001).
Schultz, R., and Barnsley, S., *The Monastery of Saint Luke of Stiris in Phocis* (London, 1901).
Sears, E., *The Ages of Man: Medieval Interpretations of the Life Cycle* (Princeton NJ, 1986).
Seeliger, S., *Pfingsten: Die Ausgiessung des Heiligen Geistes am fünfzigsten Tage nach Ostern* (Düsseldorf, 1958).
Serlio, Sebastiano, *I cinque libri d'architettura* (Venice, 1559–62).
Sharp, C., and Marson C., *Folk Songs from Somerset* (London, 1915).
Shelby, L., 'The Education of Medieval English Master Masons', *Mediaeval Studies* 32 (1970), 1–26.
—— 'The Geometrical Knowledge of Mediaeval Master Masons', *Speculum* 47 (1972), 395–421.
—— 'Geometry', in Wagner (1986), 196–217.
—— *Gothic Design Techniques* (Carbondale IL, 1977).
—— 'Mediaeval Masons' Templates', *JSAH* 30.2 (1971), 140–54.
—— 'The Role of Medieval Masons in Medieval English Buildings', *Speculum* 39 (1964), 387–403.
Shortell, E., 'The choir of Saint-Quentin: Gothic Structure, Power, and Cult', PhD thesis, Columbia University (New York, 2000).
Simpson, F., *A History of Architectural Development*, 3 vols (London, 1905–11).
Simson, O. von, *The Gothic Cathedral: Origins of Gothic Architecture and the Medieval Concept of Order* (London, 1956).

Skoblar, M., 'Early Christian Baptismal Fonts in Dalmatia', paper given at International Medieval Congress, Leeds University (2005).

Slocum, K., '*Speculum musicae*: Jacques de Liège and the Art of Musical Number', in Surles (1993), 11–37.

Smithson, A., ed., *team 10 primer* (Cambridge MA, 1968).

Speer, A., 'Is There a Theology of the Gothic Cathedral? A Re-reading of Abbot Suger's Writings on the Abbey Church of St.-Denis', in Hamburger and Bouché (2006), 65–83.

Stanley, A., *Historical Memorials of Westminster Abbey* (London, 1868).

Stewart, C., *Simpson's History of Architectural Development II: Early Christian, Byzantine and Romanesque Architecture* (London, 1954).

—— *Simpson's History of Architectural Development III: Gothic Architecture* (London, 1962).

Striker, C., 'Applied Proportions in Later Byzantine Architecture', in *Studien zur byzantinischen Kunstgeschichte. Festschrift für H. Hallensleben zum 65. Geburtstag*, eds B. Borkopp, B. Scheelewald, L. Theis (Amsterdam, 1995) 31–7.

Strzygowski, J., *Die Baukunst der Armenier und Europa* (Vienna, 1918).

Suckale, R., 'Die Rosenfenster der Ebracher Klosterkirche', *Festschrift: 700 Jahre Abteikirche Ebrach 1285–1985*, eds W. Wiemer and G. Zimmermann (Ebrach, 1985), 59–86.

Summers, N., *A Prospect of Southwell: An architectural history of the church and domestic buildings of the collegiate foundation* (London, 1974).

Surles, R., *Medieval Numerology: A Book of Essays* (New York, 1993).

Swift, E., *Hagia Sophia* (New York, 1940).

Taft, R., ed., *Liturgy in Byzantium and Beyond* (Aldershot, 1995).

—— 'The Liturgy of the Great Church: An initial synthesis of structure and interpretation on the eve of Iconoclasm', in *Liturgy* I; rev. version, *Dumbarton Oaks Papers* 34–35 (Washington DC, 1980–81), 45–75.

—— 'The Pontifical Liturgy of the Great Church according to a Twelfth-Century *Diataxis* in Codex BM Add. 34060', in *Liturgy* II, orig. in, *Orientalia Christiana Periodica* 45 (Rome, 1979), 279–307, idem 46 (Rome, 1980), 89–124.

Tatarkiewicz, W., *History of Aesthetics II: Medieval Aesthetics*, tr. R. Montgomery, ed. C. Barrett (Hague, 1970).

Texier, C., and Pullan, R., *Byzantine Architecture; Illustrated by examples of edifices erected in the East during the earliest ages of Christianity, with historical and archæological descriptions* (London, 1864).

Thomson, R., 'Architectural Symbolism in Classical Armenian Literature', *Journal of Theological Studies*, New Series 30 (1979), 102–14.

Thorndike, L., *A History of Magic and Experimental Science* (New York, 1923–34).

Trachtenberg, M., *Dominion of the Eye: Urbanism, Art, and Power in Early Modern Florence* (Cambridge, 1997).

Ueberwasser, W., 'Nach rechtem Masz: Aussagen über den Begriff des Maszes in der Kunst des XIII.-XVI. Jahrhunderts', *Jahrbuch der preussischen Kunstammlungen* 56 (Berlin, 1935), 250–72.

Ullman, B., 'Geometry in the Mediaeval Quadrivium', *Studi di bibliografia e di storia in onore di Tammaro de Marinis* 4 (Verona, 1964), 263–85.

Uspensky, T., ed., *Zapiski imperatorskago novorossiskago universiteta* 59 (1893), 420–23.

Van Nice, R., *Saint Sophia in Istanbul. An architectural survey* (Washington DC, 1965).

Velte, M., *Die Anwendung der Quadratur und Triangulatur bei der Grund- und Aufrissgestaltung der gotischen Kirchen* (Basle, 1951).

Venturi, R., *Complexity and Contradiction in Architecture* (New York, 1966).

Verzone, P., *From Theodoric to Charlemagne: A history of the Dark Ages in the West*, tr. P. Waley (London, 1968).

Viollet-le-Duc, E., *Le dictionnaire raisonné de l'architecture française du XIe au XVIe siècle*, 10 vols (Paris 1858–68).

Vregille, B. de, 'Aldebald the Scribe of Cluny and the Bible of Abbot William of Dijon', in Hunt (1971), 85–97.

Vitruvius, tr. Giocondo, G., *De architectura* (Venice, 1511).

Wagner, D., *The Seven Liberal Arts in the Middle Ages* (Bloomington IN, 1986).

Warren, J., 'Greek Mathematics and the Architects to Justinian', *AARP*, Art and Archaeology Research Papers (London, 1976).

Whittick, A., *Symbols, Signs and their Meaning* (London, 1960).

Williams, W., 'William of Dijon: A Monastic Reformer of the Early XIth Century', *Downside Review* 52 (New Series 33) (1934).

Wilson, C., *The Gothic Cathedral: The Architecture of the Great Church 1130–1530* (London, 1992).

Wilson, N., *Scholars of Byzantium* (London, 1983).

Wittkower, R., *Architectural Principles in the Age of Humanism*, 4th edn (London, 1988).

Wu, N., ed., *Ad Quadratum: The Practical Application of Geometry in Medieval Architecture* (Aldershot, 2002).

—— 'Laying out Reims after Lunch', paper given at International Congress on Medieval Studies, Western Michigan University (2007).

Yorke, B., ed., *Bishop Æthelwold: His Career and Influence* (Woodbridge, 1997).

Zenner, M-T., ed., *Villard's Legacy: Studies in Medieval Technology, Science and Art in Memory of Jean Gimpel* (Aldershot, 2004).

Index

(Main entries for numbers are given in word form. References to illustrations are in *italics*).